Handbook of Research in Social Studies Education

This *Handbook* outlines the current state of research in social studies education—a complex, dynamic, challenging field with competing perspectives about appropriate goals, and on-going conflict over the content of the curriculum. Equally important, it encourages new research needed to move the field forward to foster the civic competence which advocates for the social studies have long claimed as a fundamental goal.

In considering how to organize the *Handbook*, the editors searched out definitions of social studies, statements of purpose, and themes that linked (or divided) theory, research, and practices and established criteria for topics to include. Each chapter meets one or more of these criteria: research activity since the last Handbook that warrants a new analysis, topics representing a major emphasis in the NCSS standards, and topics reflecting an emerging or re-emerging field within the social studies. The volume is organized around seven themes:

- Continuity and Change in Social Studies
- Civic Competence in Pluralist Democracies
- Social Justice and the Social Studies
- Assessment and Accountability
- Teaching and Learning in the Disciplines
- Information Ecologies: Technology in the Social Studies
- Teacher Preparation and Development

Comprehensive and up to date, the *Handbook of Research in Social Studies Education* is an essential resource for the social studies education community, including university faculty, graduate students, teachers, school and district administrators, and state, local, regional, and national agencies who conduct and support research related to social studies education.

Linda S. Levstik is Professor in the Department of Curriculum and Instruction at the University of Kentucky.

Cynthia A. Tyson is Associate Professor in the School of Teaching and Learning at The Ohio State University.

Handbook of Research in Social Studies Education

Edited by

Linda S. Levstik
University of Kentucky
Cynthia A. Tyson
The Ohio State University

Routledge
Taylor & Francis Group

NEW YORK AND LONDON

First published 2008
by Routledge
270 Madison Ave, New York, NY 10016

Simultaneously published in the UK
by Routledge
2 Park Square, Milton Park, Abingdon, Oxon OX14 4RN

Routledge is an imprint of the Taylor & Francis Group, an informa business

© 2008 Taylor and Francis

Typeset in Sabon by EvS Communication Networx, Inc.
Printed and bound in the United States of America on acid-free paper by Edwards Brothers, Inc.

Library of Congress Cataloging in Publication Data
Handbook of research in social studies education / edited by Linda S. Levstik, Cynthia A. Tyson.
p. cm.
1. Social sciences—Study and teaching—Handbooks, manuals, etc. 2. Civics—Study and teaching—Handbooks, manuals, etc. I. Levstik, Linda S. II. Tyson, Cynthia A., 1957-
LB1584.H2748 2008
300.71—dc22
2007037618

ISBN 10: 0-8058-5535-1 (hbk)
ISBN 10: 0-8058-5536-X (pbk)
ISBN 10: 0-203-93022-3 (ebk)

ISBN 13: 978-0-8058-5535-7 (hbk)
ISBN 13: 978-0-8058-5536-4 (pbk)
ISBN 13: 978-0-203-93022-9 (ebk)

To social studies researchers investigating the "habits of mind" that inform civic engagement, enrich human experience, and build community in an increasingly diverse, complex and fascinating world.

Contents

Contributors

EDITORS

Linda S. Levstik is Professor in the Department of Curriculum and Instruction at the University of Kentucky. Professor Levstik received the Jean Dresden Grambs Career Research Award from the National Council for the Social Studies in 2007. Her research on children's and adolescents' historical thinking in the United States, New Zealand, and Ghana appears in a number of journals, including *Theory and Research in Social Education, Teachers College Record, The American Educational Research Journal*, and *The International Review of History Education*, as well as books. She is co-author with Keith C. Barton of *Doing History: Investigating with Children in Elementary and Middle Schools 3rd Edition* (Erlbaum, 2005), *Teaching History for the Common Good* (Erlbaum, 2004), *Researching History Education* (Routledge, 2008), and with Christine Pappas and Barbara Kiefer of *An Integrated Language Perspective in the Elementary School* (4th ed., Longman, 2005). Prior to earning a PhD from The Ohio State University, she taught in public and private elementary and middle schools.

Cynthia A. Tyson, PhD is an Associate Professor in the School of Teaching and Learning at The Ohio State University and a former elementary school teacher. Her research interests focus on the development of cultural competence and sociopolitical consciousness in early childhood social studies education, and the use of children's literature in civic education. The historical and political underpinnings of race and ethnicity are also at the core of her teaching and research agendas. She has worked extensively as an educational consultant (social studies and literacy) within the state of Ohio and has begun collaborative research initiatives, both nationally and internationally, exploring frameworks for teaching for social justice. She has presented numerous papers at national meetings and conferences, including NCSS and the affiliate College University Faculty Assembly (CUFA). Dr. Tyson has served as Chair of CUFA, has served on the Carter G. Woodson Committee, and is currently the chair of the recently formed NCSS Social Justice Community. She has participated in a special series of presentations at NCSS, entitled *Theory to Practice: Teaching in Urban Schools*, published articles in *Theory and Research in Social Education, Social Education, Social Studies and the Young Learner*, and *Educational Researcher* as well as other books and journals.

CHAPTER AUTHORS

Susan Adler is Professor of Education and Chair of the Division of Curriculum and Instructional Leadership at the University of Missouri-Kansas City. Dr. Adler has published numerous articles on social studies teacher education, edited a volume entitled *Critical Issues in Social Studies Teacher Education*, and co-authored *Cultural Foundations of Education*. She taught middle school social studies for nine years before earning her doctorate in Curriculum and Instruction at the University of Wisconsin with an emphasis in social studies education. She has worked extensively with pre-service and in-service teachers, both on-campus and in school based workshops. She is a past president of the National Council of the Social Studies as well as the Missouri Council for the Social Studies. Dr. Adler has served as Senior Visiting Fellow at the National Institute of Education in Singapore.

Janet Alleman is a Professor in the Department of Teacher Education at Michigan State University. She is author and coauthor of a range of publications, including *Children's Thinking About Cultural Universals* and a three-volume series entitled *Social Studies Excursions, K-3*. In addition to serving on a host of committees at the state and national levels, she has been a classroom and television teacher, actively working in school settings, and has taught at over a dozen international sites.

Theresa Alviar-Martin is a PhD candidate in the Division of Educational Studies at Emory University and research fellow of the Center for the Advancement and Study of International Education (CASIE). For 13 years, she taught in international schools in Bangkok, Hong Kong, and Manila, and a refugee camp in Bataan, the Philippines. Her dissertation, *Seeking Cosmopolitan Citizenship: A Comparative Case Study of Two International Schools*, examines how social studies programs educate youth for overlapping cultural, local, national, and global identities. Other research interests include comparative and international political socialization, the integration of multicultural and global education, human rights education, teacher education, and mixed methods research.

James A. Banks is Kerry and Linda Killinger Professor in Diversity Studies and Director of the Center for Multicultural Education at the University of Washington, Seattle. He is a past President of the American Educational Research Association (AERA) and a past President of the National Council for the Social Studies (NCSS). Professor Banks is a specialist in social studies education and in multicultural education, and has written more than 100 articles and written or edited 20 books in these fields. His books include *Diversity and Citizenship Education: Global Perspectives*, *Teaching Strategies for Ethnic Studies*, *Cultural Diversity and Education: Foundations, Curriculum and Teaching*, and *Race, Culture and Education: The Selected Works of James A. Banks*.

Keith C. Barton is Professor of Teacher Education at the University of Cincinnati. Professor Barton's research focuses on the development of children's understanding of history in national and cross-national contexts. His work appears in *AERJ, Journal of Curriculum Studies, Teachers College Record, Theory and Research in Social Education, Social Education*, and *Phi Delta Kappa* as well as in a variety of other national and international publications. He is coauthor with Linda S. Levstik of *Doing History: Investigating with Children in Elementary and Middle Schools* (Erlbaum, 2005), *Teaching History for the Common Good* (Erlbaum, 2004), and *Researching History Education* (2008) and is editor of *Research Methods in Social Studies Education: Contemporary Issues and Perspectives* (Information Age Publishing).

Kathy Bickmore (PhD Stanford University, 1991) is Associate Professor of Curriculum Studies and Teacher Development at the Ontario Institute for Studies in Education (OISE),

University of Toronto, Canada. She teaches (graduate and teacher education) and conducts research about education for constructive conflict, conflict resolution, equity, inclusive democracy, and safer schools for all in public school contexts. Her work appears in books such as *Handbook of Conflict Management, Challenges and Prospects for Canadian Social Studies, How Children Understand War and Peace,* and journals such as *Conflict Resolution Quarterly, Theory and Research in Social Education, Curriculum Inquiry, Alberta Journal for Educational Research, Journal of Peace Education, Canadian Journal of Education.* She is Guest Editor of a theme issue of *Theory and Research in Social Education* (Peacebuilding Citizenship Education, 2004).

Jere Brophy is a University Distinguished Professor of Teacher Education at Michigan State University. Author, coauthor, or editor of more than 20 books and 250 scholarly articles, chapters, and technical reports, he is well known for his research on teacher expectations, teacher-student relationships, teacher effects on student achievement, classroom management, student motivation, and, most recently, elementary social studies curriculum and instruction. He was a member of the Task Force on Social Studies Teaching and Learning that prepared the National Council for the Social Studies position statement entitled "A Vision of Powerful Teaching and Learning in the Social Studies: Building Social Understanding and Civic Efficacy."

Margaret Smith Crocco is Professor and Coordinator of the Program in Social Studies at Teachers College, Columbia University. She taught high school social studies for 8 years, as well as American Studies, Women's Studies, and American history at the college level. At Teachers College, where she has worked since 1993, she teaches a course called "Women of the World: Issues in Teaching," and "History of American Social Thought" the methods course, as well as doctoral and master's level seminars. Her research interests include gender, technology, and urban education as they relate to social studies.

S. G. Grant is Associate Professor of Social Studies Education in the Department of Learning and Instruction at the University of Buffalo. His research interests lie at the intersection of state curriculum and assessment policies and teachers' classroom practices, with a particular emphasis in social studies. In addition to publishing papers in both social studies and general education journals, he has published *History Lessons: Teaching, Learning, and Testing in High School Classrooms* (Erlbaum, 2003) and, most recently, *Measuring History: Cases of State-Level Testing Across the United States* (Information Age Publishing, 2006).

Carole L. Hahn is the Charles Howard Chandler Professor of Educational Studies at Emory University, where she teaches courses in social studies education and comparative education. She is also an Advisory Professor at the Hong Kong Institute of Education. Professor Hahn received the Jean Dresden Grambs Career Research Award from the National Council for the Social Studies in 2005. Earlier she received the Jubilee Prize of the Danish Secondary Teachers' Union for her book *Becoming Political: A Comparative Perspective on Citizenship Education* (State University of New York Press, 1998). She was the U.S. National Research Coordinator for the 30-nation Civic Education Study of the International Association for the Evaluation of Educational Achievement (IEDA). She is a past president of the National Council for the Social Studies.

Robert J. Helfenbein is Assistant Professor of Teacher Education at Indiana University-Purdue University Indianapolis, adjunct faculty in the Department of Geography, and a researcher in the Center for Urban and Multicultural Education in the School of Education. A former middle and high school social studies teacher, his current research interests include qualitative studies of youth and school with a focus on critical geography, cultural studies of education, urban education and youth culture, and contemporary curriculum theory.

Diana Hess is Associate Professor of Curriculum and Instruction at the University of Wisconsin-Madison. She teaches courses for undergraduate and graduate students in social studies education, social studies research, and democratic education. Since 1998 she has been researching what young people learn from deliberating highly controversial political and legal issues in schools.

Mark Hofer is an Assistant Professor of Educational Technology in the School of Education at the College of William and Mary. His research focuses on studying the effective integration of technology in K–12 social studies classrooms and working with teachers to develop their technological pedagogical content knowledge. He is the recipient of the National Technology Leadership Award in Social Studies Education co-sponsored by the College and University Faculty Assembly (CUFA) and the Society of Technology and Teacher Education (SITE) in 2005 and 2007. His research has appeared in the *Journal of Computing in Teacher Education, Social Studies and the Young Learner, The Social Studies, Contemporary Issues in Technology and Teacher Education,* and is the co-creator of the Historical Scene Investigation Project (www.hsionline.org) and the Digital Directors Guild (www.ddguild.org). He is also a contributing editor for *Social Studies Research and Practice.*

Steven L. Miller is Associate Professor of social studies and global education at The Ohio State University. Economic education is among Miller's areas of specialization. He started the Central Ohio Center for Economic Education at OSU in 1978, served as its director until 1993, and remains senior faculty associate of the center. Miller, a former teacher of high school economics and government, has considerable experience in instructional methodology and developing curriculum in the social studies, especially economics. Among his books are *Economic Education for Citizenship; Economics and National Security: Supplementary Lessons for High School Courses* (co-author and editor), and *Master Curriculum Guide, Part II: Teaching Strategies for High School Economics Courses* (co-author). His recent research interests include the relationship among citizenship, civics, and economics. In 2003, he was named a Social Studies Educator of the Year by the Ohio Council for the Social Studies. Miller played a key role in Education for Democratic Citizenship in Poland, a program to reform civic education in Poland undertaken by the Polish Ministry of National Education, the Open Society Foundation in Poland, and the Mershon Center. In a similar program, he twice led teams of academic specialists to Lithuania. Miller has also worked with educators in Bulgaria as part of an economic education program conducted by the Ministry of Education and the Universities of Delaware and Cincinnati. Miller has been one of the American Faculty in the National Council on Economic Education's Training of Trainers Program since 1996. This program has taken Miller to Moscow, St. Petersburg, Riga, Bishkek, Tashkent, Almaty, Bucharest, Kiev, and Minsk, among other cities. Miller has been to nations of the former Soviet Union and Central and Eastern Europe 41 times. Most recently as part of this program, Miller has worked in South Africa and Mexico.

Diem Nguyen is a Doctoral Candidate in the College of Education at the University of Washington, Seattle. She studies with Dr. James A. Banks. Her research focuses on immigrant youth's education and social adaptation.

Walter C. Parker is Professor of Education and adjunct professor of Political Science at the University of Washington in Seattle. He focuses on social studies education, civic education, and public-school curriculum politics. His books include *Social Studies in Elementary Education* (2005), *Teaching Democracy* (2003), *Education for Democracy* (2002), *Educating the Democratic Mind* (1996), and *Renewing the Social Studies Curriculum* (1991). He is the editor of the "Research and Practice" column for the journal, *Social Education.*

A. Yao Quashiga. Dr. Quashiga of the University of Education, Winneba (Ghana) was born at Keta in the Volta Region of Ghana to Edmun Nyaletashie Quashiga and Agnes Abia Atakpa—all of blessed memory. He was educated at Keta Secondary School. He obtained the Bachelor's Degree from the University of Cape Coast, Ghana, and holds a Master's Degree from Carleton University, Ottawa, Canada, and a Doctorate in Education from the University of Kentucky, Lexington. After serving at Winneba as Department Head, he is now a lecturer. He has published in the United States and Ghana on global education and social studies/environmental education.

Cinthia Salinas is Assistant Professor in Curriculum and Instruction at the University of Texas at Austin. Her research work in the social studies includes an examination of the use of teacher knowledge in high stakes testing contexts, which has appeared in S. G. Grant's *Measuring History* and most recently in *Anthropology and Education Quarterly*. In addition, her work addressing historical thinking opportunities in elementary bilingual/ESL classrooms and more critical multicultural approaches in high school social studies late arrival immigrant classrooms has been published in *Social Studies and the Young Learner, The Social Studies*, and *Multicultural Perspectives.*

Avner Segall is Associate Professor in the College of Education at Michigan State University. His research and teaching incorporate critical theory/pedagogy and cultural studies in order to critically examine education and its consequences. He is author of *Disturbing Practice: Reading Teacher Education as Text* (Peter Lang, 2002) and co-editor of *Social Studies— The Next Generation: Re-searching in the Postmodern* (Peter Lang, 2006).

Kathleen Owings Swan is an Assistant Professor of Social Studies Education at the University of Kentucky. She researches ways of effectively integrating technology into the K–12 social studies classroom. She is the recipient of the National Technology Leadership Award in Social Studies Education co-sponsored by the College and University Faculty Assembly (CUFA) and the Society of Technology and Teacher Education (SITE) in 2005, 2007, and 2008. Her research has appeared in the *International Journal of Social Education, Social Education, The Social Studies, Contemporary Issues in Technology and Teacher Education,* and is the co-author of the Historical Scene Investigation Project (www.hsionline.org) and the Digital Directors Guild (www.ddguild.org). She is also a contributing editor for *Social Studies Research and Practice.*

Stephen J. Thornton is Professor and Chair of the Department of Secondary Education at the University of South Florida. Thornton taught grades 7–12 social studies and English in an Australian boarding school for 6 years. He received his PhD from Stanford University. He is the author of *Teaching Social Studies That Matters: Curriculum for Active Learning* (Teachers College Press, 2005), which won a Readers' Choice award from the American Library Association, and co-editor of *The Curriculum Studies Reader*, (2nd ed.; Routledge, 2004). He is currently working on two new projects—one about geography in school programs and the other about teaching social studies to English Language Learners—as well as a new edition of the *Curriculum Reader.*

Phillip J. VanFossen is the James F. Ackerman Professor of Social Studies Education and Director of the Ackerman Center for Democratic Citizenship in the College of Education at Purdue University, where he teaches courses in elementary and secondary social studies education. He is also the Associate Director of the Purdue University Center for Economic Education (and holds a courtesy appointment in the Krannert School of Management at Purdue) where he teaches introductory economics courses for the Economics department. A former middle and high school social studies teacher, VanFossen is Chair of the Advisory Board of EconEdLink, the National Council on Economic Education's MarcoPolo online resource site. He has coauthored four curriculum monographs for the National Council on Economic Education. VanFossen serves on the editorial boards of three journals, is economics advisor for the Harcourt textbook series, *Horizons*, and is Consulting Editor for the Cobblestone publication, *Appleseeds*. He has published articles on Internet use and economic and social studies education in *Theory and Research in Social Education, Social Education, The International Journal of Social Education, The International Journal of Educational Media, The Senior Economist, The Southern Social Studies Journal* and *Economics for Kids*, and has twice been a guest editor for *Social Studies and the Young Learner*. His research interests include how social studies teachers use the Internet in their teaching, and in 2001 he co-authored *Using Internet Primary Sources to Teach Critical Thinking in Government, Economics and World Issues* (Greenwood Press). VanFossen also has an interest in the intersection between civic education and economic education and, since 1991, has conducted more than two dozen workshops and inservice training seminars and given numerous invited lectures on curriculum development and teacher training in economic education in eastern European and Baltic countries.

Stephanie van Hover is Associate Professor of Social Studies Education at the Curry School of Education of the University of Virginia. She serves as the program coordinator and faculty advisor for secondary social studies education. She teaches social studies methods courses at the secondary level as well as doctoral seminars. Formerly a teacher in Fort Lauderdale, Florida, she earned her doctorate in social studies education from the University of Florida. Her dissertation, a historical biography in curriculum history, examined Deborah Partridge Wolfe's contributions to social education. Her other research interests include the teaching and learning of history within a high-stakes teaching context as well as the professional development of history teachers. Reports of her research have been published in several books and journals, including *Theory and Research in Social Education, Journal of Social Studies Research, International Journal of Social Education,* and the *Social Studies Forum*.

Rahima Wade, EdD is Professor of Elementary Social Studies at The University of Iowa. Rahima has authored over 50 journal articles and four books on community-based social studies education. Rahima is the John Glenn Scholar for Service-Learning in Teacher Education, and she has served as project director for ten grants on community service-learning and civic education in social studies K–12 and teacher education.

Angene H. Wilson is Professor Emeritus at the University of Kentucky, where she worked with secondary social studies and served as Associate Director of International Affairs from 1990–1996. Her major area of research is the impact of international experience on students, teachers, and schools. She published articles in a number of journals, most recently in *The International Social Studies Forum* and *Theory Into Practice,* and a book, *The Meaning of International Experience for Schools* (Praeger, 1993). Among early Peace Corps volunteers, she taught history in Liberia from 1962–1964, later taught at teacher-training colleges in Sierra Leone and Fiji, and served as a Fulbright Scholar in Ghana in 1997.

Guichun Zong is Associate Professor in the Department of Secondary and Middle Grades Education at Kennesaw State University. Deeply influenced by her trips to the *USS Arizona* Memorial in Pearl Harbor; the Holocaust Museum in Washington, D. C.; the Nanjing Massacre Memorial in Nanjing, China; and the Hiroshima Peace Park of Japan, Dr. Zong's primary teaching and research interests are developing pedagogies that enhance cross-cultural communication and global understanding. She has published in such journals as *Social Education* and *Theory and Research in Social Education*.

Acknowledgments

We would like to thank the following reviewers for their careful readings and thoughtful responses to each chapter: Keith C. Barton (University of Cincinnati), Margaret Crocco (Teachers College, Columbia University), Merry Merryfield (Ohio State University), Stephen J. Thornton (University of South Florida), Stephanie van Hover (University of Virginia), O.L. Davis (University of Texas), John Lee (University of Georgia), Paulette Dillard (Auburn University), David Hicks, Patricia Avery (University of Minnesota), Letitia Finkel (University of Alaska), Geneva Gay (University of Washington), Judy Alston (Ashland University), Jeffrey Passe (UC Charlotte), Bev Armento (University of Georgia), Jean Craven (University of New Mexico), Lynn Boyle-Baise (Indiana University), and Elizabeth Yaeger (University of Georgia). In addition, we would like to thank Jane Arrington, graduate student at the University of Kentucky, for her able assistance throughout this project.

Finally, we are especially grateful to our editor, Naomi Silverman, whose patience and support made this book possible.

Preface

Social studies is the integrated study of the social sciences and humanities to promote civic competence. . . The primary purpose of social studies is to help young people develop the ability to make informed and reasoned decisions for the public good as citizens of a culturally diverse, democratic society in an interdependent world. (National Council for the Social Studies, 1994, vii)

In considering how a new *Handbook of Research in Social Studies Education* might be organized, we looked not only to the previous *Handbook of Research on Social Studies Teaching and Learning* (1991), but also to National Council for the Social Studies (NCSS) position statements, publications, and committee structures, to the arguments of critics and proponents of the field, and to the work of scholars who identify themselves with the field. We searched out definitions of social studies, statements of purpose, and themes that linked (or divided) theory, research, and practice. As the chapters that follow demonstrate, social studies is a complex, challenging, and largely under-researched field. Given its many disciplinary roots, competing perspectives about appropriate goals, and ongoing conflict over the content of the social studies curriculum, social studies will no doubt remain complex, challenging, and, one hopes, dynamic. It need not remain under-researched. We hope that this *Handbook* will not only outline the present state of things, but encourage the kind of new research needed to move the field forward and foster the civic competence that advocates for the social studies have long claimed as a fundamental goal of the field.

The *Handbook* includes chapters on areas of the social studies that met one or more of the following criteria:

- Research activity since the last *Handbook* warrants a new analysis.
- The topic represents a major emphasis in the NCSS standards.
- The topic represents an emerging or reemerging field within the social studies.

Given these criteria, we commissioned considerably fewer chapters than has been the case in the past. All chapters were reviewed by social studies scholars, and, in some cases, reviewers concluded that there was insufficient research to justify inclusion. The *Handbook* is divided into parts based on several broad themes.

Part I, Change and Continuity in Social Studies, includes a historic overview of social studies curriculum (Thornton); consideration of a historically neglected aspect of the social studies, primary education (Brophy & Alleman); and a review of current classroom practices (Levstik).

Part II, Civic Competence in Pluralist Democracies, is the largest section of the *Handbook*, including attention to civic education in national (Parker) and international (Hahn &

Alviar-Martin) contexts, service learning (Wade), democratic discourse (Hess), and multicultural education (Banks & Diem).

Part III, Social Justice and the Social Studies, includes an overview of research on social justice issues (Bickmore) as well as specific attention to gender and sexual orientation (Crocco) and global education (Zong, Wilson, & Guashiga).

Part IV, Assessment and Accountability, offers an overview of research on the impact of assessment and accountability at various levels of social studies teaching and learning (Grant & Salinas).

Part V, Teaching and Learning in the Disciplines, describes research on learning history (Barton), geography (Segall & Helfenbein), and economics (Miller & VanFossen).

Part VI, Information Ecologies: Technology in the Social Studies, provides an overview of research on information ecologies in school settings (Swan & Hofer).

Part VII, Teacher Preparation and Development, includes two chapters. The first examines research on teachers' preparation (Adler), and the second considers professional development for experienced teachers (van Hover).

The *Handbook* offers an overview of the state of social studies research. Because some areas of the social studies curriculum are so rarely the subject of investigation, however, they do not appear in this volume. New work in media and archaeology, for instance, suggests growth for the future. In the meantime, we hope that this volume provides useful information for beginning and experienced researchers in the field.

1 Introduction

Linda S. Levstik

University of Kentucky

Cynthia A. Tyson

The Ohio State University

In 1994, after decades of debate regarding the goals and purposes of social studies, the National Council for the Social Studies (NCSS) reiterated its commitment to civic competence as the "ability to make informed and reasoned decisions for the public good" in "a culturally diverse, democratic society...[and] interconnected world" (NCSS, 1994). While the 1994 definition briefly alludes to the place of "coordinated, systematic study drawing upon...traditional academic disciplines," the curriculum standards document developed to accompany the new definition organizes the field around themes (also identified as *strands*) rather than disciplines.[1] Most themes include organizing questions (i.e., "How can individual rights be protected within the context of majority rule?"), connections between organizing questions and civic competence, and grade-appropriate "performance expectations." Rather than offer one more in an almost endless supply of content standards, NCSS chose to shift focus "from content...to method" (p. 158). Accordingly, the "guiding vision" behind the standards places disciplinary content within a coherent citizen education curriculum engaging "students in the difficult process of confronting ethical and value-based dilemmas [encouraging] students to speculate, think critically, and make personal and civic decisions based on information from multiple perspectives" (p. 159). Citizenship goals and purposes rather than (though not exclusive of) disciplinary structures would guide curriculum planning. To this end, NCSS offered an addendum to their standards, a "vision of powerful teaching and learning in the social studies" (p. 156).

"Vision statements" in diffuse and relatively loosely-defined fields such as social studies offer some insight into the issues and questions with which scholars contend, and that is certainly the case here.[2] The NCSS (1994) statement defines some terms common to the field (social understanding, civic efficacy), attempts to clarify the civic purposes and goals of social studies, identifies "key features of ideal social studies teaching and learning" (p. 162) and outlines the conditions necessary for "developing and maintaining powerful social studies programs" (p. 171). Accordingly, powerful teaching and learning in the social studies would mean that

> teachers model fundamental democratic principles in their classrooms, discuss them as they relate to curriculum content and current events and make them integral to the school's daily operations....[S]ocial studies programs also prepare students to connect knowledge with beliefs and action using thinking skills that lead to rational behavior in social settings....[and] develop social and civic participation skills that prepare students to work effectively in diverse groups to address problems by discussing alternative strategies, making decisions, and taking action: To pursue social and civic agendas through persuasion, negotiation, and compromise; and to participate actively in civic affairs." (pp. 160–161)

1

Given the perspective outlined above, research in social studies might be expected to focus on connections among content, method, and civic behaviors with diverse populations and in international context, on the challenges of persuasion, negotiation, and compromise in various classroom and community settings, and on the complexities of active participation and rational behavior in civic affairs. As Daniel Pearlstein (1996) noted, community and democracy may both be worthy but not always overlapping educational goals. Community, for instance, is always somewhat ambiguous, marking borders and exclusions that create social inequalities on the one hand, and fostering citizen involvement and facilitating demands for justice on the other. Yet many social studies educators share the progressive ideal of a public school as a "hub, indeed engine, of democratic community life" (Pearlstein, 1996, p. 634). It is worth considering, then, what such a perspective illuminates or obscures, and the extent to which research might help us understand and, to the extent possible, work with its affordances and mitigate its constraints.

In a field whose goals include developing citizens who can draw on history and the social sciences to inform decision-making, we might also expect research to investigate the relationship between disciplinary ways of knowing and informed decision-making. And, given the emphasis on making decisions in an interdependent world, we might hope that research helps us understand how social studies might prepare globally responsible citizens. Saying that the world is interdependent has become so unremarkable as to be a cliché. Recognizing interdependence, however, offers little help in working across borders, sorting out local, national, and global interests, recognizing fundamental differences as well as similarities, or having enough information and understanding to participate intelligently and humanely in related decision making. What experiences prepare students to recognize others' perspectives, or encourage them to care enough to take others' perspectives into account, much less do so without abandoning individually or communally important social values (NCSS, p. 166)?

Finally, social studies exists within social, cultural, and political contexts where different aims and purposes take precedence or elicit controversy at different times. The National Council for the Social Studies may advocate for a particular version (or vision) of social studies, but alternative approaches arise in professional training and development programs, disciplinary standards, state assessment frameworks, and local interests (Adler, 1991; Grant, 2003; Segall, 2002). Scholarship in social studies has always included attention to these contending aims and interests. Indeed, one could argue that the field suffers from too much attention to defending itself against its critics and not enough to the kind of research that might help the field realize the lofty aims espoused by its proponents. The reviews of research included in this handbook suggest that without a firmer research base, social studies' educators' expressed intent will continue to exceed their empirical reach.

PROMOTING CIVIC COMPETENCE

To some extent, the research published in social studies journals between 1995 and 2007 reflects the emphases laid out by the National Council for the Social Studies. More articles in *Theory and Research in Social Education (TRSE)*, the primary research journal in the field, focus explicitly on aspects of civic education than on any other topic. The same holds true for social studies research published in general education journals such as *The American Educational Research Journal (AERJ)*, *Teachers College Record*, and the *Journal of Curriculum and Supervision*. As represented in these journals, research related to civic education falls into five broad categories. The first focuses on the development of civic ideas and inclinations within the United States' pluralist democracy. This body of work includes historical and philosophical studies as well as investigations of students' and teachers' civic attitudes and understandings and classroom practices within the United States. A second category investigates civic ideas, attitudes, and values in cross-national context. While scholarship in this category focuses largely on Western democracies, it provides insight into the impact of differing Western contexts on civic education and suggests interesting research possibilities in other parts of the world. A third category of scholarship concentrates on democratic discussion and decision making. Most studies in this category locate discussion and decision making in the context of engagement with controversial issues in the classroom and in the larger (usually national) society. Research in a fourth category falls under the rubric of "service learning"—an approach that seeks to ground civic action in informed, evidence-based decision making and includes studies of civic participation—activity (usually local) designed to enhance the "common good." Finally, a fifth category examines the connections between citizenship education, cosmopolitanism, and multicultural education.

Scholarship related to race, culture, and ethnicity appears regularly in social studies research journals as well as in general education journals. Between 1995 and 2007, for instance, three research journals, *TRSE, AERJ,* and *Teachers College Record* devoted a combined total of seven special issues or sections of their journals to some aspect of diversity, educating for multicultural competence, or race/ethnicity-based achievement gaps in the United States. In addition *Social Education* and *Social Studies* offered an array of articles and special issues devoted to aspects of teaching or learning about race, culture, and ethnicity. Despite this attention, empirical studies lag well behind theoretical and philosophical scholarship in the field. While a lack of research does not preclude fine teaching, curriculum development, or learning in individual instances, it certainly hinders informed decision-making in classrooms and in public policy. Perhaps this would not be as critical a weakness if research in other aspects of the social studies offered evidence regarding the differential impact of teaching and learning across populations. Unfortunately, as the reviews of research in this volume make clear, too few studies offer much help in this regard.

Again, there is considerable overlap across the categories in this section, but we commissioned separate chapters for each in order to do justice to their complexity as well as to their prominence in the social studies literature. Ultimately, civic competence develops in the context of particular and increasingly pluralist societies. Conceptions of race, class, gender, ethnicity, sexual orientation, religion, and region, among other "differences" challenge the old progressive/Deweyan notion of society as "a number of people held together because they are working along common lines, in a common spirit, and with reference to common aims" (Pearlstein, 1996, p. 632). Indeed, as Pearlstein (1996) argues, "issues of class conflict and racial exclusion are not unfortunate lapses that can be easily excised from progressive pedagogy. Rather, they are central to its formulation of activity, child-centeredness, culture, and democratic participation" (p. 645). As any number of critics argue, silence on issues of difference supports social inequities and undermines civic competence (see for instance, Banks, 1996; Bickmore, 2003; Boyle-Baise, 2004; Gay, 200; Ladson-Billings, 2001; and Thornton, 2005). What, then, can social studies scholarship contribute regarding the *plurality* of democratic citizenship?

We organized the third section of this volume around several categories of scholarship: research, theory, and philosophical arguments for educating for social justice, scholarship related to gender and sexual orientation, and, finally, scholarship related to global education. We recognize deep connections across these categories and with the Banks and Diem chapter in the previous section, deep divisions among them. The difficulties in finding language to describe the categories suggests that the boundaries between them are permeable and, in many ways, artificial. Yet each category raises different questions, uses distinctive theoretical lenses and calls us to think about distinctions that are too often lost when attending to *difference* as if it were a single, clearly defined, straight-forward category.

To some extent, everything we've discussed to this point represents attention to social justice and human rights. Indeed, we see social justice as an umbrella concept that links the strands of civic education, multicultural/cosmopolitan education, education about gender and sexual orientation, and global education. Conceptions of justice as *fairness* certainly resonate with students and might provide a beginning point in exploring the nature of social justice. On the other hand, distinguishing between equality and equity challenges almost everyone. Living in a pluralist democracy whose founding document declares life, liberty, and the pursuit of happiness *unalienable rights*, but whose history includes denying those rights at various times to various groups and individuals, challenges us to think carefully about what it means to teach for or about social justice. Over time, social studies educators have discussed, debated, and written position statements regarding social justice and human rights. The NCSS Curriculum Standards mention human rights in reference to global connections (p. xii), to individual rights (p. xi) and to civic ideals and practices (p. xii). More recently, after NCSS moved social justice from a separate committee to part of the committee on academic freedom, the College and University Faculty Assembly (CUFA), the research arm of NCSS, established a *Social Justice Committee* to offer some leadership in this area. Yet, as Kathy Bickmore points out in chapter 9 in this volume, scholarship leans more heavily towards advocacy than investigation. We know relatively little about teaching and learning about social justice, no matter how defined. What we do know, however, represents an important beginning point and raises interesting questions to consider for future scholarship, as Bickmore's chapter makes clear.

Scholarship related to gender and sexual orientation suffers from rather different issues than other issues of social justice. Between 1995 and 2007, articles focusing on gender appeared sixth most often in *TRSE*.[3] Prior to 1995, *TRSE* published at least one special issue focusing on gender; the first special issue on sexual orientation appeared in 2002. Beyond that issue, we could identify only two articles published in *TRSE* between 1995 and 2007 that included attention to sexual orientation, and in neither was sexual orientation the primary focus of the article. As Margaret Crocco points out in chapter 10, little of the scholarship on gender and sexual orientation from other fields makes its way into the social studies literature. We find this a curious omission given not only the rich work on gender and sexual orientation available in the disciplines that inform social studies, but the obvious relationship between these topics and NCSS themes, including *Individual Development and Identity* and *Power, Authority, and Governance*, for instance (NCSS, 1994). In fact, no mention of gender or sexual orientation appears in the descriptions of any themes. The performance expectations for *Individual Development and Identity* mention gender (but not sexual orientation) once each for middle and high school and not at all for elementary students. No other themes include either topic, nor do either appear in any of the examples of classroom practice. We should note here that performance expectations are written so that they *could* include gender and/or sexual orientation, but there is no attempt to make that connection clear, except, briefly, in the *Individual Development and Identity* expectations. A stronger research base might counter the silence on this area in the NCSS Curriculum Standards. Given current concern regarding male/female school performance, too, it would be useful to have a strong enough research base to inform proposed remedies for differential academic performance (see for instance, Gurian & Stevens, 2007; and Pollock, 1999).

TEACHING AND LEARNING IN THE DISCIPLINES

In a field whose goals include developing citizens who draw on history and the social sciences to inform decision-making, we might expect a rich array of research to support those goals. With the notable exception of history, this has not been the case. Between 1995 and 2007, social studies and general educational research journals published relatively little research on teaching or learning in particular social sciences. Most recently, attention to geography education seems to be increasing among geographers and social studies researchers (see Bednarz, 2000, 2004, 2006). Most of this work has appeared in journals outside of social studies education. In fact, in the last decade *TRSE* published only two articles reporting research in this area, but an increase in research presentations on geography at professional meetings and a spurt of research since 2000 bodes well for an area Segall and Helfenbein describe in chapter 14 as fundamental to understanding and acting responsibly in the world.

Economics presents a rather different problem. As Miller and VanFossen note in chapter 15, research on teaching and learning economics appears in a number of outlets outside of social studies. In the last two decades, however, only one article reporting research on economic education appeared in *TRSE*. Interestingly, general social studies journals (*Social Education, Social Studies*) offer a wide array of articles suggesting teaching strategies and resources for economics education (variously defined), state and national funding and a variety of private interest groups support professional development efforts, and the *National Assessment of Education Progress* (*NAEP*) now tests for economic literacy, yet surprisingly few reports of research appear in social studies journals. While economics may not attract much interest among social studies researchers, it remains a high-profile field for researchers outside the social studies, for curriculum developers, policy makers, and test developers. Once again, social studies education could benefit from increased research attention to this high-profile discipline.

Only a trickle of research informs our understanding of teaching and learning in other social sciences. Here, too, practitioner-oriented journals offer an array of teaching strategies intended to teach social science concepts but, overall, we know relatively little about students' concept formation, about the impact of recommended teaching practices, or about the connections between teaching, learning, and personal or civic decision-making. Recent research on primary children's thinking regarding "cultural universals" makes an important contribution in this regard, as Jere Brophy & Janet Alleman point out in chapter 3 on primary social studies, and this research suggests rich possibilities for inquiry in other settings. This work is especially important if social studies is to maintain any kind of presence in schools prior to fourth or fifth grade (Rock et al 2003).

A handful of recent work in archaeology also suggests some increase in interest in this area, more often tied to history than to anthropology, however (Davis, 2005; Levstik, Henderson, & Schlarb, 2005; Smith, McManamon, & United States National Park Service, 1991). At present, archaeology education more often appears as extra curricular work or in programs for "gifted and talented" students than as a regular feature of social studies education. Revisions in archaeology education programs, meanwhile, mark increasing attention to the relationship between archaeological and historical literacy, and to how to more effectively integrate archaeological ways of knowing into the social studies curriculum.[4] Given the high priority of multicultural education within the social studies, it is interesting that archaeology and anthropology, so focused on culture, receive so little attention in the curriculum or from educational researchers. Despite a lack of research attention to teaching or learning in anthropology, however, social studies researchers continue to adapt anthropological research techniques to educational questions. Indeed, "naturalistic" and "quasi-naturalistic" research methodologies continue to dominate the research literature in social studies, although mixed methodology studies appear to be on the increase (see Barton, 2005).

Given the importance of history and the social sciences to the aims of social studies education, the field requires a richer, deeper research base across the disciplines. In this regard, the rapid growth of research in history education can be informative. We know more about teaching and learning history than any of the other social sciences. History is the second most common subject of social studies research—just behind civic education. Between 1995 and 2007, *TRSE* published close to 40 studies[5] related to history education, and additional history-related research appeared in other national and international educational research journals. During the same period, articles about teaching and learning history dominated other social studies journals as well. *The Social Studies*, for instance, published more than 45 articles related to history research and (more commonly) history teaching. In addition to a steady stream of articles on history teaching and learning, the *International Journal of Social Studies* published a special issue on research on historical thinking in 2006. In the United States, the *American Historical Association* and the *Organization of American Historians* offered special sessions at their annual meetings as well as publications reporting research and suggesting strategies aimed at improving collegiate and pre-collegiate history education.

Relative to other social sciences, national history in the United States is a high-profile discipline—assessed by *NAEP*, currently funded through the Teaching American History (TAH) grant initiative, subjected to legislative scrutiny, media attention, and public controversy.[6] Public schools commonly teach national history at elementary, middle, and secondary levels and most states mandate some form of state history at one or more of these levels. Given the emphasis on national history, a degree of scholarly attention should not be surprising. Interestingly, however, the wealth of available scholarship on history is relatively recent. In the 1991 *Handbook on Research in Social Studies*, Downey and Levstik described the then-current research base as thin—more suggestive than definitive. As Keith Barton's chapter in this volume makes clear, that is no longer the case. Interestingly, though, research in history education exploded despite relatively little federal funding (the recent TAH grants program primarily funds professional development for K–12 teachers, not research).

Why other disciplines have not managed similar growth is puzzling. The historical and current prevalence of history (as opposed to other social sciences) in the K–12 curriculum probably accounts for some of the difference, but perhaps equally significantly, history education attracts an international audience. While not all countries include social studies in their curriculum, and some define it very differently than do U. S. educators, just about everyone studies history at some point in their schooling (Barton & Levstik, 2004; Grant, 2003). In consequence, researchers can more easily consider the influence of different local, national, and international contexts on history teaching and learning. Cross-national work fosters a rich and varied dialogue about the nature of historical thinking, about effective curriculum development, pedagogy, and assessment, and about the relationship between history education and participatory citizenship in national and international contexts (see Barton, chapter 14, this volume). Rapid communication, fostered in large measure by the Internet, coupled with relatively easy travel also makes it easier for scholars to establish and maintain international collaborations.

Similar opportunities obtain in other disciplines within social studies, most notably in geography, as Segal and Helfenbein point out. Federal funding has long supported professional development in geography and economics, suggesting that a core of experienced teachers might be interested in collaborative research opportunities. Indeed, researchers have begun to build a critical mass of scholarship related to teaching and learning in several social sciences, often working outside of the social studies. Geographers and economists have been interested in research on pre-collegiate teaching and learning for some time now and, as the work reported in this volume suggests, collaboration between social studies educators and other social scientists has produced interesting scholarship. Similar collaborative efforts with other social scientists require relatively low start-up costs but offer significant benefits for social studies research.

SOCIAL STUDIES CURRICULUM AND ASSESSMENT

Linda Darling-Hammond and John Bransford (2005) describe social studies as an "extreme" case of curricular diffusion. Social studies educators' long-lasting discussion regarding the scope, sequence, and purpose of social studies means that generalizations about the field can be elusive. Is social studies an umbrella term for disciplinary study in history and the social sciences? A review of course offerings in many middle and high schools would support such a conclusion. Since 1995 *TRSE* published 12 articles specifically addressing social studies curriculum, most in reference to teaching a particular social science discipline. Or, perhaps social studies more closely approximates an integrated study drawing on history and the social sciences to investigate "the individual and social demands of associated living" (see Thornton, chapter 2, this volume). Examining some elementary curriculum plans might suggest this as an apt description of social studies, but enough variation exists between and within grade levels, across regions, and from one moment to the next to belie such easy assumptions. This is particularly the case in regard to elementary classrooms where, as Brophy and Alleman explain in this volume, children may encounter social studies only as a content vehicle for some other subject—usually reading. Further complicating the curricular picture, teachers may implement mandated curricula as inquiry, as single or competing narratives, or as compendia of information, among other approaches.

We commissioned two chapters focused on curricular issues. In the first chapter, Stephen J. Thornton provides a historical analysis of social studies curriculum, arguing that social studies educators continually juggle competing demands for continuity and reform. While a cursory review of other analyses of the social studies curriculum highlights the consistency with which the scope, sequence, aims and purposes of the field are described as unclear, diffuse, or atypical (see Darling-Hammond & Bransford, 2005), Thornton offers a different perspective, noting historical patterns that belie the assumption that social studies too often drifts among diffuse aims and purposes. Thornton's broad analysis of social studies curriculum is paired with a more specific case study of primary social studies. Squeezed for space in a school day largely devoted to literacy and mathematics, primary social studies too often either disappears or devolves into a pastiche of holiday celebrations and national myths and legends with occasional forays into reinforcing socially acceptable behaviors. As a consequence, primary social studies represent the most fragile portion of the social studies curriculum—easily ignored, omitted or reduced to insignificance. *Social Studies and the Young Learner* marks one attempt by NCSS to bolster elementary social studies, but relatively few articles in the journal report empirical research. Over the period from 1995 to 2007 the research journal, *TRSE*, averaged only slightly over one article per year reporting research on primary or elementary social studies. In chapter 3, Brophy and Alleman review the current state of primary social studies and offer an alternative to the status quo based on research on young children's conceptions of "cultural universals."

A small body of research examines social studies classroom practices across grade levels. *NAEP* data suggests that textbook-based instruction predominates, but Levstik (chapter 4) notes that we really know very little about predominant patterns in regard to classroom climate, pedagogical techniques employed or resources used in social studies classroom. Researchers in different areas of the social studies certainly describe class-rooms where students engage in interesting and intellectually challenging work with social studies content, or where social studies content seems to be disappearing from the curriculum, but we have few longitudinal or large-scale studies that might help us trace patterns of adoption, use, or persistence over time of various instructional approaches.

High-stakes assessments and No Child Left Behind (NCLB) legislation drive cur-riculum and instruction in many schools and classrooms in the United States. Indeed, assessments not only drive instruction, they often determine whether any instruction occurs at all. Where untested, social studies too often ends up untaught (Rock et al., 2003). If testing ensures inclusion, then what kinds of assessments encourage what kinds of teaching and learning? How can educators use (or work around) high-stakes assess-ment to ensure high-quality instruction in social studies? Given the power of assessment in the current political context of schooling, we might expect more research attention to this area. Unfortunately, as Grant and Salinas (chapter 12) suggest, "a well-conceived, well-supported theory specific to social studies assessment and accountability has yet to surface." Their review of the research raises interesting questions about what such a theory might include, how it, too, might be assessed, and how teachers might use assess-ment in constructive ways.

INFORMATION ECOLOGIES

Imagine human experience separate from technologies. From flint knapping to text messaging, technologies mediate human interaction with and adaptation to the environ-ment. Yet conversations about technology too often focus on access to and the use of specific tools rather than on what Nardi and O'Day (1999) call *information ecologies* or systems of people, practices, values, and technologies situated in particular local environments. Thinking about a classroom, for instance, as an information ecology focuses less on a particular tool and more on the human activities served by that tool in specific local contexts. Nardi & O'Day (1999) argue that an ecological metaphor serves in important ways. First:

> An ecology responds to local environmental changes and local interventions. An ecology is a place that is scaled to individuals. We can all name the ecologies we belong to and participate in. In an ecology, we are not cogs in sweeping sociological processes. Instead, we are individuals with real relationships to other individuals. The scale of an ecology allows us to find individual points of leverage, ways into the system, and avenues of intervention. (p. 2)

Second, "there is an urgency in the notion of ecology, because we all are aware of the possibility of ecological failure due to environmental destruction" (p. 6).

Educators' sense of urgency in regard to technology, their concern that tools and technologies might destroy classroom environments is, Nardi and O'Day suggest, well-placed. The pace of change requires constant adaptation, constant decision-making about what technologies to employ and to what ends, and a constant and often steep learning curve if educators are to develop and maintain classrooms as healthy informa-tion ecologies.

The NCSS theme, *Science, Technology, & Society*, addresses information ecologies as a field of study for K–12 students:

> Young children can learn how technologies form systems and how their daily lives are intertwined with a host of technologies... By the middle grades, students can

begin to explore the complex relationships among technology, human values, and behavior... [and high school students] will need to think more deeply about how we can manage technology so that we control it rather than the other way around.[7] (p. 28)

Given this emphasis on information ecology, we commissioned a chapter examining the research base for building ecologies whose aims and goals relate to social studies teaching and learning. Researchers might focus on a system itself, on diversity within a system, on key elements of the ecology, or on adaptation, but some social studies content or purpose had to motivate the study.

As Swan and Hofer (chapter 16) note in their chapter in this volume, attention to technology use in social studies education increased between 1995 and 2006. As has been the case with so many of the themes outlined in the NCSS standards, however, the body of published work leans more heavily towards advocacy and practical use suggestions than to investigations of the information ecologies themselves. Given the relative recency of attention to technology in social studies, this probably should not be surprising. As the various reviews of research in this volume point out, however, other long-standing themes within social studies have not advanced much beyond advocacy. It is heartening then, to note an increase in research related to technology and especially an increase in studies examining the complexity of information ecologies where social studies aims and purposes are "keystone species."

TEACHER DEVELOPMENT

Linda Darling-Hammond and John Bransford (2005) pose three questions intended to guide the preparation of teachers "equipped to help all students achieve to their greatest potential" (p. 2):

1. What kinds of *knowledge* do effective teachers need to have about their subject matter and about the learning processes and development of their students?
2. What *skills* do teachers need in order to provide productive learning experiences for a diverse set of students, to offer informative feedback on students' ideas, and to critically evaluate their own teaching practices and improve them?
3. What *professional commitments* do teachers need to help every child succeed and to continue to develop their own knowledge and skills, both as individuals and as members of a collective profession (pp. 2–3)?

Well-prepared teachers, they explain, become "adaptive experts," adding to their knowledge, skills, and professional commitments over the course of their teaching careers. While professional development must be sustained over time to ensure increasing expertise at addressing students' needs, all teachers, they argue, must be prepared "to serve adequately the very *first* students they teach" (Darling-Hammond & Bransford, 2005, p. 3). Thornton (2005) suggests, too, that teachers' role as curricular-instructional gatekeepers, daily enacting curriculum, necessitates careful attention to how teachers view the purposes of their teaching. Along with Darling-Hammond and Bransford, Thornton argues that initial preparation must lay the foundation for *immediate* as well as career-long high-quality practice.

Social studies presents particular problems in regard to professional development. As Stodolsky and Grossman (1995) note, the field is more loosely structured than, say, mathematics. Not only does social studies require some degree of subject matter expertise across several disciplines, but its aims and purposes are contested and may not be broadly shared nor fully understood by many practitioners. Students seem equally confused, expressing interest in social studies topics, but rating the subject poorly in relation to other school subjects (Thornton, 2005). Perhaps, as John Goodlad (1984) argued, social studies loses just what appeals to students—its "intrinsically human character"—as it enters the classroom. Drawing a relationship between social studies' loose structure and student disinterest, Thornton (2005) suggests that "because the proper scope and sequence of social studies is less apparent" to educators and curriculum developers it too often degenerates "into a flood of information" rather than coherent, substantive academic engagement (p. 5). Under these circumstances, empirically based initial preparation and professional development would seem especially important for social studies teachers, and both are reflected in professional journals as well as the NCSS curriculum standards. Given the distinct but equally important goals of initial preparation and later professional development, then, we commissioned separate chapters to address the research in each area. Susan Adler revisits work on initial preparation begun in her chapter in the last *Handbook* (Shaver, 1991). Stephanie van Hover considers career-long professional development, noting that "diffusion" marks professional development in much the same ways that it does other aspects of teaching and learning social studies. Both suggest that professional development could benefit from more focused research so that all students could be assured competent teachers who become increasing expert over the course of their careers.

CONCLUSION

Any review of social studies research captures a moment in time—not a beginning or an end—but an extension of a conversation among educators. Because social studies has been more loosely defined and has a more tenuous foothold in the schools than some fields, a solid research base is crucial to informed deliberation about the goals and purposes of teaching and learning in the field. At present the research base continues to be uneven, characterized by gaps where we can say little to nothing about how children and adolescents learn, how teachers conceptualize their work, or how they operationalize their conceptions, but also by areas of intense scrutiny. Contributors to this volume highlight this high-quality work, often accomplished despite underfunding, a shrinking presence in some schools, and very public conflicts over the nature and purpose of the field and its related disciplines. They also point out the places where advocacy outmatches evidence, where initial findings need further investigation, and where theory development is needed. The breadth of the social studies—all of time and the entire world—means that social studies educators face considerable challenges in building a coherent research base. This can result in paralyzing impossibility or invigorating possibility. Overall, we hope that this volume supports the latter by critically examining existing work and suggesting useful directions for novice as well as experienced social studies researchers.

NOTES

1. The 10 themes that form the framework of the social studies standards as outlined in *Expectations of Excellence* (1994) are: Culture; Time, Continuity, and Change; People, Places, and Environments; Individual Development and Identity; Individuals, Groups, and Institutions; Power, Authority and governance; Production, Distribution, and Consumption; Science, Technology, and Society, Global Connections, and Civic Ideals and Practices. While particular academic disciplines may be emphasized in a theme, most are presented as cutting across disciplinary boundaries. It should be noted here that the themes are currently under revision.

2. For a more complete discussion of the impact of ill-defined subject matter on curricular activity, see Stodolsky and Grossman (1995).
3. We categorized articles by reviewing titles and abstracts. It is likely that more articles dealt with gender than such a review might imply, but titles and abstracts suggest the relative importance that scholars attached to gender in their research. Based on titles and abstracts, the most common topics published in *TRSE* were, in descending order: civic education, history teaching and learning, diversity, teacher development, technology, gender, and teaching and learning in elementary social studies. Other topics appeared considerably less often (five or fewer times in a 10-year period).
4. Newly revised to put more emphasis on concept development, Project Archaeology curriculum materials are currently being field tested (J. Moe, personal communication, October 25, 2006).
5. Other research in *TRSE* may not have mentioned history in the title or abstract but may have included history as part of a broader focus on social studies, so the number reported here may underrepresent the emphasis on history.
6. In 2006, for instance, the Florida legislature mandated a history curriculum devoid of interpretation, declaring that historical study should stick to "facts" rather than interpretation. Other state legislatures have mandated or banned an array of historical topics and argued over labels given to historical places or events. For a discussion of some of these issues, see Leigh Neihardt (2006).
7. The idea that human/technology interaction could be one-way (humans control technologies or technologies control humans) is, we suggest, a limited conception of the role of technology in human experience. For further discussion from different disciplinary perspectives, see Ian Hodder (2002), Bonnie Nardi and Vicki O'Day (1999), Michael Schiffer (1995), and James Wertsch (1998).

REFERENCES

Adler, S. A. (1991). The education of social studies teachers. In J. Shaver (Ed.), *Handbook of research on social studies teaching and learning* (pp. 197–209). New York: Macmillan.

Banks, J. A. (1996). *Multicultural education, transformative knowledge and action: Historical and contemporary perspectives.* New York: Teachers College Press.

Barton, K.C. (2005). Primary sources in history: Breaking through the myths. *Phi Delta Kappan, 86,* 745–753.

Barton, K. C., & Levstik, L. S. (2004). *Teaching history for the common good.* Mahwah, NJ: Erlbaum.

Bickmore, K. (2003). Conflict resolution education: Multiple options for contributing to just and democratic peace. In W. Pammer & J. Killian (Eds.), *Handbook of conflict management.* Marcel-Dekker.

Bednarz, R. S. (2006). Environmental research and education in US Geography. *Journal of Geography in Higher Education, 30*(2), 237–50.

Bednarz, R. S., & Bednarz, S. W. (2004). Geography Education: The glass is half full and it's getting fuller. *The Professional Geographer, 56*(1), 22–27.

Bednarz, S. W. (2000). Geography education research in the *Journal of Geography,* 1988–1997. *International Research in Geographical and Environmental Education, 9*(2), 128–140.

Boyle-Baise, M. (2004). *Multicultural service learning: Educating teachers in diverse communities.* New York: Teachers College Press.

Darling-Hammond, L., & Bransford, J. (Eds.) (2005). *Preparing teachers for a changing world: What teachers should learn and be able to do.* San Francisco: Jossey-Bass.

Davis, M. E. (2005). *How students understand the past: From theory to practice.* Lanham, MD: AltaMira Press.

Hodder, I. (2002). *Archaeological theory today.* Cambridge: Polity Press.

Gay, G. (2000). *Culturally responsive teaching: Theory, practice, and research.* New York: Teachers College Press.

Goodlad, J. (1984). *A place called school.* New York: McGraw-Hill.

Grant, S. G. (2003). *History lessons: Teaching, learning, and testing in U.S. high school classrooms.* Mahwah, NJ: Erlbaum.

Gurian, M., & Stevens, K. (2007). *The minds of boys: Saving our sons from falling behind in school and life.* San Francisco: Jossey-Bass.

Ladson-Billings, G. (2001). *Crossing over to Canaan: The journey of new teachers in diverse classrooms.* San Francisco: Jossey-Bass.

Levstik, L. S., Henderson, A. G., & Schlarb, J. (2005). Digging for clues: An archaeological exploration of historical cognition. In R. Ashby, P. Gordon, & P. Lee (Eds.), *The International Review of History Education* (vol. 4, pp. 37–53). London: Taylor and Francis.

Nardi, B. A., & O'Day, V. L. (1999). Information ecologies: Using technology with heart. *First Monday.* Retrieved November 19, 2006, from: http://www.firstmonday.org/issues/issue4_5/nardi_chapter4.html

National Council for the Social Studies (NCSS) (1994). *Expectations of excellence: Curriculum standards for social studies.* Washington, DC: Author.

Neihardt, L. A. (October, 2006). Florida Legislation Mandates How to Teach History, *Academe.* Retrieved November 19, 2006, from: http://www.aaup.org/AAUP/pubsres/academe/2006/SO/NB/Florida+Legislation+Mandates+How+to+Teach+History.htm

Pearlstein, D. (1996). Community and democracy in American schools: Arthurdale and the Fate of progressive education. *Teachers College Record, 97*(4), 625–650.

Pollock, W. (1999). *Real boys : Rescuing our sons from the myths of boyhood.* New York: Owl Books.

Segall, A. (2002). *Disturbing practice: Reading teacher education as text.* New York: Peter Lang.

Shaver, J. P. (1991). *Handbook of research on social studies teaching and learning.* New York: Macmillan.

Schiffer, M. (1995). *Behavioral archaeology: First principles.* University of Utah Press.

Smith, S., & McManamon, F. P. (1991). *Intrigue of the past: Investigating archaeology. A teacher's activity guide for fourth through seventh grades.* Washington, DC: United States Department of the Interior, Bureau of Land Management.

Stodolsky, S., & Grossman, P. (1995). **The impact of subject matter on curricular activity: An analysis of five academic subjects.** *American Educational Research Journal, 32*(2), 227–249.

Thornton, S. J. (2005). *Teaching social studies that matters: Curriculum for active learning.* New York: Teachers College Press.

Wertsch, J. (1998). *Mind as action.* Oxford: Oxford University Press.

Part I

Continuity and change in social studies

2 Continuity and change in social studies curriculum

Stephen J. Thornton

University of South Florida

Since the social studies curriculum holds potential to shape young peoples' world views, there has always been pressure to preserve this or change that. Accounting for continuity and change, however, depends on how one defines what one wants to preserve or change as well as how deeply one looks. Care is therefore imperative in defining what we mean by *social studies* and specifying at what level we look for continuity or change. It could also be that continuity, which may lack obvious drama, attracts less attention than change (Cuban, 1979, p. 175). But this may not translate into continuity being any the less significant for explaining what has happened to the social studies curriculum (hereafter, *curriculum*).

A key proviso to note about continuity and change is that curriculum reformers invariably conceive plans that are, in Herbert Kliebard's (1995) words, "more ambitious and grandiose than one could possibly expect in practice." The diffusion of these ideas, however, may still be broader than the limited number of sites where they are adopted in their entirety. They may also be incorporated "within the existing framework of the curriculum" (p. ix) or, I would add, their influence may have spread via teacher education programs. Moreover, while a curriculum specifies aims and a framework for its accomplishment, aims can be realized through a variety of means, and a framework is a general plan, not a script.

In this chapter I explore curriculum continuity and change as it is manifest in different "curriculum ideologies" (Eisner, 2002) . But at the same time I recognize that continuity and change coexist insofar as new ideas are typically incorporated into existing curricular arrangements. In practice, wholesale substitution of one curriculum scheme for another has been rare. This makes it important to describe exactly what we mean by one curriculum ideology or another; otherwise discussion can be at cross-purposes.

THE MEANINGS OF SOCIAL STUDIES AND OF CHANGE

In the United States social studies is a course of study taught in elementary and secondary schools that is concerned particularly with geography, history, and civics (Parker, 1991, p. v). Harold Rugg (1941) noted that "all the materials that have to do with how people live together" (p. 194) are the proper subject matters of social studies (see also Marshall & Goetz, 1936, p. 2; National Education Association, 1994, p. 9); John Dewey (1944) observed along the same lines that the individual social studies, such as geography and history, "are only emphases in a common topic, namely, the associated life of men" (p. 211). But, so defined, what should the curriculum contain—that is,what should be taught to whom, when, and in what order?

More particularly, is education for associated life best accomplished through emphasis on the traditional academic subjects, what I call a *social science* view of social studies? Or, while drawing on the disciplines where appropriate, should disciplinary boundaries be disregarded to focus directly on the individual and societal dimensions of associated life, what I call a *social education* view? Since the birth of the social studies field in the opening decades of the 20th century, curriculum planners have gone back and forth in how they have answered these questions (Thornton, 2005). Teachers of the social studies, too, seem divided about which position is sounder (National Commission on Social Studies in the Schools, 1991, p. 4).

Some educators (e.g., Evans, 2004) have portrayed struggles over the curriculum, in effect struggles over continuity and change, as "wars"; insofar as this is an apt metaphor, there has been no clear victor. Rather the fortunes of social science and social education (and whatever ideologies they have carried with them at various times, of which more below) have waxed and waned depending on the era in question, the level of schooling considered, whether the school serves the privileged or the poor, and so forth. By the opening years of the 21st century, neither view had secured a monopoly on the K–12 social studies curriculum.

Significantly, it seems a mistake to look for a simple pattern of one view ascendant, followed by the other view ascendant (Thornton, 2004). Most minds do not seem to change that much. Rather, what seem like big swings of the "pendulum" may represent little more than policies or problems that temporarily secure attention and possibly return in hybrid form some years later (Beyer, 1994; Hertzberg, 1971; Muessig, 1987; J. J. White, 1988). Nel Noddings (2005) captures one variant of this theme:

> When things are too discipline-centered, traditional, and teacher-centered, progressives hope for a swing of the pendulum toward more flexible, present-oriented, and child-centered ways. When that has been accomplished (or threatens to be accomplished), traditional thinkers hope and work for a swing that will return schools to the discipline-centered ways they prefer. Swings of the pendulum have rarely represented changes in minds and hearts, except in the case of a few students in teacher education; the changes have been and can only be shifts in power. (p. xiv)

In this chapter, my analysis of curriculum continuity and change dwells on the *official* curriculum—that is, the curriculum devised in advance by authorities beyond the classroom, which is intended to guide curricular-instructional gatekeepers (Thornton, 1991), normally teachers, in planning and implementing instructional programs. As gatekeepers, teachers actively shape an instructional program. Teachers can and do interpret what counts as successful passage through the gate, open the gate wide or narrow, based on what they believe students can or should profit from on the other side, allow innovation through or block it based on their estimation of its educational or practical worth, and so forth. Communities, students, educational publishers, and administrators, as well as other entities, also serve as gatekeepers (see Ross, 1997). But while it exerts an influence on all dealt with here, gatekeeping is not my dominant concern in this chapter.

Rather I focus on items one to four of what the National Council for the Social Studies' first curriculum bulletin (Michener, 1939) identified as the *six principal problems* to be addressed in designing a comprehensive program in social studies education: (1) deciding on objectives, (2) constructing courses, (3) selecting and arranging materials, (4) determining what methods to use, (5) preparing teachers, and (6) evaluation of the foregoing (p. 1). The content of this chapter, therefore, overlaps with the topics of curriculum diffusion (e.g., Turner & Haley, 1975), instruction (Cuban, 1991), and systematic studies of classroom activity structures (Stodolsky, 1988), but it is not interchangeable with any of those topics.

The evidence on the official curriculum is easier to trace than the evidence on what happens to it in and beyond classrooms. Analysis of the latter mostly relies on observation and interview studies, from which the evidence is "spotty" (Cuban, 1991, p. 198). Reliance on the official curriculum—based on sources such as the diffusion of textbooks, survey data, school site visits, and prescribed curricula—presents a more definitive view of curriculum continuity and change than it is possible to reconstruct about what occurs in classrooms. But this definitiveness, it should not be forgotten, comes at the expense of assuming that official curriculum actually reached the classroom level. This can be misleading, as many innovations scarcely affect day-to-day classroom routines (Shaver, 1979). Moreover, the ways in which the same curriculum can be interpreted vary widely (Grant & Gradwell, 2005; Stodolsky, 1999; Thornton, 2006).

Still there is a long research tradition that assumes the official curriculum as revealed by surveys, for instance, tells us what people are thinking about it (Smith, 1986, p. 28) and thus provides useful perspectives on curriculum patterns (e.g., Gross, 1951, 1977; Hahn, 1985; Weiss, 1978). Similarly textbook analysis shows what opportunities for content and method are likely to be available in schools (Palmer, 1965; Wade, 1993). Analyses of textbooks have been a special favorite as textbooks have been, and still are, regarded as the main source of social studies instruction. These analyses can, then, reveal webs of meaning that otherwise may not be apparent (e.g., Anyon, 1983; Billington, 1966; Elson, 1964; FitzGerald, 1979; Foster & Nicholls, 2005; Herz, c. 1978; Moreau, 2003; Walworth, 1938).

Largely restricting attention to the official curriculum may simplify matters, but it by no means implies it is unchallenging to track continuity and change. For one thing, there are diverse and potentially contradictory influences on the official curriculum—some of which should be apparent below. Furthermore, researchers have frequently employed inconsistent units of analysis in their studies of change. For example, if we take the larger amount of space now (e.g., Clark, Allard, & Mahoney, 2004; Clark, Ayton, Frechette, & Keller, 2005) devoted to women in textbooks relative to 40 or more years ago, we might conclude there has been positive change in the direction of gender equity. But other indicators suggest the opposite. For example, if we took how much time and attention boys often receive relative to girls in the enacted curriculum of classrooms, we might see continuity in how girls are "shortchanged " (American Association of University Women, 2004; Beard & Beard, 1921, p. vi).

In the remainder of this chapter, I first analyze the character of the social science and social education positions, attempting to explicate their principles and problems. Then I explore two illustrative eras—roughly from the 1920s till around World War II and from the late 1950s till the early 1970s—when one position or the other enjoyed special visibility, not necessarily ascendance in practice, and describe what it looked like. Exploration of these two eras also reveals how fragmentary the evidence is and, hence, may suggest to readers questions for further research. For example, rather than merely asking did the New Social Studies movement (see below) succeed or fail, we could ask what it looked like. Where did it spread? At what levels did it change things? I conclude that neither continuity nor change has prevailed in the curriculum and perhaps neither will, which seems to imply we need to live with curricular compromises.

SOCIAL STUDIES AS SOCIAL SCIENCE

As noted, history, geography, and civics or government have traditionally been the mainstay social studies; however, economics, sociology, anthropology, psychology, current events or problems, and even archaeology have also been offered. This deceptively straightforward descriptive statement is often taken to mean that the curriculum should consist of what scholars in each of the social science fields currently judge significant. But, as Dorothy Fraser (1962) once pointed out, "It is frequently hard for the scholar to understand that, even it were desirable to do so, his discipline cannot be given the kind of development that he considers minimal because of the limited amount of school time available for the entire social studies field" (p. 73). Moreover, current scholarship could yield a virtually unlimited number of instructional programs (see Thornton, 2005, p. 31).

The difficulties of devising school curriculum from the disciplines in higher education were thrown into relief during national standards-making in the 1990s. For example, while the historical profession vigorously defended the history standards from neoconservative assault, its defense boiled down to the standards being based upon the best recent historical scholarship. The historical profession does not appear to have questioned "that its work over recent decades" (Nash, Crabtree, & Dunn, 1997, p. 238) was the rightful centerpiece for formulating educational aims and for teacher education (see also Symcox, 2002). Lauren Sosniak (1999) has asked, however, "Is there any good reason to constrain the possibilities of K–12 education because the order created for 'disciplines of knowledge' at the post-secondary level is useful at that level?" (pp. 190–191). Even in higher education, organizing knowledge into the traditional disciplines is increasingly questioned. For instance, the dean of Columbia's School of International and Public Affairs (Anderson, 2003) noted that, by the end of the 20th century, researchers expressed "growing qualms about the utility" of the "disciplinary templates" (p. 53) as they "were as much artifacts of university departmental organization as they were genuine research traditions" (p. 37).

Even when the disciplines are accepted on faith as the building blocks of the curriculum, major questions remain unanswered. For example, the boundaries of the social sciences are not always clearly delineated in the school curriculum, such as in, say, the combination of a civics and U. S. history in one course. To make matters still more complicated, it is questionable whether civics *is* an academic subject or discipline, as it has frequently drawn on other disciplines, such as economics and sociology, as well as its presumed base, government or political science (Hertzberg, 1981, p. 2). What is more, does a disciplinary approach imply scarcely more than a number of currently significant topics, as sometimes seen in course syllabi issued by states, or does it imply we should teach the structure of the social science in question, as during the New Social Studies movement of the 1960s (Schwab, 1968)?

But whatever form courses primarily organized around one or more social science do take, clearly they have always been justified by claims that they serve purposes beyond the academic content and methods of the disciplines themselves. For example, historians and educators alike have long extolled, as the director of a major national study during World War II reported (Wesley, 1944), the uses of American history for educating "loyal citizens," "intelligent voters," "good neighbors," and "stable, well-rounded individuals" (p. 14). It is specious to claim that any social science can be taught for "its own sake" as, whether consciously or not, *some* decision must be made to determine what out of the universe of possible content is most suitable for the scarce time available in the school curriculum (Levstik, 1996, p. 23; Thornton, 2001a). Whether recognized as such or not, these are educational decisions, as the academic disciplines are silent on which parts of them young people ought to study.

Thus Edgar Wesley's (1937) oft-quoted definition of the social studies as "the social sciences simplified for pedagogical purposes" (p. 6) is properly understood as distinguishing the social sciences as a branch of knowledge from those parts of them selected for study in general education. As Linda Levstik (1996) noted, using the case of history, but in a point applicable to other social sciences as well: "It is not enough for us to simply accept historians' views of history.... [If we want to] better consider how history contributes to the larger goals of social studies" (pp. 30-31). Others have made much the same point since the early days of the social studies field (e.g., Brophy, Alleman, & O'Mahony, 2000, p. 294; Dewey, 1990, p. 151; Hunt, 1935; Popkewitz, 1977; Tyler, 1949, p. 26).

In terms of curriculum ideologies, the social sciences can, of course, be variously oriented. If we take the case of American history, the most widely taught social studies course, one recurring and important function has been to construct a "unifying" national narrative (see Barton & Levstik, 2004; Billington, 1966; FitzGerald, 1979; Moreau, 2003). Often this unity has come at the cost of attacks on certain topics or beliefs in American history, branding them as divisive or subversive or both. Censorship may result. Sometimes censorship has been effective enough that some topics or beliefs simply no longer appear in the curriculum. For example, Frances FitzGerald (1979) noted 1940's "business groups and right-wing citizens' groups attacked ... liberal textbooks" for alleged anti-free enterprise bias: "By 1950 or so, the merely conservative groups had been so successful that they had nothing more to complain about: the texts had become reflections of the National Association of Manufacturers viewpoint" (p. 37). A more recent case of censorship is the war in Iraq, which appears to go unmentioned in school programs (Flinders, 2005).

Of course, these kinds of attacks have been more acute at some times than others, but they appear to have always been present to some degree in the history of social studies (see Cornbleth & Waugh, 1995; Crocco, 2005; Nelson & Stanley, 1985; Pierce, 1926; Rugg, 1941). Proponents of such unity (e.g., Gabler & Gabler, 1982; Nevins, 1942; Schlesinger, 1993) have not necessarily had identical motives, but they believe the forces of American nationalism should be bolstered by the curriculum. In doing so, these proponents may appropriate key American beliefs, such as *freedom*, for their cause. Thus, even though the meaning of freedom has altered and been contested throughout American history (see Foner, 1998), self-proclaimed opponents of disunity may assign freedom an arbitrary meaning to steel their cause. It is sometimes overlooked that the construction of national "community," in practice, has served the interests of some social groups rather than others (Anyon, 1983; Crocco, 2001; Ladson-Billings, 2005; Levstik, 1990; Noddings, 1996; Thornton, 2003).

Plainly, there is no necessity that history or the other social sciences must take traditional or conservative forms in school programs. In the early 20th century, for instance, Charles and Mary Beard (1927) produced history textbooks that were, in Margaret Crocco's words (1997), "commensurate with the democratic achievement of the nation" (p. 12), as well as civics texts (Beard & Beard, 1921) that exemplified the progressive impulse. More recent educators, too, have seen the potential of teaching the contemporary "new" social and cultural history (see Foner, 1997) for "the common good" (Barton & Levstik, 2004) or seen educational promise when they look at "democratic" deliberation in civics classes (Parker, 2003).

Whether progressive or conservative, any social science is taught through some curricular frame and, in that sense, is never entirely ideologically neutral. In a democratic society, responsible educators strive for balance among reasonable viewpoints. They provide access to sufficient information so that students can make up their own minds after critical reflection (see National Council for the Social Studies, 1992).

Before leaving this section, it should be pointed out that in one sense the social sciences, as the standard subject matters of the great bulk of the curriculum, represent an important source of curricular continuity. But once more, questions arise of what levels one looks at for change and what we mean by social sciences in the curriculum. For instance, the high-school American history course has remained relatively unchanged since the early 20th century if we look at its mainstay status in the curriculum or its form as a survey. On the other hand, we could point to significant changes in its content, such as a new emphasis on international affairs after World War I (Merideth, 1947, p. 51) or greater attention to women and people of color since the 1960s and 1970s (Thornton, 2001c, pp. 186–192; 2005, pp. 32–39). Similarly, as taken up in the next section, the strong social studies movement of the 1910's (see Saxe, 1991; Singleton, 1980) did not necessarily mean the established subject matters, especially geography and history, were supplanted. Rather, while their arrangement in use, or method, may have changed and greater emphasis was afforded the recent than the distant past, geography and history remained curricular mainstays (see Jenness, 1990, pp. 78–88; H. Johnson, 1940, pp. 83–84; Watras, 2004, pp. 197–198; Wesley, 1944, p. 28). In the next section where we look at social education, however, its curricular fortunes have fluctuated more than history, geography, and civics.

SOCIAL STUDIES AS SOCIAL EDUCATION

One way of conceiving the social education position is as identifying the individual and social demands of associated living and then deciding what material from the social sciences (and collateral material) is relevant to those demands. Writing from this perspective, Noddings (2003) points out:

> History, geography, and natural history offer the promise of self-understanding on the level of groups and whole societies, and self-understanding is crucial to both citizenship and personal happiness. Notice, however, that I would contradict myself if I now said that we have justified history and geography in the curriculum. We've done no such thing. We have justified a careful search through history and geography for topics that may enhance the "associated life of men." Simply being *about* the associated life of men is not sufficient justification for including a topic in the curriculum. (p. 255)

This approach can shape curriculum decision-making in social education. In geography, for instance, priority would be assigned "the residences, pursuits, successes, and failures of men [as these] are the things that give geographic data their reason for inclusion in the material of instruction" (Dewey, 1944, p. 211). Speaking more generally of the educational significance of the social sciences, Dewey (1991) believed that sound social education depended less on which social science was selected (or if they were integrated) than on whether it is "taught in connection with things that are done, that need to be done, and how to do them" (p. 185). This "problems" method, with its Deweyan emphasis on "thinking rather than recalling," Edwin H. Reeder (1935) reflected, "brought about some very important changes in the teaching of the social studies" (p. 46).

Taking the subject of history as an illustration, Dewey (1990) considered that "existing society is both too close to the child and too complex to be studied." Therefore, meaningful historical instruction "must be an indirect sociology—a study of society which lays bare its process of becoming and its modes of organization" (p. 151). Vivid accounts of this kind of problem-based instruction in history and correlated geography from his celebrated Lab School at the University of Chicago document how this could work in practice (e.g., Mayhew & Edwards, 1966, pp. 310–335). A generation later, related experimentation was continued by, among others, teacher educators Lucy Sprague Mitchell (1991) in New York City and Corinne Seeds (Crocco, Munro, & Weiler, 1999) in Los Angeles. Speaking of her method of geography teaching, for instance, Mitchell (1991) pithily wrote, "It is *using* facts; not merely knowing them" (p. 5).

As instruction in history and geography at Dewey's Lab School suggests, social education is consistent with discipline-based instruction (Metcalf, 1989; Reeder, 1933, 1935). Nonetheless, we might expect disciplinary boundaries to be crossed in social education as rich material arouses wide-ranging student curiosity. Today's proponents of the disciplines may insist, of course, that such interdisciplinary perspectives will naturally arise with, say, history as it is now conceived by scholars. But social educators arrive at crossing disciplinary boundaries for educational reasons, not merely the contemporary interests of academicians. While the interests of social scientists have sometimes overlapped with the progressive impulses of social educators, as in the 1920s and 1930s (Thornton, 1996), in other periods, such as the 1950s and 1960s, they have not (Shaver, 1977, p. 349; Weisberger, 1962, p. 130).

In addition to its fluid relationship with the academic disciplines, social education emphasizes the importance of the student's choice in what he or she studies. Choice is important for at least four reasons. First, different students have different aptitudes. Social educators respect these individual differences where possible in order to capitalize on how individual students most effectively learn (Crabtree, 1983; Eisner, 1982; Krug & Anderson, 1944). Second, choice in what students study is associated with their motivation to learn (Barton & Levstik, 2004, p. 232; Branom & Branom, 1921, p. 165; Dewey, 1963, p. 67; Thornton, 2005, pp. 24–25). Third, choice enhances how inclusive a curriculum can be. As Jane Roland Martin (2002) argues, a one-size-fits-all curriculum inevitably, given limited available instructional time, narrows the scope of what is included in the curriculum, often limiting it to shared knowledge reflecting the interests of elites. Only by broadening the curriculum can the voices of all communities in a diverse nation such as the United States find their way into school programs. Fourth, choice offers young people valuable experience in making decisions for themselves and, as Noddings points out, such experience is important in order for them to learn how to make well-informed decisions in a democratic society (Thornton, 2005, p. ix).

Thus far in this section on the character of social education I have been speaking of its humanistic form, most associated with Dewey (Hertzberg, 1989, p. 82; Jenness, 1990, pp. 73–75). At least a few words are also needed on a related form that developed from progressive-era doctrines of scientific management (see Callahan, 1962) and social efficiency (see Snedden, 1924). This movement is sometimes referred to as administrative progressivism (Cuban, 1979, pp. 168–171).

Efficiency was to be secured through scientific curriculum making—tracking, standardized testing, minimization of waste—and aimed at prediction and social control, all of which ran against the Deweyan grain (Flinders & Thornton, 2004, pp. 2–4). While contemporaneously engaged at Teachers College, Columbia University with Dewey, leading social efficiency educator David Snedden (1932; 1935) well illustrated what administrative progressivism could mean for social education.

Snedden contended that social studies as social science was largely irrelevant to the demands of contemporary living and, hence, unjustified in occupying scarce space in school programs (see also Thorndike, 1940). Instead, he called for "functional civic education." Taken to its extreme, functional social education "favors sociology, economics, current events, and other 'practical' and easily tested subjects, and…history is often regarded as impractical and irrelevant" (Hertzberg, 1989, p. 81). Along the same lines, in 1920's Los Angeles, scientific curriculum maker Franklin Bobbitt (1922) screened social studies objectives by the extent to which they would contribute to "a comprehensive list of human abilities and characteristics which appear to be generally needed by the citizens of Los Angeles" in adulthood (p. 4).

Administrative progressivism outlived Snedden and Bobbitt. In the 1980's, for instance, Hazel Hertzberg (1989) observed that this form of social education "exercises a powerful, even dominant, influence in our own time" (p. 80). Since then, its prominence has increased with the rise of content standards and associated mandatory standardized testing (Grant, 2003; Stanley & Longwell, 2004; Vinson & Ross, 2001).

The assumptions and procedures of administrative progressivism became, over time, embedded in numerous social studies policies and practices. A "latent effect," as Michael Apple (2000) observes, "has been the gradual framing of educational issues largely in terms of the conservative agenda" (p. 71). Curriculum and evaluation, for instance, came to be conceived in terms of the administrative progressives' linear means-ends model of schooling. Thus, New Social Studies guru Edwin Fenton (1967) promoted discovery learning, with all it implied for open-ended instruction, yet still adopted, without apparent self-consciousness, a means-end scheme of pre-set behavioral objectives and continuous evaluation to judge if "students have achieved the objectives we have set for them" (p. 24). Administrative progressivism, all in all, should be considered one significant source of curricular continuity. For example, whether taking the form of instructional objectives in the 1960s and 1970s or content standards today, emphasis on behaviorist and easily measured learning tasks slants the curriculum toward exposition rather than problem-solving and individualistic expression (Eisner, 2002, pp. 108–122).

Before closing this section on the character of social education, it should be underscored that both the Deweyan and conservative social efficiency strands share a belief that the demands of social living should be the *starting* point for curriculum makers selecting subject matter (Thornton, 2005, p. 28), and not vice-versa. From this perspective geography became the study of the earth as the home of human activity. Nineteenth century school geography underscored mental discipline, so that map study, for instance, involved the recall of physical features and political boundaries. Writing for the American Historical Association's Commission on the Social Studies, however, the distinguished geographer Isaiah Bowman (1934) noted that "advance in geographical teaching is not made... by absorbing a body of fixed data and doctrine" (p. 217). Rather the new map study stressed relationships between human economic and political livelihood and the earth (Schulten, 2001, pp. 122–129). This approach suited administrative progressives who saw it as a "practical" curricular track "to make a living in business" (Bowman, 1934, p. 200). In an admittedly different way, it also fitted with a humanistic perspective. Dewey (1990) wrote that: "It is through occupations determined by this environment that mankind has made its historical and political progress" (p. 19).

Strangely, this attention to social goals as a filter for subject matter selection strikes observers such as FitzGerald (1979) as substituting a progressive view of "the social good" (p. 174) for content. But FitzGerald evidently fails to see that the same criticism can also be made of her (see Hertzberg, 1981, pp. 146–147). The "truth," which she admits having imbibed from 1950's American history textbooks (p. 7), was every bit as much a version of "social good." As with consensus historians of the Cold War (see below), whom she cites approvingly, FitzGerald seems to "[stand] beyond... [her] own narrative" as an "ironist" (Gewen, 2005, p. 31). For example, what course of action is being suggested when FitzGerald observes of 1970s textbooks, "As for Teddy Roosevelt, he now champions the issue of conservation instead of charging up San Juan Hill" (p. 9)?

The choice is not, in other words, whether some view of social good is implied by curriculum materials, or whether they will contain content (how could any curriculum material be formulated without content?). Rather, in a democratic society, the choice concerns what possibilities for social good through what subject matter are made available and with what allowance for balance so students can make up their own minds. As should be evident in the next sections, whichever view of social studies has been emphasized, its content suggests *some* version of social good. Of course, it cannot be assumed that curriculum makers have always striven for balance as well.

SOCIAL EDUCATION AT HIGH TIDE

There are various estimates of when social education, and progressive education more generally, thrived, but the 1910s seems the early point and the late 1940s the end point (Cuban, 1979; Eisner, 2002, p. 72; Foshay, 1990, p. 33). Even at its height, however, the effects of social education were apparently shallow in most places. Social education probably had greatest influence at middle- and upper-class suburban and private elementary schools and more so at the lower than upper grades (Cuban, 1979, p. 171). Nevertheless, social education appears to have had considerable influence on textbooks and other curriculum materials (Tanner, 1988, pp. 130–132) , which suggests broad diffusion. But what did social education look like?

Although too large a question to answer comprehensively here, I adumbrate four possible elements of social education—more the humanistic rather than administrative, to be sure—to illustrate. First, social education affected the content of established courses such as American history. Traditional emphases on war, diplomacy, and politics gave way to more "economic and social topics such as education, industry, labor, trade, and commerce" (Merideth, 1947, p. 54). In this regard, Dewey (1944) had called economic history "more democratic" than political history as "the one thing every individual *must* do is live" (p. 215). Political history was not ignored, but it was "interwoven into the larger fabric of American life" (Wesley, 1944, p. 65). The textbooks produced by the Beards (e.g., 1927) and Rugg (see Bisland, 2004, p. 211; Buckingham, c. 1935; Kliebard, 1995, pp. 174–177; Thornton, 2001b) were leaders in using history to explain present living conditions and current events as well as placing the U. S. experience in its international setting. The Beards, too, unusually for their time, defined history to be inclusive of the experience of women on its own terms—that is, not just when women took on traditionally masculine roles or supported men (Crocco, 1997).

Second, social education created new courses. Community Civics and Problems of Democracy (POD) are probably the clearest examples. The latter, conceived by the National Education Association 1916 committee (National Education Association, 1994), had by the end of the following decade an enrollment second only to American history (Singleton, 1980). POD was intended to draw on economics, sociology, and political science to address the compelling issues of contemporary life in the United States. It was to be the capstone social studies course to educate citizens for decision-making in a democratic society.

Third, progressive emphasis on democratic living was heightened by the challenges posed by fascism and communism in the 1930s. *Democratic human relations* became an explicit arm of social education. Hilda Taba was probably its most prominent exponent (Bernard-Powers, 1999; Foshay, 1990). She paid particular attention to improving relations between the various ethnic and cultural groups that made up American society. She (Taba & Van Til, 1945) was impatient with indirect approaches to "intergroup" relations and was a leader in devising social education to attack the problem directly (or, at minimum, doing the same through altering existing courses like American history). Although possibly tame-sounding to 21st-century ears, Taba and her colleagues took on the Anglo-Saxon norm that had long been tacitly equated with being American (FitzGerald, 1979, p. 77). Programs were launched in dozens of communities across the nation in the 1940s. In Akron, Ohio, for example, one group of American history pupils studied "the attitudes of majority toward minority groups" (Dimond, 1945, pp. 99–100).

Fourth, methods in the curriculum sometimes moved away from traditional reliance on the teacher and single textbook toward more independent work. Projects and activity, rather than passive recitation, were recommended for students (Branom & Branom, 1921; Reeder, 1935). A variety of reference materials and tangible objects as well as enhanced school libraries, were substituted for the use of a single basic textbook series (Foshay, 1990, p. 33). Supplemental social studies texts were also developed. Perhaps the best-known was *Building America,* which "was conceived to provide for the thoughtful examination of socioeconomic problems" in junior and senior high schools. By 1945, sales of the monthly paperback texts had reached more than a million copies per issue. Topics included *Youth Faces the World, Women, Italian Americans, Our Water Resources,* and *Advertising* (Tanner, 1988, pp. 131–133). As with the attacks on Rugg's highly popular textbooks of the 1930s, which led to their expulsion from the schools (Thornton, 2001b), right-wing criticism led to a sharp decline in sales, and in 1948 *Building America* ceased publication. Parenthetically, attacks on progressive education generally (e.g., Hofstadter, 1966) and social education in particular (e.g., Leming, Ellington, & Porter, 2003), sometimes boldly negative, have continued into the 21st century.

SOCIAL STUDIES AS SOCIAL SCIENCE: THE NEW SOCIAL STUDIES

There is no time here to explore in any depth what developed between the high tide of social education and the rise of the New Social Studies (NSS). Suffice it to say that the social context of education altered greatly, as did thinking within education and the social sciences. Significant among these social changes were postwar prosperity, conformity engendered by the Cold War and McCarthyism, a growing proportion of young people attending college, conservative determination to stem expansion of the New Deal, suburbanization and its accompanying White flight from the cities and considerable political indifference to urban and minority populations, and emphasis on traditional gender roles—Margaret Mead (*Interview with Margaret Mead,* 1977) called the United States in the 1950s the "most married country in the world."

Commensurate changes in historical scholarship also followed World War II. School history, long the dominant social study, was inevitably affected by a new generation of historical interpretation that supplanted the progressive history practiced by the likes of the Beards. Consensus or neoconservative history underscored, not the divisions and problems of American society, but its alleged absence of fundamental conflict (Novick, 1988, pp. 333–335). None of these changes boded well for problem-centered, activity-oriented, social studies. To the contrary, there was agitation to stress a college-preparation curriculum slanted to the traditional academic subjects (Hampel, 1986, p. 73). The perception that the U. S. was falling behind the Soviet Union following Sputnik amplified existing calls for academic excellence, which critics charged was being slighted by social education. Even before the NSS was born in the early 1960s, it seems no coincidence that the 1958 National Council for the Social Studies yearbook (Price, 1958) was devoted to "new viewpoints in the social sciences" (see also American Council of Learned Societies & National Council for the Social Studies, 1962). Similarly the titles and content emphasis of two other yearbooks by the same organization, a decade apart, also speak to this shift from an educational focus to a disciplinary one: *Geographic Approaches to Social Education* (Kohn, 1948) and *New Viewpoints in Geography* (James, 1959).

The text that inspired a national curriculum reform movement, of which the NSS was part, was Jerome Bruner's (1960) *The Process of Education.* Bruner popularized the notion of *structure* or "how things are related" (p. 7). He said a curriculum centered on structure was more intellectually powerful than a curriculum based on information because concepts did not become dated as quickly as information; moreover, concepts transferred to new information in a way in which facts did not. Therefore, the curriculum should be designed to promote discovery learning, where students worked out for themselves how things were related, rather than being told, as in traditional expository instruction. Bruner wanted to reduce the existing—and undesirable in his view—gap between the kind of intellectual activity in which young people engaged and the disciplinary scholar in higher education: "intellectual activity is everywhere the same, whether at the frontier of knowledge or in a third grade classroom" (p. 14). Bruner thought all this suggested "the use of our best minds in devising curricula" (p. 19), which in social studies meant geographers, historians, anthropologists, and the like.

Heady days followed. A revolution was called for to replace allegedly tired and intellectually pallid social studies with a rigorous alternative (Keller, 1961). In social studies Bruner's ideas spurred activity in areas that had traditionally played secondary roles to history, such as geography, anthropology, sociology, and economics. The latter subjects lent themselves easily to Bruner's essentially scientific model. But Bruner also fitted in history to his template. For instance, he suggested that a student might better understand "the [Cold War] ideological struggle" if he or she "could grasp...the weariness of Europe at the close of the Thirty Years' War and how it created the conditions for a workable but not ideologically absolute Treaty of Westphalia" (p. 25).

The NSS reformers put their main efforts into systematic development of curriculum materials. These materials typically came in the form of packages, designed to replace or supplement the existing curriculum, but sharing a goal of redirecting instruction from surveying the material to more "analytic" or "discovery episodes" (Massialas & Zevin, 1967). *The High School Geography Project* was representative insofar as it developed units of instruction that made no attempt to cover the ground of established geography survey courses. Rather it looked at geographic principles employing methods similar to those used in higher education (Patton, 1970), an approach that, incidentally, continues to be recommended by geographic educators (e.g., R. Fraser & Stoltman, 2001, p. 322). For an overview of dozens of NSS projects, see the account by John Haas (1977).

Taught as planned, the NSS projects, like social education methods, placed great demands on the subject-matter facility of teachers. These demands were generally not ones for which teachers had been (or are) well prepared (Thornton, 2005, p. 92). NSS reformers hoped that thoroughly designed curriculum packages would compensate for the inadequacy of teacher education (e.g., G. F. White, 1970, p. 1), but this does not seem to have commonly worked out. Teachers who belonged to professional organizations and who were department chairs—presumably better prepared than average—embraced NSS projects more than average teachers (Turner & Haley, 1975, pp. 41–42).

Still, even at the time, there was appreciation that the success of the NSS was likely to vary depending on what one considered to be meaningful change (e.g., G. F. White, 1970, p. 2). In the mid-1970s Haas (1977) contended that "perhaps five percent of social studies classrooms were affected by the NSS, and that the greatest impact was on selected suburban schools" (p. 79). In the mid-1980s Carole Hahn (1985) offered a more complicated perspective. While conceding that NSS projects "never reached widespread use" (p. 221), the figures she provides show varying levels of use of different projects, many beyond 5%, suggesting how difficult it is to provide definitive answers as to the effects of the NSS (p. 222). Moreover, certainly the disciplinary message of NSS found its way into textbooks (FitzGerald, 1979, pp. 162–165), and the major curriculum projects were introduced in social studies methods courses (Gross, 1984), but the effects of both developments on school curriculum are largely undocumented.

CONCLUSION

NSS peaked in the mid-1960s. In response to what FitzGerald called "a chorus of protests against the white, male, middle-class orientation" (p. 3) of the curriculum, a new movement calling for a more relevant curriculum emerged (e.g., Kownslar, 1974). With its echoes of social education, the relevance movement was short-lived; however, by introducing areas of study such as multicultural education and gender relations (e.g., Banks, 1970; Grambs, 1976), it has had lasting effects. Similar developments also contributed to making staple courses such as American history (e.g., Downey, 1982) and world history (Merryfield & Wilson, 2005, pp. 69–84) more inclusive. In the latter case, for instance, world regions, such as Sub-Saharan Africa—once viewed, if at all— through Eurocentric lens moved toward treatment in rounded terms.

Nonetheless a "basic" skills movement (Lunstrum & Irvin, 1981) owing much to the efficiency movement, which gained momentum as the 1970s wore on, was to be the dominant force in the curriculum down to the 21st century. Eventually this movement spawned content standards. These were devised in the 1990s by groups dominated by social scientists, packing in more material reflective of their present interests than the curriculum could bear without being swamped (Gagnon, 2005). Thus, the movement came to link, in a way Snedden, for example, would have found odd, the social science disciplinary perspective with administrative progressivism.

Since the 1970s it has become, once more, difficult to answer whether the curriculum has been marked more by change or continuity. Again, what looks to be a straightforward empirical question turns out to be a question that depends on how one defines curriculum and at what level one looks for change (Noddings, 1979, p. 298). Conservative, even reactionary, political forces have plainly acted as stumbling blocks to transformative change (Cornbleth, 2001; T. Johnson & Avery, 1999), resulting in charges that the changes that have taken place are superficial or partial in, for example, curricular treatment of gender relations (Noddings, 2002, pp. 51–52) or inclusion of people of color (Ladson-Billings, 2005). Moreover, gains by disadvantaged groups, such as women, in formulating social studies policies have not necessarily been maintained (Crocco, 2004; Levstik, 2005).

Gauging change and continuity in other respects is also challenging to generalize about. For example, in courses and methods, the basics movement may have helped secure the position of some secondary-school courses (Marker & Mehlinger, 1992, pp. 839–840), but emphasis on the basics of reading and math has undermined a substantive role for social studies in the elementary, especially primary, grades (Gross, 1977; Hahn, 1985; Manzo, 2005). Similarly, changes in methods and media have occurred, such as use of primary sources in history instruction (Barton, 2005) or digital technology (Bolick, 2004), but their effects on the curriculum can be mechanistic rather than transformative.

Finally, it seems unlikely that in the near future either a cultural transmission or more critical version of social studies will secure a monopoly on the curriculum. As noted, both approaches can take place through either social science or social education. One function of social studies has been, and doubtless will continue to be, promoting cultural continuity, providing "a measure of what is permanent in a nation's life" (Wesley, 1944, p. 14). On the other hand, social and scholarly changes, not to mention the demands of decision-making in a democratic society, compel social studies to critique the traditions it transmits. As I believe the anthropological perspective of Jane White (e.g., 1989) demonstrates, both of these functions can co-exist in a defensible curriculum. In these circumstances of compromise, the task of social studies educators seems to be reconciling the competing imperatives of social adaptation usually associated with curriculum continuity and social reconstruction usually associated with curriculum change.

REFERENCES

American Association of University Women. (2004). How schools shortchange girls: Three perspectives on curriculum. In D. J. Flinders & S. J. Thornton (Eds.), *The curriculum studies reader* (2nd ed., pp. 205–228). New York: RoutledgeFalmer.

American Council of Learned Societies & National Council for the Social Studies (Eds.). (1962). *The social studies and the social sciences.* New York: Harcourt, Brace & World.

Anderson, L. (2003). *Pursuing truth, exercising power: Social science and public policy in the 21st century.* New York: Columbia University Press.

Anyon, J. (1983). Workers, labor, and economic history, and textbook content. In M. W. Apple & L. Weis (Eds.), *Ideology and practice in schooling* (pp. 37–60). Philadelphia: Temple University Press.

Apple, M. W. (2000). Standards, markets, and curriculum. In B. M. Franklin (Ed.), *Curriculum and consequence: Herbert M. Kliebard and the promise of schooling* (pp. 55–74). New York: Teachers College Press.

Banks, J. A. (1970). *Teaching the black experience: Methods and materials.* Belmont, CA: Fearon.

Barton, K. C. (2005). Primary sources in history: Breaking through the myths. *Phi Delta Kappan, 86,* 745–753.

Barton, K. C., & Levstik, L. S. (2004). *Teaching history for the common good.* Mahwah, NJ: Erlbaum.

Beard, C. A., & Beard, M. R. (1921). *American citizenship* (rev. ed.). New York: Macmillan.

Beard, C. A., & Beard, M. R. (1927). *The rise of American civilization.* New York: Macmillan.

Bernard-Powers, J. (1999). Composing her life: Hilda Taba and social studies history. In M. S. Crocco & O. L. Davis, Jr. (Eds.), *"Bending the future to their will": Civic women, social education, and democracy* (pp. 185–206). Lanham, MD: Rowman & Littlefield.

Beyer, B. K. (1994). Gone but not forgotten—Reflections on the New Social Studies. *The Social Studies, 85,* 251–256.

Billington, R. A. (1966). *The historian's contribution to Anglo-American misunderstanding.* New York: Hobbs, Dorman.

Bisland, B. M. (2004). *The Hanna and Rugg social studies textbooks for elementary school: A comparative content evaluation.* Unpublished doctoral dissertation, Columbia University, New York.

Bobbitt, J. F. (1922). *Curriculum-making in Los Angeles.* Chicago: University of Chicago Press.

Bolick, C. M. (2004). Technology and social studies teacher education: A framework. In S. Adler (Ed.), *Critical issues in social studies teacher education* (pp. 131–144). Greenwich, CT: Information Age.

Bowman, I. (1934). *Geography in relation to the social sciences.* New York: Scribner's.

Branom, M. E., & Branom, F. K. (1921). *The teaching of geography emphasizing the project, or active, method.* Boston: Ginn.

Brophy, J., Alleman, J., & O'Mahony, C. (2000). Elementary school social studies: Yesterday, today, and tomorrow. In T. L. Good (Ed.), *American education: Yesterday, today, and tomorrow* (pp. 256–312). Chicago: National Society for the Study of Education.

Bruner, J. S. (1960). *The process of education.* Cambridge: Harvard University Press.

Buckingham, B. R. (c. 1935). *Rugg course in the classroom: The junior-high-school program.* Chicago: Ginn.

Callahan, R. E. (1962). *Education and the cult of efficiency: A study of the forces that have shaped the administration of the public schools.* Chicago: University of Chicago Press.

Clark, R., Allard, J., & Mahoney, T. (2004). How much of the sky? Women in American high school history textbooks from the 1960s, 1980s, and 1990s. *Social Education, 68,* 57–62.

Clark, R., Ayton, K., Frechette, N., & Keller, P. J. (2005). Women of the world, re-write: Women in American world history high school textbooks from the 1960s, 1980s, and 1990s. *Social Education, 69,* 41–45.

Cornbleth, C. (2001). Climates of constraint/restraint of teachers and teaching. In W. B. Stanley (Ed.), *Critical issues in social studies research for the 21st century* (pp. 73–95). Greenwich, CT: Information Age.

Cornbleth, C., & Waugh, D. (1995). *The great speckled bird: Multicultural politics and education policymaking.* New York: St. Martin's.

Crabtree, C. (1983). A common curriculum in the social studies. In G. D. Fenstermacher & J. I. Goodlad (Eds.), *Individual differences and the common curriculum* (pp. 248–281). Chicago: National Society for the Study of Education.

Crocco, M. S. (1997). Forceful yet forgotten: Mary Ritter Beard and the writing of history. *The History Teacher, 31,* 9–31.

Crocco, M. S. (2001). The missing discourse about gender and sexuality in the social studies. *Theory into Practice, 40,* 65–71.

Crocco, M. S. (2004). Women and the social studies: The long rise and rapid fall of feminist activity in the National Council for the Social Studies. In C. Woyshner, J. Watras, & M. S. Crocco (Eds.), *Social education in the twentieth century: Curriculum and context for citizenship* (pp. 142–159). New York: Peter Lang.

Crocco, M. S. (Ed.). (2005). *Social studies and the press: Keeping the beast at bay.* Greenwich, CT: Information Age.

Crocco, M. S., Munro, P., & Weiler, K. (1999). *Pedagogies of resistance: Women educator activists, 1880–1960.* New York: Teachers College Press.

Cuban, L. (1979). Determinants of curriculum change and stability, 1870–1970. In J. Schaffarzick & G. Sykes (Eds.), *Value conflicts and curriculum issues: Lessons from research and experience* (pp. 139–196). Berkeley: McCutchan.

Cuban, L. (1991). History of teaching in social studies. In J. P. Shaver (Ed.), *Handbook of research on social studies teaching and learning* (pp. 197–209). New York: Macmillan.

Dewey, J. (1944). *Democracy and education.* New York: Free Press.

Dewey, J. (1963). *Experience and education.* New York: Collier Books.

Dewey, J. (1990). *The school and society; and, The child and the curriculum.* Chicago: University of Chicago Press.

Dewey, J. (1991). The challenge of democracy to education. In J. A. Boydston (Ed.), *The later works, 1925–1953* (Vol. 11, pp. 181–190). Carbondale, IL: Southern Illinois University Press.

Dimond, S. E. (1945). Practices in social studies courses. In H. Taba & W. Van Til (Eds.), *Democratic human relations: Promising practices in intergroup and intercultural education in the social studies* (pp. 87–126). Washington, DC: National Council for the Social Studies.

Downey, M. T. (Ed.). (1982). *Teaching American history: New directions.* Washington, DC: National Council for the Social Studies.

Eisner, E. W. (1982). *Cognition and curriculum: A basis for deciding what to teach.* New York: Longman.

Eisner, E. W. (2002). *The educational imagination: On the design and evaluation of school programs* (3rd ed.). Upper Saddle River, NJ: Merrill Prentice Hall.

Elson, R. M. (1964). *Guardians of tradition: American schoolbooks of the nineteenth century.* Lincoln: University of Nebraska Press.

Evans, R. W. (2004). *The social studies wars: What should we teach the children?* New York: Teachers College Press.

Fenton, E. (1967). *The new social studies.* New York: Holt, Rinehart and Winston.

FitzGerald, F. (1979). *America revised: History schoolbooks in the twentieth century.* Boston: Little, Brown.

Flinders, D. J. (2005). Adolescents talk about the war in Iraq. *Phi Delta Kappan, 87,* 320–323.

Flinders, D. J., & Thornton, S. J. (Eds.). (2004). *The curriculum studies reader* (2nd ed.). New York: Routledge Falmer.

Foner, E. (1998). *The story of American freedom.* New York: Norton.

Foner, E. (Ed.). (1997). *The new American history* (rev. ed.). Philadephia: Temple University Press.

Foshay, A. W. (1990). Textbooks and the curriculum during the Progressive Era. In D. L. Elliot & A. Woodward (Eds.), *Textbooks and schooling in the United States* (pp. 23–41). Chicago: National Society for the Study of Education.

Foster, S., & Nicholls, J. (2005). America in World War II: An analysis of history textbooks from England, Japan, Sweden, and the United States. *Journal of Curriculum and Supervision, 20,* 214–233.

Fraser, D. M. (1962). *Current curriculum studies in academic subjects.* Washington, DC: National Education Association.

Fraser, R., & Stoltman, J. P. (2001). Teaching methods in physical geography: Bridging tradition and technology. In J. Brophy (Ed.), *Subject-specific instructional methods and activities* (pp. 315–345). Oxford: Elsevier Science.

Gabler, M., & Gabler, N. (1982). Mind control through textbooks. *Phi Delta Kappan, 64,* 96.

Gagnon, P. A. (2005, March). Educating democracy: Are we up to it? *National Council for History Education Occasional Paper.*

Gewen, B. (2005, June 5). Forget the Founding Fathers: In the constantly changing narrative of American history, a globalized history is only the latest twist. *New York Times Book Review,* pp. 30–33.

Grambs, J. D. (Ed.). (1976). *Teaching about women in the social studies: Concepts, methods, and materials.* Washington, DC: National Council for the Social Studies.

Grant, S. G. (2003). *History lessons: Teaching, learning, and testing in U. S. high school classrooms.* Mahwah, NJ: Erlbaum.

Grant, S. G., & Gradwell, J. M. (2005). The sources are many: Exploring history teachers' selection of classroom texts. *Theory and Research in Social Education, 33,* 244–265.

Gross, R. E. (1951). Trends in the teaching of U. S. history in the senior high schools of California. *California Journal of Secondary Education, 26,* 263–267.

Gross, R. E. (1977). The status of the social studies in the public schools of the United States: Facts and impressions of a national survey. *Social Education, 41,* 194–200, 205.

Gross, R. E. (1984). Is there a method to our madness or a madness to our method? *The Social Studies, 75,* 158–165.

Haas, J. D. (1977). *The era of the New Social Studies.* Boulder, CO: ERIC Clearinghouse for Social Studies/Social Science Education, and Social Science Education Consortium.

Hahn, C. L. (1985). The status of the social studies in the public schools of the United States. *Social Education, 49,* 220–223.

Hampel, R. L. (1986). *The last little citadel: American high schools since 1940.* Boston: Houghton Mifflin.

Hertzberg, H. W. (1971). *Historical parallels for the sixties and seventies: Primary sources and core curriculum revisited.* Boulder, CO: Social Science Education Consortium.

Hertzberg, H. W. (1981). *Social studies reform, 1880–1980.* Boulder, CO: Social Science Education Consortium.

Hertzberg, H. W. (1989). History and progressivism: A century of reform proposals. In P. Gagnon & The Bradley Commission on History in Schools (Eds.), *Historical Literacy: The Case for History in American Education* (pp. 69–99). New York: Macmillan.

Herz, M. F. (c. 1978). *How the Cold War is taught: Six American history textbooks examined.* Washington, DC: Ethics and Public Policy Center, Georgetown University.

Hofstadter, R. (1966). *Anti-intellectualism in American life.* New York: Vintage.

Hunt, E. M. (1935). Scholars' history versus school history. *The Social Studies, 26,* 513–517.

Interview with Margaret Mead. (1977, January 11). *San Francisco Examiner,* p. 14.

James, P. E. (Ed.). (1959). *New viewpoints in geography.* Washington, DC: National Council for the Social Studies.

Jenness, D. (1990). *Making sense of social studies.* New York: Macmillan.

Johnson, H. (1940). *Teaching of history in elementary and secondary schools with applications to allied studies* (rev. ed.). New York: Macmillan.

Johnson, T., & Avery, P. G. (1999). The power of the press: A content and discourse analysis of the U.S. history standards as presented in selected newspapers. *Theory and Research in Social Education, 27,* 447–471.

Keller, C. R. (1961). Needed: Revolution in the social studies. *Saturday Review, 44,* 60–61.

Kliebard, H. M. (1995). *The struggle for the American curriculum* (2nd ed.). New York: Routledge.

Kohn, C. F. (Ed.). (1948). *Geographic approaches to social education.* Washington, DC: National Council for the Social Studies.

Kownslar, A. O. (Ed.). (1974). *Teaching American history: The quest for relevancy.* Washington, DC: National Council for the Social Studies.

Krug, E., & Anderson, G. L. (Eds.). (1944). *Adapting Instruction in the social studies to individual differences.* Washington, DC: National Council for the Social Studies.

Ladson-Billings, G. (2005). Differing concepts of citizenship: Schools and communities as sites of civic development. In N. Noddings (Ed.), *Educating citizens for global awareness* (pp. 69–80). New York: Teachers College Press.

Leming, J., Ellington, L., & Porter, K. (Eds.). (2003). *Where did social studies go wrong?* Washington, DC: Fordham Foundation.

Levstik, L. S. (1990). From the outside in: American children's literature from 1920–1940. *Theory and Research in Social Education, 18,* 327–343.

Levstik, L. S. (1996). NCSS and the teaching of history. In O. L. Davis, Jr. (Ed.), *NCSS in retrospect* (pp. 21–34). Washington, DC: National Council for the Social Studies.

Levstik, L. S. (2005). Woman as force in social education. In L. M. Burlbaw & S. L. Field (Eds.), *Explorations in curriculum history* (pp. 193–200). Greenwich, CT: Information Age.

Lunstrum, J. P., & Irvin, J. L. (1981). Integration of basic skills into social studies content. *Social Education, 45,* 169–177.

Manzo, K. K. (2005, March 16). Social studies losing out to reading, math. *Education Week,* pp. 1, 16–17.

Marker, G., & Mehlinger, H. D. (1992). Social studies. In P. W. Jackson (Ed.), *Handbook of research on curriculum* (pp. 830–851). New York: Macmillan.

Marshall, L. C., & Goetz, R. M. (1936). *Curriculum-making in the social studies: A social process approach.* New York: Scribner's.

Martin, J. R. (2002). *Cultural miseducation: In search of a democratic solution.* New York: Teachers College Press.

Massialas, B. G., & Zevin, J. (1967). *Creative encounters in the classroom: Teaching and learning through discovery.* New York: Wiley.

Mayhew, K. C., & Edwards, A. C. (1966). *The Dewey School: The laboratory school of the University of Chicago, 1896–1903.* New York: Atherton Press.

Merideth, D. (1947). Changing content of American history courses. In R. E. Thursfield (Ed.), *The study and teaching of American history* (pp. 35–57). Washington, DC: National Council for the Social Studies.

Merryfield, M. M., & Wilson, A. (2005). *Social studies and the world: Teaching global perspectives.* Silver Spring, MD: National Council for the Social Studies.

Metcalf, L. E. (1989). An overview of the Deweyan influence on social studies education. *International Journal of Social Education, 3*(3), 50–54.

Michener, J. A. (1939). The problem of the social studies. In J. A. Michener (Ed.), *The future of the social studies: Proposals for an experimental social-studies curriculum* (pp. 1–5). Cambridge: National Council for the Social Studies.

Mitchell, L. S. (1991). *Young geographers: How they explore the world and how they map the world* (4th ed.). New York: Bank Street College of Education.

Moreau, J. (2003). *Schoolbook nation: Conflicts over American history textbooks from the Civil War to the present.* Ann Arbor: University of Michigan Press.

Muessig, R. H. (1987). An analysis of developments in geographic education. *Elementary School Journal, 87,* 519–530.

Nash, G. B., Crabtree, C., & Dunn, R. E. (1997). *History on trial: Culture wars and the teaching of the past.* New York: Knopf.

National Commission on Social Studies in the Schools. (1991). *Voices of teachers: Report of a survey on social studies.* Dubuque, IA: Kendall/Hunt.

National Council for the Social Studies. (1992). *Alan F. Griffin on reflective teaching: A philosophical approach to the subject-matter preparation of teachers of history.* Washington, DC: Author.

National Education Association. (1994). The social studies in secondary education. In M. R. Nelson (Ed.), *The social studies in secondary education: A reprint of the seminal 1916 report with annotations and commentaries.* Bloomington, IN: ERIC Clearinghouse for Social Studies/Social Science Education.

Nelson, J. L., & Stanley, W. B. (1985). Academic freedom: 50 years standing still. *Social Education, 49,* 662–664, 666.

Nevins, A. (1942, June 21). American history for Americans. *New York Times.*

Noddings, N. (1979). NIE's national curriculum development conference. In J. Schaffarzick & G. Sykes (Eds.), *Value conflicts and curriculum issues: Lessons from research and experience* (pp. 291–312). Berkeley, CA: McCutchan.

Noddings, N. (1996). On community. *Educational Theory, 46,* 245–267.

Noddings, N. (2002). *Educating moral people: A caring alternative to character education.* New York: Teachers College Press.

Noddings, N. (2003). *Happiness and education.* Cambridge, UK: Cambridge University Press.

Noddings, N. (2005). *The challenge to care in schools: An alternative approach to education* (2nd ed.). New York: Teachers College Press.

Novick, P. (1988). *That noble dream: The "objectivity question" and the American historical profession.* Cambridge, UK: Cambridge University Press.

Palmer, J. R. (1965). Selection and use of textbooks and audio-visual materials. In B. G. Massialas & F. R. Smith (Eds.), *New challenges in the social studies: Implications of research for teaching* (pp. 155–189). Belmont, CA: Wadsworth.

Parker, W. C. (1991). *Renewing the social studies curriculum.* Alexandria, VA: Association for Supervision and Curriculum Development.

Parker, W. C. (2003). *Teaching democracy: Unity and diversity in public life.* New York: Teachers College Press.

Patton, D. J. (Ed.). (1970). *From geographic discipline to inquiring student: Final report on The High School Geography Project.* Washington, DC: Association of American Geographers.

Pierce, B. L. (1926). *Public opinion and the teaching of history in the United States.* New York: Knopf.

Popkewitz, T. S. (1977). The latent values of the discipline-centered curriculum. *Theory and Research in Social Education, 5*(1), 41–60.

Price, R. A. (Ed.). (1958). *New viewpoints in the social sciences.* Washington, DC: National Council for the Social Studies.

Reeder, E. H. (1933). Method in geography. In *The teaching of geography* (pp. 315–331). Bloomington, IL: Public School Publishing.

Reeder, E. H. (1935). John Dewey and the activist movement. In E. B. Wesley (Ed.), *The historical approach to methods of teaching the social studies* (pp. 38–49). Philadelphia: McKinley.

Ross, E. W. (1997). The struggle for the social studies curriculum. In E. W. Ross (Ed.), *The social studies curriculum: Purposes, problems, and possibilities* (pp. 3–19). Albany: State University of New York Press.

Rugg, H. (1941). *That men may understand: An American in the long armistice.* New York: Doubleday, Doran and Co.

Saxe, D. W. (1991). *Social studies in schools: A history of the early years.* Albany: State University of New York Press.

Schlesinger, A. M., Jr. (1993). *The disuniting of America: Reflections on a multicultural society.* New York: Norton.

Schulten, S. (2001). *The geographical imagination in America, 1880–1950.* Chicago: University of Chicago Press.

Schwab, J. J. (1968). The concept of the structure of a discipline. In L. J. Hebert & W. Murphy (Eds.), *Structure in the social studies* (pp. 43–56). Washington, DC: National Council for the Social Studies.

Shaver, J. P. (1977). Needed: A Deweyan rationale for social studies. *The High School Journal, 60,* 345–352.

Shaver, J. P. (1979). The usefulness of educational research in curricular/instructional decision-making in social studies. *Theory and Research in Social Education, 7*(3), 21–46.

Singleton, H. W. (1980). Problems of Democracy: The revisionist plan for social studies education. *Theory and Research in Social Education, 8,* 89–104.

Smith, D. L. (1986). Survey research. In C. Cornbleth (Ed.), *An invitation to research in social education* (pp. 28–39). Washington, DC: National Council for the Social Studies.

Snedden, D. (1924). History studies in schools: For what purposes? *Teachers College Record, 25,* 1–14.

Snedden, D. (1932). *Educations for political citizenship: A critical analysis of certain unsolved problems of school educations towards superior memberships in democratic political societies.* New York: Bureau of Publications, Teachers College, Columbia University.

Snedden, D. (1935). The effect upon methods of a changing curriculum: With special reference to the social studies. In E. B. Wesley (Ed.), *The historical approach to methods of teaching the social studies* (pp. 9–19). Philadelphia: McKinley.

Sosniak, L. A. (1999). Professional and subject matter knowledge for teacher education. In G. A. Griffin (Ed.), *The education of teachers* (pp. 185–204). Chicago: National Society for the Study of Education.

Stanley, W. B., & Longwell, H. (2004). Ideology, power, and control in social studies teacher education. In S. Adler (Ed.), *Critical issues in social studies teacher education* (pp. 189–229). Greenwich, CT: Information Age.

Stodolsky, S. S. (1988). *The subject matters: Classroom activity in math and social studies.* Chicago: University of Chicago Press.

Stodolsky, S. S. (1999). Is teaching really by the book? In M. J. Early & K. J. Rehage (Eds.), *Issues in curriculum: A selection of chapters from past NSSE yearbooks* (pp. 141–168). Chicago: National Society for the Study of Education.

Symcox, L. (2002). *Whose history? The struggle for national standards in American classrooms.* New York: Teachers College Press.

Taba, H., & Van Til, W. (Eds.). (1945). *Democratic human relations: Promising practices in intergroup and intercultural education in the social studies.* Washington, DC: National Council for the Social Studies.

Tanner, D. (1988). The textbook controversies. In L. N. Tanner (Ed.), *Critical issues in curriculum* (pp. 122–147). Chicago: National Society for the Study of Education.

Thorndike, E. L. (1940). Who should study economics? In H. F. Clark (Ed.), *Economic education* (pp. 101–104). Washington, DC: National Council for the Social Studies.

Thornton, S. J. (1991). Teacher as curricular-instructional gatekeeper in social studies. In J. P. Shaver (Ed.), *Handbook of research on social studies teaching and learning* (pp. 237–248). New York: Macmillan.

Thornton, S. J. (1996). NCSS: The early years. In O. L. Davis, Jr. (Ed.), *NCSS in Retrospect* (pp. 1–7). Washington DC: National Council for the Social Studies.

Thornton, S. J. (2001a). From content to subject matter. *The Social Studies, 92,* 237–242.

Thornton, S. J. (2001b). Harold Rugg, 1886–1960. In J. R. Palmer (Ed.), *Fifty Modern Thinkers on Education* (pp. 10–15). London: Routledge.

Thornton, S. J. (2001c). Legitimacy in the social studies curriculum. In L. Corno (Ed.), *A century of study in education: The centennial volume* (pp. 185–204). Chicago: National Society for the Study of Education.

Thornton, S. J. (2003). Silence on gays and lesbians in social studies curriculum. *Social Education, 67,* 226–230.

Thornton, S. J. (2004). Citizenship education and social studies curriculum change after 9/11. In C. A. Woyshner, J. Watras & M. S. Crocco (Eds.), *Social education in the twentieth century: Curriculum and context for citizenship* (pp. 210–220). New York: Peter Lang.

Thornton, S. J. (2005). *Teaching social studies that matters: Curriculum for active learning.* New York: Teachers College Press.

Thornton, S. J. (2006). What is history in U. S. history textbooks? In J. Nicholls (Ed.), *School history textbooks across cultures: International debates and perspectives* (pp. 15–25). Oxford: Symposium Books.

Turner, M. J., & Haley, F. (1975). *Utilization of new social studies curriculum programs.* Boulder, CO: ERIC Clearinghouse for Social Studies/Social Science Education, and Social Science Education Consortium.

Tyler, R. W. (1949). *Basic principles of curriculum and instruction.* Chicago: University of Chicago Press.

Vinson, K. D., & Ross, E. W. (2001). In search of the social studies curriculum: Standardization, diversity, and a conflict of appearances. In W. B. Stanley (Ed.), *Critical issues in social studies research for the 21st century* (pp. 39–71). Greenwich, CT: Information Age.

Wade, R. C. (1993). Content analysis of social studies textbooks: A review of ten years of research. *Theory and Research in Social Education, 21,* 232–256.

Walworth, A. (1938). *School histories at war: A study of the treatment of our wars in the secondary school history textbooks of the United States and its former enemies.* Cambridge: Harvard University Press.

Watras, J. (2004). Historians and social studies educators, 1893–1998. In C. Woyshner, J. Watras & M. S. Crocco (Eds.), *Social education in the twentieth century: Curriculum and context for citizenship* (pp. 192–209). New York: Peter Lang.

Weisberger, B. A. (1962). United States history. In *High school social studies perspectives* (pp. 127–150). Houghton Mifflin: Boston.

Weiss, I. R. (1978). *National survey of science, mathematics, and social studies education.* Research Triangle Park, NC: Center for Educational Research and Evaluation, supported by National Science Foundation.

Wesley, E. B. (1937). *Teaching the social studies: Theory and practice.* New York: Heath.

Wesley, E. B. (1944). *American history in schools and colleges: The report of the Committee on American History in Schools and Colleges of the American Historical Association, the Mississippi Valley Historical Association, the National Council for the Social Studies.* New York: Macmillan.

White, G. F. (1970). Assessment in midstream. In D. J. Patton (Ed.), *From geographic discipline to inquiring student: Final report on The High School Geography Project* (pp. 1–2). Washington, DC: Association of American Geographers.

White, J. J. (1988). Searching for substantial knowledge in social studies texts. *Theory and Research in Social Education, 16,* 115–140.

White, J. J. (1989). The power of politeness in the classroom: Cultural codes that create and constrain knowledge construction. *Journal of Curriculum and Supervision, 4,* 298–321.

3 Early elementary social studies

Jere Brophy
Janet Alleman

Michigan State University

This chapter focuses on research on social studies in early elementary (K–3) classrooms, especially work that has appeared in the 15 years since publication of the *Handbook of Research on Social Studies Teaching and Learning* (Shaver, 1991). It synthesizes noteworthy developments in the status of social studies in the schools, models of curriculum and instruction, and research on early social education.

Until recently, reviewers agreed that there was little scholarly work to report in these areas, and what did exist was mostly discouraging. Armento (1993) noted that elementary social studies tends to be defined by the textbook series, which combine the holidays-heroes-history curriculum that goes back to the late 19th century with the expanding communities curriculum that developed several decades later. Students tended not to like or learn much of lasting value from this curriculum (Zhao & Hoge, 2005), and would-be reformers periodically called for replacing it entirely or at least improving it by reducing its breadth to focus in more depth on powerful ideas, incorporating more activities calling for higher order thinking, including more global and multicultural content, and shifting emphasis from reading textbooks and filling out worksheets to engaging in a broader range of discourse genres (discussion and debate, role play, collaboration) and learning activities (work with primary sources and cultural artifacts, inquiry and synthesis activities).

These reform proposals sometimes led to marginal adjustments in the textbook series (such as inclusion of more basic concepts from the disciplines), but they did not replace the traditional curriculum or even get established as viable alternatives. Even if they were widely perceived as feasible and desirable (often they were not), proposed reforms usually were limited to relatively general guidelines and did not include attempts at full curriculum development. As a result, the elementary curriculum has changed little since the 1960s.

Cuban (1991), Finkelstein, Nielsen, and Switzer (1993), Haas and Laughlin (2001), and Seixas (2001) sounded many of the same themes. Marker and Mehlinger (1992) added that, despite scholarly criticism, textbooks tend to be popular with teachers, who lean on them heavily because they usually do not know much about social studies. Others also have observed that elementary teachers lack a big-picture perspective on social studies as a coherent K-12 subject, so they often are vague about its purposes and uncertain about how to teach it. Many of them downgrade its importance in the curriculum or offer fragmented programs because they select activities for convenience or student interest rather than for their value as means of accomplishing clearly formulated social education goals (Atwood, 1986; Brophy, Alleman, & O'Mahony, 2000; Thornton, 2005). Marker and Mehlinger also noted the relative absence of observational research. They concluded that social studies educators have spent too much time trying to define the field and arguing about its purposes and goals, but not enough time looking at what happens in classrooms.

Most of these themes emphasized by previous reviewers still apply in 2008. However, early social education has begun to receive more attention, for both good and ill. Some of this reflects outside influences, notably spillover from the "culture wars" and from new curriculum standards and high-stakes testing programs. There also has been more activity within the community of social studies educators. The NCSS now publishes *Social Studies and the Young Learner* and distributes books (Haas & Laughlin, 1997; Krey, 1998) aimed at elementary teachers and videos showing teaching in the early grades, and more scholars have begun to focus on early social education. Observational studies have become much more frequent, although most have been confined to one or a few classrooms (Brophy, Alleman, & O'Mahony, 2000; Seixas, 2001).

REDUCED SOCIAL STUDIES PRESENCE IN THE CURRICULUM

An alarming recent trend has been reduction in the time devoted to social studies in the elementary grades, especially the primary grades (NCSS, 1989). Houser (1995) noted that elementary social studies had been "put on the back burner," attributing the problem to competition for resources, low student interest, and an uneven curriculum. More recent reports have noted an acceleration of this trend, due primarily to high-stakes testing in reading, writing, and mathematics. Social studies is being taught an average of only 1–2 hours per week in Grades K–3 and only 2–3 hours per week in Grades 4–6 (Howard, 2003; Pascopella, 2005; VanFossen, 2005). In many classrooms, it is not taught at all as a separate subject but integrated into some of the reading and writing activities included within the literacy curriculum. This integrated approach usually does not systematically address the purposes and goals (social knowledge, civic efficacy) traditionally associated with social studies (Alleman & Brophy, 1993, 1994).

High-stakes testing programs create both problems and potential for social studies. In states where testing is restricted to literacy and mathematics, the typical result is substantial increase in time devoted to these two subjects, at the expense of everything else. However, if social studies is included in a state's testing program, it receives more attention, teaching time, and resources (e.g., inservice training programs). Also, as debates about standards and testing have escalated to the national level because of the *No Child Left Behind Act*, policymakers have become more aware that testing programs tend to narrow the curriculum by focusing emphasis on what is tested (Thomas, 2005).

Furthermore, unhappiness with American students' performance on national and international tests in history, geography, and civics has led to calls for more and better teaching in these areas, and even to the passage in 2005 of a law mandating yearly instruction in the U.S. Constitution. Thus, as the standards and testing movement continues to play out, it could lead to an increase in time devoted to social studies. However, this probably would be framed in terms of teaching the disciplines (primarily history, geography, and civics/political science), not social studies as a subject with its own unique purposes and goals. Worse, emphasis probably would be placed on teaching disconnected factual information instead of big ideas and their applications.

THE "CULTURE WARS" AND THE EXPANDING COMMUNITIES CURRICULUM

The culture wars that have divided American society in recent decades have included debates and reform proposals relating to social studies in general and history in particular (Cornbleth & Waugh, 1999; Evans, 2004; Symcox, 2002). Most of these focused on the secondary grades, but the spillover included attacks on the expanding communities curriculum that had become the de facto national curriculum throughout much of the twentieth century and into the twenty-first. Hanna (1963) had rationalized the expanding communities approach as being (a) logical, in starting with the self and family and then moving outward toward progressively wider human communities (neighborhood, community, state, region, nation, world), and (b) convenient, in allowing for a holistic, coordinated approach to the study of people living in societies.

This sequence also meshed well with developmental stage theories popular at the time, and publishers and teachers liked it because it proved flexible enough to accommodate most emerging topics and issues. Its rationale was criticized occasionally for being rooted in discredited ideas (e.g., that children relive the cultural history of the human race as they develop) and being sequenced according to adult rather than child logic (e.g., the concept of a state is just as abstract as the concept of a nation, so there is no need to study the state first; in fact, it might be better to study the nation first to provide framework for understanding what a state is) (Akenson, 1989; LeRiche, 1987, 1992; Wade, 2002). However, no one offered a fully developed alternative, so it stayed in place.

Part of the conservative agenda for the schools involves replacing this pandisciplinary social studies curriculum with a history curriculum (Gagnon, 1989). In the elementary grades, this would require eliminating the expanding communities sequence and most of the geographical and social science content subsumed within it. Consequently, history curriculum advocates have singled out the expanding communities sequence for special attention, not only criticizing it for being based on invalid developmental notions, but also blaming it for all of the perceived problems with the elementary curriculum (content is boring, trivial, lacking in substance, repetitious, etc.) (Frazee & Ayers, 2003; Ravitch, 1987).

In essence, the argument for replacing a pandisciplinary social studies curriculum with a history curriculum rests on unfounded assertions that history has very high curricular value, but geography and the social sciences do not. Thus, calls for replacing pandisciplinary social studies with just history courses make no more sense than would calls for replacing it with just sociology courses or replacing the science curriculum with just biology courses. The history curriculum advocates apparently recognize this at some level, because even though they controlled the development of California's History-Social Science Framework (California Department of Education, 1997), its guidelines for the primary grades do not call for a complete shift to a history curriculum. Instead, both that framework and the Houghton-Mifflin textbook series developed to conform to it incorporate a great many of the topics addressed in the traditional curriculum.

Even though arguments for replacing pandisciplinary social studies with a history curriculum are not persuasive, some of the criticisms of the traditional curriculum are valid. Social studies educators ought to address these, and in the process, proactively articulate a convincing rationale for pandisciplinary early social studies. To do so, one must distinguish the intended curriculum from the textbook series and the scheme for sequencing the content from the content itself.

First, criticizing the textbook series is not the same as criticizing the envisioned curriculum and its underlying rationale. Critics inside and outside of social studies agree that the primary textbooks contain very little content, and that what is there is often trite and already familiar to students (Alter, 1995; Brophy, 1992; Haas, 1991; Larkins, Hawkins, & Gilmore, 1987; Ravitch, 1987). However, these are criticisms of the instructional materials that the major publishers have developed based on the traditional rationale, not criticisms of the rationale itself. The same rationale could provide the basis for developing much more powerful instructional materials.

Second, although critics have established that there is no need to organize the curriculum within the expanding communities sequence, that sequence is simply a way of arranging the content. Its categories refer primarily to the levels of analysis at which content is addressed, not to the content itself. Although there is some material on families in first grade, on neighborhoods in second grade, and on communities in third grade, the topics of most lessons are human social activities that are carried out within families, neighborhoods, and communities. These activities tend to be structured around cultural universals—basic needs and social experiences found in all societies, past and present (food, clothing, shelter, communication, transportation, government, etc.). In short, the traditional curriculum is mostly about fundamental social aspects of the human condition related to satisfaction of culturally universal needs and wants, not about expanding communities.

Given the lack of research support for the expanding communities sequence and the baggage now associated with the term *expanding communities curriculum*, perhaps social studies educators should avoid that term and shift to terms such as *traditional* or *pandisciplinary*. This would allow the rationale for the traditional curriculum to be shifted (really, returned) from the expanding communities sequence to introducing students to the social aspects of the human condition (in general, and in their country and locale, in particular). Arguments about content then would focus on its relative value in providing a sound basis for developing fundamental understandings about the human condition, not about which discipline it comes from or how it fits within the expanding communities sequence.

The expanding communities sequence would no longer be seen as essential to the primary curriculum, although it would remain a possible option (it is not logically or psychologically necessary, but neither is any other organizational scheme, and 75 years of experience with it have shown that it offers several advantages). Even if the sequence is not used, it still is advisable to scaffold primary students' initial processing of new topics by helping them connect with relevant prior knowledge and experience, and to continue to facilitate such connections as instruction moves away from the here and now.

OTHER CURRICULAR DEVELOPMENTS

Instructional resources

Textbook series remain problematic. Because of mergers and acquisitions in the industry, only a few major publishers now offer K–6 textbook series, and with social studies on the back burner, they have little incentive to undertake wholesale revisions or even frequent updates. They have addressed some of the criticisms of their series, but improvements are notable mostly at the middle and upper grades. There is still very little content in the texts for the primary grades, and neither the content nor the suggested activities go very far toward establishing a coherent social studies program.

In contrast, there has been a welcome proliferation of alternative instructional materials, children's literature, and internet websites suitable for use as texts or bases for activities in social studies. However, few primary teachers have clear enough visions of social studies to enable them to make good use of these resources. Furthermore, fewer than 1% are members of social studies organizations or attend their meetings with any regularity (Finkelstein, Nielsen, & Switzer, 1993; Haas & Laughlin, 2001; VanFossen, 2005).

The National Council for the Social Studies (1994) has developed content and process standards that should help teachers to focus social studies instruction on big ideas and their applications. These can be used either as building blocks around which to develop instructional units (Krey, 1995) or as checklists against which to assess the scope and balance of unit plans developed on some other basis (Alleman & Brophy, 1995).

Alternative curricula

In recent years, two alternative primary curricula have been developed and made available through sources other than the publishers of K–6 elementary series. Of these, the Core Knowledge curriculum overlaps with the visions put forth by history curriculum advocates, and the Cultural Universals curriculum overlaps with the traditional curriculum.

Core Knowledge curriculum   The Core Knowledge curriculum is rooted in the ideas of E.D. Hirsch, Jr. (1987), who proposed cultural literacy as the basis for curriculum development. He produced a list of over 5,000 items of information that he believed should be acquired in elementary school to equip students with a common base of cultural knowledge. However, his list was not an ideal content base because it was fragmented and dubiously extensive (e.g., knowing that Alexander's horse was named Bucephalus), emphasizing breadth of coverage of disconnected details over development of connected knowledge structured around powerful ideas.

However, educators inspired by Hirsch later developed the Core Knowledge curriculum (Core Knowledge Foundation, 1999), in which the social studies strands are built around historical studies. First graders study ancient Egypt and the early American civilizations (Mayas, Incas, Aztecs). Second graders study ancient India, China, and Greece, along with American history up to the Civil War. Third graders study ancient Roman Byzantium, various Native American tribal groups, and the 13 English colonies prior to the American Revolution.

The Core Knowledge curriculum is a considerable improvement over Hirsch's list as a content base for primary social studies. However, it focuses on the distant past. A version of the traditional approach that begins with students' familiar environments but then moves to the past, to other cultures, and to the future constitutes a better rounded and more powerful introduction to social education than an exclusive focus on the past. Such a curriculum would equip students with many more concepts and principles that they could use to understand and explain their social experiences, thus providing them with bases for appreciating the value of social studies and developing related self-efficacy perceptions.

Cultural universals curriculum   Working within the rationale described above, Alleman and Brophy (2001, 2002b, 2003b) developed instructional units on nine cultural universals: food, clothing, shelter, communication, transportation, family living, money, government, and childhood around the world. These units address many of the same topics addressed in the traditional curriculum, but with greater focus on big ideas. This approach provides a sound basis for developing fundamental understandings about the human condition, because: (a) activities relating to cultural universals account for a considerable proportion of everyday living and are the focus of much human social organization and communal activity, so until children understand the motivations and causal explanations that underlie these activities, they do not understand much of what is happening around them all the time; (b) children from all social backgrounds begin accumulating direct personal experiences with most cultural universals right from birth, so content on these topics is easier to connect to their prior knowledge and develop in ways that stay close to their experience; (c) because such content is inherently about humans taking action to meet basic needs and wants, it lends itself well to presentation within narrative formats; (d) narratives focused on humans engaged in goal-oriented behavior provide frequent opportunities to introduce basic disciplinary concepts and principles, to explore causal relationships, and to make explicit some of the social intentions and economic or political processes that children usually do not recognize or appreciate; (e) because it focuses on people taking actions to meet basic needs and pursue common wants, students are likely to view the content as relevant and to appreciate follow-up activities as authentic (because they will have applications to life outside of school); and (f) although the lessons often deal with life in the past or in other cultures, they focus on commonalities (people pursuing familiar needs and wants), so they highlight similarities rather than differences and thus promote empathy to help counteract the tendencies toward presentism and chauvinism that are common in young children's thinking about the past and about other cultures (Brophy & Alleman, 2006; Davis, Yeager, & Foster, 2001).

Literacy adaptations

In recent years, textbook series have begun including literature selections, with mixed results (Alleman & Brophy, 1994). In addition, literacy materials (children's tradebooks) and instructional techniques have been integrated into primary social studies.

Tradebooks as teaching resources   Tradebooks for children have broadened from traditional forms of children's fiction to include other genres more useful as resources for social studies teaching. These include narrative works such as biographies and factually based stories about life in the past or in other cultures, as well as informational texts on geographical and social science topics. We view the use of well chosen tradebooks as a welcome enrichment of primary social studies, so long as it amounts to an incorporation of children's literature into social studies and not an expansion of literacy at the expense of social studies.

Each year, the May/June issue of *Social Education* includes an annotated review of children's tradebooks that have special potential as social education resources. In addition, social educators have been publishing guidelines for selecting and using tradebooks as bases for social studies lessons (Field, 2003; Hicks, 1996; Houser, 1999; Kim & Garcia, 1996; Lamme, 1994; Marra, 1996; McGowan & Powell, 1996; Sullivan, 1996; Tunnell & Ammon, 1993). McGowan, Erickson, and Neufeld (1996) summarized the arguments and evidence relating to incorporation of children's literature into early social studies. They concluded that the arguments were persuasive, but the available evidence was thin and inconclusive.

Storypath   A different form of integration of literacy into social studies is represented by the Storypath curriculum developed by McGuire (1997a). Storypath combines constructivist learning principles with the narrative format to engage the class in developing stories related to social studies topics. The teacher provides needed scaffolding (primarily by posing questions), but the students develop the story during both whole-class discussions and pair or small-group brainstorming and writing activities. In a kindergarten example (Fulwiler & McGuire, 1997), the teacher began by reading a description of a neighborhood and then inviting the students to elaborate the setting in which the story would take place. Next, the students imagined and developed profiles of families living in the neighborhood. Third, they developed a plot (about mobilizing to deal with litter, speeding cars, and other problems) and fleshed out its unfolding. Finally, they developed a conclusion that was logical to the story, provided closure, and made for a satisfying experience.

Storypath involves a great deal of oral and written construction, in which students access their prior knowledge to construct a story that incorporates responses to the teacher's questions (which are designed to ensure that the activity promotes social studies purposes and goals). Unit summaries for the primary grades address topics such as families in their neighborhoods, the community's business district, a safari to Kenya, and the Wampanoags' Thanksgiving.

Curricular integration

Curricular integration is a topic of perennial interest, as it applies both within social studies (arguments for pandisciplinary content vs. separate courses in history, geography, and the social sciences) and within the larger curriculum (arguments for integrating social studies with other subjects, especially literacy). In recent years, spillover from both high-stakes testing and the culture wars have created external pressures for more of the latter form of integration (Hinde, 2005).

Many primary teachers have been salvaging what they can of the social studies curriculum by including within their literacy curriculum reading selections and writing assignments that connect to social education themes. From a social studies perspective, this is better than nothing, but it is not a coherent curriculum structured around social education goals. It does support progress toward literacy goals: Frequent reading of informational texts (primarily trade books with science or social studies themes) leads to better progress in literacy than a literacy curriculum focused heavily on fiction (Duke, 2000; Pappas, 1993).

Those who would replace pandisciplinary social studies typically envision a celebratory history curriculum that subsumes traditional civic and character education themes. Along with biographies and historical fiction, it would include frequent exposures to myth, lore, fables, folk tales, and fairy tales. From a social education perspective, this is counterproductive. Myth and lore may be worth studying as literature (i.e., within the literacy curriculum), but usually not as social studies. Stories about Paul Bunyan or Pecos Bill might be interesting to children, and the story of George Washington and the cherry tree might be a convenient fiction to use when teaching them about honesty. However, these are fictions, not historical accounts of actual events. At ages when children are struggling to distinguish what is true and continuing from what is false or fleeting, an emphasis on myth and lore is likely to interfere with their efforts to construct a reality-based model of the world. Further, most of the content of myth and lore reflects the thematic preoccupations and entertainment needs of pre-modern agrarian societies, not the social education needs of contemporary Americans. And, finally, a wealth of authentic children's literature, both nonfiction and factually accurate historical and cultural fiction, is available for introducing today's children to the human condition in ways that connect to their prior knowledge and experience (Brophy & Alleman, 2007; Seefeldt, 1993).

VISIONS OF POWERFUL TEACHING

In addition to curricular developments, there have been developments in ideas about making social studies teaching more powerful (meaningful, memorable, applicable). Some are rooted in generic notions about powerful teaching in any subject, while others are more specific to powerful teaching in social studies.

Teaching for understanding

One generic influence has been renewed appreciation of the importance of teaching for understanding, particularly by connecting instruction to prior knowledge, structuring the content around big ideas, and developing these ideas in depth with emphasis on their connections and applications (Bransford, Brown, & Cocking, 1999; Newton, 2000). Critiques of textbooks routinely bemoan their lack of focus around big ideas and disparage their content as parades of disconnected facts or even "trivial pursuit." International comparisons have heightened awareness of American texts and curriculum guidelines as "mile-wide but inch-deep" (Schmidt et al., 2001). Critics of the social studies activities suggested in textbooks or observed in classrooms have noted that they lack grounding in big ideas that would provide a basis for authentic applications (Brophy & Alleman, 1991). If the content base for an activity is listing the state birds or alphabetizing the state capitals, teachers cannot enrich it to make it more authentic. They need to shift to a different content base—big ideas with more potential for authentic application. These and related ideas about teaching for understanding are elaborated in the process guidelines in the NCSS (1994) vision statement, which depict powerful social studies teaching as meaningful, value-based, integrative, challenging, and active.

Research on children's thinking about social studies topics   An important component of teaching for understanding is connecting with students' prior knowledge. To do so, one needs information about common trajectories in children's knowledge in different domains. There has been noteworthy growth recently in developing such information in the social domain.

Brophy and Alleman (2006) studied developments in children's thinking about nine cultural universals commonly addressed in primary social studies. They found that, although children do accumulate some knowledge about these topics through everyday experience, this knowledge is mostly tacit, limited in scope, poorly connected, and frequently distorted by naïve ideas or outright misconceptions. It focuses on easily observable forms and functions of objects and actions, without understanding of less obvious cause-and-effect relationships and explanations. For example, most children can distinguish among business clothes, work clothes, and play clothes; but they think of cloth as a solid akin to plastic or leather, not realizing that it is a fabric woven from threads. Similarly, they recognize *tipis* as one type of Native American home, but usually are not aware that the plains tribes who constructed tipis did so because they were nomadic societies who needed portable housing. Lacking this knowledge (and more generally, knowledge about nomadic societies that must move periodically because they depend on hunting and gathering practices that deplete resources if they stay in one place too long), when asked why some tribes lived in tipis, the children said that the people were poor and couldn't afford better housing, were small families that didn't need bigger housing, liked to cook and the smoke would go out the top, or needed a use for animal skins that otherwise would be wasted.

Other studies have addressed children's developing knowledge about economics, history, politics and government, social class, and world cultures. Most of the findings have been synthesized in four books (Barrett & Buchanan-Barrow, 2005; Berti & Bombi, 1988; Brophy & Alleman, 2006; Furnham & Stacey, 2001) and in other chapters in this handbook.

Incorporating constructivist teaching

Another recent trend affecting social studies is enthusiasm for constructivist theories of learning and approaches to teaching. The image of a teacher scaffolding co-construction of understandings within a collaborative learning community is more attractive than the image of a teacher lecturing to mostly passive listeners. Similarly, the image of students collaborating in pairs or groups during inquiry or decision-making activities is more attractive than the image of students silently filling out worksheets. However, not everything involving discussion or hands-on activity serves worthwhile curricular purposes or helps students to construct significant understandings. Misguided constructivist notions can lead to students making pyramids from sugar cubes, Native American necklaces from macaroni, or Conestoga wagons from popsicle sticks, without learning anything significant about Egypt, Native American cultures, or the frontier (Frazee & Ayers, 2003).

Textbooks and other publications by social studies educators often advocate constructivist teaching (Grant, 1997; Scheurman, 1998) and some suggest learning activities for the primary grades (Levstik, 1993; Levstik & Smith, 1996). However, there are limits to the feasibility of constructivist teaching in early social studies, especially when introducing students to new content (propositional knowledge). Here, presentation of information in the early stages of lessons or units may be required to establish a common knowledge base before moving on to activities calling for processing and applying this knowledge.

Nuthall (2002, 2004) noted that effective discussion depends on students sharing a base of knowledge that can be referred to without explanation or elaboration. He found that, even at the intermediate grades, widespread possession of mutually shared knowledge is relatively uncommon in social studies unless it relates to an experience that all of the students have recently shared. Consequently, relatively few students make consistent contributions to discussion, and momentum is frequently interrupted because students cannot respond or communicate misconceptions. Furthermore, many students remember the misconceptions expressed by peers rather than the target conceptions that the teacher was attempting to develop.

The problems reported by Nuthall occur even more frequently in the early grades because: (a) the students are young learners with as-yet only partially developed skills for learning through speaking and listening and undeveloped skills for learning through reading and writing; and (b) their prior knowledge about social studies topics is usually very limited and poorly articulated, so that questions frequently fail to produce responses, or they elicit irrelevant or invalid statements (Brophy, 2006).

Analyses of social studies lessons taught by Barbara Knighton illustrate how information presentation and constructivist teaching can be blended in ways that address the limitations of young learners, yet encourage them to personalize and apply their learning. When introducing a new topic, she asks students to tell what they wonder or would like to learn about it (which yields mostly useful questions) but usually does not ask them to tell what they think they know about it (which yields many misconceptions). She provides basic information during whole-class instruction early in a lesson or unit, then follows up with small-group or partner activities that allow students to draw on what they know or have experienced. Most information is communicated using an informal, narrative style that includes frequent opportunities for students to ask or respond to questions. Following (or even between) such segments of whole-class lessons, Knighton will instruct her students to "turn to your partner and share your ideas," or "talk with your table group to decide what you think was the most important idea." In addition, most lessons include home assignments calling for students to collaborate with their parents in carrying out some activity relating to what was learned that day in class (Alleman, Brophy, & Knighton, 2003).

Narrative teaching style Much of children's knowledge is organized and retained within narrative structures that more closely resemble stories than the conceptual structures of the social sciences (Bruner, 1990). Knighton takes advantage of her young learners' familiarity with the narrative structure by transmitting new information using an informal, narrative style. She typically begins with examples from her own life, then connects to examples from her students' lives, then extends to talk about the concepts or principles as they apply in society generally, as they developed in the past, and as they play out in other cultures. Most of this content is related within the context of talking about people engaged in goal-oriented behavior for reasons that the students can understand. This helps them to retain the narrative structure and many of the particulars as meaningful and connected knowledge.

Co-construction of learning resources   A noteworthy component of many of Knighton's lessons is the co-construction of learning resources such as visual displays (timelines, posters, graphs, or outlines). The discourse that occurs during the construction process allows her to focus on the big ideas that she wants to emphasize and to develop a common vocabulary for talking about them. Once the resource is constructed and used to synthesize big ideas emphasized in that day's lesson, it is posted for reference in future lessons and follow-up activities.

TEACHING DISCIPLINE-BASED CONTENT

Some of the recent research and scholarship targeted for the primary grades has focused on the learning and teaching of history, geography, or one of the social sciences. We will not attempt systematic coverage of these contributions because other chapters focus on the separate social studies disciplines, but we do want to call attention to a few noteworthy developments.

Works on history teaching emphasize that primary students are interested in and capable of learning historical content (especially when it is presented within narrative structures with emphasis on big ideas rather than as chronologies overloaded with names, dates, and other details) and that the content should counteract children's predispositions toward presentism by fostering empathy with the people being studied (Cooper, 1995; Seefeldt, 1993). Barton and Levstik (2004) synthesized these and related ideas about teaching history to young children, and Levstik and Barton (2005) offered instructional plans, lesson analyses, and other guidelines for fleshing them out within an inquiry approach. Other sources also emphasized the value of exposing students to varied data sources and providing them with opportunities to conduct historical inquiry, to synthesize and communicate their findings, and to learn from listening to or reading biography and historical fiction as well as conventional textbooks (Fertig, 2005; Harmes & Lettow, 1994; Lamme, 1994; Sunal & Haas, 1993).

Articles suggesting historical activities for primary students often recommended engaging them in research on their own personal or family history or on local history (Hickey, 1999; Leigh & Reynolds, 1997; McBee, Bone, Mossop, & Owens, 1998; Rose, 2000; Schwartz, 2000). These and other sources also commonly suggested using a variety of primary sources, photos, and physical artifacts (Barton, 2001; Field, Labbo, Wilhelm, & Garrett,1996; Haas, 2000; Hickey, 1997). Barton (2005) cautioned that historical artifacts need to be used for appropriate purposes within well-designed lessons. He gave examples of ways that such sources can be used unproductively.

Timelines continue to be recommended for representing chronological sequences, although it is important to keep them relatively simple. Alleman and Brophy (2003a) described lessons in which the teacher co-constructed timelines with her students. Masterman and Rogers (2002) analyzed the affordances and constraints of alternative chronological representations (circular clocks, horizontal or vertical timelines, meandering paths taken by time travelers in computer-mediated games).

Social educators commonly note that television brings non-western lands and cultures into the home early, so that if one waits until the sixth grade to begin teaching world geography and cultures with an emphasis on human commonalities, it may be too late to overcome the ethno-centrism that has developed in the meantime (Merryfield & Wilson, 2005). They also emphasize the importance of conveying an *insider's* perspective on cultural practices, as well as conveying a balanced picture of the culture, rather than overemphasizing the exotic. As Merryfield (2004) put it, "If Japanese students made quilts, ate southern fried chicken and Boston baked beans, and sang 'Old Mac-Donald had a farm,' would they have acquired information that leads to understanding of Americans today?" (p. 270).

Anthropologists often advocate using examples of cultural diversity to "make the familiar strange" and "make the strange familiar." For example, people in some countries use chopsticks instead of forks, wear white instead of black at funerals, or bow rather than shake hands. Most such differences are means for accomplishing the same ends (bringing food to the mouth, expressing grief, performing a greeting ritual as a prelude to social interaction). Many are explainable with reference to economic resources or cultural practices. Sources of guidelines on these and other ideas for teaching about cultures include Cunha (2001), Haas (2001), Marra (1996), and Payne and Gay (1997).

Social studies educators tend to favor exposing students to multiple perspectives in respectful ways, as evidenced by the NCSS (1994) standards and the statement on education and diversity from the Multicultural Education Consensus Panel (Banks et al., 2005). They call for infusing global and multicultural perspectives throughout the curriculum rather than planning special units that address global or multicultural topics, but otherwise wall them off from the rest of the curriculum. They also emphasize fostering empathy and emphasizing commonalities over differences when teaching about people in other cultures. Merryfield (2004) presented five strategies for engaging elementary students in substantive culture learning, Sullivan (1996) offered principles for using tradebooks in ways that counter stereotypes, and Field (2003) provided suggestions and tradebook references for using children's literature to teach about Mexico.

Economics educators often recommend using children's literature as a vehicle for teaching economic concepts and principles (Kehler, 1998; Suiter & Meszaros, 2005; VanFossen, 2003). The most powerful and lasting economics lessons, however, are likely to involve experiential learning in which students are engaged in economic activities or decision-making followed by debriefing discussions focusing on key principles (Laney, 2001; Laney & Schug, 1998). For example, children can come to understand and appreciate the concept of opportunity cost through activities that call for them to make decisions about allocating their time or money and then to discuss the trade-offs (e.g., when you allocate some time or money to one purpose, you simultaneously forego opportunities to use it for another purpose).

Economics educators and organizations have developed series of lessons that provide experiential economics learning for primary-grade students. These include the Kinder-Economy (Kourilsky, 1992), Children in the Marketplace (NCEE, 2005), Money Savvy Kids (Schug & Hagedorn, 2005), and Small-Size Economics (Skeel, 1988).

Primary teachers often dislike teaching about government, probably because traditional approaches featured relatively dry and abstract lessons on topics such as how a bill becomes a law. Students tend to respond positively, however, when taught about why governments are needed and what they do for their people (i.e., provide facilities and services that are too big in scope, expense, and so on, for individuals to provide for themselves). This can be brought home to students by taking them through a typical day in their lives and underscoring the role of governments in facilitating their activities (Alleman & Brophy, 2002a).

Lesson plans and children's literature resources for teaching about government, and especially the presidency, are plentiful, but they often focus on the trivial and stop well short of genuine civic education. This produces outcomes like the one reported by Haas (2004): A middle school student who had completed a report on President Reagan recalled only three facts: Reagan was called "the Gipper"; he had a sense of humor; and he loved jelly beans. For ideas about teaching about the presidency and presidential elections, see Haas (2004), McGuire (1997b), www.Bensguide.gpo.gov/3-5/election/index.html, or www.kidsvotingusa.org.

Many states now require instruction relating to core democratic values. This is a welcome development, but much of this instruction is relatively stilted, focusing on definitions and preparation for state tests. Information on how core values can be defined and taught meaningfully at different grade levels can be found at the website of the Michigan Department of Education: www.michigan.gov.mde.

Instruction in civic content increases civic knowledge but usually has negligible effects on attitudes and dispositions related to civic and political participation. However, both sets of outcomes are likely when students frequently discuss issues, hear and explore alternative views, and feel comfortable expressing their own opinions because the teacher maintains a classroom atmosphere that supports this kind of thoughtful discourse (Torney-Purta, Hahn, & Amadeo, 2001). Social studies educators have published guidelines and case studies indicating that social issues, including controversial ones, can be addressed safely and productively in primary classrooms (Bickmore, 1999; Houser, 1996; Houser & Overton, 2001; Ochoa-Becker, Morton, & Autry, 2001).

TECHNOLOGY

Despite the recent emphasis on technology in general, and computers and the Internet in particular, very few primary teachers make much use of technology for teaching social studies (VanFossen, 2004), probably because of perceived developmental readiness constraints. Technologically mediated learning experiences, especially those involving conducting inquiry via the Internet, require reading-comprehension, direction-following, and self-regulated learning skills that most K–3 students do not yet possess. However, some websites and technology applications are suitable for use in the primary grades, at least by teachers with sufficient access to computers and technological support.

For example, Keypals sites make it possible for individual students to write to one another online or submit contributions to a group bulletin board, and for classes to exchange group letters or work together on projects (Finegan-Stoll, 1998). Another possibility is WebQuest sites, which eliminate the need to search for information by providing self-contained modules that scaffold Internet-based content to an inquiry process that results in a product or project (Webquest, 2007). Teachers can preview and control the content to which their students will be exposed. Many WebQuests are suitable for the primary grades, such as one that invites third graders to learn about a day in the life a Japanese child. For information about WebQuests in early social studies and links to useful websites, see VanFossen (2004).

CONCLUSION

Our status report on primary social studies has yielded a mixed picture. The short-term outlook is discouraging because of the widespread reduction or even elimination of the subject as an independent component of the K–3 curriculum. Increasing awareness of this problem has created concerns that expand beyond the social education community, however, so there is some basis for optimism about the future. There also is reason to celebrate the increased research and scholarly attention that has focused on primary social studies in recent years. However, to date most of these publications have featured standards, models, guidelines, or suggested lessons, but not formal presentation of empirical data. Empirical research is still very rare in early social studies, especially studies documenting the effects of particular curricula or instructional methods on the social knowledge and civic efficacy outcomes of greatest interest to social educators.

REFERENCES

Akenson, J. (1989). The expanding environments in elementary education: A critical perspective. *Theory and Research in Social Education, 17,* 33–52.

Alleman, J., & Brophy, J. (1993). Is curriculum integration a boon or a threat to social studies? *Social Education, 57,* 287–291.

Alleman, J., & Brophy, J. (1994). Trade-offs embedded in the literary approach to early elementary social studies. *Social Studies and the Young Learner, 6*(3), 6–8.

Alleman, J., & Brophy, J. (1995). NCSS social studies standards and the elementary teacher. *Social Studies and the Young Learner, 8*(1), 4–8.

Alleman, J., & Brophy, J. (2001). *Social studies excursions, K-3. Book One: Powerful units on food, clothing, and shelter.* Portsmouth, NH: Heinemann.

Alleman, J., & Brophy, J. (2002a). How to make government a class favorite. *Social Studies and the Young Learner, 15*(1), 6–10.

Alleman, J., & Brophy, J. (2002b). *Social studies excursions, K-3. Book Two: Powerful units on communication, transportation, and family living.* Portsmouth, NH: Heinemann.

Alleman, J., & Brophy, J. (2003a). History is alive: Teaching children about changes over time. *Social Studies, 94,* 97–110.

Alleman, J., & Brophy, J. (2003b). *Social studies excursions, K-3. Book Three: Powerful units on childhood, money, and government.* Portsmouth, NH: Heinemann.

Alleman, J., Brophy, J., & Knighton, B. (2003). Co-constructing classroom resources. *Social Studies and the Young Learner, 16*(2), 5–8.

Alter, G. (1995). Transforming elementary social studies: The emergence of a curriculum focused on diverse, caring communities. *Theory and Research in Social Education, 23,* 355–374.

Armento, B. (1993). Reform revisited: The story of elementary social studies at the crest of the 21st century. In V. Wilson, J. Litel, & G. Wilson (Eds.), *Teaching social studies: Handbook of trends, issues, and implications for the future* (pp. 25–44). Westport, CT: Greenwood.

Atwood, V. (1986). Elementary social studies: Cornerstone or crumbling mortar? In V. Atwood (Ed.), *Elementary school social studies: Research as guide to practice* (Bulletin No. 79, pp. 1–13). Washington, DC: National Council for the Social Studies.

Banks, J., Cookson, P., Gay, G., Hawley, W., Irvine, J., Nieto, S., Schofield, J., & Stephan, W. (2005). Education and diversity. *Social Education, 69,* 36–40.

Barrett, M., & Buchanan-Barrow, E. (Eds.). (2005). *Children's understanding of society.* Hove, England: Psychology Press.

Barton, K. (2001). A picture's worth: Analyzing historical photographs in the elementary grades. *Social Education, 65,* 278–283.

Barton, K. (2005). Primary sources in history: Breaking through the myths. *Phi Delta Kappan, 86,* 745–753.

Barton, K., & Levstik, L. (2004). *Teaching history for the common good.* Mahwah, NJ: Erlbaum.

Berti, A., & Bombi, A. (1988). *The child's construction of economics.* Cambridge: Cambridge University Press.

Bickmore, K. (1999). Elementary curriculum about conflict resolution: Can children handle global politics? *Theory and Research in Social Education, 27,* 45–69.

Bransford, J., Brown, A., & Cocking, R. (Eds.). (1999). *How people learn: Brain, mind, experience, and school.* Washington, DC: National Academy Press.

Brophy, J. (1992). The de facto national curriculum in U.S. elementary social studies: Critique of a representative example. *Journal of Curriculum Studies, 24,* 401–447.

Brophy, J. (2006). Graham Nuthall and social constructivist teaching: Research-based cautions and qualifications. *Teaching and Teacher Education, 22,* 529–537.

Brophy, J., & Alleman, J. (1991). Activities as instructional tools: A framework for analysis and evaluation. *Educational Researcher, 20*(4), 9–23.

Brophy, J., & Alleman, J. (2006). *Children's thinking about cultural universals.* Mahwah, NJ: Erlbaum.

Brophy, J., & Alleman, J. (2007). *Powerful social studies for elementary students* (2nd ed.). Belmont, CA: Thomson Wadsworth.

Brophy, J., Alleman, J., & O'Mahony, C. (2000). Elementary school social studies: Yesterday, today, and tomorrow. In T. Good (Ed.), *American education: Yesterday, today, and tomorrow* (99th Yearbook of the National Society for the Study of Education, Part II, pp. 256–312). Chicago: University of Chicago Press.

Bruner, J. (1990). *Acts of meaning.* Cambridge, MA: Howard University Press.

California Department of Education. (1997). *History-social science framework for California public schools: Kindergarten through grade 12.* Sacramento, CA: Author.

Cooper, H. (1995). *History in the early years.* New York: Routledge.

Core Knowledge Foundation. (1999). *The Core Knowledge sequence.* Charlottesville, VA: Core Knowledge Foundation. Available at http://www.coreknowledge.org.

Cornbleth, C., & Waugh, D. (1999). *The great speckled bird: Multicultural politics and education policymaking.* Mahwah, NJ: Erlbaum.

Cuban, L. (1991). History of teaching in social studies. In J. Shaver (Ed.), *Handbook of research on social studies teaching and learning* (pp. 197–209). New York: Macmillan.

Cunha, S. (2001). Teaching methods in cultural geography: Making a world of difference. In J. Brophy (Ed.), *Subject-specific instructional methods and activities* (pp. 347–372). New York: Elsevier Science.

Davis, O. L., Jr., Yeager, E., & Foster, S. (Eds.). (2001). *Historical empathy and perspective taking in the social studies.* New York: Rowman & Littlefield.

Duke, N. (2000). 3.6 minutes per day: The scarcity of informational texts in first grade. *Reading Research Quarterly, 35,* 202–225.

Evans, R. (2004). *The social studies wars: What should we teach the children?* New York: Teachers College Press.

Fertig, G. (2005). Teaching elementary students how to interpret the past. *Social Studies, 96,* 2–8.

Field, S. (2003). Using children's literature and the universals of culture to teach about Mexico. *The Social Studies, 96,* 123–127.

Field, S., Labbo, L., Willhem, R., & Garrett, A. (1996). To touch, to feel, to see: Artifact inquiry in the social studies classroom. *Social Education, 60,* 141–143.

Finegan-Stoll, C. (1998). Keypals for young children. *Social Studies and the Young Learner, 11*(1), 28–29.

Finkelstein, J., Nielsen, L., & Switzer, T. (1993). Primary elementary social studies instruction: A status report. *Social Education, 57,* 64–69.

Frazee, B., & Ayers, S. (2003). Garbage in, garbage out: Expanding environments, constructivism, and content knowledge in social studies. In J. Leming, L. Ellington, & K. Porter (Eds.), *Where did social studies go wrong?* (pp. 111–123). Washington, DC: Thomas B. Fordham Foundation.

Fulwiler, B., & McGuire, M. (1997). Storypath: Powerful social studies instruction in the primary grades. *Social Studies and the Young Learner, 9*(3), 4–7.

Furnham, A., & Stacey, B. (2001). *Young people's understanding of society.* New York: Routledge.

Gagnon, P. (1989). Democracy's Half-told story: What American hstory textbooks should add. Washington, DC: Education for Democracy Project of the American Federation of Teachers, 1989. ED 313 305.

Grant, S. G. (1997). A policy at odds with itself: The tension between constructivist and traditional views in the New York State Social Studies Framework. *Journal of Curriculum and Supervision, 13,* 92–113.

Haas, M. (1991). An analysis of the social science and history concepts in elementary social studies textbooks Grades 1–4. *Theory and Research in Social Education, 19,* 211–220.

Haas, M. (2000). *A Street Through Time* used with powerful instructional strategies. *Social Studies and the Young Learner, 13*(2), 20–23.

Haas, M. (2001). Strategies for increasing achievement in geography. In R. Cole (Ed.), *More strategies for educating everybody's children* (pp. 87–100). Baltimore: Association for Supervision and Curriculum Development.

Haas, M. (2004). The presidency and presidential elections in the elementary classroom. *Social Education, 68,* 340–346.

Haas, M., & Laughlin, M. (Eds). (1997). *Meeting the standards: Social studies readings for K-6 educators.* Washington, DC: National Council for the Social Studies.

Haas, M., & Laughlin, M. (2001). A profile of elementary social studies teachers and their classrooms. *Social Education, 65,* 122–126.

Hanna, P. (1963). Revising the social studies: What is needed? *Social Education, 27,* 190–196.

Harmes, J., & Lettow, L. (1994). Criteria for selecting picture books with historical settings. *Social Education, 58*, 152–154.

Hickey, M.G. (1997). Bloomers, bellbottoms, and hula hoops: Artifact collections aid children's historical interpretation. *Social Education, 61*, 293–299.

Hickey, M. G. (1999). *Bringing history home: Local and family history projects for Grades K-6.* Boston: Allyn & Bacon.

Hicks, S. (1996). Promoting civic competence using children's tradebooks: Ideas for pre K-4 classrooms. *Social Education, 60*, 216–219.

Hinde, E. (2005). Revisiting curriculum integration: A fresh look at an old idea. *Social Education, 96*, 105–111.

Hirsch, Jr., E. D. (1987). *Cultural literacy: What every American needs to know.* New York: Houghton Mifflin.

Houser, N. (1995). Social studies on the back burner: Views from the field. *Theory and Research in Social Education, 23*, 147–168.

Houser, N. (1996). Negotiating dissonance and safety for the common good: Social education in the elementary classroom. *Theory and Research in Social Education, 24*, 294–312.

Houser, N. (1999). Critical literature for the social studies: Challenges and opportunities for the elementary classroom. *Social Education, 63*, 212–215.

Houser, N., & Overton, S. (2001). Reconciling freedom and control in the early grades: Toward a critical consciousness for a freedom of choice. *Theory and Research in Social Education, 29*, 582–616.

Howard, R. (2003). The shrinking of social studies. *Social Education, 67*, 285–288.

Kehler, A. (1998). Capturing the "economic imagination": A treasury of children's books to meet content standards. *Social Studies and the Young Learner, 11*(2), 26–29.

Kim, C., & Garcia, J. (1996). Diversity and tradebooks: Promoting conceptual learning in social studies. *Social Education, 60*, 208–211.

Kourilsky, M. (1992). *KinderEconomy: A multidisciplinary learning society for primary grades.* New York: Joint Council on Economic Education.

Krey, D. (1995). Operationalizing the thematic strands of social studies for young learners. *Social Studies and the Young Learner, 8*(1), 12–15.

Krey, D. (1998). *Children's literature in social studies: Teaching to the standards* (Bulletin No. 95). Waldorf, MD: National Council for the Social Studies.

Lamme, L. (1994). Stories from our past: Making history come alive for children. *Social Education, 58*, 159–164.

Laney, J. (2001). Enhancing economic education through improved teaching methods: Common sense made easy. In J. Brophy (Ed.), *Subject-specific instructional methods and activities* (pp. 411–435). New York: Elsevier Science.

Laney, J., & Schug, M. (1998). Teach kids economics and they will learn. *Social Studies and the Young Learner, 11*(2), 13–17.

Larkins, A., Hawkins, M., & Gilmore, A. (1987). Trivial and noninformative content of elementary social studies: A review of primary texts in four series. *Theory and Research in Social Education, 15*, 299–311.

Leigh, A., & Reynolds, C. (1997). Little windows to the past. *Social Education, 61*, 45–47.

LeRiche, L. (1987). The expanding environments sequence in elementary social studies: The origins. *Theory and Research in Social Education, 15*, 137–154.

LeRiche, L. (1992). The political socialization of children in the expanding environments sequence. *Theory and Research in Social Education, 20*, 126–140.

Levstik, L. (1993). Building a sense of history in a first-grade classroom. In J. Brophy (Ed.), *Advances in research on teaching* (Vol. 4, pp. 1–31). Greenwich, CT: JAI Press.

Levstik, L., & Barton, K. (2005). *Doing history: Investigating with children in elementary and middle schools* (3rd ed.). Mahwah, NJ: Erlbaum.

Levstik, L., & Smith, D. (1996). "I've never done this before": Building a community of historical inquiry in a third-grade classroom. In J. Brophy (Ed.), *Advances in research on teaching: Teaching and learning history* (Vol. 6, pp. 85–114). Greenwich, CT: JAI Press.

Marker, G., & Mehlinger, H. (1992). Social studies. In P. Jackson (Ed.), *Handbook of research on curriculum* (pp. 830–851). New York: Macmillan.

Marra, D. (1996). Teaching to the national geography standards through children's picture books. *Journal of Geography, 95*, 148–152.

Masterman, E., & Rogers, Y. (2002). A framework for designing interactive multimedia to scaffold young children's understanding of historical chronology. *Instructional Science, 30*, 221–241.

McBee, R., Bone, K., Mossop, G., & Owens, C. (1998). Common threads: Teaching immigration in elementary classrooms. *Social Education, 62*, 417–419.

McGowan, T., Erickson, L., & Neufeld, J. (1996). With reason and rhetoric: Building the case for the literature-social studies connection. *Social Education, 60*, 203–207.

McGowan, M., & Powell, J. (1996). An annotated bibliography of resources for literature-based instruction. *Social Education, 60*, 231–232.

McGuire, M. (1997a). *Storypath foundations: An innovative approach to teaching social studies.* Chicago: Everyday Learning.

McGuire, M. (1997b). *The presidential election.* Chicago: Everyday Learning.

Merryfield, M. (2004). Elementary students in substantive culture learning. *Social Education, 68*, 270–273.

Merryfield, M., & Wilson, A. (2005). *Social studies and the world: Teaching global perspectives* (Bulletin No. 103). Silver Spring, MD: National Council for the Social Studies.

National Council on Economic Education. (2005). *Children in the marketplace: Lesson plans in economics for grades 3 and 4* (2nd ed.). Washington, DC: Author.

National Council for the Social Studies. (1989). Social studies for early childhood and elementary school children: Preparing for the 21st century (a report from NCSS Task Force on Early Childhood/Elementary Social Studies). *Social Education, 53*, 14–22.

National Council for the Social Studies. (1994). *Expectations of excellence: Curriculum standards for social studies.* Washington, DC: National Council for the Social Studies.

Newton, D. (2000). *Teaching for understanding: What it is and how to do it.* New York: Routledge/Palmer.

Nuthall, G. (2002). Social constructivist teaching and the shaping of students' knowledge and thinking. In J. Brophy (Ed.), *Social constructivist teaching: Affordances and constraints* (pp. 43–79). New York: Elsevier.

Nuthall, G. (2004). Relating classroom teaching to student learning: A critical analysis of why research has failed to bridge the theory-practice gap. *Harvard Educational Review, 74*, 273–306.

Ochoa-Becker, A., Morton, M., & Autry, M. (2001). A search for decision making in three elementary classrooms: A pilot study. *Theory and Research in Social Education, 29*, 261–289.

Pappas, C. (1993). Some insights from kindergarteners' pretend readings of stories and information books. *Journal of Reading Behavior, 25*, 97–129.

Pascopella, A. (2005). Staying alive: Social studies in elementary schools. *Social Studies and the Young Learner, 17*(3), 30–32.

Payne, H., & Gay, S. (1997). Exploring cultural universals. *Journal of Geography, 94*, 220–223.

Ravitch, D. (1987). Tot sociology or what happened to history in the grade schools. *American Scholar, 56*, 343–353.

Rose, S. (2000). Fourth graders theorize prejudice in American history. *International Journal of Historical Learning, Teaching, and Research, 1*(1), 1–11.

Scheurman, G. (1998). From behaviorist to constructivist teaching. *Social Education, 62*, 6–9.

Schmidt, W., McKnight, C., Houang, R., Wang, H., Wiley, D., Cogan, L., & Wolfe, R. (2001). *Why schools matter: A cross-national comparison of curriculum and learning.* San Francisco: Jossey-Bass.

Schug, M., & Hagedorn, E. (2005). The Money Savvy Pig goes to the big city: Testing the effectiveness of an economics curriculum for young children. *Social Studies, 96*, 68–71.

Schwartz, S. (2000). My family's story: Discovering history at home. *Social Studies and the Young Learner,12*(3), 6–9.

Seefeldt, C. (1993). History for young children. *Theory and Research in Social Education, 21*, 143–155.

Seixas, P. (2001). Review of research on social studies. In V. Richardson (Ed.), *Handbook of research on teaching* (4th ed., pp. 545–565). Washington, DC: American Educational Research Association.

Shaver, J. (Ed.). (1991). *Handbook of research on social studies teaching and learning.* New York: Macmillan.

Skeel, D. (1988). *Small-Size Economics: Lessons for the primary grades.* Glenview, IL: Scott, Foresman.

Suiter, M., & Meszaros, B. (2005). Teaching about saving and investing in the elementary and middle school grades. *Social Education, 69*, 92–95.

Sullivan, J. (1996). Real people, common themes: Using tradebooks to counter stereotypes. *Social Education, 60*, 399–401.

Sunal, C., & Haas, M. (1993). *Social studies and the elementary/middle school student.* Fort Worth, TX: Harcourt Brace Jovanovich.

Symcox, L. (2002). *Whose history? The struggle for national standards in American classrooms.* New York: Teachers College Press.

Thomas, R.M. (2005). *High-stakes testing: Coping with collateral damage.* Mahwah, NJ: Erlbaum.

Thornton, S. (2005). *Teaching social studies that matters: Curriculum for active learning.* New York: Teachers College Press.

Torney-Purta, J., Hahn, C., & Amadeo, J. (2001). Principles of subject-specific instruction in education for citizenship. In J. Brophy (Ed.), *Subject-specific instructional methods and activities* (pp. 373–410). New York: Elsevier Science.

Tunnell, M., & Ammon, R. (Eds.). (1993). *The story of ourselves: Teaching history through children's literature.* Portsmouth, NH: Heinemann.

VanFossen, P. (2003). Best practice economic education for young children? It's elementary! *Social Education, 67,* 90–94.

VanFossen, P. (2004). Using WebQuest to scaffold higher-order thinking. *Social Studies and the Young Learner, 16*(4), 13–16.

VanFossen, P. (2005). "Reading and math take so much of the time . . . ": An overview of social studies instruction in elementary classrooms in Indiana. *Theory and Research in Social Education, 33,* 376–403.

Webquest (2007). Retrieved November 19, 2007, from: http://webquest.org/index.php.

Wade, R. (2002). Beyond expanding horizons: New curriculum directions for elementary social studies. *Elementary School Journal, 103,* 115–130.

Zhao, Y., & Hoge, J. (2005). What elementary students and teachers say about social studies. *Social Studies, 96,* 216–221.

4   What happens in social studies classrooms?

Research on K–12 social studies practice

Linda S. Levstik

University of Kentucky

When students enter social studies classrooms, what happens? And, are social studies classrooms very different from a decade ago or half a century ago? In 1991, a survey conducted by the Council of State Social Studies Specialists (CSSS) of social studies offerings in K–12 classrooms in the United States revealed only slight shifts in patterns that prevailed throughout most of the previous 90 years of the 20th century (Svengalis, 1992). A decade later, however, a parallel study (Dye & Huffman, 2003) noted reductions in social studies course offerings, especially at the elementary level.

PATTERNS OF COURSE OFFERINGS

Patterns of course offerings in elementary social studies continue to reflect the expanding environments curriculum (starting with self and family and moving to community, state, and nation) prevalent through much of the 20th century. Sixth graders tend to study world regional geography, with seventh graders facing some form of world history and eighth graders marching their way through pre-20th-century American history. Although ninth-grade patterns vary considerably, tenth graders are likely to take world history, eleventh graders to take post-Reconstruction through 20th-century U.S. history, and twelfth graders to take civics or government with a smattering of electives in economics, psychology or, less often, sociology or anthropology (Dye & Huffman, 2003; Patrick, 1992).

As Brophy (1993) and Barton and Levstik (2004) note in reviewing studies of teacher practice, the same course may be enacted in very different ways, depending on individual teachers' goals, their sense of the purpose behind instruction in a particular discipline or area of the social studies, and the particular setting in which instruction takes place. Brophy (1993) further notes that the elementary teachers in the studies he reviewed emphasized student engagement and affective outcomes rather than content-specific goals or social critique. Even teachers who engaged elementary students in inquiries that included discussion of the moral dimensions of content tended to make fewer attempts to address controversies or provide "countersocialization" than might social studies scholars (p. 222). Further, Brophy argues that classroom studies make clear that "exemplary" social studies teachers vary considerably one from another:

> [T]hey often show maverick tendencies, being noteworthy for unusual or even unique approaches that are fueled by their personal interests in the subject and suited to their orientations and beliefs about what is involved in teaching it. These maverick tendencies of exemplary teachers call into question the feasibility and desirability of standardized curriculum guidelines and texts, even at the local level. (p. 225)

As a result, attempts to mandate particular forms of instruction within mandated course offerings should be viewed with considerable caution as more likely to inhibit exemplary teachers than mitigate the problems presented by weaker ones.

Attention to course offerings remains strong, however, in part as a means of gauging the strength of social studies across the nation. As a result, exceptions to national patterns take on particular significance, as the cases of California and Florida make clear. Rather than a social studies curriculum, California moved to a history/social science framework. The California framework emphasizes history from the primary grades on, beginning with "then and now" comparisons and emphasizing "people who make a difference" (California, 1988).[1] Two years after California adopted its framework, Florida moved to a curriculum focused on geography and history in an integrated program emphasizing literature and the arts, global comparisons, and the multiethnic character of Florida and the United States (Florida, 1990). Recent concern regarding the history curriculum, however, has led to legislative attempts to limit instruction in history to "facts" rather than interpretation (c.f. Organization of American Historians, 2006). State-level restructuring of social studies curricula continue in other states and continue to inspire concern and controversy (Leming, Ellington, & Porter-Magee, 2003; Rock et al., 2004; Stern, 2003).

RESTRUCTURED SOCIAL STUDIES

Several studies of curricular reform offer some insight into what happens in "restructured" classrooms, a generally under-researched aspect of social studies teaching and learning. In their study of New York City schools, Crocco and Thornton (2002) describe an inconsistent effect on social studies in restructured urban secondary schools. At one end of the instructional continuum, they found that the tendency to replace social studies with humanities courses (combined English and history) diluted social studies content. Restructured schools tended to have less experienced teachers, curriculum tended to be more fragmented, and social studies goals were often sacrificed to English goals. At the same time, administrators put less emphasis on content or lesson planning and provided less mentoring to their novice teachers, even though teachers would be expected to manage more complicated interdisciplinary instruction.

In a parallel study in a private school, Meister and Nolan (2001) investigated a group of secondary teachers faced with mandated integration of content. Over 3 years the teachers struggled with imposed changes, a history of "adopt and abandon" reforms, and subject matter loyalties. The researchers found that teachers with more "defined, unitary, and sequential" content were less likely to adapt to integrated instruction (p. 608). English and history teachers were better able to create integrative themes, but still worried about losing content that they considered important.

More experienced teachers better managed the challenges of restructured curricula, more often emphasizing depth over breadth in their instruction (Crocco & Thornton, 2002). They adapted changing standards to their own instructional goals, and provided more coherent instruction for their students. As Howard (2003) notes, these findings raise considerable concern in regard to urban schools where over 50% of beginning teachers leave within 5 years, and 16% do not even complete their first year. As a result, urban students rarely benefit from more experienced teaching. Indeed, 80% of urban districts in the United States employ non-certified teachers, 12% of whom have no training whatsoever. Further, close to half of *all* teachers will be retiring in the next decade (Howard, 2003). As a result, urban students are considerably less likely to encounter experienced teachers than might their suburban peers. Further complicating matters the teaching force in the United States is about 90.7% "White" with a student population predicted to be 46% "people of color" by 2040. Although schools across the country will be affected by changing demographics, urban schools may face more challenges as they seek to find and keep ambitious teachers who provide coherent, interesting and worthwhile social studies instruction in the context of shifting standards- and assessment-driven curricula and controversies over what constitutes legitimate social studies content (Grant, 2004; Nelson, 2001).

Controversies and uncertainties regarding content rise to the surface in the face of restructuring with sometimes frightening consequences for social studies educators. Nelson (2001), for instance, examines the controversy surrounding New York City's move to implement a "Rainbow Curriculum." The Rainbow Curriculum grew out of attempts to better reflect the student population in a system where over 100 languages are spoken and more than half the students live in homes where languages other than English are spoken (Nelson, 2001). Opponents to the new curriculum focused primarily on books and curricular suggestions regarding families with gay or lesbian parents. The ensuing conflict reduced the Rainbow Curriculum to rubble. Nelson argues that this controversy grew out of a more general erosion of public confidence in the legitimacy of public schools as "guardians of children's intellectual and moral development..." (p. 216).

The Rainbow Curriculum fits into a larger framework of controversy regarding aspects of the social studies curriculum and related school practices including the place of the Pledge of Allegiance and "revisionist" history (Bennett, 2004; OAH, 2006; Westheimer, 2007). Disputes about the appropriate (and legal) uses of the Pledge of Allegiance persist in remarkably similar form over time, generally focusing on enforced recitation and education for some form of patriotism (Rethinking Schools, 2007; Westheimer, 2007). To a large extent, concern about so-called revisionist history also focuses on patriotism and fear that attention to "warts and all" national history will not only detract from a traditional national narrative of progress, but weaken students' pride in national accomplishments and support for perceived national goals (Leming, Ellington & Porter-Magee, 2003; Stern, 2003.). While this concern is not exclusive to school history—Smithsonian exhibits have also been criticized on these grounds—it has taken rather odd turns in schools. When Florida's state legislature declared that school history should stick to "facts" and skip interpretation, for instance, historians across the country pointed out the absurdity of this position (OAH, 2006). Nonetheless, explaining the factual basis of new interpretations (revisionist history) and the interpretive basis of traditional narratives failed to mollify critics and history curricula in Florida and elsewhere remain hotly contested.

In response to these and other concerns about social studies curricula, some states mandate attention to specific units (i.e., national symbols, Irish Famine, Holocaust), while others suggest broad periodizations (Early National Period, Reconstruction), themes (Human Rights, Families Around the World) or skills (map reading, document analysis, conflict resolution). Only a small body of research investigates the impact of most of these curricular mandates. In 2001, for instance, a team of teachers, historians, and teacher educators investigated the impact of a unit on the "Great Irish Famine" as part of New York State's Human Rights curriculum (MacCurtain et al., 2001). Developers tested the use of differentiated texts on the famine (texts at varying reading/interest levels) in 4th- through12th-grade units in urban and suburban schools. They concluded that the use of differentiated texts supported complex conceptual understandings across diverse populations regardless of students' differing views on immigration, their varying levels of interest, or their level of academic achievement. Investigators did note, however, that implementation varied depending on the dynamics of particular classrooms and on students' ability to "locate themselves within the lessons" (p. 258). The presence of immigrant students in different classrooms, for instance, seemed to correlate with brisker classroom discussion and more skepticism regarding the trustworthiness of government sources. Interestingly, too, suburban students who had more practice in group work managed group tasks more easily than did their urban peers, but their discussions and debate tended to be less wide ranging. The researchers speculated that group work was so common in the suburban classrooms that students responded to it in a somewhat pro forma way, while urban students more used to direct instruction found the opportunity for discussion and debate invigorating.

Overall, research on mandated social studies curricula shows substantial variation across contexts and grade levels. In one study in New York, for instance, Gerwin and Visone (2006) found teachers of elective courses more likely to focus on historical analysis and employ "richer" use of primary sources than did those teaching state-tested secondary history courses. Grant's (2004) and Crocco and Thornton's (2002) work in the same state suggests some caution here. Grant (2004) found that some teachers in state-tested classes felt more or less stymied by testing depending on their ideas about the purpose of history instruction, and Crocco and Thornton (2002) found that more experienced teachers adapted mandated change to meet their own instructional styles more easily than did less experienced teachers.

The impact of testing on elementary social studies appears much starker. Von Zastrow and Janc (2004), for instance, found that in the wake of No Child Left Behind legislation (NCLB), with its emphasis on reading and mathematics, Indiana schools averaged less than eighteen minutes a day on social studies. A 3-year study (Rock et al., 2004) in North Carolina, mirrored these findings. In that study, a mere 23% of the elementary teachers taught social studies on a daily basis all year. Even though social studies was supposed to be integrated into reading, teachers received minimal professional development to prepare them for meeting social studies as well as literacy goals. Preparation time was also found to be minimal, and the integration of social studies into other curricular areas ended up marginalizing social studies content.

INTEGRATED INSTRUCTION

The issue of the impact of curricular integration on social studies is an important one, especially at the elementary level. While replacing social studies with humanities courses or other forms of integration remains relatively rare at the secondary level, integrated units of instruction have a long history in elementary schools, dating back at least to Dewey and the progressive education movement. Integrated units are also a common feature of middle school programs (see, for instance, Atwell, 1990; Pappas, Kiefer, & Levstik, 2005). Prior to NCLB, the literature on integrated instruction, especially for elementary and middle level education, remained generally positive, drawing on sociocultural theories to argue for the importance of contextualized learning (Atwell, 1990; Meier, 1995; Young, 1994; Chang-Wells & Wells, 1992). While few advocates of integrated instruction claim that the approach is easier than more traditional textbook pedagogies, research in classrooms where student inquiry forms the basis for content integration argue that integration units motivate interest and support deeper concept development (Levstik & Smith, 1996; Young, 1994; Wells & Chang-Wells, 1992). In general, however, these approaches to integration *begin* with questions or topics from social studies or science and employ mathematics, reading, and writing as tools in an inquiry (Levstik, 1993; Levstik & Barton, 2005; Pappas, Kiefer, & Levstik, 2005). Recent alarm over losing social studies to integrated instruction, however, rests primarily on different premises: (1) Teachers are unprepared to enact integrated curricula in any subject-sensitive way, and (2) Claims of integrated instruction mask real reductions in instructional time for social studies.

One of the problems with evaluating these claims lies in an interesting shift regarding the meaning of integrated instruction. Is, for instance, a humanities course necessarily "integrated"? And if so, on what grounds? What about a combined English/history class? A thematic unit drawing on various disciplines? Or a reading lesson whose text is historical fiction? As researchers investigating this area point out, problems may lie at least as much with the uncertainty of instructional goals as with a particular curricular label (Barton & Levstik, 2004; Crocco & Thornton, 2002; Meister & Nolan, 2001; Sosniak & Stodolsky, 1993).

In any case, no recent studies of mandated integrated instruction note systematic training for teachers. As noted earlier, quite the opposite appears to be the case (see, for instance, Crocco & Thornton, 2002, Rock et al., 2004). Further, at the elementary level, pressure to devote more and more time to reading and mathematics combined with less concern with social studies content on some administrators' and teachers' parts may well result in little more than a few reading lessons with social studies themes. School administrators may claim that students learn social studies as they read literature with social studies themes, but the content they encounter may be disjointed—a happenstance of reading choices rather than social studies aims and goals—or ignored as teachers focus on reading goals. And, finally, the habits of mind associated with the various social science disciplines and the larger citizenship goals of social studies may well disappear in favor of literacy or mathematics skill development. While none of this is entirely new—social studies has historically lagged behind reading and mathematics instruction in elementary classrooms—it does appear that current high-stakes testing pushes social studies even further into the curricular shadows.

On a more positive note, investigations in elementary classrooms suggest that when teachers are committed to teaching social studies, they can and do engage their students with substantial social studies content in integrated or thematic units and in the context of literacy instruction. Sosniak and Stodolsky (1993) and Levstik (1993, 1996) for instance, both studied classrooms where social studies was regularly integrated into other aspects of the curriculum. In each case, teachers emphasized social studies as the content under study, with literacy and mathematics as tools to support that study. In Sosniak and Stodolsky's (1993) investigation, the reading series, *Open Court*, provided social studies themes that the teacher made fundamental parts of classroom discussion. In Levstik's (1993, 1996) studies, teachers did not use a reading series, but organized instruction around social studies and science themes. Instruction in literacy and mathematics occurred in the context of studying social studies and science topics, but each subject also received separate instructional attention as particular skills or processes were needed. In each of these cases, teachers preferred subject integration—it bought them time and they thought the integration benefited students in regard to literacy (providing reasons to read and write) and social studies (providing worthwhile content and important themes). In each of these studies, too, researchers documented student interest and growing facility with aspects of social studies content. All three studies, however, were conducted prior to implementation of *NCLB* legislation. MacCurtain et al.'s (2001) study suggests that teachers committed to social studies goals continue to integrate curriculum in ways that honor social studies aims and purposes, but Rock et al. (2004) caution that too few elementary teachers share these commitments.

In Rock et al.'s (2004) study, integration in the context of high-stakes tests in North Carolina emphasized reading and mathematics, but not social studies. Rock and her colleagues conclude that when teachers see social studies as less important than other curricular areas, are uninvolved in curriculum decision making, or feel pressure to focus only on tested content areas, integration is a misnomer. Social studies content may appear in reading materials, but it rarely appears in classroom discourse, in students' expressed interest, or in teachers' curricular planning. In these cases, claims of integration disguise the elimination of any substantive content aside from reading and mathematics and significantly reduce or eliminate instructional time for social studies. This is particularly troublesome in light of recent National Assessment of Educational Progress (NAEP, 2002, 2007) results demonstrating a correlation between instructional time and test performance. Fourth graders whose teachers spent more than 180 minutes per week on social studies, for instance, scored significantly higher on the U.S. history assessment than did those whose teachers spent less time teaching social studies. Further, several instructional activities (reading the text, using primary sources, using technology) were positively associated with student performance at all three tested grade levels on the U.S. history test (fourth, eighth, and twelfth grade). Not only does this finding reinforce the importance of time spent teaching social studies, but of time spent on activities specific to social studies (rather than peripheral to reading). NAEP data on instructional activities only includes frequencies as recalled by teachers and students, not the instructional contexts for these activities, making it difficult to judge what students do with primary documents or technology—or the textbook. The reliance on social studies textbooks reported by NAEP does suggest, though, that integrated instruction is not the primary instructional approach in most classrooms at any level—instruction remains tied to social studies textbooks (or, the only instruction that teachers and students recall as social studies is text-based).

CLASSROOM TEXTS

After reviewing 10 years of research on textbook use, Wade (1993) concluded that 70%–90% of social studies instructional time in the decade she reviewed was textbook based. Given the prevalence of text-based instruction, it would be quite useful to know more about the texts themselves, teachers' use of them, and their impact on student understanding. Unfortunately, Wade found that most textbook analyses for the period she reviewed were biased, superficial, and poorly written, leaving educators with little basis for selecting one over another. Most of these analyses focused on secondary texts (60%), and U.S. history texts (40%), but few either identified the bases for selecting the texts for review or clearly defined their analytical categories and 68% failed to identify *any* unit of analysis. Analysts generally criticized publishers for offering broad coverage rather than depth in textbook treatments, but few suggested ways to address the problems they described. In fact, most of the critics arguing for more depth argued for increased coverage of one topic or another without suggesting what might be omitted. Three years after Wade's review, Dillabough and McAlpine (1996) offered an even more withering attack on "the cultural politics of methodology in text evaluation research" (p. 167). They focused particular attention on problems with cultural "outsiders" evaluating the level and quality of textbook attention to minority groups, arguing for inclusion of previously missing voices, not just in the textbooks themselves, but in textbook analyses.

Fewer such analyses have appeared in more recent years. Instead, recent studies focus more on how accessible texts are for readers, how "considerate" they are, or the ways in which they help or inhibit student understanding (McCabe, 1993). Among the most influential of these, Beck and McKeown's (1994) and Beck, McKeown, Sinatra, and Loxterman's (1991) investigations of fifth-grade American history texts report that explanations are often so simplified that students struggle to make sense of historical events and that the texts are interrupted so often that students lose narrative cohesion. In one study (Beck et al., 1991), researchers took textbook passages and revised them, and presented 85 fourth- and fifth-grade students with text materials revised according to text-processing protocols. Students were asked to recall what they had read and answer questions on the material. Those who read the revised text recalled more material and answered more questions correctly than students who read the original text. Researchers also used interview data to examine students underlying reasoning as they dealt with each type of text.

Another study by Roth, Hasbach, Hoekwater, et al. (1993) examined how students learned to analyze social studies texts in a U.S. history curriculum organized around what the researchers considered "powerful" concepts related to history and students' own lives. In this instance, students' careful text analyses led to improved comprehension of issues related to social justice and human rights. Despite their apparent ubiquitousness in K–12 classrooms, however, surprisingly few other studies focus on how teachers use texts. Kon (1995) investigated teachers' curricular decision making in response to a newly adopted social studies text and found that teachers' responses were more varied than had been expected. Three patterns emerged: Teachers viewed the text as the curriculum, others made active use of the text, but did not regard it as their primary teaching resource, and a third group considered the text of limited usefulness. Kon found that the most powerful influence on each groups' approach to the new text was teachers' beliefs about how students learned. This finding parallels recent research (Levstik & Kern, 2006) regarding the influence of teachers' beliefs about student learning on their willingness to engage students in more inquiry-oriented historical work.

Overall, then, most of our information about textbook use comes from occasional studies and NAEP data. In the 2007 NAEP report for U.S. history, fourth-grade students who reported reading their social studies text everyday outperformed those doing so weekly or monthly. Given the lack of information on what else fourth graders might be doing in the way of social studies, this finding should be read with some caution. If, as previous research suggests (Kon, 1995; Wade, 1993), textbooks remain the primary instructional tool in social studies, the NAEP finding may reflect time devoted to instruction rather than to the effectiveness of a particular instructional approach. It would be useful, however, to know more about how teachers use this prominent feature of social studies education.

Another feature of textbook-based instruction, Teachers' Guides, are also little researched. One study (Alter, 1995) found that the guides offered little help to teachers interested in building "diverse, caring [learning] communities" but I found no other studies that considered how (or if) teachers used the references to other sources, strategies for differential instruction, or enhancement activities in the Guides (p. 355).

Textbooks are not the only texts that students encounter in social studies classrooms. The push to include fiction and non-fiction in social studies instruction has a long history in the field. The National Council for the Social Studies in collaboration with the Children's Book Council offers a yearly list of fiction and non-fiction for use by social studies teachers and *Social Studies and the Young Learner* publishes a number of articles on how to use literature to enhance elementary social studies. Most of this literature is advocacy rather than empirical studies of literature use in classrooms, the impact of fiction or non-fiction on children's concept development, or motivational issues related to the use of literature in the social studies curriculum.[2] Given the push to integrate social studies through reading at the elementary level, it is worth considering what the existing literature might suggest about the affordances and constraints of literature-based curricula. To begin with, most of the research has focused on fiction—particularly historical fiction. Levstik's (1995) summary of the then-existing research describes several features of children's response to historical fiction: moralizing history, developing historical judgment and the need for teacher mediation. She notes that because historical fiction elicits a moral response (identifying with a particular perspective or perspectives), even when students recognize different historical perspectives represented in the text, the protagonist's "truth" has considerable power and generally requires teacher mediation if students are to consider alternatives to a literary interpretation. Further, while most children's long experience with narrative allows them to bring narrative schema to bear in making sense out of narrative-based social studies content, it also leads to narrative conflations—simplifying to make the narrative work—or reconfigurations—reorganizing information to fit narrative schema rather than historical evidence, and a tendency to interpret the past solely in terms of individual motivation (Barton, 1996; Levstik & Barton, 2005; VanSledright & Brophy, 1992; Wills, 1995). Tyson (2002), however, found that, with teacher mediation, narrative could be used to motivate collective as well as individual social action.

Very little research investigates the uses or impact of non-fiction. Pappas' (1991, 1992) and Levstik's (1993) studies of children's response to non-fiction suggests once again that with teacher mediation, students respond positively to non-fiction and use it to inform their inquiries into various topics in social studies and science. One approach to a more analytical response to literature is suggested by Segall (1999) who argues that instruction in history should focus on *how* particular versions of the past came to be constructed and passed on rather than presenting past events as if accounts were unproblematic.

In sum, no text is unproblematic, although textbooks and literary texts may present rather different problems. In the case of literary texts, however, their very accessibility brings with it considerable responsibility that might be easily missed, especially in the so-called integration filtering into elementary classrooms. In order for literary texts to meet social studies aims and purposes, the existing research suggests that teacher mediation is essential. Without purposeful attention to how texts are constructed, to alternative perspectives, and analysis of the social studies content as well as the literary merit of particular texts, students are likely to misconstrue social studies content. Hoping for students to understand social studies in any meaningful way simply by literary happenstance cannot be supported by current research.

CLASSROOM CONTEXTS

Most of what we know about classroom climate or pedagogical practices comes to us in bits and pieces in studies of other aspects of social studies. As Harwood (1991) noted, social studies classroom climate is an under-researched area confined largely to civic education. Some recent studies of classroom climate, however, extend beyond civic education, using questionnaires and scales with interview follow-up to consider the impact of cooperative learning (Lee, Ng, & Phang, 1999; Lee, Chew, Ng, & Hing, 1999) technology (Mucherah, 2003), teacher behaviors and social studies content (Shindler, Jones, Taylor, & Cadenas, 2004) that affect climate (Antosca, 1997), and the relationship between student perceptions of social climate and academic self-concept (Byers, 2000; Raider-Roth, 2005). Studies by Lee and colleagues (Lee, Ng, & Phang, 1999; Lee, Chew, Ng, & Hing., 1999), for instance, found that cooperative learning did not significantly affect classroom climate in the Singapore classrooms under study, but did benefit low-performing students. In fact, students identified as low performing on the pre-test in the cooperative learning experimental group matched the performance of high performing students in the experimental group and outperformed both low and high performing students in the control group on post-tests.

In his study of student perceptions of classroom climate, Byers (2000) found that there was a statistically significant match between students' self-perception and the perceived classroom social climate. Byer used multiple scales and interview data with 185 eighth-grade U.S. history students in western Mississippi. Among the 60% African American and 40% European American students, perceptions of involvement and affiliation were positively correlated with positive academic self-perception. These findings are similar to those of Raider-Roth (2005). Drawing on a growing body of research on knowledge formation in schools, Raider-Roth examined how sixth-grade students "read" their relationships with teachers and peers and shared or repressed their academic understanding or knowledge in response. While Raider-Roth's research argues that children are astute observers of their environments, constantly picking up on clues regarding the trustworthiness of teachers and peers, Antosca's (1997) study suggest quite the opposite for teachers. In investigating classroom climate among eighth graders, Antosca describes teachers who seemed largely unaware of behaviors that negatively influence the learning environment. As teachers ignored negative student behaviors, other students' expressed negative perceptions of the classroom climate.

A fairly extensive qualitative research literature suggests that not all teachers are as tone-deaf as those in Antosca's studies. These studies may not use the term "classroom climate" but they certainly investigate the relationships among teachers, students, and social studies content. Many of these studies are cited in other chapters in this volume, but a few bear mentioning here. Gaudelli's (2003) research, for instance, offers an in-depth look at the complexities of globalizing secondary social studies instruction. He notes the moments when teachers and students make it work, and the points where they seem to work at cross-purposes. Wade's (2007) work combining history and service learning offers a number of case studies of engaging inquiry-oriented instruction in social studies classrooms and Grant (2004) provides careful examinations of two secondary history teachers and the curricular choices they make, the classroom climates they create, and their students' responses. Each teacher creates a very different classroom, but Grant argues that each is an example of "ambitious teaching and learning"—the coming together of smart teachers, curious students, and powerful ideas. Although Grant does not suggest a "one size fits all" model for ambitious teaching and learning, he does outline some basic characteristics of classrooms where both are more likely to happen: teachers who know their subject(s) and students well, know "when to push and when to support, when to praise and when to prod...and how to create space for themselves and their students in an environment that may never appreciate either of their efforts" (p. 211). Grant's research points out the need for further investigation of ambitious teaching and learning in other contexts. A number of investigations already exist in regard to history and civics/citizenship education but fewer indepth studies inform our understanding of classroom contexts for other aspects of the social studies.

As previously noted, we can glean some information about instructional activities from NAEP data, but only in regard to U.S. history, civics, and geography. The most recent data for U.S. history (NAEP, 2007), for instance, associates several instructional activities with test performance. The fourth-grade textbook use mentioned earlier is one example, but at the eighth-grade level, students whose teachers reported using primary historical documents (letters, diaries, or essays written by historical figures) on a weekly basis out-performed those whose teachers did so less frequently. The data does not provide information on how primary documents were used (stand-alone "sourcing" activities, in the context of historical inquiry, presented as part of a lecture or class discussion?). Interestingly, the NAEP data indicates a slight drop in performance when eighth graders reported daily use of primary documents.

Further, on the NAEP U.S. history assessment, students who reported reading historical literature (biographies, historical stories) at least a few times a year outperformed those who did not, and eighth and twelfth graders scored better if they made more extensive use of computers for research and report writing than did peers who had fewer such experiences.[3] At a bear minimum these findings suggest that instructional time and some variety in pedagogical strategies increases the likelihood that students will recall some historical information. What we cannot determine from NAEP history data is what any of these activities actually look like in classrooms.

The NAEP civics assessment (2002) offers a few more statistics on the frequency of specific topics during social studies (the question asks for occurrence during social studies or "during this school year" rather than during civics in particular). In descending order, the most often cited topics include:

Your community	68% of students
The President and leaders of our country	58%
Rights and responsibilities of citizens	56%
Rules and law of our government	53%
Elections and voting	43%
How people try to solve disagreements	43%
How our government works	41%

Again, there is no way to know *how* students experienced any specific topic, but the three most commonly reported activities include filling out worksheets (87%), reading from a textbook (77%), and "memorizing material you have read" (61%). More than half the students also report watching media, discussing current events, and writing reports. Only 19% report taking part in debates or panel discussions, and only slightly more write letters regarding public affairs (26%) or have visits about local affairs from community members (31%). Even assuming that students may underreport some activities, these data suggest that students' experiences in social studies classrooms have changed little between the last assessment (NAEP, 1994) and 2001 when the NAEP data was collected.

Finally, the NAEP (2001) geography assessment shows patterns of performance similar to history and civics (improvement at fourth and eighth grade, no change at twelfth). Only two classroom activities showed a statistically significant correlation with test scores in geography. Computer use at least once or twice a month correlated with higher test scores at eighth and twelfth grades as did frequency of study about other cultures.

CONCLUSIONS

On the surface, little appears to have changed in social studies classrooms since the 1992 review by the Council of State Social Studies Supervisors. Patterns of instruction persist, with textbooks still predominating, but with some teachers drawing on other resources, and engaging students in the kind of inquiry social studies scholars and NCSS standards tend to call for. Upon closer inspection, though, fault lines begin to appear. Restructuring and high-stakes testing take a toll on social studies, especially among more inexperienced teachers who may be afraid to expand beyond test guidelines and textbook narratives, or who struggle to manage in newly integrated courses. At the elementary level, social studies appears to be in even more trouble. Few elementary teachers perceive themselves as experts in regard to social studies. Moreover, as high-stakes assessment focuses on reading and mathematics, social studies too often disappears entirely, almost disappears as it is integrated into reading programs, or survives at such a low level students are as likely to misunderstand as understand it. Again, individual teachers continue to perform admirably, but we have little idea of how often this happens. Case studies make it clear that interesting and exciting things can and do happen for some students in some classrooms, but there seems to be little institutional support to ensure that more students experience this kind of instruction. What we do know is that teachers matter and that teaching is influenced by teachers' sense of purpose, their understanding of students' capabilities, and their expectations regarding institutional support.

NOTES

1. For further discussion of the affordances and constraints of "then and now" comparisons for young children, see Ashby and Lee, 2004; Barton and Levstik, 2004, and Levstik (in press).
2. For further discussion of the impact of literature on middle school students' thinking about taking social action, see Tyson (2002).
3. For advocacy regarding the uses of literature in social studies, see Krey (1998) *Children's literature in social studies: Teaching to the standards*. NCSS Bulletin 95. Washington, DC: National Council for the Social Studies,

REFERENCES

Alter, G. (1995). Transforming elementary social studies: The emergence of a curriculum focused on diverse, caring communities. *Theory and Research in Social Education, 23*(4), 355–374.

Ashby, R., & Lee P. (2004). Developing a concept of historical evidence: Students' ideas about testing singular factual claims. *International Journal of Historical Learning, Teaching and Research, 4*(2), Retrieved April 1, 2006, from: http://www.centres.ex.ac.uk/historyresource/journal8/ashby.pdf.

Antosca, D. (1997). Classroom climate in middle school eighth grades. Dissertation, University of Massachusetts at Amhearst. Retrieved April 1, 2006, from: http://scholarworks.umass.edu/dissertations/AAI9721428/.

Atwell, N. (1990*). In the middle: New understandings about reading, writing, and learning*. Portsmouth, New Hampshire: Boynton-Cook.

Barton, K. C. (1996). Narrative simplifications in elementary children's historical understanding. In J. Brophy (Ed.). *Advances in research on teaching, Vol. 6. Teaching and learning history* (pp. 51–83). Greenwich, CT: JAI Press.

Barton, K. C., & Levstik L.S. (2004). *Teaching history for the common good*. Mahwah, NJ: Erlbaum.

Beck, I. L., & McKeown, M. G. (1994). Outcomes of history instruction: Paste-up accounts. In J. F. Voss & M. Carretero (Eds.), *Cognitive and instructional processes in history and the social sciences* (pp. 237–256). Hillsdale, NJ: Erlbaum.

Beck, I. L., McKeown, M. G., Sinatra, G. M., & Loxterman, J. A. (Summer, 1991). *Reading Research Quarterly, 26*(3), 251–276.

Bennett, L. J. (2004). Classroom recitation of the Pledge of Allegiance and its educational value: Analysis, review, and proposal. *Journal of Curriculum and Supervision, 20*(1), 56–75.

Brophy, J. (1993). Findings and issues: The cases seen in context. In J. Brophy (Ed.), *Advances in research on teaching, Vol. 4: Case studies of teaching and learning in social studies* (pp. 219–232). Greenwich, CT: JAI Press.

Byers, J. L. (2000). Measuring the effects of students' perceptions of classroom social climate on academic self-concept. Paper presented at the Annual Meeting of the Louisiana Educational Research Association (ERIC #:ED429088).

California State Board of Education (1988). *History-social science framework for California public schools kindergarten through grade twelve*. Sacramento: California State Board of Education.

Chang-Wells, G. L., & Wells, G. (1992). *Constructing knowledge together: Classrooms as centers of inquiry and literacy*. Portsmouth, NH: Heinemann.

Crocco, M., & Thornton, S. J. (2002). Social studies in the New York City public schools: A descriptive study. *Journal of Curriculum and Supervision, 17*(3), 206–231.

Dillabough, J., & McAlpine, L. (1996). Rethinking research processes and praxis in the social studies: The cultural politics of methodology in text evaluation research. *Theory and Research in Social Education, 24*(2), 167–203.

Dye, P., & Huffman, L. (2003). National survey of National survey of course offerings in social studies, kindergarten-grade 12, 2002–2003. Council of State Social Studies Specialists. Retrieved March 1, 2007, from: http://www.cs4online.org/survey.html.

Florida Commission on Social Studies Education (1990). *Connections, challenges, choices: Florida K-12 Social Studies Program of Study.* Tallahassee: Florida Department of Education.

Gaudelli, W. (2003). *World class: Teaching and learning in global times.* Mahwah, NJ: Erlbaum.

Gerwin & Visone (2006). The freedom to teach: Contrasting history teaching in elective and state-tested courses. *Theory and Research in Social Education, 34*(2), 259–282.

Grant, S. G. (2004). *History lessons: Teaching, learning, and testing in U.S. high school classrooms.* Mahwah, NJ: Erlbaum.

Harwood, A. (1991). The difference between "democracy sucks," and "I may become a politician." Paper presented at the Annual Meeting of the American Educational Research Association.

Howard, T. (2003).Who receives the short end of the shortage? Implications of the U.S. teacher shortage on urban schools. *Journal of Curriculum and Supervision, 18*(2), 142–160.

Kon (1995) . Teachers' curricular decision making in response to a new social studies textbook. *Theory and Research in Social Education, 23*(2), 121–146.

Lee, C. K., Ng. M., & Phang, R. (1999). A school-based study of cooperative learning and its effects on social studies achievement, attitude towards the subject and classroom climate in four social studies classrooms. Paper presented at the Annual Meeting of the American Educational Research Association.

Lee, C. K., Chew, J., Ng, M., & Hing, T. S. (1999). Teachers' use of cooperative learning in their classrooms: Case studies of four elementary school teachers. Presented at the Annual Meeting of the American Educational Research Association.

Leming, J., Ellington, L., & Porter-Magee, K. (2003). Where did social studies go wrong? Fordham Foundation. Retrieved April 1, 2007 from: http://www.edexcellence.not/foundation/about/individual_detail.cfm?id=287.

Levstik, L. S. (1993). Building a sense of history in a first-grade classroom. In J. Brophy (Ed.), *Case studies of teaching and learning in social studies* (Vol. 4, pp. 1–31). Greenwich, CT: JAI Press.

Levstik, L. S. (1995). Narrative constructions: Cultural frames for history. *The Social Studies, 86*(3), 113–116.

Levstik, L. S. (in press). Thinking about the past: The research base. In C. Berkin, M. Crocco, & B. Winslow (Eds.), *Teaching women's studies.* Oxford University Press.

Levstik, L. S., & Barton, K.C . (2005). *Doing history: Investigating with children in elementary and middle schools.* Mahwah, NJ: Erlbaum.

Levstik, L. S., & Smith, D. (1997). "I've never done this before": Building a community of inquiry in a third-grade classroom. In J. Brophy (Ed.), *Advances in research on teaching: Vol. 6. Teaching and learning history* (pp. 85–114). Greenwich, CT: JAI Press.

Levstik, L., & Kern, K.(2006). Thinking outside the box: Teachers engaging with historical interpretation. Paper presented at the Annual Meeting of the College and University Faculty Assembly of the National Council for the Social Studies.

MacCurtain, M., Murphy, M., Singer, A., Costello, L., Gaglione, R., Miller, S., Smith, D. C., Tella, A., & Williams. N. (2001) Text and Context: Field testing the New York state Great Irish Famine curriculum. *Theory and Research in Social Education, 29*(2), 238–260.

McCabe, P. (1993). Considerateness of fifth-grade social studies texts. *Theory and Research in Social Education, 21*(2), 128–142.

Meier, D. (1995). *The power of their ideas: Lessons for America from a small school in Harlem.* Boston: Beacon Press.

Meister, D., & Nolan, J. (2001). Out on a limb on our own: Uncertainty and doubt moving from subject-centered to interdisciplinary teaching. *Teachers College Record, 103*(4), 608–633.

Mucherah, W. (2003). The influence of technology on the classroom climate of social studies classrooms: A multidimensional approach. *Learning Environments Research, 6*(1), 37–57.

National Assessment of Educational Progress (2007). 2006 Civics Assessment. Retrieved July 12, 2007, from: http://nces.ed.gov/pubsearch/pubsinfo.asp?pubid=2007476.

National Assessment of Educational Progress (2002). 2001 Geography Assessment. Retrieved April 1, 2007 from: http://nces.ed.gov/nationsreportcard/geography/.

National Assessment of Educational Progress (2007). 2006 U.S. History. Retrieved July 12, 2007 from: http://nces.ed.gov/nationsreportcard/ushistory/.

Nelson, M.R. (1998). Are teachers stupid?: Setting and meeting standards in social studies. *The Social Studies, 89*(2), 66–69.

Nelson, M. R. (2001). No pot of gold at the end of the rainbow. *Journal of Curriculum and Supervision, 16*(3), 206–227.

Organization of American Historians (2006). Education reform and the history wars in Florida. Retrieved April 1, 2007 from: http://www.oah.org/pubs/nl/2006aug/newsprof.html.

Pappas, C. (1991). Fostering full access to literacy by including information books. *Language Arts, 68*, 449–462.

Pappas, C. (1993). Is narrative primary? Some insights from kindergartners' pretend readings of stories and information books. *Journal of Reading Behavior, 25*, 97–126.

Pappas, C., Kiefer, B., & Levstik, L. (2005). An integrated language perspective (4th ed.). New York: Allyn &Bacon/Longman.

Patrick, J. J. (1992). Topics in the social studies curriculum, grades K-12. In P. B. Urmacher (Series Ed.), *Social studies: Curriculum resource handbook*, (pp. 65–82). Krauss International.

Raider-Roth, M. (2005). Trusting what you know: Negotiating the relational context of classroom life. *Teachers College Record, 107*(4), 587–628.

Rethinking Schools. (2007). Foundation: Don't think, just salute. Retrieved April 1, 2007, from: http://www.rethinkingschools.org/archive/17_01/Ford171.shtml.

Rock, T. C., Heafner, T., O'Connor, K., Passe, J., Oldendorf, S., Good, A., & Byrd, S. (2004). One state closer to a national crisis: A report on elementary social studies education in North Carolina schools. *Theory and Research in Social Education, 34*(4), 455–483.

Roth, K. J., Hasback, C., Hazelwood, C., Hoekwater, E., Master, J., & Woodham, P. (1993, February). *Many voices: Learning to teach social studies* (Series No. 86). East Lansing: Institute for Research on Teaching, The Center for the Learning and Teaching of Elementary Subjects, Michigan State University.

Segall, A. (1999). Critical history: Implications for history/social studies education. *Theory and Research in Social Education, 27*(3), 358–374.

Shindler, J. V., Jones, A. F., Taylor, C., & Cadenas, H. G. (2004). Does seeking to create a better classroom climate lead to student success or improved teaching? Examining the relationship between pedagogical choices and classroom climate in urban secondary schools. A paper presented at the Annual Meeting of the American Educational Research Association. Retrieved April 1, 2007, from: http://www.calstatela.edu/centers/schoolclimate/research/aera2004.html.

South Carolina Department of Education. Palmetto Achievement Challenge Test (PACT) Scores: Social Studies: 2003. Available at: http://www.myscschools.com/tracks/testsco res/pact/2003/.

South Carolina Department of Education. Palmetto Achievement Challenge Test (PACT) Scores: Social Studies: 2000. Available at: http://www.myscschools.com/tracks/testsco res/pact/2004/.

Sosniak, L., & Stodolsky, S. (1993). Making connections: Social studies education in an urban fourth-grade classroom. In J. Brophy (Ed.). Advances in research on teaching (Vol. 4, pp. 71–100). Grenwich, CT: JAI Press Inc.

Stern, S. M. (2003). Effective State Standards for U.S. History: A 2003 Report Card. Fordham Institute. Retrieved on April 1, 2007, from: http://www.edexcellence.not/foundation/about/individual_detail.cfm?id=167.

Svengalis, C. M. (1992). National survey of course offerings in social studies, kindergarten-grade 12, 1991–1992. Washington, DC: Council of State Social Studies Specialists.

Tyson, C. (2002) Get up offa that thing: African American Middle School students respond to literature to develop a framework for understanding social action. 30,1, 42–65.

VanSledright, B., & Brophy, J. (1992). Storytelling, imagination, and fanciful elaboration in children's historical reconstructions. *American Educational Research Journal, 29,* 837–859.

von Zastrow, C., & Janc, H. (2004). *The condition of the liberal arts in America's public schools.* Washington, DC: Council for Basic Education.

Wade, R. C. (2007). *Community action in history: The CiviConnections model of service-learning.* Bulletin 106. Silver Springs, MD: NCSS.

Wade, R. C. (1993). Content analysis of social studies textbooks: A review of ten years of research. *Theory and Research in Social Education, 21*(3), 232–256.

Westheimer, J. (2007). *Pledging allegiance: The politics of patriotism in America's schools.* New York: Teachers College Press.

Wills, J. S. (1995). Who needs multicultural education? White students, U.S. history, and the construction of a usable past. *Anthropology and Education Quarterly, 27*, 365–389.

Young, K. A. (1994). *Constructing buildings, bridges and minds: Building an integrated curriculum through social studies.* Portsmouth, NH: Heinemann.

Part II

Civic competence in pluralist democracies

5 Knowing and doing in democratic citizenship education

Walter C. Parker

University of Washington

Among the most interesting questions to ask of democratic citizenship education is the curriculum one: What outcomes are desired, and what is the plan for reaching them? Put differently, what kind of citizens do we want schools to cultivate, and how might these organizations go about that work? The question is at once philosophical (e.g., Dewey, 1985a), historical (e.g., Crocco, 1999), cultural (Ladson-Billings, 2004), sociological (e.g., Counts, 1932), critical (Cherryholmes, 1988), and pedagogical (e.g., Banks, 1997). It is deeply contextual—particular to time, place, and circumstance—and it goes to the heart of the purposes of schooling. Instructional questions are subordinate to it, as are organizational and developmental questions. In the simultaneity of school practice, where everything happens at once, these cannot be separated neatly, of course. But they can be asked one at a time, and doing so affords a degree of clarity, avoiding what Dewey (1927, p. 83) called "the great bad." By this he meant "the mixing of things which need to be kept distinct."

I will address the curriculum question in this review essay and argue that democratic citizens need both to *know* democratic things and to *do* democratic things. I will also argue that a proper democratic education proceeds in both directions in tandem. Arguing this requires dropping the hackneyed either/or debate between the two and replacing it with a more pertinent curricular question: *Which* participatory experiences in combination with the study of *what?* I will begin with a brief review of curriculum contexts—what Schwab (1973) called the curriculum milieu[1]—and then turn to the literature on knowing and doing democracy. To show that instructional questions are, albeit secondary, never far off, I will represent the knowing/doing tension with a pedagogic case: classroom discussion. I will draw a distinction between two kinds of classroom discussion, seminar and deliberation. Each emphasizes one side of the tension. The two together are not a complete democratic education, certainly, but they do cover a lot of curricular territory, and they display the two emphases at work on the ground in classroom practice. As well, they reveal the uncertain boundaries between, indeed the interdependence of, knowing and doing.

CONTEXTS

I begin by clarifying two categories in the opening paragraph: *schools* and *we*. By schools I am referring to elementary and secondary schools in nations that are trying to be liberal democracies and are formally organized as such (e.g., the U.S., Mexico, Japan, South Africa, France): Popular sovereignty is practiced through elections that are held to standards of fairness; majority power is constitutionally constrained; government power is limited; and civil liberties are protected by government power.[2] These are principles or ideals, and there are, to varying degrees across nations, serious gaps between principles and conditions on the ground. There are no ideal democracies anywhere; the focus shifts, therefore, to the struggles to close the gaps and the defensive moves by elites to protect the status quo.[3] In most of the established democracies of Europe and North America, the middle class is more or less content with the degree to which the actually-existing democracy accords with democratic ideals, and historically oppressed groups challenge this status quo, targeting the persistence of civic inequality and also, to a much lesser extent, economic injustice (Fraser & Honneth, 2004; Green, 1990).

Who are *we* in the curriculum question? This raises the question of legitimate educational authority: Who, in a society that is trying to be a democracy, has the right to educate citizens? That is, who has the legitimate authority to plan that part of the school curriculum that concerns the formation of democratic citizens—the next generation of governors? In a political democracy, *we* are autonomous citizens who together compose *we the people*—governors of the commonwealth—and in that capacity practice self-government (popular sovereignty). We elect school boards that, in turn, form schools, hire teachers and principals, choose curricula, and so forth. In a cultural democracy (Rosaldo, 1997; Kymlicka, 1995), we additionally are reflexive about cultural pluralism—our religious and ethnic differences. This *we* directs the schools to engage in culturally relevant pedagogy and, in this and other ways, to embrace difference and dialogue, avoid segregation, and eschew assimilation beyond what is needed for political democracy (e.g., tolerance).

The authority question centrally concerns power, which has been treated widely and passionately in the literature—from Aristotle (1958) and Hobbes (1976) to Foucault (1980) and Butler (1997). Let me briefly review three perspectives on the authority question as it applies to curriculum planning: cultural, social, and economic.

Citizenship education, generally, is authorized by dominant cultures who seek the continuance of their members' social status, social vision, and self regard. As Gonçalves e Silva (2004) writes of the curriculum milieu in Brazil, "those who have the power to govern and influence public policy do so following principles that guarantee the protection of their own interests. In this way, their values, desires, and everything they find useful are imposed on everyone" (p. 186). And in the United States:

> (T)hree compromises—the three-fifths, the 20-year extension of the slave trade, and the fugitive slave clause—are the terrain over which citizenship in America has been configured. The three compromises not only served to subordinate peoples of African descent but also confirmed superiority of Whites in the form of the doctrine of White supremacy...(B)y inscribing White supremacy...the laws of the land created a racial hierarchy that made every non-White group less worthy and less eligible for citizenship. (Ladson-Billings, 2004, p. 110)

Citizenship education in these milieus is not solely under the command of privileged groups, however, but also of marginalized groups who struggle for access to power and, in the case of oppressed groups, a decent and respected life. Subaltern, community-based schools "educate through the very process of confronting interests that disavow and disrespect them," writes Gonçalves e Silva (2004, p. 193). She is referring to the informal education that occurs within the resistance struggles of these groups. The freedom schools of the civil rights movement are the historical exemplar in the U.S. (Chilcoat & Ligon, 1994; Horton & Freire, 1990). Such schools educate youth and adults alike through, on the one hand, the process of confronting an education system that maintains their oppression and the regime elites who slowly make concessions and, on the other, mobilizing resources for alternative educational sites where a serious education can proceed.[4]

A second perspective focuses on social roles in the everyday. Here the concern is not the contention between dominant and subordinate cultural groups but between parents and educators and between both of these and citizens. (Because these are roles, not persons, they overlap.) The question, recall, is who has the legitimate authority to plan that part of the school curriculum that concerns the formation of democratic citizens? Parents may claim that they have a natural right to exclusive educational authority—natural because, first, the children in question are their children (the ownership assumption), and second because parents are naturally concerned to maximize the welfare of their children (the altruistic assumption). Both assumptions are specious, as both educators and citizens are quick to point out. Parents may have given birth to children, or they may be their legal guardians, but that does not establish possession (children could be and have been imagined to belong to the gods, the state, or the village, for example). The frequency of child abuse and neglect undermines the second assumption, as does the propensity of at least some families to teach racist, sexist, authoritarian, and other values that contradict the democratic ethos, particularly the bedrock democratic values of civic equality, popular sovereignty, tolerance, and freedom.

Neither professional educators nor democratic citizens are inclined, as parents sometimes may be, to claim exclusive educational authority because that would be unambiguously undemocratic. Rather, both groups claim a seat at the deliberative table, alongside parents. where curricular policy is developed in a democratic society. Gutmann (1999) has developed a comprehensive portrayal of this role contention as part of her presentation of a democratic theory of education, and she concludes that collective moral argument and decision making (deliberation) among the various educational roles is the most democratically justifiable approach to the authority question.

A third perspective on the authority question focuses on the macroeconomic transition currently underway. National political economies in Europe and North America especially—and to varying degrees around the world—are shifting from one regime of accumulation to another—from fordism or keynesianism to post-fordism or neo-liberalism (Fischman, Orvitz, & Ball, 2003; Harvey, 1989; Larner, 2000; Mitchell, 2003; Ong, 1999). In uneven and incomplete ways, this is a transition from nationalism to globalism; however, national power remains strong alongside transnational corporate power (Sparke, in press). Centrally, this is a historical transition *from* an articulation of capital, labor, government, and market, in such a way that a modified market system exists in symbiosis with a welfare state; *to* global networks, flexible arrangements within and between labor and capital, and a greater withdrawal of governments from markets. Society becomes subordinated, not to government, but to free enterprise, and the nation-state gives way to, and exists largely to support, the market-state. Pertinent to our curriculum question, a new kind of citizen is called forth: the enterprising, self-reliant citizen (Rose, 1992; Ong, 1999). We are morphing, from a "we the people" who celebrate our diversity to a "we the entrepreneurs" who strategically advantage ourselves on the new playing field. Multiculturalism shifts from a rights-oriented, inclusion-seeking educational movement to a strategic, competitive advantage in the global marketplace (e.g., knowing to bow when doing business in Japan).

ENLIGHTENED POLITICAL ENGAGEMENT

Because of these conditions and numerous others at different scales and registers,[5] planning the education of the next generation of governors is inevitably a contentious affair. Dominant groups typically win these battles while making the aforementioned concessions, but struggles do persist, both between mainstream and marginalized groups and within them. The curriculum arguments generally have had two objects: (a) whether study (knowing) or practice (doing) should be emphasized in the democratic citizenship curriculum, and (b) what to study and what to practice. Both are content selection controversies (Binder, 2002; Evans, 2004; Gagnon, 1996; Hirsch, 1996; Hunt & Metcalf, 1955; Kliebard, 2004; Massialas, 1996; Oliver, 1957; Rugg, 1939; Rutter & Newmann, 1989; Thornton, 2005; Zimmerman, 2002).

The study and practice of democracy have a common end: what we could call enlightened political engagement (Nie, Junn, & Stehlik-Barry, 1996), reflective citizen participation (Newmann, 1989), or, simply, wise political action. These are synonymous terms, and each synthesizes study and practice. Let us deploy the first, *enlightened political engagement*, and flesh out the two dimensions: *democratic enlightenment* and *political engagement*. The latter dimension, political engagement, refers to the action or participation dimension of democratic citizenship, from voting to campaigning, boycotting, and protesting. Democratic enlightenment refers to the knowledge and commitments that inform this engagement: for example, knowledge of the ideals of democratic living, the ability to discern just from unjust laws and actions, the commitment to fight civic inequality, and the ability and commitment to deliberate public policy in cooperation with disagreeable others. Without democratic enlightenment, participation cannot be trusted: The freedom marchers of the Civil Rights Movement participated, but so did Hitler's thugs and so did (and do) the Klan, anti-plural (monotheistic) fundamentalists, and so forth. Political engagement without democratic enlightenment can be worse than apathy. Enlightened political engagement is not easily achieved, and it is never achieved for all time; one works at it continually (path), in concert with others (participation), and intentionally with others who are of different ideology, perspective, or culture (pluralism).[6]

Judgment or principled reasoning is required to distinguish between enlightened and unenlightened political engagement (Arendt, 1958; Beiner, 1984; Kohlberg, 1980; Parker, 1996b; Rawls, 1971; Young, 1990). Judgment is required because drawing that distinction is not a matter of applying rules or algorithms. Reasonable people of good judgment may disagree vehemently about which course of action is wise in a given circumstance. Should the majority be permitted to do whatever it wishes? Of course not. That would surely undermine democratic ideals, as political theorists from Aristotle (1958) and Madison (1937) to King (1963), Phillips (1991), and Gutmann (1999) have argued well. But should corporate power be restrained and wealth be redistributed? Should groups have rights, or are rights only for individuals? Should voting be required? Should ex-felons be disenfranchised? These are highly contested issues among democratic citizens.

School attendance itself (measured simply in years—what political scientists call "educational attainment"—irrespective of educational achievement) has been shown consistently to be the best predictor of enlightened political engagement in adults. Converse wrote in 1972 that "the relationship is always in the same direction": positive. Table 5.1 presents the correlations between years of schooling and seven variables of enlightenment and engagement based on this and more recent studies (Nie et al., 1996). In this scheme, there are five variables associated with the knowing side of the coin and five associated with the doing side, and there is some overlap. These correlations are based on survey research, which has unique strengths and weaknesses, but I feature them to clarify the two dimensions—to better draw the distinction between the knowing and doing sides of the coin and their relationship. Consider tolerance, for example. The citizen who knows that tolerance of diversity is crucial to making a democracy work possesses knowledge that is directly consequential for living together cooperatively in a pluralist society. This knowledge should, for example, restrain her from advocating a state religion or the incarceration of political dissidents—both standard practices in authoritarian states. It should help her also to grasp the wisdom of reciprocity—to argue not only for her own rights, but for the rights of others, especially those with

Table 5.1 Correlations between seven citizenship outcomes, by dimension and years of formal education completed

Citizenship outcome	Correlation	Dimension
Knowledge of principles of democracy	.38	Democratic enlightenment
Knowledge of current political leaders.	29	Political engagement
Knowledge of other current political facts	.37	Both
Political attentiveness	.39	Both
Participation in difficult political activities	.29	Political engagement
Frequency of voting	.25	Both
Tolerance	.35	Democratic enlightenment

Note: From *Education and democratic citizenship in America*, by N. H. Nie, J. Junn, and K. Stehlik-Barry, 1996, University of Chicago Press.

whom she disagrees or whose cultural life she finds repugnant. What could otherwise be a kind of political engagement dedicated to self-aggrandizement at the expense of the common good—also known as *idiocy* (Parker, 2005)—is moderated by a grasp of democratic principles and one's obligations to the political community.

Why does school attendance predict enlightened political engagement? Schools are both curricular and civic spaces; a child who is coming to school from the private worlds of family and faith community is being exposed, perhaps for the first time, to a public space. Public spaces are different from family spaces in one key way—their "numerous and varied interests" (Dewey, 1985a, p. 89). Playtime must be negotiated with a greater number and variety of others; new norms are introduced, and others must be improvised by the children themselves; a broader array of adults is orchestrating and supervising both work and play; groupwork requires planning and division of labor; students are expected to work with other students whether they are friends or kin or neither; and elaborate status dynamics pervade work and play (e.g., Cohen & Lotan, 1997; Piaget, 1965; Wenger, 1998). This social topography, with its buzzing variety of interactions and practices, does not exist at home, or at church, temple, or mosque, but in public places where people who come from numerous private worlds and social positions are congregated on common ground with shared interests (e.g., learning, graduating). Schools are public places where multiple social perspectives and personal values are brought into face-to-face contact around both shared interests and all the matters that arise in the friction of social interaction (Parker, 2005).[7]

But the curriculum matters, too (Avery, 2000; Hahn, 1998; Niemi & Junn, 1998; Torney-Purta & Richardson, 2002). Educators who labor to shape school curriculum toward critical and democratic ends may find the school-attendance data annoying. After all, it ignores the "savage inequalities" (Kozol, 1992) between schools and the variable practices within them on both the social (e.g., class meetings) and the academic (e.g., required readings) fronts (Gay, 2000; Oakes, 1985). Educators care about the inequalities between affluent and impoverished schools, for example (not all schools are alike), and the differences between high and low tracks in the same school (not all classes are alike). Educators care about teaching quality, building leadership, availability of curriculum materials, funding, the local policy context, and the battle against racist and sexist practices embedded within the culture of the school. The currency of educators is not description, as with survey researchers, but prescription—reform, renewal, transformation. Political scientists subsume education within the concept *political socialization*, and therein are concerned with *un*conscious social reproduction; educators are concerned to intervene in history and to intentionally shape society's future—that is, with *conscious* social production (Gutmann, 1999). And therein are the two points of contention regarding the production of enlightened political engagement with which I am concerned in this chapter: (a) whether study (knowing) or practice (doing) should be emphasized, and (b) what to study and what to practice.

SEMINAR AND DELIBERATION

I have argued elsewhere (Parker, 2003, 2005, 2006) that the school curriculum can afford opportunities for students to learn enlightened political engagement by exploiting school attendance—that is, by developing the public potential of schools to educate citizens, not only in the academic curriculum but also in the social curriculum. Compared to home life, as we have seen, schools are like crossroads or cities. They have the two essential assets for cultivating democrats: diversity and shared problems. When these resources are mobilized, every student has the opportunity to learn the tolerance, respect, sense of justice, and knack for governing with others *whether one likes them or not*. If the favorable conditions, both social and psychological, are marshaled, students will develop some degree of enlightened political engagement, and perhaps give birth to critical consciousness: the ability to cut through conventional wisdom. Put differently, schools are probably the most fertile sites in contemporary society—where so many life spaces are private, and so few are public—for helping students move through puberty to citizenship. Schools cannot work miracles, of course—they are embedded in society and its norms and prejudices—but they can make a difference, and it is within this degree of freedom that educators do their work.

Puberty in this context references the ancient Greek meaning: the transition to public consciousness. From what? From *idiocy*. Idiocy shares with idiom and idiosyncratic the root *idios*, which means private, separate, distinct. *Idiotic* was in the Greek vernacular a term of reproach meaning selfish. When a person's behavior was concerned myopically with private, separate things and unmindful of the commonwealth, the person was believed to be a like a rudderless ship—without consequence save for the danger it posed to others. The meaning of idiocy achieves its force when contrasted with politês (citizen) or public. Here we have the private, unenlightened, and unengaged individual versus the enlightened, engaged citizen (Parker, 2005).

Cultivating the democratic potential of schools requires three interventions. Here I synthesize research on intergroup relations and prejudice reduction (Aronson, Blaney, Stephan, Sikes, & Snapp, 1978; Pettigrew, 2004) with Dewey's (1985a, b) understanding of growth and experience. First, increase the variety and frequency of interaction among students who are culturally, linguistically, and racially different from one another. Classrooms sometimes do this naturally, but if the school itself is homogenous—or if the school is diverse, but curriculum tracks are keeping groups of students apart—then this first intervention is undermined. It is not helping that resegregation has intensified in recent years despite an increasingly diverse society (Orfield, 2001). Second, orchestrate these contacts so that competent dialogue is fostered. In schools, competent dialogue is speaking and listening to one another about texts and problems. Third, clarify the distinction between purposeful dialogue and bull sessions and between open (inclusive) and closed (exclusive) exchanges. In other words, expect, teach, and model competent, inclusive discussion.

Purposeful classroom discussion is a species of cooperative inquiry, the desired outcomes of which rely on the expression and consideration of diverse views. Schwab (1978, p. 126) saw that "discussion is not merely a device, one of several possible means by which a mind may be brought to understanding of a worthy object. It is also the *experience* of moving toward and possessing understanding." Bridges (1979) clarified the pedagogical force of discussion:

> The distinctive and peculiar contribution which discussion has to play in the development of one's knowledge or understanding...is to set alongside one perception of the matter under discussion the several perceptions of other participants...challenging our own view of things with those of others. (p. 50)

Bridges' description points to the basic circumstance of discussion—it is a shared situation with a shared purpose—and to the potential of that circumstance to encourage participants to consider others' interpretations of the topic at hand and, in that broadened horizon, to reconsider their own readings, thereby widening and deepening their own understanding. This is why some have argued that discussion is not only an instructional means, but a curriculum goal; both learners and democratic citizens need to be capable and willing discussants. This is teaching *with* and *for* discussion (Parker & Hess, 2001; also Larson, 2000; Wilen & White, 1991).

Two kinds of classroom discussion, seminar and deliberation (Parker, 2003, 2006), emphasize respectively democratic enlightenment and political engagement, or democratic knowing and doing. Seminars encourage students to see the world more deeply and clearly, thanks largely to the selection of the seminar's text and to multiple interpretations that are brought to bear by the various discussants. Deliberations encourage discussants to think together, with and across their differences, as do seminars, but now the discussion is aimed at deciding which course of action to take to solve a shared problem.

The work of seminars concerns the seminar's text and the multiple interpretations that are brought to bear by the various discussants (Haroutunian-Gordon, 1991). By *text* is meant any semipermanent or nontransitory cultural product, such as a painting, script, book, or article; but it also includes *events*—cultural products that are transitory and non-permanent, such as performances, riots, and demonstrations (Cormack, 1992). In a seminar, facilitator and participants interpret a text together, and they speak and listen to learn. One needs to interpret with others in order to compare interpretations and, as Bridges put it, challenge one's own view of things with the views of others. See Table 5.2.

Like seminars, deliberations are social occasions that provide opportunities for discussants to think, speak, and listen together, with and across their differences, about a chosen topic. But in deliberations, learning is not the goal. It occurs as an intended side-effect, but it is not the goal. Rather, participants speak and listen to decide (Dillon, 1994). The purpose is to decide which course of action to take in order to solve (or in some other way address) a shared problem. This can be a classroom or school matter (e.g., recess disputes, attendance policy, dress code, curriculum tracking, girls' and boys' sports funding), a national or world problem (e.g., immigration policy, the coming water shortage), an academic controversy (e.g., why Rome fell, the literary canon), or other problem where a shared decision is needed and controversy arises over which

Table 5.2 Two kinds of purposeful discussion compared on three dimensions

	Seminar	*Deliberation*
Purpose	Reach an enlarged understanding of a powerful text.	Reach a decision on what a "we" should do about a shared problem.
Subject matter	Ideas, issues, and values in a text or performance	Alternative courses of action related to a controversial issue.
Opening question (heuristics)	What does this mean? What is happening?	What should we do? What's the best alternative?

Note: From *Teaching Democracy: Unity and Diversity in Public Life*, by W. C. Parker, 2003, Teachers College Press.

alternative is best. The focal point of the discussion is the controversy about what to do.

The work of deliberation is finding and weighing alternative courses of action. One needs to do this work with others for three reasons: democracy, quality, and social knowledge. First, the problem is actually shared, so the decision-making should be shared, too (popular sovereignty). Second, the array of alternatives that a diverse group generates, assuming participants are both speaking and listening, will be broader than one generated by an individual working in isolation. The resulting decision will be better than if many alternatives were overlooked. Third, within that broader array will be alternatives stemming from social positions that are more or less different from one's own, thereby developing one's own social knowledge (of social positions and their relations) while also contributing to a better and fairer solution. In deliberation, one speaks and listens to decide, but one learns along the way, too, because the listener is exposed to and has the opportunity to understand the primary and secondary discourses of the participants (Gee, 1996; Young, 1997; Williams, 2000). Social betterment and social knowledge, then, are the desired fruits of deliberation and the outcomes that make it worth the trouble.

Seminars and deliberations display the distinction between the world-revealing (enlightening) and world-changing (engaging) functions of conversation. The two are complementary—one can barely be imagined without the other—and then only in the way that courses are divided sequentially into units and units into lessons (wisely, teachers don't try to accomplish everything at once; recall Dewey's "great bad"). An eighth-grade class might hold a seminar on the Pledge of Allegiance (what are its meanings?) followed by a deliberation on whether they should recite it daily at school; a 12th-grade class might hold a series of seminars on the Earth Charter,[8] and then deliberate whether (and which) changes in U.S. domestic and foreign policy are warranted. The horizon-broadening function of seminars helps to provide an enlightened platform for public decision making, and vice versa. This two-way street is Dewey's "double movement of reflection" (1985b, p. 242), involving induction and deduction, which is at the heart of his pragmatic "method of intelligence" for educating a democratic community (Stanley, 2005).

ISSUES

I turn now to two issues that bear on seminar and deliberation as pedagogies that represent a knowing-and-doing curriculum geared to enlightened political engagement. These are, first, contention over text selection and, second, blurring the boundaries between knowing and doing. The latter will include a discussion of social positioning and perspective.

DISCUSS WHAT?

Text selection is a key site of contention. *Which* texts and problems should be interpreted in a seminar and deliberated in a deliberation? Kliebard (2004), Zimmerman (2002), and Evans (2004) capture a good many of the curriculum debates pertinent to democratic citizenship education across the 20th century, and Hess (2005) has studied how teachers' own political views shape their selection of topics. In 1994, when the several national curriculum standards were published for history, civics and government, geography, and integrated social studies, curriculum conflict intensified again (Appleby, Hunt, & Jacob, 1994; Cornbleth & Waugh, 1995; Nash, Crabtree, & Dunn,

2000; Symcox, 2002; Thornton, 2005), and a new volley of criticism was directed at the alleged liberalism and anti-patriotism of social studies teaching and curriculum materials (e.g., Cheney, 1994; Finn, 2003).

Seminars are particularly liable to criticism from the political left because of their past association with the *Great Books of the Western World* curriculum (Adler, 1982; Hutchins, 1952) and with the eurocentrism of the Western literary canon generally (Said, 1993). Meanwhile, deliberations are liable to criticism from the political right because they so often feature social problems relevant to the experience of students as the focus of study. Hunt and Metcalf's (1955) curriculum featured social taboos, Oliver and Shaver's (1974) featured six arenas of public conflict (e.g., race and ethnicity; religion and ideology), and the famous Problems of Democracy curriculum (Commission on the Reorganization of Secondary Education, 1916) promoted the study of social problems through several disciplinary lenses. For example, immigration would be studied economically, sociologically, and politically (p. 54). Both seminar and deliberation have been criticized from the political right because they are discussion forums and, therefore, reduce the amount of teacher lecture (Finn, 2003).

Parents have challenged educators' text selections mainly on religious grounds, where texts related to sex education, global climate change, and the teaching of evolution are concerned, but also on racial and cultural grounds, where Eurocentrism has been alleged. The curriculum challenges of creationists and Afrocentrists have been documented by Binder (2002), whose study at once captures the parent-educator-citizen dynamic as well as the dominant/subordinate group dynamic. Afrocentrists and creationists both mounted challenges to established educational practices and, to date, both have been largely unsuccessful.

KNOWING AND DOING

Leaving aside the conflict over *what* to discuss during discussions—the content of democratic enlightenment and the topics for policy deliberation—let us turn to a second issue. It was noted earlier that students do learn during deliberation, though that is not its primary purpose; similarly, they engage one another during seminar, though that is not its primary purpose. Seminar has thus far represented the knowing (enlightenment) side of the coin, and deliberation the doing (engagement) side. But this oversimplifies while masking the converse: What does one learn in deliberation and what does one do in seminar?

The primary purpose of seminar is to achieve an enlarged understanding of the issues, ideas, and values in the text at hand, be it a print work, a work of visual art, a music selection, an event, whatever. As we have seen, a student's understanding grows as a consequence of setting alongside one interpretation of the text under discussion the several interpretations of other students and, thereby, having one's initial interpretation challenged by the views of others (Bridges, 1979). At the heart of the learning that seminar affords, therefore, is the collaborative work of the discussion group. If the text is fuel, the groupwork is the furnace. Here is how one prominent seminar leader approaches it:

> Seminars demand rigorous thinking by all the participants, not mere mastery of information. They require no predetermined notion of what particular understandings will be enlarged or what routes to greater understanding will be followed. The conversation moves along in accordance with what is said by the participants, rather than deference to a hard and fast lesson plan. Seminars are inhospitable to competition for right answers, particularly given the principal aim in engaging

students in critical thinking about complex, multisided matters. Instead, they join participants in a collaborative quest for understanding, in mutual testing of each other's responses to the text. (Gray, 1989, p. 18)

Accordingly, what is done in seminar, the action that is taken, is communication across difference (Habermas, 1990). Students exchange emotions and ideas with one another, both speech and silence, whether they like one another or not. It is precisely this activity—not its content—that draws criticism from both the right and left. Finn (2003) derides discussion pedagogy for aiming to make students into "mini pundits," forming and presenting opinions rather than learning facts on which to base them. While "there is nothing wrong" with students deliberating alternatives, he continues, it would be better for them "to learn as much as the teacher can teach them" (p. 12). Pragmatically, teachers use it rarely because this activity runs counter to their chief purpose, which is covering content and controlling students (Barton & Levstik, 2004). Critics on the cultural left, meanwhile, are pessimistic about whether such dialogue is even possible, given the power differential across groups and their social positions. The discourse patterns that emerge during seminars can and too often do reinforce rather than disrupt systemic relations of inequality (Boler, 2004; Delpit, 1988). A form of discursive bullying can arise when dominant students out-shout or simply out-talk students who are drummed into acquiescence, and when particular issues are not allowed space in the discussion, such as race, religion, and bullying.

Seminar, then, is about doing something as much as it is about knowing something. And it is the doing, as much as the knowing, that draws fire from critics.

Deliberation is ostensibly a form of doing democracy directly by collectively determining public policy. Whether this is a classroom rule in kindergarten, a school attendance policy in high school, or a U. S. foreign policy deliberation as developed by the popular *Choices for the 21st Century* program,[9] cooperative rule making—popular sovereignty—is democratic activity at its heart. But much is learned too. Specifically, deliberators learn the problem at hand, the alternatives that are weighed, and the social positions and perspectives of the discussants. I consider each briefly.

Problems   Five-year-olds in a kindergarten classroom are discussing a rule their teacher (Paley, 1992) has proposed: Shouldn't we have a rule that says you can't tell one another not to play with you? As they discuss the proposal and its alternatives, students are exposed to the problem of exclusion in their midst and learn that some children are typically excluded while others are typically the "bosses." Meanwhile, high school students in Denver are discussing whether the state of Colorado should permit physician-assisted suicide (Miller & Singleton, 1997; Parker, 2001). They learn a good deal about the issue thanks to the background reading they completed prior to the discussion. They learn the distinction between state and federal law on this matter; they compare societies that prevent and allow the practice; and they learn about the frequency of the practice in places that allow and forbid it.

Alternatives   The alternative courses of action are the primary subject matter of a deliberation. Deliberation involves, most centrally, *comparing* alternatives (the *liber* in deliberation derives from the Latin for scale); accordingly, participants hold the array of alternatives in mind along with the details of each alternative. Among those details are the consequences of an alternative's implementation—to the extent they can be predicted and imagined—and these consequences are weighed against those of the competing alternatives. One of the kindergartners above complained that if the rule was implemented, an unacceptable consequence would be put into effect: Play would cease to be play; play would become work. And one of the high school students argued that if physician-assisted suicide was made legal, then some doctors would "start killing people off"—the people they didn't like.

Social position and perspective   All of us are thrown into unchosen historical situations (Sartre, 1948; Young, 1997). None of us chooses our birthplace or the race, social class, language, or religion of our parents. We are positioned in already structured fields of power and privilege. Once we begin to examine our found situation, we see that it has located us closer to some individuals (in my case, fellow working-class WASPS in the church group of which I was a member, for example) and simultaneously farther from others who were positioned differently (wealthy WASPS living in other neighborhoods, poor Whites, Jews, Catholics, Muslims, and African Americans, for example—and all this only in the U.S. context). That is, people are positioned closer to persons similarly thrown and farther from persons who were thrown elsewhere. Furthermore, the groups into which we are thrown are not equal; they are positioned differently in the socio-economic hierarchy and the related status hierarchies of race, gender, language, sexual orientation, and religion.

Being positioned in one way rather than another adds up to a unique social perspective—a point of view, vantage point, frame of reference. Where one is positioned matters in terms of how one sees the world and what one attends to in it. Young's (1997) portrayal of this relationship between position and perspective manages to account for the force of positioning while avoiding determinism:

> A social perspective is a certain way of being sensitive to particular aspects of social life, meanings, and interactions, and perhaps less sensitive to others. It is a form of attentiveness that brings some things into view while possibly obscuring others.... Perspective is a way of looking at social processes without determining what one sees. (pp. 394–395; also Code, 1991; Epstein & Shiller, 2005; Mitchell & Parker, in press)

A social perspective, then, is a shared way of looking at situations that is grounded in a shared social position. But it is does not automatically predict what one sees. Sharing the same social perspective with others creates a bond of sorts, an affinity of being similarly positioned and—perhaps due to similar experiences in that location—a sense of solidarity and, sometimes, even agreement on what should be done about particular problems. Drawing this distinction between perspective (point of view) and identity (subjectivity) is practically useful because it acknowledges group membership while arguing against stereotyping (and essentializing) or "the tendency to interpret groups as fixed, closed, and bounded" (Young, 1997, p. 398).

This is perhaps too long a way of getting to the third point about what is learned in deliberation. The array of positions and related perspectives and identities gathered in a deliberation that involves diversely positioned participants advantages that deliberation, I argue, in three ways. The first of these, already mentioned, is related to the learning of alternatives: A greater number and variety of alternatives will be included in the deliberation. More heads—more social positions and perspectives—are better than one because more alternatives can be culled from the members' diverse experiences and perspectives. As Williams (2000) writes, "pluralism enhances deliberation because it expands the number of alternative understandings of a problem we can entertain in attempting to resolve it" (pp. 131–132). Second, more is learned in the deliberation than simply the greater variety of alternatives. How? Each participant's knowledge of perspectives and identities is enlarged. This includes social knowledge about life as it is lived and viewed from other positions. One's social horizon is broadened; one's knowledge of the society in which one lives is deepened. Third, the presence of multiple perspectives increases the likelihood that dominant norms and practices will be subjected to observation and critique. What is not seen by members of one group may be brought sharply into focus by members of another. The student above who told her classmates that physicians might use the assisted-suicide law to kill people they didn't like was herself positioned in a vulnerable group (she was a young Latina woman in an urban high school) and recognized that physicians are members of society's power elite. Similarly, the kindergarten children most favorably disposed to Ms. Paley's proposed rule were those who most frequently felt the sting of exclusion from play.

Summing up, knowing and doing are both accomplished in both seminar and deliberation. While the purpose of each directs the work toward enlightenment or decision making respectively, both, in fact, involve both. Much is learned in deliberation about the problem itself; the alternatives from which a choice must be made; and the other people involved in the discussion, their social perspectives and identities. And much is done dialogically in seminar because the work of textual interpretation is carried out in a rich group context.

CONCLUSION

What kind of citizens do we want schools to cultivate and how might schools go about that work? I have argued here that we want citizens who are both democratically enlightened and democratically engaged, and, accordingly, that there is both a knowing and a doing dimension to this work. These dimensions are, practically speaking, inseparable; at least, there is no use arguing for one over the other in school practice. Engaged citizens who don't know what they're doing is not the goal; nor is the prospect of knowledgeable citizens who are disengaged from the problems of living together. I have tried to show that two kinds of classroom discourse, seminar and deliberation, each emphasize one of these dimensions yet contain both, making them promising pedagogies in the education of democratic citizens.

Diversity matters in both knowing and doing, in both enlightenment and engagement, in both seminar and deliberation—in both revealing the world and solving its problems. Without the diversity afforded by a varied social environment—such as a school—growth is stunted, idiocy encouraged, civic consciousness narrowed, and decisions impoverished. Diversity and shared problems are the essential resources schools afford to the education of democratic citizens. If we are to be serious about this work, and practical, then what are needed are demanding courses of study, seminars on powerful texts, and a multitude of deliberative forums in which democracy and difference can be experienced directly and decisions made about what to do.

NOTES

1. Schwab's formulation was apolitical, but still seminal in acknowledging that the other commonplaces—students, teachers, and subject matters—do not exist in a social vacuum. It was apolitical but not asocial.
2. See Zakaria (1997) as well as the annual evaluation of nation-states conducted by Freedom House. The former distinguishes between liberal and illiberal democracies; the latter rates democracies by how liberal they are, using two scales of measurement: political rights and civil liberties. Available at www.freedomhouse.org.
3. See discussions of the gap between principles and conditions in Gutmann (2004), Habermas (1990), and King (1963).
4. The social movement literature sheds light on how subaltern groups *produce* knowledge in the process of contention. See Eyerman & Jamison (1991).

5. Not addressed here are additional contextual factors such as the religious awakening occurring currently in the U.S. and elsewhere along with the intensification of tensions between faith, science, democracy, and schooling; nor the hyperconsumption of northern societies and how their curriculum theorizing is thus biased toward materialism and their environmental education rendered feckless.
6. Path, participation, and pluralism are three "'advanced' ideas about democracy" (Parker, 1996a).
7. This is a somewhat different explanation than the one given by Nie et al. (1996). Theirs emphasizes the positive correlation of school attendance and access to political resources plus the positive correlation of school attendance and knowledge of democracy.
8. Available at www.earthcharter.org/. The secretariat is in San Jose, Costa Rica,
9. Available at www.choices.edu.

REFERENCES

Adler, M. J. (1982). *The Paideia proposal.* New York: Macmillan.

Appleby, J., Hunt, L., & Jacob, M. (1994). *Telling the truth about history.* New York: Norton.

Arendt, H. (1958). *The human condition.* Chicago: University of Chicago Press.

Aristotle. (1958). *The politics of Aristotle* (E. Barker, Trans.). New York: Oxford University Press.

Aronson, E., Blaney, N. T., Stephan, C., Sikes, J., & Snapp, M. (1978). *The Jigsaw classroom.* Beverly Hills, CA: Sage.

Avery, P. (2000). Review of the book *Civic education: What makes students learn. Theory and Research in Social Education, 28,* 290–295.

Banks, J. A. (1997). *Educating citizens in a multicultural society.* New York: Teachers College Press.

Barton, K. C., & Levstik, L. S. (2004). *Teaching history for the common good: Theory and research for teaching about the past.* Mahwah, NJ: Erlbaum.

Beiner, R. S. (1984). *Political judgment.* Chicago: University of Chicago Press.

Binder, A. (2002). *Contentious curricula: Afrocentrism and creationism in American public schools.* Princeton, NJ: Princeton University Press.

Boler, M. (Ed.). (2004). *Democratic dialogue in education: Troubling speech, disturbing silence.* New York: Peter Lang.

Bridges, D. (1979). *Education, democracy and discussion.* Atlantic Highlands, NJ: Humanities Press.

Butler, J. (1997). *Excitable speech.* New York: Routledge.

Cheney, L. V. (1994, October 20). The end of history. *Wall Street Journal,* p. A26.

Cherryholmes, C. H. (1988). *Power and criticism: Poststructural investigations in education.* New York: Teachers College Press.

Chilcoat, G. W., & Ligon, J. A. (1994). Developing democratic citizens: Mississippi 'freedom schools' as a model for social studies instruction. *Theory and Research in Social Education, 22,* 128–175.

Code, L. (1991). *What can she know? Feminist theory and the construction of knowledge.* Ithaca: Cornell University Press.

Cohen, E. G., & Lotan, R. A. (1997). *Working for equity in heterogeneous classrooms: Sociological theory in practice.* New York: Teachers College Press.

Commission on the Reorganization of Secondary Education of the National Education Association — Committee on Social Studies. (1916). *The social studies in secondary education (Bureau of Education bulletin no.28).* Washington, D. C.: Author.

Converse, P. E. (1972). Change in the American electorate. In A. Campbell & P. E. Converse (Eds.), *The human meaning of social change* (pp. 263–337). New York: Russell Sage Foundation.

Cormack, M. J. (1992). *Ideology.* Ann Arbor: University of Michigan Press.

Cornbleth, C., & Waugh, D. (1995). *The great speckled bird: Multicultural politics and education policymaking.* New York: St. Martin's Press.

Counts, G. S. (1932). *Dare the school build a new social order?* New York: John Day.

Crocco, M. (Ed.). (1999). *"Bending the future to their will": Civic women, social education, and democracy.* Lanham, MD: Roman & Littlefield.

Delpit, L. D. (1988). The silenced dialogue: Power and pedagogy in educating other people's children. *Harvard Educational Review, 58*(3), 280–298.

Dewey, J. (1927). *The public and its problems.* Chicago: Swallow.

Dewey, J. (1985a). *Democracy and education* (Vol. 9) J. A. Boydston (Ed.). Carbondale: Southern Illinois University Press.

Dewey, J. (1985b). *How we think, and selected essays* (Vol. 6) J. A. Boydston (Ed.). Carbondale: Southern Illinois University Press.

Dillon, J. T. (Ed.). (1994). *Deliberation in education and society.* Norwood: Ablex.

Epstein, T., & Shiller, J. (2005). Perspective matters: Social identity and the teaching and learning of national history. *Social Education, 69*(4), 201–204.

Evans, R. W. (2004). *The social studies wars.* New York: Teachers College Press.

Eyerman, R., & Jamison, A. (1991). *Social movements: A cognitive approach.* University Park: Pennsylvania State University Press.

Finn, C. E. (Ed.). (2003). *Terrorists, despots, and democracy: What our children need to know.* Washington, DC: Thomas B. Fordham Foundation.

Fischman, G., Gvirtz, S., & Ball, S. (Eds.). (2003). *Crisis and hope: The educational hopscotch of Latin America.* New York: Falmer.

Foucault, M. (1980). *Power/knowledge: Interviews and other writings* (C. Gordon Ed. & Trans.). New York: Routledge.

Fraser, N., & Honneth, A. (Eds.). (2004). *Redistribution or recognition? A political-philosophical exchange.* London: Verso.

Gagnon, P. (1996). History's role in civic education. In W. C. Parker (Ed.), *Educating the democratic mind* (pp. 241–262). Albany: State University of New York Press.

Gay, G. (2000). *Culturally responsive teaching.* New York: Teachers College Press.

Gee, J. P. (1996). *Social linguistics and literacies: Ideology in discourses* (2nd ed.). Philadelphia: Routledge.

Gonçalves e Silva, P. B. (2004). Citizenship and education in Brazil: The contribution of Indian peoples and blacks in the struggle for citizenship and recognition. In J. A. Banks (Ed.), *Diversity and citizenship education: Global perspectives* (pp. 185–214). San Francisco: Jossey-Bass.

Gray, D. (1989). Putting minds to work. *American Educator, 13*(3), 16–23.

Green, A. (1990). *Education and state formation.* London: Macmillan.

Gutmann, A. (1999). *Democratic education* (2nd ed.). Princeton, NJ: Princeton University Press.

Gutmann, A. (2004). Unity and diversity in democratic multicultural education. In J. A. Banks (Ed.), *Diversity and citizenship education: Global perspectives* (pp. 71–95). San Francisco: Jossey-Bass.

Habermas, J. (1990). *Moral consciousness and communicative action.* Cambridge, MA: MIT Press.

Hahn, C. L. (1998). *Becoming political.* Albany: State University of New York Press.

Haroutunian-Gordon, S. (1991). *Turning the soul.* Chicago: University of Chicago Press.

Harvey, D. (1989). *The condition of postmodernity.* Oxford: Blackwell.

Hess, D. E. (2005). How do teachers' political views influence teaching about controversial issues? *Social Education, 61*(1), 47–48.

Hirsch, E. D. J. (1996). *The schools we need and why we don't have them.* New York: Doubleday.

Hobbes, T. (1976). *Leviathan.* New York: Dutton.

Horton, M., & Freire, P. (1990). *We made the road by walking: Conversations on education and social change.* B. Bell, J. Gaventa, & J. Peters (Eds.). Philadelphia: Temple University Press.

Hunt, M. P., & Metcalf, L. E. (1955). *Teaching high school social studies.* New York: Harper & Brothers.

Hutchins, R. M. (1952). *The great conversation: The substance of a liberal education.* Chicago: Encyclopedia Britannica.

King, M. L., Jr. (1963). *Why we can't wait.* New York: Mentor.

Kliebard, H. M. (2004). *The struggle for the American curriculum, 1893–1958* (3rd ed.). New York: Falmer.

Kohlberg, L. (1980). High school democracy and educating for a just society. In R. L. Mosher (Ed.), *Moral education: A first generation of research and development* (pp. 20–57). New York: Praeger.

Kozol, J. (1992). *Savage inequalities.* New York: HarperPerennial.

Kymlicka, W. (1995). *Multicultural citizenship: A liberal theory of minority rights.* Oxford: Clarendon.

Ladson-Billings, G. (2004). Culture versus citizenship. In J. A. Banks (Ed.), *Diversity and citizenship education: Global perspectives* (pp. 99–126). San Francisco: Jossey-Bass.

Larner, W. (2000). Neo-liberalism: Policy, ideology, governmentality. *Studies in Political Economy, 63*, 5–26.

Larson, B. E. (2000). Classroom discussion: A method of instruction and a curriculum outcome. *Teaching and Teacher Education, 16*(5), 661–677.

Madison, J. (1937). The federalist no. 10. In J. Madison, A. Hamilton & J. Jay (Eds.), *The federalist* (pp. 53–62). New York: Modern Library.

Massialas, B. G. (1996). Criteria for issues-centered content selection. In R. W. Evans & D. W. Saxe (Eds.), *Handbook on teaching social issues* (pp. 44–50). Washington, DC: National Council for the Social Studies.

Miller, B., & Singleton, L. (1997). *Preparing citizens: Linking authentic assessment and instruction in civic/law-related education.* Boulder: Social Science Education Consortium.

Mitchell, K. (2003). Educating the national citizen in neoliberal times: From the multicultural self to the strategic cosmopolitan. *Transactions of the Institute of British Geographers, 28*(4), 387–403.

Mitchell, K., & Parker, W. C. (in press). I pledge allegiance to…. Flexible citizenship and shifting scales of belonging. *Teachers College Record.*

Nash, G. B., Crabtree, C., & Dunn, R. E. (2000). *History on trial.* New York: Vintage.

Newmann, F. M. (1989). Reflective civic participation. *Social education, 53*(6), 357–360, 366.

Nie, N. H., Junn, J., & Stehlik-Barry, K. (1996). *Education and democratic citizenship in America.* Chicago: University of Chicago Press.

Niemi, R. G., & Junn, J. (1998). *Civic education: What makes students learn.* New Haven, CT: Yale University Press.

Oakes, J. (1985). *Keeping track: How schools structure inequality.* New Haven, CT: Yale University Press.

Oliver, D. W. (1957). The selection of content in the social sciences. *Harvard Educational Review, 27*, 271–300.

Oliver, D. W., & Shaver, J. P. (1974). *Teaching public issues in the high school.* Logan: Utah State University Press.

Ong, A. (1999). *Flexible citizenship: The cultural logics of transnationality.* Durham, NC: Duke University Press.

Orfield, G. (2001). *Schools more separate: Results of a decade of resegregation.* Cambridge, MA: Harvard University Civil Rights Project. Retrieved January 26, 2005, from: www.civilrightsproject.harvard.edu/research/deseg/separate_schools01.php.

Paley, V. G. (1992). *You can't say you can't play.* Cambridge: Harvard University Press.

Parker, W. C. (1996a). "Advanced" ideas about democracy: Toward a pluralist conception of citizen education. *Teachers College Record, 98*(1), 104–125.

Parker, W. C. (Ed.). (1996b). *Educating the democratic mind.* Albany: State University of New York Press.

Parker, W. C. (2001). Classroom discussion: Models for leading seminars and deliberations. *Social Education, 65*(2), 111–115.

Parker, W. C. (2003). *Teaching democracy: Unity and diversity in public life.* New York: Teachers College Press.

Parker, W. C. (2005). Teaching against idiocy. *Phi Delta Kappan, 86*(5), 344–351.

Parker, W. C. (2006). Public discourses in schools: Purposes, problems, possibilities. *Educational Researcher, 35*(8), 19–29.

Parker, W. C., & Hess, D. (2001). Teaching with and for discussion. *Teaching and Teacher Education, 17*(3), 273–289.

Pettigrew, T. F. (2004). Intergroup contact: Theory, research, and new perspectives. In J. A. Banks & C. A. M. Banks (Eds.), *Handbook of research on multicultural education* (2nd ed., pp. 770–781). San Francisco: Jossey-Bass.

Phillips, A. (1991). *Engendering democracy.* University Park, PA: Pennsylvania State University Press.

Piaget, J. (1965). *The moral judgment of the child.* New York: Free Press.

Rawls, J. (1971). *A theory of justice.* Cambridge: Harvard University Press.

Rosaldo, R. (1997). Cultural citizenship, inequality, and multiculturalism. In W. Flores & R. Benmayor (Eds.), *Latino cultural citizenship: Claiming identity, space, and rights* (pp. 27–38). Boston: Beacon.

Rose, N. (1992). Governing the enterprising self. In P. Heelas & P. Morris (Eds.), *The values of the enterprise culture: The moral debate* (pp. 141–164). New York: Routledge.

Rugg, H. O. (Ed.). (1939). *Democracy and the curriculum: The life and program of the American school.* New York: Appleton-Century.

Rutter, R. A., & Newmann, F. M. (1989). The potential of community service to enhance civic responsibility. *Social Education, 53*(6), 371–374.

Said, E. W. (1993). *Culture and imperialism*. New York: Knopf.

Sartre, J. (1948). *The wall* (L. Alexander, Trans.). New York: New Directions.

Schwab, J. J. (1973). The practical 3: Translation into curriculum. *School Review, 81,* 501–522.

Schwab, J. (1978). Eros and education: A discussion of one aspect of discussion. In I. Westbury & N. Will (Eds.), *Science, curriculum, and liberal education: Selected essays* (pp. 105–132). Chicago: University of Chicago.

Sparke, M. (in press). *Introduction to globalization: The ties that bind*. London: Blackwell.

Stanley, W. B. (2005). Social studies and the social order: Transmission or transformation? *Social Education, 69*(5), 282–286.

Symcox, L. (2002). *Whose history: The struggle for national standards in American classrooms.* New York: Teachers College Press.

Thornton, S. J. (2005). *Teaching social studies that matters*. New York: Teachers College Press.

Torney-Purta, J., & Richardson, W. K. (2002). An assessment of what 14-year-olds know and believe about democracy in 28 countries. In W. C. Parker (Ed.), *Education for democracy: Contexts, curricula, and assessments* (pp. 185–210). Greenwich, CT: Information Age.

Wenger, E. (1998). *Communities of practice: Learning, meaning, and identity*. New York: Cambridge University Press.

Wilen, W. W., & White, J. J. (1991). Interaction and discourse in social studies classrooms. In J. P. Shaver (Ed.), *Handbook of research on social studies teaching and learning* (pp. 483–495). New York: Macmillan.

Williams, M. S. (2000). The uneasy alliance of group representation and deliberative democracy. In W. Kymlicka & W. Norman (Eds.), *Citizenship in diverse societies* (pp. 124–152). Oxford: Oxford University Press.

Young, I. M. (1990). *Justice and the politics of difference*. Princeton, NJ: Princeton University Press.

Young, I. M. (1997). Difference as a resource for democratic communication. In J. Bohman & W. Rehg (Eds.), *Deliberative democracy: Essays on reason and politics* (pp. 383–406). Cambridge, MA: The MIT Press.

Zakaria, F. (1997). The rise of illiberal democracy. *Foreign Affairs, 76*(6), 22–43.

Zimmerman, J. (2002). *Whose America? Culture wars in the public schools*. Cambridge, MA: Harvard University Press.

6 International political socialization research

Carole L. Hahn
Theresa Alviar-Martin

Emory University

In recent years, there has been much interest in civic education internationally. As the number of democratic nations increased in Latin America, Africa, and Central and Eastern Europe, policy makers have focused on how to instill democratic beliefs and values in youth. In older democracies, policy makers have been concerned about how to stimulate youth civic-political engagement. Within Europe, politicians and educators have been interested in developing a European identity. Additionally, interest in civic education has intensified as a consequence of globalization; national policy makers want to know how their youth "measure up" to peers in other countries in terms of their knowledge in the civic and political arena, as well as in other areas such as literacy, mathematics, and science. Accompanying this multifaceted interest in civic education and civic-political outcomes has been an increase in political socialization research internationally.

In the 1960s and 1970s, political scientists, political psychologists, and social studies education researchers in the United States (and to a lesser extent Western Europe) studied the processes by which young people acquired their civic-political knowledge, skills, attitudes, and behaviors. At the time, scholars sought to identify the links between particular inputs (messages from family, school, and media) and outputs (student knowledge, attitudes, and behaviors) in the belief these would predict adult orientations (for a review of the early studies see Ehman, 1980). Students were viewed as passive recipients of information about formal political institutions and processes.

Since that early period, political socialization researchers shifted their focus to include young people's orientations to engagement in civil society, as well as with the traditional avenues for political participation. Additionally, researchers have been influenced by constructivist theories of cognitive psychologists, and as a result, today they view youth as actively constructing meaning of the civic-political arena within nested contexts of face-to-face social interactions and wider ecologies of community, nation, and world (Conover & Searing, 2000, Haste & Torney-Purta, 1992; Lave & Wenger, 1991; Torney-Purta, Schwille, & Amadeo, 1999). To depict the ecological systems in which youth construct individualized meanings of the civic-political world, the Civic Education Study of the International Association for the Evaluation of Educational Achievement, better known as IEA, developed the Octagon Model (Torney-Purta et al., 1999).

Although the Octagon model was developed with input from scholars in different countries, for the most part, the scholars came from societies whose political systems are rooted in the European Enlightenment, which places a high value on individual rights and participation—government of the people and by the people, as well as for the people.[1] Because most of the research we discuss comes from such societies, we believe the model is a useful framework for examining the research. However, it is important to realize that it may not be applicable to research from other cultural traditions.

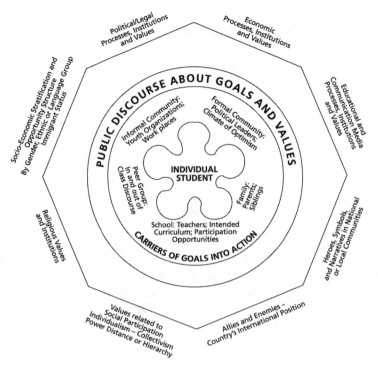

Figure 6.1 Octagon model (Torney-Purta et al., 1999).

For example, case studies of civic education in 12 Asian-Pacific countries reveal that civic-political values that underlie Western political socialization research are not universally held (Lee, Grossman, Kennedy, & Fairbrother, 2004). Rather, when scholars shift the center of concern from West to East, they can see that within Asia there is much diversity in civic education and political socialization, as well as diversity in religion, values, and economic and political systems (Lee et al, 2004). In Asia, researchers tend to focus more on moral and/or civic education than political education.

Thus, it is important that scholars and readers not generalize about political socialization beyond the countries and cultures in which data were collected. Furthermore, readers should realize that when researchers conduct a study, they examine variables that are meaningful in their particular cultural context. Researchers from other traditions might ask other questions and focus on other variables. The research that was available to us for this review was limited to reports in English language journals and conferences. Even the research on Asian and African students of which we are aware was reported in English-language journals and conducted by researchers whose education was at least partially completed in the United States, the United Kingdom, or Australia; consequently, it is not surprising that these researchers used variables and concepts that are prevalent in the West.

Despite these limitations, we believe there are several advantages to viewing political socialization from a comparative and international perspective. First, we believe that social studies educators will find research conducted in other countries interesting as it reveals the variety of cultural contexts in which youth learn about the social and political world. Second, comparative and international studies can serve as a kind of quasi-experimental laboratory. One can see the effects of different policies and practices in a way that might not be possible within a single nation. Third, by stepping out of one's familiar surroundings and looking at social studies and citizenship education in different national settings one can view her or his own taken-for-granted assumptions with fresh eyes. We hope this chapter will serve these purposes.

We have organized this chapter into two broad sections.[2] First, we discuss studies done in particular regions. Second, we discuss the large-scale IEA cross-national study of civic education. Within each section, we begin by discussing research on K–12 student knowledge, attitudes, and civic-political orientations—whenever possible making links to agents of socialization (school, family, media, and other influences). Because we believe teachers are keys to the creation of environments in which students construct their civic-political views, and because this section of the *Handbook* is concerned with teaching as well as learning, we discuss studies of teacher beliefs and practices. Finally, we synthesize major findings from our review and make recommendations for needed research, policy, and practice.

RESEARCH FROM PARTICULAR COUNTRIES IN REGIONS

As international interest in citizenship education has grown, a number of scholars have written case studies of civic education in their respective countries for edited volumes (Arthur, Davies, & Hahn, 2008; Cogan & Derricott, 1998; 2000; Cogan, Morris, & Print, 2002; Ichilov, 1998; Kennedy, 1997; Lee & Fouts, 2005; Lee et al., 2004; Torney-Purta et al., 1999). To produce their case studies, researchers examined policy documents, surveyed previous research, and described the history of civic education in their societies. In some cases, researchers examined textbooks, interviewed teachers and students in focus groups, and/or made observations in a sample of schools. The case studies describe both the intended and the implemented curriculum of civic education and are important for understanding the differing contexts in which political socialization occurs. We will not try to summarize the case studies, which would be an impossible task, but encourage readers to read them for countries of particular interest to them. In this chapter, we discuss empirical studies of student learning and teachers' role in political socialization.

Research from Western Europe

Throughout Europe, there has been much recent interest in education for citizenship, in part growing out of the European Union's desire to create a European identity. Varied initiatives add a European dimension to existing national programs in citizenship education. In 2005 the European Union celebrated the Year of Citizenship, drawing attention to shared issues in a region in which countries have very different approaches to education for citizenship. For example, France, Germany, and the Scandinavian countries have traditionally educated young people for their roles as democratic citizens, whereas England, Portugal, and the Netherlands have, for the most part, not expected schools to deliberately educate for citizenship (Banks, 2004; Hahn, 1998; Torney-Purta et al., 1999). However, in recent years there has been a convergence in the idea that schools should play some role in educating young people for democracy, participation, and respect for diversity and human rights (Roland-Levy & Ross, 2003; Ross, 2001). It is within this changing context that recent political socialization researchers have conducted studies in Europe.

The varied ways in which students in different countries within this region are politically socialized was revealed in Hahn's (1998) study of adolescents' political attitudes, beliefs, and experiences in Denmark, England, Germany, and the Netherlands, as well as the United States.[3] Danish schools were expected to model democracy, providing young people with many opportunities for decision-making and teaching lessons in social science and history. In contrast, at the time of the study citizenship education was relegated to the position of a cross-curricular theme in the English national curriculum and it was only minimally evident in schools Hahn observed. The policy in the Netherlands varied from one year to the next, but for the most part, Dutch students received little deliberate citizenship education. In Germany students were exposed to courses that were quite similar to American social studies throughout their schooling. Differences in civic education tended to reflect the differing civic cultures in these particular countries, leading Hahn to conclude that even within similar Western democracies "there is no one form of democracy and there is no one way of teaching for democracy" (Hahn, 1998, p. 236).[4] Hahn (1998) was particularly interested in the role of controversial issues discussion in classes and the development of political attitudes. Drawing on her observational data, she illustrated differences in pedagogical cultures and the distinct ways in which controversial issues were examined in each country. Importantly, both across and within countries, students who reported discussing diverse views in classrooms with supportive climates expressed the highest levels of political interest, efficacy, and trust. Subsequent studies yielded similar conclusions, as we discuss later.

Since the time of Hahn's (1998) study, England has undergone major reforms in education for citizenship. Parliament passed legislation that required schools to provide education for citizenship from 2002 onward to all students at key stages 3 and 4 (ages 8–11 and 14–16). In the English context, education for citizenship is conceived as having three dimensions: social and moral responsibility, community involvement, and political literacy. It is left up to each school to decide how it will meet the statutory requirement.[5]

The National Foundation for Educational Research (NFER) has been monitoring the implementation of the new policy in the Citizenship Education Longitudinal Study.[6] Preliminary findings from the longitudinal study provide some insight into political socialization in England. The researchers reported that students' development of citizenship was associated with personal, family, and community characteristics (Cleaver, Ireland, Kerr, & Lopes, 2005). For example, the number of home literacy sources (books in the home, a proxy for socioeconomic status in this and other studies) correlated with student knowledge, feelings of empowerment, levels of trust, engagement, community attachment, and commitment to volunteering, participation, and political engagement (Cleaver et al., 2005). Although there were no gender differences in civic/political knowledge, boys expressed greater political interest and girls were more likely to expect to vote. Additionally, students were more likely to say that a good adult citizen obeys the law than to say a good citizen follows politics in the media. Similarly, more students defined good citizenship as obeying the law, belonging to a community, and working together than as voting, politics, and government (Ireland, Kerr, Lopes, Nelson, & Cleaver, 2006).

In 2005, the Nestle Social Research Program interviewed a random sample of youth 11–21 years old in England, Scotland, and Wales (Haste, 2005). The researchers found that from a quarter to half of young people were civically engaged by helping in the community and/or "making their voices heard." The researchers identified six distinct profiles of engagement among youth. Three of the profiles reflected involvement with the political and social system: the political activist, the community helper, and those exhibiting concern about social control. In contrast, three other types reflected degrees of disengagement from politics, and within this, varying levels of disillusion and alienation. Youth were most likely to be currently engaged and to anticipate later civic engagement, to trust government, and to have a sense that they could be effective, if they perceived that they were consulted about the development of school rules and policies, involved with planning their class-work, and were encouraged to make up their own minds about issues. Being encouraged by the school to become involved with the community was associated with actively participating in helping (Haste, 2005).

Other researchers in the United Kingdom conducted case studies of individual schools' implementation of citizenship education (Osler, 2005; Watchorn, 2005). Some case study authors described student participation in school decision making (Hannam, 2001, 2005) and programs that celebrate diversity and respect for human rights (Osler, 2005; Osler & Starkey, 2005).

One study of English teachers was part of a larger cross-national study of teachers' perceptions that we draw on throughout this chapter (Lee & Fouts, 2005). The researchers found that a majority of sampled teachers in England defined a good citizen as one who showed "concern for the welfare of others," "moral behavior" and "tolerance for diversity" (Davies, Gregory, & Riley, 2005).[7] Conversely, the fewest teachers in the English sample indicated that they thought "patriotism," "knowledge of government," and "knowledge of the world community" characterized qualities of good citizenship (Davies et al., 2005). Although the researchers used non-representative samples of teachers, the findings are consistent with student perceptions found in the longitudinal study mentioned earlier (Ireland et al., 2006).

Research in Central and Eastern Europe

Other authors have described programs to teach democracy, national and European identity, and tolerance for diversity in new democracies in Central and Eastern Europe, as well as in the older democracies in Western Europe (Roland-Levy & Ross, 2003; Ross, 2001). After the fall of the Soviet Union, countries in Central and Eastern Europe undertook numerous programs to develop democratic citizens. Various projects developed curriculum materials in civic education and prepared teachers to teach the new content using participatory democratic pedagogy (Avery, Freeman, Greenwalt, & Trout, 2006; Bishop & Hamot, 2001; Craddock, 2005; Torney-Purta et al., 1999; Vontz, Metcalf, & Patrick, 2000). Evaluations of several of those projects yield insights into the process of political socialization of youth in post-Communist societies.

First, evaluators of these projects, like evaluators of special programs in the United States,[8] found that specifically designed programs increased student knowledge, but had only modest effects on student attitudes. For example, an experimental program, *We Are Citizens of Ukraine,* was developed as one of several curricular options for a new 9th- or 10th-grade civics course that met 1 hour per week. Designed to reflect the Ukrainian context, it focused on social, economic, and cultural factors important for democracy in Ukraine (Craddock, 2005). The lessons utilized active teaching-learning methods to counter the Soviet educational legacy of didactic lectures and to teach skills necessary for democratic citizenship, such as group cooperation and decision making. The course culminated with a problem-based social action learning activity. The evaluators of the project found that students in the treatment group, who used the new curriculum, significantly outperformed a control group on a test of civic knowledge that emphasized knowledge of democracy.[9] Importantly, the evaluators found a large difference between the treatment and control group students on a scale that asked students about the topics they had studied in school. Students who participated in the project were more likely than other students to report that in school they learned about the importance of voting, how to act to protect the environment, to contribute to solving problems in the community, to understand people who have different ideas, and to cooperate in groups with other students. Further, students in the treatment group, as compared to control group students, reported greater frequency of discussions with teachers about national and international politics, and they were more likely to say teachers present several sides of issues and encourage students to express their views. Additionally, students in the treatment group were more supportive of rights for women and immigrants than students in the comparison group. In short, this study demonstrated that a specifically designed curriculum combined with teacher preparation in active pedagogy could increase secondary students' civic knowledge and democratic attitudes in one country—Ukraine. Similarly, researchers studying the effects of using *Project Citizen* in Bosnia identified several positive outcomes. Students who participated in the program possessed better research skills, were more efficacious, participated in political activities at a higher rate, contacted political officials at higher rates, and paid more attention to politics than their peers who did not participate (Soule, 2002).[10]

In another evaluation of a project designed to promote democratic teaching and learning methods, evaluators studied the use of the *Deliberating Democracy* project in Azerbaijan, the Czech Republic, Lithuania, and three cities in the United States (Avery et al., 2006). The heart of the program was the use of structured academic controversy (SAC) to guide student deliberations about social and political issues. Using this approach, in groups of four, students present one side of an issue, listen to an alternative view, and subsequently reverse roles. Finally, the small groups develop a consensus about what they think would be the best approach to an issue. The project staff developed student materials that addressed issues from teenage curfews to the death penalty. They also conducted workshops to give teachers practice in using the strategy. Initial indications were that students who participated in the program said that they learned about issues, increased in the frequency with which they discussed national and international issues with their teachers, and they liked hearing different points of view and having students express their ideas. Importantly, both teachers and students found the method relatively easy to learn and it combined active student learning with an open climate for discussion.

Studies of teachers in the Czech Republic and Russia provide further information about civic education in Central and Eastern Europe.[11] Bishop (1999) found that sampled teachers in the Czech Republic defined citizenship as a social, rather than a political, concept. For more than half of Czech respondents, citizenship meant belonging to a community. Additionally, the Czech teachers perceived citizenship as a role that makes explicit one's rights, without attention to correspondent duties and they seemed to see citizenship as a passive role, to be received "from above" (Bishop, 1999, p. 67).[12]

Ellis and Brown (2005) reported that a sample of Russian teachers indicated concern for the "fall of morality" taking place in society.[13] The respondents said that in order to reverse societal moral decline, teachers needed to focus on developing moral principles and students' sense of integrity and that the family, and not the schools, might be the best avenue for developing citizenship (Ellis & Brown, 2005). They said that their own beliefs and attitudes about citizenship (formed during the years of communism) had come from family rather than school. Bishop's (1999) and Ellis and Brown's (2005) findings point to avenues for exploration as teachers grapple with conceptions of citizenship in nations transitioning towards democracy.

Research from Canada and Australia

Social studies and civic educators in Canada and Australia have been active in international discussions of civic education. Several have written histories of civic education in their country, noting particularly: the evolution of "citizenship" distinct from being a subject of the British monarch; the place of First Nations and aboriginal peoples in discussions of citizenship and citizenship education; the early emphasis on assimilation of immigrants that was later replaced with a multicultural view; and recent reforms to foster citizenship education in a multicultural global context (Joshee, 2004; Nicholas, 1996; Osborne, 1996; Print, Kennedy, & Hughes, 1999; Sears, Clarke, & Hughes, 1999). In Canada, researchers have interviewed samples of children and youth to ascertain their understanding of civic concepts, such as freedom of religion, freedom of speech, and due process rights (Hughes & Sears, 1996); ethnic diversity and rights of ethnic minorities (Peck & Sears, 2005); and civic participation (Chareka & Sears, 2005). They emphasize the importance of educators' understanding the prior knowledge that students' bring to the classroom.[14]

In Australia, researchers assessed student political knowledge and attitudes in two different states at a time when few students received deliberate instruction in civic education. Print (1995) found that on average students in New South Wales had a very low level of political knowledge.[15] Importantly, students who had taken an optional course in Commerce that included a unit on Parliament and politics scored higher on a test of political knowledge than students who had not taken the course.

In Victoria, as in New South Wales, no subject was required of all students that included civics content. Mellor (1998) estimated that only about 15% of students enrolled in a subject from the integrated learning area Studies in Society and the Environment (SOSE, combining history, geography, politics, and environmental studies), and for many of them, there was little attention to political issues. Interestingly, most students Mellor studied said that they were most likely to discuss issues, current events, and politics in their English class; fewer than 3% named SOSE.[16] Additionally, Mellor found that the students she studied reported a less open climate for classroom discussion and expression of views and lower levels of political interest than had students in Hahn's (1998) study, with the exception of Dutch students, who also had not had deliberate civic education. The Victoria students also reported low levels of political efficacy, political trust, and civic tolerance (willingness to extend rights to disliked groups). Both Mellor (1998) and Print (1995) concluded that without specific attention to civic education, students in Australia were not developing the knowledge and attitudes needed to be effective citizens of a democracy. Mellor argued that adding a content-based approach, however, would not be sufficient; she emphasized the importance of participatory pedagogy in the teaching and learning of democratic processes.

In a recent national study of young Australians' (ages 15–25) attitudes toward voting and other forms of civic-political engagement, researchers found that many youth were alienated from traditional forms of politics, expressing negative views of politicians and lack of trust in the electoral process (Print, Saha, & Edwards, 2005). However, a significant number of young people expressed interest in political issues; many had participated in some form of protest related to issues that were important to them, such as the environment, the war in Iraq, and refugees. The researchers concluded, as did Haste (2005) in the United Kingdom, that many young people are active and civically engaged, despite their lack of faith in politicians and the ballot box.

Australian teachers, in the cross-national study of teachers discussed earlier, echoed Mellor's skepticism of a content-based approach to civic education (Lee & Fouts, 2005). Prior (2005) found that the Australian teachers he surveyed cited "concern for the welfare of others" as most important to good citizenship, followed by practicing "moral behavior," and "tolerance for diversity."[17] Sampled teachers, thus, considered acquiring knowledge per se as peripheral to their conception of a good citizen. Rather, they viewed knowledge as contributing to social concerns and participatory democracy. Teachers in other regions who participated in this study reported similar perceptions, as will be seen throughout this chapter.

Research from Asia

Scholars writing about education for citizenship in Asia tend to emphasize the moral and personal dimensions of citizenship—sometimes in addition to and other times in place of the political dimensions of citizenship. In addition, some scholars and policy makers in parts of Asia have focused on national education to instill patriotism. That is not to say that they have no interest in critical reflection and participation, but the students and teachers they study tend to give lower priority to those aspects of citizen-ship education than do their counterparts in Western liberal democracies.

Several scholars have written about the history of civic education in Hong Kong (Lee, 1999; Leung & Ng, 2004; Morris & Morris, 1999).[18] Hong Kong is an interesting case because it reflects a mix of Eastern and Western cultures and people hold diverse views of their national identity, thinking of themselves as Chinese, Hong Kongese, or Hong Kong Chinese. Recent curricular reforms that emphasize moral education along with civic education and national education to promote identity with China are controver-sial among civic educators. Leung and Ng (2004) argue that the reforms reflect "re-depoliticized approaches" prevalent under British colonialism. Kennedy (2005) argues that moral education alongside civic education reflects modern Confucian humanism as the good person is the foundation for a good society and is similar to values or charac-ter education in Australia and the United States. Additionally, Kennedy argues that the concern for national identity in the Hong Kong curriculum can be viewed within the global discourse about multiple cultural and civic identities.

Fairbrother (2003) examined political socialization in Hong Kong and Mainland China. Whereas Mainland China promoted an ideology of patriotism in the 1990s, Hong Kong promoted an ideology of depoliticization, so that students would not develop political sentiments toward the nation. Reflective of these differing approaches, university students in Mainland China exhibited higher levels of patriotism and nation-alism than did university students in Hong Kong.[19] Further, Mainland students said that secondary schools—through the curriculum and extra-curricular activities—had the most influence on their political beliefs, followed by family. In contrast, the Hong Kong students reported that the media had the most influence, followed by secondary school. Somewhat surprisingly, there were no significant differences between the two groups of students' perception that teachers allowed differences of opinion on national affairs. Several of the Mainland students recalled their politics teachers' use of debate and discussion having an important influence on them. Fairbrother (2003) concluded that policy makers in both societies had been largely effective in achieving their goals, as Mainland students tended to express high levels of patriotism and nationalism and the Hong Kong students expressed neutral and ambivalent feelings with respect to nationalism and patriotism. However, in both societies there were some students who exhibited resistance to the state by holding attitudes that were contrary to the intended goal. Critical thinking expressed as "skepticism" detracted from some Mainland Chi-nese students' nationalism, whereas in Hong Kong the primary factor that contributed to feelings of patriotism was a sense of "curiosity" about the nation, leading some students to seek information on their own. Future researchers might explore resistance to the school's efforts at political socialization among other samples in Asian countries and in societies such as the United States, France, and Germany where the state claims to promote reflective citizenship.[20]

Other studies in Asia yielded findings that offer interesting comparisons to ones obtained in the United States and Western Europe. In one study of activist students in Hong Kong, Leung (2006) found that students' views of the good citizen included both conservative elements (obeying the law, doing ones best) and more radical ones (partici-pating in demonstrations, opposing unreasonable laws). The young activists attributed their political interest to teachers they respected who used experiential learning activities and encouraged students to discuss controversial issues in an open classroom climate for discussion.[21] In another study, Leung (2003) examined the effects of a service learn-ing project that began as a charity-type activity but was transformed into advocacy.[22] This study is an important complement to research conducted in the United States and Europe on the effects of service learning and projects in which students examine local problems and propose solutions to policy makers (Billig, 2000; Billig, Root, & Jesse, 2005; Vontz, Metcalf, & Patrick, 2000).

Researchers working in another Chinese society—Taiwan—studied the effects of an issues-centered approach to social studies on grade 8 and 11 students' civic attitudes (Liao, Liu, & Doong, 1998). Students explored teen issues such as whether 16-year-olds should have drivers' licenses for scooters, as well as questions dealing with national political and social policies. The Taiwanese students who participated in the issues-centered project, like their counterparts in the United States (Hahn, 1996), exhibited enhanced civic participation attitudes, concern about social/political issues, reasoned thinking, and perspective-taking abilities (Liao et al., 1998).

Another study that included students from China and Japan, along with students from the United States and Mexico, provides interesting data about gender and politics in differing cultural and economic contexts (Mayer & Schmidt, 2004). Using samples of convenience and multivariate analysis, the researchers found that boys in grades 7–9 in selected schools in Guangzhou and Michigan, and to a lesser extent, in Oaxaca, Mexico, had higher levels of political interest than girls. However, there was no significant gender difference in political interest in the Tokyo sample. Although most sampled students said politics was "for boys," girls in the two developing countries—China and Mexico—were less likely to view politics as a man's domain than were girls in the Japanese and U.S. samples. In Guangzhou—but not in the other samples—the more a girl perceived that politics was a male domain, the less interest she had in politics. In all four samples, the frequency of political discussion with a parent was associated with youths' political interest.

Turning from students to teachers, Lee (2005) examined the civic conceptions of teachers in Hong Kong and two cities in Mainland China, as part of the cross-national study of teachers discussed earlier (Lee & Fouts, 2005).[23] Like their counterparts in England and Australia, sampled teachers in the Chinese cities primarily characterized good citizens as "socially aware" or "socially concerned" (Lee, 2005). Unlike teachers from the two Western democracies, however, teachers from the three Chinese cities ranked highly "fulfillment of family responsibilities," reflecting beliefs in filial piety prevalent in Confucian societies.[24]

Research from Africa and the Middle East

Cross nationally, students acquire many ideas about citizenship, democracy, and political institutions and processes from school history lessons (Hahn, 1999; Torney-Purta et al., 1999). Because another chapter in this *Handbook* addresses history education, we have not discussed it here. One study of the meanings that students make from official and unofficial histories, however, is particularly relevant because researchers focused on students' conceptions of citizenship (Levstik & Groth, 2005). Noting that the objectives of Ghana's national curriculum were for students to become "good citizens" who are "able to make rational decisions and solve personal and societal problems," the researchers found that students they interviewed emphasized the importance of self-rule—Ghanaians ruling Ghana—without acknowledging that citizens, as well as the government, might exercise that rule.[25] Students articulated clear expectations that their government provide political and economic stability and foster unity and diversity; they did not, however, mention that citizens had a role in maintaining democracy. It remains for future researchers to ascertain whether historic, cultural, pedagogical, developmental, or other factors suggested by the researchers may be most important in understanding how young people in Ghana, other African countries, and other regions construct conceptions of citizenship, but this study makes an important contribution.

In South Africa, as in Central and Eastern Europe, civic education projects were undertaken that partnered local educators with non-governmental organizations in the West to develop curriculum materials and prepare teachers in democratic methods of civic education. *Street Law South Africa* is one such project. Project staff trained university student volunteers in democracy education to enable them to teach the curriculum *Democracy for All* (DFA) to students in grades 11 and 12 across the country (Finkel & Ernst, 2005).[26] The curriculum included topics of law, human rights, and democracy. Accompanying teacher guides recommended using interactive classroom activities such as role playing, debates, educational games, group discussions, mock trials, and student presentations. To measure the effects of the program, researchers interviewed black and "coloured" secondary students who participated in the program and other students, some of whom had other civics training from their regular high school teachers and some of whom had no exposure to a civic education course. The researchers found that exposure to civic education, either through DFA or a regular civics course, had relatively strong effects on student political knowledge. Importantly, moving from no exposure, to monthly exposure, to weekly civics instruction, and finally to daily instruction led to consistent increases in student knowledge (Finkel & Ernst, 2005).[27]

Similar to experimental studies conducted in Eastern European countries, Finkel and Ernst (2005) found that exposure to a civic education program alone did not affect attitudes. However, if the credibility—or perceived quality—of the teacher and the pedagogy that was used were taken into account, then civic instruction could affect student civic attitudes (Finkel & Ernst, 2005). Students who rated their civic education instructor as knowledgeable, interesting, likeable, understandable, and inspiring had positive attitudes in the areas of civic duty and institutional trust.[28] Teaching methods were even more important to influencing student attitudes than perceived teacher quality. Students who reported their teachers used games, mock trials, role playing or simulations, mock elections, and artistic work reported higher scores on the tolerance, institutional trust, civic skills, and approval of legal behavior scales than students who did not report such experiences.[29] Additionally, the more students reported engaging in group projects and making presentations, the more they increased in political tolerance, civic duty, and approval of legal behavior. Further, this study indicated that black and "coloured" South African secondary students who were exposed to civic education and experienced participatory learning activities did increase their willingness to extend rights to disliked groups—even racists.

Later, Kubow (2007) studied teachers' beliefs about democracy in South Africa and Kenya. The teachers with whom she spoke defined democracy in terms of equality, particularly sex equity, and freedom of thought and speech as experienced in homes, schools, and communities. Their conceptions were informed by global/Western rights-oriented discourses and local/indigenous values of compassion, communalism, and concern for the interests of the community.

With respect to research from the Middle East, most of the political socialization research has focused on Israeli students (Eisikovits, 2005; Ichilov, 1998; Perlinger, Canetti-Nisim, & Pedahzur, 2006). Notably, like researchers in other countries, Perlinger and colleagues found that having had a civics course was associated with higher civic knowledge, but alone did not affect attitudes. Further, among students who took a course in civics, those who perceived an open climate for discussion reported higher levels of political efficacy, political participation, and democratic orientations than did students without an open classroom climate (Perlinger et al., 2006). We discuss additional research on Israeli students later in the section on the IEA Civic Education Study. We located one small-scale study of teachers in Iran, in which the researcher compared the reported practices of a sample of middle school teachers in Tehran with those of a similar sample in Ohio (Dezfooli, 2005).[30]

We hope that in the future we will find more political socialization studies from Africa and the Middle East regions. We think this will happen if comparative education scholars conduct empirical studies of civic learning, if evaluators of projects to promote democracy gather data on student learning, and if political scientists and social studies researchers in Middle Eastern and African countries focus their attention on the civic-political development of youth.

In summarizing research from varied countries in different regions, we find that deliberate civic education can increase student knowledge. Additionally, when students perceive their teachers to have high credibility, civic instruction incorporates active, participatory learning activities, and there is an open climate for discussion, then students may develop democratic attitudes. These findings and others have been further explored in a large-scale cross-national study of students and teachers that we discuss next.

THE IEA CIVIC EDUCATION STUDY

Much of the information that is available on young people's civic-political knowledge, attitudes, and experiences internationally comes from the IEA Civic Education Study, which we mentioned when we introduced the Octagon Model of student learning. Researchers in over 30 countries gathered information from 1995 to 2000 on civic education and youth political knowledge, attitudes, and experiences in the most extensive political socialization study to date. The project produced four international reports and researchers in several countries produced national reports. In addition, since the completion of the study, researchers have conducted important secondary analyses using the international data set. Because the IEA study is such a rich source of information about political socialization internationally, we discuss it at length.

In the first phase of the IEA study, researchers in 24 countries collected data for case studies on what 14- to 15-year-old-students in their countries were intended or likely to learn in three domains: (1) democracy, political institutions, and rights and duties of citizens; (2) national identity and national history; and (3) social cohesion and diversity (Torney-Purta et al., 1999).[31] The case studies provided valuable information about the contexts in which young people experienced their political socialization in the 1990s, as well as provided the basis from which questionnaires were developed for the second phase of the study. Most of the studies that we discuss in this chapter use the data set generated in phase 2 of the study.

In the second phase, questionnaires were administered to representative samples of 14-year-old students (in grades 8 or 9) in 28 countries in 1999.[32] In addition, school administrators completed school questionnaires and up to three teachers in each school completed a teacher questionnaire. In all, more than 90,000 students completed surveys that measured student knowledge (civic content and skills), attitudes, and experiences (Torney-Purta, Lehmann, Oswald, & Schulz, 2001).[33] The following year, similar questionnaires were administered to an older population in 16 countries (Amadeo, Torney-Purta, Lehmann, Husfeldt, & Nikolova, 2002).[34] In the next sections we summarize selected findings from the international report of 14-year-olds and from some of the secondary analyses that explore processes and outcomes of political socialization. We conclude this section by synthesizing research on teachers as gleaned from IEA case studies and the IEA teacher questionnaire.

Cross-national student perspectives

The main international report for the IEA Civic Education Study compared mean scores on a variety of scales for 14-year olds in 28 countries. Here we highlight some of the key findings.

Civic knowledge   Students from the following countries scored above the international average on the test of student knowledge: Poland, Finland, Cyprus, Greece, Hong Kong, the United States, Italy, the Slovak Republic, Norway, and the Czech Republic (Torney-Purta et al., 2001).[35] A regression analysis yielded three variables that predicted civic knowledge in most countries: a student's expected level of future educational attainment (those who expected to complete university were more likely to score high on the knowledge test than those who thought they would soon be leaving school); home literacy resources (books and newspapers); and student perceptions of an open classroom climate for discussion.[36]

Perceptions of the good citizen.   Students were asked whether they thought it was important that "an adult who is a good citizen..." engage in a number of activities. Responses fell into two factors: conventional citizenship (a good citizen...obeys the law, votes, knows the country's history, engages in political discussion, joins a political party) and social-movement related citizenship (a good citizen... takes part in activities to help the community, protect the environment, and/or promote human rights). Most students said that obeying the law and voting were the most important civic activities and joining a political party and discussing political issues the least important. Young people in most countries tended to agree that social-movement related activities were important. Female students in about one third of the countries, including the United States, were more likely than their male peers to say that social-movement activities are important to good citizenship (Torney-Purta et al., 2001).

Civic attitudes.   Students were asked about their attitudes toward the nation, trust in government institutions, attitudes toward rights for women and immigrants, and other social and political issues. Most of the 14-year-olds indicated positive attitudes toward their country, and across countries, most students reported trusting courts and the police more than the national and local governments; they trusted political parties the least. Most students in the study held generally positive attitudes toward rights for women and immigrants.[37] In all 28 countries, young women, on average, were more supportive of economic and political rights for women than were their male peers. Additionally, in 23 countries, young women were more supportive of rights for immigrants than were young men (Torney-Purta et al., 2001).[38]

Civic-political actions or experiences.   The IEA survey asked about a variety of student experiences, finding, for instance, that across countries, 14-year-old students reported obtaining information about national and international events primarily from television, rather than newspapers or radio. Confidence in the effectiveness of school participation—through student government and joining groups to influence school policy—was especially high in Cyprus, Greece, and Portugal.[39]

Students were also asked about the classroom climate for discussion, including whether students were encouraged to express their opinions, whether they felt comfortable doing so when they differed from the other students and teacher, and whether the teacher presents multiple sides of issues. Students in Colombia, Greece, Norway, and the United States were most likely to say that they had experienced open classroom climates (Torney-Purta et al., 2001).[40]

Young people were the most likely to expect that as adults they would vote and collect money for a charity. Very few students expected to participate in protests, join a political party, write letters to newspapers, or be a candidate for office. The researchers found that civic knowledge and having learned about the importance of voting in school were the strongest predictors of expected voting, among those in a regression model (Torney-Purta et al., 2001). To a lesser extent watching television news, an open classroom climate, expected years of education, and participation in a school/student council were also positively associated with students' expectations of voting in many countries.

The international report contains much further information about youth within particular countries, which we do not have space to elaborate on here. We turn next to secondary analyses that used this large data set to further explore political socialization.

Secondary analyses of the IEA data

Since the publication of the main reports of the IEA study, researchers have examined relationships among variables, comparing percentage responses to particular items on scales, conducting regression analyses to identify related variables, and using multi-level modeling techniques to account for individual students being nested within classes within schools within countries.

Civic knowledge.   Schulz (2002) and Barber (2005) used multi-level regression analysis to identify the variables in the IEA data set that contribute to differences in students' knowledge and civic skills. Schulz explored whether particular student-level, school-level, and country-level factors in 27 countries (excluding Cyprus) had an effect on knowledge. He found that overall 66% of the variance in student knowledge scores existed between students, 25% between schools, and only 9% between countries. Schultz emphasized that although most of the variance in civic knowledge is found at the student-level, the amount of between-school variance differs among countries. In Scandinavian countries, there was little difference between schools on civic knowledge and the between-school variance in English-speaking countries was comparatively low. In contrast, in countries where students are tracked into different schools according to their abilities the between-school variance in civic knowledge was much higher, as in Russia, Bulgaria, Germany, and the Czech Republic.

The explained variance in student knowledge at the student level ranged from 5% (in Colombia) to 32% (in Slovenia) (Schulz, 2002). At the student level, gender effects were the highest in Denmark, Norway, Sweden, Germany, Switzerland, Portugal, and the Czech Republic. Although gender did not appear important in the bivariate analysis of knowledge used in the international report, when other factors were controlled, gender did appear to be important in some countries, with male students scoring higher than female students. Additionally on the student level, home literacy resources had a strong and significant effect in all countries, except Hong Kong and Colombia. Use of another language at home, another student-level variable, also had a strong effect on civic knowledge in most countries.

Further, at the student level, an individual's perception of an open classroom climate for discussion was significantly related to student knowledge (Schulz, 2002). However, as Schulz cautioned, this could mean either that when students feel they can openly express diverse opinions, they learn more—or it could mean that students with lower levels of knowledge are less likely to participate in discussions and do not notice that there are opportunities to do so. Somewhat surprisingly, political discussion with parents and reported frequency of media use did not have very strong effects on civic knowledge in most countries—when all other factors were held constant.[41]

At the school level, average home literacy resources (indicating socioeconomic status) had an effect on civic knowledge in the United States, Germany, Switzerland, Italy, Chile, and Colombia (Schulz, 2002). The effect of an open classroom climate was generally stronger in countries with schools that are segregated by ability. In countries where schools do not show a large variation in test performance, such as the Scandinavian countries, average classroom climate had a smaller association with test scores than in countries with greater variation.

Also at the school level, Barber (2005) found that in England the average socio-economic status, the head teacher's (principal's) perception of the students' attitudes towards the school, and student perceptions of an open classroom climate were related to students' level of civic knowledge. Additionally, racial and religious tolerance within a school, as reported by the school administrator, influenced whether an open classroom climate for discussion was associated with civic knowledge. School socioeconomic status and the overall attitude of students towards school were related to the effectiveness of discussion with peers on civic knowledge (Barber, 2005).

Although few social studies researchers have yet used multilevel modeling, we believe it will become increasingly important in the future as researchers look at differences in student knowledge, attitudes, and experiences both within and across countries. These methods provide insights into the importance of context, revealing that policies that have a positive effect on student learning under particular conditions may not have the same effect in other classes, schools, or countries.

Anticipated civic engagement.   Several researchers used regression analyses to identify variables associated with students' expected levels of civic engagement. For example, Torney-Purta and Richardson (2004), using data from Australia, England, Norway, and the United States, found that predictors of students' anticipating that they would be actively engaged citizens in four ways (voting and getting information about candidates before voting, joining a political party, volunteering in the community, and participating in a non-violent protest march) were: civic knowledge, students' confidence in their ability to participate, and whether their schools emphasized elections and voting. With respect to anticipated volunteering, the most important predictors were: learning in school about community problems, confidence in school participation, and current experiences with an organization that helps in the community (Torney-Purta & Richardson, 2004).

In another study using data from five differing countries—Bulgaria, Chile, Colombia, England, and the United States—Torney Purta, Richardson, and Barber (2004) explored this line of inquiry further. They found that different types of civic engagement were associated with different types of school-related and out-of-school political socialization experiences. First, expecting to be an informed voter was primarily associated with school curricular emphases and civic knowledge. Second, expecting to be an adult citizen who takes public positions on political issues and joins a political party was primarily associated with experiences at home, such as discussion with parents, and a sense of internal political efficacy. Third, expected volunteering in the community was related to in-school experiences such as studying about the community in school (Torney-Purta et al., 2004). It remains for other researchers using data from other countries to determine whether these relationships are found in many countries. Most importantly, it remains for future researchers using longitudinal designs to determine whether expectations of civic behavior held by 14-year-olds turn in to reality when students reach adulthood.

Perceptions of citizenship and civic attitudes.   Several researchers analyzed student responses to particular items on IEA scales. For example, Hahn (2005, 2006) and Kennedy, Hahn, and Lee (2008) looked at the importance students in England, Germany, Australia, Hong Kong, and the United States attached to engagement in conventional political and social movement-related activities. Students in different societies varied in the importance they gave to particular behaviors, reflecting differences in cultural and historic factors in school and society. Nevertheless, students across these five societies ranked behaviors in the same order of importance. Within each sample, the highest percentages of students said that voting (conventional citizenship) and participating in activities to help the community (social-movement citizenship) were the most impor-tant, followed by working with groups to help the environment and human rights. At the next level of priority, students ranked respecting government representatives and knowing the country's history—both passive behaviors. Across these differing societ-ies, students were less likely to say that a good citizen keeps up with political news and engages in political discussions, apparently not thinking of citizens as having a respon-sibility to stay informed and regularly engage in discussions of public issues. Finally, in all five societies students were the least likely to say that a good citizen joins a political party.

On other attitude scales, too, students in different societies gave similar rankings to particular items. Across the five societies, students were most likely to support educa-tional rights for immigrants and the least likely to say that immigrants should have the right to keep their language (Hahn, 2005, 2006; Kennedy et al., 2008).

Other researchers used scale scores to examine predictors of student attitudes. For example, Torney-Purta and Barber (2004a) found that three school-related variables were associated with positive attitudes toward rights for ethnic minorities and immi-grants.[42] In countries where students said that in school they learned about cooperation and diversity, students were more supportive of rights for minorities and immigrants than in countries where students did not recall studying about cooperation and diver-sity.[43] Additionally, in countries where students said they had confidence in school par-ticipation and where they reported that in classrooms they were encouraged to express diverse views, students reported high levels of support for rights for minorities.[44]

Experiences. As noted earlier, researchers have long been interested in the role of media in political socialization. Comparing percentages of student responses to media-related items on the IEA survey from Chile, Portugal, and the United States, research-ers found that in Chile fewer than one quarter of the 14-year-olds reported that their families received a daily newspaper compared with half of students in Portugal and the United States (Amadeo, Torney-Purta, & Barber, 2004). In all three countries, the students who reported watching the most television news had the highest average scores on the IEA test of civic knowledge (Amadeo et al., 2004). Similarly, students who reported frequently reading news about their country in newspapers had higher average levels of civic knowledge. Additionally, students who said they frequently read the newspaper for news about their country were the most likely to anticipate they would vote as adults.

As important as the findings are of the positive correlation between students' reported news consumption and civic knowledge in three countries, a few cautions are in order. We do not know the cause and effect relationships. We do not know if the habits of fol-lowing news in the media increased students' civic knowledge or, alternatively, if more knowledgeable students find it easier to follow media news and are, therefore, more likely to read newspapers and watch television news. Second, we do not yet know if these relationships are found in other countries or age groups. Third, we do not know if news consumption patterns at age 14 are predictive of lifelong news habits or of civic engagement in adulthood. Clearly, more research along these lines is needed.

Within country analyses from the IEA CivEd study

A number of researchers have used the IEA data to look at relationships among vari-ables within a single country. Although it was not possible to examine results for ethnic groups cross-nationally, it is possible to examine results in terms of subgroups within national populations, such as African American and Hispanic students in the United States and Afro-Caribbean and Asian students in England.

Using the Israeli data from the upper secondary part of the IEA study, Ichilov (2005) compared results for 11th graders enrolled in Arab state schools, Hebrew state schools, and Hebrew religious schools. In particular, she examined differences in political discussions, attitudes toward the nation, and political efficacy, concluding that rifts within Israeli society are evident among students as young as 16-years old.

Overall Israeli 11th graders reported that they did not discuss politics a great deal. However, the Israeli Palestinian Arab students reported discussing politics with parents, friends, and teachers more than did either group of Jewish students (Ichilov, 2005). In terms of anticipated experiences, like students in other countries discussed earlier, Israeli students were most likely to expect to participate in conventional political activities such as voting. The Jewish students from both religious and secular schools expected to undertake more conventional political activity than did the students in Arab schools. In contrast, the Arab students, more than either group of Jewish students, were more likely to expect to be actively engaged in politics, to participate in social causes, and to engage in illegal protest actions. Perhaps not surprisingly, the Israeli Palestinian Arab youth tended not to identify with Israel's flag and national anthem, not to express love for the country, and not to be proud of the country's history. In contrast, both groups of Jewish students reported positive attitudes on most items on the national pride scale. Interestingly, the Israeli Palestinian Arab students were more politically efficacious than the Jewish students, which Ichilov attributed to the timing of political leaders' discussions as part of a "peace process" that were occurring at the time. She noted that in 2001 a new civics curriculum was introduced in the hopes of inculcating a common Israeli civic identity and instilling values of pluralism and respect for diversity, but it was clear from this study that the program would face challenges in a deeply divided society.

The authors of the U.S. national report found that students who attend schools with many students from low income backgrounds scored significantly lower on the civic knowledge test than students from schools with more affluent student bodies (Baldi, Perie, Skidmore, Greenberg, & Hahn, 2001). Additionally, students whose parents had low levels of education scored lower than students whose parents had more education. Similarly, Torney-Purta and Barber (2004b) found large differences in civic knowledge between students who came from homes with few literacy resources and who did not expect to go to college and students with many home literacy resources and who expected to go to college. They emphasized that it is precisely because students who do not plan to go to college and who are from low-income families have the least civic knowledge that civics should be taught before many students leave school at age 16.

Additionally, U. S. students who reported having social studies every day scored higher on the test of civic knowledge than students with less frequent social studies instruction (Baldi et al., 2001). Further, students who reported studying particular topics in school (U.S. Constitution, how laws are made, Congress, political parties, and the courts) performed better on the civic knowledge test than students without such instruction (Torney-Purta & Barber, 2004b). This reinforces a point made by Junn and Niemi (1998) in their analyses of national assessments in civics/government that social studies instruction in general, and civics/government lessons or courses in particular, have a positive effect on student knowledge. This point was also made by researchers who conducted studies in Ukraine and South Africa, as we noted earlier (Craddock, 2005; Finkel & Ernst, 2005). The national reports for Australia and England provide additional insights by looking at relationships among variables within a single country (Kerr et al., 2002; Mellor, Kennedy, & Greenwood, 2001), as do the reports from Italy, Germany, and Norway, which are written in their respective national languages.

Clearly, the IEA Civic Education Study provides much useful information for understanding political socialization within and between national contexts at the end of the 20th century. Researchers will continue to "mine the data" for fresh insights and they will use the instruments developed for the study with other populations in the future as Craddock (2005) and Watchorn (2005) did. At the time of this writing, planning had begun for another IEA study that would enable researchers to compare student knowledge, attitudes, and experiences at different points in time. In the next section, we move from student perspectives to the role of teachers and teaching in political socialization as gleaned from the IEA study.

Research on teachers and teaching from the IEA study

In a classic review of political socialization research in the United States, Ehman (1980) concluded that teachers' attitudes and behaviors can affect how students make meaning of political knowledge, develop civic attitudes and skills, and form expectations of civic participation. With this in mind, in this section we draw on information from the phase 1 case studies and teacher data from phase 2 related to teacher preparation and practice, teacher confidence, and teacher influence on students' civic knowledge.[45]

Teaching preparation and practice. Internationally, civic education teachers come to the field with a wide variety of subject-matter backgrounds. For example, in Italy, many civic education teachers hold degrees in Italian literature, philosophy, and education (Losito, 1999). Because of their lack of subject-specific preparation, Italian teachers tend not to pay attention to civic education and are not able to deliver lessons with complex, student-centered formats, according to the author of the Italian case study (Losito, 1999). The inadequacy of teacher preparation was echoed by case study authors in Hong Kong, Hungary, and the Czech Republic (Lee, 1999; Matrai, 1999; Valkova & Kalous, 1999). Mintrop (2002) argued that where teachers are not well prepared, civic education is likely to consist of "common-place knowledge, norms, and practical wisdom" rather than a formal, codified body of knowledge (Mintrop, 2002, p. 67). However, not all civic-related teachers are poorly prepared in the subject they teach. In Finland, teachers of civic-related subjects usually majored in history or social studies in the university, have a masters' degree, and are well qualified to teach their subject (Ahonen & Virta, 1999). In sum, the preparation of civic education teachers varies greatly from one country to another and may affect teacher practice.

IEA case study authors in Italy, Hungary, the Czech Republic, and Hong Kong, reported that the most widespread instructional practice in civic education was the transmission of factual knowledge through lectures and recitation, and teachers in many countries reported using the textbook or syllabus as guiding material and worksheets (Losito & Mintrop, 2001; Mintrop, 2002). Nevertheless, in some countries, many teachers said that students were also taught using group work. Importantly, teachers in Chile, Greece, Hong Kong, Italy, Lithuania, Poland, Romania, and Slovenia reported use of controversial issues discussion in contrast to other teachers who avoid presenting issues where strong difference of opinion exists (Lee, 1999; Losito, 1999; Mintrop, 2002).

Teacher confidence and student knowledge. The IEA teacher questionnaire included a measure to assess teacher confidence in teaching specific topics. For each country Losito and Mintrop (2001) computed a score based on teachers' level of confidence. They found that teacher confidence in the Belgium and Hong Kong samples was relatively low, whereas it was relatively high in Australia, Cyprus, Germany, Greece, Romania, and the Slovak Republic. Across countries, most teacher respondents said they felt confident teaching about their nation's history, citizens' rights, human rights, equal opportunities, media, and environmental concerns. Conversely, they felt least confident teaching topics related to international relations, economic issues, trade unions, international problems, and social welfare.

In a recent study, researchers synthesized results from the IEA Teacher Confidence scale with country reports and student data (Alviar-Martin, Randall, Usher, & Engelhard, 2008). Using Differential Item Functioning (DIF) analysis for each of the scale's 20 topics, the researchers examined teacher confidence in Germany, Hong Kong, Italy, and the United States.[46] They found that teachers from the United States expressed most confidence teaching issues that raised little controversy, such as the judicial system and dangers of propaganda (Alviar-Martin et al., 2008). They also indicated confidence in teaching about cultural differences and minorities, but little confidence in teaching about social welfare. Across the four settings, teachers who held degrees in civic-related subjects were more confident than those who did not hold civic-related degrees.[47]

Importantly, Torney-Purta, Richardson, and Barber (2005), using IEA teacher data from eight countries, found teachers' experience and confidence in teaching civic-related subjects related to their students' civic knowledge and attitudes in eight countries. Teachers in Australia, Finland, and the United States expressed greater confidence in teaching about political topics than did teachers in the Czech Republic, England, Hungary, and Norway. Similar to Alviar-Martin and her colleagues' (2008), they found teachers had high confidence in countries where teachers had high levels of education and training. Teachers in the Czech Republic and Hungary, where new curricula were introduced and former political education teachers were replaced after the end of communism, showed low levels of confidence. English teachers' lack of confidence may have been based on a situation where teachers had little background in education for citizenship, yet they were newly required to deliver the subject to students. In Norway, where a relatively low percentage of teachers held degrees in civic-related subjects and most lacked in-service education, teachers showed a low level of confidence. An important finding from this study was that teachers' educational experience was positively related to students' civic knowledge only in the United States (Torney-Purta et al., 2005).

In summarizing information from students and teachers in the IEA study, what emerges is that a deliberate program of civics instruction benefits both students and teachers. Students who experience specific civic preparation score higher on tests of civic knowledge and in some cases have more positive attitudes about citizenship. Teachers who are prepared academically or trained professionally to teach citizenship show higher confidence in their ability to teach the subject to their students.

In concluding this section, we need to remember that as extensive as the IEA study is, it does not tell us all we need to know about political socialization internationally. We do not yet know if similar results would obtain from samples in countries that did not participate in the study or even within the participating countries for students of other ages or at other time periods. Importantly, the study contains much information about what is happening, but provides little answers as to how or why students construct meanings of the political world. In the future, we need to continually assess student and teacher perspectives from large representative samples, such as IEA studies use, and we need qualitative studies that can provide insights about how political socialization occurs in particular contexts.

CONCLUSIONS

Clearly, research in political socialization has gone global. The internationalization of the field presents new avenues for both research and practice.

First, focusing on research, what do we know from research and what do we need to know? Looking at small-scale studies in different regions and the large-scale IEA study, we know that: 1) In varied countries, students and teachers tend to view citizenship as a passive role, with little emphasis on active participation. This is likewise reflected in teaching strategies; 2) Civic-political knowledge tends to be correlated with socioeconomic status—in some countries it is associated with gender; 3) Civic political attitudes vary considerably by gender; 4) Deliberate planned civic-political instruction can increase student knowledge; 5) When such instruction is delivered through participatory active learning strategies, students develop political interest, efficacy, and trust—and they are more willing to extend rights to diverse groups; 6) An open classroom climate for discussion facilitates civic knowledge, political interest, efficacy and trust, and positive attitudes towards rights for diverse groups; 7) Experiences in school are important to developing student intentions to become actively engaged citizens (voting and volunteering); and 8) Confidence in school participation is often associated with positive civic attitudes (toward women and immigrants).

What do we need to know? What are some lines of inquiry that future researchers might explore? Several questions that might be addressed are: 1) How do different students in the same classes and schools perceive their civic instruction and experiences similarly and differently? 2) Why is it that young men and young women seem to have different civic attitudes? In what ways does gender intersect with race, ethnicity, social class, and other markers of identity? 3) Do knowledge, attitudes, and anticipated behaviors of 14-year-olds persist into adulthood? 4) Do skepticism, curiosity, or other dispositions prompt some students to resist particular civic-political messages? 5) Are civic-political knowledge, skills, and values affected more by service learning programs that enable students to examine alternative public policies than those limited to charity? How do multicultural and global perspectives influence how teachers and students think about "citizenship," and how do these views change with transnational populations, with multiple levels of identity, or situated in diverse cultural contexts? 6) Do teachers' differing perceptions of "the good citizen" lead them to implement curricular guidelines differently—and what is the effect on student learning? 7) In what ways do external factors influence teachers when preparing their lessons, such as the presence or absence of examinations, textbooks, syllabi and official curricula, as well as society's perceptions of controversial issues discussion in classrooms, and what effect does that have on youth political socialization?

Remembering that research findings in one context are not directly applicable to another cultural context, we believe findings from varied studies can provide hypotheses for studies in other contexts and there may be potential implications for policy and practice in contexts similar to those where the research was conducted. For example, because teaching deliberately towards civic education has had positive effects on student knowledge in varied countries, policy makers might make citizenship knowledge a distinct curricular aim and require particular subjects to address it, as well as having it as a school wide goal. Because instruction with participatory pedagogy and open classroom climates, combined with civic content and high teacher credibility, has had a positive influence on students' civic attitudes in many countries, both pre-service and in-service teacher education programs should teach teachers to use such strategies and to provide an open climate in a manner that fits their civic and pedagogical cultures. This need is further reinforced by research on the importance of teacher confidence and teacher credibility from across regions. Curriculum developers might develop materials that draw on cases and strategies that have been used in different countries. Video clips of teachers effectively managing student-centered learning and controversial issues discussions in different countries could be used in professional development programs so that teachers can see that there are many ways to design and execute lessons that facilitate students' development of democratic skills and participatory attitudes as well as knowledge. Across nations, civic educators can explore how students may increase involvement in actual democratic practices, through student government, service-learning, and civic action. In societies experiencing cultural diversification, there seems to be some attention to political and social tolerance, but global migration trends indicate a need for civic educators in all nations to confront issues of social cohesion and diversity. This becomes a more pressing concern with the growing recognition of human rights. European countries have taken steps to incorporate human rights into mainstream civic curriculum, but some Asian and African scholars argue that emphasizing individualistic human rights reflects a Eurocentric worldview. We wonder if a human rights framework can ultimately provide civic educators and political socialization researchers with a common discourse.

As a consequence of globalization, social studies educators have greater opportunities to interact with international scholars and to benefit from the research and experiences of colleagues in many countries. As they learn about varied practices, policies, and research, it is our belief that they can gain new insights for approaching the challenges they face. Sharing research in political socialization internationally is one step in the process of enhancing teaching and learning globally.

NOTES

1. Twenty-one of the 24 countries that participated in the IEA study were located in Europe or the Americas. The remaining three societies were Australia, Israel, and Hong Kong. Australia and Israel are culturally connected to European civic-political cultures and Hong Kong, which was a British colony until 1997, bridges Western and Eastern cultures.
2. We have included empirical studies of elementary and secondary teaching and learning of civic and political knowledge, skills, and attitudes. Due to space limitations, we did not try to survey the many studies of identity and attachment to various communities (cultural, national, regional, and global) or research on youth activism that is relevant to citizenship education. Also, we did not include studies of higher education or adult citizenship education.
3. In the years 1986–1995, Hahn (1998) surveyed students in secondary schools, interviewed teachers and students, and observed classes that were similar to social studies in the United States. She purposefully selected schools in different regions of each country that reflected the types of secondary schools in each country, such as *Realschulen, Gymnasien,* and *Gesamptshulen* in Germany, and state schools and an independent boarding school in England. For the quantitative part of the study, she compared student mean responses to seven scales for samples in each country. For the qualitative part of the study, she identified themes from fieldnotes of observations and interviews.
4. Given these contextual differences, Hahn (1998) found that Danish students in the study had comparatively high levels of political interest and efficacy; in contrast students who attended English state schools and schools in the Netherlands reported low levels of political interest and efficacy. Political trust was low among students in all of the countries. Hahn (1998) also explored issues related to gender and to students' willingness to extend rights to diverse groups. For the most part, she found no gender differences in political attitudes and both young men and women reported positive attitudes toward women in government, with the women being more enthusiastically supportive than the men. Sample students in all five countries were willing to extend political and civic rights to diverse groups, except for groups that were racist. Similarly, anthropologists studied the ways in which young people in England, Germany, and the Netherlands, as well as France are enculturated to their civil identity (Schiffauer, Baumann, Kastoryano, & Vertovic, 2004).
5. In 2003, 71% of schools reported that they delivered citizenship in personal, social, and health education (PSHE) lessons and school assemblies. Citizenship education was also being delivered in religious education, history, geography, and English. Only about one-third of schools said they delivered citizenship through a dedicated timeslot, such as one or two lessons a week in a subject like Citizenship Studies. In 2007, policy makers added to the earlier guidance for schools the expectation that citizenship education should promote community cohesion.
6. In one component of the study, researchers are studying a nationally representative sample of schools over time (Kerr, Ireland, Lopes, Craig, with Cleaver, 2004). In 2002, year 7 students in the sampled schools completed questionnaires measuring their knowledge, attitudes, and experiences. The cohort of students will be assessed again when they are in years

9, 11, and 13 (or equivalent), providing one of very few nationally representative longitudinal data sets that exist internationally. In addition, case study data are being collected from a sub-sample of the schools in the longitudinal study and NFER researchers have also been assessing a cross sectional sample of students in years 8, 10, and 12 every 2 years since 2002.

7. Questionnaires were administered to 679 teachers in 64 primary schools and 11 secondary schools in Yorkshire, London, and Cambridgeshire. Additionally, 40 teachers in five primary and five secondary schools were interviewed.

8. For a summary of early research see Ehman, 1980. Since that time, researchers in the United States studied the programs *Kids Voting* (McDevitt & Chaffee, 2000), *Project Citizen* (Tolo, 1998; Vontz, Metcalf, & Patrick, 2000), *We The People* (Broudy, 1994) and *Tolerance for Diversity* (Avery, Bird, Johnstone, Sullivan, & Thalhammer, 1992).

9. The treatment group for the research contained 509 students in 23 schools that were randomly selected from the 674 schools that had used the curriculum. The control group consisted of 506 students in 23 schools that were randomly selected from schools that had not used the curriculum. The researchers used the released items from the knowledge test of the IEA Civic Education Study, enabling them to compare the performance of 14-year-olds in Ukraine (both with and without the particular curriculum project) with those of students in Central and East European countries that participated in the IEA study.

10. Similarly, in a study in Indonesia, students who participated in *Project Citizen* increased their political participation more than did a comparable group of students who had not been exposed to the program (Soule & Nairne, 2006). Across these studies, researchers found no gender differences in political knowledge.

11. Bishop's study (*N* = 43) focused on one city and two rural towns in the Czech Republic.

12. In other studies of Czech civic educators' conceptions of democracy, Bishop and Hamot (2001) found that most teachers equated democracy with representative government, rather than a way of life or citizen participation. Czech curriculum writers who participated in a workshop in the United States emphasized tolerance and decision-making as central features of democracy.

13. Questionnaires were completed by 681 elementary and secondary teachers from 22 schools in Russia, of which 529 teachers came from 17 urban schools (Moscow) and 152 teachers from five rural schools (in Plotrinovskaya). In addition, interviews were conducted with 53 of the teachers.

14. Using non-representative samples, these researchers do not attempt to generalize to a wider population. Rather, using a phenomenographic approach, they aim to identify qualitatively different ways in which different individuals perceive civic phenomena.

15. Print (1995) administered a political knowledge test to year 9 and 10 students in Sydney, New South Wales, where no specific school subject addressed civic goals.

16. Mellor (1998) replicated Hahn's (1998) study, administering questionnaires to 633 students in six secondary schools that were purposefully selected to represent different approaches to civic education and differing school ethos.

17. Prior (2005) surveyed 377 teachers in 14 schools (12 coeducational state schools and two private girls schools) within 50 km of Melbourne, in the state of Victoria. He also interviewed 25 of the surveyed teachers.

18. Historically, Hong Kong schools were influenced by the struggle between the Kuomintang and the Communist Party in the 1920s, the policy of depoliticization under British colonial rule from the 1950s to the 1980s, then, in the late 1980s and 1990s, increased attention to civic education to instill in youth respect for "one country, two systems" when the territory was handed over from Britain to China (Leung, 2004).

19. Fairbrother (2003) administered a survey to more than 500 university students in 14 universities in Mainland China and Hong Kong and he interviewed 10 university students in each society. The patriotism factor included emotional attachment to the nation and its symbols and a sense of duty to the nation. The nationalism factor included concern for national interests over international interests, and viewing the nation as superior to others.

20. Fairbrother (2003) uses the term "the state" to refer to the power of the government apparatus and its branches, such as the Communist Party, public schools, and the police, which seek to maintain power.

21. The importance of teacher credibility was found by researchers working in South Africa and the United States (Ernst & Finkel, 2005; Goldenson, 1978) and the importance of an open classroom climate for discussion of issues was found in many studies discussed in this chapter.

22. Leung (2003) purposefully selected a secondary school that had experienced such a change. He interviewed the civic education teacher and three of the students who participated in the activity that began as a beach clean up project and evolved into a project to collect signatures for a petition to stop the building of an incinerator. He found that the experience had an impact on students' self esteem and self efficacy, their knowledge, perspective-taking abilities, and action.

23. Lee's (2005) sample included 81 teachers from Guangzhou and 502 from Hangzhou in China and 733 teachers from Hong Kong. Some of the Guangzhou and Hong Kong teachers were interviewed (the number was not reported).

24. In another study, Leung and Print (2002) surveyed teachers in the 417 secondary schools in Hong Kong to measure teachers support for different theoretical types of nationalistic education. Most teachers said they understood nationalistic education to mean cultural nationalism (knowing about and feeling affection for the cultural aspects of China), using words such as homeland, culture, and customs. However, most said they would like to see content related to cosmopolitan (concern for all humankind) and civic nationalism (rights to participate in governing), as well as cultural nationalism.

25. The sample included 150 students in four parochial junior secondary schools in different parts of Ghana.

26. Street Law, South Africa, based at the University of Natal's Centre for Socio-Legal Studies adapted the U.S. curriculum *Street Law* to the South African context. The samples for the study contained 261 students exposed to the curriculum, 124 students enrolled in regular civic education courses, and 215 students who had no exposure.

27. Moreover, the researchers found that civic education in school mattered as much to civic knowledge as did exposure to mass media, student age and grade level, whether students came from a family that discussed politics often, and whether members of their family were politically active.

28. These students said it was important for a citizen to vote, pay taxes, and take part in political decisions; they had a good deal of trust in the legal system, the press and media, the church, the president, the police, the national government, and the African National Congress; and they communicated their ideas with others better than other high school students they knew. The positive correlation between democratic civic attitudes and teacher credibility reinforces other research in the United States (Goldenson, 1978) and Hong Kong (Leung, 2006).

29. These students were willing to extend free speech rights, the right to vote, and the right to organize peacefully to racists; and they agreed that an ordinary citizen should try to influence politics and the decisions of elected officials by voting, joining groups to solve problems, taking part in peaceful protests against government policies, and contacting officials.

30. Dezfooli's samples of convenience contained middle school teachers who taught a variety of subjects. The Tehran teachers said the democratic practice they used the most was encouraging individual responsibility by assigning students responsibilities in group activities and asking them to voice their views in the classroom. The Tehran teachers, like those in Ohio, reported using decision-making and problem-solving activities less than other strategies.

31. The researchers examined curriculum documents and textbooks. Several conducted focus group interviews with students and teachers and some conducted surveys and telephone interviews with experts in civic education. Some researchers conducted cross-case analyses of the case studies (Steiner-Khamsi, Torney-Purta & Schwille, 2002).

32. Researchers selected schools from nationally stratified sampling frames. Within schools they randomly selected an intact non-tracked class (preferably for a civic-related subject) for testing.

33. Responses to items were factor analyzed and Rasch scores were computed.

34. Because it was not possible to obtain comparable samples in terms of age or educational track at the upper secondary level, comparisons cannot be made across countries. The data are useful, however, for comparing the knowledge and attitudes of two age groups within a single country.

35. The differences in means among these countries, for the most part, were not statistically significant; however, the means of this "high performing group" did differ significantly from samples at and below the international mean.

36. Because regression analyses are correlations, it is important to understand that if one variable "predicts" another, this means it predicts the outcome, in this case a civic knowledge score; it does not indicate a cause and effect relationship.

37. Nevertheless, there were some notable differences cross-nationally. In Cyprus, Norway, Sweden, and the United States, students on average scored above the international mean

on both the Rights for Women and the Rights for Immigrants scales. Countries where support for both groups' rights was below the international average were Bulgaria, Estonia, Hungary, Latvia, Lithuania, and the Slovak Republic.

38. In a secondary analysis using the international data set, girls were also more willing than boys to ensure rights for minorities and anti-democratic groups (Kennedy, 2006). However, most girls like most boys were more likely to guarantee rights to women, immigrants, and minorities than to anti-democratic groups.

39. In contrast, confidence in school participation was particularly low in Germany, Hungary, Latvia, and Switzerland. In 16 countries, female students were more likely than their male peers to have high confidence in school participation. In the other countries, there were no significant gender differences on this scale.

40. In contrast, students in Belgium (French), Bulgaria, and Slovenia were least likely to perceive their classroom climates to be open for discussion. In 23 of the countries, female students perceived the classroom climate to be more open than did their male peers. In the other five countries, there were no significant gender differences in perceptions of classroom climate for discussion (Torney-Purta et al., 2001).

41. Additionally, at the student level expected further education was a strong predictor of knowledge in all countries, whereas participation in a school council or extracurricular organizations had a positive effect on civic knowledge in only a few countries. Conversely, time spent outside of the home "hanging out" was a negative predictor of knowledge in most countries. Similar to Schulz (2002), Barber (2005) found that among student-level characteristics, socioeconomic status and individual perceptions of an open classroom climate for discussion influenced student knowledge in England.

42. They used data from 23 European countries, Australia, and the United States.

43. Students in Cyprus, Portugal, Greece, Poland, and the United States scored high on both these scales.

44. Similarly, using hierarchal linear modeling, other researchers found that classroom climate and confidence in school participation were important to support for immigrants' rights and women's rights at the school level—when other variables were controlled (Cheong & Hahn, 2008).

45. In each school, three teachers who taught subjects covered in the students' test of civic knowledge completed questionnaires. Although the teachers were not representative of teachers of civic-related subjects in their country, they did teach in a representative sample of schools in the country.

46. Teachers in Hong Kong expressed less confidence than other teachers in the sample in dealing with topics relating to national constitutions, national history, and civil and human rights. German and Italian teachers in the sample expressed most confidence teaching citizens' rights and obligations, different political systems, and human and civil rights. German teachers expressed least confidence in teaching about dangers of propaganda and manipulation; whereas Italian teachers said they were most confident teaching about trade unions.

47. This finding contradicted the international report, which used data from 27 countries (Losito & Mintrop, 2001).

REFERENCES

Ahonen, S., & Virta, A. (1999). Towards a dynamic view of society: Civic education in Finland. In J. Torney-Purta, J. Schwille, & J. A. Amadeo (Eds.). *Civic education across countries: Twenty four national case studies from the IEA civic education project* (pp. 229–256). Amsterdam: The International Association for the Evaluation of Educational Achievement.

Alviar-Martin, T., Randall, J., Usher, E. L., & Engelhard, G. (2008). Teaching civic topics in four societies: Examining national context and teacher confidence. *The Journal of Educational Research.*

Amadeo, J.A., Torney-Purta, J., Lehmann, R., Husfeldt, V., & Nikolova, R. (2002). *Civic knowledge and engagement: An IEA study of upper secondary students in sixteen countries.* Amsterdam: International Association for the Evaluation of Educational Achievement.

Arthur, J., Davies, I., & Hahn, C. L. (2008). *Handbook on education for citizenship and democracy.* London: SAGE Publishing.

Avery, P. G., Bird, K., Johnstone, S., Sullivan, J. L., & Thalhammer, K. (1992). Exploring political tolerance with adolescents. *Theory and Research in Social Education, 20,* 386–420.

Avery, P. G., Freeman, C., Greenwalt, K., & Trout, M. (2006, April). The deliberating in a democracy project. A paper presented at the American Educational Research Association meeting, San Francisco.

Baldi, S., Perie, M., Skidmore, D., Greenberg, E., & Hahn, C. L. (2001). *What democracy means to ninth-graders: U.S. results from the international IEA Civic Education Study.* Washington, DC: National Center for Education Statistics, U.S. Department of Education. Available at: http://nces.ed.gov/pubsearch/pubsinfo.asp?pubid=2001096 (accessed January 9, 2008).

Banks, J. A. (Ed.) (2004). *Diversity and citizenship education: Global perspectives.* San Francisco: Jossey-Bass.

Barber, C. (2005, March). The effects of learning climate, socioeconomic status, and discussion on students' civic knowledge in England: Looking beyond uniform effects. Paper presented at the annual meeting of the Comparative and International Education Society, Stanford, CA.

Billig, S. (2000). Research on k-12 school based service learning: The evidence builds. *Phi Delta Kappan, 81,* 658–664.

Billig, S., Root, S., & Jesse, D. (2005). *The impact of participation in service-learning on high school students' civic engagement.* College Park: University of Maryland, Center for Information and Research on Civic Learning and Engagement.

Bishop, J. (1999). Conceptions of democracy, citizenship, and civic education in the Czech Republic: A comparison of teachers and students in three types of secondary schools. Unpublished Ph.D. dissertation. The University of Iowa.

Bishop, J. J., & Hamot, G. E. (2001). Democracy as a cross-cultural concept: Promises and problems. *Theory and Research in Social Education, 29,* 463–487.

Broudy, R. A. (1994, March). Secondary education and political attitudes: Examining the effects on political tolerance of the "We the People" curriculum. Paper presented at the meeting of the Comparative and International Education Society, San Diego, CA.

Cheong, Y. F., & Hahn, C. L. (2008). Student beliefs, school experiences and ninth graders political attitudes. Unpublished paper.

Cleaver, E., Ireland, E., Kerr, D., & Lopes, J. (2005). *Citizenship education longitudinal study: Second cross sectional survey 2004: Listening to young people: Citizenship education in England.* London: Department for Education and Skills.

Cogan, J. J., & Derricott, R. (2001) (Eds.). *Citizenship education for the 21st century: An international perspective on education.* London: Kogan Page.

Cogan, J. J, Morris, P., & Print, M. (2002) (Eds.). *Civic education in the Asia-Pacific region: Case studies across six societies.* New York: RouledgeFalmer.

Conover, P. J., & Searing, D. D. (2000). A political socialization perspective. In L. M. McDonnell, P. M. Timpane, & R. Benjamin (Eds.). *Rediscovering the democratic purposes of education* (pp. 91–126). Lawrence: University Press of Kansas.

Chareka, O., & Sears, A. (2005). Discounting the political: Understanding civic participation as private practice. *Canadian and International Education, 34,* 50–58.

Craddock, A. (2005, November). *Education for Democracy in Ukraine: Student learning through a US-Ukraine civic education partnership.* Paper presented at the College and University Faculty Assembly meeting of the National Council for the Social Studies, Kansas City, MO.

Davies, I., Gregory, I., & Riley, S. C. (2005). Teachers' perceptions of citizenship in England. In W. O. Lee & J. T. Fouts (Eds.), *Education for social citizenship: Perceptions of teachers in the USA, Australia, England, Russia, and China* (pp. 131–174). Aberdeen: Hong Kong University Press.

Dezfooli, N. A. (2005). Middle school teachers' perceived level of incorporation of democratic values in classroom practice: A comparison between Iran and the United States. Unpublished master's thesis. Bowling Green State University, Ohio.

Ehman, L. H. (1980). The American school in the political socialization socialization process. *Review of Educational Research, 50,* 99–119.

Eisikovits, R. A. (2005). Perspectives of young immigrants from the former USSR on voting and politics in Israel. *Theory and Research in Social Education, 33,* 454–475.

Ellis, M. J., & Brown, C. (2005). Teachers' perceptions of citizenship in Russia. In W. O. Lee & J. T. Fouts (Eds.), *Education for social citizenship: Perceptions of teachers in the USA, Australia, England, Russia, and China* (pp. 175–208). Aberdeen: Hong Kong University Press.

Fairbrother, G. (2003). *Toward critical patriotism: Student resistance to political education in Hong Kong and China.* Hong Kong: Hong Kong University Press.

Finkel, S. E., & Ernst, H. R. (2005). Civic education in post-Apartheid South Africa: Alternative paths to the development of political knowledge and democratic values. *Political Psychology, 26*, 333–364.

Goldenson, A. R. (1978). An alternative view about the role of the secondary school in political socialization. *Theory and Research in Social Education, 6*, 44–72.

Hahn, C. L. (1996). Research on issues-centered social studies. In R. Evans & D. W. Saxe (Eds.), *Handbook on issues-centered teaching and learning* (pp. 25–44). Washington, DC: National Council for the Social Studies.

Hahn, C. L. (1998). *Becoming political: Comparative perspectives on citizenship education.* Albany: State University of New York Press.

Hahn, C. L. (1999). Challenges to civic education in the United States. In J. Torney-Purta, J. Schwille, & J. A. Amadeo (Eds.). *Civic education across countries: Twenty four national case studies from the IEA civic education project* (pp. 583–607). Amsterdam: The International Association for the Evaluation of Educational Achievement. ERIC document reproduction service, ED 431 705.

Hahn, C. L. (2005). Diversity and human rights learning in England and the United States. In A. Osler (Ed.), *Teachers, human rights, and diversity: Educating citizens in multicultural societies* (pp. 23–40). Stoke on Trent, UK: Trentham Books.

Hahn, C. L. (2006). Citizenship education and youth attitudes: Views from England, Germany, and the United States. In H. Ertl (Ed.), *Cross-national attraction in education: Accounts from England and Germany* (pp. 129–154). Oxford, UK: Symposium Books.

Hannam, D. (2001). *The Hannam report: A report to the DfEE.* London: Community Service Volunteers. Available at http://www.csv.org.uk/Resources/Educational+Publications (accessed January 9, 2008).

Hannam, D. (2005, Spring). Education for democracy and education through democracy. *Teaching Citizenship*, (No. 10), 21–28.

Haste, H. (2005). *My voice, my vote, my community: A study of young people's civic action and inaction.* London: Nestle Social Research Programme.

Haste, H., & Torney-Purta, J. V. (1992). *The development of political understanding: A new perspective.* San Francisco: Jossey-Bass.

Hughes, A., & Sears, A. (1996). Macro and micro level aspects of a programme of citizenship education research. *Canadian and International Education, 25*(2), 17–30.

Ichilov, O. (1998) (Ed.).*Citizenship and citizenship education in a changing world.* London: The Woburn Press.

Ichilov, O. (2005). Pride in one's country and citizenship orientations in a divided society. *Comparative Education Review, 49*, 44–61.

Ireland, E., Kerr, D., Lopes, J., Nelson, & Cleaver, E. (2006). *Active citizenship and young people: Opportunities, experiences, and challenges in and beyond school. Citizenship education longitudinal study fourth annual report* (pp. 127–156). London: Department for Education and Skills.

Joshee, R. (2004). Citizenship and multicultural education in Canada: From assimilation to social cohesion. In J. A. Banks (Ed.), *Diversity and citizenship education: Global perspectives* (pp. 127–156). San Francisco: Jossey-Bass

Kennedy, K. J. (Ed.). (1997). *Citizenship education and the modern state.* Washington, DC: Falmer Press.

Kennedy, K. J. (2005). Reframing civic education for new citizenships. In K. Kennedy (Ed.), *Changing schools for changing times: New directions for the school curriculum in Hong Kong* (pp. 131–150). Hong Kong: The Chinese University Press.

Kennedy, K. J. (2006). The gendered nature of students' attitudes to minority groups: Implications for teacher education. *Citizenship and Teacher Education, 2*, 55–65.

Kennedy, K. J., Hahn, C. L., & Lee, W. O. (2008). Constructing citizenship: Comparing the views of students in Australia, Hong Kong, and the United States. *Comparative Education Review.*

Kerr, D., Ireland, E., Lopes, J., & Craig, R. with Cleaver, E. (2004). *Citizenship education longitudinal study second annual report: Making citizenship education real.* London: Department for Education and Skills.

Kerr, D., Lines, A., Blenkinsop, S., & Schagen, I. (2002). *England's results from the IEA international citizenship education study: What citizenship and education mean to 14 year olds.* DfES Research Brief 375. London: Department for Education and Skills.

Kubow, P. K. (2007). Teachers' constructions of democracy: Intersections of Western and Indigenous knowledge in South Africa and Kenya. *Comparative Education Review, 51*, 307–328.

Lave, J., & Wenger, E. (1991). *Situated learning: legitimate peripheral participation.* Cambridge: Cambridge University Press.

Lee, W. O. (1999). Controversies of civic education in political transition: The case of Hong Kong. In J. Torney-Purta, J. Schwille, & J. Amadeo (Eds.), *Civic education across countries: Twenty-four case studies from the IEA civic education project* (pp. 313–340). Amsterdam: International Association for the Evaluation of Educational Achievement.

Lee, W. O. (2005). Teachers' perceptions of citizenship in China. In W. O. Lee & J. T. Fouts (Eds.), *Education for social citizenship: Perceptions of teachers in the USA, Australia, England, Russia, and China* (pp. 209–246). Aberdeen: Hong Kong University Press.

Lee, W. O., & Fouts, J. T. (2005). *Education for social citizenship: Perceptions of teachers in the USA, Australia, England, Russia, and China.* Aberdeen: Hong Kong University Press.

Lee, W. O., Grossman, D. L., Kennedy, K., & Fairbrother, G. P. (Eds.). (2004). *Citizenship education in Asia and the Pacific: Concepts and issues.* Comparative Education Research Centre, The University of Hong Kong, Hong Kong: Kluwer Academic.

Leung, Y. W. (2003). Citizenship education through service-learning: From charity to social justice. *Education Journal, 31,* 95–115.

Leung, Y. W. (2006, April). How do they become socially/politically active?: Case studies of Hong Kong secondary students' political socialization. *Citizenship Teaching and Learning, 2,* 51–67.

Leung, Y. W., & Ng, S. W. (2004). Back to square one: The "re-depoliticizing" of civic education in Hong Kong. *Asia Pacific Journal of Education, 24,* 43–60.

Leung, Y. W., & Print, M. (2002). Nationalistic education as the focus for civics and citizenship education: The case of Hong Kong. *Asia Pacific Education Review, 3,* 197–209.

Levstik, L. S., & Groth, J. (2005). "Ruled by our own people": Ghanaian adolescents' conceptions of citizenship. *Teachers' College Record, 107,* 563–586.

Liao, T., Liu, M., & Doong, S. (1998). [In Chinese] *The impact of issues-centered approach on students' civic participation attitudes for grade 8 and 11 students.* Research report. Taiwan: National Science Council.

Losito, B. (1999). Italy: Educating for democracy in a changing democratic society. In J. Torney-Purta, J. Schwille, & J. Amadeo (Eds.), *Civic education across countries: Twenty-four case studies from the IEA civic education project* (pp. 395–498). Amsterdam: International Association for the Evaluation of Educational Achievement.

Losito, B., & Mintrop, H. (2001). The teaching of civic education. In J. Torney-Purta, R. Lehmann, H. Oswald, & W. Schulz (Eds.), *Citizenship and education in twenty eight countries; Civic knowledge and engagement at age fourteen* (pp. 158–173). Amsterdam: The International Association for the Evaluation of Educational Achievement.

Mayer, J., & Schmidt, H. (2004). Gendered political socialization in four contexts: Political interest and values among junior high school students in China, Japan, Mexico, and the United States. *The Social Science Journal, 41,* 393–407.

Matrai, Z. (1999). In transit: Civic education in Hungary. In J. Torney-Purta, J. Schwille, & J. Amadeo (Eds.), *Civic education across countries: Twenty-four case studies from the IEA civic education project* (pp. 341–370). Amsterdam: International Association for the Evaluation of Educational Achievement.

McDevitt, M., & Chaffee, S. (2000). Closing gaps in political communication and knowledge: Effects of a school intervention. *Communication Research, 27,* 259–292.

Mellor, S. (1998). *What's the point?: Political attitudes of Victorian year 11 students.* Melbourne: The Australian Council for Educational Research.

Mellor, S., Kennedy, K., & Greenwood, L. (2002). *Citizenship and democracy: Australian students' knowledge and beliefs—the IEA civic education study of fourteen year olds.* Melbourne: Australian Council for Educational Research. Available at http://www.acer.edu.au/research/_reports/Civics_citizenship.html (accessed January 9, 2008).

Mintrop, H. (2002). Teachers and civic education instruction in cross-national comparison. In G. Steiner-Khamsi, J. Torney-Purta, & J. Schwille (Eds.), *New paradigms and recurring paradoxes in education for citizenship: An international comparison* (pp. 61–83). Kidlington, UK: Elsevier Science Ltd.

Nicholas, A. B. (1996). Citizenship education and aboriginal people: The humanitarian art of cultural genocide. *Canadian and International Education, 25*(2), 59–107.

Osler, A. (Ed.). (2005). *Teachers, human rights, and diversity: Educating citizens in a multicultural society.* Stoke-on-Trent, UK: Trentham.

Osler, A., & Starkey, H. (2005). *Changing citizenship: Democracy and inclusion in education.* Berkshire, UK: Open University Press.

Osborne, K. (1996). Education is the best national insurance: Citizenship education in Canadian schools: Past and present. *Canadian and International Education, 25*(2), 31–58.

Peck, C., & Sears, A. (2005). Unchartered territory: Mapping students' conceptions of ethnic diversity. *Canadian Ethnic Studies, 37,* 101–120.

Perlinger, A., Canetti-Nisim, D., Pedahzur, A. (2006). Democratic attitudes among high school pupils: The role played by perceptions of class climates. *School Effectiveness and School Improvement, 17,* 119–140.

Print, M. (1995). *Political understanding and attitudes of secondary students.* Canberra, AU: Department of the Senate, Parliament House.

Print, M., Kennedy, K., & Hughes, J. (1999). Reconstructing civic and citizenship education in Australia. In J. Torney-Purta, J. Schwille, & J. A. Amadeo (Eds.), *Civic education across countries: Twenty four national case studies from the IEA civic education project* (pp. 37–59). Amsterdam: The International Association for the Evaluation of Educational Achievement. ERIC document reproduction service, ED 431 705.

Print, M., Saha, L., & Edwards, K. (2005). *Youth electoral study, report one, Enrolment and voting.*

Prior, W. (2005). Teachers' perceptions of citizenship in Australia. In W. O. Lee & J. T. Fouts (Eds.), *Education for social citizenship: Perceptions of teachers in the USA, Australia, England, Russia, and China* (pp. 93–130). Aberdeen: Hong Kong University Press.

Roland-Levy, C., & Ross, A. (2003). *Political learning and citizenship in Europe.* Stoke-on-Trent, UK: Trentham.

Ross, A. (Ed.). (2001). *Learning for a democratic Europe: Proceedings of the third conference of the children's identity and citizenship in Europe thematic network.* London: Institute for Policy Studies in Education, University of North London.

Schulz, W. (2002, April). Explaining differences in civic knowledge: Multi-level regression analysis of student data from 27 countries. Paper presented at the annual meeting of the American Educational Research Association, New Orleans. ERIC Reproduction Services, ED 465 762.

Sears, A., Clarke, G. M., & Hughes, A. S. (1999). Canadian citizenship education: The pluralist ideal and citizenship education for a post-modern state. In J. Torney-Purta, J. Schwille, & J. A. Amadeo (Eds.), *Civic education across countries: Twenty four national case studies from the IEA civic education project* (pp. 111–135). Amsterdam: The International Association for the Evaluation of Educational Achievement. ERIC document reproduction service, ED 431 705.

Schiffauer, W., Baumann, G., Kastoryano, R. Vertovec, S. (2004). *Civil enculturation: Nation state, school, and ethnic differences in the Netherlands, Britain, Germany, and France.* New York: Berghahn Books.

Soule, S. (2002, September). Creating a cohort committed to democracy? Civic education in Bosnia and Hertzegovina. Paper presented at the annual meeting of the American Political Science Association, Boston.

Soule, S., & Nairne, J. (2006, April). Are girls checking out? Gender and political socialization in transitioning democracies. Paper presented at the annual meeting of the Midwestern Political Science Association, Chicago.

Steiner-Khamsi, G., Torney-Purta, J., Schwille, J. (Eds.). (2002). *New paradigms and recurring paradoxes in education for citizenship.* Amsterdam: Elsevier Science (JAI Press).

Tolo, K. W. (1998). *An assessment of We the People...Project Citizen: Promoting citizenship in classrooms and communities.* Austin, TX: Lyndon B. Johnson School of Public Affairs, University of Texas.

Torney-Purta, J., & Barber, C. (2004a, October). *Democratic school participation and civic attitudes among European adolescents: Analysis of data from the IEA civic education study.* A paper prepared for the Conference on Education for Democratic Citizenship, 2001–2004, Strasbourg, France: Council of Europe.

Torney-Purta, J., & Barber, C. (2004b, June). *Strengths and weaknesses in US students' knowledge and skills: Analysis from the IEA civic education study.* CIRCLE Fact Sheet. Available at http://www.civicyouth.org (accessed August 1, 2005).

Torney-Purta, J., Lehmann, R., Oswald, H., & Schulz, W. (2001). *Citizenship and education in twenty eight countries; Civic knowledge and engagement at age fourteen.* Amsterdam: The International Association for the Evaluation of Educational Achievement. Available at http://www.wam.umd.edu/~iea (accessed October 10, 2005).

Torney-Purta, J., & Richardson, W. (2004). Anticipated political engagement among adolescents in Australia, England, Norway, and the United States. In J. Demaine (Ed.), *Citizenship and political education today* (pp. 41–58). Basingstoke, UK: Palgrave, Macmillan.

Torney-Purta, J., Richardson, W., & Barber, C. (2004, August). *Trust in government-related institutions and civic engagement among adolescents: Analysis of five countries from the IEA civic education study.* CIRCLE Working Paper 17. Silver Spring, MD: The Center for Information and Research on Civic Learning & Engagement, the University of Maryland. Available at http://www.civicyouth.org (accessed October 10, 2005).

Torney-Purta, J., Richardson, W. K., & Barber, C. (2005). Teachers' educational experience and confidence in relation to students' civic knowledge across countries. *International Journal of Citizenship and Teacher Education, 1*(1), 32–57.

Torney-Purta, J., Schwille, J., & Amadeo, J. A. (Eds.). (1999). *Civic education across countries: Twenty four national case studies from the IEA civic education project.* Amsterdam: The International Association for the Evaluation of Educational Achievement.

Valkova, J., & Kalous, J. (1999). The changing face of civic education in the Czech Republic. In J. Torney-Purta, J. Schwille, & J. A. Amadeo (Eds.), *Civic education across countries: Twenty four national case studies from the IEA civic education project* (pp. 179–202). Amsterdam: The International Association for the Evaluation of Educational Achievement.

Watchorn, E. J. (2005). Citizenship in school. Unpublished D.Phil. thesis, University of Oxford, Oxford, UK.

Vontz, T. S., Metcalf, K. K., & Patrick, J. J. (2000). *Project Citizen and the civic development of adolescent students in Indiana, Latvia, and Lithuania.* Bloomington, IN: The ERIC Clearinghouse for Social Studies/Social Science Education.

7 Service-learning

Rahima Wade

The University of Iowa

Creating informed and active public citizens is one of the professed goals of social studies education (Barr, Barth, & Shermis, 1977; NCSS, 1979; Parker, 1989, Shaver, 1977). As Ferguson (1991) wrote, "it follows that the success or failure of social studies may be gauged by the extent to which the citizenry takes a reflective and active part in the political and social life of the community" (p. 385). Yet young adults in the United States do not vote or engage in political involvement in great numbers. Many social studies scholars are deeply concerned about this fact, realizing that a democracy lacking in participation by the majority of its constituents is a democracy at risk. Bellah and his colleagues (1985) concluded, "We have failed at every level; we have put our own good, as individuals, as groups, as a nation, ahead of the common good" (p. 285). For a thriving democracy, we need a majority of citizens willing to participate in community life and to contribute to decisions from the local to the international level that affect their own lives and the wellbeing of society as a whole (Barber, 2004).

This chapter examines the contributions made by community service-learning toward these goals. Service-learning—the integration of community-based service experiences and academics combined with structured reflection—is an increasingly prevalent strategy for civic education in our nation's K–12 schools and teacher education programs. As Barber (1992) maintains, the concept of *service* is central to the civics curriculum if students are to realize the obligations engendered in democratic citizenship. This chapter begins, then, with a definition of service-learning and a rationale for its centrality in social studies education. Following a brief discussion of the limitations in research on service-learning, I provide the reader with a picture of the prevalence of service-learning in U.S. schools. The research findings are divided into three aspects of the literature on K–12 student outcomes: (a) academic and intellectual, (b) social and personal, and (c) civic and political. The first two areas are addressed briefly while the third is explored in some depth, given the alignment of these service-learning outcomes with social studies' goals. As teachers' training in service-learning is very important in terms of providing students with high quality service-learning experiences, a brief discussion of the research on service-learning in social studies teacher education is also included. The chapter concludes with suggestions for further directions in research on service-learning in the social studies.

SERVICE-LEARNING DEFINED

Service-learning programs take a variety of shapes and forms, making defining service-learning a challenging task. Definitions reflect various opinions about the nature of service-learning (philosophy of education, curricular strategy, or program design) and its purposes (e.g., personal growth, social skills development, civic competence) (Billig, 2000). In recognition of the need for a widely agreed-upon definition of service-learning and a set of standards by which to judge programs, a diverse group of service-learning educators nationwide, the Alliance for Service-Learning in Education Reform (ASLER), established the following definition, which, despite persisting differences of opinion, is widely used:

> Service-learning is a method by which young people learn and develop through active participation in thoughtfully-organized service experiences: that meet actual community needs, that are coordinated in collaboration with the school and community, that are integrated into each young person's academic curriculum, that provide structured time for a young person to think, talk, and write about what he/she did and saw during the actual service activity, that provide young people with opportunities to use newly acquired academic skills and knowledge in real life situations in their own communities, that enhance what is taught in the school by extending student learning beyond the classroom, and that help to foster the development of a sense of caring for others. (1993, p. 1)

The components of curriculum integration and reflection are, in fact, what distinguish service-learning from community service. In service-learning programs, service projects serve as the basis of learning opportunities. From this perspective, youth are seen as capable, productive, and essential contributors to their communities; and their contributions are seen as opportunities for citizenship education. To maximize the potential for service and learning, then, high quality service-learning programs include the following essential elements: thoughtful preparation, respectful collaboration, meaningful service, curriculum integration, structured reflection activities, evaluation of both service and learning, student ownership, and community celebration (ASLER, 1993; Billig, 2000; Conrad & Hedin, 1991; Giles, Honnet, & Migliore, 1991; Maryland Student Service Alliance, 1995).

While in almost all cases service-learning projects have a goal of promoting active citizenship (and thus could be thought of as enhancing the goal of social studies), social studies educators can develop activities especially suited to their curricula. For example, elementary students could study the historical buildings in their community and work on restoring one site. High school students might conduct a voter registration drive, making presentations to groups who are typically underrepresented in the voter pool. As part of a unit on immigration, middle school students could interview recent immigrants in their community and take care of young children while their parents study for their U.S. citizenship tests. In all of these projects, the service experience becomes the motivation and central activity for connecting social studies knowledge and attitudes with civic skills and behaviors.

A RATIONALE FOR SERVICE-LEARNING
IN THE SOCIAL STUDIES

The primary role of social studies is to prepare youth for civic competence (Clark, 1990; Merryfield & Subedi, 2001); yet traditional social studies instruction has not been effective in creating informed and active citizens. The decline in high school and college students' interest in civic life over the last 40 plus years has been well documented. Compared with earlier generations of Americans, young people today are less informed about politics, vote less often, and indicate lower levels of civic obligation (Bennett & Bennett, 1990; Bennett & Rademacher, 1997; Teixeira, 1992). Recent research on civic education, while contesting earlier findings on the ineffective nature of schools' attempts to shape students' political attitudes and behaviors, has also focused attention on the ways in which civics is taught, highlighting, in particular, opportunities for participation (Emler, 1992; Niemi & Junn, 1998). Thus, offering students the opportunity to engage in civic involvement through service in the community has been one response to the apparent inefficacy of traditional civics instruction (Riedel, 2002), and service-learning has been promoted as a relevant strategy in this regard (Ehrlich, 1999).

Social studies is especially well situated to play a major role in the growing national service movement. Although social studies educators differ in their views about what constitutes citizenship (Shermis & Barth, 1982), many have asserted that an essential component of civic education is students' active involvement in the social and political life of the community (Engle & Ochoa, 1988; Eyler & Giles, 1999; Parker & Jarolimek, 1984; Pratte, 1988; Rutter & Newmann, 1989; Schug & Beery, 1984). Moreover, the history of social studies education reveals a legacy of service and community activism (Wade & Saxe, 1996), from the early work of Arthur Dunn and the 1916 Social Studies Committee through numerous National Council for the Social Studies' publications (NCSS, 1979, 1980, 1989, 1994), including the recent position statement, *Service-Learning: An Essential Component of Citizenship Education* (NCSS, 2001).

LIMITATIONS IN SERVICE-LEARNING RESEARCH

In her keynote address at the First Annual Conference on Service-Learning Research, Janet Eyler asserted, "For a field that engenders so much passion in practitioners and that we believe transforms students by engaging their hearts as well as their minds, there is remarkably little evidence of strong impact and even less evidence about the kinds of practices that lead to the effects we desire" (2002, p. 5). Service-learning research is typically characterized by one or more of the following: program evaluations conducted primarily or solely to meet reporting requirements, one-shot efforts such as dissertations, lack of control groups or tracking of participants over time, self-report data, and a wide variance in program quality (Billig, 2000; Eyler, 2002). Studies that draw on large national samples are plagued by the fact that developmental gains are dependent on factors that cannot be controlled, including the variety of activities construed as "service," the diverse focus of program goals, and the inconsistency in the context within which service is conducted (Blythe, Saito, & Berkas, 1997; Metz & Youniss, 2005). Conrad (1991) noted additional methodological problems, such as research being conducted by service-learning advocates, atypical samples, brevity of programs, and difficulty in identifying the appropriate dependent variables.

An additional challenge when examining the research on whether or not service-learning contributes to civic and/or political outcomes is the conceptual confusion about the terms *service, service-learning, civic,* and *citizenship*. Definitions of *politics* and *political participation* are also contested (Walker, 2002). Campbell (2004) distinguishes between civic and political participation in the following way: Civic participation consists of "non-remunerative publicly spirited collective action that is not motivated by the desire to affect public policy," and political participation is seen as "those activities by private citizens that are more or less directly aimed at influencing the selection of governmental personnel and/or the actions they take" (p. 7).

In this review, I have adopted a broad focus in regard to these terms in an effort to be inclusive of the variety of research focused on civic and political outcomes. Thus, I have chosen to include civic knowledge, attitudes, skills, values, and behaviors that apply to civic life generally or politics in particular. Where possible, I have been specific in the review as to which outcomes researchers were examining. However, in some studies, this is not specified beyond the generic civic or political terms. In regard to whether studies have focused on community service or service-learning (the latter including reflection and an academic component), I have attempted to focus primarily on service-learning, except in those cases where seminal studies and reviews conducted in the 1970s or 1980s (which often included both service and service-learning) are concerned. Searches for relevant research studies and reviews of the research included the use of ERIC, Google Scholar, several service-learning and social studies listserves, and inquiries to the National Service-Learning Clearinghouse.

While some scholars may take issue with such an inclusive approach to the literature, I do so here for several reasons that, I hope, militate against conceptual fuzziness. First there are relatively few research studies on service-learning in social studies specifically. Second, research on service-learning is still in its infancy. An inclusive approach will assist in revealing those aspects of the literature that point to potentially relevant findings and opportunities for further research.

PREVALENCE OF SERVICE-LEARNING

Service-learning has surged in popularity over the last decade, becoming an increasingly prevalent practice in the nation's K–12 schools (Billig, 2000; Skinner & Chapman, 1999; Stagg, 2004). According to a National Center for Educational Statistics report, 64% of public schools, including 83% of high schools, offered service activities recognized by or arranged by the school, and about a third organized service-learning as part of the curriculum, including almost half of high schools (Skinner & Chapman, 1999). As of February 2004, approximately 4.7 million K–12 students in 23,000 public schools are involved in some variety of service-learning (Stagg, 2004) and 24% of public high schools in the United States require community service or service-learning as a prerequisite for high school graduation (Scales & Rochlkepartain, 2004).

Research has not kept up with the exponential growth in service-learning practice, however. Given the prevalence of service experiences in our nation's schools, understanding what types of student outcomes can be reasonably expected from students' service involvement and what factors contribute to these outcomes is of paramount importance. While scholars have observed that personal factors contribute to or are associated with positive student outcomes from service, this review will focus on the research on student outcomes in regard to academic, personal, social, civic, and political development and the program factors associated with these outcomes.

ACADEMIC AND INTELLECTUAL DEVELOPMENT

Service learning activity shows some positive effects on variables related to academic success (e.g., non-disruptive school conduct, subject matter test scores, grade point average, school engagement, and commitment to school) (Scales, Blythe, Berkas, & Kielsmeier, 2000). Additional academic variables positively influenced, according to some studies, include motivation to learn and student attendance rates (Billig, 2000). However, most scholars acknowledge that academic achievement is not the primary goal in most service-learning programs, and research results in this area are mixed and inconclusive (Billig, 2000; Galston, 2001; Raskoff & Sundeen, 2001; Scales et al., 2000; Shumer, 1999; Wade & Saxe, 1996). Typically, teachers who engage in service-learning projects are more concerned with students' social and emotional growth as a result of their service experience.

Wade and Saxe (1996) assert that the match between service-learning activities and tests or subject matter assessments is critical in fostering strong academic achievement outcomes. For example, programs that employ cross-age tutoring appear to be particularly effective in contributing to academic achievement (Cohen, Kulik, & Kulik, 1982; Hedin, 1987). Root (1997) further notes that when the service activity is carefully matched with course content, academic gains are greater (internships in a local government office as part of a civics course, for example). Also noteworthy is the finding that time spent on service outside of the classroom does not seem to reduce academic achievement, even though students are spending less time in the classroom (Alt & Medrich, 1994; Waterman, 1993). Additional factors that appear to positively influence student outcomes include in-depth reflection, greater hours of service—studies have posited 10, 30, 35, and 50 as the key number of hours (Scales et al., 2000; Shumer, 1999; Wade & Saxe, 1996)—and older age of students—more positive effects for late high school students (Melchior, Frees, LaCava, Kingsley & Nahas, 1999; Wade & Saxe, 1996).

PERSONAL AND SOCIAL DEVELOPMENT

Service-learning researchers generally agree that the area of personal and social development is the strongest outcome for K–12 students (Billig, 2000; Conrad, 1991; Raskoff & Sundeen, 2000, 2001; Scales & Blythe, 1997; Scales et al., 2000; Wade, 2000; Wade & Saxe, 1996). Findings include positive associations between service-learning and increased self-esteem, social responsibility, identity development, and career awareness (Shumer & Belbas, 1996). Students involved in service-learning activities are also less likely to engage in risk behaviors and are more positive in relating with culturally diverse groups (Billig, 2000). Overall, then, service-learning enhances students' concern for others and their sense of duty towards others (Billig, 2000).

Wade and Saxe (1996) note that, while not all studies have resulted in positive personal and social student outcomes, many have shown gains in self-esteem, competence, or general self-worth, and most have revealed modest gains in social responsibility. Alt and Medrich (1994) asserted that, while studies of voluntary service programs tend to show only small increases in self-confidence and improved self-image, "these data confirm a consensus of opinion expressed by teachers and students about positive gains in this area" (p. 9). Conrad and Hedin (1989) also noted that reviews of studies found evidence that moral and ego development are enhanced through service activities.

CIVIC AND POLITICAL OUTCOMES

There is evidence that service-learning can be a particularly effective method of civic education if attention is paid to the intended democratic outcomes in the design of programs and curricula (Battistoni, 2000; Hepburn, 2000). Perry and Katula (2001) assert that service-learning favorably influences citizenship-related cognitive understanding, and Billig (2000) notes that it helps develop students' sense of civic responsibility and their citizenship skills. However, these claims are not guaranteed; the findings in the area of civic and political outcomes are mixed (Alt & Medrich, 1994; Billig, 2000; Conrad & Hedin, 1989; Hepburn, 2000; Raskoff & Sundeen, 2000; Wade, 1997).

Political efficacy

The role of political efficacy has received relatively little attention in the research on service-learning (Perry & Katula, 2001). However, several studies have led to positive findings. Conrad and Hedin (1981) found that students in service-learning programs showed greater gains in valuing community involvement than students in control groups (though no indication was given of the magnitude or significance of these findings). Wilson (1974) found that students in a community-based alternative school who engaged in political and social action made significant gains in political efficacy, as did students who completed fieldwork regarding the political structure of their city in Button's (1973) research. A study of high school students in a Boston area public school revealed that the mandatory service graduation requirement led to significant civic outcomes for those students deemed in the "less inclined to serve" groups (Metz & Youniss, 2005). The students showed significant improvement on three of the four measures: intention to vote in the future, intention to volunteer and join civic organizations in the future, and civic interest and understanding. While students already predisposed to service involvement measured high on these factors throughout the 2-year study, Metz and Youniss (2005) concluded that, "for students who might otherwise not do service, the requirement had a positive impact" (p. 431).

However, in several other studies service participation did not lead to statistically significant changes in political efficacy (Wade & Saxe, 1996). For example, in Newmann and Rutter's (1983) study, service participation failed to elicit changes in political efficacy, plans for future participation, or future social/institutional affiliation. Similarly, in a study of a year-long community service program, Corbett (1977) saw no significant gains in political efficacy, and Davidson (1995) reported that most of the high school students she interviewed saw no relationship between service activities and their responsibilities of citizenship or their future political involvement.

Several studies have looked at the effect of service-learning on voting behavior and found no significant relationship (Jastrzab, Blomquist, Masker, & Orr, 1996; Rosenthal, Feiring, & Lewis, 1998; Verba, Schlozman, & Brady, 1995). Metz, McLellan and Youniss (2003) also found that high school students' service experiences were not predictive of intention to vote in the future. Indeed, the NASS (1999) asserted that there is no significant statistical relationship between volunteering and voting.

Political knowledge

Only a few studies have looked at service-learning's ability to contribute to students' political knowledge. Hamilton and Zeldin (1987) found that students who volunteered in local government internships increased their knowledge of local government and their sense of competence in political work more than students in traditional government courses. An investigation into the effectiveness of the *Youth for Justice* violence prevention program found that students demonstrated a significantly higher level of knowledge about law and governance after participating in a program that combined law-related classroom lessons, training in mediation and negotiation, and service-learning, as compared with control group youth (Pereira & Rodriquez, 1997).

Understanding the research on political outcomes

A reasonable hypothesis when considering all of these findings is that programs focused specifically on political issues or local government (and most service-learning programs do not have this focus) may be more likely than other types of service-learning programs to lead to increased political efficacy and knowledge (Hepburn, 2000; Wade, 1997). On the other hand, as Metz and his colleagues (2003) found, service related to social causes (as opposed to other types of service) positively relates to concern for social issues, future intended service, and future unconventional civic activities (boycott, demonstration, working on a political campaign).

Wade and Saxe's (1996) explanation of the often weak relationship between service and political involvement is that "when programs promote an individualistic, charitable conception of service and do not tie their activities to political issues or organizations, participants are unlikely to gain on this dimension" (p. 346). Other scholars have observed service-learning's emphasis on individual development and the resultant lack of changes on civic and political measures (Chi, 2002; Newmann & Rutter, 1983; Walker, 2002). In practice, service-learning often neglects a focus on the root causes that create the need for service in the first place. Levison (1986) notes that, while service-learning increases students' awareness of problems, the lack of focus on the root causes of the problems results in limited development of skills, knowledge, or attitudes to work on changing public policy. Echoing this shortcoming, Billig (2000) posited that "to achieve stronger civic responsibility outcomes, it is necessary for the teacher to help students make explicit connections with social or citizenship issues" (p. 662).

Galston (2001) concludes that the evidence suggests that students who participate in high quality programs that integrate community service with systematic reflection on their experience are more likely to develop an understanding of political context and governing institutions, to think of themselves as politically efficacious, and to become civically and politically engaged. Indeed, research by Westheimer and Kahne (2000) found compelling evidence that when service is accompanied by rigorous analysis and/ or related social issues, students do develop civic knowledge, skills and attitudes. Furthermore, Riedel (2002) found that "exposure to the wider political and social context of class material and opportunities to engage in political action" (p. 518) (e.g., working on public campaigns or elections) led to significant gains in civic obligation. Marks' (1994) research revealed that the single most powerful influence on positive outcomes in regard to citizenship and political efficacy was the amount of time spent thinking about social and political issues in classroom discussions and assignments.

Time spent on service is also a key factor. In a study based on data from 4,000 high school students, Niemi, Hepburn, and Chapman (2000) concluded that a minimum of 35 hours of service was associated with gains in students' political knowledge, participatory skills, and feelings of understanding politics. In a pre- and post-test study of mostly ninth graders, students who contributed 40 or more hours of service showed greater increases in positive attitudes toward social responsibility and civic involvement than students who participated in fewer hours of service (Blyth et al., 1997). Research on selected high quality programs funded by Learn and Serve America reveals that high school service-learning has a better chance of enduring effects if students participate in school-organized service for several years (Melchior, 1998).

The complexity of structuring curriculum to promote students' sense of political and civic efficacy goes beyond the amount of time spent on service. Kahne and Westheimer (2002) found that when students' sense of efficacy grows, their commitment to future civic involvement grows as well, but "when students become frustrated or come to believe that problems are intractable, their commitment appears to decline" (p. 3). Thus, even in the most extensive service-learning programs, students might not gain in political efficacy unless teachers carefully construct experiences in which students can contribute to and witness some measure of positive change.

Several other studies shed light on additional factors that may contribute to the impact of high school service experience on future political involvement. In a study of a year-long service-learning program as part of a mandatory social justice course at a Catholic high school, Yates and Youniss (1998) found that face–to-face struggles with issues of poverty and homelessness, coupled with frequent opportunities for written reflection and class discussion, led to students' consideration of political issues and helped to define students' emerging sense of participatory identity. Similarly, Morgan and Streb (2001) found that when high school students' voice and ownership in a service-learning experience increase, so do political efficacy and participation.

In sum, there are many factors that influence service-learning's ability to enhance polit-ical outcomes. If political knowledge is the goal, then programs must carefully connect government or politically oriented service experiences with academic content. Significant time needs to be spent on service, and in-depth reflection on political issues is important. Increasing students' investment in their service and learning by giving them voice and ownership is also a plus. Also, it is important to note that teachers are key in designing service-learning experiences with explicit political outcomes. Finally, attention must be paid to students' sense of success, or frustration may lead to decreased political efficacy.

Civic outcomes

Several of the previously cited studies examined service-learning's ability to enhance civic outcomes beyond the political realm (e.g., civic knowledge, skills, and disposi-tions). Again, in this area of study, research findings are mixed. A study funded by the Center for Information and Research on Civic Learning and Engagement (CIRCLE) makes clear some of the complexities involved in investigating the relationship between service-learning and civic outcomes for students. The CIRCLE study compared more than 1,000 high school students who participated in service-learning programs with those who did not participate (Billig, Root, & Jesse, 2005). Subjects in the study were matched, based on similar demographics and student achievement profiles, with stu-dents in conventional social studies classes. More than half of the students were Latino; high schools in the study were from the southeast, north central, and western parts of the United States. While the researchers measured a broad range of outcomes including academic success and other school-related factors, several of the primary foci pertinent to this study were civic knowledge, behaviors, and dispositions.

Although service-learning students in the CIRCLE study scored higher than com-parison students on several outcomes, most of the differences were not statistically sig-nificant. Acknowledging that there were substantial differences in the quality of the programs, the researchers concluded that "[s]ervice-learning is effective when it is imple-mented well, but it is no more effective than conventional social studies classes when the conditions are not optimal" (2005, p. 1). The factors deemed optimal included: more extensive time in the program, number of years of teaching experience (and especially longer experience using service-learning), program quality as it supports several essen-tial elements of service-learning, high student engagement in service-learning, inten-tional focus on civics and government, and the type of service project. As has been found in other studies, students who engaged in political or civic action (such as circu-lating a petition or organizing a community forum) scored highest on civic knowledge and dispositions. Additional qualitative data analyses of three sites at which students had statistically significantly higher scores on measures of civic knowledge, skills, and dispositions revealed that student voice, cognitive challenge, and students' affective connections to people whom they served were instrumental in programs that produced the strongest civic outcomes.

In a comprehensive review of research studies on service-learning, Billig (2004) con-cluded that most studies of service-leaning and its impact on various measures of civic engagement show that service-learning has positive results, particularly in regard to civic skills and dispositions. Mixed results are most likely due to a low quality program and/or programs that do not intentionally focus on civic outcomes.

Civic and political participation

In regard to civic and political participation, several service-learning researchers have observed that public school service experience is an important predictor of future civic involvement (Astin, Sax, & Avalos, 1999; Perry & Katula, 2001; Wade & Saxe, 1996; Youniss, McLellan, & Yates 1997). Furthermore, the schools play a critical role, as it is often a teacher who invites students to get involved in service (Schervish, Hodgkinson, Gates, & Associates, 1995). "Regardless of race or ethnic background, if individuals are asked to volunteer they are more than three times as likely to volunteer than if they are not asked" (Schervish et al., 1995). Two studies by Independent Sector reveal that early community service experience is a strong predictor of volunteering for both teens and youth (Hodgkinson & Weizman, 1992a, 1992b). Another national survey of youth views further affirms the importance of school-based service-learning. The Wirthlin Group (1995) found much higher involvement in youth community service when schools placed emphasis on its importance.

Several retrospective studies confirmed that highly politically active high school students became more politically active adults as compared to the general population (Beane, Turner, Jones, & Lipka, 1981; Fendrich, 1993; McAdam, 1989; Rosenhan, 1970; Sturges, Barfoo, Friesen, Weaver, & Wood, 1977; Youniss, McLellan, & Yates, 1997). These studies involved interviewing adults about their experiences in service and service-learning as youth. Participants often interpreted their early service experience as having a profound and ongoing influence that helped them define their political identities (Yates & Youniss, 1998). In particular, they mentioned participating as a cohort, being encouraged and supported by respected adults, and having opportunities to reflect upon and debrief their service experiences. Sturges et al. (1977) found that politically active high school students who protested school and societal issues were more politically active as adults, as measured by voting, supporting candidates, and supporting issues not unlike those they addressed in high school. In a more recent review, Youniss et al. (1997) found that high school students who participated in community service or school governance were more likely than were non-participants to be engaged in community organizations and voting 15 or more years later.

Overall, the research findings on the positive effects of service-learning on civic and political participation are more promising than those on civic and political efficacy, knowledge, skills, or attitudes. When service-learning experiences engage youth in extensive and well-planned experiences in their communities, they are more likely to contribute to students' future civic and political participation as adults.

SERVICE-LEARNING IN SOCIAL STUDIES TEACHER EDUCATION

As several studies described above indicate, teacher expertise in designing high quality service-learning experiences, including both knowledge of the elements of quality service-learning and the number of years implementing service-learning in the classroom, is a key factor in promoting positive student outcomes. Thus, training in service-learning as part of a teacher education program may be likely to increase the effectiveness of service-learning in K–12 classrooms.

Only a few studies have been conducted on service-learning in social studies teacher education (one in a methods course, several in student teaching). There are more studies focused specifically on the use of service-learning as a means for college students developing multicultural competency and social justice understanding. (These studies include, but are not limited to, social studies pre-service teachers). It is important to note that almost all studies focusing on pre-service teachers were conducted by teacher educators on their own service-learning programs and rely on participants' self-reports (e.g., journals, interviews, course papers). The discerning reader will note that such studies tend to tilt toward positive outcomes.

Social studies methods course

Service-learning in a social studies methods course led to positive changes on several dimensions. Teacher education students participated in service-learning experiences in community agencies working with children in need (e.g., disabilities, single parent families, second language learners) for at least 15 hours over the course of the semester. Several class discussions and reflection assignments facilitated students' learning from their service experience. More than 70% of the students reported increases in self-knowledge (understanding themselves as both teachers and community service providers), self-efficacy (belief in their abilities to make a difference in children's lives), knowledge about serving, personal connections with the children they served, and having fun or other good feelings in association with service (Wade, 1995).

Student teaching

Several studies on service-learning during student teaching have revealed positive findings. Dinkelman (2001) found that service-learning was a powerful and effective experience during the student teaching semester, leading to first-hand experience in delivering instruction that engaged student interest and fostered critical thinking, and Harwood (1999) found that service-learning contributed to pre-service teachers becoming more issues-centered. Wade and Yarbrough (1997), in a study of 255 student teachers from three Midwestern universities, found that service-learning contributed to student teacher empowerment and enhanced relationships between student teachers and cooperating teachers. Student teacher initiative and leadership in the design and conduct of the service-learning project appear to be key factors contributing to positive outcomes (Wade & Yarbrough, 1997).

Multicultural education

Boyle-Baise, in concert with several colleagues, has engaged in substantial work on investigating the strengths and challenges of engaging college students (including, but not limited to, pre-service social studies teachers) in service-learning for multicultural competency (Boyle-Baise, 1998, 2002; Boyle-Baise & Efiom, 2000; Boyle-Baise & Kilbane, 1999; Boyle-Baise & Langford, 2004; Boyle-Baise & Sleeter, 2000; Wade, Boyle-Baise, & O'Grady, 2001). While acknowledging that service-learning is not a panacea, a review of studies in this area show consistent and substantial positive outcomes when students' engage in service-learning experiences, including increased awareness of diverse youth, increased acceptance or affirmation of others and increased awareness of self and personal beliefs (Wade et al., 2001).

Social justice education

Findings are mixed in regard to teacher education students' abilities to think about the larger societal contexts influencing people's lives. Several studies have noted service-learning's contribution to teacher education students' complexity of thinking about social problems (Batchelder & Root, 1994; Vadeboncoeur, Rahm, Aquilera, & LeCompte, 1996). However, studies note little change in pre-service teachers' social activism, their tendency to question stereotypes, and their interest in and commitment to social justice (Boyle-Baise, 1998; Boyle-Baise & Efiom, 2000; Hones, 1997; Vadeboncoeur et al., 1996; Wade & Raba, 2003). In light of these findings, some scholars suggest emphasizing social change over charity and offering in-depth structured reflection opportunities to counteract student teachers' resilient attitudes, especially toward children and families of color (Wade, 2000). Wade, and colleagues (2001), for instance, suggest four principles for developing high quality service-learning experiences for multicultural and social justice goals. These include strong partnerships between teacher education programs and community agencies, respect for community partners' expertise, critique of the status quo and myths about children and families, and involving teacher education students in activism with children and families of color.

Thus, while service-learning in social studies teacher education has not led to questioning the status quo or being committed to social justice, experiences in methods and student teaching have resulted in several positive outcomes for pre-service teachers. High quality service-learning experiences that engage students in meaningful service with children and families, as well as effective reflection on these experiences, have the potential to deepen students' understanding of diversity, increase their knowledge of themselves and others, and enhance their self-efficacy in terms of making a difference in children's lives.

FUTURE DIRECTIONS FOR RESEARCH ON SERVICE-LEARNING IN SOCIAL STUDIES

If service-learning is to more consistently achieve the goals its advocates claim for it, the field needs a richer and deeper research base. Considerable research is needed on the impact of service-learning in social studies education and service-learning aimed at political and civic outcomes. This review points to several program factors that could be tested further (e.g., time spent on service, reflection, connecting service and politics). In particular, the field will benefit from high quality studies that include control groups with multiple measures of assessment. It is essential that studies provide clear definitions for key terms (e.g., citizenship, political efficacy, service-learning) and in-depth descriptions of program elements such as program goals, time spent on service, student voice and leadership, and teacher expertise, among others. Only with studies that fulfill these criteria will social studies scholars attain a deeper understanding of service-learning's potential to contribute to the development of informed and active citizens.

REFERENCES

Alt, M. N., & Medrich, E. A. (1994). Student outcomes from participation in community service. Prepared for the U.S. Department of Education Office of Research, Berkeley, CA: MPR Associates.

Alliance for Service Learning in Education Reform (ASLER). (1993). *Standards of quality for school-based service-learning.* Chester, VT: Author.

Astin, A. W, Sax, L. J., & Avalos, J. (1999). Long-term effects of volunteerism during the undergraduate years. *Review of Higher Education, 21*(2), 187–202.

Barber, B. (1992). *An aristocracy of everyone: The politics of education and the future of America.* New York: Ballantine.

Barber, B. (2004). *Strong democracy: Participatory politics for a new age.* Berkeley: University of California Press.

Barr, R. D., Barth, J. L., & Shermis, S. S. (1977). *Defining the social studies.* Arlington, VA: National Council for the Social Studies.

Batchelder, T. H., & Root, S. (1994). Effects of an undergraduate program to integrate academic learning and service: Cognitive, prosocial and identity outcomes. *Journal of Adolescence, 17,* 341–356.

Battistoni, R. (2000). Service learning and civic education. In S. Mann & J. J. Patrick (Eds.), *Education for civic engagement in democracy: Service learning and other promising practices.* Bloomington, ID: ERIC Clearinghouse for Social Studies/Social Science Education.

Beane, J., Turner, J., Jones, D., & Lipka, R. (1981). Long-term effects of community service programs. *Curriculum Inquiry, 11,* 143–155.

Bellah, R. N., Madsen, R. Sullivan, W. M., Swidler, A., & Tipton, S. M. (1985). *Habits of the heart: Individualism and commitment in American life.* New York: Harper and Row.

Bennett, L. M., & Bennett, S. E. (1990). *Living with leviathan: Americans coming to terms with big government.* Lawrence: University Press of Kansas.

Bennett, S. E., & Rademacher, E. W. (1997). The age of indifference revisited: Patterns of political interest, media exposure, and knowledge among Generation X. In S. C. Craig & S. E. Bennett (Eds.), *After the boom: The politics of Generation X* (pp. 21–42). Lanham, MD: Rowman & Littlefield.

Billig, S. H. (2000). Research on K-12 school-based service-learning: The evidence builds. *Phi Delta Kappan, 81*, 658–664.

Billig, S. H. (2004). Heads, hearts, and hands: The research on K-12 service-learning. In *Growing to Greatness 2004.* St. Paul, MN: National Youth Leadership Council.

Billig, S., Root, S., & Jesse, D. (2005). *The impact of participation in service-learning on high school students' civic engagement.* Denver, CO: RMC Research Corporation and Center for Information and Research on Civic Learning and Engagement (CIRCLE).

Blythe, D., Saito, R., & Berkas, T. (1997). A quantitative study of the impact of service learning programs. In A. Waterman, (Ed.), *Service learning: Applications from the research.* Mahwah, NJ: Erlbaum.

Boyle-Baise, M. (1998). Community service-learning for multicultural education: An exploratory study with preservice teachers. *Equity and excellence in education, 31*(2), 52–60.

Boyle-Baise, M. (2002). *Multicultural service-learning: Educating teachers in diverse communities.* New York: Teachers College Press.

Boyle-Baise, M., & Efiom, P. (2000). The construction of meaning: Learning from service learning. In C. O'Grady (Ed.), *Integrating service-learning and multicultural education in colleges and communities.* Mahwah, NJ: Erlbaum.

Boyle-Baise, M., & Kilbane, J. (2000). What really happens? A look inside service-learning for multicultural teacher education. *Michigan Journal of Community Service Learning, 7,* 54–64.

Boyle-Baise, M., & Langord, J. (2004). There are children here: Service learning for social justice. *Equity & Excellence in Education, 37*, 55–66.

Boyle-Baise, M., & Sleeter, C. E. (2000). Community-based service learning for multicultural teacher education. *Educational Foundations, 14*(2), 33–50.

Button, C. (1973). The development of experimental curriculum to effect the political socialization of Anglo, black and Mexican American adolescents. *Dissertation Abstracts International, 33,* 4787A–4788A.

Campbell, D. E. (2004). What you do depends on where you are: Community heterogeneity and participation. Paper presented at the Annual Meeting of the Midwest Political Science Association, Chicago.

Chi, B. S. (2002). Teaching the 'heart and soul' of citizenship: Service-learning as citizenship education. Unpublished doctoral dissertation, University of California, Berkeley.

Clark, T. (1990). Participation in Democratic Citizenship Education. *The Social Studies, 81* (5), 206–209.

Cohen, P. A., Kulik, J. A., & Kulik, C-L. C. (1982). Educational outcomes of tutoring: A meta-analysis of findings. *American Educational Research Journal, 19*, 237–248.

Conrad, D. (1991). School-community participation for social studies. In J. P. Shaver (Ed.), *Handbook of research on social studies teaching and learning* (pp. 540–548). New York: Macmillan.

Conrad, D., & Hedin, D. (1981). *National assessment of experiential education: A final report.* St. Paul: University of Minnesota, Center for Youth Development and Research.

Conrad, D., & Hedin, D. (1989). *High school community service: A review of research and programs.* Madison, WI: National Center on Effective Secondary Schools, Wisconsin Center for Educational Research, University of Wisconsin-Madison.

Conrad, D., & Hedin, D. (1991). School-based community service: What we know from research and theory. *Phi Delta Kappan, 72*(10), 754–757.

Corbett, F. C. (1977). The community involvement program: Social service as a factor in adolescent moral psychological development. Unpublished doctoral dissertation, The University of Toronto.

Davidson, M. L. (1995). The influences of mandatory service learning on the attitudes toward political involvement of a selected group of secondary school students. Unpublished doctoral dissertation, University of Maryland.

Dinkelman, T. (2001). Service-learning in student teaching. *Theory and Research in Social Education, 29*(4), 617–639.

Ehrlich, T. (1999). Civic education: Lessons learned. *PS: Political Science and Politics, 32*(2), 245–250.

Emler, N. (1992). Childhood origins of beliefs about institutional authority. *New Directions in Child Development, 56,* 65–78.

Engle, S., & Ochoa, A. (1988*). Education for democratic citizenship: Decision making in the social studies.* New York: Teachers College Press.

Eyler, J. (2002). Stretching to meet the challenge: Improving the quality of research to improve the quality of service-learning. In S. H. Billig & A. Furco (Eds.), *Service-learning through a multi-disciplinary lens.* Greenwich, CT: Information Age Publishing.

Eyler, J., & Giles, D. E., Jr. (1999). *Where's the learning in service-learning?* San Francisco: Jossey-Bass.

Fendrich, J. (1993). *Ideal citizens.* Albany: State University of New York Press.

Ferguson, P. (1991). Impacts on social and political participation. In J. P. Shaver (Ed.), *Handbook of research on social studies teaching and learning* (pp. 385–399). New York: Macmillan.

Galston, W. A. (2001). Political knowledge, political engagement, and civic education. *Annual Review of Political Science, 4,* 217–234.

Giles, D., Honnet, E. P., & Migliore, S. (1991). *Research agenda for combining service and learning in the 1990's.* Raleigh, NC: National Society for Experiential Education.

Hamilton, S. F., & Zeldin, R S. (1987). Learning civics in the community. *Curriculum Inquiry, 17,* 407–420.

Harwood, A. M. (1999, November). Developing pre-service teachers' knowledge of issues through service-learning. Paper presented to the College and University Faculty Assembly at the annual meeting of the National Council for the Social Studies, Orlando, Florida.

Hedin, D. (1987). Students as teachers: A tool for improving school. *Social Policy* 17(3), 42–47.

Hepburn, M. A. (2000). Service learning and civic education in the schools: What does recent research tell us? In S. Mann & J. J. Patrick (Eds.), *Education for civic engagement in democracy: Service learning and other promising practices.* Bloomington: Indiana University, ERIC Clearinghouse for Social Studies/Social Science Education.

Hodgkinson, V. A., & Weizman, M. S. (1992a). *Giving and volunteering in the United States.* Washington, DC: Independent Sector.

Hodgkinson, V. A., & Weizman, M. S. (1992b). *Giving and volunteering among American teenagers 12 to 17 years of age.* Washington, DC: Independent Sector.

Hones, D. (1997). Preparing teachers for diversity: A service-learning approach. Paper presented at the Annual Meeting of the American Educational Research Associaton, Chicago, IL.

Jastrzab, J.,Blomquist, J., Masker, J., & Orr, L. (1996). *Impacts of service: Final report on the evaluation of American conservation and youth service corps.* Washington, DC: Corporation for National and Community Service.

Kahne, J., & Westheimer, J. (2002). *The limits of efficacy: Educating active citizens for a democratic society.* New York: Surdna Foundation, Inc.

Levison, L. (1986). *Community service programs in independent schools.* Boston, MA: National Association of Independent Schools.

Marks, H. (1994). The effect of participation in school-sponsored community service programs on student attitudes toward social responsibility. Unpublished doctoral dissertation, University of Michigan.

Maryland Student Service Alliance. (1995). *Maryland's best practices: An improvement guide for school-based service-learning.* Baltimore: Maryland Department of Education.

McAdam, D. (1989). The biographical consequences of activism. *American Sociological Review, 54,* 744–759.

Melchior, A. (1998). *National evaluation of Learn and Serve America School-based programs: Final report.* Waltham, MA: Brandeis University Center for Human Resources and Abt Associates.

Melchior, A., Frees, J., LaCava, L., Kingsley, C. & Nahas, J. (1999). *Summary Report: National Evaluation of Learn and Serve America.* Waltham, MA: Center for Human Resources, Brandeis University.

Merryfield, M. & Subedi, B. (2001). Decolonizing the mind for world-centered global education. In W. Ross (Ed.), *The social studies curriculum* (pp. 277–290). Albany: State University of New York Press.

Metz, E., McLellan, J., & Youniss, J. (2003). Types of voluntary service and adolescents' civic development. *Journal of Adolescent Research, 18*(2), 188–203.

Metz, E. C., & Youniss, J. (2005). Longitudinal gains in civic development through school-based required service. *Political Psychology, 26*(3), 413–437.

Morgan, W., & Streb, M. (2001). Building citizenship: How student voice in social-learning develops civic values. *Social Science Quarterly, 82*(1), 154–169.

National Association of Secretaries of State. (1999). *New Millenium Project – Part 1: American youth attitudes on politics, citizenship, government, and voting.* Washington, DC: Author.

NCSS (1979). Revision of the National Council for the Social Studies curriculum guidelines. *Social Education, 43,* 261–273.

NCSS (1980). *National Council for the Social Studies essentials of social studies.* Washington, DC: Author.

NCSS (1989). *Social studies for citizens of a strong and free nation – Report of the National Council for the Social Studies task force on scope and sequence.* Washington, DC: Author.

NCSS (1994). *National Council for the Social Studies curriculum standards for the social studies.* Washington, DC: Author.

NCSS (2001). Service-learning: An essential component of citizenship education. *Social Education, 65*(4), 240–241.

Newmann, F. M., & Rutter, R. A. (1983). *The effects of high school community service programs on students' social development.* Madison: Wisconsin Center for Educational Research, University of Wisconsin.

Niemi, R. G., & Junn, J. (1998). *Civic education: What makes students learn?* New Haven, CT: Yale University Press.

Niemi, R., Hepburn, M., & Chapman, C. (2000). Community service by high school students: A cure for civic ills? *Political Behavior, 22,* 45–69.

Parker, W. (1989). Participatory citizenship: Civics in the strong sense. *Social Education, 53,* 353–354.

Parker, W., & Jarolimek, J. (1984). *Citizenship and the critical role of the social studies.* Washington, DC: National Council for the Social Studies.

Patrick, J. J. (2000). Introduction to education for civic engagement in democracy. In S. M. A. J. J. Patrick (Ed.), *Education for Civic Engagement in Democracy: Service Learning and Other Promising Practices.* Bloomington: Indiana University, ERIC Clearinghouse for Social Studies/Social Science Education.

Pratte, R. (1988). *The civic imperative: Examining the need for civic education.* New York: Teachers College Press.

Pereira, C., & Rodriguez, K. (1997). Linking violence prevention and good social studies. *Social Education, 61*(5), 282–287.

Perry, J., & Katula, M. C. (2001). Does service affect citizenship? *Administration and Society, 33,* 330–333.

Raskoff, S. A., & Sundeen, R. A. (2000). Community service programs in high schools. *Law and Contemporary Problems, 62*(4), 73–111.

Raskoff, S. A., & Sundeen, R. A. (2001). Cultural diversity and high school community service: The relationships between ethnicity and students' perceptions. *Nonprofit and Voluntary Sector Quarterly, 30*(4), 720–746.

Riedel, E. (2002). The impact of high school community service programs on students' feelings of civic obligation. *American Politics Research, 30*(5), 499–527.

Root, S. (1997). School-based service: A review of research for teacher educators. In J. A. Erickson & J. B. Anderson (Eds.), *Learning with the community: Concepts and models for service-learning in teacher education.* Washington, DC: American Association of Higher Education.

Rosenhan, D. L. (1970). The natural socialization of altruistic autonomy. In J. Macauley & L. Berkowitz (Eds.), *Altruism and helping behaviors* (pp. 251–268). Orlando, FL: Academic Press.

Rosenthal, S., Feiring, C., & Lewis, M. (1998). Political volunteering from late adolescence to young adulthood: Patterns and predictors. *Journal of Social Issues, 54*(3), 477–493.

Rutter, R. A., & Newmann, F. M. (1989). The potential of community service to enhance civic responsibility. *Social Education, 53,* 371–374.

Scales, P. C., Blyth, D. A., Berkas, T. H., & Kielsmeier, J.C. (2000). The effects of service-learning on middle school students' social responsibility and academic success. *Journal of Early Adolescence, 20*(3), 332–358.

Scales, P. C., & Blyth, D. A. (1997). Effects of service-learning on youth: What we know and what we need to know, *Generator,* 6–9.

Scales, P. C., & Rochlkepartain, E. (2004). *Community service and service-learning in U.S. public schools: Findings from a national survey.* Minneapolis: Search Institute.

Schervish, P. G., Hodgkinson, V. A., Gates, M. & Associates. (1995). *Care and community in modern society: Passing on the tradition of service to future generations.* Washington, DC: Independent Sector.

Schug, M. C., & Beery, R. (1984). *Community study: Applications and opportunities.* Washington, DC: National Council for the Social Studies.

Shaver, J. P. (Ed.) (1977). *Building rationales for citizenship education.* Washington, DC: National Council for the Social Studies.

Shermis, S., & Barth, J. (1982). Teaching for passive citizenship: A critique of philosophical assumptions. *Theory and Research in Social Education, 10,* 17–37.

Shumer, R. (1999). Service, social studies, and citizenship: Connections for the new century. *ERIC Digest.*

Shumer, R., & Belbas, B. (1996). What we know about service learning. *Education and Urban Society, 28,* 208–223.

Skinner, R., & Chapman, C. (1999). *Service-learning and community service in K-12 public schools.* Washington, D.C.: National Center for Education Statistics.

Stagg, A. (2004). *Service-learning in K-12 public education.* College Park, MD: CIRCLE, School of Public Affairs.

Sturges, A., Barfoo E., Friesen, D., Weaver, R., & Wood, F. (1977, March). High school graduates of the stormy 1960's: What happened to them? Paper presented at the Annual Conference of the Association of Supervision and Curriculum Development, Houston, TX.

Teixeira, R. A. (1992). *The disappearing American voter.* Washington, DC: Brookings Institution.

Vadeboncoeur, J., Rahm, J., Aquilera, D., & LeCompte, M. D. (1996). Building democratic character through community experiences in teacher education, *Education and Urban Society, 28*(2), 189–207.

Verba, S., Schlozman, K. L., & Brady, H. E. (1995). *Voice and equality, civic voluntarism in American politics.* Cambridge, MA: Harvard University Press.

Wade, R. (1995). Developing active citizens: Community service-learning in social studies teacher education. *The Social Studies,* 122–128.

Wade, R. (Ed.). (1997). *Community service-learning: A guide to including service in the public school curriculum.* Albany: State University of New York Press.

Wade, R. (2000). Service-learning for multicultural teaching competency: Insights from the literature for teacher educators. *Equity and Excellence in Education, 33*(3), 21–30.

Wade, R., Boyle-Baise, L., & O'Grady, C. (2001). Multicultural service-learning in teacher education. In J. B. Anderson, K. J. Swick, & J. Yff (Eds.), *Service-learning in teacher education: Enhancing the growth of new teachers, their students, and communities.* Washington, DC: American Association of Colleges of Teacher Education.

Wade, R., & Raba, S. (2003). The Chicago experience: Border crossing for social studies preservice teachers. *Theory and Research in Social Education, 31*(2), 153–173.

Wade, R., & Saxe, D. (1996). Community service-learning in the social studies: Historical roots, empirical evidence, critical issues. *Theory and Research in Social Education, 24*(4), 331–359.

Wade, R., & Yarbrough, D. B. (1997). Community service-learning in student teaching: Toward the development of an active citizenry. *Michigan Journal of Community Service-Learning,* 42–55.

Walker, T. (2002). Service as a pathway to political participation: What research tells us. *Applied Developmental Science, 6*(4), 183–188.

Waterman, A. (1993). Conducting research on reflective activities in service learning. In H. C. Silcox, (Ed.), *A how-to guide to reflection.* Philadelphia: Brighton Press.

Westheimer, J., & Kahne, J. (2000, January 26). Service learning required. *Education Week.* Retrieved from: http://wwweducationweek.org/ew/ew.

Wilson, T. C. (1974). An alternative community-based secondary education program and student political development. *Dissertation Abstracts International 35,* 5797A.

Wirthlin Group. (1995). *The Prudential spirit of youth community survey.* Newark, NJ: Prudential.

Yates, M., & Youniss, J. (1998). Community service and political identity development in adolescents. *Journal of Social Studies, 54,* 495–512.

Youniss, J., McLellan, J. A., & Yates, M. (1997). What we know about engendering civic identity. *American Behavioral Scientist, 40,* 620–632.

8 Controversial issues and democratic discourse

Diana Hess

University of Wisconsin–Madison

For almost a century, various advocates of the social studies have called for the infusion of controversial issues into the curriculum. In the early 20th century, teachers were encouraged to focus on the "problems of democracy." By the 1960s, curriculum was introduced that focused on a "jurisprudential" approach to analyzing historic and contemporary policy issues. More recently, the teaching of "controversial public issues" has come to describe a social studies lesson, unit, course, or curriculum that engages students in learning about issues, analyzing them, deliberating alternative solutions, and often taking and supporting a position on which solutions may be based.

Just as different labels have been used to describe this type of social studies, different definitions of what constitutes an "issue" have been advanced. For example, in an approach advanced in the early 1950s, Hunt and Metcalf (1955) advocate the inclusion of issues related to "taboo" topics (such as sexuality and racism) in the curriculum, while Oliver and Shaver's approach (1966) focuses on policy issues that include the weighing and balancing of competing "democratic" values (such as liberty and equality). Some issues are defined as inherently public, while others, such as the moral dilemmas in Kohlberg's approach (1981), are personal decisions for an individual to consider. In addition, other dimensions of how "issues" are conceptualized and defined include time (an issue of the past, the present, or possibly the future), place (local, state, national, global), and scope (ranging from broad perennial issues to more narrowly focused "case" issues).

Along with the multiple definitions of what constitutes a controversial issue in social studies, a plethora of rationales exist for why such issues should be included in the curriculum. The most frequently articulated reason for including controversial issues in the curriculum is the connection between learning how to deliberate controversial issues, especially those that focus on public problems, and participating effectively in a democratic society. This connection hinges on a definition of democracy that requires people to engage in high-quality public talk. For example, Mansbridge (1991) posits that, "Democracy involves public discussion of common problems, not just silent counting of individual hands" (p. 122). Those who hold this conception of democracy advance the inclusion of controversial issues in the school curriculum as a form of authentic instruction to prepare young people to participate fully and competently in a form of political engagement that is important in "the world outside of school" (Newmann & Wehlage, 1995). Other rationales for controversial issues in the social studies curriculum do not focus on developing students' competence in discussing issues per se; instead, learning about controversial issues acts as a vehicle for other outcomes, such as developing an understanding and commitment to democratic values, increasing interest in engagement in public life, learning important content, improving critical thinking, and building more sophisticated interpersonal skills. Finally, many social studies educators support controversial issues instruction because it is highly engaging to students and may enhance their affective assessments of social studies classes.

While there is no shortage of theoretical and practical claims about what young people *could* or *should* learn from a social studies curriculum with at least some focus on controversial issues, to date, we do not have a clear understanding of what students *do* learn and why. As Hahn (1996) points out in her review of the research on issues-centered education, one of the central problems with researching what students learn from controversial issues is that there are so many different approaches, and virtually all of them are embedded in a course of study that includes a number of other components as well. This makes it difficult to identify precisely what influence the study of controversial issues has on the outcomes that many of its proponents hope will be achieved. Moreover, it is highly unusual to find schools or school districts that have infused controversial issues in the curricula in a systematic way that ensures that students will have multiple opportunities throughout a number of school years to engage in issues-centered social studies. Consequently, researchers often study the effects of one issues-centered course and find, not surprisingly, that even exceptionally well-taught courses do not result in huge gains on measurable outcomes (Hahn & Tocci, 1990; Hess & Posselt, 2002). Just as it would not be prudent to expect students to learn how to write well in a one-semester course, it is clearly problematic to expect a relatively short course to help students achieve many of the challenging, complex, and sophisticated outcomes that we expect from issues-centered social studies, such as the ability to develop and critique whether sufficient evidence exists to support a particular position.

Notwithstanding these definitional ambiguities and research challenges, the historic support for controversial issues in social studies clearly continues. In fact, evidence indicates that the advocacy for such an approach to social studies has become more widespread and mainstream. For example, the broadly disseminated Civic Mission of the Schools Report (2003) makes only six research-based recommendations for improving civic education in the United States (Carnegie Corporation of New York & CIRCLE). One of these is to "incorporate discussion of current local, national, and international issues and events into the classroom, particularly those that young people view as important to their lives" (pp. 26–27). This recommendation is based on accumulated evidence from research dating back to the 1970s, which indicates that teaching young people about controversial issues in a supportive classroom environment that encourages the analysis and critique of multiple and competing viewpoints is positively correlated with important civic outcomes (p. 41). The Civic Mission of the Schools report summarizes the civic power of controversial issues discussions in a bold and straightforward manner:

> Studies that ask young people whether they had opportunities to discuss current issues in a classroom setting have consistently found that those who did participate in such discussions have a greater interest in politics, improved critical thinking and communications skills, more civic knowledge, and more interest in discussing public affairs out of school. Compared to other students, they also are more likely to say that they will vote and volunteer as adults. (p. 8)

In this chapter, I describe recent research in controversial issues teaching and learning in the United States. I seek to build on the excellent existing research reviews of social studies scholars on this topic (Hahn, 1991, 1996) by concentrating on research about controversial issues teaching and learning since 1990. Since the vast majority of research on controversial issues in social studies focuses on the discussion of such issues,

I also concentrate on that pedagogical approach instead of other potential approaches, such as simulations and writing assignments. I set the stage by exploring the prevalence of controversial issues in the social studies. Then, I turn to the key players in this enterprise—teachers—and explain what factors and forces encourage or inhibit teachers from including controversial issues in their curriculum, as well as what teachers who are unusually skillful at this type of social studies teaching do in practice. Next, I focus on student learning, first by explaining the various student outcomes that advocates of controversial issues teaching advance, and then by analyzing and evaluating the extent to which the research supports these claims. What becomes clear is that although we know quite a bit about controversial issues teaching and learning, there is much that we do not understand. Consequently, I conclude the chapter with recommendations for future research.

THE PREVALENCE OF CONTROVERSIAL
ISSUES IN SOCIAL STUDIES

Although many teachers and their students report that social studies classes are rich with controversial issues, it remains extremely difficult to assess how many and with what frequency students learn about controversial issues in their courses. Some evidence indicates that the vast majority of teachers report an emphasis on such issues in their curricula. For example, Engel (1993) surveyed 337 secondary social studies and English teachers in eight counties in a Midwestern state about their views on the examination of controversial issues in their classrooms, finding that 75% of the teachers report spending up to 25% of class time examining controversial issues. Students also report that their social studies classes include a focus on controversial issues. In an Internet-based survey of more than 1,000 15- to 25-year-olds, 69% report that they often (48.3%) or sometimes (28.7%) discussed political and social issues on which people have different opinions in social studies classes (Andolina, Jenkins, Keeter, & Zukin, 2002). Similarly, in the 1999 International Association for the Evaluation of Educational Achievement (IEA) study of civic education (Torney-Purta, Lehmann, Oswald, & Schultz, 2001), 75% of the 2,811 ninth graders from 124 nationally representative public and private schools in the United States report that their social studies classes included the discussion of controversial issues.

However, in another survey given to 278 randomly selected public high school social studies teachers in Florida, Phillips (1997) reports that while 63% of the teachers say they experienced controversial issues instruction in their own pre-collegiate education, only 23% say they discuss controversial issues with their students more than 25% of the time. Moreover, in the first phase of the IEA study that involves the development of a detailed case study of civic education in the United States based on multiple data sources, researchers find "little evidence in our focus groups of such an approach [issues-centered instruction] being widely used" (Hahn, 1999, p. 593).

Additionally, although discussion is often advocated as a key vehicle for the study of controversial issues, fairly large-scale observational studies involving middle and high school social studies classes report virtually no classroom discussion (Nystrand, Gamoran, & Carbonara, 1998). Moreover, most of the discussions that do occur do not focus on controversial issues (Kahne, Rodriguez, Smith, & Thiede, 2000). Martin Nystrand and his colleagues analyzed discourse in 106 middle and high school social studies classes, each observed four times throughout the school year, reporting that "despite considerable lip service among teachers to 'discussion,' we found little discussion in any classes" (Nystrand et al., 1998, p. 36). To account for this, Nystrand explains that teachers typically conflate some form of recitation (such as the familiar IRE pattern of teacher-initiated question, student response, and teacher evaluation) with discussion. Defining discussion as the free exchange of information among three or more participants (which may include the teacher), the researchers note that they did observe some discussions, but that 90.33% of what they viewed involved no discussion, and the remaining discussion time was brief: on average, 42 seconds per class in eighth-grade classes and 31.2 seconds per class in ninth-grade classes. Kahne and his colleagues (2000) share a similar report in their observations of 135 middle and high school social studies classes in the Chicago Public Schools, finding that controversial issues receive scant attention. In over 80% of the classes there was no mention of a social problem, and even when problems were mentioned, there was rarely any discussion of possible solutions, connections to modern times, or action.

Clearly, a contradiction exists within the literature. Although many teachers and students report social studies classes as being rich with controversial issues discussion, when researchers observe social studies classes they rarely find discussion of any sort and little attention to controversial issues. These perplexing and contradictory findings have significant implications because much of the research about the effects of a curriculum rich with controversial issues is correlational and hinges on students' self reports of whether they experience this type of social studies instruction.

Many young people say they are in classes with discussion of controversial issues, and based on that, researchers report positive correlations between discussion and other valued civic outcomes. For example, in the IEA study students were asked whether their "teachers encourage us to discuss political or social issues about which people have different opinions" and whether "students bring up current political events for discussion in class." These items were part of open classroom climate construct that measures the "extent to which students experience their classrooms as places to investigate issues and explore their opinions and those of their peers" (Torney-Purta et al., 2001, p. 138). The IEA researchers report that an open classroom climate for discussion is a significant predictor of civic knowledge, support for democratic values, participation in political discussion, and political engagement, as measured by whether young people say they will vote when they are legally able. Similarly, Andolina and her colleagues (2002) find that young people who report participating in open discussions in high school are much more likely to engage in a variety of civic and political behaviors, such as following political news, signing petitions, and participating in boycotts. It is difficult to identify what might account for the difference between what students report occurs in their classes and what researchers who have conducted observational studies in many classrooms report. It may simply be a definitional problem. Researchers report that students and teachers alike tend to conflate classroom talk with discussion (Larson, 1997; Hess & Ganzler, 2006), which may account for why so many teachers and students report the inclusion of controversial issues discussion in their classes. Evidence to support this explanation can be gleaned from Richardson's study (2006) about what high school students think IEA survey questions mean. Richardson finds that the majority of students do not make a distinction between a controversial issue and a current event, and that discussion is defined broadly to include any talk with a teacher—even if it occurs outside of class (p. 171).

In the first phase of a 4-year mixed method study involving 260 high school students in 15 schools, researchers report that discussions of issues are not necessary in order for students to label their classroom climate as open (Hess & Ganzler, 2006). As long as some opportunities exist for students to voice their views on issues or topics, coupled with a teacher who students perceive as non-indoctrinating and non-authoritarian, students tend to say the climate is open. These students may mean that they feel free to voice their opinions, which presumes that there are opportunities for opinions to be voiced. That is, an open classroom climate is not a proxy for issues discussions, but instead means that students are in classrooms with at least some modicum of a democratic ethos where students believe they can talk and there is some inclusion of issues. While discussion experts do not equate classroom talk with discussion (see Nystrand et al., 1998; Parker, 2003), it appears that students do.

The implications of this finding are potentially far-reaching since the primary basis for the claim that controversial issues discussions affect political engagement is based on students' assessment of whether they are in an open classroom climate (e.g., one that includes issues discussions). Yet it may be that such discussions are not the variable that matters, but instead what is necessary is simply a sense from students that they are in a classroom where they can speak, and occasionally things are said about issues. If so, then the current scale researchers use to assess an open classroom climate does not distinguish between students who are in issues-rich discussion classes and those who are simply in classes with student talk. This raises the possibility that in classes that include more robust and frequent full-fledged issues discussions, the effects on students' political engagement may be above and beyond what occurs when students are in classes they simply perceive as open.

TEACHERS' BELIEFS AND PRACTICES

Even though it is unclear how prevalent controversial issues are in social studies classes, a number of recent studies investigate the beliefs and practices of teachers who do include controversial issues in the curriculum. While it is clear that teaching students to discuss controversial issues is an extremely complex enterprise that can be implemented successfully in a variety of ways, some similarities among teachers who achieve this appear to matter if such instruction is to be effective. This section of the chapter is divided into two parts: teachers' beliefs and practices. The belief section focuses on three key questions: Why do teachers include controversial issues in their courses? What criteria do teachers use to select which issues students will discuss? How do teachers conceptualize their role as it relates to the disclosure of their own views on the issues to their students? The second section on teacher practices examines how teachers who are particularly skillful teach their students to participate more effectively in controversial issues discussions.

The literature suggests that the primary reason teachers include controversial issues in their courses is because it aligns with their conceptions of democracy and the purpose of schooling. For example, Rossi's (1995) in-depth case study of a teacher who has created a course that focuses primarily on discussion using the Oliver and Shaver (1966) approach illustrates how the teacher links public talk about public problems to a healthy democracy because he sees a connection between such talk and good public policy. The teacher, Mr. Lansbury, directs the entire course toward the goal of teaching students how to participate in policy talk. Similarly, in two other case studies of middle and high school teachers, the primary reason given for infusing the curriculum with controversial issues is a belief that students need to learn how to analyze and take positions on such issues in order to participate effectively in a democracy (Hess, 2002; Hess & Posselt, 2002).

However, while teachers agree on why students should learn controversial issues, there is decidedly less agreement about what constitutes a controversial issue, and which issues are appropriate to include in the curriculum. In one study (Hess, 2002), the researcher asks middle and high school teachers to analyze a list of topics that sparked controversy in society (such as abortion, gay rights, and affirmative action), and finds significant disagreement about whether some topics give rise to legitimate matters of controversy. For example, one teacher argued that gay rights issues were not controversial. Instead, he characterized them as human rights issues for which there were answers he wanted his students to build and believe. Other teachers made the same point with respect to other issues, suggesting that one threshold criterion that teachers use to select issues is based on their personal views of whether they think the issue is legitimately in the public square.

Considerable evidence also suggests that many teachers, especially those with less experience, will not select issues that may be upsetting to the community or to students, or are simply deemed "too hot to handle." For example, in a survey described above, Phillips (1997) finds that teachers ranked abortion as the most controversial issue and were unwilling to include it in the curriculum; they also were reticent to include issues about pornography or creationism in fear of community reprisals. Another frequently cited reason for keeping an issue out of the curriculum is that the discussion of it may be particularly upsetting to some students. For example, one teacher refused to include issues about gay rights in her classes because she feared students may not talk about them with sensitivity and that gay students in her class may feel uncomfortable (Hess, 2002).

Regardless of what issues teachers include in the curriculum, they must make a decision about whether to disclose their own views on the issues to their students. Although a number of frameworks for how to think through the question of disclosure have been proposed (Kelly, 1986; Hess, 2005), until recently, no research existed that probed how teachers made sense of this critical question. Miller-Lane and his colleagues (2006) begin to fill this gap with their study of four middle and eight high school social studies teachers in a rural county located in a northeastern state. By selecting teachers from the same community, the researchers seek to understand how teachers' perceptions of community norms would influence their decisions about disclosure. The teachers were presented with Kelly's (1986) framework of four difference stances that could be taken on the disclosure issue, including committed partiality in which the teacher fosters discussion, is committed to disclosing, and encourages students to do the same, and neutral impartiality in which teachers foster discussion, but are committed to not disclosing their own views to students. All but three of the teachers rejected disclosure of their position in favor of the role of an impartial facilitator. It is notable that all of the middle school teachers supported this position, and just over half of the high school teachers agreed. The teachers rejected disclosure because they were concerned that the tolerant environment they were trying to create in their classrooms would not exist in the larger community, and they feared a community backlash that would make it difficult to include such issues in the curriculum. The teachers recognized that teaching is not value neutral, but they preferred to disclose their commitment to a set of transcendent values such as tolerance, justice, and equality rather than disclose a point of view on a particular controversial issue.

In a recent study of six high school government courses in upstate New York, Niemi and Niemi (2007) report that while five teachers did not explicitly share their opinions on controversial issues (including who they will vote for in hotly contested elections), they are hardly neutral or silent about their views on the political system and their assessment of individual politicians, They found that educators regularly made cynical and derogatory remarks about political leaders (in one especially stunning example the superintendent of the school districts poked his head into the classroom and asked, "Are you talking about Hilary Rotten Clinton?" (p. 43) and communicate cynicism and impoverished and thin views of how individuals can or should participate politically. Niemi and Niemi raise concerns that teachers' willingness to share their own cynicism about the political system and political leaders may be a form of "teacher disclosure" that is anti-thetical to the goals of democratic education:

> But the extent to which teachers made derogatory comments about the knowl-
> edge and ability of ordinary citizens, about political leaders, about governmental

institutions, and about political processes (campaigns, law-making) was at times overwhelming. That a presidential debate made you "dumber," that Kermit the Frog was the best candidate, that our "wonderful" Congress was "idiotic," and so on, hardly suggest healthy, serious-minded criticism. That teachers and even a superintendent resorted to name-calling is even more indicative of a degree of cynicism greater than one might wish for among those teaching about democratic governance. (Niemi & Niemi, 2007, p. 56)

In summary, teachers' beliefs about what constitutes an issue, what issues should be included in the curriculum, and whether they should disclose their own views, illustrates that most teachers do not include issues in the curriculum because they want to indoctrinate students into a particular point of view. Instead, they seek a way to engage students in talking about their own views within the bounds of community norms. Of course, an argument can be made that the determination of what constitutes an issue or not is a de facto form of indoctrination, since the decision may influence whether students think a particular topic has multiple sides or one agreed-upon answer. However, few teachers will state explicitly that they include controversial issues in the curriculum because they want students to form a particular perspective.

The concern about not indoctrinating students is evident also in the pedagogical practices of teachers who appear especially skillful at teaching students to discuss controversial issues. Many of the teachers showcased in case studies that examine their practice in some detail appear especially interested in involving their students in the examination and critique of multiple and conflicting points of view in an atmosphere that minimizes intimidation (Bickmore, 1993; Rossi, 1995; Brice, 2002; Hess 2002; Hess & Posselt, 2002; Beck, 2003).

While tremendous variance occurs among the practices of the teachers in these studies, the central tendencies that emerge are deliberately teaching students discussion skills and distinguishing between "bull sessions" and analytic discussions by working to ensure that students have an understanding of key background information so they are prepared to participate. These teachers also attend to the careful teaching and monitoring of civil norms so the discussions do not become so heated that students feel intimidated, and they use a variety of discussion models, group configurations, and facilitating moves to encourage the greatest possible number of students to participate verbally. Finally, the teachers encourage students to confront each issue and evaluate and critique multiple and competing perspectives. Bickmore (1993) labels this "conflictual pedagogy" and finds that it engages students when used in combination with "conflictual content" that presents students with differing points of view on important issues.

In spite of these consistencies, no single model or style of controversial issues discussion emerges out of studies of these skillful teachers. Some teachers prefer students to talk in small groups, others in large groups or as a whole class. The teachers also make different decisions about whether to require all students to participate verbally in every discussion or to encourage this participation in more subtle ways. Key differences also emerge in the manner of assessment and evaluation of students' performance in controversial issues discussion. Teachers who formally evaluate their students' participation also tend to be much more explicit about the kind of talk that is valued. For example, Rossi (1995) finds that the teachers who use the Public Issues Model used direct instruction to ensure that students understood the different discussion moves valued in the model, such as asking questions about value conflicts, reasoning by analogy, and distinguishing between factual and definitional issues. Additionally, Hess (2002) finds a tension between authenticity and accountability when analyzing the different assessment and evaluation practices of teachers. One reason not to formally evaluate students' participation is that it caused the discussions to be less authentic because, as one teacher said, "it was paying kids to talk" (p. 32). Conversely, teachers who did formally evaluate their students believed it enabled them to hold students accountable and communicated alignment between what they value (e.g., high quality issues talk) and what they assess. Thus, while no one model or approach to effective controversial issues teaching exists, it appears that skillful teaching in this realm is marked by a combination of explicit teaching of discussion skills so students know what they are aiming for, adequate preparation so students have enough information to talk about, and the creation of an environment that will encourage students to want to participate.

WHAT STUDENTS LEARN FROM CONTROVERSIAL ISSUES

Although many teachers include controversial issues in their curriculum because they want students to be more effective participants in the kinds of public discourse that healthy democracies require, this approach to social studies has also been advocated as a way to promote other important student outcomes. Specifically, advocates advance issues discussions as a way to teach students the meaning of democratic values and enhance their commitment to those values, increase students' understanding of important social studies content, improve students' critical thinking skills, and build their interpersonal skills, especially their ability to work well in groups. Issues advocates also suggest a positive relationship between this form of instruction, interest in politics, and actual political and civic engagement.

Research on the development of democratic values provides strong support for the inclusion of controversial issues in social studies. The strongest line of research in this area involves the relationship between issues discussions (and other forms of conflictual pedagogy) and the development of tolerance, as examined in a study of 338 middle and high school students (Avery, Bird, Johnstone, Sullivan, & Thalhammer 1992). Defining tolerance as the willingness to extend civil liberties to groups with whom one disagrees, the researchers worked with a group of teachers to develop a 4-week unit that involved a variety of active learning strategies, many focusing on controversial issues related to freedom of expression. Using a quasi-experimental design with control and experimental classes, the researchers find that the curriculum causes most students to move from mild intolerance to mild tolerance, regardless of their previous achievement levels in schools, their gender, or their socioeconomic status (SES). Moreover, in a follow-up 4 weeks later, these gains do not dissipate. However, for a small number of students who demonstrated low levels of self-esteem and high levels of authoritarianism (N = 22), the curriculum actually causes them to become less tolerant. While this backlash effect is troubling, it is significant that the effect of the curriculum for most students is increased tolerance.

Given the increased emphasis on standardized tests in social studies and other subjects, many teachers report that it is hard for them to justify spending time on issues discussions unless they can show a link to enhanced content knowledge. However, much of the content that students might learn from issues discussions is not what is typically covered on the standardized tests, which research shows are powerfully shaping decisions social studies teachers make about what and how to teach. It is reasonable to expect high quality issues discussion to cause students to build content understanding. David Harris (1996) explains the rationale for this claim: "The effort to produce coherent language in response to a question of public policy puts knowledge in a meaningful context, making it more likely to be understood and remembered" (p. 289). However, it is difficult to design studies to assess what impact issues discussions have on students' content knowledge because the content students might learn varies with each issue.

Notwithstanding this obstacle, some researchers try to avoid the problem by developing content-related outcomes that might be achieved regardless of the content of the issues students discuss. For example, to test what difference the discussion of public issues has on what students learn, researchers implement a study that compares high school students who learned about the background of an issue and then discussed it in classrooms with teachers trained in the public issues approach against high school students who were exposed to the same background but did not discuss the issue (Johnston, Anderman, Milne, Klenk, & Harris, 1994). The background was delivered via a Channel One news program that focused on differing views on a public issue related to the news. Students in both classes participated in a constructed dialogue session before and after viewing the program and then took an assessment to measure their ability to analyze a public issues discussion. This instrument was designed to assess whether students' critical thinking skills as applied to public issues improved. Students in both classes also took a test on their knowledge of current events. The students in the experimental group scored higher on the current events test and also showed more improvement in their ability to analyze public issues discussions. However, their discussion skills as measured by the post-show constructed dialogue sessions did not improve relative to the control group.

There is also evidence that students in government classes that include local issues learn more about how change could be brought about in their communities. Kahne and his colleagues (in press) use a quasi-experimental design to assess what effect a curriculum that includes learning about problems in the community, learning how local government works to address these problems, and learning about issues the students find personally relevant promotes various civic norms, knowledge of social networks, and trust. Personal relevance was the strongest predictor of civic outcomes with significant relationships to all outcomes they measured. With respect to social networks, students were much more likely to say that they know who to contact if they have concerns about their community, know what resources are available to help with them with a community project, and know how to work effectively with organizations in their community when they were in classes that included a focus on issues that the students considered personally relevant to their lives (p. 14).

HOW ISSUES DISCUSSION INFLUENCES WHAT STUDENTS DO

Although the student outcomes previously described are often viewed as important by social studies educators, they pale in comparison to the claim that participation in issues discussions can influence students' actual civic and political engagement. A quasi-experimental longitudinal study of the impact of Kids Voting USA, an interactive curriculum that includes classroom discussions of controversial issues (McDevitt & Kiousis, 2006) shows students who participated in the curriculum were much more likely to engage in acts associated with deliberative democracy than students without such exposure. It is important to note that although the curriculum has a number of components, three were found to have the most dramatic influence on the long-term civic development of young people: frequent classroom discussions of election issues, teacher encouragement for expressing opinions, and student participation in get-out-the-vote drives (p. 3). In terms of impact, the study shows the positive effects of the curriculum on media use, political knowledge, issues discussions with friends and family and the size of discussion network, some deliberative habits, volunteering, campus activism, and some forms of conventional and unconventional political activism.

To summarize, there is evidence that participating in controversial issues discussions can build pro-democratic values (such as tolerance), enhance content understanding, and cause students to engage more in the political world. However, it is crucial to point out that much more research is needed to understand the causal pathways between issues discussions and these outcomes. Moreover, as Avery and her colleagues report (1992), for a minority of students, issues discussions appear to have the opposite impact of what curriculum developers intend.

HOW STUDENTS EXPERIENCE CONTROVERSIAL ISSUES DISCUSSIONS

Even though there is evidence that participating in discussions of controversial issues has positive effects on outcomes that many social studies educators value, it is important to recognize that classrooms are complicated social spaces experienced differentially by students. Rossi (1995) reports that some of the students in Mr. Lansbury's controversial issues course found it engaging and relevant, while some others thought it was dull. Similarly, Hess and Posselt (2002) report that even though the vast majority of the students in the two classes they studied liked the issues discussions and became better and more frequent participants as a consequence of the course, for some students this was not the case. In particular, for students who were wary of their peers' judgment, especially from classmates they perceived as popular and powerful, the controversial issues discussions provoked anxiety and anger. Other students began the course with these fears and became more comfortable over time as they gained confidence in their ability to contribute to the discussions and found that doing so did not provoke negative judgments from their classmates. However, Hemmings' study of discussions in two high school classes (2000) illustrates how sociocultural divisions within each class influenced how and why students participated. She found that there were deep divisions based on race and class that were masked by students' displays of tolerance.

Hemmings' finding raises a troubling challenge for teachers who want to include controversial issues discussions in their courses. Much of the theory supporting issue discussion is based on the idea that it is important to see diversity as a deliberative strength (Gutmann, 1999; Parker, 2003). By this logic, controversial issues in classrooms with students who are similarly situated would not yield much because there would not be enough difference of opinion to produce a meaningful consideration of competing perspectives. Simply put, the possibility that students will come to respect and value the opinions of others as a consequence of the discussions cannot be realized if they are not given the opportunity to deliberate in a heterogeneous group. But just as diversity can be a deliberative strength, it can also re-inscribe social divisions if students feel they are being silenced or simply do not want to voice opinions that differ from the majority. Moreover, David Campbell's analysis (2005) of the IEA data from the United States suggests an inverse relationship between exposure to controversial issues and racial diversity in a class. Specifically, he finds that African Americans and Anglos are more likely to report issues discussions as the proportion of students in a class who share their racial identify rises—what he calls the "racial solidarity effect" (p. 16).

While most of the research about how issues discussions work are based in classrooms and involve face-to face discussion, there are a number of researchers who are investigating how students experience on-line discussions. One study compares students' experiences in both formats—face-to-face and online (Larson, 2003) and finds that the online format sparked the participation of some students who often were silent in classroom discussions. However, there were drawbacks to online discussion, too. In particular, the online discussions took longer for students because they had to read the postings. More significantly, Larson noted that many students simply responded to the teacher's prompts instead of to their classmates' comments—creating an online environment akin to IRE that included few of the hallmarks of effective issues discussions.

It should not be a surprise that students experience controversial issues discussions in different ways—certainly, that is the case for virtually all pedagogical practices. However, the fact that students' participation in controversial issues discussions are typically public makes it important to create a classroom environment that is interpreted by students as welcoming, otherwise discussions may reify some of the inequalities that exist in the deliberative world outside of school. That being said, even though Campbell's research (2005) suggests that teachers may be more likely to engage students in issues discussions in racially homogeneous classrooms, it is important for students to learn how to discuss issues in heterogeneous groups, which is why Parker (2003) argues that tracking practices in schools are harmful to issues deliberations. Moreover, in classrooms where students have strong ideological differences that are activated by the teacher through controversial issues discussions, there is evidence that students begin to see political conflict as a normal and necessary part of democracy (Hess & Ganzler, 2006). This normalization of conflict is linked to enhanced political engagement (Hibbing & Theiss-Morse, 2001). Researchers routinely report that discussions in which students air and examine strong and genuine differences of opinion in a civil climate are also highly engaging to students (McDevitt & Kiousis, 2006; Rossi, 1995; Hess & Posselt, 2002; Hess & Ganzler, 2006); which may account for the pathway that exists from discussion to political engagement.

RECOMMENDATIONS FOR FUTURE RESEARCH

While we are beginning to build a more robust understanding of what influence participation in controversial issues discussions has on many of the civic and political outcomes that have long been the hallmark of social studies, it is clear that we have many questions left to address.

I began this chapter by describing a troubling contradiction in the existing literature about the prevalence of issues discussions in social studies. Students often report learning in an open classroom climate that includes the discussion of issues, but large-scale observational evidence suggests that may not be the case. It is essential that researchers examine this contradiction in detail, in differing school contexts, and over time to determine what is actually happening in classrooms gauged as open (or not) by students. Moreover, it would be extremely helpful if researchers could assess the effects of the relative quantity and quality of issues discussions. For example, it may be that a relatively minor focus on issues has large civic education pay-offs, which could encourage teachers who are feeling pressured by standardized tests to include some opportunities for students to engage in issues discussions.

Given the plethora of research that shows positive correlations between self-reported exposure to issues discussions in schools and later expected or actual political engagement, it is important engage in research similar to the Kids Voting USA study (McDevitt & Kiousis, 2006) to examine the ways in which issues discussions *cause* political and civic engagement.

We know very little about how teachers learn how to infuse issues discussions in social studies courses, although many of the teachers showcased in the literature as especially skillful at this form of teaching report specialized professional developments and lots of practice (Rossi, 1995; Hess, 2002; Hess & Posselt, 2002). It is important to investigate what influence various forms of issues-focused teacher education and professional development have on whether and how teachers include issues in their classes.

Also, a number of pedagogical practices related to issues discussions spark enormous controversy. For example, the question about whether teachers should disclose their own views on issues often creates heated debates. But we know virtually nothing about what students think about whether they want to hear their teachers' views. It would also be helpful to know what influence a teacher's decision about disclosure has on how students' perceive the classroom environment. While many people believe that a teacher who discloses his/her views may indoctrinate students, there is no evidence that this is the case. Researchers need to explore the ways in which teachers' views influence students in order to assess the pros and cons of teachers' disclosure decisions.

At its very heart, the concept of deliberative democracy is the presumption that the diversity of views that exist in multicultural societies, such as the United States, is an asset that needs to be fostered and nurtured, both in public spaces such as classrooms, and in the political world outside of school. There are teachers who are exceptionally good at putting this presumption into practice in extremely diverse communities. We need research that helps all of us understand what motivates them, how they conceptualize issues teaching, and what they do to make it work. The teaching of controversial issues is often recommended because it is *authentic* to the world we live in—a world that is also *authentically* diverse. For this reason, we need to build on what we know about controversial issues teaching and learning because it holds great promise as an *authentic* form of democratic education.

REFERENCES

Andolina, M. W., Jenkins, K., Keeter, S., & Zukin, C. (2002). Searching for the meaning of youth civic engagement: Notes from the field. *Applied Developmental Science, 6*(4), 189–195.

Avery, P. G., Bird, K., Johnstone, S., Sullivan, J. L., & Thalhammer, K. (1992). Exploring political tolerance with adolescents. *Theory and Research in Social Education, 20*(4), 386–420.

Beck, T. (2003). If he murdered someone, he shouldn't get a lawyer: Engaging young children in civics deliberation. *Theory and Research in Social Education, 3*(3), 326–346.

Bickmore, K. (1993). Learning inclusion/inclusion in learning: Citizenship education for a pluralistic society. *Theory and Research in Social Education, 21*, 341–84.

Brice, L. (2002). Deliberative discourse enacted: Task, text, and talk. *Theory and Research in Social Education, 30*(1), 66–87.

Campbell, D. E. (2005). Voice in the classroom: How an open classroom environment facilitates adolescents' civic development. Center for Information and Research on Civic Learning and Engagement, *CIRCLE Working Paper 28.*

Carnegie Corporation of New York and the Center for Information and Research on Civic Learning and Engagement (CIRCLE). (2002). *The civic mission of the schools.*

Engel, S. L. (1993). Attitudes of secondary social studies and English teachers toward the classroom examination and treatment of controversial issues. PhD dissertation, University of Illinois at Urbana-Champaign. Retrieved August 3, 2006, from: ProQuest Digital Dissertations database (Publication No. AAT 9329022).

Gutmann, A. (1999). *Democratic education* (2nd ed.). Princeton, NJ: Princeton University Press.

Hahn, C. L. (1991). Controversial issues in social studies. In J. Shaver (Ed), *Handbook of research on social studies teaching and learning* (pp. 470–480). New York: Macmillan.

Hahn, C. L. (1996). Research on issues-centered social studies. In R.W. Evans & D.W. Save (Eds.), *Handbook on teaching social issues* (pp. 26–39). Washington, DC: National Council for the Social Studies.

Hahn, C. L. (1999). The IEA Civic education project: National and international perspectives. *Social Education, 63*, 425–431.

Hahn, C. L., & Tocci, C. M. (1990). Classroom climate and controversial issues discussions: A five nation study. *Theory and Research in Social Education, 18*(4), 344–362.

Harris, D. (1996). Assessing discussion of public issues: A scoring guide. In R. W. Evans & D. W. Save (Eds), *Handbook on teaching social issues* (pp. 289–297). Washington, DC: National Council for the Social Studies.

Hemmings, A. (2000). High school democratic dialogues: Possibilities for praxis. *American Educational Research Journal, 3*(1), 67–91.

Hess, D. (2002). Teaching controversial public issues discussions: Learning from skilled teachers. *Theory and Research in Social Education, 30*(1), 10–41.

Hess, D. (2005). How do teachers' political views influence teaching about controversial issues? *Social Education, 69*(1), 47–48.

Hess, D., & Ganzler, L. (2006). How the deliberation of controversial issues in high school courses influences students' views on political engagement. Presentation at the Annual Meeting of the American Educational Research Association, San Francisco, CA.

Hess, D., & Posselt, J. (2002). How High School Students Experience and Learn from the Discussion of Controversial Public Issues. *Journal of Curriculum and Supervision, 17*(4), 83–314.

Hibbing, J. R., & Theiss-Morse, E. (2001). Process preferences and American politics: What the people want government to be. *American Political Science Review, 95*(1), 145–153.

Hunt, M. P., & Metcalf, L. E. (1955). *Teaching high school social studies: Problems in reflective thinking and social understanding.* New York: Harper and Row.

Johnston, J., Anderman, L., Milne, L., Klenck, L., & Harris, D. (1994). Improving civic discourse in the classroom: Taking the measure of Channel One. *Research Report 4.* Ann Arbor: Institute for Social Research, University of Michigan.

Kahne, J., Rodriguez, M., Smith, B., & Thiede, K. (2000). Developing citizens for democracy? Assessing opportunities to learn in Chicago's social studies classrooms. *Theory and Research in Social Education, 28*(3), 311–338.

Kahne, J., Chi, B., & Middaugh, E. (in press). Building social capital for civic and political engagement: The potential of high school government courses. *Canadian Journal of Education.*

Kelly, T. (1986). Discussing controversial issues: Four perspectives on the teacher's role. *Theory and Research in Social Education, 14*(2), 113–138.

Kohlberg, L. (1981). *The philosophy of moral development: Moral stages and the ideas of justice.* San Francisco: Harper and Row.

Larson, B. E. (1997). The Makah: Exploring controversial issues through structured classroom discussion. *Social Studies and the Young Learner, 10*(1), 10–13.

Larson, B. E. (2003). Comparing face-to-face discussion and electronic discussion: A case study for high school social studies. *Theory and Research in Social Education, 31*(3), 347–397.

Mansbridge, J. (1991). Democracy, deliberation, and the experience of women. In B. Murchland (Ed.), *Higher education and the practice of democratic politics: A political education reader* (pp. 122–135). Dayton: Kettering Foundation. (Eric Document 350909).

McDevitt, M., & Kiousis, S. (2006). Experiments in political socialization: Kids voting USA as a model for civic education reform. Center for Information and Research on Civic Learning and Engagement. *CIRCLE Working Paper 49.*

Miller-Lane, J., Denton, E., & May, A. (2006). Social studies teachers' views on committed impartiality and discussion. *Social Studies Research and Practice, 1*(1), 30–44.

Newmann, F. M., & Wehlage, G.G. (1995). *Successful school restructuring: A report to the public and educators.* Madison: University of Wisconsin, Center on Effective Secondary Schools.

Niemi, N., & Niemi, R. (2007). Partisanship, participation, and political trust as taught (or not) in high school history and civics classes. *Theory and Research in Social Education, 35*(1), 32–61.

Nystrand, M., Gamoran, A., & Carbonara, W. (1998). *Towards an ecology of learning: The case of classroom discourse and its effects on writing in high school English and social studies.* Albany: National Research Center on English Learning and Achievement.

Oliver, D. W., & Shaver, J.P. (1966). *Teaching public issues in the high school.* Logan: Utah State University Press.

Parker, W. C. (2003). *Teaching democracy: Unity and diversity in public life.* New York: Teacher's College Press.

Phillips, J. P. (1997). Florida teachers' attitudes toward the study of controversial issues in public high school social studies classrooms. PhD dissertation, The Florida State University. Retrieved August 3, 2006, from: ProQuest Digital Dissertations database. (Publication No. AAT 9813696).

Richardson, W. K. (2006). Combining Cognitive Interviews and Social Science Surveys: Strengthening Interpretation and Design. In K. C. Barton (Ed.), *Research Methods in Social Studies Education: Contemporary Issues and Perspectives.* Greenwich: Information Age Publishing.

Rossi, J. A. (1995). In-depth study in an issues-oriented social studies classroom. *Theory and Research in Social Education, 23*(2), 88–120.

Torney-Purta, J., Lehmann, R., Oswald, H., & Schultz, W. (2001). *Citizenship and education in twenty-eight countries: Civic knowledge and engagement at age fourteen.* Amsterdam: International Association for the Evaluation of Educational Achievement.

9 Diversity and citizenship education
Historical, theoretical, and philosophical issues[1]

James A. Banks
Diem Nguyen

University of Washington

The increasing racial, ethnic, cultural, language, and religious diversity in nation-states throughout the world raises new and complex questions about educating students for effective citizenship. Since World War II, nation-states throughout the Western world have become more diversified because of worldwide immigration. In European nations such as the United Kingdom, France, and the Netherlands, the demographic make-up has become more diverse because groups from their former colonies in Asia, Africa, and the West Indies immigrated to Europe to satisfy labor needs and to improve their economic status (Banks, 2004a; Banks & Lynch, 1986).

Although the United States has been diverse since its founding, the ethnic texture of the nation has changed dramatically since the Immigration Reform Act was enacted in 1965. During most of its history prior to the mid-1960s, most of the immigrants to the United States came from Europe. However, most came from nations in Latin America and Asia between 1991 and 2000 (U.S. Census Bureau, 2000b). Between 1991 and 2000, 67% of the documented immigrants to the United States came from nations in Asia and Latin America; 14.6% came from nations in the Caribbean and Africa. Only 15% came from European nations. The U.S. Census Bureau (2000b) projects that ethnic groups of color will make up 50% of the U.S. population in 2050. In 2004, students of color made up 43% of the students in U. S. public schools (Dillon, 2006).

In the context of sweeping demographic changes and increasing racial, ethnic, cultural, language, and religious diversity, it is critical that we rethink questions related to citizenship and citizenship education in democratic multicultural nation-states such as the United States, the United Kingdom, Canada, and France (Banks, 2006b). Democratic multicultural nation-states should find ways to foster civic communities that incorporate the rich and diverse cultures of its citizens while at the same time cultivating a set of shared values, ideals, and goals that unify and make structural inclusion into the commonwealth possible for diverse groups.

Most conceptions of citizenship and citizenship education were consistent with the dominant assimilationist and Anglo-conformity ideology in American society prior to the Civil Rights and ethnic revitalization movements of the 1960s and 1970s. A major goal of citizenship education in Western democratic nation-states that embraced an assimilationist conception of citizenship was to create nation-states in which all groups shared one dominant mainstream culture. Although the aim was to have one shared culture, assimilation worked differently for various racial and ethnic groups. Assimilationist policies eventually resulted in the structural inclusion of the large numbers of

---

[1] Parts of this chapter are adapted, with permission of the publishers, from J. A. Banks (2004). Teaching for social justice, diversity, and citizenship in a global world. *The Educational Forum*, 68(4), pp. 296–305; and from J. A. Banks (Ed.) (2004). *Diversity and citizenship education: Global perspectives*. San Francisco: Jossey-Bass, pp. 3–16.

Southern, Central, and Eastern European immigrants who arrived in the United States in the late 1800s and early 1900s after an initial period of discrimination (Bennett, 1988; Higham, 1972). However, many racial and ethnic groups were denied the basic rights granted to other citizens. These groups included immigrants from Asia, Latin America, and other non-European nations—as well as African Americans who came to America in chains and indigenous groups such as Native Americans, Native Alaskans, and Native Hawaiians (Franklin, 1976; Jacobson, 1998; Kwong & Miscevic, 2005). Assimilation resulted in *structural inclusion* for European immigrants and *structural exclusion* for people of color (Franklin, 1976; M. Gordon, 1964).

The major educational theories and practices related to citizenship and citizenship education during the late 1800s and early 1900s were assimilationist oriented. In 1909 Ellwood Patterson Cubberley, the noted educational scholar and leader, stated that assimilating immigrants into the dominant Anglo culture was an important goal of schools. Cubberley believed that the schools should "break up these groups" and amalgamate them as "part of the American race" and "implant in their children…the Anglo-Saxon conception of righteousness, law and order, and popular government" (pp. 15–16).

Many scholars and educators in the first decades of the 20th century believed that assimilation was an inevitable and desirable goal of American society. Park, the eminent sociologist at the University of Chicago, conceptualized the experiences of immigrant and indigenous groups as a "race-relations cycle" that consists of four inevitable stages: *contact, conflict, accommodation*, and *assimilation* (cited in Alba & Nee, 2003, p. 20). Park's theory predicted that all immigrant groups would experience a similar process of adaptation which included conflicts and problems in their initial contact with the new culture and eventual accommodation and assimilation into the mainstream culture. Missing in his linear progression theory is a discussion of racialization and how institutional racism excludes people of color from structural inclusion into the mainstream society.

Since the 1970s a rich literature related to diversity and citizenship education has evolved (Banks, 2004a; Burke, 2002; Gutmann, 1999; Kymlicka, 1995; Taylor, Gutmann, Rockefeller, Walzer, & Wolf, 1992). In this chapter, we focus on the literature that conceptualizes ways in which multicultural nation-states can balance unity and diversity, i.e., how they can construct a unified nation-state while individuals from diverse racial, ethnic, cultural, and religious groups are provided opportunities to maintain important aspects of their cultural traditions, values, languages, and behaviors.

We define an ethnic group as an involuntary group that shares a common culture, social practices, ancestry, history, and a sense of community (Jenkins, 1997). Race is socially constructed to categorize people based on physical characteristics that have no biological basis (Omi & Winant, 1994).

THE CONSTRUCTION OF RACE AND CITIZENSHIP IN THE UNITED STATES

The history of citizenship construction in the United States is closely tied to the construction of race. As a socially constructed category, race has been used as a tool to classify and sort people. Racial classifications have important implications for a group's social, economic, and political status as well as for individual members of these groups. Brodkin (1998) makes a conceptual distinction between *ethnoracial assignment* and *ethnoracial identity* that is helpful in considering the relationship between citizenship identification and citizenship education. She defines ethnoracial assignment as "popularly held classifications and their deployment by those with national power to make them matter economically, politically, and socially to the individuals classified" (p. 3). Ethnoracial identities are defined by individuals themselves "within the context of ethnoracial assignment" (p. 3). Arab Americans, for example, who are citizens of the United States, and have a strong national identity as Americans are sometimes viewed by fellow American citizens as non-Americans (Gregorian, 2003).

Race has been and remains a significant factor in every aspect of American life (Jacobson, 1998; Omi & Winant, 1994), including education (Hatcher & Troyna, 1993; Ladson-Billings, 2004; Olsen, 1997) and the popular media, art, and entertainment industries (Cortés, 2000; Giroux, 1996). Race is used to both define and divide Americans. Morrison (1992) states that race has become "metaphorical," and "a way of referring to and disguising forces, events, classes and expressions of social decay and economic division far more threatening to the body politic than biological 'race' ever was..." (p. 63).

Racialization has worked through U.S. institutions and policies—including citizenship formation—in powerful ways and has significantly influenced who can become a citizen and has defined the rights and protection designated to each racial group. While racialization privileges people of European descent and has created and sustained a majority White race, it has consistently isolated and excluded ethnic groups of color (Castles, 2000; Jacobson, 1998; Ladson-Billings, 2004).

The categories and criteria for determining who is White and non-White have changed over time to reflect the historical and social contexts (Jacobson, 1998; U.S. Census Bureau, 2000a). Becoming White is not an either/or process but is a process in which racial identities change "across contexts and time" (Lopez, 1966, p. 106). Groups that were once classified as legally non-White are now classified as White (Jacobson, 1998; Lopez, 1996). The U.S. Census Bureau legally classifies Arab Americans as White. However, in these post-September 11 and heightened national security times their legal racial category does not protect them from racial profiling or from being targets of public scrutiny (Nguyen, 2005).

Racialization has combined the cultures, customs, histories, and languages of different European ethnic groups to create an image of uniformity and commonality—a monolithic White racial group (Jacobson, 1998). The flexible context of the White racial category allows it to expand and change over time to maintain its majority status, as it has done throughout U.S. history. In the late 1920s the White racial category expanded to include European ethnic groups that were earlier classified as non-White (Jacobson). Irish, Italians, Poles, and other European immigrants who were categorized as separate racial groups in the late 1800s became White (Brodkin, 1998; Jacobson, 1998). The White racial category was also expanded after World War II to incorporate Jews (Brodkin, 1998).

While racialization has benefited the members of the White dominant group, it has marginalized people of color and has often been used to deny them full citizenship rights. Historically, as different immigrant groups arrived in the U.S.—such as the Southern, Central, and Eastern European immigrants, Jews, and Asian immigrants—they were perceived as very different from and as potential threats to the dominant Anglo-Saxon race and culture. These immigrant groups were given limited rights and access to society and some—such as the Chinese immigrants—could only live in segregated neighborhoods and could only obtain jobs that were unwanted by other groups (Kwong & Miscevic, 2005). Over time, European immigrants were granted full membership into the White majority race while immigrants of color and indigenous groups such as Native Americans and Native Hawaiians—as well as African Americans—were assigned minority status.

ASSIMILATIONIST APPROACHES TO CITIZENSHIP

White majority group dominance has resulted in an assimilationist model of citizenship and citizenship education in the United States in which minority ethnic groups have become structured into a social, cultural, economic, and political hierarchy (Castles & Davidson, 2000; Kymlicka, 1995). Citizenship involves having membership in what Parsons (1966) calls a societal community. This membership means "having access to society's resources and capacities that allow for social mobility and comfort. Thus, access to health care services, education, employment, and housing without discrimination are part of social citizenship" (Ladson-Billings, 2004, p. 101). Assimilationist approaches to citizenship and citizenship education have not been effective in helping to integrate ethnic and immigrants groups of color into the larger societal community. Assimilationist approaches to citizenship have been implemented "without the structural inclusion of ethnic and cultural groups into the mainstream society and without these groups attaining social and economic equality" (Banks, 2004a, p. xx).

Castle and Miller (2003) define assimilation as the process of integrating racial and ethnic minorities—particularly immigrants—"into society through a one-sided process of adaptation: immigrants are expected to give up their distinctive linguistic, cultural or social characteristics and become indistinguishable from the majority population" (p. 250). Assimilation assumes that over time, there is a decline in ethnic, cultural, and social differences. Alba and Nee (2003) explain, "Individuals' ethnic origins become less and less relevant in relation to the members of another ethnic group (typically, but not necessarily, the ethnic majority group), and individuals on both sides of the boundary see themselves more and more as alike" (p. 11).

The melting pot notion of assimilation is popular in the American imagination and is embraced by many educational practitioners in the United States. However, as Gordon (1964) points out, the melting pot concept of assimilation is a "loose and illogical" explanation which "may envisage the culture of the immigrants as melting completely into the culture of the host society without leaving any cultural trace at all" (p. 125). In the case of multiethnic nation-states such as the United States, the melting pot concept is a myth because prejudice, racism, and discrimination persist. Assimilation has, in fact, worked to sort minorities into the bottom rungs of the racial and socio-economic hierarchy while helping to maintain the social, economic, and political interests of the dominant group (Ong, 1999). As has been observed, people of color such as African Americans and Native Americans stuck to the bottom of the mythical melting pot.

Racialization, assimilation, and citizenship formation create social and political pitfalls for people of color as they seek citizenship. The assimilationist process requires minority groups to conform to the dominant culture and to adopt the dominant language while racialization excludes them from full citizenship participation. Whiteness is a criterion for full citizenship. Whiteness "allows an almost seamless melding of the cultural and the civic for the dominant group" (Ladson-Billings, 2004, p. 113). This "seamless melding" permits Whites to switch their racial identity to national identity, such as in the United States where White is often viewed as synonymous with "American." The American identity allows Whites to be "viewed as more loyal, more patriotic, and more committed to the public good. Citizens of color in the United States frequently are accused of being ethnocentric and less patriotic" (Ladson-Billings, 2004, p. 113) while White Americans are rarely viewed as being un-patriotic and un-American. The connection between being *White* and *American* is one of the many White privileges in U. S. society that McIntosh (2001) insightfully describes.

A HISTORY OF DEFENDING CULTURAL DIVERSITY AND PLURALISM

Philosophers and educators in the United States have been arguing for the right of ethnic and cultural minorities to maintain important aspects of their cultures and languages since the first decades of the 1900s. Randolph Bourne (1916), Julius Drachsler (1920) and Horace M. Kallen (1924)—of immigrant backgrounds themselves—argued that the European immigrants who were entering the United States in large numbers had a right to retain parts of their cultures, ethnicities, and languages while enjoying full citizenship rights. The German Americans who arrived in the United States in the late 1800s, for example, advocated for ethnic group rights. Many German immigrants rejected the melting pot idea, refused to conform to the Anglo racial category, retained their ethnic identity, and practiced their language and culture (Tolzmann, 2000). In the process of retaining their ethnic identity while adapting to life in the United States, they created a unique German American identity.

The right to exercise cultural democracy and cultural freedom within the nation-state—such as was done by the German Americans in the late 1800s—is an essential component of a political democracy (Drachsler, 1920). In the first decades of the 1900s, a number of influential educators in New York City implemented several initiatives that promoted diversity in order to improve race relations and to increase the academic achievement of European American students. Rachel Davis DuBois established school ethnic heritage programs for European immigrant groups (C.A.M. Banks, 2005). Carter G. Woodson (1933/1977) made a case for cultural democracy when he argued that a curriculum for African American students should reflect their history and culture and harshly criticized the absence of Black history in the curriculum. He stated that schools, colleges, and universities were "mis-educating" Black students because they were not teaching them about African cultures and civilizations.

Scholars of color who were deeply influenced by the Civil Rights and ethnic revitalization movements of the 1960s and 1970s strongly challenged assimilation as the inevitable and desirable goal of intergroup and race relations in the United States (B. Gordon, 2001; King, 2004; Ladson-Billings, 2004; Sizemore, 1972). These theorists argued that racial and ethnic groups of color such as African Americans and Mexican Americans who had experienced high levels of cultural assimilation were still denied structural assimilation and full citizenship rights. Being White in the United States remained an essential criterion for full citizenship no matter how culturally assimilated an individual of color became. Consequently, scholars argued that individuals from diverse racial, ethnic, and cultural groups should be able to maintain aspects of their community cultures while attaining full citizenship rights. Citizens should not have to abandon important parts of their cultures and languages in order to have full citizenship rights.

The ethnic revitalization movements of the 1960s and 1970s that took place in the U.S. echoed throughout the world. French and Indians in Canada, West Indians and Asians in Britain, Indonesians and Surinamese in the Netherlands, and Aborigines in Australia joined the series of ethnic movements, expressed their feelings of marginalization, and worked to make the institutions within their nation-states responsive to their economic, political, and cultural needs. Indigenous peoples and ethnic groups within the various Western nations—such as American Indians in the United States, Aborigines in Australia, Maori in New Zealand, African Caribbean in the United Kingdom, and Moluccans in the Netherlands—want their histories and cultures to be reflected in their national cultures and in the school, college, and university curriculum (Eldering & Kloprogge, 1989; Gillborn, 1990; Smith, 1999). Multicultural education was developed, in part, to respond to the concerns of ethnic, racial, and cultural groups that feel marginalized within their nation-states (Banks & Banks, 2004). When the nation-state recognizes diverse groups it enables them to feel an integral part of the national civic culture. State recognition of diverse groups also provides opportunities for them to engage with one another and to work collectively to decrease discrimination and racism. Reducing racism and working towards equal rights for all groups are important goals for multicultural democratic nation-states.

142 James A. Banks and Diem Nguyen

DIVERSITY AND ASSIMILATIONIST THEORIES OF CITIZENSHIP

Both assimilationist and diversity theories related to citizenship and citizenship education exist today, just as both existed in the early decades of the 1900s. There is, however, an important difference between then and now. Today, diversity theories have
more legitimacy and are more influential in both the United States and around the world
than they were in the first decades of the twentieth century. Arthur Schlesinger, Jr.
(1991), Diane Ravitch (1990), Dinesh D'Souza (1991), and Nathan Glazer (1997) have
constructed widely disseminated and influential arguments that promote Anglo-conformity and assimilation in U. S. schools, colleges, and universities. However, Glazer
concedes that diversity issues in the school might help underachieving minority students
to increase their academic achievement.

During the 2000s, several thoughtful sociologists conceptualized assimilation in more
complex ways than it had been described in the past. These theorists include Portes and
Rumbaut (2001) who problematize assimilation by conceptualizing it as a process of
segmented assimilation "where outcomes vary across immigrant minorities and where
rapid integration and acceptance into the American mainstream represent just one possible alternative" (p. 45). In other words, Mexican immigrants might assimilate into
African American inner-city culture rather than into White mainstream middle-class
culture. Assimilation continues to exist as a theory and practice in society writ large
and in educational settings. However, theorists are recognizing the myriad and complex
ways in which diversity and assimilation interact. Most immigrants and people of color
live in neighborhoods and attend schools that are populated primarily by people of color
(Suárez-Orozco, 2001). The daily exchanges and encounters between diverse cultures
and groups in many low-income urban neighborhoods and schools reflect the social
interactions, relationships, and tensions among these communities. Many immigrants
and people of color have few opportunities to assimilate into the dominant White mainstream culture because they have few sustained interactions with the dominant culture
and community (Wilson, 1996). However, the idea that low-income and marginalized
groups of color will assimilate into the mainstream culture is still a widespread expectation among educators and the general American population.

REDEFINING CITIZENSHIP AND CITIZENSHIP
EDUCATION IN A MULTICULTURAL NATION-STATE

A citizen may be defined as a "native or naturalized member of a state or nation who
owes allegiance to its government and is entitled to its protection." This is the definition of citizen in *Webster's Encyclopedic Unabridged Dictionary of the English Language* (1989, p. 270). This same dictionary defines citizenship as the "state of being
vested with the rights, privileges, and duties of a citizen" (p. 270). Absent from these
minimal definitions of citizen and citizenship are the rich discussions and meanings of
citizen and citizenship in democratic, multicultural societies that have been developed
by scholars such as Kymlicka (1995), Castles and Davidson (2000), Gutmann (1999),
Rosaldo (1999), and Ong (1999). These scholars state that citizens within democratic
multicultural nation-states endorse the overarching ideals of the nation-state such as
justice and equality, are committed to the maintenance and perpetuation of these ideals, and are willing and able to take action to help close the gap between their nation's
democratic ideals and practices that violate those ideals, such as social, racial, cultural,
and economic inequality.

An important goal of citizenship education in a democratic multicultural society is
to help students acquire the knowledge, attitudes, and skills needed to make reflective

decisions and to take actions to make their nation-states more democratic and just (Banks, 1997; Banks, 2006c). To become thoughtful decision makers and active citizen, students need to master social science knowledge, to clarify their moral commitments, to identify alternative courses of action, and to act in ways consistent with democratic values (Banks & Banks, with Clegg, 1999; Banks, 2006c). Gutmann (2004) states that democratic multicultural societies are characterized by *civic equality, toleration*, and *recognition*. Consequently, an important goal of citizenship education in multicultural societies is to teach toleration and recognition of cultural differences. Gutmann views deliberation as an essential component of democratic education in multicultural societies. Gonçalves e Silva (2004) states that citizens in a democratic society work for the betterment of the whole society, and not just for the rights of their particular racial, social, or cultural group:

> A citizen is a person who works against injustice not for individual recognition or personal advantage, but for the benefit of all people. In realizing this task—shattering privileges, ensuring information and competence, acting in favor of all—each person becomes a citizen. (p. 197)

Becoming a citizen is a *process* that takes place over time. Education can greatly facilitate this process as well as help students develop civic consciousness and agency (Gonçalves e Silva, 2004).

Developing multiple views of citizenship

While scholars and educators agree that schools need to help students acquire the knowledge, skills, and attitudes needed to function in a democratic society, it is important to discuss how complex and difficult this process of citizenship formation becomes in a multicultural nation-state. The current leading theories on citizenship in Western nation-states are grounded in the liberal notion of citizenship, which privileges individual rights and identity over group rights (Cogan, 1998; Patterson, 1977). The liberal theory of citizenship "assumes that group attachments will die of their own weight within a modernized, pluralistic democratic society if marginalized and excluded groups are given the opportunity to attain structural inclusion into the mainstream society" (Banks, 2006b, p. 7). Liberal assimilationist approaches to citizenship have been practiced in United States during most of its history, yet structural exclusion of minority groups of color continues.

Since the 1960s and 1970s ethnic revitalization movement, theorists have been re-examining and questioning liberal conceptions of citizenship (Benhabib, 2004; Castle & Davidson, 2000; Gordon, 1964; Young, 1989). The structural exclusion of many racial, ethnic, and language groups in nation-states throughout the Western world—and the increasing levels of diversity in these nation-states—have created serious concerns and questions among scholars and theorists regarding ways in which democratic multicultural nation-states can provide cultural recognition and rights to diverse groups while maintaining national unity. Kymlicka (1995) argues that the current conditions of many marginalized racial and ethnic groups in Western nation-states demand a policy change in which individuals belonging to these groups have both individual rights as well as group rights. These group rights—which should co-exist with universal human rights—include the right to practice community cultures and religions, the right to land claims that resulted from broken treaties, and right to use community languages (Banks, 2006b; Kymlicka, 1995). Kymlicka uses "multicultural citizenship" to describe citizenship in nations that have implemented policies incorporating universal human rights, individual rights, and group differentiated rights.

Diversity and unity is a difficult issue in most nation-states around the world. In the discussion of his citizenship identity in Japan, Murphy-Shigematsu (2004) describes how complex and contextual citizenship identification is within a multicultural nation-state such as Japan. Becoming a legal citizen of a nation-state does not necessarily mean that an individual will attain structural inclusion into the mainstream society and its institutions or will be perceived as a citizen by most members of the dominant group within the nation-state. A citizen's racial, ethnic, cultural, class, language, and religious characteristics often significantly influence whether she is viewed as a citizen within her society. It is not unusual for their fellow American citizens to assume that Asian Americans born in the United States emigrated from another nation. They are sometime asked, "What country are you from?"

Categorizing and perceiving groups as having minority status—which prevents many of them from full participation in the societal community—threatens the core values of democratic multicultural nations such as justice and equality. A nation-state that does not structurally include all cultural groups into the national culture runs the risk of creating alienation and causing groups to focus on specific concerns and issues rather than on the overarching goals and policies of the nation-state.

THE STAGES OF CULTURAL IDENTITY AND CITIZENSHIP EDUCATION

Students from racial, ethnic, cultural, and language minority groups that have historically experienced institutionalized discrimination, racism, or other forms of marginalization often have a difficult time accepting and valuing their own ethnic and cultural heritages. Developing *self-acceptance* is a prerequisite to the acceptance and valuing of others (Banks, 2004a). Teachers should be aware of and sensitive to the stages of cultural development that all of their students—including mainstream students, students of color and other marginalized groups of students—may be experiencing and facilitate their identity development.

In 1976, Banks developed the *Stages of Ethnicity Typology* to help teachers, practitioners, scholars, and researchers to conceptualize diversity *within* ethnic groups and to construct strategies that will help students acquire identifications with groups beyond their community cultures. Banks (2006a) later expanded the typology to make it more inclusive so that it could be used with groups other than ethnic groups, such as gender groups, social-class groups, and groups related to sexual orientation. He changed its name to the *Stages of Cultural Identity* (see Figure 9.1). Banks' typology has been used in a number of research studies and as a tool to facilitate classroom discussions (see, for example, Tomlinson, 1996; Mallette, Bean, & Readence, 1998).

Banks hypothesizes that students need to reach Stage 3 of the typology, *Cultural Identity Clarification*, before we can expect them to embrace other cultural groups or attain thoughtful and clarified national or global identifications. The typology is an ideal-type concept. Consequently, it does not describe the actual identity development of any particular individual. Rather, it is a framework for thinking about and facilitating the identity development of students who approximate one of the stages.

During Stage 1—*Cultural Psychology Captivity*—individuals internalize the negative stereotypes and beliefs about their cultural groups that are institutionalized within the larger society and may exemplify cultural self-rejection and low self-esteem. Cultural encapsulation and cultural exclusiveness, and the belief that their ethnic group is superior to others, characterize Stage 2—*Cultural Encapsulation*. Often individuals within this stage have newly discovered their cultural consciousness and try to limit participation to their cultural group. They have ambivalent feelings about their cultural group

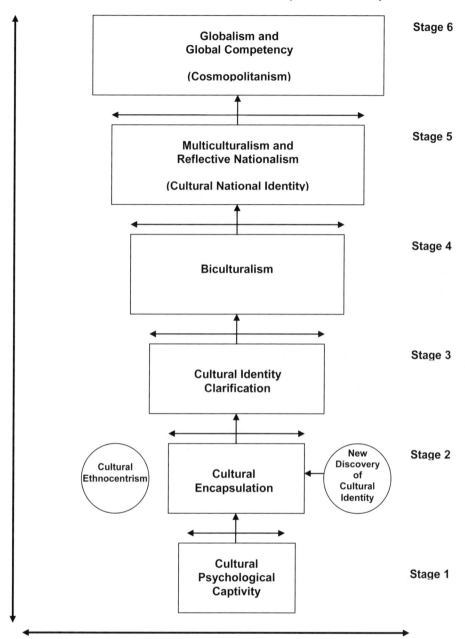

Figure 9.1 The stages of cultural identity: A typology. Copyright ©2007 by James A. Banks.

and try to confirm, for themselves, that they are proud of it. In Stage 3—*Ethnic Identity Clarification*—individual are able to clarify their personal attitudes and cultural identity and to develop clarified positive attitudes toward their cultural group. In this stage, cultural pride is genuine rather than contrived. Individuals within Stage 4—*Biculturalism*—have a healthy sense of cultural identity and the psychological characteristics to participate successfully in their own cultural community as well as in another cultural community. They also have a strong desire to function effectively in two cultures.

Stage 5—*Multiculturalism and Reflective Nationalism*— individuals have clarified, reflective, and positive personal, cultural, and national identifications and positive attitudes toward other racial, cultural, and ethnic groups. At Stage 6—*Globalism and Global Competency*—individuals have reflective and clarified national and global identifications. They have the knowledge, skills, and attitudes needed to function effectively within their own cultural communities, within other cultures within their nation-state, in the civic culture of their nation, as well as in the global community. Individuals within Stage 6 exemplify cosmopolitanism and have a commitment to all human beings in the world community (Nussbaum, 2002, p. 4). Gutmann (2004) states that the primary commitment of these individuals is to justice, not to any particular human community.

The Bellagio Project: Reforming citizenship education

Citizenship education needs to be changed in significant ways because of the increasing diversity within nation-states throughout the world and the quests by racial, ethnic, cultural, and religious groups for cultural recognition and rights (Banks, 2004a; Castles, 2004). The Center for Multicultural Education at the University of Washington (http://depts.washington.edu/centerme/home.htm) has implemented a project to reform citizenship education so that it will advance democracy as well as be responsive to the needs of cultural, racial, ethnic, religious, and immigrant groups within multicultural nation-states. The first part of this project consisted of a conference, "Ethnic Diversity and Citizenship Education in Multicultural Nation-States," held at the Rockefeller Foundation's Study and Conference Center in Bellagio, Italy, June 17–21, 2002 (hereafter "Bellagio Conference"). The conference, which was supported by the Spencer and Rockefeller Foundations, included participants from 12 nations: Brazil, Canada, China, Germany, India, Israel, Japan, Palestine, Russia, South Africa, the United Kingdom, and the United States. The papers from this conference are published in *Diversity and Citizenship Education: Global Perspectives* (Banks, 2004a).

One of the conclusions of the Bellagio Conference was that world migration and the political and economic aspects of globalization are challenging nation-states and national borders. At the same time, national borders remain tenacious; the number of nations in the world is increasing rather than decreasing. The number of UN member states increased from 80 in 1950 to 191 in 2002 (Castles, 2004). Globalization and nationalism are coexisting and sometimes conflicting trends and forces in the world today (Banks et al., 2005).

Globalization is "a dynamic process of increasing interactions and interdependencies among people and systems on the Earth" (Banks et al., 2005, p. 18). Although globalization influences important aspects of social and cultural life, it is driven primarily by economic and political interests (Delanty, 2000). Through the advances of technology, communications, and improved transportation systems, globalization has blurred some of the economic and political boundaries between nation-states as it stimulates free trade ventures and global migration patterns; simultaneously, it has worked to preserve more cultures, languages, and ethnic groups that were bound for extinction (Delanty, 2000). As an economic, political, and social force, globalization has worked to bring cultures and countries closer together while at the same time helping to widen the gaps between groups within and across different nation-states (Burbules & Torres, 2000). Across the world, globalization has helped to create more opportunities for social, economic, and political elites while worsening work and living conditions for those at the bottom of the social and economic ladder.

Because of globalization and worldwide migration, educators around the world should rethink and redesign citizenship education courses and programs to take into consideration the influence of globalization on social, cultural, economic, and political structures within and across nation-states. Citizenship education should help students acquire the knowledge, attitudes, and skills needed to function in their nation-states as well as in a diverse global society that is experiencing rapid globalization and quests by racial, ethnic, cultural, language, and religious groups for recognition and inclusion. Citizenship education should also help students to develop a commitment to act to change the world to make it more just.

Another conclusion of the Bellagio Conference is that citizenship and citizenship education are defined and implemented differently in various nations and in different social, economic, and political contexts. It is also a contested idea in nation-states throughout the world. However, there are shared problems, concepts, and issues, such as the need to prepare students in various nations to function within as well as across national borders. The conference also concluded that these shared issues and problems should be identified by an international group that would formulate guidelines for dealing with them.

In response to the Bellagio Conference recommendations, the Center for Multicultural Education at the University of Washington created an International Consensus Panel, which was supported by the Spencer Foundation and the University of Washington. The Consensus Panel constructed four principles and identified ten concepts for educating citizens for democracy and diversity in a global age. These principles and concepts constitute Table 9.1. In addition to an International Consensus Panel that drafted the manuscript for the publication—*Democracy and Diversity: Principles and Concepts for Educating Citizens in a Global Age* (Banks et al., 2005)—an International Review Panel made up of scholars and practitioners from 17 nations around the world reviewed the manuscript. It was then revised by the Consensus Panel to incorporate the comments and suggestions made by the Review Panel. *Democracy and Diversity* also includes a checklist that enables schools to determine to the extent to which the princi-

Table 9.1 Principles and concepts for teaching democracy and diversity

Principles
Section I   Diversity, Unity, Global Interconnectedness, and Human Rights
   1. Students should learn about the complex relationships between unity and diversity in their local communities, the nation, and the world.
   2. Students should learn about the ways in which people in their community, nation, and region are increasingly interdependent with other people around the world and are connected to the economic, political, cultural, environmental, and technological changes taking place across the planet.
   3. The teaching of human rights should underpin citizenship education courses and programs in multicultural nation-states.

Section II   Experience and Participation
   4. Students should be taught knowledge about democracy and democratic institutions and provided opportunities to practice democracy.

Concepts
   1. Democracy
   2. Diversity
   3. Globalization
   4. Sustainable Development
   5. Empire, Imperialism, Power
   6. Prejudice, Discrimination, Racism
   7. Migration
   8. Identity/Diversity
   9. Multiple Perspectives
  10. Patriotism and Cosmopolitanism

ples and concepts are reflected in their institutions. This publication can be downloaded as a PDF at http://depts.washington.edu/centerme/home.htm

BALANCING CULTURAL, NATIONAL, AND GLOBAL IDENTIFICATIONS

An important challenge for educators in multicultural nation-states is to "respect and acknowledge the community cultures and knowledge of students while at the same time helping to construct a democratic public community with an overarching set of values to which all students will have a commitment and with which all will identify" (Banks, 2004b, p. 12). Citizenship education should enable students from diverse groups to experience cultural freedom and empowerment.

In the global community in which we live, it is critical that schools help students to develop a delicate balance of *cultural, national, and global identifications and allegiances* (Banks, 2004b). Citizenship education should help students to develop thoughtful and clarified identifications with their cultural communities and their nation-states. It should also help them to develop clarified global identifications and deep understandings of their roles in the world community. Strong, positive, and clarified cultural identifications and attachments are a prerequisite to cosmopolitan beliefs, attitudes, and behaviors. It is not realistic to expect Puerto Rican students in New York City to have a strong allegiance to U. S. national values or deep feelings for dying people in Afghanistan or Iraq if they feel marginalized and rejected within their community, their school, and in their nation-state. We must nurture, support, and affirm the identities of students from marginalized cultural, ethnic, and language groups if we expect them to endorse national values, become cosmopolitans, and work to make their local communities, the nation, and the world more just and humane.

Global education should have as major goals helping students to develop understandings of the interdependence among nations in the world today, clarified attitudes toward other nations, and reflective identifications with the world community. Cultural, national, and global experiences and identifications are interactive and interrelated in a dynamic way (Banks, 2004b). Developing identifications and connections with local, national, and the global community is a long-term process that requires discussion, interactions, and deliberation with other people within and across racial, ethnic, cultural, and religious communities. One of the main goals of citizenship education in a democratic multicultural nation-state is to help students to learn how to act to improve their own local communities, nation, and the global community (Osler & Starkey, 2005; Osler & Vincent, 2002).

Cultural, ethnic, racial, language, and religious diversity exists in most nations in the world. One of the challenges to diverse democratic nation-states is to provide opportunities for different groups to maintain aspects of their community cultures while building a nation in which these groups are structurally included and to which they feel allegiance. A delicate balance of diversity and unity should be an essential goal of democratic nation-states and of teaching and learning in democratic societies (Banks et al., 2001). Unity must be an important aim when nation-states are responding to diversity within their populations. They can protect the rights of minorities and enable diverse groups to participate only when they are unified around a set of democratic values such as justice and equality (Gutmann, 2004).

Citizenship education must be transformed in the 21st century to respond to the deepening racial, ethnic, cultural, language, and religious diversity in nation-states around the world. Citizens in a diverse democratic society should be able to maintain attachments to their cultural communities as well as participate effectively in the national civic culture. Diversity and unity should coexist in diverse and democratic nation-states and the rights of groups should be balanced with the needs of the local community, the nation-state, and the global community.

REFERENCES

Alba, R., & Nee, V. (2003). *Remaking the American mainstream: Assimilation and contemporary immigration*. Cambridge. MA: Harvard University Press.

Banks, C. A. M. (2005). *Improving multicultural education: Lessons from the intergroup education movement*. New York: Teachers College Press.

Banks, J. A. (1976). The emerging stages of ethnicity: Implications for staff development. *Educational Leadership*, 34(3), 190–193.

Banks, J. A. (1997). *Educating citizens in a multicultural society*. New York: Teachers College Press.

Banks, J. A. (Ed.). (2004a). *Diversity and citizenship education: Global perspectives*. San Francisco: Jossey-Bass.

Banks, J. A. (2004b). Introduction: Democratic citizenship education in multicultural societies. In J. A. Banks (Ed.), *Diversity and citizenship education: Global perspectives* (pp. 3–16). San Francisco: Jossey-Bass.

Banks, J. A. (2006a). *Cultural diversity and education: Foundations, curriculum, and teaching* (5th ed.). Boston: Allyn and Bacon.

Banks, J. A. (2006b, April). Educating students for cosmopolitan citizenship in a diverse and changing world. Paper presented at the Center for Advanced Study in the Behavioral Sciences, Stanford, CA.

Banks, J. A. (2006c). *Race, culture, and education: The selected works of James A. Banks*. London & New York: Routledge.

Banks, J. A., & Banks, C. A. M. (Eds.). (2004). *Handbook of research on multicultural education* (2nd ed.). San Francisco: Jossey-Bass.

Banks, J. A., Banks, C. A. M., with Clegg, A. A. Jr. (1999). *Teaching strategies for the social studies: Decision-making and citizen action* (5th ed.). New York: Longman.

Banks, J. A., & Lynch, J. (Eds.). (1986). *Multicultural education in Western societies*. London: Holt.

Banks, J. A., Cookson, P., Gay, G., Hawley, W. D., Irvine, J. J. , Nieto, S., Schofield, J. W., & Stephan, W. G. (2001). *Diversity within unity: Essential principles for teaching and learning in a multicultural society*. Seattle: Center for Multicultural Education, University of Washington.

Banks, J. A., Banks, C. A. M., Cortés, C. E., Hahn, C., Merryfield, M., Moodley, K., Osler, A., Murphy-Shigematsu, S., & Parker, W. C. (2005). *Democracy and diversity: Principles and concepts for educating citizens in a global age*. Seattle: Center for Multicultural Education, University of Washington.

Benhabib, S. (2004). *The rights of others: Aliens, residents, and citizens*. New York: Cambridge University Press.

Bennett, D. H. (1988). *The party of fear: From nativist movements to the new right in American history*. Chapel Hill: The University of North Carolina Press.

Bourne, R. S. (1916, July). Trans-national America. *The Atlantic Monthly*, 118, 86–97.

Brodkin, K. (1998). *How Jews become White folks and what that says about race in America*. New Brunswick: Rutgers University Press.

Burbules, N. C., & Torres, C. A. (2000). Globalization and education: An introduction. In N. C. Burbules & C. A. Torres (Eds.), *Globalization and education: Critical perspectives* (pp. 1–26). New York: Routledge.

Burke, J. (2002). *Mestizo democracy: The politics of crossing borders*. College Station: Texas A & M University Press.

Castles, S. (2000). *Ethnicity and globalization*. Thousand Oaks, CA: Sage.

Castles, S. (2004). Migration, citizenship, and education. In J. A. Banks (Ed.), *Diversity and citizenship education: Global perspectives* (pp. 17–48). San Francisco: Jossey-Bass.

Castles, S., & Davidson, A. (2000). *Citizenship and migration: Globalization and the politics of belonging*. New York: Routledge.

Castles, S., & Miller, M. J. (2003). *The age of migration: International population movements in the modern world* (3rd ed.). New York: Guilford.

Cogan, J. J. (1998). Citizenship education for the 21st century: Setting the context. In J. J. Cogan & R. Derricott (Eds.), *Citizenship for the 21st century: An international perspective on education* (pp. 1–20). London: Kogan Page.

Cortés, C. E. (2000). *The children are watching: How the media teach about diversity.* New York: Teachers College Press.

Cubberley, E. P. (1909). *Changing conceptions of education.* Boston: Houghton Mifflin.

Delanty, G. (2000). *Citizenship in a global age: Society, culture, politics.* Philadelphia: Open University Press.

Dillon, S. (2006, August 27). In schools across U. S., the melting pot overflows. *New York Times,* vol. CLV [155] (no. 53,684), pp. A7 & 16.

D'Souza, D. (1991). *Illiberal education: The politics of race and sex on campus.* New York: The Free Press.

Drachsler, J. (1920). *Democracy and assimilation.* New York: Macmillan.

Eldering, L., & Kloprogge, J. (1989). *Different cultures, same school: Ethnic minority children in Europe.* Amsterdam: Swets & Seitlinger.

Franklin, J. H. (1976). *Racial equality in America.* Chicago: The University of Chicago Press.

Gillborn, D. (1990). *Race, ethnicity, and education.* London: Unwin Hyman.

Giroux, H. (1996). Doing cultural studies: Youth and the challenge of pedagogy. In P. Leistyna, A. Woodrum, & S. A. Sherblom (Eds.), *Breaking free: The transformative power of critical pedagogy* (pp. 83–108). Cambridge, MA: Harvard University Press.

Glazer, N. (1997). *We are all multiculturalists now.* Cambridge, MA: Harvard University Press.

Gonçalves e Silva, P. B. (2004). Citizenship and education in Brazil: The contribution of Indian peoples and Blacks in the struggles for citizenship and recognition. In J. A. Banks (Ed.), *Diversity and citizenship education: Global perspectives* (pp. 185–218). San Francisco: Jossey-Bass.

Gordon, B. M. (2001). Knowledge construction, competing critical theories, and education. In J. A. Banks & C. A. M. Banks (Eds.), *Handbook of research on multicultural education* (1st ed., pp. 184–199). San Francisco: Jossey-Bass.

Gordon, M. M. (1964). *Assimilation in American life.* New York: Oxford University Press.

Gregorian, V. (2003). *Islam: A mosaic, not a monolith.* Washington, D.C.: Brookings Institution Press.

Gutmann, A. (1999). *Democratic education.* Princeton, NJ: Princeton University Press.

Gutmann, A. (2004). Unity and diversity in democratic multicultural education: Creative and destructive tensions. In J. A. Banks (Ed.), *Diversity and citizenship education: Global perspectives* (pp. 71–96). San Francisco: Jossey-Bass.

Hatcher, R., & Troyna, B. (1993). Racialization and children. In C. McCarthy & W. Crichlow (Eds.), *Race, identity, and representation in education* (pp. 109–125). New York: Routledge.

Higham, J. (1972). *Strangers in the land: Patterns of American nativism 1860–1925.* New York: Atheneum.

Jacobson, M. F. (1998). *Whiteness of a different color: European immigrants and the alchemy of race.* Cambridge, MA: Harvard University Press.

Jenkins, R. (1997). *Rethinking ethnicity: Arguments and explorations.* London: Sage.

Kallen, H. M. (1924). *Culture and democracy in the United States.* New York: Boni and Liveright.

King, J. E. (2004). Culture-centered knowledge: Black studies, curriculum transformation, and social action. In J. A. Banks & C. A. M. Banks (Eds.), *Handbook of research on multicultural education* (2nd ed., pp. 349–378). San Francisco: Jossey-Bass.

Kwong, P., & Miscevic, D. (2005). *Chinese America: The untold story of America's oldest new community.* New York: New Press.

Kymlicka, W. (1995). *Multicultural citizenship: A liberal theory of minority rights.* New York: Oxford University Press.

Kymlicka, W. (2004). Foreword. In J. A. Banks (Ed.), *Diversity and citizenship education: Global perspectives* (pp. xiii–xviii). San Francisco: Jossey-Bass.

Ladson-Billings, G. (2004). Culture versus citizenship: The challenge of racialized citizenship in the United States. In J. A. Banks (Ed.), *Diversity and citizenship education: Global perspectives* (pp. 99–126). San Francisco: Jossey-Bass.

Lopez, I. F. H. (1996). *White by law: The legal construction of race.* New York: New York University Press.

Mallette, M. H., Bean, T. W., & Readence, J. E. (1998). Using Banks' typology in the discussions of young adult, multiethnic literature: A multicase study. *Journal of Research and Development in Education, 31*(4), 193–204.

McIntosh, P. (2001). White privilege: Unpacking the invisible knapsack. In P. S. Rothenberg (Ed.), *Race, class, and gender in the United States* (pp. 163–168). New York: Worth Publishers.

Morrison, T. (1992). *Playing in the dark: Whiteness and the literary imagination.* Cambridge, MA: Harvard University Press.

Murphy-Shigematsu, S. (2004). Expanding the borders of the nation: Ethnic diversity and citizenship education in Japan. In J. A. Banks (Ed.), *Diversity and citizenship education: Global perspectives* (pp. 303–332). San Francisco: Jossey-Bass.

Nguyen, T. (2005). *We are all suspects now: Untold stories from immigrant communities after 9/11.* Boston: Beacon Press.

Nussbaum, M. (2002). Patriotism and cosmopolitansim. In J. Cohen (Ed.), *For love of country* (pp. 2–17). Boston: Beacon Press.

Olsen, L. (1997). *Made in America: Immigrant students in our public schools.* New York: The New Press.

Omi, M., & Winant, H. (1994). *Racial formation in the United States: From the 1960s to the 1990s* (2nd ed.). New York: Routledge.

Ong, A. (1999). *Flexible citizenship: The cultural logics of transnationality.* Durham, NC: Duke University Press.

Osler, A., & Starkey, H. (2005). *Changing citizenship: Democracy and inclusion in education.* New York: Open University Press.

Osler, A., & Vincent, K. (2002). *Citizenship and the challenge of global education.* Stoke-on-Trent, UK: Trentham Books.

Parsons. T. (1966). Full citizenship for the Negro American? A sociological problem. In T. Parsons & K. B. Clark (Eds.), *The Negro American* (pp. 709–754). Boston: Houghton Mifflin.

Patterson, O. (1977). *Ethnic chauvinism: The reactionary impulse.* New York: Stein & Day.

Portes, A., & Rumbaut, R. G. (2001). *Legacies: The story of the immigrant second generation.* Berkeley: University of California Press.

Ravitch, D. (1990). Multiculturalism: E pluribus plures. *The American Scholar, 593,* 337–354.

Rosaldo, R. (1999). Cultural citizenship, inequality, and multiculturalism. In R. D. Torres, L. F. Miron, & J. X. Inda (Eds.), *Race, identity, and citizenship* (pp. 253–263). Malden, MA: Blackwell Publishers.

Schlesinger, A. M. Jr. (1991). *The disuniting of America: Reflections on a multicultural society.* Knoxville, TN: Whittle Direct Books.

Sizemore, B. A. (1972). Is there a case for separate schools? *Phi Delta Kappan, 53*(5), 281–284.

Smith, L. T. (1999). *Decolonizing methodologies: Research and indigenous peoples.* New York: Zed Books.

Suárez-Orozco, M. (2001). Globalization, immigration, and education: The research agenda. *Harvard Educational Review, 71*(3), 345–366.

Taylor, C., with Gutmann, A., Rockefeller, S. C., Walzer, M., & Wolf, S. (1992). *Multiculturalism and "The politics of recognition."* Princetown, NJ: Princeton University Press.

Tolzmann, D. H. (2000). *The German-American experience.* New York: Humanity Books.

Tomlinson, L. M. (1996). *Teachers' application of Banks' typology of ethnic identity development and curriculum goals to story content and classroom discussion: Phase two.* Athens: National Reading Research Center, University of Georgia.

U.S. Census Bureau (2000a). *Overview of race and Hispanic origin.* Retrieved September 14, 2006 from http://www.census.gov/prod/2001pubs/c2kbr01-1.pdf

U.S. Census Bureau (2000b). *Statistical abstract of the United States: 2000* (120th ed.). Washington, DC: U.S. Government Printing Office.

Webster's encyclopedic unabridged dictionary of the English language (1989). New York: Portland House.

Wilson, W. J. (1996). *When work disappears: The world of the new urban poor.* New York: Knopf.

Woodson, C. G. (1933/1977). *The mis-education of the Negro.* New York: AMS Press. (Original work published 1933)

Young, I. M. (1989). Polity and group difference: A critique of the ideal of universal citizenship. *Ethics, 99,* 250–274.

Part III
Social justice and the social studies

10 Social justice and the social studies

Kathy Bickmore

OISE, University of Toronto

Social justice is a supremely appropriate goal for social education. Three related dimensions of democratic social interaction, in schools and societies, facilitate (or impede) social justice:

- *Processes:* voicing, listening, advocacy, persuasive reasoning, dialogue, dissent, discussion, negotiation, deliberation, consensus-building, decision-making;
- *Institutional governance frameworks:* civil, legal, and political protections and mechanisms for appropriate and consistent treatment of persons and problems, including power sharing and rights;
- *Substantive equity:* practice of fairness—openness, accessibility, inclusivity, impartiality, non-repression, non-discrimination, equivalent status—for all, across individual and social differences (in effect, the personal and political, culturally and socially just conditions that democratic processes and institutions seek to achieve).

My (rather daunting) purpose in this chapter is to examine theory and research about how social studies education might contribute to democratization—that is, facilitate the development of citizenship that embodies and fosters movement toward democratic social justice.

Although the relevant evidence is complex and somewhat contested, there seem to be escalating patterns of social fracture and disengagement from democratic governancein many parts of the world (e.g., Mátrai, 2002; Print, 1998; Salomon & Nevo, 2002; Tawil & Harley, 2004; Torney-Purta, 1999). The first challenge for citizenship educators is that we directly influence neither this citizen action and inaction, nor the surrounding collective citizenship cultures that make up a society. We merely shape learning experiences, through which we hope to help the knowledge, skill, motivational, and experiential "ingredients" of socially just democracy to take root in the student participants. Teachers' and students'/citizens' agency is shaped and constrained by the currents of power surrounding their social positions, identities, and contexts, as well as by their education. Furthermore, all learning experiences are deeply and inevitably influenced by the power-laden discourses through which teachers and students/citizens communicate.

Democratic social justice describes behavior, not merely ideals or beliefs. Understanding, believing in, or even knowing how to achieve equity, freedom, or transparent decision-making is not sufficient to make them happen: They also require patterns of action/participation. Our project in social education is essentially to add some important ingredients to an uncertain social soup. I can't possibly offer here simple truths from research that would tell each of us how to get there—even if, from our diverse viewpoints, we all agreed what democratic social justice goals we were actually seeking.

Yet many scholarly sources do offer insights that can facilitate the movement of social education toward social justice. One theme to be pursued in this chapter is the participation of diverse students (current and future citizens) in social studies and how this might (and often doesn't) facilitate their capacity and motivation to engage in socially just interaction and in advocacy for social justice.

Some democratic processes, some institutional frameworks for citizenship and governance, and some principles and protections for equity surely exist in many societies, but no existing social system has achieved clear, uncontested social justice for all. Thus democratization requires social change. Change (that disrupts the social order) provokes, or raises to the surface, uncertainty and conflict. "Conflict" does not necessarily mean fighting, violence, or repression: Conflict refers not just to symptoms, but to the underlying disagreement, opposition, injustice, struggle, or problem, which may be interpreted and handled in a whole range of constructive or destructive ways (Curle, Freire, & Galtung, 1974; Galtung, 1996). Democratic processes and institutional arrangements are themselves approaches to handling conflict, especially to making decisions in the context of conflicting interests, needs, and viewpoints. Thus a second theme in this chapter is to examine how students may gain experience in constructively encountering, comprehending, and handling conflict.

A key challenge in citizenship education for social justice is teacher expertise and confidence. Subject matter and pedagogies that attend to significant conflicts among differing global and local interests are complex, uncertain, and sometimes controversial (Kelly & Brandes, 2001; Parker, 2004; Simon, 2001). A further challenge is to understand myriad kinds of intersecting identities and justice issues—for example, in relation to gender, ethno-cultural/racial diversity, international disparities, heterosexism, and inter-religious biases (e.g., Ayers, Hunt, & Quinn, 1998; Boler & Zembylas, 2003; Freire, 1998; Van Galen, 2004). These topics are themselves social science (and moral and political) content, much of which was not taught to teachers when they were students.

The choice and interpretation of such subject-matter is especially complicated in relation to today's populations of diverse students with global reach (e.g., Banks & Banks, 1995; Bickmore, 1999; Cochran-Smith, 1995; Harris, 1996). Twenty-first century students affect, and are more clearly affected by, a much wider world than students of past generations (e.g., Elkind, 1995; Kirkwood-Tucker, 2004; Thornton, 2005; Torres, 1998). Furthermore, it is challenging to provide students (who begin with unequal social status and incommensurate prior knowledge bases) equal opportunities to succeed. In the context of student diversity and globalization, teaching for social justice may require more substantive knowledge, more skills, and greater comfort with openness and uncertainty than teaching towards the status quo and an unquestioned, dominant "common sense." This can feel overwhelming, especially for novice teachers, given the social pressures, practicalities, and sanctions at work in the life of a teacher (Bigelow et al., 2002; Ladson-Billings, 2004b). For teachers as well as student learners, knowledge and comfort zones are shaped by our formal and informal learning experiences, by the discourses we use to think, and by our actual participation (practice) and the feedback it elicits. Thus the third thread through this chapter is the question of how teachers may develop capacity and confidence to teach complex, conflictual, globally-relevant subject matter in equitable, inclusive, and dialogic ways.

Students' (and teachers') awareness, their ways of thinking, being and behaving, are not completely autonomous. We all are shaped by cultural patterns, including language, which embody and reinforce implicit hierarchies of power. Dominant discourse encodes and reinforces certain relations of power through its presumptions, for example in the ways it recognizes, denies, normalizes, or constructs as "other" certain identities and behavior (e.g. Butler, 1999; Ellsworth, 1997). The various identities we "perform," and the language we use, shape what we each come to believe is natural and possible. Mass public media, shaped predominantly by the powerful, reinforce expectations about "normal" relationships, families, and sexuality through unquestioned performances such as politicians' use of their spouses on the campaign trail, sexualized images used in advertisements, and so forth (Epstein & Johnson, 1998). As Applebaum (2004) and Cary (2001) argue, young citizens can learn to be relatively critical, self-reflexive participants in cultural rituals and popular media, consciously questioning and influencing—though inevitably also influenced by—the discourses around them.

Notions of social difference, gender, national identity, and conflict are (re-)shaped by the dominant and alternative narratives that surround us (Funk & Said, 2004; Ichilov, 2005; Luwisch, 2001). For example, the discourses of multiculturalism evolved differently in the US and Canada, with ramifications for each community's assumptions about equity and citizenship (Joshee, 2004). Reva Joshee argues that the Canadian government's recent discursive turn toward a language of social cohesion reflects an interest in presenting public institutions as benevolent and (yet) reducing the state's role in redressing inequalities. Similarly, dominant discourses about violence tend to direct attention and resources toward management of symptoms (direct, overt violence) instead of toward recognizing and confronting the social-structural sources of violence, such as repression, exclusion, and social injustice (Lederach, 2004). Unless questioned and juxtaposed to alternative stories, such dominant discourses direct the critical gaze away from social institutions and those they privilege and, instead, place primary responsibility for oppression and violence on individuals. Thus the task of social justice citizenship education is not simply to build procedural and substantive knowledge, but to facilitate constructive questioning (deconstruction) of the sources, shape, and drivers of that knowledge.

I will weave the three threads of citizen engagement and preparation, conflict, and teacher capacity development through three facets of social studies (and social justice in) education: *processes* and skill development for justice in conflictual human relations, *substantive knowledge* about conflict and justice questions embedded in subject matter, and engaged agency in the unjust *institutional contexts* beyond the classroom. Clearly, these facets intersect, since real teaching is (at least) three-dimensional. However, for conceptual manageability, I review educational research that emphasizes each aspect in turn, after some attention to the question of conflict that connects them all.

CONFLICT AND/IN POLITICS: DESTRUCTIVE AND CONSTRUCTIVE

The word "politics" often refers, in prevalent discourse, to destructive conflict—intra-organizational tensions, corrupt leadership, scheming. To try to reverse this incentive toward cynicism and disengagement, political education in social studies often idealizes the politics of governance and inter-group interaction, preaching tolerance and the power of the democratic process. Such avoidance or palliative care is insufficient to handle social ills and build social harmony, and is even counter-productive if school knowledge thereby appears naïve and irrelevant to students steeped in public media images of dirty dealing and social tensions. Clearly, some kind of practice with recognizing and handling social/political conflict in constructive ways is essential to social justice social studies. Social justice education theory makes clear that any teaching is inevitably political—that is, that it has ramifications for the distribution of power even (or especially) when denying that—although the spaces for teacher, student, and citizen agency in relation to the workings of this power are understood differently.

Social conflict can be confronted in social studies classrooms, with positive consequences, although unfortunately it most often is not (e.g., Anyon, 1978; Fine, 1995;

Hahn, 1996; McNeil, 1986; Merelman, 1990; Sears & Hughes, 1996; Soley, 1996; Tupper, 2005; Wilson, Haas, Laughlin, & Sunal, 2002). Social education scholars prioritize various overlapping kinds of knowledge for social justice citizenship. All include elements of conflict management:

- skills and values for toleration and dialogue across social/ideological diversities and conflicts;
- familiarity with political issue deliberation processes, interpersonally and in/through political systems;
- experience with diverse cultural communities' and social movements' leadership for change;
- critical inquiry and reasoning;
- analysis of conflict, interests, and power;
- capacity and willingness to look below the surface of discourse for the differential power it conceals.

The above skills/knowledge are tools for two different dimensions of social justice: access (equipping diverse students to navigate and impact the management of public controversies through dominant political institutions) and transformation (building upon diverse students' and communities' distinctive dynamic and multidimensional cultural knowledge to overcome inequities and build a new, inclusive social order).

On one hand, citizen disengagement from collective-level politics (including formal governance) would leave disproportionate power in the hands of the over-privileged few. Replacing explicit education about the political system with attempts to encourage individual harmony values, for example, could easily leave students ill-equipped to handle actual social/political conflicts and leave the currently-unjust social order unshaken. Elizabeth Frazer (2003) argues that what she sees as an "anti-political" individual values approach in current British citizenship education denies the importance of negotiating real social conflicts through democratic political processes.

> Real political societies are full of friction....No wonder, perhaps, that many ideal models of politics are focused on the ideal of reasoned settlement, harmonious social relations, rational cooperation and the constraint of power by right. Yet this emphasis on nonviolent conciliation can foster the illusion that politics is less antagonistic than it really is. Further, it can foster the illusion of the non-necessity of politics....But politics is non-optional. In political societies we all have to encounter fellow citizens who are strangers (not liked, not loved, not known; also 'different'...). These strangers may be antagonists. The aim of political education must be to enable people to participate in these webs of political relations....It is not the case that getting the politics right is simply a matter of getting the values right. (Frazer, 2003)

Social education research (cited below) reinforces and extends Frazer's argument, showing that capacity-building for engagement in handling controversial public issues is both crucial for fostering social justice citizenship and feasible to carry out effectively in social studies classrooms.

On the other hand, a narrow emphasis on skills for engaging in formal public civil-legal issues and institutions could also limit social justice capacity building and, in fact, reinforce unjust systems. The interests of elite White men dominate such institutions in most of the Western world: Recognition of, and skills for participating in, more private community/cultural action and self-determination (often led by and for women, poor and working class people, and people of color) is another essential part of social justice citizenship education (e.g., Bear Nicholas, 1996; Mansbridge, 1998). Gloria Ladson-Billings (2004a) cites and builds on the early work of Marshall and Parsons in calling for a "new citizenship" education that attends to social and cultural concerns (such as access to resources and opportunities and self-determination) as well as legal and political concerns. Like feminist political scientist Mary Dietz (1989), she suggests that oppressed and marginalized peoples have long contributed as citizens in this wider sense, even when (and sometimes because) they have been excluded from formal politics. Ladson-Billings challenges (U.S.) social education to enable students to recognize fluid, multidimensional, local, and global cultural/racial loyalties, and to "narrow the distance between what the United States says it stands for (through its founding documents) and what it currently practices" (Ladson-Billings, 2004a, p. 122).

Along compatible lines, Peggy McIntosh calls for less emphasis in social studies on individual heroism and more emphasis on the processes of making and mending the fabric of culture—for example, providing basic human necessities and sustaining the ecosystems that form the basis for human life.

> Within patriarchy...Behind the scenes of what is presented to us as 'history,' women make and mend the fabric of society. Lower-caste men are likewise expected to make and mend the fabric. Those who wield the most public power are seen to be the leaders of citizens, but in fact the alternative fabric of day-to-day maintenance of citizens exists in a world more or less out of sight of public discussions....The nurturance of each generation depends on this lateral, ongoing way of sustaining life in the world. (McIntosh, 2005, p. 25)

Thus social justice citizenship processes include rebuilding equitable social/cultural relationships. This requires capacities of heart as well as capacities of mind; experience with constructive, equitable coexistence among plural cultural identities as well as formal political processes.

PROCESSES AND SKILLS FOR JUSTICE AND CONSTRUCTIVE CONFLICT MANAGEMENT

Next, I offer three examples of social studies approaches that emphasize participatory processes and skill development relevant to building social justice: inspiring the imagination through literature and drama, community service/action learning, and deliberation about social problems and controversial public issues. I conclude this section with a caution about the role of student-centered process and skill-based approaches in students' development of social justice awareness and agency.

Some exemplary social education approaches emphasize engaging the imagination through discussion of the social justice concerns; alternative narratives; and viewpoints embodied in literature, poetry, writing, and drama (e.g., Bickmore, 1999; Bigelow, 2003; Damico & Riddle, 2004; McCall, 2004; Sandmann, 2004; Tyson & Hinton-Johnson, 2003). Such methods show tremendous promise for social justice citizenship education because of the ways these media and activities can inspire emotional engagement, empathy, and awareness of alternative narratives of experience (Day, 2002; Rossi, 2003; Russell, 2002; Slack, 2001; S. Smith & Fairman, 2005). In contexts where there is high-stakes testing of literacy, it may also be easier to find classroom time for these approaches, compared with less literacy-focused approaches. At the same time, further careful research is needed to understand which factors make what kinds of difference in such social education. Megan Boler (1997) shows, in a teacher education context, how the well-intended use of multicultural narratives can lead student readers to develop "passive empathy"—essentially the illusion that they understand—while leaving them uninformed about the actual contexts and causes of injustice and the ways they are implicated in the persistence of such injustices. Role play, when students are insufficiently prepared to actually make sense of unfamiliar perspectives, carries a similar risk of reinforcing misconceptions rather than provoking careful thought or inquiry. Cynthia Tyson (2002) articulates criteria for selecting literature likely to inspire constructive social justice conversations. Consistent with Boler's argument, these criteria include selecting stories in which social justice problems are acted upon by the characters in ways that stimulate debate and social critique and that model possible ways to resist, rather than passive empathy.

Another type of social education potentially very relevant to social justice citizenship is community service or social action learning. These approaches directly confront the core challenge of citizenship—diverse individuals' engagement, responsibility, and agency to make a difference in local and wider communities. They aim to develop students' awareness and skills by having them take responsibility for improving the lot of some of their fellow humans in some particular way—through project work outside the school, or in initiatives such as international relief fundraising (Kirkwood-Tucker, 2004) or school community anti-violence efforts (Bickmore, 2001; Wals, 1999). *Service* (whose implicit learning is unplanned and could run in many directions) is distinguished from *service-learning*, which includes explicit guidance for inquiry, problem-solving, and reflection about the relevant social, political, and/or ecological problems (e.g., Battistoni, 1997; Boyle-Baise & Slecter, 2000; Wade, 2001a). For example, the province of Ontario, Canada requires 30 hours of community service as a condition of high school graduation, but there is no infrastructure for helping students to make sense of the social-structural causes and ramifications of the problems they confront (www.edu.gov. on.ca/eng/document/curricul/policy.html).

Service-learning scholars often broaden notions of community involvement to include social action and political advocacy with and on behalf of marginalized groups, in addition to what is typically understood as service (Patricia Avery, 1994; Wade, 2001b). Kahne and Westheimer's influential article (1996) shows how having relatively privileged students engage in "charity" toward those "less fortunate," without helping them to critically investigate the reasons for social problems, can reinforce their sense of superiority and help to reify the unjust social order. After reviewing the available evidence, Cipolle (2004) concludes that service-learning *can* be a counter-hegemonic (social justice building) practice, although often it is not.

A key element of all of the above approaches, that also stands on its own as a core procedural knowledge-building component of social studies, is to facilitate students' practice with a constellation of democratic processes and skills. These include dialogue, conflict analysis and resolution, constructive discussion of controversial issues, deliberation, and decision-making. Social justice citizenship applies such processes to various shapes and sizes of interpersonal, political, global, historical, and current social questions and problems. Democratic processes are not generic, simple, or technical: questions of unequal power, cultural norms and values, identity and difference, equitable access and voice are inseparable from the processes people use to communicate and make decisions together (e.g., Bickford, 1996; Freire, 1970; Ross, 1993; Young, 1998). Such capacities are not sufficient by themselves to equip citizens for social justice building—for one thing, the power imbalances that make such processes challenging are often ignored—but they are definitely a necessary condition. Social change requires conflict management. Students/citizens are likely to gain capacity in democratic processes when they have opportunities to practice these processes, preferably with guidance and feedback. Matters of conflict and fairness are intrinsically interesting and, as well, are all around us in society, so school knowledge is also more engaging and credible when students have opportunities to practice handling conflicting perspectives. In classrooms where students have opportunities to discuss social and political issues in an open manner, they are more likely to be interested, engaged, and well-informed about politics and the world around them (Hahn, 1996; Hess & Posselt, 2002; Torney-Purta, Lehmann, Oswald, & Schultz, 2001). Unfortunately, as mentioned above, such pedagogy is relatively rare in the world's classrooms.

One set of social education approaches that can be effective in building students' competence with processes and skills relevant to social justice citizenship is conflict-resolution education. Well-implemented conflict resolution education programs, including peer mediation and curriculum initiatives, have been shown to increase social skills, reduce aggression, and increase understanding of alternate ways of handling conflict (Jones, 2004). As with service learning, however, interpretation and implementation of conflict resolution education is highly varied. It may or may not enhance social justice: Some conflict resolution education can reinforce the status quo by privileging high-status students and/or imposing dominant culture norms (Bickmore, 2001, 2003; Lederach, 1995). There is less robust evidence about the effects of directly democratic conflict resolution education processes, such as restorative justice circles and class meetings, but such processes look tremendously promising. Such initiatives guide students and teachers to handle in a dialogic, fair, and non-punitive manner the conflict and justice issues that arise, and simultaneously guide students participants' development of social bonds and reasoning skills (e.g., Angell, 2004; Claasen & Claasen, 2004; Palazzo & Hosea, 2004; Zachariah, 2004).

There are a number of interesting lines of research on fostering constructive dialogue and deliberation on controversial issues in the context of classroom academic work. As with service learning and conflict resolution, some such integrated conflict education initiatives explicitly and self-critically confront social justice issues, whereas others emphasize more generic discussion and deliberation principles that do not attend to the particular challenges of socially-structured power imbalance. One influential approach is the creative controversy model promoted by David and Roger Johnson and their associates, in which paired students prepare and present opposing viewpoints on academically-relevant issues to another pair, then reverse roles, and eventually seek consensus on key points (e.g., Avery, Johnson, & Johnson, 1999; Stevahn & Johnson, 1996). Approaches that are more directly grounded in social studies and citizenship curricula often focus on pivotal justice issues, current and/or past, that have been faced by legislatures and especially courts (Hahn, 1998; Hess, 2002; Parker, 1997; Parker & Hess, 2001; Wilson, Haas, Laughlin, & Sunal, 2002). Students who participate in curricula that present citizen actions in the context of dialogue about meaningful, value-laden questions, rather than studying generic structures and obligations, are more likely to support and intend engagement in such actions (see also Jonsson & Flanagan, 2000; Williamson et al., 2003).

A related set of approaches focuses directly on inter-group prejudice and peace-building dialogue (e.g., McCauley, 2002; McCully, O'Doherty, & Smyth, 1999; Mlamleli, Mabelane, Napo, Sibiya, & Free, 2000; Stephan, 1999). Although the links between knowledge and attitude (and between those and behavior) can be uneven and difficult to document, it appears that well-facilitated dialogue and cooperation initiatives, in supportive institutional environments that equalize differential status, can help to reduce inter-group hostility (Tal-Or, Boninger, & Gleicher, 2002). Thus, clearly, conflict management skills and processes can be taught and learned, even in environments of inequity and inter-group conflict, and these skills can have direct ramifications for student/citizen behavior.

Skills, processes, and relationships of engagement are essential elements of democracy, and student-centered processes are crucial to developing these ingredients of social justice citizenship. At the same time, such processes never exist without content. The language used, the topics and perspectives addressed and ignored, embody relations of unequal power and depend on students' and teachers' prior knowledge. In the interests of leveling hierarchy, students may be given autonomy to participate in activities and discuss issues with neither sufficient explicit guidance nor grounding in knowledge bases that equitably represent subaltern as well as dominant perspectives. Such activity is thereby likely to reinforce unfounded and uncritical assumptions about the world. Further, such inadequately-guided activity can reinforce inequities in educational success—leaving codes of power and academic knowledge implicit, thus disproportionately inaccessible to less-privileged students (Delpit, 1995; Nykiel-Herbert, 2004). In a study of the diverse meanings-in-practice of student engagement in a few Canadian schools, Vibert and Shields (2003) show that students left to autonomously choose research or action projects virtually never chose projects that questioned official knowledge: Socially or politically critical possibilities had not been made visible or available to those students through prior instruction or experience.

SUBSTANTIVE KNOWLEDGE FOR CONFLICT AND SOCIAL JUSTICE EDUCATION

Especially in resource-poor communities, textbooks (albeit generally focused on uncritical master narratives and fragmented information overloads) often make up a huge proportion of the implemented curriculum (e.g., Milligan, 2003; Tupper, 2005). Even relatively-available supplementary resources (such as those on the Internet and in newspapers and those distributed by development initiatives) can be shallow and uncritical of social injustices. Any transformation in social studies curriculum depends heavily on teachers' academic and professional preparation (which is also limited by resource constraints, including in-service teacher time). Thus infusion of social justice in social studies can be fraught with wishes that are difficult to fulfill.

If social justice citizenship education relied fundamentally on how teachers teach, more than on what teachers know (and know how) to teach, the challenge would be difficult, but in many ways more manageable. Initiatives to recruit diverse teachers and facilitate their peer-centered capacity development (comparable to the kinds of pedagogy advocated above for use with students) could make a world of difference. The postmodern context has extended both global accessibility and respect for alternative (including critical and subaltern) knowledge. Yet at the same time, the need for teachers to develop the kinds of substantive knowledge bases that can invite and guide socially-critical questioning and debate is probably more important, and more difficult to remedy, than is often acknowledged in social education research. It requires sophisticated content knowledge for teachers to handle complex topics in a student-centered and open (constructively conflictual) manner in light of global diversity and justice concerns (Kymlicka, 1998, 2003; Parker, 2004; Thornton, 2005).

Kevin Kumashiro explains why and how, to be anti-oppressive, teaching must challenge the partial nature of both curriculum resources and students' prior knowledge, facilitating "learning to unearth the oppressive tendencies and anti-oppressive possibilities inherent" in each school subject (2004, p. 27). This requires raising questions about the stories underlying geographic, political, and historical phenomena, and thereby "disrupting the repetition of comforting knowledges" (p. 47). This disruption, in turn, provokes the desire and the need for further knowledge building.

Kathy Simon (2001) shows that moral questions (about how people should act) and existential questions (about one's place in the world and life's meaning) are barely discussed in many high school classrooms—even though such discussions are generally regarded by students to be their best learning experiences. On the rare occasions when these questions are confronted, the discussion is typically uninformed by academic evidence.

> ... high school history courses are mostly about answers, not about questions. What if history curriculum and pedagogical strategies were conceived so that they put struggling with ambiguities at their center? ... such an orientation might have opened up an opportunity for students to delve deeply, marshalling facts to support their opinions. (Simon, 2001, p. 70)

This passage illuminates the multidirectional intersections among knowledge, pedagogical process, and discourse that shape citizenship education.

Keith Barton and Linda Levstik (2004) develop this line of reasoning in relation to history education. They show how prevailing teaching approaches can give students the false impression that historical events were inevitable and universally agreed upon by a narrow range of relevant actors—thereby masking pluralist contexts, dissent, and the important role of citizen action. They demonstrate how, instead, history teaching can be organized around guiding students' practice with well-grounded deliberation about options, constraints and consequences of human action in real contexts—democratic citizenship preparation.

Official curriculum materials and textbooks (which guide teachers' as well as students' in-school knowledge development) often not only gloss over or censor social justice relevant information, but also are downright inaccurate. For example, Karen Riley and Samuel Totten (2002) critique several U.S. state-endorsed human rights and Holocaust curricula, pointing to shallow analysis, inattention to context and multiple actors/ factors shaping events, and also historical inaccuracy. Paulette Patterson Dilworth's research (2004) finds similar kinds of problems, along with a few shining alternatives, in the multicultural content of social studies curricula implemented in selected U.S. classrooms. Robert Nash (2005) cites U.S. Supreme Court decisions ensuring schools' right and responsibility to teach about multiple world religions in a balanced fashion, yet laments that such topics are typically avoided or presented in woefully misleading ways.

As Laura Finley (2003) asks, for example, "how can I teach peace when the book only covers war?" The substantive knowledge needed for building social justice (including just peace) is not merely a matter of adding information about marginalized people and human rights violations, as if the basic story were the same: Knowledge transformation that would open the way for social justice would significantly change both which knowledge is developed and how it is interpreted and juxtaposed with other information (Bickmore, 2004b; Pang & Valle, 2004; Woyshner, 2002). However, primary ignorance (not even knowing that one doesn't know) is much more daunting than secondary ignorance. What makes dominant discourse hegemonic is the way it builds an understanding of the status quo as natural or common sense, masking or closing down openings for re-thinking. Teachers' capacity to discern that some information, topics, or language for questioning are missing or misleading, knowing where (and why) to find alternatives, and bringing these into the classroom, is a necessary precondition for students to develop such capacity in the classroom.

Such knowledge-building can be and has been facilitated, certainly. For example, Tom Murray (2004) describes the process and significance of using in-depth guided oral history inquiry to teach about the Vietnam War from multiple perspectives. Another teacher describes a grade 7 media studies unit about sexism (Espinosa, 2003). The Canadian International Development Agency recently made available online a substantial anthology of teacher-scholars' resource materials on teaching for global justice citizenship (Evans & Reynolds, 2005). Tyrone Howard (2004) discusses intermediate students' development of both capacity and interest in social studies through working with an excellent teacher whose in-depth knowledge and commitment enabled her to facilitate "counterstorytelling" and dialogue on matters of race and racism.

In these cases, teachers' consciousness that certain topics and understandings were missing or misleading in their curricular materials, and of how to begin acquiring alternative information, enabled them to co-learn with students. One place teachers may acquire such knowledge (about how and what to question) is in their own citizenship activity: However, most teachers are not necessarily themselves the kinds of active citizens or social justice advocates that curriculum writers might hope to foster (Myers, 2004).

Global and local events can crack through educators' shells of conflict avoidance and motivate new learning to inform social justice efforts in curriculum. For example, the September 11, 2001, attacks on the United States, and the subsequent rash of intolerance and violent reaction, motivated a remarkable amount of new study and curriculum resource development. As many have noted, war is the devil's geography teacher. In another case, local incidents of intolerance caused teachers in a rural area to become concerned about their own lack of sufficient subject matter knowledge and motivated a series of in-service workshops about Holocaust education (Wolpow, Johnson, & Wognild, 2002). Margaret Crocco and Judith Cramer (2005) and Toni Fuss Kirkwood-Tucker (2004) describe interactive teacher education pedagogies, grounded in carefully-chosen Internet-based and United Nations information, designed to build critical, gender-equitable international perspectives. A collaboration among social studies and English educators from a university and seven British Columbia secondary schools yielded insights for participants about different ways to implement a concern for social justice in the classroom (Brandes & Kelly, 2000). For many teachers, there is already a clear motivation to learn, embedded in the "deep-seated sense of ambiguity" they feel toward prevailing curricula that reflect fragmented information and a "mythic structure of modernism" amid "postmodern realities" (Richardson, 2002, p. 135).

Paradoxically, the initiatives that show the most promise in overcoming teachers' felt need for deeper subject matter preparation for social justice citizenship education do not involve simple knowledge dissemination. Quantity of knowledge cannot substitute for quality of knowledge, nor for confidence (agency) in interpreting that knowledge. The teacher development opportunities that seem to offer this quality tend to be relatively horizontal, built around experiences of dissent and dialogue among peers (Little, 1993).

Such dialogue need not deny expertise. For example, Foster, Lewis, and Onafowara (2005) describe an initiative that might appear to rely on a top-down approach—teachers from schools with underachieving African-American students observing master teachers teaching their students in an after-school program. Yet key components of this initiative include dissonance (watching their own students doing things they didn't know they were capable of doing) and dialogue (opportunities for questioning and problem-solving debriefing among the teachers). Richardson (2002) describes a collaborative teacher action research group that confronted together the challenge of finding legitimate spaces for teaching pluralist and dynamic citizenship within the existing Alberta curriculum, facilitating learning by surfacing the participants' deeply conflicting interpretations of national identity. Simon (2001) advocates creating a culture of transparency and dialogue among school staff members through school-wide inquiry, built on acknowledgement that the curriculum inevitably has moral ramifications that are not (and should not be) neutral: "controversy is inevitable when people talk about things that matter to them" (p. 219). Instead of shying away from such controversy, it can serve as the motivation, frame, and quality-control mechanism of teacher development.

INSTITUTIONAL CONTEXTS: ENGAGED AGENCY FOR SOCIAL JUSTICE?

Last but not least, educators are citizens of our own schools, communities, nations, and world, responsible to do our part to confront social, structural, and institutional injustices beyond the classroom. In particular, citizenship is modeled and practiced in the implicit and informal curriculum of school social relationships, including especially the climate of competition or equity; the sanctioning of violence, dissent, and (dis)obedience; and the opportunities for democratic engagement and input by students, faculty, and staff into school and community matters (Bickmore, 2004a).

As Amy Gutmann (2004, p. 89) explains, "democratic education at its best is a product of many public deliberations reiterated over time." Public recognition of diversity in curriculum and equitable treatment in classrooms, important as they are, are by themselves insufficient because they do not remedy preexisting injustice. Democratic disagreements are inevitable and can be constructive opportunities to improve equity, for example, in policies regarding religious expression, discipline, or implementation of conflict resolution processes. Teachers' active citizenship participation at times can be overwhelmed by the daunting demands of directly classroom-related work, yet their insights and voices are needed as advocates for equitable working and learning environments.

Schooling is by no means always a benign force for social justice. It can promote (or resist) violence—for example, in dehumanizing and inequitable punishment; condoning sexual and homophobic abuse; or indoctrination into militarism, violent masculinities, or hatred of the "other" (Bush & Saltarelli, 2000; Callender & Wright, 2000; Davies, 2004; Harber, 2004; McCadden, 1998). Through explicit and implicit expectations and reward structures, school and classroom climates can exacerbate or alleviate the status competition and prejudice that underlie most harassment and social exclusion (Aronson, 2000; Bickmore, 2002; Gordon, Holland, & Lahelma, 2000). Educators shape and limit (in)equitable opportunities for diverse students to escape their traditional role and to practice making a difference themselves, for example in student governance, conflict resolution and anti-bias peer leadership, or initiatives to address social and environmental problems (Bickmore, 2001, 2003; Close & Lechmann, 1997). Social justice initiatives inside social studies classrooms will not be successful unless they also help to redress inequities in students' opportunities for educational success (Ghosh, 2004; Maynes & Sarbit, 2000). In an international study, Akiba, LeTendre, Baker, and Goesling (2003) found that (independent of violence rates outside schools) school systems that reduced the variance between most-successful and least-successful students (for example by de-emphasizing tracking and offering remedial help) also had lower rates of overt physical violence than more competitive systems. Thus the responsibility for social justice building extends not only to students' and teachers' explicit learning, but also to educators' roles in shaping the school and school system's human rights climate (Opffer, 1997; Osler & Starkey, 1998; G. A. Smith, 2004).

CONCLUSION

Social studies can contribute to social justice by educating for pluralist, equitable democratic citizenship. Socially just democracy requires inclusive democratic conflict management processes—such as dialogue, dissent, and negotiation—and awareness of the ways viewpoints are shaped by power-laden discourse in school and society. Also, it requires democratized governance and human relations practices in schools and communities, especially to improve mechanisms and opportunities for oppressed and marginalized people to experience respect and success in school and beyond.

Open, equitable classroom discussion of important political and moral issues is a necessary, although by itself insufficient, condition for students' development of social justice citizenship capabilities and motivations. To give such pedagogies life and meaning for democratization requires broadening educators' international, pluralistic, critical knowledge bases, and also broadening teachers' own participation as citizens in advocating for redress of inequities in curriculum and school processes. To facilitate moving more classrooms and schools toward such social justice achievements, new and continuing teachers need ample opportunity and support to engage in challenging, dialogic, problem-solving learning with professional colleagues. The circle is unbroken: Teachers' participation in discussion-rich learning about crucial issues, viewpoints, and options can facilitate their capacity to engage diverse students, equitably and effectively, in dialogic learning for social justice citizenship.

REFERENCES

Akiba, M., LeTendre, G., Baker, D., & Goesling, B. (2003, Winter). Student victimization: National and school system effects on school violence in 37 nations. *American Educational Research Journal, 39*(4), 829–853.

Angell, A. (2004). Making peace in elementary classrooms: A case for class meetings. *Theory and Research in Social Education, 32*(1), 98–104.

Anyon, J. (1978). Elementary social studies textbooks and legitimating knowledge. *Theory and Research in Social Education, 6*(3), 40–55.

Applebaum, B. (2004). Social justice education: Moral agency and the subject of resistance. *Educational Theory, 54*(1), 59–72.

Aronson, E. (2000). *Nobody left to hate: Teaching compassion after Columbine.* New York: Worth Publishers.

Avery, P. (1994). The future of political participation in civic education. In M. Nelson (Ed.), *The Future of the Social Studies* (pp. 47–52). Boulder, CO: Social Science Education Consortium.

Avery, P., Johnson, D., & Johnson, R. (1999). Teaching an understanding of war and peace through structured academic controversies. In A. Raviv et al. (Eds.), *How children understand war and peace* (pp. 260–280). San Francisco: Jossey-Bass.

Ayers, W., Hunt, J. A., & Quinn, T. (Eds.). (1998). *Teaching for social justice.* New York: New Press and Teachers College.

Banks, C. M., & Banks, J. (1995). Equity pedagogy: An essential component of multicultural education. *Theory Into Practice, 34*(3), 152–158.

Barton, K., & Levstik, L. (2004). *Teaching history for the common good.* Mahwah, NJ: Erlbaum.

Battistoni, R. (1997). Service learning and democratic citizenship. *Theory Into Practice, 36*(3), 150–156.

Bear Nicholas, A. (1996). Citizenship education and Aboriginal people: The humanitarian art of cultural genocide. *Canadian and International Education, 25*(2), 59–107.

Bickford, S. (1996). *The dissonance of democracy.* Ithaca, NY: Cornell University Press.

Bickmore, K. (1999). Elementary curriculum about conflict resolution: Can children handle global politics? *Theory and Research in Social Education, 27*(1), 45–69.

Bickmore, K. (2001). Student conflict resolution, power 'sharing' in schools, and citizenship education. *Curriculum Inquiry, 31*(2), 137–162.

Bickmore, K. (2002). How might social education resist (hetero)sexism? Facing the impact of gender and sexual ideology on citizenship. *Theory and Research in Social Education, 30*(2), 198–216.

Bickmore, K. (2003). Conflict resolution education: Multiple options for contributing to just and democratic peace. In W. Pammer & J. Killian (Eds.), *Handbook of Conflict Management* (pp. 3–32). New York: Marcel-Dekker.

Bickmore, K. (2004a). Discipline for democracy? School districts' management of conflict and social exclusion. *Theory and Research in Social Education, 32*(1), 75–97.

Bickmore, K. (2004b). Education for peacebuilding citizenship: Teaching the dimensions of conflict resolution in social studies. In A. Sears & I. Wright (Eds.), *Challenges and prospects for Canadian social studies* (pp. 187–201). Vancouver: Pacific Educational Press.

Bigelow, B. (2003). Teaching Gulf War II: Lessons that encourage Ss to question the official story on Iraq. *Rethinking Schools, 17*(3), 10–11.

Bigelow, B., Christensen, L., Swope, K., Dawson, K., Karp, S., Levine, D., et al. (2002). Teaching to make a difference: Advice to new Ts from Ts who've been there. *Rethinking Schools,* 13–17.

Boler, M. (1997). The risks of empathy: Interrogating multiculturalism's gaze. *Cultural Studies, 11*(2), 253–273.

Boler, M., & Zembylas, M. (2003). Discomforting truths: The emotional terrain of understanding difference. In P. Trifonas (Ed.), *Pedagogies of difference: Rethinking education for social change* (pp. 110–136). Halifax: Fernwood.

Boyle-Baise, M., & Sleeter, C. (2000). Community-based service learning for multicultural teacher education. *Educational Foundations, 14,* 33–50.

Brandes, G. M., & Kelly, D. (2000). Placing social justice at the heart of teacher education: Reflections on a project in process. *Exceptionality Education Canada, 10*(1-2), 75–94.

Bush, K., & Saltarelli, D. (2000). *The two faces of education in ethnic conflict: Towards a peacebuilding education for children.* Florence, Italy: UNICEF Innocenti Research Centre.

Butler, J. (1999). *Gender Trouble: Feminism and the subversion of identity* (2nd ed.). London: Routledge.

Callender, C., & Wright, C. (2000). Discipline and democracy: Race, gender, school sanctions and control. In M. Arnot & J. Dillabough (Eds.), *Challenging democracy: International perspectives on gender, education and citizenship* (pp. 216–237). London: Routledge.

Cary, L. (2001). The refusals of citizenship: Normalizing practices in social educational discourses. *Theory and Research in Social Education, 29*(3), 405–430.

Cípolle, S. (2004). Service learning as a counter-hegemonic practice: Evidence pro and con. *Multicultural Education, 11*(3), 12–23.

Claasen, R., & Claasen, R. (2004, Winter). Creating a restorative discipline system: Restorative justice in schools. *The Fourth R,* 9–12.

Close, C., & Lechmann, K. (1997). Fostering youth leadership: Students train students and adults in conflict resolution. *Theory Into Practice, 36*(1), 11–16.

Cochran-Smith, M. (1995). Uncertain allies: Understanding the boundaries of race and teaching. *Harvard Educational Review, 65*(4), 541–570.

Crocco, M. S., & Cramer, J. (2005). Women, WebQuests, and controversial issues in the social studies. *Social Education, 69*(4), 143–148.

Curle, A., Freire, P., & Galtung, J. (1974). What can education contribute towards peace and social justice? Curle, Freire, Galtung panel. In M. Haavelsrud (Ed.), *Education for peace: Reflection and action* (pp. 64–97). Keele, UK: University of Keele.

Damico, J., & Riddle, R. (2004). From answers to questions: A beginning teacher learns to teach for social justice. *Language Arts, 82*(1), 36–46.

Davies, L. (2004). *Education and conflict: Complexity and chaos.* London: Routledge/Falmer.

Day, L. (2002). Putting yourself in other people's shoes: The use of Forum Theatre to explore refugee and homeless issues in schools. *Journal of Moral Education, 31*(1), 21–34.

Delpit, L. (1995). *Other people's children: Cultural conflict in the classroom.* New York: New Press.

Dietz, M. (1989). Context is all: Feminism and theories of citizenship. In J. K. B. Conway, S., & J. Scott (Ed.), *Learning about women* (pp. 1–24). Ann Arbor: University of Michigan Press.

Dilworth, P. P. (2004). Multicultural citizenship education: Case studies from social studies classrooms. *Theory and Research in Social Education, 32*(2), 153–186.

Elkind, D. (1995). School and family in the postmodern world. *Phi Delta Kappan, 77*(1), 8–14.

Ellsworth, E. (1997). *Teaching positions: Difference, pedagogy, and the power of address.* New York: Teachers College Press.

Epstein, D., & Johnson, R. (1998). Sexualities, nationalities, and schooling. In *Schooling Sexualities.* Buckingham, UK: Open University Press.

Espinosa, L. (2003). Seventh graders and sexism: A new teacher helps her students analyze gender stereotypes in the media. *Rethinking Schools, 17*(3), 17–19.

Evans, M., & Reynolds, C. (2005). *Educating for global citizenship in a changing world: A teacher's resource handbook.* Toronto and Ottawa: Ontario Institute for Studies in Education of University of Toronto and Canadian International Development Agency (available online).

Fine, M. (1995). *Habits of mind: Struggling over values in America's classrooms*. San Francisco: Jossey-Bass.

Finley, L. (2003). How can I teach peace when the book only covers war? *Online Journal of Peace and Conflict Resolution, 5*(1), 150–165.

Foster, M., Lewis, J., & Onafowora, L. (2005). Grooming great urban teachers. *Educational Leadership, 62*(6), 28–32.

Frazer, E. (2003). Citizenhip education: Anti-political culture and political education in Britain. In A. Lockyer, B. Crick, & J. Annette (Eds.), *Education for citizenship: Issues of theory and practice* (pp. 64–77). Aldershot, Hants, UK: Ashgate.

Freire, P. (1970). *Pedagogy of the oppressed*. New York: Seabury Press.

Freire, P. (1998). *Pedagogy of freedom: Ethics, democracy, and civic courage*. Lanham, MD: Rowman & Littlefield.

Funk, N., & Said, A. A. (2004). Islam and the West: Narratives of conflict and conflict transformation. *International Journal of Peace Studies, 9*(1), 1–28.

Galtung, J. (1996). *Peace By Peaceful Means: Peace and Conflict, Development, & Civilization*. London: Sage Publications & International Peace Research Assn.

Ghosh, R. (2004). Public education and multicultural policy in Canada: The special case of Quebec. *International Review of Education, 50*(5-6), 543–566.

Gordon, T., Holland, J., & Lahelma, E. (2000). *Making spaces: Citizenship and difference in schools*. London: MacMillan.

Gutmann, A. (2004). Unity and diversity in democratic multicultural education: Creative and destructive tensions. In J. Banks (Ed.), *Diversity and Citizenship Education: Global Perspectives* (pp. 71–96). San Francisco: Jossey-Bass/ Wiley.

Hahn, C. (1996). Empirical research on issues-centered social studies. In R. Evans & D. Saxe (Eds.), *Handbook on issues-centered social studies* (Vol. 93, pp. 25–41). Washington, DC: National Council for the Social Studies.

Hahn, C. (1998). *Becoming political: Comparative perspectives on citizenship education*. Albany: State University of New York Press.

Harber, C. (2004). *Schooling as violence: How schools harm pupils and societies*. London: Routledge-Falmer.

Harris, I. (1996). From world peace to peace in the 'hood: Peace education in a postmodern world. *Journal for a Just and Caring Education, 2*(4), 378–395.

Hess, D. (2002, Winter). Discussing controversial public issues in secondary social studies classrooms: Learning from skilled teachers. *Theory and Research in Social Education, 30*(1), 10–41.

Hess, D., & Posselt, J. (2002). How high school students experience and learn from the discussion of controversial public issues. *Journal of Curriculum and Supervision, 17*(4), 283–314.

Howard, T. (2004). Does race really matter? Secondary students' construction of racial dialogue in the social studies. *Theory and Research in Social Education, 32*(4), 484–502.

Ichilov, O. (2005). Pride in one's country and citizenship orientations in a divided society. *Comparative Education Review, 49*(1), 44–61.

Jones, T. (2004). Conflict resolution education: The field, the findings, and the future. *Conflict Resolution Quarterly, 22*(1-2), 233–267.

Jonsson, B., & Flanagan, C. (2000). Young people's views on distributive justice, rights, and obligations: A cross-national study. *International Social Science Journal (164)*, 195–208.

Joshee, R. (2004). Citizenship and multicultural education in Canada: From assimilation to social cohesion. In J. Banks (Ed.), *Diversity and citizenship education: Global perspectives* (pp. 127–156). San Francisco: Jossey-Bass/ Wiley.

Kahne, J., & Westheimer, J. (1996). In service of what? The politics of service learning. *Phi Delta Kappan, 77*, 592–598.

Kelly, D., & Brandes, G. M. (2001). Shifting out of 'neutral:' Beginning teachers' struggles with teaching for social justice. *Canadian Journal of Education, 26*(4), 437–454.

Kirkwood-Tucker, T. F. (2004). Empowering teachers to create a more peaceful world through global education: Simulating the United Nations. *Theory and Research in Social Education, 32*(1), 56–74.

Kumashiro, K. (2004). *Against common sense: Teaching and learning toward social justice*. New York: Routledge.

Kymlicka, W. (1998). The theory and practice of Canadian multiculturalism. 2004

Kymlicka, W. (2003). Two dilemmas of citizenship education in pluralist societies. In A. Lockyer, B. Crick, & J. Annette (Eds.), *Education for democratic citizenship: Issues of theory and practice* (pp. 47–63). Aldershot, Hants, UK: Ashgate.

Ladson-Billings, G. (2004a). Culture versus citizenship: The challenge of racialized citizenship in the United States. In J. Banks (Ed.), *Diversity and citizenship education: Global perspectives* (pp. 99–126). San Francisco: Jossey-Bass/ Wiley.

Ladson-Billings, G. (2004b). Foreward. In K. Kumashiro (Ed.), *Against common sense: Teaching and learning toward social justice* (pp. xiii–xxviii). New York: Routledge.

Lederach, J. P. (1995). *Preparing for peace: Conflict transformation across cultures.* Syracuse, NY: Syracuse University Press.

Lederach, J. P. (2004). The challenge of the 21st century. Retrieved November 14, 2004, from http://www.xs4all.nl/~conflic1/pbp/part1/1_justpe.htm.

Little, J. W. (1993). Teachers' professional development in a climate of educational reform. *Educational Evaluation and Policy Analysis, 15*(2), 129–151.

Luwisch, F. E. (2001). Understanding what goes on in the heart and the mind: Learning about diversity and co-existence through storytelling. *Teaching and Teacher Education, 17,* 133–146.

Mansbridge, J. (1998). Feminism and democracy. In A. Philipps (Ed.), *Feminism and politics* (pp. 142–158). New York: Oxford University Press.

Mátrai, Z. (2002). National identity conflicts and civic education: a comparison of five countries. In G. Steiner-Khamsi, J. Torney-Purta & J. Schwille (Eds.), *New paradigms and recurring paradoxes in education for citizenship: An international comparison* (pp. 85–104). Amsterdam: JAI/ Elsevier Science.

Maynes, B., & Sarbit, G. (2000). Schooling children living in poverty: Perspectives on social justice. *Exceptionality Education Canada, 10*(1-2), 37–61.

McCadden, B. M. (1998). Why is Michael always getting timed out? Race, class and disciplining other people's children. In R. E. Butchart & B. McEwan (Eds.), *Classroom discipline in American schools: Problems and possibilities for democratic education* (pp. 109–134). Albany: State University of New York Press.

McCall, A. (2004). Using poetry in social studies classes to teach about cultural diversity and social justice. *The Social Studies, 95*(4), 172–176.

McCauley, C. (2002). Head first versus feet first in peace education. In G. Salomon & B. Nevo (Eds.), *Peace education: The concept, principles, and practices around the world* (pp. 247–258). Mahwah, NJ: Erlbaum.

McCully, A., O'Doherty, M., & Smyth, P. (1999). The speak your piece project: Exploring controversial issues in Northern Ireland. In L. Forcey & I. Harris (Eds.), *Peacebuilding for adolescents* (pp. 119–138). New York: Peter Lang.

McIntosh, P. (2005). Gender perspectives on educating for global citizenship. In N. Noddings (Ed.), *Educating citizens for global awareness* (pp. 22–39). New York: Teachers College Press.

McNeil, L. (1986). *Contradictions of control: School structure and school knowledge.* New York: Routledge.

Merelman, R. (1990). The role of conflict in children's political learning. In O. Ichilov (Ed.), *Political socialization, citizenship education, and democracy* (pp. 47–65). New York: Teachers College Press.

Milligan, J. (2003). Teaching between the cross and the crescent moon: Islamic identity, postcoloniality, and public education in the Southern Philippines. *Comparative Education Review, 47*(4), 468–492.

Mlamleli, O., Mabelane, P., Napo, V., Sibiya, N., & Free, V. (2000). Creating programs for safe schools: Opportunities and challenges in relation to gender-based violence in South Africa. *McGill Journal of Education, 35*(3), 261–277.

Murray, T. (2004). Citizenship education about war and peace: A study of the Vietnam War through oral history. *Theory and Research in Social Education, 32*(1), 113–117.

Myers, J. P. (2004). *Pedagogy and politics: Educating for democratic citizenship in Brazil and Canada.* Unpublished doctoral dissertation, OISE/UT, Toronto.

Nash, R. (2005). A letter to secondary teachers: Teaching about religious pluralism in the public schools. In N. Noddings (Ed.), *Educating citizens for global awareness* (pp. 93–107). New York: Teachers College Press.

Nykiel-Herbert, B. (2004). Mis-constructing knowledge: The case of learner-centred pedagogy in South Africa. *Prospects, 34*(3), 249–265.

Opffer, E. (1997). Toward cultural transformation: Comprehensive approaches to conflict resolution. *Theory Into Practice, 36*(1), 46–52.

Osler, A., & Starkey, H. (1998). Children's rights and citizenship: Some implications for the management of schools. *International Journal of Children's Rights, 6,* 313–333.

Palazzo, D., & Hosea, B. (2004, Winter). Restorative justice in schools: a review of history and current practices. *The Fourth R, 1* & 7–8.

Pang, V. O., & Valle, R. (2004). A change in paradigm. *Theory and Research in Social Education, 32*(4), 503–522.

Parker, W. (1997). The art of deliberation. *Educational Leadership, 54*(5), 18–21.

Parker, W. (2004). Diversity, globalization, and democratic education: Curriculum possibilities. In J. Banks (Ed.), *Diversity and citizenship education: Global perspectives* (pp. 433–458). San Francisco: Jossey-Bass/Wiley.

Parker, W., & Hess, D. (2001). Teaching with and for discussion. *Teaching and Teacher Education, 17*, 273–289.

Print, M. (1998). From civic deficit to critical mass: The new civics education. 2005, Retrieved from http://www.abc.net.au/civics/teach/articles/mprint/mprint1.htm.

Richardson, G. (2002). *The death of the good Canadian: Teachers, national identities, and the social studies curriculum.* New York: Peter Lang.

Riley, K., & Totten, S. (2002). Understanding matters: Holocaust curricula and the social studies classroom. *Theory and Research in Social Education, 30*(4), 541–562.

Ross, M. (1993). *The management of conflict: Interpretations and interests in comparative perspective.* New Haven, CT: Yale University Press.

Rossi, J. A. (2003, July/August). Teaching about international conflict and peacemaking at the grassroots level. *The Social Studies*, 149–157.

Russell, J. (2002). Moral consciousness in a community of inquiry. *Journal of Moral Education, 31*(2), 141–153.

Salomon, G., & Nevo, B. (Eds.). (2002). *Peace education: The concept, principles, and practices around the world.* Mahwah, NJ: Erlbaum.

Sandmann, A. (2004). Literature that promotes justice for all. *Social Education, 68*(4), 254–259.

Sears, A., & Hughes, A. (1996). Citizenship education and current educational reform. *Canadian Journal of Education, 21*(2), 123–142.

Simon, K. (2001). *Moral questions in the classroom.* New Haven, CT: Yale University Press.

Slack, D. B. (2001). Fusing social justice with multigenre writing. *English Journal, 90*(6), 62–66.

Smith, G. A. (2004). Cultivating care and connection: Preparing the soil for a just and sustainable society. *Educational Studies, 36*(1), 73–92.

Smith, S., & Fairman, D. (2005). The integration of conflict resolution into the high school curriculum: The example of Workable Peace. In N. Noddings (Ed.), *Educating citizens for global awareness* (pp. 40–56). New York: Teachers College Press.

Soley, M. (1996). If it's controversial, why teach it? *Social Education, 60*(1), 9–14.

Stephan, W. (1999). *Reducing prejudice and stereotyping in schools.* New York: Teachers College Press.

Stevahn, L., & Johnson, R. (1996, April). Integrating conflict resolution training into academic curriculum units: Results of recent studies. Paper presented at the American Educational Research Association, New York.

Tal-Or, N., Boninger, D., & Gleicher, F. (2002). Understanding the conditions necessary for intergroup contact to reduce prejudice. In G. Salomon & B. Nevo (Eds.), *Peace education: The concept, principles, and practices around the world* (pp. 89–107). Mahwah, NJ: Erlbaum.

Tawil, S., & Harley, A. (Eds.). (2004). *Education, conflict and social cohesion.* Geneva: UNESCO/ International Bureau of Education.

Thornton, S. (2005). Incorporating internationalism into the social studies curriculum. In N. Noddings (Ed.), *Educating citizens for global awareness* (pp. 81–92). New York: Teachers College Press.

Torney-Purta, J. (1999). *Civic education across countries: 24 national case studies from the IEA civic education project.* Amsterdam: International Association for the Evaluation of Educational Achievement.

Torney-Purta, J., Lehmann, R., Oswald, H., & Schultz, W. (2001). *Citizenship and education in 28 countries: Civic knowledge and engagement at age 14.* Amsterdam: IEA (International Assn. for the Evaluation of Educational Achievement).

Torres, C. A. (1998). Democracy, education, and multiculturalism: Dilemmas of citizenship in a global world. *Comparative Educational Review, 42*(4), 421–447.

Tupper, J. (2005, April). *Social studies teachers speak up! Uncovering the (im)possibilities of citizenship.* Paper presented at the American Educational Research Association, Montreal.

Tyson, C. (2002). 'Get up offa that thing:' African-American middle school students respond to literature to develop a framework for understanding social action. *Theory and Research in Social Education, 30*(1), 42–65.

Tyson, C., & Hinton-Johnson, K. (2003). Once upon a time: Teaching about women and social justice. *Social Education, 67*(1), 54–57.

Van Galen, J. A. (2004). Seeing classes: toward a broadened research agenda for critical qualitative researchers. *International Journal of Qualitative Studies in Education, 17*(5), 663–684.

Vibert, A., & Shields, C. (2003). Approaches to student engagement: Does ideology matter? *McGill Journal of Education, 38*(2), 221–240.

Wade, R. (2001a). *Issue paper ... and justice for all: Community service-learning for social justice.* Denver, CO: Education Commission of the States.

Wade, R. (2001b). Social action in the social studies: From the ideal to the real. *Theory Into Practice, 40*(1), 23–28.

Wals, A. (1999). Stop the violence: Conflict management in an inner-city junior high school through action research and community problem solving. In L. Forcey & I. Harris (Eds.), *Peacebuilding for adolescents* (pp. 240–262). New York: Peter Lang.

Williamson, I., Gonzales, M. H., Avery, P., Sullivan, J., Riedel, E., & Bos, A. (2003). Collectivistic values and individualistic language as predictors of endorsement of citizenship activities among high school students. *Theory and Research in Social Education, 31*(2), 203–217.

Wilson, E., Haas, M., Laughlin, M., & Sunal, C. (2002). Teachers' perspectives on incorporating current controversial issues into the social studies curriculum. *International Social Studies Forum, 2*(1), 31–45.

Wolpow, R., Johnson, N., & Wognild, K. (2002). Designing, implementing and evaluating a teacher inservice program enabling 6th–12th grade rural teachers to integrate Holocaust studies into their curriculum. *Theory and Research in Social Education, 30*(4), 563–588.

Woyshner, C. (2002). Political history as women's history: Toward a more inclusive curriculum. *Theory and Research in Social Education, 30*(3), 354–380.

Young, I. M. (1998). Polity and group difference: A critique of the ideal of universal citizenship. In A. Phillips (Ed.), *Feminism and politics* (pp. 410–429). New York: Oxford University Press.

Zachariah, M. (2004). *Peacemaking circles: A case of participatory decision-making among teachers.* Unpublished master's thesis, OISE/University of Toronto.

11 Gender and sexuality in the social studies

Margaret Smith Crocco
Teachers College, Columbia University

INTRODUCTION

Over the last 20 years, academic discourse changed the vocabulary it used to talk about men and women as subjects for study. *Gender* replaced *sex* as the way to describe differences and similarities between men and women, reflecting new notions concerning the social and cultural construction of physical and psychological attributes. The old lexicon of *sex differences*, *sex discrimination*, and *sex equity* gave way to consideration of inter- and intra-cultural variation; a new emphasis emerged concerning the historicity of what earlier had been labeled *sex roles* and *sexual identity*. These shifts produced a focus on elasticity in considering what it means to be a man or woman, with repeated reminders by feminist academics to avoid "essentialism" (that is, seeing men or women as inherently and universally possessing a specified set of attributes).*

As postmodernism, poststructuralism, and postcolonialism—three distinct intellectual developments with different trajectories and markedly different consequences—spread within the academy, debates have emerged about whether any stable meaning could be attributed to the words *female* and *male*. At the same time, scholars introduced new fields of study around human sexuality. Changing perspectives on gender and sexuality resulted in masculinity studies, along with more widespread research and teaching about gay and lesbian history and literature. This movement—which was fueled by societal efforts to gain equity for women, gays, lesbians, and trans-sexual and transgendered individuals—led to new college courses, concentrations, and majors and, at some institutions, the reconstitution of women's studies programs as gender studies or gender and sexuality programs. Within the humanities, a "linguistic turn" characterized the academic field of history, and an "historical turn," language and literature. Within the social sciences, these changes were more muted but gradually made inroads, especially in marking the salience of language and ideology to human activity. This is not to say that these trends came to dominate these fields. They were, and remain, highly contested in many respects.

Despite such changes in the humanities and social sciences, these developments have had little perceptible impact on social studies. The situation might be characterized in the following fashion: Women working in the social studies had grown in numbers long before feminist theorizing arose in the field during the 1970s and 1980s. In social studies teaching and teacher education, men outnumbered women throughout the 20th century, but women became an increasingly visible force, serving as presidents of the National Council for the Social Studies, chairs of the College and University Faculty

*I am grateful to Lyn Reese and Karen Offen for reactions to and suggestions for this chapter.

Assembly, and editors of *Theory and Research in Social Education*, the field's premier journal, by the early 21st century.

Presumably many women in social studies shared concerns with other academic women about equity, discrimination, and inclusion, but, overall, women working in the social studies have done relatively little research on gender. During the women's movement of the 1970s and 1980s, pioneering social studies women (and a few men) labored to include women in social studies textbooks out of concern for gender-balancing the school curriculum, to serve on committees within professional organizations, and to present on gender-related topics at academic conferences. Engagement with sex equity in social studies, engagement with "sex equity," as it was called in the 70s and 80s, was relatively fleeting; attention to gender and sexuality in the last 20 years has also been slight (Crocco, 2001, 2002, 2003). Progress was made, but by century's end attention to issues of gender had waned considerably. Research, advocacy, and discussion of topics related to women's studies, masculinity studies, and sexuality were encountered only rarely within the field.

Most notably, however, the new linguistic and conceptual discourses used to discuss gender and sexuality hardly surfaced among social studies scholars, especially in relation to the central trope of the field: citizenship and citizenship education. In this chapter, I consider what the new linguistic changes might mean for research in social studies. Specifically, I pose two questions: Does the change in nomenclature from sex to gender represent a reorientation with significance to the social studies mandate of citizenship education? If so, what has this shift meant for research regarding gender and sexuality in social studies? I begin by laying out a feminist theoretical framework before turning to a review of the social studies research on gender and sexuality in the second half of the chapter.

Linguists have long argued that language is constitutive of thought. Not only is language the vehicle by which thoughts get expressed, but, more fundamentally, language—through syntax, vocabulary, and structure—provides a set of cultural affordances and constraints that facilitate or inhibit the possibilities for perceiving, conceptualizing, and acting in the world. Language provides conceptual scaffolding for thinking about issues in certain ways. In intellectual life as in politics, words matter greatly, and shifts in terminology often signal paradigmatic changes in thinking. Practically speaking, different constructions of problems can lead to different conceptualizations of solutions for those problems (Bacchi, 1999; see also, Crocco, 2006).

For example, Judith Shklar (1993) offers four distinct ways of thinking about citizenship: standing, nationality, active participation, and "ideal republican citizenship" (p.3). Where might these differing orientations lead? Recent work in the history of education suggests that citizenship's meanings have been changing towards an emphasis on private rather than public actions, economic rather than civic roles, rights rather than responsibilities (Graham, 2005; Reuben, 2005). Clearly, changing forms of emphasis on these matters, that is, changes in the definition of citizen, may lead to differing expectations for the forms citizenship education should take in public schools.

Feminist scholars (e.g., Kerber, 1998; Pateman, 1989; Siim, 2000) suggest that in reconceptualizing citizenship we need to pay particular attention to cross-cultural and historical models of women's relationship to the rights and responsibilities of citizenship. One scholar has alerted us to the "gender paradox," in which women's citizenship is constructed within democratic states in terms of both a "sameness" principle and a "difference" principle (McDonagh, 2002). The subject of citizenship education, like citizenship, is highly gendered: Women were long denied equal opportunities for education (Biklen & Pollard, 1993; Solomon, 1985); academic knowledge has long been gendered male (Minnich, 1990). Concomitantly, citizenship education has focused on the public rather than the private dimensions of life (Noddings, 1992).

In keeping with an emphasis on language, I borrow educational scholar Sandra Acker's (1994) definition of discourse traditions as "systems of representation which circulate a set of meanings" (p. 21). Such traditions can be so totalizing in their impact as to bring about a sea change in world view. For example, since the Enlightenment, a discourse of human rights, connected in many ways to women's efforts to achieve full citizenship, has been on the ascendancy in Western societies. When the United Nations adopted the Universal Declaration of Human Rights in 1949, this event marked the codification of the human rights discourse of the preceding 2 centuries. In 1995, the Beijing Conference took an additional momentous step in promulgating the notion that "women's rights are human rights." Representatives of diverse nation states at the conference affirmed their belief that women should be considered first-class citizens whose human rights warrant respect from civil society. Nevertheless, failure to implement ideals, even espoused ones, retreat from commitments, as well as resistance to notions of "cosmopolitanism" and its claims of "world citizenship" (Appiah, 2006; Cohen, 2002; Nussbaum, 1994) are also much in evidence today. Words can beget action but are not the same thing as action.

Amanda Datnow (1998) gets at the potency of language when she writes that "Discourses shape how we see the world and operate at both the conscious and unconscious levels" (p. 3). Datnow also argues that discourses must be understood within the context of what she calls the "politics of representation" (p. 5). In other words, discourses have both ideological and material effects, an idea familiar to readers of Foucault (1977). Power resides within and flows from discourse; thus, discourses can advance or impede one agenda at the expense of another.

As noted previously, the replacement of sex by gender underscores the shift from biologically based views towards culturally and historically imprinted views of how societies define what it means to be a man or a woman, heterosexual or homosexual, as well as the relational nature of these identities. In this case, changing language signals a paradigm shift: In this new lexical order, sex refers to chromosomal distinctions and their bodily manifestations; gender refers to the ways in which human societies have conceptualized and sorted the categories (social identities) and plans (attributes and roles) flowing from these physical realities. The new paradigm emphasizes variability and even ambiguity rather than universality and constancy in making distinctions between categories of humans in terms of gender and sexuality and the critical role of self-identification in determining these matters.

The last two decades have seen many feminist scholars adopt gender as a powerful analytical concept. Early on, historian Joan Wallach Scott (1986, 1996) pronounced gender a "useful category for historical analysis." As attention to women, feminism, and gender developed across the humanities, however, scholars interrogated the use of key words, with some feminist scholars wondering what denotation the label *women* held (Riley, 1988). Some voiced concerns about an "identity crisis" in feminist theory in light of post-structuralism (Alcoff, 1997) while others questioned the utility of gender itself as a concept (Hawkesworth, 1997):

> [A]n analytic category can be understood as a heuristic device that performs both positive and negative functions...As a positive heuristic gender illuminates an area of inquiry, framing a set of questions for investigation. Although it need not involve any explicit methodological commitment, gender as analytic tool identifies puzzles or problems in need of exploration or clarification and provides concepts, definitions, and hypotheses to guide research...[T]he negative heuristic of gender ...would be intimately bound up with challenges to the natural attitude. (p. 147)

Anthropologist Sherry Ortner (1996) raised questions about the direction in which these linguistic changes and postmodern influences in the academy were taking the women's movement:

> [W]e must seriously consider whether we create as many problems as we solve by insisting on "women" and "men" as bounded analytic categories in and of themselves. Do we not in fact aggravate the very problem we seek to counter—the hegemony of gender distinction as a basis for organizing social life and thought? Sexism, of course, is real enough. It is still the case...that women are disadvantaged in various ways simply by virtue of being women, while the same is not true of men. If it is *this* (italics in original) that we wish to understand, then of course we must look for "difference." Yet an over-emphasis on difference, regardless of context, can create serious mystifications in our analyses, blinding us to the disadvantages women share with many (if not indeed most) men, and allowing us to sweep under the rug the many real advantages that *some* women share with *some* men. (1996, p. 137)

Many scholars who raise concerns about postmodernist influences within women's studies remain committed to feminism as both an intellectual and political movement. Whatever problems attend the notion of gender, they (cf: Young, 1997) argue for its utility in providing a platform to organize against sexism and patriarchy. Introducing attention to gender, sexuality, and masculinity within women's studies is defensible so long as the new paradigm does not obscure the discrimination and inequitable material conditions many women continue to face worldwide. Feminist scholars (e.g., Bulbeck, 1998; Collins, 1990; Mohanty, Russo, & Torres, 1991; Spelman, 1988; Young 1997) also caution against essentialism in both the academy and politics, especially when it reinforces an action agenda based on the assumption that what all women want is what White, middle class feminists in the United States say they want.

Feminist theorizing has been particularly lively within the arts and humanities. As previously noted, such theorizing has surfaced only minimally within social studies (Crocco, 2004). Much research in the field seems to reflect feminist concerns prior to the linguistic turn, when feminists focused on charting sex differences as opposed to considering how gender and sexuality have been implicated in constructing a field in subtle and not-so-subtle ways. The presence of more women in leadership positions in social studies has occasionally surfaced equity concerns consonant with a liberal feminist framework. One might raise the question: Has the lack of attention to gender and sexuality been due to the lack of overall interest in postmodernism in the field (Segall, 2004; Cherryholmes, Heilman, & Segall, 2006)? Or is it due to the fact that attention to multicultural education over the last 15 years has eclipsed interest in what are often viewed as middle class white women's issues (Crocco, 2004)? Why has there been so little discussion of sexuality in social studies? Does this speak to the fundamental conservatism of the field? If not, then what factors are at work?

Perhaps the politics of representation—and the politics of small academic fields such as social studies and the politics of large yet low status fields such as education—help explain the fact that issues of gender have not stimulated as much intellectual interest in social studies as they have in the humanities and social sciences. Perhaps some aspect of the research preparation and traditions within social studies (Woyshner, 2005), reflecting the norms of education in general, explains the seeming lack of interest in gender by social studies scholars today. Perhaps these *lacunae* have more to do with the structure of incentives and disincentives within which many teacher educators in universities work, preoccupied as they are by accreditation, regulatory, and survival-oriented issues. Perhaps these silences reflect the ways in which social studies has conventionally been defined as a school subject (Crocco & Davis, 1999), with its heavy emphasis on traditional political rather than social history (Woyshner, 2002). Alternately scholars may believe that topics other than gender are more important, assuming that women's battles have all been fought and won. The lack of engagement with gender and sexuality within social studies research may reflect the contemporary conservative mood in the United States (Kornfeld, 2005). Finally, it is important to note that inside as well as outside the academy, gender inequities persist (Glazer-Raymo, 2007).

The advent of a new generation of social studies scholars may bring change in future patterns of engagement with gender and sexuality (Cherryholmes, Heilman, & Segall, 2006). Knowledgeable citizens recognize that the situation of women worldwide remains fragile, perilous, and uncertain and that the situation of gays, lesbians, trans-gendered and trans-sexual individuals, highly marginalized.

A NEW VISION OF CITIZENSHIP EDUCATION

In addition to changes in conceptualizing gender, new scholarship in the humanities and social sciences related to race, ethnicity, and the meaning of *difference* (inside and outside the United States) has stimulated reconsideration of the concept of citizenship. In this section, I raise questions concerning the implications of these new views of citizenship for the field.

A number of historians, political scientists, and political theorists (e.g., Cogan, 1997; Foner, 1999; Isenberg, 1998; Kerber, 1998; Keyssar, 2001; Pateman, 1989; Shklar, 1991; Smith, 1997; Williams, 1991) have illuminated the distance between American ideals and its social, legal, and juridical realities. Collectively, these histories emphasize the degree to which the promise of citizenship has been circumscribed and denied to many groups over the course of American history.

In *Civic Ideals*, Smith (1997) argues that two traditions of citizenship have vied with each other throughout American history: one liberal and expansive in nature, and the other, continuously re-inscribing exclusionary hierarchies even after their formal, albeit incomplete repudiation has occurred during more liberal periods. Smith focuses on the ways in which "ascriptive identity characteristics," chiefly race, ethnicity, gender, and sexual orientation, have defined those deemed fit to be called citizens. In over 600 pages of exhaustive research into legal and judicial history, Smith's book (1997) tells a story that debunks patriotic pieties about "freedom for all" in American life. He notes soberly at the end of the book:

> The history of U.S. citizenship policies demonstrates incontrovertibly that the legal prerogatives of the majority of the domestic population through most of the nation's past have officially been defined in conformity with those ascriptive doctrines, at least as much as purely liberal and republican ones. And many examples, like the reductions in the rights of African-Americans from the Revolution to the 1850s, and from Reconstruction to the Progressive years, as well as the new restrictions imposed on married women in 1855, Asian-Americans in the late nineteenth century, and homosexuals in the twentieth, all indicate that neither the possession nor the fresh achievement of greater equality can guarantee against later losses of status due to renewed support for various types of ascriptive hierarchy. (p. 471)

Shklar (1991) also finds conflicts over citizenship at the heart of American history. She notes, "The struggle for citizenship in America has, therefore, been overwhelmingly a demand for inclusion in the polity, an effort to break down excluding barriers to recognition" (p. 3). Similarly, Alexander Keyssar (2001) finds the history of voting to be a story similar to the one told by Smith (1997) and Shklar (1991), tacking between points of inclusion and exclusion in terms of defining who has a right to the franchise.

Against the landscape of these larger patterns, Linda Kerber (1998) has paid particular attention to the situation of women. She shows that refusal of the franchise to women was only one of many restrictions placed on them, including both the rights and duties related to citizenship. For example, into the 20th century, married women did not control their property and wages; women could be taxed but had no say in representation. Indeed, when a woman married a foreigner, she lost her citizenship. In many states, women did not gain the right to sit on juries and thus be judged by a jury of peers until after passage of the Nineteenth Amendment in 1920. In short, according to Kerber, women's rights and obligations as citizens were "negotiated" (p. xxiii), uncertain, and contingent far more than men's throughout the nation's history.

Attending to new interpretations of difference and citizenship can contribute to understanding the past and present in more complex terms and, thus, to reshaping citizenship education. Several feminist scholars working in social studies (Asher & Crocco, 2001; Bloom, 1998; Crocco, 2000; Noddings, 1992; Shields, 1999; Shinew, 2001; Stone, 1996) have already drawn upon these insights to argue for reconsideration of citizenship education. Other scholars have brought multicultural perspectives to bear on this topic (Banks, 2003, 2004; Bickmore, 1993; Gay, 1994, 1995; Houser, 2001; Howard, 2004; Marri, 2005; Pang, 2004; Parker, 1998, 2003; Tyson, 2006). Although it is true that multicultural theory generally espouses an interest in gender, in practice multicultural scholars give little attention to gender, and even less to sexuality, undoubtedly due to the demands of dealing with the central topics of race and ethnicity. Some social studies scholars (Asher & Crocco, 2001; Heilman, 2006; Merryfield, 1997; Merryfield & Subedi, 2003; Shinew, 2006) have also called for bringing postcolonialist theories into citizenship education.

Researchers interested in building upon newer considerations of citizenship might pursue three avenues of analysis: First, how has social studies' history been inflected by difference, in particular, gender, race, class, and sexual orientation? Second, to what degree is social studies theory and practice today shaped by these considerations? Third, in looking towards the future, is attention being given to issues related to gender and sexuality in informing the priorities and goals of the field and the development of future researchers and teacher educators? In pursuing any of these lines of inquiry, careful attention will need to be paid to the ways in which discourse patterns illuminate underlying normative perspectives on the salience of identity attributes to social studies education.

As the next sections show, work has begun on some of these questions. For the most part, however, social studies scholars' concerns hew more closely to concepts of sex equity circulating in the field in the 70s and 80s than to poststructuralist approaches to gender and sexuality.

RESEARCH ON GENDER IN SOCIAL STUDIES[1]

In this section, I organize review of the research on gender and social studies along the following lines: (a) student knowledge, skills, and attitudes; (b) curriculum and textbooks; (c) technology; (d) classroom practice; (e) teacher education; and (f) the history of the field. Because research into sexuality and the social studies at the K–12 level is in an early stage, I address this subject separately and only briefly at the end of this chapter.

Several limitations of the research reviewed here bear mentioning. First, most of it comes from the United States and to a lesser extent, Canada. Second, the focus is on

K–12 schooling. Third, I deal chiefly with research generated since 1990. Fourth, due to limitations within the research itself, attention to gender in the social studies remains almost exclusively attention to women; masculinity has not emerged as a major topic for study. Unavoidably, therefore, the treatment of gender here deals chiefly with differences between males and females, and not with construction of male identities or masculinities, within the context of social studies education. Likewise, the following sections also shift towards a positivistic tone, one in keeping with the nature of the research discovered.

Student knowledge, skills, and attitudes

In elementary grades, Jere Brophy and Janet Alleman (1999, 2000, 2001, 2003, 2005) have analyzed student understanding of cultural universals and interpreted their data according to gender, socio-economic status, and grade level. They studied 216 students in the early elementary years in three predominantly White but socio-economically diverse communities. Overall, their findings do not show any statistically significant differences between boys' and girls' knowledge of these topics, although on particular sub-items boys or girls did exhibit greater knowledge. For example, boys knew more about heat, water, and light (2003, p. 102). Girls and boys had a different understanding of the utility of clothing. In looking at shelter, girls were more likely to offer a color for their ideal future home than boys. Synthesizing across these disparate results, however, shows no statistically different patterns according to gender.

Brophy and Alleman's findings of macro-similarities between boys and girls, with micro-level differences at the item level, are paralleled by several other studies exploring high school students' knowledge of history. Walter and Young (1997) found that 432 high school juniors and seniors in Alberta, Canada, exhibited differences according to gender in response to certain test items. Le (1999) looked at the 10th-grade history test given as part of the National Education Longitudinal Study (NELS) of 1988, which used nationally representative samples with retesting of the same students in subsequent years. Gender differences emerged in students' answers associated with what researchers characterized as "male themes" (e.g., power, conflict, and control) and "female themes" (e.g., individual liberty, equality, social consequences of historical change, religion, and food). June Chapin (1998, 2001) also reviewed the NELS: 88 data and found gender disparities. More males than females scored in the highest and lowest categories at all grade levels, and boys showed more positive attitudes towards history, including greater participation in extra-curricular activities oriented towards history.

Similar differences have emerged in the Advanced Placement (AP) tests given nationwide. Researchers (Breland, Dannos, Kahn, Kubota, & Bonner, 1994; Mazzeo, Schmitt, & Bleistein, 1990) found that males did better on the multiple choice portions and females on the free-response sections of AP tests in U.S. History and European history. Females, however, are more likely than males to take AP U.S. History exams, and in urban schools they tend to do better. More recently, Buck, Kostin and Morgan (2002) examined AP tests in U.S. History, European History, Microeconomics, and Macroeconomics and uncovered "differential item functioning" associated with gender. In this study, male-oriented content that produced differences in performance associated with gender included business and economics, competition and conflict, sports, fame and high achievement, and politics, among others, while female-oriented content included human relationships, feelings and emotions, personality and behavior, arts and literature, verbal aggression, and religion, among others (pp. 1–2).

Finally in terms of nationwide exams of history knowledge, on the National Assessment of Educational Progress (NAEP) tests given prior to 2000, males outperformed females in 12th grade. Since that time, no statistical differences have been found between male and female performance in 4th, 8th, and 12th grades on NAEP tests in American history.

Some data (Le, 1999) indicated that boys take more history courses than girls, raising questions about the match between such courses and girls' interests. Several dissertations (Ferguson, 1993; Protano, 2003; Lawson, 1999) examining attitudes towards social studies among males and females have shown somewhat contradictory results. Clearly, however, one factor impeding infusion of female-oriented content into the social studies curriculum is the general lack of knowledge by many social studies teachers of important milestones in women's history, such as Title IX (Zittleman, 2006).

In geography, gender differences can also be found, even among young children (Wridt, 1999). The 1994 NAEP geography assessment showed males outperforming females in geography at grades 4, 8, and 12. Likewise, the Educational Testing Service Gender Study, which analyzed data from hundreds of tests and students in grades 4, 8, and 12, also reported that males surpassed females in their "geopolitical knowledge." One research project (LeVassuer, 1999) investigating geographic knowledge among 359 students in six Florida middle and high schools showed no statistically significant differences between male and female scores in geography knowledge, although more males than females and more Whites than African Americans were represented in the top achieving group. This may explain why geography bees have been so dominated by males (Hyman, 2005).

In civics, female students have made significant progress in their achievement on tests over the last 15 years, in some cases reversing pre-1990 disparities in knowledge of politics, civics, and governments vis à vis male students. As with history tests, gendered patterns can be found, albeit to a lesser extent than in the past. These differences emerge in specific categories of items on both the NAEP civics test and the Civic Education Study of the International Association for the Evaluation of Educational Achievement, or IEA. As in other subject areas, the NAEP civics tests assessed students' knowledge in grades 4, 8, and 12, while the IEA assessed knowledge, attitudes, and experiences of 14-year-olds in 28 countries in 1999.

In 1998, female students in grades 8 and 12 had higher overall average scores on NAEP civics tests than did male students, although males' achievement surpasses females' achievement at the advanced level at all three grades (Lutkus, Weiss, Campbell, Mazzeo, & Lazer, 1999; Niemi & Junn, 1998). On the IEA study, no gender differences were found among US students (Baldi, Perie, Skidmore, Greenberg, & Hahn, 2001; Torney-Purta, Lehmann, Oswald, & Schulz, 2001). On the subscale measuring civic skills, which includes abilities to distinguish fact from opinion, interpret political cartoons, and comprehend information from political texts, female students did significantly better than male students (Baldi et al., 2001).

In terms of civic attitudes, IEA researchers found no significant gender differences in terms of political interest and perceptions of good citizenship, although females have been found to be less likely than males to say that government is their favorite subject or that they enjoy civics more than other classes (Niemi & Junn, 1998). In the areas of political trust and political efficacy, however, gender differences were apparent. Female students were more likely than male students to say they trust government institutions and to agree that participation in school activities can be effective. Of further interest are differing attitudes among boys and girls concerning women's participation in government. Researchers (Hahn, 1996, 1998; Torney-Purta, 1991; Torney-Purta et al., 2001) have consistently found that female students in the United States were more likely than male students to support gender equity and rights for women, although overall support for women's political and economic equality was at 90% among both boys and girls, according to the latest research.

Research on how these attitudes inform future behavior can also be found in the IEA study. Female students are more likely than male students, according to the Civic Education Study, to vote, collect money for charities, and collect signatures for a petition (Richardson, 2004; Torney-Purta et al., 2001). Female students also were more likely to anticipate joining a political party, writing letters to newspapers about social or political concerns, or being candidates for local political office (Baldi et al., 2001; Richardson, 2004). Other studies indicate that female students in the United States are more likely to participate in community service activities (Chapin, 2001; Flanagan, Bowes, Jonson, Csapo & Sheblanova, 1998; Independent Sector, 1996). In one of the rare examples of research in social studies that breaks gender results down by race and ethnicity, June Chapin (1998, 2001) found that African American female students were the most likely to participate in political groups; Asian female students were most likely to participate in hospital auxiliaries; and White female students were most likely to participate in environmental groups as forms of civic activism. White male students participated most in youth-oriented groups. A longitudinal study about the long-term effects of participation in high school extra-curricular activities (Damico, Damico, & Conway, 1998) indicated that being a leader in high school increased the likelihood of later civic activism.

In economics, most studies use the Test of Economic Literacy (TEL) and the AP economics tests to gauge gender differences in knowledge and skills since NAEP does not test knowledge of economics. Males consistently have scored higher on the TEL than females and reported liking economics more (Walstad & Robson, 1997; Walstad & Soper, 1989). In a national sample of 12th-grade students, Heath (2001) compared those in mandated and elected economics classes. She found that males were more likely to choose economics classes than females and that in these elected classes they outperformed female students by a significant margin. When the picture in economics classes is corrected for the self-selection issue, the gender difference is actually much larger than might appear otherwise. Interestingly, Heath (2001) also found that when a female teacher taught economics, both males and females scored higher on tests of economic literacy. One other study found intriguing gender differences that may play a role in economics courses' treatment of social issues. Beutel and Marini (1995) found that female adolescents expressed greater concern than male peers for the well-being of others; concomitantly, they were less accepting of competition and materialism. Researchers also found that female adolescents placed greater emphasis on discovering the meaning and purpose of life than male adolescents. The researchers could not explain these differences by other criteria, such as religiosity or levels of perceived social support.

Curriculum and textbooks

Curriculum theorists agree that creating and delivering curriculum is a normative process. In essence, a curriculum represents truth and cultural value for students. If women's lives (or those of non-elite men) get left out of the curriculum, then students receive a message that women's stories, issues, and concerns are unimportant for history. If political and economic history crowd out social history and, by extension, women's history, then students get the message that childbearing and childrearing, subsistence agriculture, the building of a social order, and the care and maintenance of communities have had little significance over time (Bernard-Powers, 1995, 1996; Crocco, 1997; Noddings, 1992; Woyshner, 2002). Still, it is important to note that even within the context of political history, it is quite possible to infuse substantial content related to women and gender as long as one focuses on struggle and debate rather than simply on great (male) political leaders.

During the 1990s, many professional organizations promulgated curriculum standards (Center for Civic Education, 1994; NCSS, 1994; National Center for History in the Schools, 1996; National Council for Economics Education, 1997; National Council for Geography Education, 2000). Research suggests that inclusion of gender in national standards was not a high priority for the organizations or states developing curriculum frameworks. In a survey of 50 state social studies coordinators, only a few respondents indicated that school districts offered a separate course in women's studies (Hahn, Dilworth, Hughes & Sen, 1998). Respondents also indicated that teachers infused content on women and gender into the courses they taught. Nevertheless, if teachers are following standards and using textbooks, it is not clear to what extent such infusion occurs, given the almost gender-blind character of many curricular frameworks and social studies textbooks. Recent research concerning gender, world history standards, and human rights (Crocco, 2007) presents a rather gloomy picture about women's place in world history. Nevertheless, over the years, social studies journals have published quite a few articles concerning women in American and world history and geography (e.g., Christensen, 2005; Huerta & Flemmer, 2001; Hickey & Kolterman, 2006; Kohlmeier, 2005, Landorf & Pagan, 2005; Webster, 2000).

Few broad-based curriculum studies have been conducted nationwide over the last 15 years in social studies, perhaps due to the absence of federal or other funding. However, several studies of gender, textbooks, and trade books have been done. These are important since researchers consistently argue that textbooks play a critical role in the field (Baldi et al., 2001; Lutkus et al., 1999; Niemi & Junn, 1998) and that trade books are increasingly important in middle schools. Recent investigations suggest that the progress made in including gender in textbooks has been overrated (Commeyras & Alvermann, 1996; Clark, Allard, & Mahoney, 2004; Clark, Ayton, Frechette, & Keller, 2005), although recently published trade books do show signs of diversifying their representations of gender (Ensico, 1999). In the following paragraphs, I discuss studies related to curriculum and textbooks for each of the core areas of social studies.

According to Joan Wallach Scott (1997), a member of a panel organized by the Council for Basic Education to review the National History Standards (1994), the creation of curriculum standards in American and World History resulted in codifying a political approach to teaching history that "emphasizes the growth of nation-states" and "makes the systematic inclusion of women difficult" (p. 173). Since, in the past, women have been marginalized from formal political activity in most societies, approaches that emphasize traditional political history tend to obscure women's role. The NCSS standards, however, are broad enough to allow teachers so inclined to infuse gender into their teaching, although neither the social studies standards nor the curricular examples developed in tandem with them provide much incentive to do so.

In the 90s, the American Association of University Women (1992, 1998) concluded that publishers had produced social studies textbooks that were slightly more gender balanced than in the past. Recent research (Clark et al., 2004; Clark et al., 2005) has substantiated this judgment for both American and World History textbooks. Still, it is also worth noting that many large urban school systems use textbooks that are 10 or 20 years old (Ginsberg, Shapiro, & Brown, 2004), which clearly undercuts the positive impact of recent gender equity progress in textbook publishing.

Gender has had a relatively high profile in geography curriculum, perhaps due to the marked disparities in girls' and boys' achievement in this subject and federal funding to address disparities in math and science-related areas. Interestingly, feminist geographers such as Lydia Pulsipher (L. Pulsipher & A. Pulsipher, 2002) have written some of the bestselling college textbooks in this field. Over the last 10 years, a number of investigations into gender and geography have been published (e.g., Cope, 1997; Hardwick, 2000; McDowell, 1999; Self, 1994). The *Journal of Geography* (1999) devoted an entire issue to reporting about a symposium on gender and geographic education. The National Science Foundation has funded a curriculum development project called "Finding a Way:

Encouraging Underrepresented Groups in Geography" (AAUW, 1996; Sanders, 1999; *Women's Studies Quarterly*, 2001) that attempts to interest young women and students of color in developing an interest in geography by using material that is directly relevant to women's lives. The National Center for Geographic Education (2000) also produced "Pathways," a curriculum product containing learning activities, bibliographies, and background information about gender and geography designed for grades 7 to 11.

In terms of civics education, the National Standards for Civics and Government (1994) mention gender only twice (on pp. 95 and 111); nevertheless, they note gender's role, along with race and ethnicity, in shaping citizenship participation over time. A team of researchers did a content analysis of the quotations used as graphics in the margins of the civics and government standards (Gonzales, Riedel, Avery, & Sullivan, 2001). These researchers found that 90% of the highlighted quotes were made by male speakers, with 64% by European American men. Similarly, in another study of civics and U.S. history textbooks for grades seven through nine, Avery and Simmons (2001) found that European American male office holders garnered the most attention, with Martin Luther King, Jr., the only prominent exception to this pattern. Women received significantly less coverage in both civics and history textbooks. Hickey (2002) found gender differences in the understanding of the citizenship construct among 46 students she interviewed in grades six, seven, and eight.

Specifically, in civics textbooks, women were mentioned 258 times, compared to 1,899 times for men (Avery & Simmons, 2001, pp. 122–23). Several of the women mentioned were wives of presidents, including Abigail Adams and Eleanor Roosevelt; very few women of color appeared. Rarely did civic textbooks highlight women as political or governmental role models or actors, and incredibly, only one in three discussed the disparity between men and women in electoral politics (Webster, 2000). The women's suffrage movement in U.S. history is the only women's history topic that virtually all American students learn about (Hahn, 1998), reflecting the political framework in which both young adolescent boys and girls think about women's place in American history (Levstik, 1997–98). It is safe to conclude that in both history and civics courses, female students find few opportunities to study content capturing the experiences of past and present women.

Little research has examined gender within secondary-level economics curriculum. Several researchers have, however, examined college textbooks for their treatment of women, minorities, gender, and related economics topics (e.g., Feiner, 1993; Robson, 2001). Feiner (1993) looked at 16 introductory textbooks in 1991 and compared her findings to a similar study done for the 1974 to 1984 period. In 1984, the average textbook devoted 1.28% of its space to discussions of race and gender; by 1990 the coverage had risen to 1.71%, or 14.5 pages out of roughly 800 to 1,000 pages of text. Feiner scrutinized the books specifically along the lines prescribed by the *Guidelines for Avoiding Race and Gender Bias in Economics,* which were promulgated by the Committee for Race and Gender Balance in the Economics Curriculum. Her results indicated that stereotypes could still be found in photographs and text examples, and gender was often overlooked in discussions (as was race) about income and employment.

Technology

Over the last decade, promotion of technology in K–12 education has shifted emphasis from technology taught as a separate course to technology blended into academic courses. In social studies, a growing body of research and writing about technology has demonstrated the ways in which technology can be incorporated into K–12 curriculum, especially history. Much of this research has emphasized new approaches to teaching history using primary sources, which can be readily accessed on the Internet, and the extraordinary opportunities afforded by geographic information systems (GIS) in bringing sophisticated databases of information into social studies classrooms for those with the time, money, and expertise to support such curricular endeavors.

The "digital divide" (Gorski, 2003) between groups—women and men, students of color and European American students, affluent and poor students—remains underexplored, however, as a topic of research within the field. Despite efforts to remediate the digital divide in K–12 schooling, the AAUW (2000) indicates that the gendered digital divide has narrowed somewhat but has not vanished entirely. Unfortunately, only a handful of social studies researchers have looked at gender (or race or class) and its relation to technology.

Outside social studies, gender and technology investigations have been more common. For example, a meta-analysis of gender and technology research (Volman & van Eck, 2001) reports no statistically significant gender differences in attitudes towards computers; however, the researchers did report that females felt less confident and knowledgeable about their computer skills than males. This problem of female "self-efficacy" regarding computer use is widely reported in the technology literature.

A few examples of research on technology, gender, and social studies bear mention. One project investigating female self-efficacy in a technology-oriented social studies context is the GlobalEd Project, based at the University of Connecticut (www.globaled.uconn.edu). The project was designed to address perceived gender differences in leadership, decision-making styles, and values related to using technology in an international relations simulation. In research related to the project, Brown, Boyer, and Mayall (2003) report that male students who participated in the simulation scored higher on measures of technological self-efficacy than female students in both pre-tests and post-tests. Nevertheless, researchers also found that embedding technology into academic subjects, as in the GlobalEd Project, holds the potential for reducing the gender gap in technology use. Two dissertation studies (Johnson, 2005; Mayall, 2002) based on the GlobalEd project probed questions concerning gender and self-efficacy and gender and leadership, respectively, and reached similar conclusions.

Mucherah's dissertation (1999) examined the use of computers in 14 social studies classrooms in three public urban middle schools in Maryland. The researcher found significant gender differences, with boys more interested in computers than girls and more inclined to use them competitively. In another dissertation study conducted in North Carolina's secondary schools, Heafner (2002) found that teacher attributes and barriers to classroom use influenced the likelihood that technology would be adopted in teaching social studies. In this study, female social studies teachers found technology to be of greater value than did male social studies teachers. Male teachers saw technology as a useful classroom management tool and suitable chiefly for word processing. By contrast, women viewed technology as a teaching tool that held promise for supporting their constructivist teaching approaches.

A few scholars (Crocco & Cramer, 2004a, 2004b, 2005a; Owens, 1999) have offered models for considering gender in using technology in social studies teaching and teacher education. These studies are small scale but suggest ways for thinking about how to engage women in using technology in their classrooms, especially through female-oriented curriculum materials.

Classroom practice

Research on instructional practices in classrooms, especially in social studies, is notoriously thin. The social studies literature of the last decade, however, does contain a number of examples of classroom practice in which some aspect of gender is explored (e.g., Blankenship, 1990; Gaudelli, 1999; Levstik & Groth, 2002; Marri, 2003, 2005;

Singer, 1995). In certain cases, gender serves as the subject of the classroom practice being investigated (Fouts, 1990; Goetz, 2002; Levstik & Groth, 2002; Karnes, 2000; Richburg, 2002; Schur, 1995; Smith, 1997; Singer, 1995); in other cases, gender is one variable being considered in relation to a different focus for the research (Blankenship, 1990). Too often, however, gender is ignored as a dimension of difference in investigating classroom practice, teacher identity, technology use, and a whole host of other issues in social studies.

Some researchers have found that considering gender dynamics in classroom practice can improve girl students' interest in social studies (Karnes, 2000) and that gender remains a salient factor in classroom practice at all grade levels (Goetz, 2002; Levstik & Groth, 2002; Singer, 1995; Steelsmith, 1990). For example, in one classroom that Ochoa-Becker (1999) studied, boys held all the major roles; in another classroom, only the most recently certified teachers had content knowledge that allowed them to teach women's history with confidence. Singer (1995) found that social location is a complex construction and that efforts at transformative curriculum work in secondary classrooms may founder on the shoals of this complexity.

One study of 80 middle school classrooms in Connecticut (Schmurak & Ratliff, 1993) concluded that little teaching about women's history went on year round, and that pictures of only male historical figures were hung on the walls of social studies classrooms. Likewise, boys dominated discussions in the majority (65%) of these classrooms. This judgment has been reinforced by later studies of social studies classroom practice (Doyle, 1998).

Diana Hess (2002) has identified a number of ways in which males and females perceive the benefits of discussion of controversial issues differently. After a class designed to involve students in such discussions on a regular basis, male students reported that their enjoyment increased while female students spoke of gaining more confidence from the experience.

Teacher education

Social studies scholars have approached the subject of gender and teacher education from both conceptual and empirical standpoints. Over the years, many publications have offered teacher educators and practicing teachers numerous suggestions for how history could be taught in a more gender inclusive fashion (e.g., Crocco, 1997, 2000; Cruz & Groendal-Cobb, 1998; Levstik, 2001; Woyshner, 2002). However, if such suggestions have been implemented in social studies teacher education courses, we have little evidence of this fact (Bernard-Powers, 1995). Social studies scholars have also encouraged their colleagues to "read beyond our field," in an effort to become more aware of issues related to pluralism within a democracy (Boyle-Baise, Longstreet & Ochoa-Becker, 2000).

Research on textbooks in teacher education (Zittleman & Sadker, 2002) suggests that, although they are "less offensive today than they were 20 years ago, they are far from equitable" (p. 169). This study found that on average teacher education textbooks devoted only 2.5% of their content to topics related to sexism or women's experiences. The authors conclude that it seems unlikely future teachers will be prepared to teach about the experiences of women and the role of gender bias in shaping these experiences if they have not been adequately prepared to do so through their teacher preparation programs.

In a dissertation focused on social studies teacher education, Nelson (1990) studied 21 preservice teachers enrolled in a social studies methods course at the University of Minnesota in order to gauge the effects of a plan to promote gender equity in curriculum and instruction. The researcher observed teacher-training activities, analyzed instructional methods, and surveyed and interviewed students engaged in a course designed with this end in mind. She found that, with significant attention to including gender equitable approaches and materials in such courses, preservice teachers developed the skills needed to recognize content and language bias in lesson plans and to produce more equitable and inclusive instructional units. In a later dissertation, Carol Bain Hill (2003) reached a similar conclusion: Enhanced instruction about gender equity in pre-service teacher education can contribute to inclusion of women in the social studies curriculum. Hill did not find, however, that teacher education made the teachers' inter-actions with students more balanced between girls and boys.

Many other publications dealing with gender in the context of social studies teacher education are practice oriented. *Gender and Teacher Education: Exploring Essential Equity Questions across Subject Areas* includes a chapter devoted to social studies teacher education (Crocco & Libresco, 2006). Likewise, a special issue of *Social Educa-tion* focused on teaching about "Women of the World" (Merryfield & Crocco, 2003) and included a lead article by Merryfield and Subedi (2003) outlining a comprehen-sive framework for integrating women into global studies curricula. *Women's Studies Quarterly* (2000) devoted a special issue to "gender on the chalkboard," which included a syllabus for a teacher education course about women of the world (Crocco, 2000b). Otherwise, only a few articles have appeared in the social studies literature dealing with women from a global perspective (Asher & Crocco, 2001; Crocco, 2005a).

History of the field

Until the last decade, few researchers considered gender in analyzing the origins and development of the field. Several recent works, however, have provided more gender-bal-anced approaches to the foundational representations, some of which have raised ques-tions pertinent to considerations of gender and citizenship introduced earlier (Crocco, 2003, 2004; Segall, 2004; Woyshner, Watras, & Crocco, 2004). A growing body of works has addressed the contributions of individual women such as Lucy Salmon, Han-nah Adams, Mary Ritter Beard, Mary Kelty, Eleanor Roosevelt, Hilda Taba, and Ella Baker, among others, to citizenship education (e.g., Ayanru, 2003; Bair, 2001; Barton, 2005; Bohan, 1999, 2004; Crocco & Davis, 2002; Levstik, 2005; Middaugh & Perl-stein, 2005; Schwartz, 1999, 2001). Other research has offered an overview of women's place in social studies history and the role of women's organizations in contributing to social education (Crocco, 1999a, 1999b, 2002, 2004; Woyshner, 2002, 2003, 2004). Such works have laid a foundation for gender-balanced understanding and theoretically sophisticated development of the field's history.

RESEARCH ON SEXUALITY IN THE SOCIAL STUDIES

Across the academy, the advent of women's studies in the 1970s contributed to new interest in sexual identity and sexuality. Numerous publications uncovered the stories of those who had been "hidden from history" (e.g., Black, 2001; Blasius & Phelan, 1997; Duberman, Vicinus, & Chauncey, 1990; Faderman, 1981; Katz, 1992). Such work emphasized the fluid and constructed nature of sexual identities (see, for example, Smith-Rosenberg, 1975). This scholarship asserts that labels such as *lesbian* and *homo-sexual* came into widespread use only in the 20th century, but many issues remain con-tested. For example, historians differ about whether the term lesbian should be applied to the intense female bonding typical of *Boston marriages* during the 19th century. Likewise, historians have often overlooked evidence of bisexuality in literary and his-torical figures presumed to be gay or lesbian (Black, 2001).

Teaching this history and researching these topics within K–12 education, including social studies, remains relatively uncommon. The title of Kevin Jennings' chapter in E.

Wayne Ross's third edition of *The Social Studies Curriculum* (2006) captures the long-term goal of such curriculum work: "'Out' in the Classroom: Addressing Lesbian, Gay, Bisexual and Transgender (LGBT) Issues in Social Studies Classrooms." As the founder of GLSEN (Gay, Lesbian, Straight Education Network) and author of a reader on LGBT history (1994), Jennings has been a pioneer in this arena. Throughout educational research, publications on these topics and on transgendered issues in schools have begun to appear, some of which are directly tied to discourses of democracy and citizenship (e.g., Deeb-Sossa & Kane, 2007; MacGillivray, 2000; Rhoads & Calderone, 2007).

A growing number of voices (Crocco, 2001; Mayo, 2007; Thornton, 2003) have echoed Jennings' calls for inclusion of "diversity taboos" (Wade, 1995) within social studies education. Educators can now draw upon an expanded body of secondary literature, videos, and archival resources, making it possible to introduce LGBT history into American and World History courses (Crocco, 2005c). In geography, a few recent publications have also broached this subject (Elder, 1999; England, 1999), although most of this work is aimed at higher education classrooms.

Through the leadership of Editor Elizabeth Yeager, social studies crossed an important threshold in 2002 with publication of a special issue of *Theory and Research in Social Education* devoted to the problem of homophobia. Articles dealt with curriculum, classroom climate, teaching, and teacher education (Avery, 2002; Bickmore, 2002; Crocco, 2002; Franck, 2002; Levstik & Groth, 2002; McCrary, 2002; Marchman, 2002; Oesterreich, 2002; Thornton, 2002). The issue also included two book reviews—one on masculinity and schooling (Barton, 2002) and the other on lesbian and gay issues in schooling (Asher, 2002). Subsequently, Thornton (2003) published a groundbreaking article in the mass circulation journal of NCSS, *Social Education*, entitled "Silence on Gays and Lesbians in Social Studies Curriculum," which is presumably the first piece in the journal to address this topic.

A few additional publications about this subject are worthy of note: Jackie M. Blount (2004) contributed a chapter on "Same-Sex Desire, Gender, and Social Education in the Twentieth Century" to a volume on the history of social education in the 20th century (Woyshner, Watras, & Crocco, 2004). Her chapter examines the ways in which schools and curriculum have enforced heteronormativity, in part through courses in life adjustment promoting traditional gender roles, as well as by defining acceptable sexual identities for teachers. Lisa Loutzenheiser (1996) has written about "How Schools Play Smear the Queer," and more recently (2006), "Gendering Social Studies, Queering Social Education." In the latter publication, she draws upon Michael Warner (1993), a queer theorist whose work has been influential in the humanities, as well as Sumara and Davis's article (1999) propounding a queer theory of curriculum. Loutzenheiser's writing is notable on several fronts, not the least of which is her effort to link gender with race, and both of them with sex and sexuality. Other authors (Cary, 2006; Segall, 2004) deploying a postmodernist vocabulary are also featured in the publication, *Social Studies: The Next Generation* (Cherryholmes, Heilman, & Segall, 2006). Although not all chapters deal with gender and sexuality, many raise issues important to the consideration of difference in social studies.

DIRECTIONS FOR FUTURE RESEARCH

A review of the social studies literature reveals that scholars have begun to take up gender equity and multicultural education. By and large, however, scholars in the field have not drawn upon new research related to citizenship studies to reconsider social studies education either theoretically or practically. To date, multiculturalism (e.g., Banks, 2003; Gay, 1995) and critical race theory (e.g., Ladson-Billings, 2004) have been the main influences, although the emergence of these paradigms is itself largely a product of the last several decades. In sum, topics concerning girls and women, gender and sexuality have received attention in the social studies literature. Has consideration of these topics become standard practice or a prevailing concern of research in the field? Clearly not.

Judging from the publications reviewed here, it seems that most social studies scholars (male and female) considering gender and sexuality deal with these topics from a liberal feminist perspective. Their goal appears to be to encourage fairness, gender equality, and inclusion. These are important goals, which I do not mean to disparage. Unfortunately, the field's history demonstrates that attention to diversity issues, including gender, has ebbed more than flowed (Crocco, 2004) despite these critical aims.

Given the fact that the last *Handbook of Research on Social Studies Teaching and Learning* (Shaver, 1991) did not include a chapter on feminism, gender, sex equity, or sexuality, it is probably safe to say that the field has made some progress. Yet it is also clear that, if the implications of these new discourses, theories, and questions are to have a broader, less contingent impact, the field needs to give more sustained, critical, and multi-dimensional forms of attention to gender and sexuality, especially through a concerted effort at including these topics in teacher education courses as well as research.

What difference might the lack of attention to feminist theorizing, especially of a critical poststructuralist and postcolonialist sort, make to social studies? Scott (1988) suggests that a close alliance exists between feminist theorizing and the politics of change:

> I found it imperative to pursue theoretical questions in order to do feminist history…My motive was and is one I share with other feminists and it is avowedly political: to point out and change inequalities between women and men. It is a motive, moreover, that feminists share with those concerned to change the representation of other groups left out of history because of race, ethnicity, and class as well as gender. (p. 3)

For even a poststructuralist such as Scott, the ultimate goal of feminist theorizing is to provoke change in ways of thinking about women, men, and the human condition, and thereby, to stimulate social change. Adopting new theoretical frameworks and discourses will provide social studies with a powerful and provocative set of tools to help reconsider the meanings of gender and sexuality for citizenship education. If we believe gender and sexuality to be products of social, historical, and cultural construction, and if we believe in equitable education for all citizens, then social studies must attend more comprehensively and proactively to how the field—in all its dimensions—has been and continues to be shaped by gender and sexuality.

NOTES

1. Much of the section, "Research on Gender in Social Studies," draws upon research for a chapter in the *Handbook of Research on Gender Equity* (Sue Klein, Ed., 2007) written by Carole Hahn, Jane Bernard-Powers, Margaret Smith Crocco, and Christine Woyshner.
2. It is beyond the scope of this chapter to do justice to the voluminous literature in women's and gender history, as well as citizenship studies, over the last 20 years. Readers are encouraged to investigate the wealth of this material on their own.

REFERENCES

Acker, S. (1994). *Gendered education: Sociological reflections on women, teaching, and feminism.* Bristol, PA: Open University Press.

Alcoff, L. (1997). Cultural feminism versus post-structuralism: The identity crisis in feminist theory. Re-printed in Nicholson, L. (Ed.), *The second wave: A reader in feminist theory* (pp. 330–351). New York: Routledge.

American Association of University Women. (1992). *How schools shortchange women.* New York: Marlowe.

American Association of University Women. (1998). *Gender gaps: Where schools still fail our children.* New York: Marlowe.

American Association of University Women. (2000). *Tech-Savvy.* American Association of University Women Educational Foundation.

Appiah, K. A. (2006). *Cosmopolitanism: Ethics in a world of strangers.* New York: Norton.

Asher, N. (2002). Straight talk in the classroom: Discussing lesbian and gay issues in school. *Theory and Research in Social Education 30,* 313–315.

Asher, N., & Crocco, M. S. (2001). (En)gendering multicultural identities and representations in education. *Theory and Research in Social Education 29,* 129–151.

Avery, P. (2002). Political socialization, tolerance, and sexual identity. *Theory and Research in Social Education 30,* 190–198.

Avery, P. G., & Simmons, A. M. 2000/2001. Civic life as conveyed in United States civics and history textbooks. *International Journal of Social Studies, 15*(Fall/Winter), 105–130.

Ayanru, G. R. (2003). "The journey is the destination": A study of the professional career development of Dr. Dorothy June Skeel, 1932–1995. An exemplary teacher educator. (Doctoral dissertation, West Virginia University). *Dissertation Abstracts International* No. AAT3142889.

Bacchi, C. L. (1999). *Women, policy, and politics: The construction of policy problems.* London: Sage Publications.

Bair, S. D. (2001). Finding women "under the dead leaves of history": An historical analysis of the social and educational thought of Mary Ritter Beard. (Doctoral dissertation, The Pennsylvania State University). *Dissertation Abstracts International,* No. AAT 3020419.

Baldi, S., Perie, M., Skidmore, D., Greenberg, E., & Hahn, C. (2001). *What democracy means to ninth-graders: U.S. results from the international IEA civic education study.* Washington, D.C.: National Center for Education Statistics, U.S. Department of Education.

Banks, J. (2003). *An introduction to multicultural education.* Boston: Allyn & Bacon.

Banks, J. (Ed.). (2004). *Diversity and citizenship education: Global perspectives.* San Francisco: Jossey-Bass.

Barton, K. C. (2002). Masculinity and schooling. *Theory and Research in Social Education 30,* 306–13.

Barton, K. C. (2005). Mary G. Kelty: The most important social educator no one has ever heard of. In L. Burlbaw & S. Field, (Eds.), *Explorations in curriculum history* (pp. 161–185). Greenwich, CT: Information Age Publishers.

Bernard-Powers, J. (1995). Out of the cameos and into the conversation: Gender, social studies, and curriculum transformation. In J. Gaskell & J. Willinsky (Eds), *Gender in/forms curriculum: From enrichment to transformation* (pp.191–209). New York: Teachers College Press.

Bernard-Powers, J. (1996). The 'woman question' in citizenship education. In W. C. Parker (Ed.), *Educating the democratic mind* (pp. 287–308). New York: State University of New York Press.

Beutel, A. M., & Marini, M. M. (1995). Gender and values. *American Sociological Review, 60,* 436–448.

Bickmore, K. (2002). How might social education resist heterosexism? Facing the impact of gender and sexual identity ideology on citizenship. *Theory and Research in Social Education 30,* 198–217.

Biklen, S. K., & Pollard, D. (1993). *Gender and education: Ninety-second yearbook of the Society for the Study of Education* (NSSE). Chicago, IL: NSSE.

Black, A. (2001). *Modern American queer history.* Philadelphia: Temple University Press.

Blankenship, G. (1990). Classroom climate, global knowledge, global attitudes, political attitudes. *Theory and Research in Social Education, 18,* 363–386.

Blasius, M., & Phelan, S. (Eds.). (1997). *We are everywhere: A historical sourcebook of gay and lesbian politics.* New York: Routledge.

Bloom, L. R. (1998). The politics of difference and multicultural feminism: Reconceptualizing education for democracy. *Theory and Research in Social Education 26*, 30–49.

Bohan, C. H. (1999). Go to the sources: Lucy Maynard Salmon and the teaching of history. (Doctoral dissertation, The University of Texas at Austin). *Dissertation Abstracts International,* No. AAT9959457.

Bohan, C. H. (2004). *Go to the sources: Lucy Maynard Salmon and the teaching of history.* New York: Peter Lang.

Boyle-Baise, M., Longstreet, W., & Ochoa-Becker, A. S. (2000). On democracy and pluralism: An invitation to read beyond our field. *The Social Studies 91* (5), 215–220.

Breland, H., Danos, D. O., Kahn, H. D., Kubota, M. Y., & Bonner, M. W. (1994). Performance versus objective testing and gender: An exploratory study of an Advanced Placement history examination. *Journal of Educational Measurement, 31,* 275–93.

Brophy, J., & Alleman, J. (1999). *Primary-grade students' knowledge and thinking about clothing as a cultural universal.* Spencer Foundation Report. ERIC Document Reproduction Service ED 439 072.

Brophy, J., & Alleman, J. (2000). Primary-grade students' knowledge and thinking about Native American and pioneer homes. *Theory and Research in Social Education 28,* 96–120.

Brophy, J., & Alleman, J. (2001). What primary-grade students say about their ideal future homes. *Journal of Social Studies Research, 25* (2), 23–35.

Brophy, J., & Alleman, J. (2003). Primary-grade students' knowledge and thinking about the supply of utilities (water, heat, and light) to modern homes. *Cognition and Instruction, 21,* 79–112.

Brophy, J., & Alleman, J. (2005). Primary grade students' knowledge and thinking about transportation. *Theory and Research in Social Education, 33,* 218–243.

Brown, S. W., Boyer, M. A., & Mayall, H. J. (2003). The GlobalEd Project: Gender differences in a problem-based learning environment of international negotiations. *Instructional Science 31,* 255–276.

Buck, G., Kostin, I., & Morgan, R. (2002). *Examining the relationship of content to gender-based performance differences in Advanced Placement exams.* New York: The College Board.

Bulbeck, C. (1998). Re-orienting Western feminisms: Women's diversity in a postcolonial world. Cambridge: Cambridge University Press.

Cary, L. J. (2006). Within and against citizenship: Bad girls in deviant subject positions. In C. Cherryholmes, E. Heilman, & A. Segall (Eds.), *Social studies: The next generation—researching in the postmodern* (pp. 47–61). New York: Peter Lang.

Chapin, J. (1998, April). *Gender and social studies learning in the 8th, 10th, and 12th grades.* Paper presented at the annual meeting of the American Educational Research Association. San Diego, CA.

Chapin, J. R. (2001). From eighth grade social studies to young adulthood voting and community service: National education longitudinal study of 1988 eighth graders. *The International Social Studies Forum, 1,* 33–44.

Cherryholmes, C., Heilman, E., & Segall, A. (Eds.). (2006). *Social studies: The next generation—researching in the postmodern.* New York: Peter Lang.

Christensen, L. M. (2005). Women who passed the torch of freedom. *Social Studies, 6*(3), 99. Retrieved October 13, 2007, from ERIC database.

Clark, R., Allard, J., & Mahoney, T. (2004). How much of the sky? Women in American high school history textbooks from the 1960s, 1980s, and 1990s. *Social Education, 68,* 57–62.

Clark, R., Ayton, K., Frechette, N., & Keller, P. J. (2005). Women of the world, rewrite! Women in world history high school textbooks from the 1960s, 1980s, and 1990s. *Social Education, 69,* 41–47.

Cogan, J. K. (1997). The look within: Property, capacity, and suffrage in nineteenth-century America. *The Yale Law Journal, 107* (2), 473–499.

Cohen, J. (Ed.). (2002). *For love of country.* Boston: Beacon.

Collins, P. H. (1990). *Black feminist thought.* New York: HarperCollins.

Cope, M. (1997). Participation, power, and policy: Developing a gender-sensitive political geography. *Journal of Geography, 96,* 92–7.

Crocco, M. S. (1997). Making time for women's history…when your survey course is already filled to overflowing. *Social Education, 61,* 32–7.

Crocco, M. S. (2000a). Women, citizenship, and the social studies. *Educational Forum 65* (1), 52–59.

Crocco, M. S. (2000b). Teacher education and the study of women from a global perspective. *Women's Studies Quarterly, 28* (3/4), 347–350.

Crocco, M. S. (2001). The missing discourse on gender and sexuality in the social studies. *Theory into Practice, 40,* 65–71.

Crocco, M. S. (2002). Homophobic hallways: Is anyone listening? *Theory and Research in Social Education, 30,* 217–33.

Crocco, M. S. (2003). Dealing with difference in the social studies. *International Journal of Social Education,* 106–126.

Crocco, M. S. (2004). Women and the social studies. The long rise and rapid fall of feminist activity in the National Council for the Social Studies. In C. Woyshner, J. Watras, & M. S. Crocco (Eds.), *Social education in the twentieth century: Curriculum and context for citizenship* (pp. 142–160). New York: Peter Lang.

Crocco, M. S. (2005a). Teaching *Shabanu*: The challenges of using world literature in the social studies classroom. *Journal of Curriculum Studies 37,* 561–582.

Crocco, M. S. (2005b). Mary Kelty: An ironic tale of remembrance. In L. Burlbaw & S. Field. (Eds.), *Exploration in curriculum history* (pp. 185–193). Greenwich, CT: Information Age Publishers.

Crocco, M. S. (2005c). History, teaching of. In J. Sears (Ed.), *[Homo] sexualities education and youth: An encyclopedia* (Vol. 1, pp. 405–409). Westport, CT: Greenwood Publishing Co.

Crocco, M. S. (2006). Gender and social education: What's the problem? In. E.W. Ross (Ed.), *The social studies curriculum: Purposes, problems, and possibilities* 3rd ed. (pp.171–193). Albany: State University of New York Press.

Crocco, M. S. (2007, November). Speaking truth to power: Women's rights as human rights. *The Social Studies, 98,* 257–269.

Crocco, M. S., & Davis, O. L. Jr. (Eds.). (1999). *Bending the future to their will: Women, citizenship, and social education.* Lanham, MD: Rowman and Littlefield.

Crocco, M. S., & Davis, O. L. Jr. (Eds.). (2002). *Building a legacy: Women in social education 1784–1984.* Washington, DC: National Council for the Social Studies.

Crocco, M. S., & Cramer, J. F. (2004a). Technology use, women, and global studies in social studies education. *Society for Information Technology and Teacher Education International Conference 2004*(1), 4773-4780 (online proceedings).

Crocco, M. S., & Cramer, J. F. (2004b). A virtual hall of mirrors? Confronting the digital divide in urban social studies teacher education. *Journal of Computing in Teacher Education, 20,* 133–37.

Crocco, M. S., & Cramer, J. F. (2005). Women, WebQuests, and teaching controversial issues in the social studies. *Social Education, 69,* 143–148.

Crocco, M. S., Munro, P., & Weiler, K. (1999). *Pedagogies of resistance: Women educator activists 1880–1960.* New York: Teachers College Press.

Crocco, M. S., & Libresco, A.S. (2007). Gender and social studies teacher education. In D. Sadker & E. Silber (Eds.), *Gender and teacher education: Exploring essential equity questions* (pp. 109–164). Mahwah, NJ: Erlbaum.

Cruz, B. C., & Groendal-Cobb, J. L. (1998). Incorporating women's voices into the middle and senior high school history curriculum. *Social Studies, 89,* 271–75.

Damico, A., Damico, S., & Conway, M. (1998). The democratic education of women: High school and beyond. *Women in Politics, 19,* 1–31.

Datnow, A. (1998). *The gender politics of educational change.* London: Falmer Press.

Deeb-Sossa, N., & Kane, H. (2007). "It's the word of god": Students' resistance to questioning and overcoming heterosexism. *Feminist Teacher: A Journal of the Practices, Theories, and Scholarship of Feminist Teaching, 17*(2), 151–169. Retrieved October 14, 2007, from ERIC database.

Doyle, J. L. (1998). *The effects of a gender-balanced social studies curriculum on grade ten students.* (Master's thesis, Simon Fraser University, Canada). *Dissertation Abstracts International* No. AAT MQ37518.

Duberman, M., Vicinus, M., & Chauncey, G. (Eds). (1989). *Hidden from history: Reclaiming the gay and lesbian past.* New York: Meridian.

Elder, G. S. (1999). "Queerying" boundaries in the geography classroom. *Journal of Geography in Higher Education 23*(1), 86–93.

England, K. (1999). Sexing geography; teaching sexualities. *Journal of Geography in Higher Education, 23,* 94–101.

Ensico, P. (1999). Gender representations: Reaching beyond the limits we make. *New Advocate 12,* 285–97.

Faderman, L. (1981). *Surpassing the love of men: Romantic friendship and love between women from the Renaissance to the present*. New York: Morrow.

Ferguson, O. W. (1993). The effects of different instructional types on academic achievement in world history and student attitudes toward the subject. (Doctoral dissertation, University of Southern Mississippi). Dissertation Abstracts International, No. AAT 9402529.

Flanagan, C. A., Bowes, J. M., Jonson, B., Csapo, B., & Sheblanova, E. (1998). Ties that bind: Correlates of adolescents' civic commitments in seven countries. *Journal of Social Issues*, 54, 457–475.

Foner, E. (1998). *The story of American freedom*. New York: W.W. Norton.

Foucault, M. (1977). *The archaeology of knowledge*. London: Tavistock.

Fouts, J. T. (1990). Female students, female teachers, and perceptions of the social studies classroom. *Social Education 54*, 418–20.

Franck, K. (2002). Rethinking homophobia: Interrogating heteronormativity in an urban school. *Theory and Research in Social Education 30*, 274–87.

Gaudelli, W. (1999). Teacher as self: Understanding pedagogy in global education October 14, 2007, from ERIC database.

Gay, G. (1994). A synthesis of scholarship in multicultural education. *Urban monograph series*. Illinois: North Central Regional Educational Laboratory. Retrieved March 8, 2006, from ERIC database.

Gay, G. (1995). Bridging multicultural theory and practice. *Multicultural Education, 3*(1), 4–9.

Glazer-Raymo, J. (2007). Gender equality in the American research university: Renewing the agenda for women's rights. In M. A. Danowitz Sagaria (Ed.), *Women, universities and change: Revisioning gender equality in the European Union and the United States*. New York: Palgrave Macmillan.

Ginsberg, A. E., Shapiro, J. P., &Brown, S. P. (2004). *Gender in urban education: Strategies for student achievement*. Portsmouth, NH: Heinemann.

Gonzales, M. H., Riedel, E., Avery, P. G., & Sullivan, J. L. (2001). Rights and obligations in civic education: A content analysis of the National Standards for Civics and Government. *Theory and Research in Social Education, 29*(1), 109–128.

Graham, P. A. (2005). *Schooling America: How the public schools meet the nation's changing needs*. New York: Oxford University Press.

Hahn, C. L. (1998). *Becoming political: Comparative perspectives on citizenship education*. Albany, NY: State University of New York Press.

Hahn, C. L. (1996) Gender and political learning. *Theory and Research in Social Education, 24*, 8–35.

Hahn, C. L., Dilworth, P. P., Hughes, M., & Sen, T. (1998). IEA civic education project phase I: The United States—Responses to the four core international framing questions (Vol III).. Unpublished manuscript, Emory University. GA: Atlanta. ERIC Document Reproduction Service ED 444 887.

Hardwick, S. W., Bean, L. L., Alexander, K. A., & Shelly, F. M. (2000). Gender vs. sex differences: Factors affecting performance in geographic education. *Journal of Geography 99*, 238–44.

Hawkesworth, (1997). Confounding gender. *Signs: Journal of Women in Culture and Society*, 22, 649–685.

Heafner, T. L. (2002). Powerful methods: A framework for effective integration of technology in secondary social studies. (Doctoral dissertation, University of North Carolina at Greensboro). Dissertation Abstracts International, No. AAT3060354.

Heath, J. A. (2001). An econometric model of the role of gender in economic education. *American Economic Association Papers and Proceedings, 79*, 226–230.

Heilman, E. (2006). Critical, liberal, and poststructural challenges to global education. In Cherryholmes, C., Heilman, E., & Segall, A. (Eds.) *Social studies: The next generation—researching in the postmodern* (pp. 189–209). New York: Peter Lang.

Hess, D. (2002). How high school students experience and learn from the discussion of controversial public issues. *Journal of Curriculum and Supervision, 17*, 283–314.

Hewitt, W. L. (2004). "A man's gotta do what a man's gotta do!" Masculinity and manhood in social studies education. *Social Studies, 95*(2), 83. Retrieved October 13, 2007, from ERIC database.

Hickey, M. G. (2002). Why did I get an "A" in citizenship? An ethnographic study of emerging concepts of citizenship. *Journal of Social Studies Research 26*, 3–9.

Hickey, M. G., & Kolterman, D. L. (2006). Special women in my life: Strategies for writing women into the social studies curriculum. *Social Education, 70*(4), 190–196. Retrieved October 13, 2007, from ERIC database.

Hill, C. B. (2003). Gender equity in the classroom: A constant need to be reminded. (Doctoral dissertation, University of Kentucky). Dissertation Abstracts International, No.3086896.

Houser, N. O. (2001). Literature as art, literature as text: Exploring the power and possibility of a critical, literacy-based approach to citizenship education. *Equity & Excellence in Education, 34*(2), 62–74. Retrieved March 8, 2006, from ERIC database.

Howard, T. C. (2004). "Does race really matter?" Secondary students' constructions of racial dialogue in the social studies. *Theory and Research in Social Education, 32*(4), 484–502.

Huerta, G. C., & Flemmer, L. A. (2001). Latina women speak: Using oral histories in the social studies curriculum. *Social Education, 65*(5), 270–277. Retrieved October 13, 2007, from ERIC database.

Hyman, V. (2005, April 17). In geography, it's a boy's world.. Retrieved April 18, 2005, from www.startribune.com/dunamic/story.php?template+print_a&story=5348842.

Independent Sector (1996). *Giving and volunteering in the United States.* Washington, D.C.: Author.

Isenberg, N. (1998). *Sex & citizenship in antebellum America.* Chapel Hill: University of North Carolina Press.

Jennings, K. (1994). "Out" in the classroom: Addressing lesbian, gay, bisexual, and transgender (LGBT) issues in social studies curriculum. In E. W. Ross (Ed.), *The social studies curriculum: Problems, prospects, and possibilities* (3rd ed., pp. 255–282). Albany: State University of New York Press.

Johnson, P. R. (2005). Perceptions of leadership among high school students: Simulation versus face-to-face environments. (Doctoral dissertation, University of Connecticut). Dissertation Abstracts International No. UMI 3180215.

Karnes, M. (2000). Girls can be president: Generating interest in an inclusive history. *Social Studies and the Young Learner, 12* (3), M5–8.

Katz, J. N. (1992). *Gay American history: Lesbians and gay men in the USA: A documentary history.* New York: Plume.

Kerber, L. (1998). *No constitutional right to be ladies: Women and the obligations of citizenship.* New York: Hill and Wang.

Keyssar, A. (2001). *The right to vote: The contested history of democracy in the United States.* New York: Basic Books.

Kornfeld, J. (2005). Framing the conversation: Social studies education and the neoconservative agenda. *Social Studies, 96*(4), 143. Retrieved October 13, 2007, from ERIC database.

Kohlmeier, J. (2005). The power of a woman's story: A three-step approach to historical significance in high school world history. *International Journal of Social Education, 20*(1), 64–75. Retrieved October 13, 2007, from ERIC database.

Ladson-Billings, G. (2004). *Critical race theory and the social studies.* Greenwich, CT: Information Age Publishing.

Landorf, H., & Pagan, L. (2005). Unveiling the hijab. *Social Studies, 96*(4), 171. Retrieved October 13, 2007, from ERIC database.

Lawson, T. A. (1999). Teaching methodologies and gender issues impact upon students' attitudes towards the social studies discipline. (Doctoral dissertation, University of Sarasota). Dissertation Abstracts International No AAT 9920902.

Le, V. N. (1999). Identifying differential item functioning on the NELS: 88 history achievement test: CSE Technical Report. California State University Center for the Study of Evaluation.

LeVasseur, M. (1999). *Finding a way, encouraging under-represented groups in geography: An annotated bibliography.* Pathway series. Indiana, PA: National Council for Geographic Education.

Levstik, L. (1997–98). Early adolescents' understanding of the historical significance of women's rights. *International Journal of Social Education, 12* (2), 19–34

Levstik, L. (2001) Daily acts of ordinary courage: Gender-equitable practice in the social studies classroom. In P. O'Reilly, E. M. Penn, & K. DeMarrais (Eds.), *Educating young adolescent girls* (pp.189–213). Mahwah, NJ: Erlbaum.

Levstik, L. (2005). Women as a force in history. In L. Burlbaw & S. Field (Eds.), *Explorations in Curriculum History* (pp.194–203). Greenwich, CT: Information Age Publishers.

Levstik, L., & Groth, J. (2002). "Scary thing being an eighth grader": Exploring gender and sexuality in a middle school US history unit. *Theory and Research in Social Education, 30*(2), 233–254.

Loutzenheiser, L.W. (1996). How schools play smear the queer. *Feminist Teacher 10* (2), 59–65.

Loutzenheiser, L. W. (2006). Gendering social studies, queering social education. In C. Cherry-holmes, E. Heilman, & A. Segall (Eds.), *Social studies: The next generation—researching in the postmodern* (pp. 61–77). New York: Peter Lang.

Lutkus, A. D., Weiss, A. R., Campbell, J. R., Mazzeo, J., & Lazer, S. (1999). *NAEP 1998: Civics report card for the nation.* Washington, D. C.: National Center for Education Statistics, U. S. Department of Education. ED 435 583.

MacGillivray, I. K. (2000). Educational equity for gay, lesbian, bisexual, transgendered, and queer/questioning students: The demands of democracy and social justice for America's schools. *Education and Urban Society, 32*(3), 303–323. Retrieved October 14, 2007, from ERIC database.

Marchman, B. K. (2002). Teaching about homophobia in a high school civics course. *Theory and Research in Social Education 30*, 302–6.

Marri, A. R. (2005). Building a framework for classroom-based multicultural democratic education: Learning from three skilled teachers. *Teachers College Record, 107*, 1036–1059.

Mayall, H. J. (2002). An exploratory/descriptive look at gender differences in technology self efficacy and academic self-efficacy in the GlobalEd Project. (Doctoral dissertation, University of Connecticut). Dissertation Abstracts International, No. 3050198.

Mayo, J. B. (2007). Negotiating sexual orientation and classroom practice(s) at school. *Theory and Research in Social Education, 35*(3), 447–464.

Mazzeo, J., Schmitt, A., & Bleistein, C. (1990). Exploratory analyses of some possible causes for the discrepancies in gender differences on multiple-choice and free-response sections of the Advanced Placement examinations. Draft report. Princeton, NJ: Educational Testing Service, as cited in Breland, H. et al. 1994. Performance versus objective testing and gender: An exploratory study of an Advanced Placement history examination. *Journal of Educational Measurement 31*, 275–293.

McCrary, N. (2002). Investigating the use of narrative in affective learning on issues of social justice. *Theory and Research in Social Education, 30*, 255–274.

McDonagh, E. (2002). Political citizenship and democratization: The gender paradox. *American Political Science Review 96*, 535–552.

Merryfield, M. (1997). Moving the center of global education: From imperial world views that divide the world to double consciousness, contrapuntal pedagogy, hybridity, and cross-cultural competence. In W. B. Stanley (Ed.), *Social studies: Research, priorities, and prospects* (pp. 179–207). Greenwich, CT: Information Age Publishing.

Merryfield, M., & Crocco, M.S. (2003). Women of the world: A special issue of *Social Education 67*(1).

Merryfield, M., & Subedi, B. (2003). Teaching about women of the world. *Social Education 67*, 10–15.

Middaugh, E., & Perlstein, D. (2005). Thinking and teaching in a democratic way: Hilda Taba and the ethos of *Brown. Journal of Curriculum and Supervision 20*, 234–256.

Minnich, E. K. (1990). *Transforming knowledge.* Philadelphia: Temple University Press.

Mohanty, C., Russo, A., & Torres, L. (Eds.). (1991). *Third world women and the politics of feminism.* Bloomington: Indiana University Press.

National Center for History in the Schools. (1996). *National standards for history: Basic edition.* Los Angeles: University of California, Author.

National Council for the Social Studies (1994). *Curriculum standards for social studies.* Washington, DC: Author.

National Council for Geographic Education (2000). *Finding a way: Learning activities in geography for grades 7–11.* Indiana, PA: Author.

National Council on Economic Education (1997). *Voluntary national content standards in economics.* New York: Author.

National Standards for Civics and Government (1994). Available online at: http://www.civiced.org/.

Nelson, C. (1990). Gender and the social studies: Training pre-service secondary social studies teachers. (Doctoral dissertation, University of Minnesota, 1990). Dissertation Abstracts International, No. ATT 9021339.

Niemi, R., & Junn, J. (1998). *Civic education: What makes students learn.* New Haven, CT: Yale University Press.

Noddings, N. (1992). Social studies and feminism. *Theory and Research in Social Education 20*(2), 230–241.

Nussbaum, M. (1994) Patriotism and Vosmopolitanism. *Boston Review* 19:5

Ochoa-Becker, A. S. (1999). Decision making in middle school social studies: An imperative for youth and democracy. *The Clearinghouse 72* (6), 337–340.

Oesterreich, H. (2002). "Outing" social justice: Transforming civic education within the challenges of heteronormativity, heterosexism, and homophobia. *Theory and Research in Social Education 30* (2), 287–302.

Ortner, S. (1996). *Making gender: The politics and erotics of gender.* Boston: Beacon Press.

Owens, W. T. (1999). Preservice feedback about the Internet and the implications for social studies educators. *The Social Studies 90,* 133–140.

Pang, V. (2004). *Multicultural education: A caring-centered reflective approach.* New York: McGraw Hill.

Parker, W. (1998). "Advanced" ideas about democracy: Toward a pluralist conception of citizen education. *Teachers College Record, 98,* 104–125.

Parker, W. (2003). *Teaching democracy.* New York: Teachers College Press.

Pateman, C. (1989). *The disorder of women, democracy, feminism and political theory.* Stanford, CA: Stanford University Press.

Protano, R. D. (2003). Female high school students' attitude and perceptions towards the social studies discipline. (Doctoral dissertation: Fordham University). *Dissertation Abstracts International,* No. AAT 3101156.

Pulsipher, L., & Pulsipher, A. (2002). *World regional geography: Global patterns, local lives.* New York: W.H. Freeman.

Reuben, J. A. (2005). Patriotic purposes: Public schools and the education of citizens. In S. Fuhrman and M. Lazerson, (Eds.), *The public schools* (pp. 1–25). New York: Oxford University Press.

Rhoads, R. A., & Calderone, S. M. (2007). Reconstituting the democratic subject: Sexuality, schooling, and citizenship. *Educational Theory, 57*(1), 105–121. Retrieved October 14, 2007, from ERIC database.

Richardson, W. (2004). Connecting political discussion to civic engagement: The role of civic knowledge, efficacy and context for adolescents. (Doctoral dissertation. University of Maryland). *Dissertation Abstracts International,* AAT 3107254.

Richburg, R. W., Nelson, B. J., & Tochterman, S. (2002). Gender inequity: A world geography lesson. *The Social Studies, 93,* 23–30.

Riley, D. (1988). *Am I that name? Feminism and the category of "women" in history.* Minneapolis: University of Minnesota Press.

Robson, D. (2001). Women and minorities in economics textbooks: Are they being adequately represented? *Journal of Economic Education, 32,* 186–191.

Sanders, R. (1999). Introducing "white privilege" into the classroom: Lessons from Finding a Way. *Journal of Geography, 98,* 169–175.

Schur, J. B. (1995). Students as social science researchers: Gender issues in the classroom. *Social Education, 59,* 144–47.

Schwartz, S. (1999). Hannah Adams: The pioneer intellect. (Doctoral dissertation Teachers College, Columbia University) *Dissertation Abstracts International,* No. AAT 9950069.

Schwartz, S. (2001). The origins of history's mission in America's schools: A case study of Hannah Adams. *Theory and Research in Social Education, 29,* 212 –237.

Scott, J. W. (1986). Gender: A useful category for historical analysis. *American Historical Review, 91,* 1053–75.

Scott, J. W. (1988). *Gender and the politics of history.* New York: Columbia University Press.

Scott, J. W. (1996). Introduction. In J. W. Scott (Ed.), *Feminism & history* (pp. 1–13). New York: Oxford University Press.

Self, C. M. (1994). Sex-related differences in spatial ability: What every geography educator should know. *Journal of Geography, 93,* 234–243.

Segall, A. (2004). Social studies and the discourses of postmodernity. In C. Woyshner, J. Watras, & M. S. Crocco, (Eds.), *Social education in the twentieth century: Curriculum and context for citizenship* (pp.169–176). New York: Peter Lang.

Shaver, J. (1991). *Handbook of research on social studies teaching and learning.* New York: Macmillan.

Shields, P. (1999). Classroom tips: Women, history, and citizenship. *Canadian Social Studies, 33*(3), 94–95. Retrieved October 13, 2007, from ERIC database.

Shinew, D. (2001). "Disrupt, transgress, and invent possibilities": Feminists' interpretations of educating for democratic citizenship. *Theory and Research in Social Education, 29,* 488–516.

Shinew, D. (2006). Citizenship and belonging: Constructing a "sense of place and a place that makes sense." In C. Cherryholmes, E. Heilman, & A. Segall (Eds.), *Social studies: The next generation—researching in the postmodern* (pp. 77–95). New York: Peter Lang.

Shklar, J. (1991). *American citizenship: The quest for inclusion.* Cambridge, MA: Harvard University Press.

Siim, B. (2000). *Gender and citizenship: Politics and agency in France, Britain and Denmark.* Cambridge, England: Cambridge University Press.

Smith, R. M. (1997). *Conflicting visions of citizenship in U.S. History.* New Haven, CT: Yale University Press.

Smith-Rosenberg, C. (1975). The female world of love and ritual: Relations between women in nineteenth-century America. *Signs, 1,* 1–29.

Solomon, B. M. (1985). *In the company of educated women.* New Haven, CT: Yale University Press.

Spelman, E. (1988). *Inessential woman.* Boston: Beacon.

Steelsmith, S. (1990). How would you like to hear only half a story? Ideas for using biographies of historical women in the classroom. *Feminist Teacher, 5*(1), 19–23.

Stone, L. (1996). Feminist political theory: Contributions to a conception of citizenship. *Theory and Research in Social Education, 24,* 36–53.

Sumara, D., & Davis, B. (1999). Interrupting heteronormativity: Toward a queer curriculum theory. *Curriculum Inquiry 29,* 191–208.

Thornton, S. J. (2002). Does everybody count as human? *Theory and Research in Social Education 30,* 178–190.

Thornton, S. J. (2003). Silence on gays and lesbians in social studies curriculum. *Social Education 67,* 226–30.

Torney-Purta, J. (1991). Cross national research in social studies. In J. P. Shaver (Ed.), *Handbook on social studies teaching and learning* (pp. 591–601). New York: Macmillan.

Torney-Purta, J., Lehmann, R., Oswald, H., & Schulz, W. (2001*). Citizenship and education in twenty eight countries: Civic knowledge and engagement at age fourteen.* Amsterdam: The International Association for the Evaluation of Educational Achievement.

Tyson, C. (2006). From theory to practice: Teaching for social justice. *Social Studies and the Young Learner, 19*(2), 23–25.

Volman, M., & van Eyk, E. (2001). Gender equity and information technology in education: The second decade. *Review of Educational Research, 71*(4), 613–634.

Wade, R. (1995). Diversity taboos: Religion and sexual orientation in the social studies classroom. *Social Studies and the Young Learner, 7*(4), 19–22.

Walstad, W. B., & Robson, D. (1997). Differential item functioning and male-female differences on multiple-choice tests in economics. *Journal of Economic Education, 28,* 155–171.

Walstad, W. B., & Soper, J. C. (1989). What is high school economics? Factors contributing to student achievement and attitudes. *Journal of Economic Education, 20,* 23–38.

Walter, C., & Young, B. (1997). Gender bias in Alberta social studies 30 examinations: Cause and effect. *Canadian Social Studies, 31*(2), 83–86, 89.

Warner, M. & Social Text Collective. (1993). *Fear of a queer planet: Queer politics and social theory.* Minneapolis: University of Minnesota Press.

Williams, P. J. (1991). *The alchemy of race and rights.* Cambridge, MA: Harvard University Press.

Webster, G. R. (2000). Women, politics, elections, and citizenship. *Journal of Geography 99,* 1–10.

Women's Studies Quarterly (2001). Gender equity in high schools: Notes for a new century, 28(3/4).

Woyshner, C. (2002). Political history as women's history: Towards a more inclusive curriculum. *Theory and Research in Social Education 30,* 354–380.

Woyshner, C. (2003). Race, gender, and the early PTA: Civic engagement and public education, 1897–1924. *Teachers College Record, 105*(3), 520–544.

Woyshner, C. (2003–04). Women's associations and the origins of the social studies: Volunteers, professionals, and the community civics curriculum, 1890–1920. *International Journal of Social Education, 18*(2), 16–32.

Woyshner, C. (2004). From assimilation to cultural pluralism: The PTA and civic education, 1900–1950. In C. Woyshner, J. Watras, & M. S. Crocco (Eds.), *Social education in the twentieth century: Curriculum and context for citizenship* (pp. 93–109). New York: Peter Lang.

Woyshner, C. (2005). Notes toward a historiography of the social studies: Recent scholarship and future directions. In Barton, K. (Ed.), *Research methods in social studies education* (pp. 11–39). Greenwich, CT; Information Age Publishing.

Woyshner, C., Watras, J., & Crocco (Eds). (2004). *Social education in the twentieth century: Curriculum and context for citizenship.* New York: Peter Lang.

Wridt, P. (1999). The worlds of girls and boys: Geographic experience and informal learning opportunities. *Journal of Geography, 98,* 253–264.

Young, I. M. (1997) *Intersecting voices: Dilemmas of gender, political philosophy, and policy.* Princeton, NJ: Princeton University Press.

Zittleman, K. (2005). Title IX and gender issues: A study of the knowledge and perceptions of middle school teachers and students." Unpublished doctoral dissertation, American University, Washington, DC.

Zittleman, K., & Sadker, D. (2005). Title IX and gender issues: A study of the knowledge and perceptions of middle school teachers and students. Montreal, Canada. Paper presented at the annual meeting of the American Educational Research Association.

12 Global education

Guichun Zong
Kennesaw State University

Angene H. Wilson
University of Kentucky

A. Yao Quashiga
University of Winneba

On the morning of September 11, 2001, Guichun came to Angene's office to tell her that a plane had crashed into one of the World Trade Towers. Yao, who had defended his dissertation the previous week and had planned to return to Ghana the following weekend, joined us as we listened in shock to the unfolding events. We were colleagues at the University of Kentucky in social studies and global education and, because of our own transnational and cross-cultural experiences, we immediately thought about the global context.

As we complete this chapter, Guichun teaches graduate and undergraduate courses in social studies education at Kennesaw State University; Angene is recently retired from heading the secondary social studies program at the University of Kentucky; and Yao has recently completed a term as head of a social studies department of several thousand students at University of Winneba in Ghana. We have each done research in global education, and we continue to be passionate about the need for teaching toward a global perspective, for students worldwide, but perhaps especially for U.S. students because of the current power of the United States to affect the world.

Astronaut Frank Borman (as cited in Leetsma, 1979) of Apollo 8 described the context for global education when he wrote in 1968:

> The view of the earth from the moon fascinated me—a small disk, 240,000 miles away. It was hard to think that that little thing held so many problems, so many frustrations. Raging nationalistic interests, famines, wars, pestilence don't show from that distance. I'm convinced that some wayward stranger in a space-craft, coming from some other part of the heavens, could look at earth and never know that it was inhabited at all. But the same wayward stranger would certainly know instinctively that if the earth were inhabited, then the destinies of all who lived on it must inevitably be interwoven and joined. We are one hunk of ground, water, air, clouds, floating around in space. From out there it really is "one world." (Leetsma, pp. 236–237)

Looking at the world from a global perspective is not new. In terms of American universities and schools, international relations courses and area studies go back to the 1950s, and educators began to write about a global perspective and global education more than 30 years ago. A 1955 Ford Foundation report, for example, described a grant for an experimental program in foreign relations for high school seniors. In 1976 Hanvey laid out the dimensions of an attainable global perspective (perspective consciousness, state-of-the planet awareness, cross-cultural awareness, knowledge of global dynamics, and awareness of human choices), and influenced a whole generation of global educators to think beyond an international relations model positing a world of interacting nation-states. His focus on the state of the planet and global dynamics presaged our growing understanding of globalization, and his explanation of perspective consciousness opened the way to consideration of multiple perspectives. However, Hanvey (1976) did not account for the impact of Western imperialism on how, for instance, U.S. Americans see the world, and he did not call for critical decision-making or action.

Also important in the movement toward teaching from a global perspective, world history is beginning to be taught as global history, especially AP World History, which began as an Advanced Placement course in 2000 and which specifically limits European history to no more than 30% of content (2004–2005). A helpful metaphor for world history is the web; in fact, J.R. and William H. McNeill's (2003) bird's eye view of world history is entitled *The Human Web*. Now, too, the technology of the World Wide Web is a reality, and students are part of a world in which they can download a newspaper from Liberia and engage in an online project with students in Lebanon. As Thomas Friedman (2005) asserts in his recent best-seller, *The World is Flat: A Brief History of the 21st Century*, U.S. students must learn to cooperate and compete in innovation with students in other countries.

Geography, too, contributes to global education. Jared Diamond's Pulitzer Prize-winning *Guns, Germs and Steel* (1997), for instance, offers a geographically-based explanation of how the West became dominant, and his more recent *Collapse* (2005) describes the role of the environment as societies make choices that lead to success or collapse.

Social studies educators have long called for a global education in both K-12 classrooms and preservice teacher education programs (Alger, 1974; Anderson, 1991; Becker, 1979; Cushner, 1988; Hanvey, 1976; Kniep, 1989; Kirkwood, 2001; Merryfield, 1998, 2002; Myers, 2006; Thornton, 2005; Tucker, 1990, 1991; Tye & Tye, 1992; Wilson, 1993a, 1993b, 1997, 2001). The reasoning underlying such advocacy is that in an interconnected world our survival and well-being are directly related to our capacity to understand and deal responsibly and effectively with other peoples and nations and with a variety of issues that cut across national boundaries. The National Council for the Social Studies (NCSS) has shown consistent support for global education through its publications, such as *Social Studies and the World: Teaching Global Perspectives* (Merryfield & Wilson, 2005). The organization has also published a position paper stating that:

> The National Council for the Social Studies believes that an effective social studies program must include global and international education. Global and international education are important because the day-to-day lives of average citizens around the world are influenced by burgeoning international connections. The human experience is an increasingly globalized phenomenon in which people are constantly being influenced by transnational, cross-cultural, multi-cultural and multi-ethnic interactions. (NCSS, 2001)

How has this advocacy been supported by research? What has research said about teaching from a global perspective? In this chapter we focus our review on two areas: (a) theoretical inquiry and conceptualization of the field and (b) empirical research on global education in schools and in teacher education. We also suggest several areas for future research. We try, as an African proverb says, to see the world as a mask dancing, knowing that we cannot see it well if we stand in only one place. However, we acknowledge that we are limited by our own backgrounds and interests as well as our chosen focus. For example, we are not looking at the content of international studies or world history, or at how civics is taught and learned cross-culturally, and only briefly at the intersections of multicultural and global education. We are also focusing on global education in social studies. On the other hand, while all three of us are first and foremost social studies educators, we definitely recognize that teaching from a global perspective needs to be a cross-curricular effort.

THEORETICAL INQUIRY/CONCEPTUALIZING THE FIELD

How should global education be defined? What are its rationale and goals? How do we distinguish global education from other closely related fields such as international education, multicultural education, and traditional world studies (culture, geography, history)? What are the scope, focus, and direction of this emerging curriculum field?

Much published work on global education since the 1990s (Case, 1993; Dunn, 2002; Hicks, 2003; Kirkwood, 2001; Merryfield 1997, 2001, 2002; Pike, 2000; Shelby, 2000; Shapiro & Purpel, 2005; Tucker, 1991; Ukpokodu, 1999, Wilson, 1998), largely theoretical in nature, addresses these conceptual questions. Scholars are continuing the quest for greater conceptual clarity, which has not always characterized the field since its inception and throughout its development (Massialas, 1991). Despite the fact that a comprehensive theory on the goals, content, and pedagogy for global education around which consensus could build has not been fully developed in the past 15 years, numerous fresh constructs and theoretical inquiries have made significant contributions to enhance understanding of the field. Some scholars synthesized and expanded the earlier works of global education and attempted to bring clarity to the field's inconsistencies and incongruities (Case, 1993; Cross & Molnar, 1994; Hicks, 2003; Kirkwood, 2001; Lamy, 1990; Merryfield, 1997). Others, while acknowledging the foundational nature and the relevance of seminal work by global educators from the 1970s, called for a more critical look at the meaning, inevitability, and outcomes of globalization and insisted that it is time to reconceptualize education in general and global education in particular (Merryfield, 2001; O' Sullivan, 2005; Rizvi, 2004; Shapiro & Purpel, 2005; Wilson 1998).

The central rationale for global education, articulated by many scholars, rests on the necessity of preparing students for the increasing interconnectedness among people and nations that characterizes the world today. Couching their reasoning in such terms as *global village, internationalization,* and more recently and frequently, *globalization,* proponents of global education argue that the impact of dynamic multinational transactions and cross-cultural interactions brought by international trade, foreign investment, tourism, immigration, cultural exchange is felt today in virtually every local community. The instantaneous information exchange by communication technology such as the cellular phone, Internet, and satellite television has also greatly increased the way people all over the world interact. In response, many global, and more specifically social studies, educators argue that teaching from a global perspective should become an essential aspect of school curriculum in order to better prepare students to understand historical and current issues and events in an international context. This, they suggest, will better prepare students to make informed choices for the future (Anderson, 1990; Becker, 1979; Case, 1993; Cross & Molnar, 1994; Dunn, 2002; Kagan & Stewart, 2004; 2005; Kirkwood, 2001; Lamy, 1990; Merryfield, 1997; 2001; Shapiro & Purpel, 2005; Tucker, 1990; Tye & Tye, 1992).

In 1990, Lee Anderson summarized his earlier contributions to the field by calling for global education that recognized: (a) The acceleration of global interdependence can be seen through the study of history, economics, politics, demography, ecology, and other disciplines; (b) there is growing erosion of Western dominance in the world, as seen in the relative decrease in the importance of the Atlantic Basin in the global economy and the increase in importance of the Pacific Basin; (c) American hegemony is declining, as seen in its decreasing share of world production and the lessening of its commercial and financial predominance; and (d) there is globalization of American society and culture, the American economy, and American political life that is changing what needs to be taught in schools in the United States. Anderson's argument captured the essence of the rationale for teaching from a global perspective. But how should education respond to these changes that are at a global scale? What does it mean to teach from a global perspective? What knowledge, skills, and perspectives should be taught?

Core elements of global education

Case (1993) made an important contribution to the conceptual literature by identifying two interrelated dimensions of a global perspective: *substantive* and *perceptual*. Drawing upon Hanvey (1976) and Kniep (1989), Case defined the substantive elements as knowledge of cultural values and practices, global interconnections, present worldwide concerns and conditions, historic origins and past patterns of worldwide events, and the alternative and future directions. In contrast, Case's perceptual dimension included five cognitive and affective attributes: open-mindedness, anticipation of complexity, resistance to stereotyping, inclination to empathize, and non-chauvinism. He argued that achieving a global perspective requires both dimensions. From his perspective, the substance of global education—the international, cross-cultural content—can not solely define the field, but attitudes of mind are also crucial.

Kirkwood (2001) also tried to bring further clarity to the field of global education. She presented a comparative analysis of existing definitions by scholars, task forces, and professional organizations, including American Association of Colleges for Teacher Education (AACTE), the National Council for Accreditation of Teacher Education (NCATE), and the NCSS, as well as by scholars outside of the field of global education. She analyzed the various conceptualizations, compared them with the Hanvey's (1976) definition, and concluded that scholars agreed on the following essential elements in defining global education: multiple perspectives, comprehension and appreciation of cultures, knowledge of global issues, and the world as interrelated systems.

More recently, Hicks (2003) reviewed the development of global education theory and practice over the last 30 years in the United Kingdom, Canada, and United States. He identified four core elements that all global education programs should address: (a) Issues dimension, including issues such as inequality/equality, injustice/justice, conflict/peace, environmental damage/care, alienation/participation, (b) Spatial dimension, referring to exploring local-global connections that exist in relation to these issues, including the nature of both interdependency and dependency; (c) Temporal dimension, exploring the interconnections that exist between past, present and future in relation to such issues and in particular scenarios of preferred future; (d) Process dimension, a participatory and experiential pedagogy that explores differing value perspectives and leads to politically aware local-global citizenship (p. 271). Hicks' attention to very specific issues and actions stand in contrast to Case and Kirkwood.

Critical debate

While Case (1993), Kirkwood (2001), and Hicks (2003) focused more on a set of commonly agreed-upon themes in global education, others have found that the existing interpretations of the field vary considerably and sometimes conflict with each other (Cross & Molnar, 1994; Lamy, 1990; Pike 2000). As Pike noted,

> [F]or some, global education is tantamount to giving a broader geographical perspective to the social studies curriculum so as to equip students to compete more

effectively in the global marketplace. For others, it represents a fundamental evaluation of the content, organization, and purpose of schooling in line with a transformative vision of education in a planetary context. Many positions are held at
various points between these two extremes. (p. 64)

Lamy's (1990) analysis of critics and controversies surrounding global education, and
their corresponding views regarding international systems, provides insight for understanding the field from a broader social and political perspective. Similarly, Cross and
Molnar (1994) describe three distinctive perspectives toward global education coexisting and competing in U.S. schools and society: nationalist, international commerce,
and humanistic. In their view, the nationalist perspective, although recognizing that
the world is becoming interdependent, sees the evolving global society as a potential
threat to American sovereignty. Because this perspective embodies a deep-seated suspicion toward a global focus, it also resists the idea that nations must give up a degree
of sovereignty in the interests of global political, social, and economic integration. An
international commerce orientation embraces globalization but argues that a global
society should promote the values and understandings necessary to create and maintain
an international market economy. This orientation also holds that the interests of U.S.
citizens are best served when they fit into a competitive international system where
the self-interest of multinational corporations dominates. In contrast, the humanistic
orientation views the emergence of a global society as an opportunity to create an international order in which nations share, cooperate, and respect each other's cultural values; it focuses on social justice, human rights, cross-cultural understanding, peace, and
binding the earth together as one community.

Cross and Molnar (1994) trace these contending approaches to global education in
the U.S. to national debates about the United States' role in a rapidly changing global
society. "Although global village is an evocative metaphor," they note, "clarifying what
it means to be part of a global society raises difficult questions about our vision of
America, the world, and America in the world" (p. 131). Their analysis parallels Lamy's,
suggesting that differing views of global education are disputes over "images and the
realities of power, authority, and agenda setting in both domestic and international
politics (1990, pp. 12–19). However, unlike Lamy, who argued that global education
should focus on intellectual goals to avoid vagueness and ambiguity (see Lamy, 1990,
p. 55 for an excellent discussion), Cross and Molnar contend that it is important to
synthesize all three views:

> Without some synthesis of the beliefs and values embodied in the humanistic,
> nationalist, and international commerce orientations, global education curriculum
> could easily become either an empty symbolic gesture toward a global society that
> doesn't exist or an attempt to nationalize the status quo. (p. 139)

More recently, global educators in the United States have begun to draw on postcolonial scholarship such as the work of Blaut (1993), Ngugi (1993), Said (1993), and
Willinsky (1998) to reconceptualize the field of global education. In a largely conceptual and transformative article, Merryfield (2001) suggests that social studies educators
challenge the implicit assumptions about globalization underlying work in global education published in the 1970s (see, for instance, Alger, 1974; Anderson, 1979; Becker,
1979; and Hanvey, 1976). She argues that the traditional literature on global education
does not address such assumptions related to globalization as the following: Globalization is neither good nor bad but is simply the result of long-term trends in technological progress; globalization demonstrates the superiority of western capitalism,
free markets, and democracy over communism; and, finally, if schools educate young

Americans in the dynamics of globalization, they will be able to sustain American culture and world power. Merryfield further called for reconceptualizing global education and "moving the center" of the field from institutionalized divisions of people and ideas to the complexity of the interaction and synergy of the global human experience. She suggested three pedagogical processes to help teachers achieve the proposed transformation: examining how the educational legacy of imperialism shapes today's mainstream academic knowledge; illuminating world views of people on the planet who are usually omitted, marginalized or misrepresented in mainstream academic knowledge; and engaging cross-cultural experiential learning within different contexts of power.

These processes align with Wilson's (1998) call for social studies teacher educators and teachers to examine the impact of imperialism on knowledge construction in the West and to engage in what Said (1993) called contrapuntal reading, reading that looks at the overlapping, intertwined imperial experiences of the colonist and the colonized. Then teachers can begin to build a curriculum that resists reinforcing special historical privilege and attempts to accord all human beings' voice. In a similar vein, in a 2001 article, Quashigah and Wilson urged problematizing the concept of culture and emphasizing the concept of power in a dialogue across American and Ghanaian cultures about teaching from a global perspective.

Global education vs. multicultural education

As global educators seek to define their field, some also try to distinguish it from other related fields, especially multicultural education. For the most part, scholars in the United States (cf. Bennett, 1995; Merryfield, 1997; Wilson, 1997) acknowledge important links between global and multicultural education, including their mutual focus on concepts of culture and cultural differences, the recognition of the importance of knowledge, the inclusion of a call for action, and an emphasis on the human connection. Both fields emphasize developing multiple perspectives and multiple loyalties, strengthening cultural consciousness and intercultural competence, respecting human dignity and human rights, and combating prejudice and discrimination.

Ukpokodu (1999) also identifies shared purposes for global and multicultural education. Both strive to increase students' civic responsibility through broader understanding of human commonalities and diversity, and both encourage students to develop skills of informed decision making on issues of equity. Ukpokodu, however, makes an important distinction between the two fields. Global education, she argues, emerged as a response to the reality of growing interconnectedness and interdependence among nations in order to address the critical concerns and challenges that defy unilateral national solutions. Global education then focuses on learning about people and cultures of other lands. Multicultural education, in contrast, grew out of tensions around intra-national diversity and focuses on appropriate response to ethnic diversity in the United States. Citing Banks' argument (in Brandt, 1994) that teaching a unit of Japan can not be a substitute for examining Japanese internment in the United States during World War II, Ukpokodu argues that, similarly, studying a unit on Africa does not help students understand African Americans' experiences with the "stigma of past dehumanization and second-class citizenship" nor "the modern realities of ghettoization and denial of opportunity." She concludes that "it is the more direct study of ethnic groups and other minorities, and their distinctive experiences within American society, that constitute the domain of multiculturalism" (Ukpokodu, 1999, p. 299).

Dunn (2002) contends that, while multiculturalists played an important role in broadening and internationalizing curriculum, they have too often narrowly defined an international curriculum as the *study of cultures*. This approach, Dunn argues, inhibits progress toward the kind of world studies needed in the 21st century:

Many multiculturalist leaders have been so intent on demonstrating the respectability of Asian, African, and pre-1500 American civilizations and on giving them their rightful place in the school day that they have assumed the global curriculum to be mostly descriptive investigations of "other cultures" rather than the study of social processes and historical changes *in the world*. Too frequently, they have accepted the notion that 'cultures' exist as internally stable, homogeneous mechanisms. (p. 12)

In response to this concern, Dunn (2002) calls for replacing the culture-centered approach to history and social studies, which tends to organize classroom inquiry into predetermined, conventionally conceived social and cultural spaces, with a world-centered curriculum. This new world-centered curriculum, according to Dunn, would draw on the new scholarly research in the field of world history and attempt to frame good, analytical questions in order to help students understand political, economic, cultural, and environmental changes in the world. He further argues that global citizenship is compatible with patriotic national citizenship as it strives to equip students with crucial skills and knowledge to better make sense of international affairs and that patriotic citizenship in a democratic state demands a social studies curriculum that gives equal weight to national history and international studies, especially world history.

Global citizenship education

Other scholars (Banks, 2004; Davies, Evans, & Reid, 2005; Hahn, 1984; Myers, 2006; Parker, Grossman, Kubow, Kurth-Schai, & Nakayama, 1998; Tucker, 1990) have also explored citizenship in the global age. Banks' (2004) typology of citizenship provides the most thorough analysis of citizenship from a cosmopolitan perspective. His Stages of Cultural Identity Typology include: cultural psychological captivity, cultural encapsulation, cultural identity clarification, biculturalism, multiculturalism and reflective nationalism, and globalism and global competency or cosmopolitanism (Banks, 2004, p. 303).

Banks argues that worldwide trends and forces, such as globalization, increasing diversity within nation-states, and the quests by racial, ethnic, cultural, and religious groups for recognition and inclusion, require a new conception of citizenship education. From this perspective, citizens in the 21st century need the knowledge, attitudes, and skills to function in their cultural communities and beyond their cultural borders. Educators, then, should rethink and redesign citizenship education programs to help students acquire the knowledge, attitudes, and skills needed to function in their nation-states as well as in an increasingly interdependent world. Banks argues that assimilationist notions of citizenship must be transformed by multicultural citizenship and global citizenship to help students develop thoughtful and clarified identifications with their cultural communities, their nation states, and the world community (see Banks & Nguyen, this volume). Citizenship education should help students develop a deep understanding of the need to take action as citizens of the global community to help solve the world's difficult global problems. Cultural, national, and global experiences and identifications are interactive and interrelated in a dynamic way.

Banks also challenges the current conception of literacy that focuses too narrowly on so-called *basic skills* in reading, writing, and mathematics and ignores citizenship participation in national and global contexts. He argues that basic skills are essential but not sufficient in our diverse and troubled world:

Literate citizens in a diverse democratic society should be reflective, moral, and active citizens in an interconnected global world. They should have the knowledge, skills, and commitment needed to change the world to make it more just and democratic. (Banks, 2004, p. 298)

Ecological perspectives

Integrating ecological thinking into global education is another important strand in conceptualizing the field. Recent proponents of this strand take a step beyond Hanvey's (1976) notion of "state of the planet awareness" to call for shifting from an anthropo-centric philosophy to a biocentric worldview emphasizing the embeddedness of humans within the environment. This approach challenges the dualism in traditional think-ing about culture and nature and argues that the predominant Cartesian worldview encourages a dangerous separation between humans and their environment. Rather than promote a Cartesian globalism that is industrial, competitive, consumerist, and market-driven, they call for an approach that carries a planetary consciousness and promotes social justice, human rights sensitivities, peace perspectives, and environmen-tal concerns (O'Sullivan 2005; Shelby, 2000). From this perspective, adding ecological thinking to global education connotes a synergistic interplay between planetary and personal well being and speaks to the need for bridging the traditional science/humani-ties divide to involve an interdisciplinary approach that examines environmental themes and topics from cultural, ideological, natural, political, social, and spiritual aspects (Shelby, 2000). A biocentric approach is consistent with Noddings' (2005) argument for preparing students to become global citizen-carers who will protect the earth, accept pluralism, and promote peace. Noddings is especially interested in what she calls place-based education, intended to preserve the earth and its peoples.

To summarize, we have reviewed various definitions and critiques of global educa-tion and the relationship of global education to multicultural education, to citizenship, and to ecology. We believe the theoretical discussions over the last 15 years have deep-ened our understanding of the importance and complexity of global education. In our conclusions we make suggestions for further discussion.

EMPIRICAL RESEARCH

The conceptual literature provides a foundation for increasing attention to empirical research on teaching and learning from a global perspective. Researchers have examined a range of topics, including teachers' conceptualizations of global education, students' understanding of other cultures and global issues, effectiveness of global pedagogies, and the more general development of global teachers and teacher educators. This work can be divided into two broad and sometimes overlapping categories: school-based research and teacher education research. The former refers to the research that was primarily conducted in K-12 settings, while the latter refers to the research that was conducted in teacher education programs.

School-based research

Tye and Tye's (1992) pioneer study employed qualitative field-study methodologies in an effort to develop grounded theory regarding U.S. schools' and teachers' change process in the context of a university-supported professional development project on global education. The Tyes examined the meanings teachers ascribed to their experiences with global education activities and resources. They found that the majority of teachers par-ticipating in the study cited cross-cultural understanding and awareness and studies of cultures of other areas of the world as the major goals for global education. They also found that that when teachers resisted global education, they did so either because they did not understand the field, were also busy with other innovative ideas, saw global education as a frill, or perceived global education as un-American. Teachers reported that engaging in global education required relevance to the local school, recognition of the need for cross-cultural understanding, openness to new ideas, and willingness to do extra work, as well as practical guidelines for implementation and the ability to see global education as politically safe (p. 103).

Pike (1997) reports on similar research with teachers in Canada, the United Kingdom, and the United States. Based on interviews, document analysis, and observation, he found that teachers from all three countries agreed on the importance of concepts such as interdependence, connectedness, and perspectivity. They also perceived the purpose of global education as including skills and attitudinal development as well as knowledge acquisition. Beyond these broad areas of agreement, however, Pike noted distinctive national differences between American respondents and those in the U.K. and Canada. In the United States, Pike found that the future economic and political role of the United States in the global system provides a common motivation for involvement in global education, while practitioners in Canada and the United Kingdom tend to perceive global education to be in the common interests of all people and the planet as a whole. Canadian and British respondents saw personal growth, rather than national development, as a key goal, with due recognition given to the dynamic interconnections between personal and planetary health. Practitioners in these two countries also alluded to the moral responsibilities of those in richer nations toward the least affluent. These differences showed up in curricular emphases, with curriculum in the United States focused on exploring cultures and countries, while that in Canada and the United Kingdom focused more on global issues and themes. Pike did not discuss advantages, limitations, or challenges of each approach.

Merryfield's (1998) investigation of the curricular decision-making of 16 master or exemplary teachers, 67 experienced teachers, and 60 preservice teachers, all with training in global education, provides further information on U.S. teachers' decision-making in regard to global education. Data for the exemplary global educators included weekly observations and interviews over a 2-year period. Merryfield collected journals, lesson plans, and interviews from the experienced teachers in her course on global education while data on preservice teachers included weekly class essays, lesson plans, observations, and interviews. Participants in all groups agreed on:

> a guiding theory for preparing students to think with global perspectives: Teach students about their own cultures and diverse cultures through multiple perspectives and comparisons of both similarities and differences so that students understand the complexity of culture and demonstrate tolerance and respect for differences. (p. 152)

The primacy teachers gave to the study of culture corroborates Pike's findings relative to American teachers.

Teachers in all groups connected the global content to students' backgrounds, interests, and communities. They also asked students to make connections across historical periods and world regions, nations, and cultures within nations. Beyond these similarities, the responses varied. The exemplary group taught about the interconnectedness of global and local inequities, included cross-cultural experiential learning, used global issues to organize content across disciplines, emphasized higher-level thinking and research, and used a variety of strategies and resources. Among experienced teachers, two thirds expanded their curricular focus to include less commonly taught parts of the world, as well as global issues and current global events. Ten of the 67 teachers in this group recognized their students' and their own biases—for instance, seeing how racism in their schools affected how students perceived events in Africa. Unique to preservice teachers was their desire to integrate multicultural and global education. In each category, Merryfield also noted individual teachers who integrated global education with other elements of educational reform, used their own or student interests, or blended global perspectives with other subjects, such as art, or with extracurricular activities. Both the variety of teachers studied and the subsequent analysis and rich examples in each category make this study potentially useful for teachers who might see themselves in one category or another.

In another professional development study, Kirkwood (2002) looked specifically at the impact of a 3-year professional development program sponsored by the US-Japan Foundation on teaching about Japan that included a 2-week visit to the country during the summer. She found that the 33 teacher/participants in the Miami study were able to integrate teaching about Japan into various state-mandated social studies classes because of their knowledge and training and their enthusiasm and commitment to teaching about Japan. She concluded that teachers addressed

> cross-cultural understanding, acceptance of human diversity, stereotyping and scapegoating, global issues, the interconnectedness of global history, multiple perspectives, and the influence of culture on history. Teachers articulated a moral obligation to examine the U.S. nuclear bombing of Japan and other moral and ethical issues (p. 108)

Gaudelli (2003) also studied inservice teachers. Using ethnographic methods, Gaudelli investigated teachers' implementation of a state-mandated global curriculum in urban, rural, and suburban high schools in northern, central, and southern New Jersey. He noted that the curriculum, *New Jersey World History/World Cultures Curriculum*, was developed using theories of global education but did not use the world *global* in order to avoid political controversy. Instead the schools in his study used course names such as world history, world culture, and contemporary world issues. Gaudelli focused on several questions in his study:

> How do the three high schools differ in their approaches to global education? What is shared among them? How do student-to-student and teacher-to-student interactions affect learning about the world? What instructional strategies are used and how do contextual factors such as statewide assessment affect teacher choice of methodology? (p. 41)

He concluded that "contextual factors clearly matter in curriculum implementation; these are features of the school that are often beyond the control of teachers and students acting individually" (p. 62). At the urban school he found what he called "trivial pursuit pedagogy" and textbook domination, at the rural school interdisciplinary and active teaching, and at the suburban school an emphasis on course content and on individuals as cultural representatives (p. 56). Global education seemed to be more successful at the rural and suburban schools than at the urban school because the teachers, who were social studies experts, welcomed the new content. Gaudelli also identified three problems in teaching global education (nationalism, cultural relativism, and identity), explained how various teachers addressed them, and made a number of suggestions for teaching, including contrasting an American exceptionalism model with a global model and applying care theory.

Gaudelli's (2003) study is particularly interesting because it focuses on how classroom teachers without specific training in global education interpret and implement a state-mandated initiative in global education. Unlike the teachers in other studies, such as those of Tye and Tye (1992), Merryfield (1998), and Kirkwood (2002), the teachers in Gaudelli's study were not trained in global education. As more states start to introduce globally oriented curriculum, research studies that uncover the complexity of teachers' engagement with global pedagogy will be extremely helpful, especially in already stressed urban schools.

Another area of research focuses on the impact of international experience on teachers. Germain (1998), for instance, used a life history approach to investigate the in depth and transformative international experiences of six veteran teachers, four of whom lived and taught in Japan and two in China. The life history approach provides rich data on the participants' backgrounds, their experiences teaching and living abroad, their views about the impact of that experience on their pedagogy, and their perspectives about how their experiences might have been transformative for them. Germain found that international experience led the teachers to work against stereotypes, heightened their sense of empathy with immigrant and ethnic minority students, altered their pedagogy, and enhanced the authenticity of their teaching about East Asia.

Wilson (1993a), too, looked at the impact of international experience on individual teachers, as well as students. She examined her own and others' research, focusing particularly on returned Peace Corps volunteers who became teachers, teachers who participated in study tours, and high school exchange students and college students who studied abroad. Wilson concluded that international experience produced gains in substantive knowledge, perceptual understanding, personal growth, interpersonal connections, and the ability to become a cultural mediator. Wilson's work includes six case studies on specific teachers, students, and schools, including two elementary teachers with international experience, an Afghan refugee student, and an urban international studies magnet school with an International Baccalaureate program.

Other research in schools focuses more narrowly on one classroom or one topic. Merryfield (1992), for instance, describes the instructional decisions of 12 teachers as they teach the first Gulf War as a current event. She found that the teachers' decision-making processes were complex and dependent on the students in the class, especially when those classes included students from other cultures. In another study, Shapiro and Merryfield (1995) report in detail on the creation of a unit on resolving racial conflict in South Africa—from selecting the content and developing the essential questions to lesson plans and a final interdisciplinary exhibition.

In contrast to studies of teacher decision-making, another group of investigations focus on students' developing global understanding. LeSourd (1993), for example, examined 24 ten- and thirteen-year-old children's representations of people in five countries. She showed individual students photos of people in five different countries (Thailand, Pakistan, Peru, Ghana, and the former USSR) and then asked open-ended questions to elicit student representations of people depicted in the photos. The results indicated that overall students' representations emphasized austere conditions and hardships in life and the human need for security. While the 10-year-olds provided details about people's thoughts and feelings, the 13-year-olds included more information about the countries' geographic, political, and social conditions. No significant differences associated with diversity in children's own linguistic and cultural backgrounds were found, except that the children who were born outside the United States reported a slightly more pessimistic view of the circumstances of living.

Bickmore (1999) focused more specifically on 33 fourth and fifth graders in an urban classroom with a diverse multicultural population. These students responded to a social education curriculum unit that was based on conflict resolution theory and drew examples from the Hutu-Tutsi conflict in Rwanda and Zaire, bullying and exclusion conflicts on the school playground, conflicts over the appropriate development and use of water resources, and the Arab-Israeli conflict. Bickmore concluded that:

> [T]he powerful themes of social, political, and international conflict enhanced the breadth and depth of these young students' involvement in social education. Yes,

children can handle global politics, and doing so can help them to increase their capacity to handle both interpersonal conflict and academic skills. (p. 68)

Both Bickmore's and LeSourd's studies were conducted in schools located in multiethnic and low socioeconomic communities with large populations of recent immigrants. Taken together, these studies raise questions about developmental theories used to justify delaying student engagement with the content and issues of global education. Instead, they suggest that carefully scaffolded experiences can support children's construction of global-mindedness. With such a small research base, however, these studies remain more suggestive than definitive.

In addition to the qualitative studies previously described, several quantitative studies provide some insights into students' attitudes regarding global issues and people and places of the world. For example, Zevin (2003) examined how adolescents in the U.S. and Norway view their own and other countries. He used a semantic differential survey form that presented the students with sets of opposite qualities—some geographic, some political, and some social—with a 7-point Likert-type scale from which students could choose the rating that best suited their views of three countries: the United States, Norway, and Russia. Findings revealed that the vast majority of U.S. respondents saw their own country in a relatively favorable light, and the majority of Norwegian students also saw their own county and the U.S. in a positive light, but they viewed Russia with a considerable degree of mistrust and negativity. U.S. students identified television as the top source for knowledge, with teachers being second.

In another study of student attitudes, Benitez (2001) compared student attitudes after participating in an experimental globalized U.S. History course (taught by Benitez) with student attitudes after experiencing a traditional U.S. History curriculum (taught by another teacher). Using results from a pre- and post-test on patriotism, she found that students in the experimental group ($n = 55$) became more internationalistic while the control group ($n = 74$) students became more nationalistic on three dimensions of the test (anticommunism and the role of the United States in defending democracy throughout the world; ethnocentrism; and the relative importance of domestic versus international problems). She concluded that a global curriculum that showed linkages between the U.S. and other countries on issues ranging from pollution to war explained the difference between these perspectives, along with pedagogies which required students to participate in face-to-face fishbowl discussions on such issues as the death penalty, causes of inner city violence, and racism. Benetiz argued that her findings could be explained using a political socialization through cognitive dissonance model.

An earlier study by Blankenship (1990), using a global knowledge test, a global attitudes test, and a political attitudes questionnaire, combined with an observation checklist, in a survey of 202 students, found a weak relationship between student perceptions of an open classroom climate and the level of global knowledge, but a moderate relationship between an open climate and positive global attitudes. Blankenship used Hahn, Tocci, and Angell's (1988) definition of classroom climate as the degree to which students feel free to discuss controversial issues openly.

Teacher education research

Since the 1990s, the leading scholars in global education have consistently called for integrating global perspectives in both preservice preparation programs and inservice professional development initiatives to better prepare teachers to teach students about other nations, regions, and peoples. Corresponding to that call, there is a growing amount of global education literature in teacher education journals. The *Journal of Teacher Education* and *Theory into Practice*, for instance, devoted separate issues to global education in 1999 and 1993 respectively. The 1997 *Handbook for Teacher Education* (Merryfield, Jarchow, & Pickert) also focused on preparing teachers to teach global perspectives.

Although not specifically directed at social studies, most of the articles and chapters included in these three publications were written by social studies educators. Generally descriptive in nature, they include articles and book chapters addressing a range of topics, such as historical origins and intellectual foundations of global education, assessment, controversy, teacher resistance, school-university collaboration in global education, cross-cultural experiences in teacher education courses, and infusing global perspectives into a secondary social studies program. One of the articles (Johnston & Ochoa, 1993) outlined a research agenda for global education. That agenda called for research on sociopolitical influences on global education, on teacher reflection about global education, on teachers' pedagogical content knowledge and beliefs about global education, and on teachers' cognitive development in areas such as perspective taking. While that agenda is still relevant, the preponderance of the existing research focuses on teacher educators and on teacher education students.

Merryfield (2000a) focused on teacher educators to investigate whether teachers were being prepared to teach for diversity, equity, and global interconnectedness She studied profiles submitted by 80 teacher educators nominated by college deans, educational organization leaders and leaders in multicultural global education. The profiles describe experiences that shaped these teacher educators' views of multicultural and global education. Merryfield reported:

> Most of the people of color acquired an experiential understanding of discrimination and outsider status by the nature of growing up in a society characterized by White privilege and racism. However, many of the middle-class White teacher educators had their most profound experiences while living outside their own country. (p. 429)

She concluded that each educator had experiences with those different in race, ethnicity, class, language, and national origin but that many of those experiences centered upon the discrimination and injustice that comes with being treated as different. These experiences, Merryfield argued, caused critical reflection about such concepts as power and culture and led the teacher educators to understand how power affects the interpretation of human differences because they had felt first hand what it is like when difference is the reason for being placed in the center or periphery in society.

Zong (2005b) reflected on her own journey from a girl growing up in China during the Mao Era to an immigrant woman faculty member teaching in research universities in the United States. Drawing upon theory and research related to understanding lived experience (Van Manen, 1990), the influence of teachers' stories and narratives (Connelly & Clandinin, 1999), and the contribution of cross-cultural experiences to the development of multicultural and global educators (Merryfield, 2000; Wilson, 1981; 1998), she examined the impact of border-crossing experiences on her identity and pedagogy; in particular, on how she had reconciled her duality and marginality and used them as assets to advance teaching from a global perspective. She further argued that, given their cultural and linguistic background as well as their knowledge of their nations of origin and diverse cultural perspectives, immigrant professors have the unique potential to become a bridge between cultures and to make significant contributions in making colleges and universities institutions of global learning.

Several researchers have also studied their own social studies teacher education students, examining the impact of simulations and other programs as well as life experiences. Kirkwood (2004), for instance, found that using a United Nations simulation in three sections of a graduate elective course in global education with both practicing elementary teachers and preservice secondary teachers had what she identified as a positive effect. Lesson plans reflected a global education framework grounded in persistent problem themes and the interconnectedness of issues. Further, Kirkwood concluded from her field notes and videotapes that teachers grew in peace-building competence because of practice in their mock General Assembly deliberations.

Wilson (2001), too, investigated the growth toward a global perspective of 15 of her social studies methods students. Students participated in a year-long initial certification graduate program emphasizing a global perspective. Beginning with their application essays on previous cross-cultural experiences and then utilizing classroom observations, taped interviews and documents such as lesson plans and teaching philosophies, Wilson found that her students echoed some of their teachers' theories and practices, matching Merryfield's (1998) argument for connecting global content to students' experiences and expanding the curricular focus on less-taught-about parts of the world and issues. As her students talked about influences on their teaching from a global perspective, they mentioned learning specific content about the world again and again, in earlier schooling and in methods class. Nine of the 15 students mentioned a Ghanaian graduate student classmate as one of the influences on their global perspective. Finally, Wilson reported on the three students with extensive international experience, who were able to talk about their student teaching from a global perspective with particular excitement and eloquence. She wondered how more people with international experience could be attracted into teaching and how more teachers could get international experience. All but one of her 15 students reported wanting initial or continuing international experience.

Osunde, Tlou, and Brown (1996) focused more specifically on examining preservice social studies teachers' knowledge and perceptions about a single region: Africa. Their study involved the administration of a questionnaire to 100 randomly selected preservice social studies teachers from a state university in Pennsylvania and a state university in Virginia. The questionnaire listed various concepts that might be applied to Africa, and the respondents were to choose those that they considered relevant to the country. The results indicate that the concepts most often associated with Africa were wild animals, malnutrition, disease, huts, tribes, elephants, jungles, poor, deserts, villages, tigers, natives, and superstition. Other stereotypical concepts ascribed to Africa by the preservice teachers included spears, underdeveloped, illiterate, naked, witch doctors, primitive, violence, racial problems, pygmies, savages, and backward. The authors conclude that:

> [E]ven though preservice teachers are exposed to an increasing amount of information on Africa through their college courses and seminars, and even though the media now present news on Africa with more frequency, the results of our data analysis showed that a majority of the preservice social studies teachers had the same misconceptions about Africa that their grandparents and parents had several decades ago. (p. 120)

As more teacher educators begin to integrate technology into social studies teaching and learning, researchers focus more and more on the effectiveness of using electronic technologies in developing prospective and practicing teachers' global understanding and commitment to teach from a global perspective. Teacher educators have been particularly interested in exploring the potential of computer-mediated communication (CMC) in building cross-cultural understanding and promoting equity and cultural diversity in social studies and global education.

Merryfield (2000b, 2003) analyzed the strengths and weaknesses of integrating online discussions into her graduate courses in social studies and global education over several years. She compared the content and interaction patterns of online discussions with face to face discussions. Based upon content analysis of online messages and other data, including formative and summative course evaluations, she found that class discussions progressed quite differently online than face to face. This was especially the case in discussion of sensitive and controversial topics like prejudice, privilege, inequity, injustice, and imperialism. Overall, the asynchronous nature of most online pedagogy increased both depth of content and equity in participation. She further cited four ways that online pedagogy made a difference in maximizing cross-cultural learning: diffusing triggers of difference; increasing the depth of study and the meaningfulness of academic content; facilitating immediate and detailed feedback and extended discussion of ideas and resources; and creating communities of diverse learners and connections to a larger world. In her 2000 study, Merryfield noted some paradoxes in employing technologies for multicultural and global education. First, participating teachers reported that the online discussions helped them jumpstart cross-cultural interactions, tackle hard issues, and enthusiastically explore diversity of peoples' lives, but they also perceived online interaction as artificial and unreal. Second, some teachers saw the technologies as barriers that kept them from knowing their peers. Merryfield suggests that more studies, designed by researchers in both technology and multicultural and global education across many contexts, are needed to further explore the potential of electronic technologies for improving global aspects of social studies teaching and learning.

Zong (2002) studied the impact of participation in a technology-enhanced global education course on two preservice secondary teachers. The preservice teachers participated in ICONS, a worldwide simulation network that uses both synchronous and asynchronous communication characteristics of the internet to teach international negotiation and intercultural communication to university and high school students. Zong followed the two teacher candidates through their student teaching, noting the ways in which they attempted to infuse a global perspective into the student teaching. Both reported that the global education course and the ICONS simulation shaped their understanding of the importance of teaching global perspectives and prepared them to use the internet, along with other resources, to integrate global perspectives across the curriculum.

More recently Zong (2005a) reported the results of a 2-year study exploring the impact of participation in a semester-long, web-based, multinational discussion project embedded in a social studies methods course on the development of preservice elementary teachers' understanding of cultural diversity and global awareness. Drawing upon sociocultural learning theory, the study examined whether and how participation in the online project to discuss issues related to cultural diversity and global challenges with students and teachers from over 20 countries could make an impact on future teachers' understanding of global education. Data sets included the on-line discussion messages and the reflective essays written by the 60 preservice teachers at the conclusion of the project. Overall findings suggested that the CMC projects provide an authentic context to learn about other countries and cultures, global issues such as child labor in Asia and hunger and poverty in Africa, and multiple perspectives on the U.S.-led wars in Afghanistan and Iraq. The participating preservice teachers were divided, though, on the negative online messages about the United States sent by students from other countries. The project also enabled the preservice teachers to develop greater action orientation toward doing something for a better global community. The major pedagogical challenges included occasional lack of responses from participating teams from other countries, developing an appropriate assessment plan for participation and online messages, and difficulty in cyber classroom management—making sure the messages were professionally written and shared.

Both Merryfield (2000b, 2003) and Zong's (2002, 2005a) studies have demonstrated the inconclusive and sometimes contradictory impact of electronic technologies on pre-service and practicing teachers' global understanding. We share Fabos and Young's (1999) concern that the current discourse surrounding telecommunication-base projects often tends to make overly optimistic claims about learning in cultural diversity and global unity. More systematic research is clearly needed in this area.

DIRECTIONS FOR FUTURE RESEARCH

Over the past decade, there has been no other concept in social, political, and educational theory as publicly and passionately debated as globalization (Rizvi, 2004). Deep disputes have emerged with respect to the historical and cultural origins of globalization—its economic, political, and social consequences, as well as implications for educational policies and practices (Burbules & Torres, 2000; Friedman, 2000; Huntington, 1994; Klein, 2000). The tragic events of September 11, 2001, helped to reshape the discourse on global education in various ways (Rizvi, 2004; Shapiro & Purpel, 2005). Therefore, the debate about the conceptualization of global education will likely continue for the foreseeable future. In our view, the continued discussion is necessary and healthy. Conceptually, we think it is important to draw upon the current interdisciplinary scholarship on globalization to define its characteristics; seek to understand forces that produce the dynamics and interrelated effects of globalization; and assess its outcomes not merely in economic productivity, but also considering who benefits from different aspects of globalization and who does not. From this analysis, we hope a reasonable global education framework can be developed. Such a framework would help answer questions about how to determine what students will be taught about the world, what perspectives students should consider when thinking about other cultures, and what values students should attach to global interdependence.

But theory alone cannot fully inform such decision-making. The field of global education requires a stronger, richer, and deeper research base. The lack of an agreed upon conceptualization should not keep us from doing research in global education. Indeed, the agenda that Johnston and Ochoa developed in 1993, described earlier in this chapter, still has merit. We draw attention to three other possibilities: research on student thinking and learning—we hear few student voices; research that examines the long-term impact of teacher education initiatives in global education rather than just one course or year, and research in global education that is cross-national in scope.

While we have some idea about what teachers are doing or not doing in their classrooms that can be called global education, we know relatively little about what K–12 students are learning. It is hard to advocate for programming when we have little evidence of its efficacy. We urge quantitative and qualitative studies that investigate what and how students are learning about the world, both inside and outside of classrooms. Several specific possible questions follow:

- What do students learn from an online project with peers in another country?
- What do students learn from school-based international service projects?
- What do students learn from participation in specific excellent curriculum, such as those from Stanford University's SPICE and from Brown University's Choices?
- What do students learn about the world outside school through friends, media, reading, travel, and exchange experiences?
- What are the differences in learning in content and in attitudes between high school students taking the AP World History, which is no more than 30% European/West-

ern and is taught comparatively, and students taking the traditional world history course?

These research questions might be approached as smaller, "action research" studies, involving teachers as either the primary investigators or as co-investigators with global educators from intermediate agencies such as district or county offices or institutions of higher education, as well as by university researchers.

Another category in which more research might be directed is follow-up studies into teachers' beginning years. Most studies conducted by teacher educators ended at the conclusion of the course, at most during student teaching. We should examine the long-term impact of preservice and also inservice teacher education initiatives in global education.

A third area of research that we would like to see emphasized is cross-national inquiry. One model might be the previously mentioned Pike (1997) study of Canadian, British, and American teachers. Another model might be the Parker, Ninomiya, and Cogan study (1999), which used Cultural Futures Delphi procedures to interview and then survey a multinational panel from nine nations and then developed a curriculum dealing with world crises. Given the important role textbooks play in facilitating teaching and learning, it would also be fruitful to examine presentations in textbooks of certain historical topics and contemporary issues from multinational perspectives. Richard Gross's (1996) comparative study of the treatment of the United States and China in one another's textbooks is an excellent example. We agree with him that:

> in the present era of global coexistence. . .it is increasingly important that peoples and nations be helped to understand and come to grasp the realities of one another's countries. All individuals concerned with the production of textbooks need to strive to remove the overly nationalistic, one-sided, and biased statements that remain in many of the texts. (p. 134)

Still another project might involve researchers in several different countries developing common questions to study how a particular world issue—such as AIDS, conflict resolution and peace-building, environmental change, human rights, or terrorism—is taught and learned. This third area of research—cross-national research—is a crucial one for global education. As a beginning, we can learn how global educators in other countries teach about issues of ecology or justice, for example, from the issue of *Theory into Practice* entitled "Global Education/Viewed from Around the World" (2000).

In conclusion, as Pike points out:

> If the meaning of global education is to be understood at a profound level, the challenge is to find creative ways to assist practitioners in 'the removal of national borders,' not just in their curriculums but also in their thinking. (2000, p. 71)

We agree that such truly global thinking about global education is a worthy goal.

REFERENCES

Alger, C. (1974). *Your city and the world/The world and your city*. Columbus, OH: Mershon Center.

Anderson, L. F., (1979). *Schooling for citizenship in a global age*. Bloomington, IN: The Social Studies Development Center.

Anderson, L. F. (1991). A rationale for global education. In K. A. Tye (Ed.), *Global education: from thought to action* (pp. 13–34). Alexandria, VA: The Association for Supervision and Curriculum Development (ASCD).

Banks, J. (2004). Teaching for social justice, diversity, and citizenship in a global world. *The Educational Forum, 68,* 297–305.

Brandt, R. (1994). On educating for diversity: A conversation with James A. Banks. *Educational leadership, 51,* 28–31.

Becker, J. M. (Ed.) (1979). *Schooling for a global age.* New York: McGraw-Hill.

Benitez, H. (2001). Does it really matter how we teach? The socializing effects of a globalized U.S. history curriculum. *Theory and Research in Social Education, 29,* 290–307.

Bennett, C. I. (1995). *Comprehensive multicultural education.* Boston: Allyn & Bacon.

Bickmore, K. (1999). Elementary curriculum about conflict resolution: Can children handle global politics? *Theory and Research in Social Education. 27*(1), 45–69.

Blankenship, G. (1990). Classroom climate, global knowledge, global attitudes, political action. *Theory and Research in Social Education, 18,* 363–386.

Blaut, J. M. (1993). *The colonizer's model of the world.* New York: Guilford.

Burbules, N., & Torres, C. (Eds) (2000). *Globalization and education.* London: Routledge.

Case, R. (1993). Key elements of a global perspective. *Social Education, 57,* 318–325.

Connelly, F. M., & Clandinin, D. J. (1999). *Shaping professional identity: Stories of educational practice.* New York: Teachers College Press.

Cross, B., & Molnar, A. (1994). Global issues in curriculum development. *Peabody Journal of Education. 69*(2), 131–140

Cushner, K. (1988). Achieving intercultural effectiveness: Current knowledge, goals, and practices. *Education and Urban Society, 20*(2), 159–176.

Davies, I., Evans, M., & Reid, A. (2005). Globalising citizenship education? A critique of 'global education' and 'citizenship education'. *British Journal of Educational Studies, 53*(1), 66–89.

Diamond, J. (2005). *Collapse.* New York: Viking.

Diamond, J. (1997) *Guns, Germs, and Steel.* New York: Norton.

Dunn, R. (2002, October). Growing good citizens with a world-centered curriculum. *Educational Leadership,* 10–13.

Fabos, B., & Young, M. D. (1999). Telecommunications in the classroom: Rhetoric versus reality. *Review of Educational Research, 69* (3), 217–259.

Ford Foundation Annual Report (1955). *To advance human welfare.* New York.

Friedman, T. (2000). *The Lexus and the olive tree.* New York: Farrar, Straus, and Giroux.

Friedman, T. (2005). *The world is flat: A brief history of the 21st century.* New York: Farrar, Straus, and Giroux.

Gaudelli, W. (2003). *World class: Teaching and learning in global times.* Mahwah, NJ: Erlbaum.

Germain, M. H. (1998). *Worldly teachers: Cultural learning and pedagogy.* Westport, CT: Greenwood Press.

Gross, R. (1996). The United States as presented in Chinese texts. *The Social Studies, 87*(3), 133–138.

Hahn, C. (1984). Promise and paradox: Challenges to global citizenship. *Social Education, 48*(4), 240–243.

Hahn, C., Tocci, C., & Angell, A. (1998). Five nation study of civic attitudes and controversial issues discussion. Paper presented at the International Conference on the Social Studies. Vancouver, British Columbia.

Hanvey, R. G. (1976). *An attainable global perspective.* New York: Center for Global Perspectives in Education.

Hicks, D. (2003). Thirty years of global education: A reminder of key principles and precedents. *Educational Review, 55*(3), 265–275.

Huntington, S. (1994). *The clash of civilizations and the remaking of the world order.* New York: Simon and Shuster.

Johnson, M., & Ochoa, A. (1993). Teacher education for global perspectives: A research agenda. *Theory Into Practice, 32*(1), 64–68.

Kagan, S., & Stewart, V. (2005). A new world view: Education in a global era. *Phi Delta Kappan, 87*(3),184–187.

Kagan, S., & Stewart, V. (2004). Putting the world into world-class education: Introduction. *Phi Delta Kappan, 86*(3), 195–196.

Klein, N. (2000). Treats and temps. In H. Shapiro. & D. Purpel (Eds), *Critical issues in American education: Democracy and meaning in a globalizing world* (pp. 373–397). Mahwah, NJ: Erlbaum.

Kirkwood, T. F. (2001). Our global age requires global education: Clarifying definitional ambiguities. *The Social Studies, 92,* 10–15.

Kirkwood, T. F. (2002). *Teaching about Japan: Global perspectives in teacher* decision-making, context, and practice. *Theory and Research in Social Education, 30*, 88–115.

Kirkwood, T. F. (2004). Empowering teachers to create a more peaceful world through global education: Simulating the United Nations. *Theory and Research in Social Education, 32*(1), 56–74.

Kniep, W. M. (1989). Social studies within global education. *Social Education, 53*, 399–403.

Lamy, L. (1990). Global education: A conflict of images. In K. A. Tye (Ed.), *Global education: from thought to action* (pp. 49–66). Alexandria, VA: The Association for Supervision and Curriculum Development (ASCD).

Leetsma, R. (1979). Looking ahead: An agenda for action. In J. M. Becker (Ed.) *Schooling for a global age.* New York: McGraw-Hill.

LeSourd, S. (1993). Selected children's representations of people in five countries. *Theory and Research in Social Education, 21*(11), 316–340.

Massialas, B. G. (1991). Education for international understanding. In J. P. Shaver (Ed.), *Handbook of research on social studies teaching and learning* (pp. 448–458). New York: Macmillan.

McNeill, J. R., & McNeill, W.M. (2003) *The Human Web, a bird's eye view of world history.* New York: W. W. Norton.

Merryfield, M. M. (1992). Preparing social studies teachers for the twenty-first century: Perspectives in program effectiveness from a study of six exemplary teacher education programs in global education. Theory and Research in Social Education, 22, 17–46.

Merryfield, M. M. (1997). A framework for teacher education in global perspectives. In M. Merryfield, E. Jarchow, & S. Pickert (Eds.), *Preparing teachers to teach global perspectives: A handbook for teacher education* (pp. 1–24). Thousand Oaks, CA: Corwin Press.

Merryfield, M. M. (1998). Pedagogy for global perspectives in education: Studies of teachers' thinking and practice. *Theory and Research in Social Education. 26*, 342–369.

Merryfield, M. M. (2000a). Why aren't teachers being prepared to teach for diversity, equity, and global interconnectedness? A study of lived experiences in the making of multicultural and global educatiors. *Teaching and Teacher Education, 16*(4), 429–443.

Merryfield, M. M. (2000b). Using electronic technologies to promote equity and cultural diversity in social studies and global education. *Theory and Research in Social Education 28*, 502–526.

Merryfield, M. M. (2001). Moving the center of global education: From imperial world views that divide the world to double consciousness, contrapuntal pedagogy, hybridity, and cross-cultural competence. In W. Stanley (Ed.), *Critical issues in social studies research for the 21st century* (pp. 179–208). Greenwich, CT: Information Age Publishing.

Merryfield, M. M. (2002). Rethinking our framework for understanding the world. *Theory and Research in Social Education, 30*, 148–151.

Merryfield, M. M. (2003). Like a veil: Cross-cultural experiential learning online. *Contemporary Issues in Technology and Teacher Education, 3*(2), 146–171.

Merryfield, M., & Wilson, A. (2005). *Social studies and the world: Teaching global perspectives.* Washington, DC: NCSS.

Myers, J. (2006). Rethinking the socials studies curriculum in the context of globalization: Education for global citizenship in the U.S. *Theory and Research in Social Education, 34*(3), 370–394.

National Council for the Social Studies (2001). *Preparing citizens for a global community.* Retrieved May 11, 2005, from http://www.socialstudies.org/positions/global/

Ngugi wa, T. (1993). *Moving the center: The struggle for cultural freedom.* London: James Currey Ltd.

Noddings, N. (Ed.). (2005). *Educating citizens for global awareness.* New York: Columbia University Press.

Osunde, E., Tlou, J., & Brown, N. (1996). Persisting and common stereotypes in U.S. students' knowledge of Africa: A study of preservice social studies teachers. *The Social Studies, 87*(3), 119–124.

O'Sullivan, E. (2005). Education and dilemmas of modernism: Towards an ecozoic vision. In H. Shapiro & D. Purpel (Eds.), *Critical issues in American education: Democracy and meaning in a globalizing world* (pp. 339–442). Mahwah, NJ: Erlbaum.

Parker, W., Grossman, D., Kubow, P., Kurth-Schai, R., & Nakayama, S. (1998). Making it work: Implementing multidimensional citizenship. In J. Derricott (Ed.), *Citizenship for the 21st century: An international perspective on education* (pp. 135–154). London: Kogan Page.

Parker, W., Ninomiya, A., & Cogan, J. (1999). Educating world citizens: Toward multinational curriculum development. *American Educational Research Journal, 36*, 117–45

Pike, G. (1997). The meaning of global education: From proponents' vision to practitioner's perceptions. Unpublished doctoral dissertation, University of York, UK.

Pike, G., (2000). Global education and national identity: In pursuit of meaning. *Theory Into Practice, 39,* 64–74.

Quashigah, A. Y., & Wilson, A. H. (2001). A cross-national conversation about teaching from a global perspective. *Theory into Practice, XL, 1,* 55–65.

Rizvi, F. (2004). Debating globalization and education after September 11. *Comparative Education, 40*(2), 157–171.

Said, E. (1993). *Culture and imperialism.* New York: Alfred A. Knopf.

Shapiro, S., & Merryfield, M. (1995). *A case study of unit planning in the context of school reform.* In M. Merryfield & R. C. Remy (Eds.), *Teaching about international conflict and peace.* Albany: State University of New York Press.

Shapiro, H., & Purpel, D. (Eds.). (2005). *Critical issues in American education: Democracy and meaning in a globalizing world.* Mahwah, NJ: Erlbaum.

Shelby, D. (2000). A darker shade of green: The importance of ecological thinking in global education and school reform. *Theory into Practice, 3*(2), 88–96.

Thornton, S. (2005). Incorporating internationalism into the social studies curriculum. In N. Noddings (Ed.), *Educating citizens for global awareness* (81–92). New York: Columbia University Press.

Tucker, J. L. (1990). Global change and American citizenship education: The vital role of history. *Social Education, 54,* 312–315.

Tucker, J. L. (1991). Global perspectives for teachers: An urgent priority. *Journal of Teacher Education, 42,* 3–10.

Tye, B. B., & Tye, K. A. (1992). *Global education: A study of school change.* Albany: State University of New York Press.

Tye, K. A. (1999). Global education: A worldwide movement. Orange, CA: Interdependence Press.

Ukpokodu, N. (1999). Multiculturalism vs. globalism. *Social Education 63*(5), 298–300.

Van Manen, M. (1990). Researching lived experiences: Human science for an action sensitive pedagogy. Albany: State University of New York Press.

Willinsky, L. (1998). *Learning to divide the world*: Education at empire's end. Minneapolis: University of Minnesota Press.

Wilson, A. H. (1993a). *The meaning of international experience for schools.* Westport, CT: Praeger.

Wilson, A. H. (1993b). Conversation partners: Gaining a global perspective through cross-cultural experiences. *Theory into Practice, 32,* 21–26.

Wilson, A. H. (1994). The attributes and tasks of global competence. In R. D. Lambert (Ed.), *Educational exchange and global competence.* Council On International Educational Exchange.

Wilson, A. (1997). Infusing global perspectives throughout a secondary social studies program. In M. Merryfield, E. Jarchow, & S. Pickert (Eds.), *Preparing teachers to teach global perspectives: A handbook for teacher education* (pp. 1–24). Thousand Oaks, CA: Corwin Press.

Wilson, A. (1998). Oburoni outside the whale: Reflections on an experience in Ghana. *Theory and Research in Social Education, 26,* 410–429.

Wilson, A. (2001). Growing toward teaching from a global perspective: An analysis of secondary social studies preservice teachers. *The International Social Studies Forum, 1,* 127–143.

Zevin, J. (2003). Perceptions of national identity: How adolescents in the United States and Norway view their own and other countries. *The Social Studies, 94*(5), 227–231.

Zong, G. (2002). Can computer mediated communication help to prepare global teachers? An analysis of preservice social studies teachers' experience. *Theory and Research in Social Education, 30*(4), 589–616.

Zong, G. (2005a). Increasing preservice teachers' cross-cultural understanding and global awareness via computer-mediated communication. Paper presented at the National Association of Multicultural Education annual conference, Atlanta, GA.

Zong, G. (2005b). Road less traveled: An Asian woman immigrant faculty's experience practicing global pedagogy in American teacher education. In G. Li & R. Beckett (Eds.), *"Strangers" of the academy: Asian women scholars in higher education* (pp. 251–265). Sterling, VA: Stylus Publishing.

Part IV
Assessment and accountability

13 Assessment and accountability in the social studies

S. G. Grant

University of Buffalo

Cinthia Salinas

University of Texas at Austin

Social studies educators find themselves in an awkward position today vis-à-vis large-scale, standardized testing. On the one hand, many teachers worry that such tests will never approximate the kind of deep and nuanced understandings students should develop, and they object to being held responsible for assessments they have no hand in developing. At the same time, some worry that the absence of social studies from the No Child Left Behind (NCLB) agenda will condemn their school subject to second-tier status. The adage that "what gets tested gets taught" may turn out to be true though, in a different sense than has been the case in the past. The murky position in which social studies educators find themselves vis-à-vis the recent call for increased assessment and accountability is compounded when one explores the current state of theory and research on issues of assessment and accountability in the social studies.

Although assessment and accountability are well-covered in the general education literature, the social studies literature on these topics is much thinner. Far more has been written on the broad nature and impact of testing and on the nature and impact of testing on school subjects like reading and mathematics than on social studies. And within the social studies testing literature, advocacy pieces outnumber both theoretical stances and empirical studies. That ratio is changing somewhat as the number of data-based reports increases. Still, the social studies literature on testing lacks a clear theoretical frame and a solid, research-based grounding.

In this chapter, we focus on the relevant empirical and theoretical literature related to large-scale assessment and accountability in the social studies. After a brief review of the current state of standardized social studies testing, we argue that the research literature offers an ambiguous picture of the relationships between testing and student and teacher accountability. Though for different reasons, the theoretical literature on assessment and accountability is no clearer. It seems cliché to conclude that more inquiry is needed, but in this important area the case for such a conclusion seems especially strong.

THE STATE OF SOCIAL STUDIES TESTING

We begin this section by defining and delimiting the two key constructs: assessment and accountability. We, then, outline the current context of social studies testing across the United States, noting a less than certain future for teachers and students.

By itself, the term *assessment* means little because it can mean so much. Assessment typically refers to a judgment of some sort, but in the context of schooling, that judgment can refer to various situations. *Classroom* assessment may highlight a teacher's purpose as formative (judgments of students' progress made in the course of instruction that serve to inform teaching practice) or summative (judgments made at the end of an instructional period to evaluate students' growth), but it can also indicate the form in which the judgment is instantiated as, for example, multiple-choice tests, oral presentations, worksheets, and the like. *Standardized* assessment refers to any measure of students' aptitude and/or ability that is determined by an agency or organization outside the school. Some assessments, like the TerraNova tests or the Iowa Test of Basic Skills, are created by private organizations who sell their products to schools. The Educational Testing Service (ETS) is a private organization that creates a range of assessments, some of which, like the National Assessment of Educational Progress (NAEP), are commissioned by the U.S. government. Still other standardized assessments, like the various state-level achievement tests, are created by state departments of education (though typically with assistance from private testing companies). Some of these tests assess students' broad academic knowledge (i.e., the Iowa Test of Basic Skills); others are subject-specific (e.g., the New York Regents exam in U.S. history and government). Some tests (e.g., the TerraNova) are norm-referenced, meaning that individual students' scores are calculated against the mean scores of all the test-takers. Other tests (e.g., the New York Regents exam) are criterion-referenced, meaning that one or more cut-off scores are set and students are judged against those criteria. Confounding the term *assessment* even further is its use by psychologists and others in and around schools to measure factors other than academics. Thus, there are assessments of students' social aptitude, their career readiness, and the like.

From this vast landscape, we chose to focus on large-scale, standardized, social studies tests developed, administered, and scored by state departments of education and/or their designees. We chose not to explore the general tests of students' achievement that include a section on social studies (e.g., Iowa Test of Basic Skills) or tests directed toward a select student population (e.g., the Advanced Placement exams). Although they are large-scale and standardized, assessments falling into these categories are not included in this chapter because we could locate no relevant theoretical or empirical work examining them.[1] We also chose not to explore classroom assessment in this chapter largely because of our charge to look at the intersection of assessments and accountability. Although there are obvious implications for student accountability in classroom assessments, there is no corresponding implication for teacher accountability.[2]

With the assessment focus narrowed, we now turn to the construct of *accountability*. This term, too, poses some definitional and delimiting problems. We begin with the obvious: Accountability refers to the explicit rewards and/or sanctions for teachers and/or students that are attached to student test performance. For example, student accountability may take the form of a high school diploma based on passing an exam and teacher accountability may take the form of a teacher being fired for low student test scores. Such explicit consequences are part of some state accountability systems. Yet the research literature also exposes an implicit form of accountability that can manifest in teachers' thinking and practice.[3] That is, even in situations where the stakes associated with large-scale tests are minimal or even nonexistent, the presence of standardized exams can influence teachers' classroom planning, instruction, and assessment (Pedulla et al., 2003). Assessment and accountability seem to interact; however, the manifestations of that relationship are far from simple or straightforward.

THE UNCERTAIN RISE OF SOCIAL STUDIES TESTING

Although concern about Americans' understanding of history dates back to the beginnings of the last century (Paxton, 2003), social studies testing at national and state levels is a relatively recent phenomenon. The 100-year-old New York Regents testing program excepted, most large-scale assessments have focused on school subjects other than social studies. Proponents of the standards movement begun in the late 1980s embraced social studies along with other basic school subjects. New curriculum standards and course sequences emerged first; new state-level tests followed soon afterward. The increase in social studies assessment brought with it an increase in student and teacher accountability. Introduction of the No Child Left Behind legislation complicates this picture, however, as the act clearly downplays the importance of social studies.

The growth of large-scale state social studies testing is something of a moving target.[4] Since 1998, the number of state-level social studies tests has remained relatively constant; about half of the states mandate a social studies exam. Yet state policymakers add and drop social studies tests each year.

Tracking these changes in the research literature can be challenging. The best source for yearly changes in the number of state-level tests is the annual survey of state departments of education conducted by the staff of *Education Week*. The series, entitled *Quality Counts*, portrays a wide range of educational policies, conditions, and characteristics across the 50 states and District of Columbia. Since 1998, the number of states reporting standardized social studies tests has held steady at just under 50%. The stability of the 22–24 state-level tests masks two kinds of fluctuation. One is the increase in the number of states reporting standards-based testing from 1997, when 17 states reported administering standards-based exams, to 1998 when another 5 states added tests. The other kind of fluctuation reflects changes states make as they add or delete social studies tests. As we write this chapter, 23 states mandate standardized social studies tests. But in 2004, the *Quality Counts* survey shows that, over the preceding year, 3 states—Kansas, Maine, and New Hampshire—abandoned their state social studies assessments while 2 states—Tennessee and West Virginia—added new ones.

Because state policymakers administer a required social studies test does not mean, however, that explicit consequences are attached (Pedulla et al., 2003). At this writing, 10 of the 23 states that mandate a state test attach explicit stakes to student performance (Grant & Horn, 2006). These consequences typically take the form of a graduation sanction: Students are required to pass the social studies assessment (typically in combination with tests of reading, math, and sometimes others) to receive a high school diploma. The other 13 states mandate a social studies exam, but attach no particular result to students' test performance. States like Michigan require that students take a standardized social studies exam, but not passing the exam holds no consequence.

Until recently, most social studies teachers were exempt from any test-based accountability. Reading and mathematics teachers routinely found their students' test scores published, analyzed, and debated in print. Their social studies colleagues got a pass on this publicity, either because their subject was not tested or because their students' test results were ignored. As testing grows across school subjects, the publication of students' social studies test results (especially if results are disaggregated at the school level) can be viewed as a new and explicit form of teacher accountability. That sense of accountability is ratcheted up in those states that attach monetary rewards for high test performance and/or monetary and other sanctions for low scores.

The No Child Left Behind Act of 2001 muddies the social studies assessment and accountability picture. The legislation lists history (not social studies) as a core academic subject, but the call for testing students' historical knowledge is vague, and it is pushed into an undated future. This mixed message worries even NCLB proponents, who forecast decreased attention to history teaching and learning (Taylor, Shepard, Kinner, & Rosenthal, 2002; von Zastrow & Janc, 2004). Chester Finn (2003), an ardent advocate of standards-based testing, notes that "without intending to, however, NCLB may actually worsen the plight of U.S. history. By concentrating single-mindedly on reading, math, and science, it will likely reduce the priority that states, districts, and schools assign to other subject matters" (p. 5). Testing proponents like Finn are right to be worried as policymakers in each state read the NCLB tea leaves. As Burroughs (2002) notes, "state legislatures repeatedly pass and rescind laws that mandate [social studies] tests and/or define their use" (p. 315). For every state like Washington that develops a new social studies test, there are at least as many states, like Michigan, that are scaling back their tests and other states, like Maine, that are eliminating social studies tests all together. It is difficult to know, then, what the future holds of state-level social studies testing (Gaudelli, 2006).

A STATE OF AMBIGUITY, PART I: THE RELATIONSHIP BETWEEN ASSESSMENT AND ACCOUNTABILITY IN THE SOCIAL STUDIES RESEARCH LITERATURE

Despite the doom forecast by testing critics (Ohanian, 1999; Sacks, 1999) and the success predicted by testing proponents (Finn, 1995; Shanker, 1995) evident in the advocacy literature, the empirical evidence suggests an ambiguous relationship between social studies assessment and accountability. In the following sections, we explore that ambiguity on two levels—testing and student accountability and testing and teacher accountability.

Testing and student accountability

For most of a century, Americans have asked what children know about history (Paxton, 2003; Whittington, 1991). The answer—not much—has changed little (Beatty, Reese, Persky, & Carr, 1996; Lapp, Grigg, & Tay-Lim, 2002; Ravitch & Finn, 1987). Nevertheless, policymakers continue to develop new measures of students' historical understandings. At the same time, concerns around what is being tested and how have undercut any certainty in the measurement of those understandings. Further complicating these issues are two others: the relative novelty of state-level social studies testing and the incommensurate nature of state-level social studies tests. If a level of uncertainty surrounds the construction of state-level social studies testing, one imagines that there is considerable certainty on the individual student accountability side of the ledger. Simply put, students' test performance equates with either a reward (e.g., credit toward graduation) or a punishment (e.g., having to retake the test and/or course). That simple equation, however, obscures the uncertainty around social accountability. Here, the issue is largely one of incommensurate tests and the question of how the public is to know what students know.

What students know about social studies   Any review of research on testing in social studies must acknowledge the deep hole that exists around what students know. Attempts to assess students' knowledge of social studies generally and history in particular have been evident since the early 1900s. But systematic and rigorous study of what these assessments mean has been neglected. Current students may know as much as earlier generations, but that claim is based on thin evidence and still leaves unanswered the question of what knowledge is worth knowing.

Whether it's a David Letterman "man-in-the-street" interview, a *New York Times* survey, or a national test, Americans' knowledge of political, economic, social, and global events seems pitifully weak. On a 2000 survey of college seniors' knowledge of U.S. history and government, students averaged no better than 53% items correct (Paxton, 2003). This "dismal" result (p. 265) echoes the "shameful" performance of 11th graders on the 1986 National Assessment of Education Progress (Ravitch & Finn, 1987, p. 201), but it also echoes the judgment by the authors of a 1917 survey of Texas students' historical knowledge who concluded that the outcome "does not show a very thorough mastery of basic historical facts" (Paxton, 2003, p. 266). Richard Paxton and others (Whittington, 1991) who have examined the history of surveying students' knowledge conclude that contemporary students know no more than their great-grandparents, but neither do they know any less.[5] In the one study that compares students' historical knowledge over time, Dale Whittington (1991) analyzed students' performance on common items from nationally-administered social studies tests from the early 1930s to the late 1980s. The incommensurate nature of these exams posed some psychometric problems, but in the end, Whittington identified a set of 43 questions across 20 common historical categories. The result: If there ever was a golden age of students understanding history, it was well before the 1930s. Whittington concludes, "for the most part, students of the 1980s are not demonstrably different from students in their parents' or grandparents' generation in terms of their knowledge of American history" (p. 776).

Presumably there are differences between TV interviews, surveys, and nationally-administered exams and the kinds of tests state departments of education develop, the most important of which is the relationship between the assessment and the curriculum. National surveys and even national tests like the NAEP tend to focus on a scatter-plot of people, places, and events. Questions on state-level tests can also have something of a random feel (Grant, 2001), but since they are tied to a curriculum, they typically reflect ideas students have recently studied.

So what do the results of nearly 10 years of state-level testing in social studies tell us? Not much, largely because researchers have not looked deeply into students' performance on these exams. No state-level, curriculum-based test has been given longer than the 11th grade New York State Regents exam in U.S. history, and yet only a single study of student performance has been published. In that work, David Wiles (1996) observes that high-SES students typically out-perform their lower-SES peers, a finding likely to surprise no one familiar with U.S. schools (Hedges & Nowell, 1998; Horn, 2003).

To put the point on the need for more research on what students know, compare two sets of results. In the first year of the revised 10th grade New York State Global History and Geography exam, nearly 69% of the students passed state-wide (Grant, 2003) while in the first year of the new 11th grade Texas Assessment of Knowledge and Skills test in social studies, 98% of the tested students passed (Salinas, 2006). On the surface, one might conclude that Texas students know far more than their New York peers. And perhaps they do. But on a moment's reflection, one immediately realizes that passing rates alone offer little insight since the two tests are based on different curricula, ask different kinds of questions, and offer different scoring guides and cut scores.

The uncertainty of student accountability   There are many problems with standardized, state-level exams (Grant, 2003; Horn, 2006), but the difference between New York and Texas student passing rates and the questions that surround an understanding of that difference points to a key problem in determining accountability—the incommensurate nature of state-level tests (Amrein & Berliner, 2002; Gersten & Baker, 2002; Grant, 2003, 2006). That there could be important differences among national surveys, national tests, and state tests of social studies knowledge is not surprising. The fact of the matter is, however, there may be as many or more differences in social studies tests from one state to another (Buckles, Schug, & Watts, 2001; Grant & Horn, 2006). Consider the content disparity in the Texas and New York tests: 10th graders in New York are tested on the seemingly wide terrain of world history, yet world history is but one of several areas covered on the 11th grade Texas test. Such differences render any state-to-state comparisons virtually meaningless (Amrein & Berliner, 2002; Gersten & Baker, 2002; Linn, 2000, 2003b).

The relationship between state tests and individual student accountability is clear-cut: In states with a graduation requirement, for example, students who pass tests, graduate; those who don't pass, don't graduate. Since each student takes only the test administered in one state, the concern about incommensurate exams would seem not to apply. If we turn to the social nature of student accountability, however, two problems surface. One is confusion about what test scores mean from state to state. As noted above, incommensurate testing leads to incommensurate results, and so the effect of any national educational policy (such as No Child Left Behind) is problematic if measured by state-level exams. Texas taxpayers may feel that they are getting more for their money than are New Yorkers when state passing rates are compared, but the comparison itself is faulty. The second social problem with testing and student accountability involves the bigger issues of race and class. Although there is some evidence to suggest that good teaching matters more (Avery, 1999; Smith & Niemi, 2001), numerous studies demonstrate the correlation between low test scores and students who are non-White and/or from low-SES households (Hedges & Nowell, 1998; Horn, 2003; Kornhaber, Orfield, & Kurlaender, 2001). What we do not know from the research, however, is whether such patterns will result in the social accountability for *all* students.

Testing and teacher accountability

The new tests and consequences that state policymakers have created for students also affect social studies teachers. Rooted in the adage that testing can drive teaching, policymakers assume that new and presumably more ambitious tests will leverage more ambitious instruction and improved student performance. With the price tag of other interventions such as deep and sustained teacher professional development far greater than that of developing, administering, and scoring state-level exams (Grant, 1997), policymakers have yoked their hopes for standards-based reform to standardized testing.

Although the relationship between social studies teachers and testing is relatively new and unexplored, it has been more widely researched than the relationship between students and testing. The research picture that emerges, however, bedevils policymakers' assumptions in two ways. First, teachers' responses to tests, whether high-stakes or not, vary considerably. Teachers do make changes in response to new tests, but those changes typically are neither predictable nor deep. Second, although some evidence shows a correlation between teachers' practices and students' test performance, there seems to be no evidence that tests inspire more ambitious teaching. Change without improvement (Corbett & Wilson, 1991; Grant, 2003; McNeil, 2000; Mehrens, 2002) seems to be the rule.[7]

The variation in teachers' responses to state-level tests   Most observers agree: New state tests influence teachers' classroom practices. Equally evident, however, is the finding that these influences are not of a single kind; teachers seem to make the biggest changes in the content they teach and in the assessments they develop. Less evident are changes in teachers' instructional practices.

Whether promoting or damning standardized tests, the advocacy literature tends to offer sweeping generalities about test-based influences on teachers' practices (Finn, 1995; Kohn, 2000; Ohanian, 1999; Shanker, 1995). Some researchers also see pervasive influences across teachers' classroom practices (Abrams, Pedulla, & Madaus, 2003; Corbett & Wilson, 1991; Madaus, 1988; McNeil, 2000; Pedulla et al., 2003). These observers echo Smith's (M. L. Smith, 1991) claim that tests "result in a narrowing of possible curriculum and a reduction of teachers' ability to adapt, create, and diverge" and that multiple-choice testing leads to "multiple-choice teaching" (p. 10). Segall (2003) finds evidence of Smith's general claim in the social studies classes he observed. The Michigan social studies test, Segall argues, is low-stakes, yet it "impacts teaching in mostly negative ways, reducing teaching to low levels of intellectual engagement and teachers to implementers of externally designed curricula and pre-packaged materials intended to help them teach to the test" (p. 321). McNeil (2000), too, sees a test-based influence across teachers' practices. The state tests, which she argues are a part of a standardization movement, "reduced the scope and quality of course content, diminished the role of teachers, and distanced students from active learning" (p. 3).

Other researchers see small, but useful distinctions among the influences on teachers' decisions about content, instruction, and assessment. New state standards and the attendant tests appear to affect teachers' content decisions most of all (Grant, 2006; Grant et al., 2002; Segall, 2003, 2006; van Hover, 2006).[8] The social studies curriculum has long been cited as too large to teach well (Jenness, 1990), so teachers have always had to make hard choices about what content to emphasize. State tests, then, become another influence on their decisions. That influence is not always predictable, however. The narrowing effect that some researchers have noted (M. L. Smith, 1991) is countered by other reports that show teachers expanding their taught curriculum (Grant et al., 2002; Salinas, 2006; Segall, 2003, 2006; van Hover, 2006) in hopes that a shotgun approach will improve students' test performance.

The influence of state tests on teachers' classroom assessments appears more modest than on their content decisions (Fickel, 2006; Grant, 2003; Grant et al., 2002; van Hover, 2006). Numerous studies demonstrate that teachers' assessments mirror state test items (Abrams et al., 2003; Pedulla et al., 2003; Vogler, 2006), but it is less clear whether these assessments represent a change. In short, social studies teachers have long used multiple-choice, short-answer, and essay questions on their classroom exams. So, a correlation between these kinds of test items and state test items may not be much of an indication of influence. Where the influence can be detected is in states, like New York, that have introduced new types of test items, such as the Document-Based Question (DBQ). And here the evidence is quite clear: Most New York teachers are now adding DBQs to their classroom exams (Gerwin, 2004; Grant et al., 2002). That said, there is no evidence that teachers are universally abandoning alternative forms of assessment in favor of state test practice (Salinas, 2006; A. M. Smith, 2006; van Hover, 2006).

Like their content and assessment decisions, teachers' instruction can be influenced by state tests. In a survey of Mississippi teachers, Vogler (2006) reports a strong test-based impact on social studies teachers' instruction similar to that in the wider testing literature (Abrams et al., 2003; Pedulla et al., 2003). Vogler (2006) cites a teacher who claims to have given over his teaching to test preparation:

> My choice of instructional delivery and materials is completely dependent on preparation for this test. Therefore, I do not use current events, long-term projects, or creative group/corporate work because this is not tested and the delivery format is not used. All my tests reflect the testing format of the subject area tests—multiple-choice and open ended questions. (p. 273)

That said, over a quarter of the teachers Vogler surveyed (28%) report giving no more than minimal attention to preparing their students for the state exam.

This mixed result is echoed in the qualitative research base, where it appears that few teachers are giving over their classrooms to lecture, recitation, and test preparation (Gradwell, 2006; Grant & Gradwell, 2005; Segall, 2006; A. M. Smith, 2006; van Hover, 2006). This finding is something of a surprise: Given the pressures of new standards, new tests, and new consequences, one would imagine that teachers would, voluntarily or not, eliminate time-consuming teaching methods like discussion, projects, and presentations in favor of more didactic and efficient practices. Undoubtedly some are, but more striking is the wide variety of teaching strategies evident and the seeming commitment of many teachers to more ambitious practices.

Still in its infancy, research on the relationship between testing and teachers' practices is more tantalizing than coherent. Surveys suggest that tests impact teaching in fairly strong and comprehensive ways; observations and interviews offer more nuanced and complex insights into the effect of tests on teaching. Evident across all the empirical work, however, is the clear sense that teachers' responses to state tests vary not only from state to state, but from classroom to classroom. State tests carry weight, but that weight is not universally distributed.

The implications of test-based change   If researchers are of mixed minds about the kind of impact tests have on teachers, so too are they at odds about what that impact means. Although there is no evidence to support the idea that tests are inspiring more ambitious teaching, researchers offer different assessments of the import of testing on teaching.

Advocates of state-level testing invariably cite the potential for all manner of good effect (Finn, 1995; Shanker, 1995). Heubert and Hauser (1999) state the case baldly: "Large-scale assessments, used properly, can improve teaching, learning, and equality of educational opportunity" (p. 16).

The claims advocates advance are typically offered without empirical support. And this makes sense because researchers find little to support those claims (Cimbricz, 2002; Clarke, Madaus, Horn, & Ramos, 2000; Darling-Hammond & Falk, 1997; Firestone & Mayrowetz, 2000; Grant et al., 2002).[9] Even some long-time proponents of testing are now having second thoughts. For example, Popham (1999) observes that "the measuring devices being developed and distributed by the large-scale testing community are not designed to detect the differences of instruction—even first-rate instruction" (p. 14). Other researchers are more blunt: "There is, lamentably, little evidence currently available that suggests a causal link between assessment information and increased student learning" (Camilli, Cizek, & Lugg, 2001, p. 466).

When asked, teachers typically agree. Teachers generally support the idea of content standards, but they balk at the idea that state-level tests encourage more ambitious teaching and learning (Abrams et al., 2003; Pedulla et al., 2003; Sandholtz, Ogawa, & Schribner, 2004). Studies of New York social studies teachers suggest that they believe they hold their students to higher standards than do state test makers (Gradwell, 2006; Grant et al., 2002). Teachers in Texas (McNeil, 2000; Salinas, 2006), Virginia (A. M. Smith, 2006; van Hover, 2006), Michigan (Segall, 2003, 2006), Kentucky (Fickel, 2006), and Florida (Yeager & Pinder, 2006) acknowledge that, while they have made changes to accommodate new state tests, like their New York peers, they question whether those tests support the kind of teaching and learning they see as valuable. One gauge of the limited connection between state tests and more ambitious teaching can be seen in studies that show no evidence of spill-over from required and tested courses to elective, non-tested courses (Fickel, 2006; Vogler, 2006). In short, the content, instructional, and assessment changes teachers make in tested courses do not surface in elective courses. One would think that, if test-inspired changes were positive, teachers would incorporate them into their non-tested courses. Instead, the research suggests that teachers who are making the kinds of ambitious changes to their practices that correlate with higher student test performance (Avery, 1999; Lapp et al., 2002; J. Smith & Niemi, 2001) do so in spite of rather than because of the tests (Gradwell, 2006).

The uncertainty of teacher accountability   Raising the stakes associated with student test performance has consequences for teachers as well. Those consequences are hard to detail, however, because test-related consequences vary considerably from state to state. General studies of teachers suggest most are feeling some test-related pressures, and some teachers have been fired for low student scores. Perhaps because social studies tests are relatively new and are of diminished importance in an NCLB climate, there is little evidence that all social studies teachers are being held accountable to a strict set of criteria. That said, a sense of heightened accountability is developing among social studies teachers, even in states where the stakes are relatively low.

Although advocates of test-based reforms like NCLB contend that state-level assessments are essential if real change is to occur, many educators now question whether raising the stakes associated with tests will have much of an effect. Linn (2000) notes "assessment systems that are useful monitors lose much of their dependability and credibility for that purpose when high stakes are attached to them" (p. 14). Camilli and his colleagues (2001) argue that the research evidence confirms the "diminishing returns of high-stakes assessment as an educational reform strategy" (p. 466).

Getting a handle on the nature of the stakes attached to state social studies tests is difficult. Pedulla and his colleagues (2003) note that test-based consequences may be evident for districts, schools, teachers, and/or students and may yield a high, low, or medium effect on each group. When assessing the stakes associated with state tests, *Education Week* catalogs student consequences. Some states, like Texas, publish students' social studies test scores in newspapers while other states, like New York, do not. And, in some states, like Michigan, students' test performance has no obvious consequence for teachers, but high scores can result in substantial cash rewards for schools. These variations undercut any attempt to find patterns in test-related accountability for social studies teachers (Grant & Horn, 2006).

The odd thing is that a number of studies suggest that the stakes attached to state tests may not matter. For example, Firestone, Mayrowetz, and Fairman (1998) found that Maryland and Maine teachers responded to new literacy and math tests in similar fashion despite big differences in the state-mandated consequences. A similar result can be seen when comparing social studies teachers' responses in Virginia, which has a high-stakes exam (A. M. Smith, 2006; van Hover, 2006), and Michigan, which has a low-stakes test (Segall, 2003; 2006).

The variability in teachers' responses to state-tests, then, is no more predictable when accountability measures are factored in. Policymakers may hope to standardize teaching by increasing the consequences for teachers. The research suggests that the effect results in greater ambiguity rather than greater predictability.

A STATE OF AMBIGUITY, PART II: A FIELD IN SEARCH OF A THEORY OF ASSESSMENT AND ACCOUNTABILITY

Although assessment is an essential component of instructional design, the use of large-scale, state-level testing as a lever to improve classroom teaching and student learning remains unsubstantiated and intensely contested. Because history/social studies arrived late to the testing party, a paucity of research exists. With testing proponents and critics voicing loud, but largely unsubstantiated claims, the need for research-based understandings of social studies testing becomes more apparent. But if the empirical base for assessment and accountability in social studies is weak, so too is the theoretical base. Some traditional and recent theories can be applied, but research-based theories specific to social studies testing are needed.

The use of standardized tests to sort students and to rationalize school policies and decisions has a long-standing, extensively examined, and problematic history (Darling-Hammond, 1991; Kornhaber, 2004b; Shepard, 2000; Wiggins, 1998). In this section, we review two traditional theories of assessment and accountability—testing as a means of efficiently distinguishing between students and testing as a means of improving academic performance. We also review two contemporary views of assessment and accountability—testing for the promotion of student equity and testing as a means of denying student equity. After presenting these essentially generic theories, we discuss the potential for each in light of current understandings about social studies teaching, learning, and testing.

Traditional theories of testing: Efficiency and achievement

In the minds of both the general public and most educators, the theoretical justification for testing traditionally has focused on two distinct purposes. One of those purposes is rooted in the efficiency movement of the early 1900s and advances the notion that tests serve as an economical and objective means of distinguishing between students who are capable and those who are not (Kornhaber, 2004a). The other purpose tests have served is to advance student achievement. Here, the attending theory is only one step removed from behaviorism: Students who do well on exams are rewarded; those who do not are punished. Whether individually or in tandem, the lure of test-based rewards and the fear of test-based sanctions, presumably, encourage students to take their studies seriously.

Sound theories can run into reality roadblocks, however. And so it is with these generic theories once the empirical record on social studies teaching, learning, and assessment is introduced.

Testing as a means of sorting students efficiently   Kornhaber's (2004a) review of the historical assumptions underlying educational assessment offers a useful place to begin looking at the theory of tests as a means of efficiently sorting students. Beginning with Charles Darwin's and Francis Galton's grades of natural ability, and working through Yerkes and Terman's design of a classifying system for the U. S. Army, Kornharber notes that the promise of an objective and efficient testing program advanced the view that "intelligence was innate, inherited, and immutable" (p. 93). Although the assumptions of intelligence testing have proven problematic, the use of large-scale, state-level tests is still promoted in terms of efficiency.

The power of state-level exams is historically rooted in the general public's and in educators' understandings that separated assessment and instruction, while simultaneously giving assessment the function of fair and effective sorting (Wiggins, 1994). Shepard (2000) describes the current view of the efficiency paradigm as the panacea for evaluating the success and failure of public education. Analyzing this prevailing understanding of assessment, she explains how notions of Taylor's social efficiency movement and the curriculum theories advanced by Thorndike, Hull, Skinner, and Gagne fostered the development of objective-style tests and cemented the perception that "assessment needed to be an official event, separate from instruction" (p. 5). The isolation and acquisition of knowledge into atomized bits, sequenced and hierarchical and with limited transfer, is linked with the notion that tests should be frequent and isomorphic with learning and should provide external and positive motivation. The authority of the testing as a means of efficiency promotes the logic and efficiency of accountability-oriented assessments, a stance that echoes throughout state and national calls for large-scale testing.

Challenges to the theory of testing as a means of efficiency   Testing as a policy tool may make the tracking and sorting of students more efficient, but it "ignores a great many kinds of knowledge and types of performance that we expect from students and they place test-takers in a passive, reactive role, rather then engage their capacities to structure tasks, generate ideas, and solve problems" (Darling-Hammond, 1991, p. 220). With Darling-Hammond's general critique in mind, four problems arise with the idea of testing as a means of increasing school efficiency.

First, the value placed on testing for efficiency undercuts much of what researchers describe as the complexity of education (Shulman, 1987) in favor of what Shepard (2000) calls "one-skill-at-a-time test items" (p. 5). Not only do the sheer scale and costs of comprehensive, standardized testing crowd out more authentic or performance based assessment, but the premium placed on quick, efficient scoring means that judgments can easily be made. The resultant trivialization of ideas (Pahl, 2003) misrepresents subject matter disciplines and the potential of ambitious teaching and learning.

A second problem with the theory that tests promote efficiency concerns the content of state-level tests. With a premium on ease of administration and the presumed objectivity of the results, most state social studies tests emphasize a highly selective content domain (Linn, 2003a; Wiggins, 1994). Savage (2003) explains, "standardized assessments that are administered once a year over a couple of hours, contain items that have a poor curriculum match and focus on trivial content" (p. 203).

The scoring of standardized exams constitutes a third challenge to the idea that tests advance efficiency (Haney, 2004; Savage, 2003). State education officers often recalibrate cut-off scores, raising and lowering pass rates in order to accommodate changes to the test content, pilot/benchmark administrations, and political realities. For example, the Texas Assessment of Knowledge and Skills (TAKS) passing rate for students in 2004 required 22 of 55 correct responses, but in 2005 it was 25 of 55, and for 2006 the passing rate was 28 of 55 (Berlet, 2004). Such recalibrations of criterion-referenced exams can result in effectively creating a norm-referenced environment where some students will do well and others will not (Savage, 2003).

Finally, the premium placed on efficient assessments can compromise the relationship between teaching and learning. Effective instruction and learning requires robust and formative feedback; in that light, one-shot state-level tests pale (Pahl, 2003; Savage, 2003). Moreover, no evidence exists supporting the idea that large-scale testing promotes rich instructional change (Grant, 2003, 2006). State-level tests may offer a relatively inexpensive, fast, and efficient means of assessing students and holding them accountable. But efficiency seems a thin goal when one considers all that is possible in social studies classrooms.

Testing as a means of increasing student achievement   The idea that teachers and students can do more than march through a textbook is, in part, behind the theory that testing is a vehicle for improved student achievement. As noted above, one element of this theory reflects the behaviorist perspective that rewards and punishments largely determine behavior. But another element of this theory rests on a more positive premise based on the work of systemic reform theorists. From their perspective, if tests reflect rich content standards, then they can be an effective means of promoting student understanding.

The outlines of behaviorist theory are well-known, so we will resist reviewing them. Instead, we remind readers that the structures of rewarding positive behavior and punishing negative behavior are believed by many to be as germane to student assessment as they are to the most basic conditioned behavior. That the language and impact of "stakes" has been appended to the role of state-level testing seems a clear indication that behaviorist views continue to have currency.

Strict behaviorists have allies in the ranks of systemic reformers, who assert the idea that tests can advance student achievement. Advocates of systemic reform argue that, if the conditions around classrooms can be made richer, more coherent, and mutually supportive, then tests ought to be able to detect the attendant changes in teaching and learning (Fuhrman, 1993; M. Smith & O'Day, 1991). For example, if new, more rigorous content standards are created at the same time that new, more useful teacher professional development is offered and new, presumably more rigorous state tests are developed, then the results of those state tests will demonstrate that students know and can do more than previously expected.

Challenges to the theory of testing as a means of improving student achievement   Although the assumptions behind the relationship between tests and achievement seem reasonable, researchers have not been able to substantiate that relationship (Linn, 2003a; Sacks, 1999; Shepard, 2000; Whitford & Jones, 2000). For a range of reasons, researchers reject the use of a single assessment as the sole determinant for school ratings and for student promotion/retention (Heubert & Hauser, 1999; Hoffman, Assaf, & Paris, 2001; Jones, 2001; Luna & Turner, 2001; McNeil & Valenzuela, 2001).

Much of the critique of the behaviorist side of the argument echoes points made against the efficiency theory. This conclusion will surprise few close observers of schools because a major assumption of behaviorist theory is that learning can be made efficient if the right combination of incentives and penalties is offered. So, problems of a single test administration, of a selective content focus, and a changing scoring protocol are as germane to the theory of testing leading to achievement as they are to the theory of testing as a means of efficiency (Shepard, 2000). Jones (2001) concludes, "How shortsighted it is to accept test scores as the ultimate criterion of the benefits of education" (p. 27).

Systemic reform theory is equally susceptible to these critiques, but it also has been chided for one more—a Pollyannaish view of the potential for coherence and alignment in state policy. Clune (2001) and Grant (1998) challenge the key assumptions of systemic reformers that curriculum, professional development, certification, assessment, and other stars can all be arranged such that they appear mutually reinforcing to educators at all levels of schooling. If even a single policy can yield multiple interpretations, then the possibilities for rich, but inconsistent sets of interpretations only grow as more policies are added to the mix.

* * * * *

Despite a lack of empirical support, the individual students' scores generated from large-scale tests are viewed by policymakers and many in the general public as an educational panacea. Whether rooted in theories of efficiency and/or achievement, objective-style tests face a similar set of problems around what is tested, how it tested, and what these assessments can tell us about teaching and learning. The evidence that tests can deliver on the promise of efficiency is stronger than that for improving student achievement. But when one considers the complexity of the mission of American education, efficiency seems a small benefit at best.

Contemporary theories of testing: Promoting or denying equity

Skrla and Scheurich's (2004b) edited volume, *Educational Equity and Accountability*, sets an appropriate stage for the tension regarding standardized testing and its effect on linguistically and culturally diverse students. Scheurich, Skrla, and Johnson (2004) argue that "educational accountability has become the primary public space in which most of the discussion of racial inequities in public education is now occurring" (p. 15). Although many observers would agree with this claim, separate and opposing positions have developed regarding how state-level exams affect children of color as well as poor and working class White children. Some scholars have applauded the attention finally allocated towards linguistically and culturally diverse students; others rebuff accountability systems that have operationalized racist and classist schooling practices.

Testing as a means of promoting student equity   For several scholars the attention and effort now devoted to minority schools and students are immensely valuable. For example, Skrla and Scheurich (2004a) conclude "accountability has been a major driver of improved teaching and learning for children of color and children from low income families" (p. 281). From their studies of school leadership, "successful" schools, and the promise of accountability, they contend that a results-driven accountability system can be used to build a permanent culture of successful learning in minority-serving schools. Although advocates concede some of the challenges of large-scale testing, they commend the attention and resources devoted to historically marginalized students and schools. Arguing that all students now have access to high content standards, these researchers point to improved state or NAEP scores noting, "the positive change has been particularly pronounced for students of color and students from low-income homes" (Fuller & Johnson, 2004, p. 150). Although they do acknowledge equalized funding, preschool education, and class size as impacting factors, the clear catalyst, these scholars argue, is state accountability systems.

Testing as a means of denying student equity   The biggest challenge to the theory that tests promote student equity is another theory—the view that tests act as a means of denying equity.

A large number of scholars argue that the use of state-level exams, especially those with high stakes attached, furthers inequities in schools. Valencia, Valenzuela, Sloan, and Foley (2004) maintain that accountability systems that rely on high-stakes testing are treating the symptoms rather than the cause of academic inequities, and consequently are counterproductive. By equating standards-based assessment with equity, the political discourse that accompanies testing has "institutionalized a new discrimination" (McNeil, 2000, p. xxviii). Rather than attending to "the degree of segregation, the level of poverty, or the number of students...taking the SAT, and going to college," public attention is focused upon extraneous, but highly publicized, test scores (McNeil & Valenzuela, 2001, p. 4–5). Pahl (2003) asks, "why do we test statewide, when we can predict ahead of time that well-to-do school districts will score higher than poor districts?" (p. 214). These scholars and others have noted the diversion of educational expenditures, the decrease in classroom instructional time, and the creation of an artificial, test-based curriculum seem to widen the educational gaps between White middle and upper-middle class students and those in minority and poor schools (Kornhaber, 2004b; Luna & Turner, 2001; McNeil & Valenzuela, 2001).

The theory that tests disadvantage some students is embedded in two additional arguments. First, the introduction of content and testing standards divorced from students' community values ignores the notion of culturally-relevant pedagogy (Gay, 1997; Gutiérrez et al., 2002; Ladson-Billings, 1995). As school communities become increasingly linguistically and culturally diverse, standardized curricula and high-stakes exams suffer from demographic denial with "one-size-fits all ideologies" (Gutiérrez et al., 2002, p. 340). Valencia and her colleagues (2004) argue that "rather than place our faith in test-centric systems of accountability to 'leverage' more equitable, higher-quality education...there are proven means that are less top-down in nature" (p. 32). They assert that testing redirects attention that would be more useful if focused on "substantive means for achieving high academic performance" (p. 32). Second, critical theorists note the "archaeology of reform" that often layers "one reform on another without consideration of their compatibility" (Gutiérrez et al., 2002, p. 333). One description of counter-productive reforms is Newman and Chin's (2003) ethnographic study of low-income families and their negotiations between high-stakes consequences and welfare-to-work provisions. The policies, according the Newman and Chin's analysis, were mutually exclusive and forced parents to either earn income or support their children's education. Like the researchers who have examined systemic reform theory, Newman and Chin observe that policies that do not share a common ideology can create counter-productive consequences.

*   *   *   *   *

The debate over the implications of tests for student equity is likely to continue as researchers seem unable even to interpret the same data consistently.[10] This debate is also likely to continue for, while the bulk of scholarship seems to support the view that tests diminish the possibilities for real equity gains, the presence of the No Child Left Behind legislation suggests that testing will continue to be the currency by which students are evaluated.

CONCLUSION

If the arguments advanced above are on target, then the implications are pretty clear. On the one hand, a growing research base on assessment and accountability is far from sufficient. Some patterns can be seen, but they are more suggestive than definitive. On the other hand, the theoretical base on testing is even less developed. Some traditional and contemporary theories can be applied to the social studies testing context, but a well-conceived, well-supported theory specific to social studies assessment and accountability has yet to surface. That we think scholarly work on both the empirical and theoretical fronts ought to continue goes without saying.

NOTES

1. The social studies portions of general achievement tests are described in volumes such as Buros Mental Measurement, but there has been no systematic study of these sub-tests. There is a small literature on the AP exams, particularly those in U.S. History, but the pieces are largely descriptive or self-report in nature.
2. An exception is the state of Washington, which is working toward a set of state-sanctioned, classroom-based assessments.
3. Evidence of implicit notions of student accountability may exist but has not been reported in the social studies literature to date.
4. For an expanded treatment of the growth of social studies testing, see Grant and Horn (2006).
5. Paxton (2003) also points out that national assessments of students' knowledge in other school subjects show no greater advantage; students typically answer about half the questions correctly regardless of the subject matter tested.
   Whittington (1991) argues that preference is often given to test items of average difficulty (i.e., 50% of participants choose the correct response) over very easy items (i.e., 80% or more of participants choose the correct response) because they provide more discrimination among test-takers. Whittington concludes, then, an "average" score on any norm-referenced test will be around 50.
6. A particularly thorny problem is the extent to which a single test can measure what students know. Graham Nuthall and Adrienne Alton-Lee (1995) examined how students respond to standardized, test-like questions. From their analysis of how and why students choose the answers they do, Nuthall and Alton-Lee observe that "students with the same scores on the achievement test were unlikely to know, or have learned, the same content" (p. 192). In short, assuming that we know what students know from a count of right and wrong answers is problematic.
7. Vogler (2002) argues that more ambitious tests can promote more ambitious teaching, though his study did not include social studies teachers. Clarke and her colleagues (2000) observe that social studies tests were more likely to be viewed as less ambitious than those in other school subjects.

8. Firestone and his colleagues (1998) found a similar phenomenon in other school subjects.
9. See Bolgatz (2006) for an account of a classroom situation in which a teacher and a teacher-researcher used the new fifth grade New York social studies test to justify a series of ambitious classroom units.
10. See, for example, the disparate claims around the Texas "miracle" advanced by Haney (2000) and Toenjes and Dworkin (2002).

REFERENCES

Abrams, L., Pedulla, J., & Madaus, G. (2003). Views from the classroom: Teachers' opinions of statewide testing programs. *Theory Into Practice, 42*(1), 18–29.

Amrein, A., & Berliner, D. (2002). High-stakes testing, uncertainty, and student learning. *Educational Policy Analysis Archives, 10*(18), 110–123.

Avery, P. (1999). Authentic assessment and instruction. *Social Education, 63*(6), 368–373.

Beatty, A., Reese, C., Persky, H., & Carr, P. (1996). *U. S. history report card.* Washington, DC: U.S. Department of Education, Office of Educational Research and Improvement.

Berlet, L. (2004). TEA Update. *The Social Studies Texan, 20*(1), 21–26.

Buckles, S., Schug, M., & Watts, M. (2001). A national survey of state assessment practices in the social studies. *The Social Studies, 90*(4), 141–146.

Burroughs, S. (2002). Testy times for social studies. *Social Education, 66*(5), 315–319.

Camilli, G., Cizek, G., & Lugg, C. (2001). Psychometric theory and the validation of performance standards: History and future perspectives. In G. Cizek (Ed.), *Setting performance standards: Concepts, methods, and perspectives* (pp. 445–476). Mahwah, NJ: Erlbaum.

Cimbricz, S. (2002). State testing and teachers' thinking and practice: A synthesis of research. *Educational Policy Analysis Archives, 10*(2).

Clarke, M., Madaus, G., Horn, C., & Ramos, M. (2000). Retrospective on educational testing and assessment in the 20th century. *Journal of Curriculum Studies, 32*(2), 159–181.

Clune, W. (2001). Toward a theory of standards-based reform: The case of nine NSF statewide systemic initiatives. In S. Fuhrman (Ed.), *From the capitol to the classroom: Standards-based reform in the states* (pp. 13–38). Chicago, IL: University of Chicago Press.

Corbett, H. D., & Wilson, B. (1991). *Testing, reform, and rebellion.* Norwood, NJ: Ablex.

Darling-Hammond, L. (1991). The implications of testing policy for quality and equality. *Phi Delta Kappan, 73*(3), 220–225.

Darling-Hammond, L., & Falk, B. (1997). Using standards and assessments to support student learning. *Phi Delta Kappan, 79*(3), 190–199.

Fickel, L. (2006). Paradox of practice: Expanding and contracting curriculum in a high-stakes climate. In S. G. Grant (Ed.), *Measuring history: Cases of high-stakes testing across the U.S.* (pp. 75–104). Greenwich, CT: Information Age Publishing.

Finn, C. (1995). Who's afraid of the big, bad test? In D. Ravitch (Ed.), *Debating the future of American education: Do we need national standards and assessments?* (pp. 120–144). Washington, DC: Brookings Institution.

Finn, C. (2003). Forward. In S. Stern (Ed.), *Effective state standards for U.S. history: A 2003 report card.* Washington, DC: Fordham Foundation.

Firestone, W., & Mayrowetz, D. (2000). Rethinking "high stakes": Lessons from the United States and England and Wales. *Teachers College Record, 102*(4), 724–749.

Firestone, W., Mayrowetz, D., & Fairman, J. (1998). Performance-based assessment and instructional change: The effects of testing in Maine and Maryland. *Educational Evaluation and Policy Analysis, 20*(2), 95–113.

Fuhrman, S. (1993). The politics of coherence. In S. Fuhrman (Ed.), *Designing coherent education policy: Improving the system* (pp. 1–34). San Francisco: Jossey Bass.

Fuller, E. J., & Johnson, F. F. (2004). Can state accountability systems drive improvements in school performance for children of color and children from low-income homes? In L. Skrla & J. J. Scheurich (Eds.), *Educational equity and accountablity: Paradigms, policies, and politics* (pp. 133–154). New York: Routledge.

Gaudelli, W. (2006). The future of high-stakes history assessment: Possible scenarios, potential outcomes. In S. G. Grant (Ed.), *Measuring history: Cases of high-stakes testing across the U.S.* (pp. 321–334). Greenwich, CT: Information Age Publishing.

Gay, G. (1997). The relationship between multicultural and democratic education. *The Social Studies, 88*(1), 5–11.

Gersten, R., & Baker, S. (2002). The relevance of Messick's four faces for understanding the validity of high-stakes assessments. In G. Tindal & T. Haladyna (Eds.), *Large-scale assessment programs for all students: Validity, technical adequacy, and implementation* (pp. 49–66). Mahwah, NJ: Erlbaum.

Gerwin, D. (2004). Preservice teachers report the impact of high-stakes testing. *The Social Studies, 95*(2), 71–74.

Gradwell, J. M. (2006). Teaching in spite of, rather than because of, the test: A case of ambitious history teaching in New York state. In S. G. Grant (Ed.), *Measuring history: Cases of high-stakes testing across the U.S.* (pp. 157–176). Greenwich, CT: Information Age Publishing.

Grant, S. G. (1997). Opportunities lost: Teachers learning about the New York state social studies framework. *Theory and Research in Social Education, 25*(3), 259–287.

Grant, S. G. (1998). *Reforming reading, writing, and mathematics: Teachers' responses and the prospects for systemic reform.* Mahwah, NJ: Erlbaum.

Grant, S. G. (2001). When an "A" isn't enough: Analyzing the New York state global history exam. *Educational Policy Analysis Archives, 9*(39).

Grant, S. G. (2003). *History lessons: Teaching, learning, and testing in U. S. high school classrooms.* Mahwah, NJ: Erlbaum.

Grant, S. G. (Ed.). (2006). *Measuring history: Cases of high-stakes testing across the U. S.* Greenwich, CT: Information Age Publishing.

Grant, S. G., & Gradwell, J. M. (2005). The sources are many: Exploring history teachers' selection of classroom texts. *Theory and Research in Social Education, 33*(2), 244–265.

Grant, S. G., Gradwell, J. M., Lauricella, A. M., Derme-Insinna, A., Pullano, L., & Tzetzo, K. (2002). When increasing stakes need not mean increasing standards: The case of the New York state global history and geography exam. *Theory and Research in Social Education, 30*(4), 488–515.

Grant, S. G., & Horn, C. (2006). The state of state-level history testing. In S. G. Grant (Ed.), *Measuring history: Cases of high-stakes testing across the U.S.* (pp. 9–27). Greenwich, CT: Information Age Publishing.

Gutiérrez, K. D., Asato, J., Pacheco, M., Moll, L. C., Olson, K., Horng, E. L., et al. (2002). "Sounding American": The consequences of new reforms on English language learners. *Reading Research Quarterly, 37*(3), 328–347.

Haney, W. (2000). The myth of the Texas miracle in education. *Educational Policy Analysis Archives, 8*(41).

Haney, W. (2004). Response to Skrla et al. the illusion of educational equity in Texas: A commentary on "Accountability for Equity." In L. Skrla & J. J. Scheurich (Eds.), *Educational equity and accountability: Paradigms, policies, and politics* (pp. 79–89). New York: Routledge.

Hedges, L., & Nowell, A. (1998). Black-white test score convergence since 1965. In C. Jencks & M. Phillips (Eds.), *The black-white test score gap* (pp. 149–181). Washington, DC: Brookings Institute.

Heubert, J., & Hauser, R. (1999). *High stakes: Testing for tracking, promotion, and graduation.* Washington, DC: National Academy Press.

Hoffman, J. V., Assaf, L., & Paris, S. G. (2001). High stakes testing in reading and its effects on teachers, teaching, and students: Today in Texas, tomorrow? *The Reading Teacher, 54*(5), 482–492.

Horn, C. (2003). High-stakes testing and students: Stopping or perpetuating a cycle of failure. *Theory Into Practice, 42*(1), 30–41.

Horn, C. (2006). The technical realities of measuring history. In S. G. Grant (Ed.), *Measuring history: Cases of high-stakes testing across the U.S.* (pp. 57–74). Greenwich, CT: Information Age Publishing.

Jenness, D. (1990). *Making sense of social studies.* New York: Macmillan.

Jones, L. (2001). Assessing achievement vs high stakes testing: A crucial contrast. *Educational Assessment, 7*(1), 21–28.   ·

Kohn, A. (2000). *The case against standardized testing: Raising the scores, ruining the schools.* Portsmouth, NH: Heinemann.

Kornhaber, M., Orfield, G., & Kurlaender, M. (2001). *Raising standards or raising barriers? Inequality and high-stakes testing in public education.* New York: Century Foundation Press.

Kornhaber, M. L. (2004a). Appropriate and inappropriate forms of testing, assessment, and accountability. *Educational Policy, 18*(1), 45–70.

Kornhaber, M. L. (2004b). Assessment, standards, and equity. In J. Banks & C. M. Banks (Eds.), *Handbook of research on multicultural education* (pp. 91–109). San Francisco, CA: Jossey-Bass.

Ladson-Billings, G. (1995). Toward a theory of culturally responsive pedagogy. *American Educational Research Journal, 32*(2), 465–491.

Lapp, M., Grigg, W., & Tay-Lim, B. (2002). *The nation's report card: U.S. History 2001.* Washington, DC: U.S. Department of Education, Office of Educational Research and Improvement, National Center for Education Statistics.

Linn, R. (2000). Assessments and accountability. *Educational Researcher, 29*(2), 4–16.

Linn, R. (2003a). Accountability: Responsibility and reasonable expectations. *Educational Researcher, 32*(7), 3–13.

Linn, R. (2003b). Performance standards: Utility for different uses of assessments. *Educational Policy Analysis Archives, 11*(31).

Luna, C., & Turner, C. (2001). The impact of the MCAS: Teachers talk about high-stakes testing. *English Journal, 91*(1), 78–87.

Madaus, G. (1988). The influence of testing on the curriculum. In L. Tanner (Ed.), *Critical issues in curriculum: 87th yearbook of the NSSE, Part 1* (pp. 83–121). Chicago: University of Chicago Press.

McNeil, L. (2000). *Contradictions of school reform: Educational cost of standardized testing.* New York: Routledge.

McNeil, L., & Valenzuela, A. (2001). The harmful impact of the TAAS system of testing in Texas: Beneath the accountability rhetoric. In M. Kornharber & G. Orfield (Eds.), *Raising standards or raising barriers? Inequality and high stakes testing in public education* (pp. 127–150). New York: Century Foundation.

Mehrens, W. (2002). Consequences of assessment: What is the evidence? In G. Tindal & T. Haladyna (Eds.), *Large-scale assessment programs for all students: Validity, technical adequacy, and implementation* (pp. 149–177). Mahwah, NJ: Erlbaum.

Newman, K. S., & Chin, M. M. (2003). High stakes: Time, poverty, testing, and the children of the working poor. *Qualitative Sociology, 26*(1), 3–34.

Nuthall, G., & Alton-Lee, A. (1995). Assessing classroom learning: How students use their knowledge and experience to answer classroom achievement test questions in science and social studies. *American Educational Research Journal, 32*(1), 185–223.

Ohanian, S. (1999). *One size fits few: The folly of educational standards.* Portsmouth, NH: Heinemann.

Paxton, R. (2003). Don't know much about history—Never did. *Phi Delta Kappan, 85*(4), 264–273.

Pedulla, J., Abrams, L., Madaus, G., Russell, M., Ramos, M., & Miao, J. (2003). *Perceived effects of state-mandated testing programs on teaching and learning: Findings from a national survey of teachers.* Chestnut Hill, MA: National Board on Educational Testing and Public Policy.

Popham, W. J. (1999). Where large scale assessment is heading and why it shouldn't. *Educational Measurement: Issues and Practice, 18,* 13–17.

Ravitch, D., & Finn, C. (1987). *What do our seventeen year olds know?* New York: Harper & Row.

Sacks, P. (1999). *Standardized minds: The high price of America's testing culture and what we can do to change it.* Cambridge, MA: Perseus.

Salinas, C. (2006). Teaching in a high-stakes testing setting: What becomes of teacher knowledge? In S. G. Grant (Ed.), *Measuring history: Cases of high-stakes testing across the U.S.* (pp. 177–194). Greenwich, CT: Information Age Publishing.

Sandholtz, J., Ogawa, R., & Schribner, S. (2004). Standards gaps: Unintended consequences of local standards-based reform. *Teachers College Record, 106*(6), 1177–1202.

Savage, T. V. (2003). Assessment and quality social studies. *The Social Studies, 95*(5), 201–206.

Segall, A. (2003). Teachers' perceptions of the impact of state-mandated standardized testing: The Michigan Educational Assessment Program (MEAP) as a case study of consequences. *Theory and Research in Social Education, 31*(3), 287–325.

Segall, A. (2006). Teaching in the age of accountability: Measuring history or measuring up to it? In S. G. Grant (Ed.), *Measuring history: Cases of high-stakes testing across the U.S.* (pp. 105–132). Greenwich, CT: Information Age Publishing.

Shanker, A. (1995). The case for high stakes and real consequences. In D. Ravitch (Ed.), *Debating the future of American education: Do we need national standards and assessments?* (pp. 145–153). Washington, DC: Brookings Institution.

Shepard, L. (2000). The role of assessment in a learning culture. *Educational Researcher, 29*(7), 4–14.

Shulman, L. (1987). Knowledge and teaching: Foundations of the new reform. *Harvard Educational Review, 57*(1), 1–22.

Skrla, L., & Scheurich, J. J. (2004a). Conclusion: Keeping equity in the foreground. In L. Skrla & J. J. Scheurich (Eds.), *Educational equity and accountability: Paradigms, policies, and politics* (pp. 275–283). New York: Routledge Falmer.

Skrla, L., & Scheurich, J. J. (2004b). *Educational equity and accoutability: Paradigms, policies, and politics.* New York: Routledge.

Smith, A. M. (2006). Negotiating control and protecting the private: History teachers and the Virginia Standards of Learning. In S. G. Grant (Ed.), *Measuring history: Cases of high-stakes testing across the U.S.* (pp. 221–248). Greenwich, CT: Information Age Publishing.

Smith, J., & Niemi, R. (2001). Learning history in school: The impact of course work and instructional practices on achievement. *Theory and Research in Social Education, 29*(1), 18–42.

Smith, M., & O'Day, J. (1991). Systemic school reform. In S. Fuhrman & B. Malen (Eds.), *The politics of curriculum and testing* (pp. 233–267). New York: Falmer.

Smith, M. L. (1991). Put to the test: The effects of external testing on teachers. *Educational Researcher, 20*(5), 8–11.

Taylor, G., Shepard, L., Kinner, F., & Rosenthal, J. (2002). *A survey of teachers' perspectives on high-stakes in Colorado: What gets taught, what gets lost* (No. CSE Technical Report 588). Boulder, CO: National Center for Research on Evaluation, Standards, and Student Testing.

Toenjes, L., & Dworkin, A. G. (2002). Are increasing test scores in Texas really a myth, or is Haney's myth a myth? *Educational Policy Analysis Archives, 10*(17).

Valencia, R. R., Valenzuela, A., Sloan, K., & Foley, D. (2004). Let's treat the cause, not the symptoms. In L. Skrla & J. J. Scheurich (Eds.), *Educational equity and accountability: Paradigms, policies, and politics* (pp. 29–38). New York: Routledge.

van Hover, S. (2006). Teaching history in the Old Dominion: The impact of Virginia's accountability reform on seven secondary beginning history teachers. In S. G. Grant (Ed.), *Measuring history: Cases of high-stakes testing across the U.S.* (pp. 195–220). Greenwich, CT: Information Age Publishing.

Vogler, K. (2002). The impact of high-stakes, state-mandated student performance assessment on teachers' instructional practices. *Education, 123*(1), 39–55.

Vogler, K. (2006). The impact of a high school graduation examination on Mississippi social studies teachers' instructional practices. In S. G. Grant (Ed.), *Measuring history: Cases of high-stakes testing across the U.S.* (pp. 273–302). Greenwich, CT: Information Age Publishing.

von Zastrow, C., & Janc, H. (2004). *Academic atrophy: The condition of the liberal arts in America's public schools.* Washington, DC: Council for Basic Education.

Whitford, B. L., & Jones, K. (2000). *Accountability, assessment, and teacher commitment: Lessons from Kentucky's reform efforts.* Albany, NY: State University of New York Press.

Whittington, D. (1991). What have 17-year-olds known in the past? *American Educational Research Journal, 28,* 759–780.

Wiggins, G. (1994). Reconsidering standards and assessment. *Contemporary Education, 66*(1), 5–6.

Wiggins, G. (1998). An exchange of view on semantics, psychometrics, and assessment reform: A close look at 'authentic' assessments. *Educational Researcher, 27*(6), 19–22.

Wiles, D. (1996). *Networking high performance in New York's secondary education: The Regents curriculum story.* Lanham, MD: University Press of America.

Yeager, E., & Pinder, M. (2006). "Does anyone really understand this test?" Florida high school social studies teachers' efforts to make sense of the FCAT. In S. G. Grant (Ed.), *Measuring history: Cases of state-level reform across the United States* (pp. 249–272). Greenwich, CT: Information Age Publishing.

Part V
Teaching and learning in the disciplines

14 Research on students' ideas about history

Keith C. Barton

University of Cincinnati

Research on students' ideas about history has been an active field of investigation in recent decades. Over 200 empirical studies have been published since the late 1970s by scholars in a variety of countries, and this literature has included contributions from researchers in fields such as reading, educational psychology, and social studies and history education. Perhaps because of their differing disciplinary and national backgrounds, however, researchers have not always fully incorporated the findings of previous studies into their own work, and this has hindered a more comprehensive understanding of the development of students' ideas. Yet despite researchers' varied backgrounds and despite disagreements over the proper aims of history education—even over the very nature of history and historical thinking—this body of work has resulted in several consistent findings. This review summarizes results from key lines of inquiry within the field and suggests potentially productive areas for future research.

Most studies of students' ideas about history fall into three overlapping categories: (1) research on what students know about the past and how their knowledge is structured—that is, how students make connections among various aspects of the past, particularly through narrative; (2) research on students' understanding of historical evidence and their explanations for the actions of people in the past; and (3) research on the social contexts of students' ideas about history, especially the origins of their knowledge and interests, as well as the relationship between the school curriculum and other sources of historical understanding. Within each of these three areas, most studies are descriptive ones that characterize students' ideas at a given point in time, but some studies aim to assess the impact of instruction, either through brief, structured interventions or by analysis of broader, long-term classroom practices.

STUDENTS' KNOWLEDGE OF THE PAST

Students begin to accumulate historical knowledge at a young age. From the first years of schooling, they can identify some of the ways in which life was different in the past, and across the elementary grades they become increasingly familiar with changes in technology, architecture, fashion, and other aspects of everyday life, even when they have not studied these topics at school (Barton, 2002; Barton & Levstik, 1996; Downey, 1996; Harnett, 1993; Lynn, 1993; Vella, 2001). In the upper elementary grades and beyond, most students also are able to identify some long-term social and political developments, particularly those related to national history (Barton & Levstik, 1998; Epstein, 1998; Körber, 1997; P. Lee, 2004; Yeager, Foster, & Greer, 2002; Yeager & Terzian, 2007). In the United States, for example, students are likely to know abut the European settlement and expansion of North America, the political origin of the country, the expansion of rights and opportunities to previously marginalized groups, and the impact of technological changes on daily life. They may not, however, have a detailed or extensive understanding of specific people or events that exemplify those developments (McKeown & Beck, 1990; VanSledright, 1995a, 1996).

Students also are familiar with historical time from the first years of elementary school. They use language that refers to the past; they can sequence many images and events in chronological order; they know that temporal distances between past times vary; and they know that past times can be identified with dates or with a number of "years ago." At first, their engagement with historical time is very general: They group images into broad categories such as "long ago" and "very long ago"; they describe temporal distances in vague (and nonmathematical) terms; and they use only recent dates accurately. When they lack specific knowledge about historical eras and dates, students rely on a perception of material progress to sequence past times; and if asked to date those times, they may simply count backward, by years or decades, from the present (Barton, 2002; Barton & Levstik, 1996; Downey, 1996; Harnett, 1993; Hodkinson, 2004a; Hoodless, 2002; Körber, 1997; Lynn, 1993; van Boxtel & van Drie, 2004).

Over the course of the elementary grades, students' facility with historical time becomes more sophisticated: They make finer distinctions among periods; they are better able to relate events and images to other happenings from the same time; and they increasingly refer to historic times by using accurate dates and period names (Barton, 2002; Barton & Levstik, 1996; Carretero, Asensio, & Pozo, 1991; Foster, Hoge, & Rosch, 1999; Hodkinson, 2004a; Körber, 1997). (Students' understanding of dates BCE remains problematic at least through the end of elementary school, however, and sequencing of closely-spaced political events is difficult even for older adolescents.) There is no evidence that students' understanding of any of these elements, or their ability to co-ordinate them, depends either on encountering history in chronological order or simply studying more historical content. What seems to matter is that when students learn about a given time in the past, they are alerted to its temporal dimensions—how long ago it was, how far it is from other times they have studied, what else was going on at the same time, and how that time is referred to by year, decade, century, or period name (Barton, 2002; Hodkinson, 2003, 2004a, 2004b).

Students' developing knowledge of the past, however, does not consist simply of discrete pieces of information or isolated patterns. Rather, students consistently connect historical knowledge into structured narratives. When elementary students are asked to recount what they know about particular historical topics, they often respond in the form of narratives, and they tend to simplify the historical content they learn so that it better matches their expectations for the structure of stories. The particular content of these stories may include inaccuracies, conflated events, or purely fanciful details, but students strive to retain the overall narrative structure of their accounts, and they use their imaginations to fill any gaps. In addition, students are more likely to remember the core events of historical narratives—those required to maintain their story-like structure—than to recall more peripheral details (Barton, 1996; Fasulo, Girardet, & Pontecorvo, 1998; Perfetti, Britt, & Georgi, 1995; VanSledright & Brophy, 1992).

Students not only use general narrative structures to understand the past; by the middles grades they also use more specific narratives to make sense of historical trends and events. Ghanaian students, for example, describe history in terms of a national narrative that focuses on self-rule gained through ancestral sacrifice and struggle against subjugation (Levstik & Groth, 2005). Students of French heritage in Quebec explain the province's history in tragic and melancholy terms, as a one-sided and unvarying story of conquest and victimization (Létourneau & Moisan, 2004). And in the United States, students emphasize twin themes of freedom and progress: They describe how the quest for freedom motivated European settlement of North America, how uniquely American freedoms were enshrined in the U.S. Constitution, and how the nation has repeatedly solved its social and technological challenges (Barton & Levstik, 1998; Wertsch, 1994). English students also describe national history in terms of social and technological progress (P. Lee, 2004; Yeager et al., 2002), but students in both Germany and Northern Ireland are less wedded to a narrative of progress: They see some historical trends as examples of progress and others as instances of continuity or decline (Barton, 2002, 2005; Kölbl & Straub, 2001; von Borries, 1994).

Students' use of narrative sometimes leads to significant simplifications. Often, elementary students describe past times as though they involved a limited number of people and events, all operating in a restricted geographical space, and they collapse gradual and long-term processes into single, discrete events (Barton, 1996; Brophy & VanSledright, 1997). Students also frequently overlook the diverse experiences and perspectives of people at any given time in the past. Elementary students, for example, may think of each historical period as characterized by only one set of lifestyles, and this leads them to ignore the diversity found among different geographic regions or economic strata, as well as the varied experiences and perspectives that characterized different groups involved in historic events (Barton, 1996). Similarly, although students often are aware that men's and women's experiences were different in history, their perceptions of the past typically emphasize the experiences of males (Fournier & Wineburg, 1997; Levstik, 1997/1998; Waldron, 2005). However, when diversity is emphasized in curriculum requirements, instructional materials, and teaching approaches, students better understand how experiences and perspectives differed both within and among groups of people in the past (Barton, 2001b; Brophy, 1999; Brophy & VanSledright, 1997; Grant, 2001; Levstik & Groth, 2002; VanSledright, 2002c; Waldron, 2005).

Educators often assume that students, particularly those in the elementary grades, know very little about the past and cannot understand historical time. The research reviewed here indicates that such assumptions are misleading. From a young age, students know a great deal about the past and have begun to develop an understanding of historical time. Their knowledge, however, may differ from expectations of teachers or other educators: They are more likely to know about changes in social and material life than about specific people or events, and their understanding of time begins with broad sequences rather than precise dates. Similarly, older students often recognize broad historical themes and patterns even when their knowledge of specific details is vague or inaccurate. Students also tend to simplify the historical content they encounter, and this prevents them from fully recognizing the complexity and diversity of historical experiences and perspectives. None of these patterns is inevitable, though, nor are they a direct function of age; rather, instruction that specifically addresses diversity or historical time can enhance students' understanding of these elements of the subject.

IDEAS ABOUT EVIDENCE AND EXPLANATION

A great deal of research has focused on students' understanding of historical evidence and its interpretation and on their recognition that explanations of people's actions in the past depend on consideration of historical contexts. For many educators, these constitute the real "content" of history education, rather than information about particular events, time periods, or developments.

Historical accounts and the interpretation of evidence

Although students may learn a great deal of information about the past from informal sources, most do not recognize how historical accounts are developed from evidence until (and unless) they study the topic at school. Often, they appear not even to have considered the issue before studying it at school; but when pressed to explain how people today know what happened long ago, they may point to the use of material artifacts or suggest that information is handed down by word of mouth. After studying historical methods, though, students develop greater knowledge of the range of sources that can be used to develop historical accounts, and they can use such sources to make inferences about life in the past (Barton, 1997b, 2001a; Brophy & VanSledright, 1997; Cooper, 1992; Fasulo et al., 1998; Shemilt, 1980).

Even when students learn about sources used in creating historical accounts, though, they may not be critical of such sources. From elementary school through college, many students think of historical sources as providing direct and objective information about the past; they typically do not recognize the necessity of interpreting historical sources, nor do they understand how the use of sources differs from one account to another (Ashby, 2004; Ferretti, MacArthur, & Okolo, 2001; Gabella, 1994a; P. Lee & Ashby, 2000; Shemilt, 1987). When analyzing historical texts, for example, students do not automatically attend to how their authors' intentions may have influenced their creation, nor do they compare the content of sources that provide conflicting information (Afflerbach & VanSledright, 2001; Britt & Aglinskas, 2002; Foster et al., 1999; Kohlmeier, 2005b; P. Lee, 2001; Shemilt, 1980, 1987; Stahl, Britton, Hynd, McNish, & Bosquet, 1996; VanSledright, 2002b; VanSledright & Kelly, 1998; von Borries, 1997a; Wineburg, 1991a, 1991b). When asked to explain why written accounts differ, students often suggest that differences result either from limited information or from authors' personal biases or literary styles, and when asked which accounts are more reliable, they may base their decisions on the quantity (or specificity) of information provided (Ashby, 2005; Barca, 2005; Boix Mansilla, 2005; Gago, 2005; VanSledright & Afflerbach, 2005; VanSledright & Frankes, 2000; VanSledright & Kelly, 1998).

Students can learn to be more critical of historical sources, however. When instruction focuses on the factors that influence the creation of sources, students become better able to compare and critically evaluate such sources, as well as to consider the possible meanings that their authors were attempting to convey (Ashby, 2004; Barton, 1997b, 2001a; Booth, 1980; Britt & Aglinskas, 2002; Foster & Yeager, 1999; Gabella, 1994b; Hoodless, 2004; Kohlmeier, 2005b; P. Lee, Ashby, et al., 1996; VanSledright, 2002b, 2002c). In fact, simply asking students how authors' perspectives may have influenced what they wrote, or asking them to support a position on a controversial topic, leads to critical responses and comparison of sources, even in the absence of sustained classroom instruction (Britt, Rouet, Georgi, & Perfetti, 1994; Perfetti et al., 1995; Perfetti, Britt, Rouet, Georgi, & Mason, 1994; Rouet, Britt, Mason, & Perfetti, 1996; VanSledright & Kelly, 1998). Students may be less critical, however, of sources that conform to their aesthetic expectations or that match their own prior social and political commitments (Austin, Rae, & Hodgkinson, 1987; Gabella, 1994a, 1994b; Levstik, 1989; Seixas, 1993b; VanSledright, 2002b).

Yet although students can become skillful at recognizing that historical sources do not provide direct and unimpeachable information about the past, and that gaps in the historical record are inevitable, they are less adept at understanding how those partial and incomplete sources can be used to reach conclusions about history (Ferretti et al., 2001; Kohlmeier, 2005a; VanSledright & Kelly, 1998). Some students think of the process as similar to assembling a jigsaw puzzle—they imagine that small bits of information are gleaned from each source until a reasonably complete account is created (Barton, 2001a; Foster & Yeager, 1999; Voss, Wiley, & Kennet, 1998). Others, once they recognize that each source is partial in its own way, may give all sources equal weight or ignore them completely; some may even despair of the possibility of historical knowledge altogether (Barton, 1997b; P. Lee, 2001; Medina, Pollard, Schneider, &

Leonhardt, 2000; Shemilt, 1987; VanSledright, 2002a, 2002c). Some older students, though, particularly those who have had sustained classroom experience drawing conclusions from historical sources, develop a more sophisticated understanding of how accounts are developed from the purposeful selection and interpretation of fragmentary and uncertain sources, and how the use of evidence may differ from one account to another (Ashby, 2004; Kohlmeier, 2005a; P. Lee, Dickinson, & Ashby, 2001; Rouet, Favart, Britt, & Perfetti, 1997).

A number of studies have focused specifically on the effect of asking students to work with multiple sources of historical information. University undergraduates who are asked to write arguments based on multiple documents produce more analytic essays, with more causal and connective statements and greater transformation of the material, than those who work from a textbook chapter or who are asked to write a narrative or a "report" (Greene, 1993, 1994; Voss & Wiley, 1997; Wiley & Voss, 1996, 1999). At the secondary level, some research has found that students who write essays from a variety of primary and secondary sources synthesize the information into their own coherent explanations, and that they cite evidence from sources to support their views (Yeager, Foster, Maley, Anderson, & Morris, 1998). Other research, however, suggests that secondary students make little use of such sources in constructing arguments, although they may improve with practice (Stahl et al., 1996; Young & Leinhardt, 1998).

When students use multiple sources to investigate historical questions in more open-ended classroom contexts, they demonstrate a high level of engagement and report enjoying historical study (Barton, 1994; Brush & Saye, 2000; Levstik, 1993), and they may also become more critical, analytic readers who display more contextualized knowledge and higher-order reasoning (Saye & Brush, 1999; VanSledright, 2002c). However, students encounter a number of obstacles in carrying out such projects. Frequently, they are overwhelmed and frustrated by the amount of print they face, and they have no clear sense of how to read and evaluate information from differing sources; they may fail even to consult multiple sources and simply rely instead on those that are most accessible or that appear most comprehensive. Students also have difficulty synthesizing multiple sources into coherent conclusions or accounts; they may treat the entire process as a simple search for right answers, or they may invent conclusions with little or no grounding in evidence. Computer technology designed to help students locate, compare, and evaluate historical sources does little, in itself, to overcome these problems, either because students do not use the technology effectively or because the technology (particularly in the form of Internet sites) is ill-suited for instructional purposes. With or without electronic technology, improving students' participation in inquiry projects depends on modeling and assistance by teachers (Barton, 1994, 1997b; Brush & Saye, 2000, 2001; J. K. Lee & Guy, 2003; Levstik & Smith, 1996; Lipscomb, 2002; Milson, 2002; Saye & Brush, 1999, 2002; van Drie & van Boxtel, 2004; VanSledright, 2002c; VanSledright & Frankes, 2000; VanSledright & Kelly, 1998).

Explaining the actions of people in the past

Although they generally recognize, to a greater or lesser degree, that people thought, acted, and lived differently in the past than they do today, students have a limited understanding of the reasons for those differences. Sometimes, students assume that in the past people were not as intelligent or sensible as people are today. Other times, students may recognize that in the past people were similar in intelligence to people today, but they explain their actions by projecting themselves into the situation: They recognize that circumstances were different than they are now, and so they try to imagine how they themselves would respond in that setting. However, they do not clearly understand how perspectives themselves differed—how the values, attitudes, and beliefs of people in other times and places were different than their own (Ashby & Lee, 1987; Barton, 1994; Dickinson & Lee, 1984; Downey, 1996; Knight, 1989; Kohlmeier, 2006; P. Lee & Ashby, 2001; P. Lee, Dickinson, & Ashby, 1997; Shemilt, 1984).

Yet some students, particularly in the upper elementary grades and beyond, do understand that values, attitudes, and beliefs have changed over time, and they explain the lives and actions of people in the past by reference to historic perspectives rather than their own; sustained classroom attention to these issues seems to improve students' tendency to take such perspectives into account (Ashby & Lee, 1987; Barton, 1994; Dickinson & Lee, 1984; Knight, 1989, 1990; Kohlmeier, 2006; Kölbl & Straub, 2001; P. Lee & Ashby, 2001; P. Lee et al., 1997; Shemilt, 1984). However, students may initially resist entertaining historical perspectives when they conflict with their own ethical or political positions, and they can be highly judgmental of historical actions (or representations) that violate current sensibilities (Bardige, 1988; Barton, 1994; Seixas, 1994a; Seixas & Clark, 2004; VanSledright, 2002c; von Borries, 1994, 1997b).

Even when students understand that historical perspectives differed from modern ones, they rarely situate those differences within wider societal contexts. That is, although students may recognize that people in the past had different perspectives than people today, most do not see how their ideas were connected to societal institutions, nor do they recognize the role of historic beliefs and practices within larger social systems (Knight, 1989; P. Lee & Ashby, 2001; Shemilt, 1984). In fact, elementary and middle school students generally have little understanding of societal forces and institutions such as religion, government, and the economy, or of the role they play in historical change and continuity. In the primary grades, for example, students can describe changes in technology over time, but they focus almost entirely on how those changes affected individuals, rather than society at large (Brophy & Alleman, 2005; Brophy, Alleman, & O'Mahoney, 2003). Similarly, primary students may describe how precontact Native Americans lived, but they are less likely to explain the reasons for their cultural practices, and they demonstrate little understanding of the effect of the environment on Native American society (Brophy & Alleman, 2000; Brophy & VanSledright, 1997). And when older students study topics that emphasize economic and political issues, they often come away with minimal comprehension of the structural and causal relationships involved in historical events and trends. For example, they may fail to understand the political and economic relationship between England and its North American colonies or the political and economic motivations for the American Revolution (Barton, 1997a; Beck & McKeown, 1994; Beck, McKeown, & Sinatra, 1991; Brophy & VanSledright, 1997; McKeown & Beck, 1990; VanSledright, 1995a).

Students do not simply lack comprehension of historical topics that involve societal forces and institutions, however. Rather, they interpret (or misinterpret) those topics in terms of individual motivations and intentions, and they explain political, economic, and demographic processes in terms of individual psychology (Barton, 1997a; Halldén, 1986, 1993; P. Lee & Ashby, 2001; P. Lee et al., 1997; Riviére, Núñez, & Fontela, 1998; Rose, 2000). In some cases, they attribute social and cultural patterns to individual attitudes. They may believe, for example, that Native American lifestyles were due to personal preferences (Brophy & VanSledright, 1997) or that racial or gender inequality resulted from individual prejudice (rather than cultural norms, power differences, or legal and political structure), and they may believe that changes in such patterns resulted primarily from changed attitudes (Barton, 1997a; Wills, 1996). Other times, students interpret large-scale historical events as though they were the result of individual motivations or actions, and they may believe the course of history depends largely on the intentions of individuals (Barton, 1996, 1997a; Brophy & VanSledright, 1997; Carretero, Jacott, Limón, López-Manjón, & León, 1994; P. Lee & Ashby, 2001).

Students often fail to account for societal forces and institutions even when teachers or texts specifically emphasize such factors (Barton, 1997a; Beck et al., 1991; Britt et al., 1994; Halldén, 1986; Wills, 2005). Some studies, however, suggest that students better understand societal factors when instruction directly addresses these topics (Barton, 2001b; Brophy, 1999; Brophy & VanSledright, 1997; Levstik & Groth, 2002; McKeown, Beck, Sinatra, & Loxterman, 1992; Shemilt, 1980). The portion of students who emphasize personal factors in explaining historical events also decreases with age, and older adolescents and adults clearly take societal factors into account, sometimes in combination with psychological causes or the impact of individuals (Bermúdez & Jaramillo, 2001; Carretero, López-Manjón, & Jacott, 1997; Jacott, López-Manjón, & Carretero, 1998; P. Lee et al., 1997; Mosborg, 2002; Torney-Purta, 1994; von Borries & Baeck, 1997; Voss, Carretero, Kennet, & Silfies, 1994; Voss et al., 1998).

Just as educators often assume that students know little about the past or historical time, they may also dismiss students' ability to evaluate sources or explain historical actions. Again, the research reviewed here suggests that such reservations are misplaced. Although few students have considered the nature of historical sources before studying the topic at school, they can make use of common-sense notions of evidence and reliability as they become more familiar with the range of historical sources and their limitations. Students can also draw on their familiarity with present-day variations in point of view in order to makes sense of the differing perspectives of people in the past. Developing a basic facility with these elements of history seems to be a relatively straightforward undertaking. Two aspects of evidence and explanation, though, are more problematic: Students have difficulty understanding how historical accounts are constructed from fragmentary and unreliable sources, and they do not fully consider societal forces and institutions in explaining the actions of people in the past. Research suggests, however, that even these aspects of history can be effectively addressed through focused curricular content and sustained instructional attention.

SOCIAL CONTEXTS OF STUDENTS' UNDERSTANDING

Students' familiarity with history derives from a number of sources, including, but not limited to, the school curriculum. In both North America and Europe, children and adolescents report learning about the past from parents, siblings, and other relatives; from print and electronic media such as television, movies, trade books, and the Internet; from visits to museums and historic sites; and from exposure to historical artifacts within and outside the home. They often say they enjoy learning about history from these sources, and they describe themselves as seeking out historical information and having specific historical interests (Barton, 2001c; Barton & McCully, 2005; Brophy & VanSledright, 1997; Dimitriadis, 2000; Downey, 1996; Epstein, 1998; Grant, 2001; Kölbl & Straub, 2001; Levstik & Barton, 1996; Seixas, 1993a; Wineburg, 2000; Yeager & Terzian, 2007).

Students are especially interested in the lives of ordinary people, and, when studying social and political events, they are drawn to the impact of those events on individuals (Barton, 1994; Brophy & VanSledright, 1997; Halldén, 1993; Kohlmeier, 2005b; Levstik, 1986, 1989; Levstik & Groth, 2002; Levstik & Pappas, 1987; Schweber, 2003b). Students also are interested in topics that involve emotion, morality, and individual judgment, particularly under extreme circumstances, and they often like to imagine what their own responses would be if they were involved in the historical events that they study (Gabella, 1994a; Levstik, 1986, 1989; Saye & Brush, 1999; Schweber, 2003b, 2004; Wills, 1996, 2005). Secondary students may also be especially interested in modern history (Barton & McCully, 2005; Kindervater & von Borries, 1997; Lévesque,

2003) and in topics that force them to confront the "foreignness" of historic practices, such as slavery or witch hunts (Kölbl & Straub, 2001).

In school, student may not enjoy reading history textbooks (Epstein, 1994; Kindervater & von Borries, 1997), but they have more positive attitudes when teachers use them as sources of discussable ideas rather than stores of information (Sosniak & Perlman, 1990). Students also find tradebook-like texts more interesting, informative, and entertaining than traditional texts (Afflerbach & VanSledright, 2001; VanSledright & Kelly, 1998), and they are more likely to enjoy and engage with texts that have a visible author, that have a greater sense of "voice," and that focus on individuals and their reactions to events (Beck, McKeown, & Worthy, 1995; Paxton, 1997). In addition to leading to greater interest on the part of students, the use of alternatives to traditional textbooks may also increase comprehension: Students who read texts that have been rewritten to explain concepts and clarify causal connections are better able to understand and recall the content than those who read traditional textbook passages (Beck et al., 1991; McKeown et al., 1992; Voss & Silfies, 1996). Use of materials other than (or in addition to) textbooks also is associated with higher scores on achievement tests in U.S. history (Smith & Niemi, 2001).

When asked why history is important, or why it is a subject at school, many younger students do not give a clear answer, or they simply restate the question by noting that it is important to know about the past. From the upper elementary grades through secondary school, however, most students point to one or more of the following reasons for learning history: (1) History is intrinsically interesting, and many people pursue it as a hobby (such as genealogists); (2) History has utilitarian value: It could lead to a job as a teacher or museum worker, and it would be valuable for contestants on quiz shows; (3) History provides lessons for the present, particularly by identifying courses of action that should be avoided; (4) History explains how the modern world came to be (Barton, 2001c; Brophy & VanSledright, 1997; Fink, 2004; Haeberli, 2004; Huggins, 1996; Kindervater & von Borries, 1997; VanSledright, 1995b, 1997). The third and fourth of these rationales also are apparent when students make judgments about the significance of historical events, because they often explain their reasoning by noting how events provide lessons for the present or how they illustrate the origins of modern society (Barton & Levstik, 1998; Cercadillo, 2001; Seixas, 1994b, 1997; Yeager et al., 2002). In addition, many students in the United States link history to their own identities: They explain that history helps them understand not only the country's development but its origins and character, and their consistent use of first-person pronouns in discussing U.S. history attests to their identification with the nation (Barton, 2001c; Barton & Levstik, 1998; VanSledright, 1997; Yeager & Terzian, 2007).

Students' ideas about history's role in creating a sense of identity, however, vary across social and curricular contexts. African American students, for example, sometimes judge historical significance on the basis of ethnic rather than national identity (Epstein, 1998, 2000), and students in Ghana see the importance of history in relation to both ethnic and national (as well as Pan-African and international) identities (Levstik & Groth, 2005). In some countries, meanwhile, identity plays a relatively small role in the school curriculum, and students there are less likely than those in the United States to emphasize identity as a reason for studying the subject or as a criterion for judging historical significance (Cercadillo, 2001; Fink, 2004; Goalen, 1997; Seixas, 1994b). Those students may obliquely suggest the importance of identity by singling out events that affected their own country or region as interesting or important (Kindervater & von Borries, 1997; Kölbl & Straub, 2001; Lévesque, 2005; Yeager et al., 2002), or they may point to other reasons altogether for studying history—such as the importance of learning about people different than themselves (Barton, 2001c; Levstik, 2001) or remembering those who sacrificed their lives in the past (Barton, 2005). And although gender differences in students' ideas about the purpose of history have not been evident in U.S. research (Barton & Levstik, 1998), female students in other countries attribute less importance (or less personal interest and identification) to some aspects of political history than do male students, and greater importance to issues of social justice or the history of everyday life (Barton, 2005; Barton & McCully, 2005; Kindervater & von Borries, 1997; Lévesque, 2005; von Borries, Kindervater, & Körber, 1997).

The importance of students' backgrounds is particularly apparent in their appropriation of historical narratives. In Europe, for example, students in different countries emphasize varied people, events, and eras, not only when they discuss their own national histories, but also when they consider the shared topic of European history (von Borries, 1995). Even within a single nation, students' backgrounds may influence their narrative interpretations. African American students, for example, may be less likely than European Americans to point to the importance of nation-building in U.S. history and more likely to focus on the African American experience and the active denial of rights by Whites and the government (Epstein, 1998). Similarly, for some U.S. students, religiously-grounded narratives may be more important than stories of freedom and progress. Some students from Christian backgrounds, for example, see U.S. history in terms of decline rather than progress (Mosborg, 2002). Others interpret the Holocaust through narratives of religious persecution, hope and redemption, and God's abandonment of the Jewish people (Schweber, 2003a; Spector, 2005).

Students do not readily modify their prior narrative understanding when they encounter new or conflicting information (Limón & Carretero, 1999; Rosa, Blanco, & Huertas, 1998; VanSledright, 2002c). In the United States, students sometimes find it difficult to reconcile their knowledge of topics such as the Great Depression, the Vietnam War, and continuing instances of racism and sexism with the overarching historical narratives they have learned in school, and so they tend to reinterpret such events to more closely match broad themes of progress (Barton & Levstik, 1998). In other cases, students' adherence to historical narratives learned outside of school leads them to discount or transform the content of the curriculum. Quebec students' narratives, for example, are highly consistent with the general historical perspectives of adults in the province, but they do not reflect either the school curriculum or current historical scholarship (Létourneau & Moisan, 2004). In Northern Ireland, on the other hand, many students draw selectively from the curriculum in order to bolster sectarian perspectives that are consistent with the narratives they encounter outside of school (Barton & McCully, 2005). And in both Israel and the United States, some students use religiously-grounded narratives to ignore, reinterpret, or distort historical information so that it does not conflict with their prior ideas (Mosborg, 2002; Porat, 2004; Spector, 2005).

Students often are aware of disparities between the school curriculum and the history they have learned elsewhere, and members of some minority groups in the United States are particularly likely to be critical of the official curriculum and to dismiss its relevance. African American students, for example, may consider history textbooks less credible than family members, and they may fault schools for devoting too little attention to the African American experience and for overemphasizing Martin Luther King, Jr. and the theme of nonviolence (Dimitriadis, 2000; Epstein, 1998). Similarly, Mexican American students sometimes describe school history as irrelevant to their own ethnic background (Almarza, 2001). Minority students may even resent inclusion of the experiences of other marginalized groups, such as victims of the Holocaust, because they perceive it as competing with their own history (Dimitriadis, 2000; Spector, 2005).

Even when school history differs from other sources of learning, though, students do not always reject the school curriculum, nor can their responses always be easily categorized according to broad ethnic or religious groupings. In the United States, for example, students from a variety of ethnic backgrounds may accept the story of national freedom and progress, in whole or in part, and those of Cuban American heritage may be less critical of the curriculum than Mexican American students (Barton & Levstik, 1998; Yeager & Terzian, 2007). In England, students from similar religious backgrounds demonstrate a variety of ideas about history (Pomson & Hoz, 1998), and in Northern Ireland, students' ideas vary not only by religion, but by gender, school type, and geographic location (Barton & McCully, 2005). Moreover, students in Northern Ireland do not uncritically accept either school or community history but strive to reconcile the two (Barton & McCully, 2006). Finally, students' ideas about school history depend, in part, on the nature of their instruction: In the United States, when teachers focus on the contemporary relevance of history, students also note the importance of history for understanding the present. Conversely, when teachers emphasize coverage of content knowledge, students point to the need to learn a body of factual information (Evans, 1990; Grant, 2001; VanSledright, 1995b).

Research on the social context of historical learning, then, points to the importance of students' experiences outside school in developing their historical knowledge, interests, and interpretations, but such research also suggests that school, community, and personal factors interact in complicated ways to produce a variety of ideas about the nature and purpose of the subject. Students consistently describe themselves as historically interested and aware, and their interests often focus on morally charged issues and the experiences of individuals. Older students have also developed ideas about the importance of history in society, and in many cases these are tied to national, ethnic, or religious identities. For some students, school history provides a sense of identity that allows them to interpret a wide range of historical information in light of overarching themes and narratives. Others, particularly those from minority backgrounds, may consider school history irrelevant to their own identities, or they may reinterpret the content of the curriculum so that it more closely matches the narratives they have learned in their families or communities. Still others seek to integrate perspectives that they have learned in school and out, or they focus on aspects of history that have little connection to group identity. Given the central role of purpose in human learning, educators who hope to develop students' understanding of history should consider more carefully how their own goals intersect with those of their students.

DIRECTIONS FOR FUTURE RESEARCH

The greatest need in the area of research on students' ideas about history is for long-term classroom studies of how students' ideas change as a result of instruction. The research reviewed here has identified common patterns in students' understanding, and some of these stand in the way of a more complete understanding of history: Students usually explain historical events in terms of individual factors rather than societal ones, are not spontaneously critical of historical sources, do not differentiate historical perspectives from their own, have a limited understanding of diversity, and so on. Research has also established that instruction can effectively address each of these problems: Even elementary students can understand societal forces and institutions, evaluate and compare sources, recognize differences in the perspectives of people in the past, and increase their knowledge of diverse historical experiences. This body of research provides educators with an understanding of potential disparities between students' ideas and the content of the curriculum, and it reassures them that these can be addressed through classroom instruction. What it has not yet been done is provide much insight into exactly how that transformation can be accomplished.

Nearly all studies that track changes in students' ideas fall into one of two categories. The first includes quasi-experimental and case study research that compares students' ideas before and after some type of intervention—either laboratory exercises or regular classroom instruction. The second category involves cross-sectional studies that compare the ideas of students at different ages (often referred to in Britain as studies of "progression"). Both types of research focus on differences in students' ideas at two or more static points; as a result, neither illustrates the process of change itself. Although studies of progression sometimes involve careful description of students at different "levels" of understanding, they do not show how any individual student moves from one level to the next. Such studies provide educators with a better understanding of where students may go, but they offer limited information on the nature of the journey.

In addition, most case study and cross-sectional research provides only general insight into the instructional practices that lead to changes in students' ideas. During a unit built around historical fiction, for example, students may encounter a variety of literary works and engage in many different response activities—but which of those actually contributes to enhanced understanding? Similarly, over the course of their educational careers, students in Britain work with historical evidence and explanation hundreds of times, and research shows that most have a better understanding at the end of their experiences than at the beginning—but which specific methods, materials, or tasks were responsible for those changes? Quasi-experimental studies are better able to control for the effect of various tasks and materials, but in doing so they lose the ecological validity that would make them more directly useful to educators.

To increase the chance that future research will have a meaningful impact on history education, it must involve intensive, long-term research in classrooms. In order for researchers to track changes in students' ideas, they must observe and interact with students on a daily basis—listening to them as they discuss ideas in small groups or whole class discussions, watching them complete response activities and other assignments, and talking with them about their ideas. Similarly, if researchers hope to relate instructional practices to changes in students' ideas, they need to observe those practices on a regular and ongoing basis. Only then can they reach conclusions about the effect, not just of a general approach (such as inquiry or the use of writing), but of more specific components of those teaching methods. Although some classroom studies do involve this kind of careful observation, most do so on a short-term basis—sometimes for a few weeks, sometimes for only a few hours. Given the complexity of historical learning, and given that many changes in students' ideas seem to take place only after long-term and sustained instruction, brief studies are unlikely to provide the evidence necessary to reach meaningful conclusions about the effect of instructional practices.

The most useful findings also are likely to come from studies that involve collaboration between teachers and researchers in carefully planned "design experiments" (Cobb, Confrey, diSessa, Lehrer, & Schauble, 2003; VanSledright, 2002c). Such collaboration is crucial because when researchers work outside classroom contexts, they may develop interventions that are so rigorously designed or so alien to teachers' purposes that they have little chance of being implemented. Without the involvement of researchers, on the other hand, teachers are likely to engage in an eclectic variety of practices, and this makes it difficult to pin down the effect of any particular task. By working together, though, teachers and researchers can design realistic instructional plans based on systematic attention to theoretically-grounded principles. Long-term classroom studies in such settings would significantly enhance the research base for history education.

Another important area for future research involves investigating the historical learning of students from diverse backgrounds—ethnic, religious, economic, and geographic—as well as gender differences, in their ideas about history. Many researchers have used quota sampling to ensure that their data do not derive from participants of only one gender or a particular social background, but they have typically used such data to develop aggregate portraits of students' learning. When comparisons are made among such groups, the impact of social background often becomes apparent. Students' attachment to differing historical narratives affects their encounters with the stories they learn at school, for example, and their religious and political beliefs may influence their evaluation of evidence and their willingness to consider some historical perspectives. Yet there is no single way in which students negotiate the competing demands of differing historical discourses, and therefore much more research is needed to illustrate the specific ways in which students of given backgrounds learn history both in and out of school. The impact of gender, meanwhile, is still largely unknown: Although reported data often show differences in males' and females' historical interests or interpretations, few researchers have explored these differences in depth or attempted to explain them theoretically.

The field also would benefit from greater attention to the variety of contexts in which students encounter the past. Studies have consistently shown that students' experiences outside school influence their understanding of history, but this research has almost always been conducted within school settings, and researchers' techniques for eliciting students' ideas tend to resemble school tasks: Students are typically presented with materials and asked to engage in exercises designed by adult authorities. As a result, very little is known about how children and adolescents engage with the past in contexts that are less formal or scholastic—listening to relatives' stories, watching television documentaries, discussing politics with peers, viewing a museum display, or attending a commemorative event. Exploring students' learning in these contexts could best be accomplished by in-depth qualitative research, perhaps conducted as part of extensive ethnographic studies, rather than through investigations that focus solely on history.

Finally, future studies of students' ideas about history would benefit from greater conceptual clarity in the design and reporting of research (VanSledright, Kelly, & Meuwissen, 2005), particularly with regard to the theoretical frameworks that guide researchers' questions, methods, and interpretation of findings. There is no single perspective on the meaning of evidence, narrative, significance, explanation, or most other elements of historical learning (or even on what elements constitute such learning), and researchers sometimes indiscriminately mix components of differing—even contradictory—frameworks. Unless researchers are clear about which theoretically-grounded definitions they attach to such concepts, their empirical work is unlikely to reach its full potential. This kind of conceptual clarity necessarily requires familiarity with previous scholarship. New studies advance the field only when researchers situate their questions, methods, and findings within the context of work that has already been done. Although published studies these days are more likely to cite a common body of scholarship than in the past, citations do not always cross disciplinary or geographic boundaries easily, and researchers sometimes fail to recognize that they are investigating questions that have been addressed by colleagues in other countries or outside their own disciplinary specialties.

SUMMARY

Educators should be encouraged by the consistency with which research shows that young people actively participate in the process of constructing meaning from their encounters with history. They should also be pleased to know that formal instruction can have an impact on students' developing ideas. On the other hand, research demonstrates that some aspects of the subject can be problematic: Some students may have trouble reconciling school history with the narratives they have learned outside school, for example, and they do not easily develop complete understandings of the use of evidence or of the impact of societal factors on the actions and perspectives of people in the past. The most important research in the future, therefore, would involve identifying the diversity of ideas that students from different backgrounds bring to the classroom and exploring the effect of specific instructional practices on their understanding. Such work would not only contribute to academic scholarship on students' ideas about history, but might also lead to practical classroom applications.

REFERENCES

Afflerbach, P., & VanSledright, B. A. (2001). Hath! Doth! What? Middle graders reading innovative history text. *Journal of Adolescent & Adult Literacy, 44*, 696–707.

Almarza, D. J. (2001). Contexts shaping minority language students' perceptions of American history. *Journal of Social Studies Research, 25*, 4–22.

Ashby, R. (2004). Developing a concept of historical evidence: Students' ideas about testing singular factual claims. *International Journal of Historical Learning, Teaching and Research, 4*(2), Retrieved August 15, 2005, from http://www.ex.ac.uk/historyresource/journal2008/Ashby.doc.

Ashby, R., & Lee, P. (1987). Children's concepts of empathy and understanding in history. In C. Portal (Ed.), *The history curriculum for teachers* (pp. 62–88). London: Heinemann.

Austin, R., Rae, G., & Hodgkinson, K. (1987). Children's evaluation of evidence on neutral and sensitive topics. *Teaching History, 49*, 8–10.

Barca, I. (2005). "Till new facts are discovered": Students' ideas about objectivity in history. In R. Ashby, P. Gordon & P. Lee (Eds.), *International review of history education, Vol. 4: Understanding history: Recent research in history education* (pp. 68–82). New York: RoutledgeFalmer.

Bardige, B. (1988). Things so finely human: Moral sensibilities at risk in adolescence. In C. Gilligan, J. V. Ward, & J. M. Taylor (Eds.), *Mapping the moral domain* (pp. 87–110). Cambridge: Harvard University Press.

Barton, K. C. (1994). *Historical understanding among elementary children*. Unpublished doctoral dissertation, University of Kentucky, Lexington.

Barton, K. C. (1996). Narrative simplifications in elementary children's historical understanding. In J. Brophy (Ed.), *Advances in research on teaching: Vol. 6. Teaching and learning history* (pp. 51–83). Greenwich, CT: JAI Press.

Barton, K. C. (1997a). "Bossed around by the Queen": Elementary students' understanding of individuals and institutions in history. *Journal of Curriculum and Supervision, 12*, 290–314.

Barton, K. C. (1997b). "I just kinda know": Elementary students' ideas about historical evidence. *Theory and Research in Social Education, 25*, 407–430.

Barton, K. C. (2001a). Primary children's understanding of the role of historical evidence: Comparisons between the United States and Northern Ireland. *International Journal of Historical Learning, Teaching and Research, 1*(2), 21–30. Retrieved August 15, 2005, from http://www.ex.ac.uk/historyresource/journal2002/BARTON.doc.

Barton, K. C. (2001b). A sociocultural perspective on children's understanding of historical change: Comparative findings from Northern Ireland and the United States. *American Educational Research Journal, 38*, 881–913.

Barton, K. C. (2001c). "You'd be wanting to know about the past": Social contexts of children's historical understanding in Northern Ireland and the United States. *Comparative Education, 37*, 89–106.

Barton, K. C. (2002). "Oh, that's a tricky piece!": Children, mediated action, and the tools of historical time. *Elementary School Journal, 103*, 161–185.

Barton, K. C. (2005). "Best not to forget them": Adolescents' judgments of historical significance in Northern Ireland. *Theory and Research in Social Education, 33*, 9–44.

Barton, K. C., & Levstik, L. S. (1996). "Back when God was around and everything": The development of children's understanding of historical time. *American Educational Research Journal, 33*, 419–454.

Barton, K. C., & Levstik, L. S. (1998). "It wasn't a good part of history": Ambiguity and identity in middle grade students' judgments of historical significance. *Teachers College Record, 99*, 478–513.

Barton, K. C., & McCully, A. W. (2005). History, identity, and the school curriculum in Northern Ireland: An empirical study of secondary students' ideas and perspectives. *Journal of Curriculum Studies, 37,* 85–116.

Barton, K. C., & McCully, A. W. (2006, March). Secondary students' perspectives on school and community history in Northern Ireland. Paper presented to the European Social Science History Conference, Amsterdam.

Beck, I. L., & McKeown, M. G. (1994). Outcomes of history instruction: Paste–up accounts. In J. F. Voss & M. Carretero (Eds.), *Cognitive and instructional processes in history and the social sciences* (pp. 237–256). Hillsdale, NJ: Erlbaum.

Beck, I. L., McKeown, M. G., & Sinatra, G. M. (1991). Revising social studies text from a text–processing perspective: Evidence of improved comprehensibility. *Reading Research Quarterly, 26,* 251–276.

Beck, I. L., McKeown, M. G., & Worthy, J. (1995). Giving a text voice can improve students' understanding. *Reading Research Quarterly, 30,* 220–238.

Bermúdez, A., & Jaramillo, R. (2001). Development of historical explanation in children, adolescents and adults. In A. Dickinson, P. Gordon, & P. Lee (Eds.), *International review of history education, Vol. 3: Raising standards in history education* (pp. 146–167). Portland, OR: Woburn Press.

Boix Mansilla, V. (2005). Between reproducing and organizing the past: Students beliefs about the standards and acceptability of historical knowledge. In R. Ashby, P. Gordon & P. Lee (Eds.), *International review of history education, Vol. 4: Understanding history: Recent research in history education* (pp. 98–115). New York: RoutledgeFalmer.

Booth, M. (1980). A modern world history course and the thinking of adolescent pupils. *Educational Review, 3,* 245–257.

Britt, M. A., & Aglinskas, C. (2002). Improving students' ability to identify and use source information. *Cognition and Instruction, 20,* 485–522.

Britt, M. A., Rouet, J.–F., Georgi, M. C., & Perfetti, C. A. (1994). Learning from history texts: From causal analysis to argument models. In G. Leinhardt, I. L. Beck, & C. Stainton (Eds.), *Teaching and learning in history* (pp. 47–84). Hillsdale, NJ: Erlbaum.

Brophy, J. (1999). Elementary students learn about Native Americans: The development of knowledge and empathy. *Social Education, 63,* 38–45.

Brophy, J., & Alleman, J. (2000). Primary grade students' knowledge and thinking about Native American and pioneer homes. *Theory and Research in Social Education, 28,* 96–120.

Brophy, J., & Alleman, J. (2005). Primary grade students' knowledge and thinking about transportation. *Theory and Research in Social Education, 33,* 219–243.

Brophy, J., Alleman, J., & O'Mahony, C. (2003). Primary–grade students' knowledge and thinking about food production and the origins of common foods. *Theory and Research in Social Education, 31,* 10–50.

Brophy, J., & VanSledright, B. A. (1997). *Teaching and learning history in elementary schools.* New York: Teachers College Press.

Brush, T. A., & Saye, J. W. (2000). Implementation and evaluation of a student–centered learning unit: A case study. *Educational Technology Research and Development, 48*(3), 79–100.

Brush, T. A., & Saye, J. W. (2001). The use of embedded scaffolds with hypermedia–supported student–centered learning. *Journal of Educational Multimedia and Hypermedia, 10,* 333–356.

Carretero, M., Asensio, M., & Pozo, J. I. (1991). Cognitive development, historical time representation and causal explanations in adolescence. In M. Carretero, M. Pope, R. J. Simons, & J. I. Pozo (Eds.), *Learning and instruction, Vol. 3: European research in an international context* (pp. 27–48). Oxford: Pergamon Press.

Carretero, M., Jacott, L., Limón, M., López–Manjón, A., & León, J. A. (1994). Historical knowledge: Cognitive and instructional implications. In J. F. Voss & M. Carretero (Eds.), *Cognitive and instructional process in history and the social sciences* (pp. 357–376). Hillsdale, NJ: Erlbaum.

Carretero, M., López–Manjón, A., & Jacott, L. (1997). Explaining historical events. *International Journal of Educational Research, 27,* 245–253.

Cercadillo, L. (2001). Significance in history: Students' ideas in England and Spain. In A. Dickson, P. Gordon, & P. Lee (Eds.), *International review of history education: Vol. 3. Raising standards in history education* (pp. 116–145). Portland, OR: Woburn Press.

Cobb, P., Confrey, J., diSessa, A., Lehrer, R., & Schauble, L. (2003). Design experiments in educational research. *Educational Researcher, 32*(1), 9–13.

Cooper, H. (1992). *The teaching of history.* London: David Fulton.

Dickinson, A. K., & Lee, P. J. (1984). Making sense of history. In A. K. Dickinson, P. J. Lee, & P. J. Rogers (Eds.), *Learning history* (pp. 117–153). London: Heinemann.

Dimitriadis, G. (2000). "Making history go" at a local community center: Popular media and the construction of historical knowledge among African American youth. *Theory and Research in Social Education, 28,* 40–64.

Downey, M. T. (1996). *Writing to learn history in the intermediate grades. Final report.* Berkeley, CA: National Center for the Study of Writing and Literacy, School of Education, University of California. ERIC Document Reproduction Service No. ED 397 422.

Epstein, T. L. (1994). *American Revised* revisited: Adolescents' attitudes towards a United States history textbook. *Social Education, 58,* 41–44.

Epstein, T. L. (1998). Deconstructing differences in African–American and European–American adolescents' perspectives on U.S. History. *Curriculum inquiry, 28,* 397–423.

Epstein, T. L. (2000). Adolescents' perspectives on racial diversity in U.S. history: Case studies from an urban classroom. *American Educational Research Journal, 37,* 185–214.

Evans, R. W. (1990). Teacher conceptions of history revisited: Ideology, curriculum, and student belief. *Theory and Research in Social Education, 18,* 101–138.

Fasulo, A., Girardet, H., & Pontecorvo, C. (1998). Seeing the past: Learning history through group discussion of iconographic sources. In J. F. Voss & M. Carretero (Eds.), *International review of history education, Vol. 2: Learning and reasoning in history* (pp. 132–153). Portland, OR: Woburn Press.

Ferretti, R. P., MacArthur, C. D., & Okolo, C. M. (2001). Teaching for historical understanding in inclusive classrooms. *Learning Disability Quarterly, 24,* 59–71.

Fink, N. (2004). Pupils' conceptions of history and history teaching. *International Journal of Historical Learning, Teaching and Research, 4*(2), Retrieved August 15, 2005, from http://www.ex.ac.uk/historyresource/journal2008/Fink.doc.

Foster, S. J., Hoge, J. D., & Rosch, R. H. (1999). Thinking aloud about history: Children's and adolescent's responses to historical photographs. *Theory and Research in Social Education, 27,* 179–214.

Foster, S. J., & Yeager, E. A. (1999). "You've got to put together the pieces": English 12–year-olds encounter and learn from historical evidence. *Journal of Curriculum and Supervision, 14,* 286–317.

Fournier, J. E., & Wineburg, S. S. (1997). Picturing the past: Gender differences in the depiction of historical figures. *American Journal of Education, 105,* 160–185.

Gabella, M. S. (1994a). The art(s) of historical sense. *Journal of Curriculum Studies, 27,* 139–163.

Gabella, M. S. (1994b). Beyond the looking glass: Bringing students into the conversation of historical inquiry. *Theory and Research in Social Education, 22,* 340–363.

Gago, M. (2005). Children's understanding of historical narrative in Portugal. In R. Ashby, P. Gordon, & P. Lee (Eds.), *International review of history education, Vol. 4: Understanding history: Recent research in history education* (pp. 83–97). New York: RoutledgeFalmer.

Goalen, P. (1997). Cross current: History and national identity in the classroom. *History Today, 47*(6), 6–8.

Grant, S. G. (2001). It's just the facts, or is it? The relationship between teachers' practices and students' understandings of history. *Theory and Research in Social Education, 29,* 65–108.

Greene, S. (1993). The role of task in the development of academic thinking through reading and writing in a college history course. *Research in the Teaching of English, 27,* 46–75.

Greene, S. (1994). Students as authors in the study of history. In G. Leinhardt, I. L. Beck, & C. Stainton (Eds.), *Teaching and learning in history* (pp. 137–170). Hillsdale, NJ: Erlbaum.

Haeberli, P. (2004). Relating to history: An empirical typology. *International Journal of Historical Learning, Teaching and Research, 5*(1), Retrieved March 15, 2006, from http://www.centres.ex.ac.uk/historyresource/journal2009/papers/haeberlirev.doc.

Halldén, O. (1986). Learning history. *Oxford Review of Education, 12,* 53–66.

Halldén, O. (1993). Learners' conceptions of the subject matter being taught: A case from learning history. *International Journal of Educational Research, 19,* 317–325.

Harnett, P. (1993). Identifying progression in children's understanding: The use of visual materials to assess primary school children's learning in history. *Cambridge Journal of Education, 23,* 137–154.

Hodkinson, A. (2003). "History howlers": Amusing anecdotes or symptoms of the difficulties children have in retaining and ordering historical knowledge? Some observations based upon current research. *Research in Education, 70,* 21–31.

Hodkinson, A. (2004a). Does the English Curriculum for History and its Schemes of Work effectively promote primary-aged children's assimilation of the concepts of historical time? Some observations based on current research. *Educational Research, 46,* 99–119.

Hodkinson, A. (2004b). Maturation and the assimilation of the concepts of historical time: A symbiotic relationship or uneasy bedfellows? An examination of the birth-date effect on educational performance in primary history. *International Journal of Historical Learning, Teaching and Research, 4*(2), Retrieved Autumn 15, 2005, from http://www.ex.ac.uk/historyresource/journal2008/hodkinson.doc.

Hoodless, P. A. (2002). An investigation into children's developing awareness of time and chronology in story. *Journal of Curriculum Studies, 34,* 173–200.

Hoodless, P. A. (2004). Spotting the adult agendas: Investigating children's historical awareness using stories written for children in the past. *International Journal of Historical Learning, Teaching and Research, 4*(2), Retrieved August 15, 2005, from http://www.ex.ac.uk/historyresource/journal2008/Hoodless.doc.

Huggins, M. (1996). An analysis of the rationales for learning history given by children and teachers at Key Stage 2. *The Curriculum Journal, 7,* 307–321.

Jacott, L., López–Manjón, A., & Carretero, M. (1998). Generating explanations in history. In J. F. Voss & M. Carretero (Eds.), *International review of history education, Vol. 2: Learning and reasoning in history* (pp. 294–306). Portland, OR: Woburn Press.

Kindervater, A., & von Borries, B. (1997). Historical motivation and historical-political socialization. In M. Angvik & B. von Borries (Eds.), *Youth and history: A comparative European survey on historical consciousness and political attitudes among adolescents, Vol. A: Description* (pp. 62–105). Hamburg, Germany: Körber–Stiftung.

Knight, P. (1989). A study of children's understanding of people in the past. *Educational Review, 41,* 207–219.

Knight, P. (1990). A study of teaching and children's understanding of people in the past. *Research in Education, 44,* 39–53.

Kohlmeier, J. (2005a). The impact of having ninth graders "do history." *The History Teacher, 38,* 499–524.

Kohlmeier, J. (2005b). The power of a woman's story: A three–step approach to historical significance in high school world history. *International Journal of Social Education, 20,* 64–80.

Kohlmeier, J. (2006). "Couldn't she just leave"? The relationship between consistently using class discussions and the development of historical empathy in a ninth grade world history course. *Theory and Research in Social Education, 34,* 34–57.

Kölbl, C., & Straub, J. (2001). Historical consciousness in youth: Theoretical and examplary empirical analysis. *Forum: Qualitative Social Research, 2*(3), Retrieved August 15, 2005, from http://www.qualitative–research.net/fqs–texte/2003–2001/2003–2001koelblstraub–e.htm.

Körber, A. (1997). Chronological knowledge, historical associations and historico–political concepts. In M. Angvik & B. von Borries (Eds.), *Youth and history: A comparative European survey on historical consciousness and political attitudes among adolescents, Vol. A: Description* (pp. 106–152). Hamburg, Germany: Körber–Stiftung.

Lee, J. K., & Guy, C. W. (2003). High school social studies students' uses of online historical documents related to the Cuban Missile Crisis. *The Journal of Interactive Online Learning, 2,* 1–15.

Lee, P. (2001). History in an information culture. *International Journal of Historical Learning, Teaching and Research, 1*(2), Retrieved August 15, 2005, from http://www.ex.ac.uk/historyresource/journal2002/LEE.doc.

Lee, P. (2004). "Walking backwards into tomorrow": Historical consciousness and understanding of history. *International Journal of Historical Learning, Teaching and Research, 4(1),* Retrieved August 15, 2005, from http://www.ex.ac.uk/historyresource/journal2007/Lee2015–2012–2004.doc.

Lee, P., & Ashby, R. (2000). Progression in historical understanding among students ages 7–14. In P. N. Stearns, P. Seixas, & S. Wineburg (Eds.), *Knowing, teaching, and learning history: National and international perspectives* (pp. 199–222). New York: New York University Press.

Lee, P., & Ashby, R. (2001). Empathy, perspective taking, and rational understanding. In O. L. Davis, Jr., E. A. Yeager, & S. J. Foster (Eds.), *Historical empathy and perspective taking in the social studies* (pp. 21–50). Lanham, MD: Rowman & Littlefield.

Lee, P., Dickinson, A. K., & Ashby, R. (1997). "Just another emperor": Understanding action in the past. *International Journal of Educational Research, 27,* 233–244.

Lee, P., Dickinson, A. K., & Ashby, R. (2001). Children's ideas about historical explanation. In A. Dickinson, P. Gordon, & P. Lee (Eds.), *International review of history education, Vol 3: Raising standards in history education* (pp. 97–115). Portland, OR: Woburn Press.

Létourneau, J., & Moisan, S. (2004). Young people's assimilation of a collective historical memory: A case study of Quebeckers of French–Canadian heritage. In P. Seixas (Ed.), *Theorizing historical consciousness* (pp. 109–128). Toronto: University of Toronto Press.

Lévesque, S. (2003). "Bin Laden is responsible; it was shown on tape": Canadian high school students' historical understanding of terrorism. *Theory and Research in Social Education, 31*, 174–202.

Lévesque, S. (2005). Teaching second–order concepts in Canadian history: The importance of "historical significance." *Canadian Social Studies, 39*(2), Retrieved August 15, 2005, from http://www.quasar.ualberta.ca/css/Css_2039_2002/ARLevesque_second–order_concepts.htm.

Levstik, L. S. (1986). The relationship between historical response and narrative in a sixth–grade classroom. *Theory and Research in Social Education, 14*, 1–19.

Levstik, L. S. (1989). Historical narrative and the young reader. *Theory into Practice, 28*, 114–119.

Levstik, L. S. (1993). Building a sense of history in a first–grade classroom. In J. Brophy (Ed.), *Case studies of teaching and learning in social studies* (Vol. 4, pp. 1–31). Greenwich, CT: JAI Press.

Levstik, L. S. (1997/1998). Early adolescents' understanding of the historical significance of women's rights. *International Journal of Social Education, 12*, 19–34.

Levstik, L. S. (2001). Crossing the empty spaces: Perspective taking in New Zealand Adolescents' understanding of national history. In O. L. Davis, Jr., E. A. Yeager, & S. J. Foster (Eds.), *Historical empathy and perspective–taking in the social studies* (pp. 69–96). Lanhan, MD: Rowman and Littlefield.

Levstik, L. S., & Barton, K. C. (1996). "They still use some of their past": Historical salience in children's chronological thinking. *Journal of Curriculum Studies, 28*, 513–576.

Levstik, L. S., & Groth, J. (2002). "Scary thing, being an eighth grader": Exploring gender and sexuality in a middle school U. S. history unit. *Theory and Research in Social Education, 30*, 233–254.

Levstik, L. S., & Groth, J. (2005). "Ruled by our own people": Ghanaian adolescents' conceptions of citizenship. *Teachers College Record, 107*, 563–586.

Levstik, L. S., & Pappas, C. C. (1987). Exploring the development of historical understanding. *Journal of Research and Development in Education, 21*, 1–15.

Levstik, L. S., & Smith, D. (1996). "I've never done this before": Building a community of inquiry in a third–grade classroom. In J. Brophy (Ed.), *Advances in research on teaching: Vol 6. Teaching and learning history* (pp. 85–114). Greenwich, CT: JAI Press.

Limón, M., & Carretero, M. (1999). Conflicting data and conceptual change in history experts. In W. Schnotz, S. Vosniadou, & M. Carretero (Eds.), *New perspectives on conceptual change* (pp. 137–159). New York: Pergamon.

Lipscomb, G. B. (2002). Eighth graders' impressions of the Civil War: Using technology in the history classroom. *Education, Communication & Information, 2*, 51–67.

Lynn, S. (1993). Children reading pictures: History visuals at Key Stages 1 and 2. *Education 3-13, 21*(3), 23–29.

McKeown, M. G., & Beck, I. L. (1990). The assessment and characterization of young learners' knowledge of a topic in history. *American Educational Research Journal, 27*, 688–726.

McKeown, M. G., Beck, I. L., Sinatra, G. M., & Loxterman, J. A. (1992). The contribution of prior knowledge and coherent text to comprehension. *Reading Research Quarterly, 27*, 78–93.

Medina, K., Pollard, J., Schneider, D., & Leonhardt, C. (2000). *How do students understand the discipline of history as an outcome of teachers' professional development?* ERIC Document Reproduction Service No. ED 466 465.

Milson, A. J. (2002). The internet and inquiry learning: Integrating medium and method in a sixth grade social studies classroom. *Theory and Research in Social Education, 30*, 330–353.

Mosborg, S. (2002). Speaking of history: How adolescents use their knowledge of history in reading the daily news. *Cognition and Instruction, 20*, 323–358.

Paxton, R. J. (1997). "Someone with like a life wrote it": The effects of a visible author on high school history students. *Journal of Educational Psychology, 89*, 235–250.

Perfetti, C. A., Britt, M. A., & Georgi, M. C. (1995). *Text–based learning and reasoning: Studies in history*. Hillsdale, NJ: Erlbaum.

Perfetti, C. A., Britt, M. A., Rouet, J.–F., Georgi, M. C., & Mason, R. A. (1994). How students use texts to learn and reason about historical uncertainty. In J. F. Voss & M. Carretero (Eds.), *Cognitive and instructional processes in history and the social sciences* (pp. 257–283). Hillsdale, NJ: Erlbaum.

Pomson, A. D. M., & Hoz, R. (1998). Sought and found: Adolescent's "ideal" historical conceptions as unveiled by concept mapping. *Journal of Curriculum Studies, 20,* 319–337.

Porat, D. A. (2004). It's not written here, but this is what happened: Students' cultural comprehension of textbook narratives on the Israeli–Arab conflict. *American Educational Research Journal, 41,* 963–996.

Riviére, A., Núñez, B. B., & Fontela, F. (1998). Influence of intentional and personal factors in recalling historical texts: A developmental perspective. In J. F. Voss & M. Carretero (Eds.), *International review of history education, Vol. 2: Learning and reasoning in history* (pp. 214–226). Portland, OR: Woburn Press.

Rosa, A., Blanco, F., & Huertas, J. A. (1998). Uses of historical knowledge: An exploration of the construction of professional identity in students of psychology. In J. F. Voss & M. Carretero (Eds.), *International review of history education, Vol. 2: Learning and reasoning in history* (pp. 61–78). Portland, OR: Woburn Press.

Rose, S. L. (2000). Fourth graders theorize prejudice in American history. *International Journal of Historical Learning, Teaching and Research, 1*(1), Retrieved August 15, 2005, from http://www.ex.ac.uk/historyresource/journal2001/roseed–kw.doc.

Rouet, J.–F., Britt, M. A., Mason, R. A., & Perfetti, C. A. (1996). Using multiple sources of evidence to reason about history. *Journal of Educational Psychology, 88,* 478–493.

Rouet, J.–F., Favart, M., Britt, M. A., & Perfetti, C. A. (1997). Studying and using multiple documents in history: Effects of discipline expertise. *Cognition and Instruction, 15*(1), 85–106.

Saye, J. W., & Brush, T. A. (1999). Student engagement with social issues in a multimedia–supported learning environment. *Theory and Research in Social Education, 27,* 472–504.

Saye, J. W., & Brush, T. A. (2002). Scaffolding critical reasoning about history and social issues in multimedia–supported learning environments. *Educational Technology Research and Development, 50*(3), 77–96.

Schweber, S. (2003a). "Especially special": Learning about Jews in a fundamentalist Christian school. *Teachers College Record, 105,* 1693–1719.

Schweber, S. (2003b). Simulating survival. *Curriculum Inquiry, 33,* 139–188.

Schweber, S. (2004). *Making sense of the Holocaust: Lessons from classroom practice.* New York: Teachers College Press.

Seixas, P. (1993a). Historical understanding among adolescents in a multicultural setting. *Curriculum Inquiry, 23,* 301–327.

Seixas, P. (1993b). Popular film and young people's understanding of the history of Native American-White relations. *The History Teacher, 26,* 351–370.

Seixas, P. (1994a). Confronting the moral frames of popular film: Young people respond to historical revisionism. *American Journal of Education, 102,* 261–285.

Seixas, P. (1994b). Students' understanding of historical significance. *Theory and Research in Social Education, 22,* 281–304.

Seixas, P. (1997). Mapping the terrain of historical significance. *Social Education, 61,* 22–27.

Seixas, P., & Clark, P. (2004). Murals as monuments: Students' ideas about depictions of civilization in British Columbia. *American Journal of Education, 110,* 146–171.

Shemilt, D. (1980). *History 13-16 evaluation study.* Edinburgh, Scotland: Holmes McDougall.

Shemilt, D. (1984). Beauty and the philosopher: Empathy in history and classroom. In A. K. Dickinson, P. J. Lee, & P. J. Rogers (Eds.), *Learning history* (pp. 39–83). London: Heinemann.

Shemilt, D. (1987). Adolescent ideas about evidence and methodology in history. In C. Portal (Ed.), *The history curriculum for teachers* (pp. 39–61). New York: Falmer.

Smith, J., & Niemi, R. G. (2001). Learning history in schools: The impact of course work and instructional practices on achievement. *Theory and Research in Social Education, 29,* 18–42.

Sosniak, L. A., & Perlman, C. L. (1990). Secondary education by the book. *Journal of Curriculum Studies, 22,* 427–442.

Spector, K. (2005). *Framing the holocaust in English class: Secondary teachers and students reading Holocaust literature.* Unpublished doctoral dissertation, University of Cincinnati, Cincinnati, OH.

Stahl, S. A., Britton, B. K., Hynd, C., McNish, M., & Bosquet, D. (1996). What happens when students read multiple source documents in history? *Reading Research Quarterly, 31,* 430–456.

Torney–Purta, J. (1994). Dimensions of adolescents' reasoning about historical issues: Ontological switches, developmental processes, and situated learning. In J. F. Voss & M. Carretero (Eds.), *Cognitive and instructional processes in history and the social sciences* (pp. 103–122). Hillsdale, NJ: Erlbaum.

van Boxtel, C., & van Drie, J. (2004). Historical reasoning: A comparison of how experts and novices contextualise historical sources. *International Journal of Historical Learning, Teaching and Research, 4*(2), Retrieved August 15, 2005, from http://www.ex.ac.uk/historyresource/journal2008/boxteldrie.doc.

van Drie, J., & van Boxtel, C. (2004). Enhancing collaborative historical reasoning by providing representational guidance. *International Journal of Historical Learning, Teaching and Research, 4*(2), Retrieved August 15, 2005, from http://www.ex.ac.uk/historyresource/journal2008/drieandboxtel.doc.

VanSledright, B. A. (1995a). "I don't remember—the ideas are all jumbled in my head": 8th graders' reconstructions of colonial American history. *Journal of Curriculum and Supervision, 10*, 317–345.

VanSledright, B. A. (1995b). The teaching-learning interaction in American history: A study of two teachers and their fifth graders. *Journal of Social Studies Research, 19*, 3–23.

VanSledright, B. A. (1996). Studying colonization in eighth grade: What can it teach us about the learning context of current reforms. *Theory and Research in Social Education, 24*, 107–145.

VanSledright, B. A. (1997). And Santayana lives on: Students' views on the purposes for studying American history. *Journal of Curriculum Studies, 29*, 529–557.

VanSledright, B. A. (2002a). Confronting history's interpretive paradox while teaching fifth graders to investigate the past. *American Educational Research Journal, 39*, 1089–1115.

VanSledright, B. A. (2002b). Fifth graders investigating history in the classroom: Results from a researcher-practitioner design experiment. *Elementary School Journal, 103*, 131–160.

VanSledright, B. A. (2002c). *In search of America's past: Learning to read history in elementary school.* New York: Teachers College Press.

VanSledright, B. A., & Afflerbach, P. (2005). Assessing the status of historical sources: An exploratory study of eight US elementary students reading documents. In R. Ashby, P. Gordon & P. Lee (Eds.), *International review of history education, Vol. 4: Understanding history: recent research in history education* (pp. 1–20). New York: RoutledgeFalmer.

VanSledright, B. A., & Brophy, J. (1992). Storytelling, imagination, and fanciful elaboration in children's historical reconstructions. *American Educational Research Journal, 29*, 837–859.

VanSledright, B. A., & Frankes, L. (2000). Concept- and strategic-knowledge development in historical study: A comparative exploration in two fourth-grade classrooms. *Cognition & Instruction, 18*, 239–283.

VanSledright, B. A., & Kelly, C. (1998). Reading American history: The influence of multiple sources on six fifth graders. *Elementary School Journal, 98*, 239–265.

VanSledright, B. A., Kelly, T., & Meuwissen, K. (2005). Oh, the trouble we've seen: Researching historical thinking and understanding. In K. C. Barton (Ed.), *Research methods in social studies education: Contemporary issues and perspectives* (pp. 207–233). Greenwich, CT: Information Age Publishing.

Vella, Y. (2001). Extending primary children's thinking through the use of artefacts. *International Journal of Historical Learning, Teaching and Research, 1*(2), Retrieved August 15, 2005, from http://www.ex.ac.uk/historyresource/journal2002/VELLA.doc.

von Borries, B. (1994). (Re-)constructing history and moral judgment: On relationships between interpretations of the past and perceptions of the present. In J. F. Voss & M. Carretero (Eds.), *Cognitive and instructional processes in history and the social sciences* (pp. 339–355). Hillsdale, NJ: Erlbaum.

von Borries, B. (1995). Exploring the construction of historical meaning: Cross-cultural studies of historical consciousness among adolescents. In W. Bos & R. H. Lehmann (Eds.), *Reflections on educational achievement: Papers in honour of T. Neville Postlethwaite to mark the occasion of his retirement from his chair in comparative education at the University of Hamburg* (pp. 25–59). New York: Waxmann Münster.

von Borries, B. (1997a). Concepts of historical thinking and historical learning in the perspectives of German students and teachers. *International Journal of Educational Research, 27*, 211–220.

von Borries, B. (1997b). Political attitudes and decisions based on historical experiences and analyses. In M. Angvik & B. von Borries (Eds.), *Youth and history: A comparative European survey on historical consciousness and political attitudes among adolescents, Vol. A: Description* (pp. 153–180). Hamburg, Germany: Körber-Stiftung.

von Borries, B., & Baeck, O. (1997). Linkages of three time levels: Interpretations of the past, perceptions of the present and expectations of the future. In M. Angvik & B. von Borries (Eds.), *Youth and history: A comparative European survey on historical consciousness and political attitudes among adolescents, Vol. A: Description* (pp. 181–202). Hamburg, Germany: Körber-Stiftung.

von Borries, B., Kindervater, A., & Körber, A. (1997). Summary: Problems and results of the cross-cultural comparison. In M. Angvik & B. von Borries (Eds.), *Youth and history: A comparative European survey on historical consciousness and political attitudes among adolescents, Vol. A: Description* (pp. 206–234). Hamburg, Germany: Körber-Stiftung.

Voss, J. F., Carretero, M., Kennet, J., & Silfies, L. N. (1994). The collapse of the Soviet Union: A case study in causal reasoning. In J. F. Voss & M. Carretero (Eds.), *Cognitive and instructional processes in history and the social sciences* (pp. 403–429). Hillsdale, NJ: Erlbaum.

Voss, J. F., & Silfies, L. N. (1996). Learning from history text: The interaction of knowledge and comprehension skill with text structure. *Cognition and Instruction, 14*, 45–68.

Voss, J. F., & Wiley, J. (1997). Developing understanding while writing essays in history. *International Journal of Educational Research, 27*, 255–265.

Voss, J. F., Wiley, J., & Kennet, J. (1998). Student perceptions of history and historical concepts. In J. F. Voss & M. Carretero (Eds.), *International review of history education, Vol. 2: Learning and reasoning in history* (pp. 307–330). Portland, OR: Woburn Press.

Waldron, F. (2005). "A nation's schoolbooks wield a great power": How the Romans are depicted in Irish history textbooks. In C. Morgan (Ed.), *Inter– and intracultural differences in European history textbooks* (pp. 257–290). Berlin: Peter Lang.

Wertsch, J. V. (1994). Struggling with the past: Some dynamics of historical representation. In J. F. Voss & M. Carretero (Eds.), *Cognitive and instructional processes in history and the social sciences* (pp. 223–238). Hillsdale, NJ: Erlbaum.

Wiley, J., & Voss, J. F. (1996). The effects of "playing historian" on learning in history. *Applied Cognitive Psychology, 10*, S63–S72.

Wiley, J., & Voss, J. F. (1999). Constructing arguments from multiple sources: Tasks that promote understanding and not just memory for text. *Journal of Educational Psychology, 92*, 301–311.

Wills, J. S. (1996). Who needs multicultural education? White students, U. S. history, and the construction of a usable past. *Anthropology and Education Quarterly, 27*, 365–389.

Wills, J. S. (2005). "Some people even died": Martin Luther King, Jr., the civil rights movement and the politics of remembrance in elementary classrooms. *International Journal of Qualitative Studies in Education, 18*, 109–131.

Wineburg, S. S. (1991a). Historical problem solving: A study of the cognitive processes used in the evaluation of documentary and pictorial evidence. *Journal of Educational Psychology, 83*, 73–87.

Wineburg, S. S. (1991b). On the reading of historical texts: Notes on the breach between school and academy. *American Educational Research Journal, 28*, 495–519.

Wineburg, S. S. (2000). Making historical sense. In P. N. Stearns, P. Seixas, & S. Wineburg (Eds.), *Knowing, teaching, and learning history* (pp. 306–325). New York: New York University Press.

Yeager, E. A., Foster, S. J., & Greer, J. (2002). How eighth graders in England and the United States view historical significance. *Elementary School Journal, 103*, 199–210.

Yeager, E. A., Foster, S. J., Maley, S. D., Anderson, T., & Morris, J. W. I. (1998). Why people in the past acted as they did: An exploratory study in historical empathy. *International Journal of Social Education, 13*, 8–24.

Yeager, E. A., & Terzian, S. (2007). "That's when we became a nation": Urban Latino adolescents and the designation of historical significance. *Urban education.*

Young, K. M., & Leinhardt, G. (1998). Writing from primary documents: A way of knowing history. *Written Communication, 15*, 25–68.

15 Research on K–12 geography education

Avner Segall

Michigan State University

Robert J. Helfenbein

Indiana University-Purdue University

In the last two decades a series of efforts have aimed to revive and transform K–12 geography education. Alarmed by reports about the geographic illiteracy of young American (e.g., *A Nation at Risk*, 1984; National Geographic Society, 1988), politicians, business leaders, geographers, and educators initiated calls for reform in geography education (Binko & Neubert, 1996; Salter, 1986). A number of legislative, organizational, and curricular initiatives helped put geography back on the "map" and produce what some (Bettis, 1995; Boehm, 1997) have termed a "renaissance" in geographic education. The first of these initiatives was the publication of *Guidelines for Geographic Education* in 1984, identifying the five themes of geography and providing the first clear content and skills framework for K–12 education (Petersen, Natoli, & Boehm, 1994). In 1989, President Bush and the nation's state governors included geography as one of the five "core subjects" in the National Education Goals. Those were later signed into law by President Clinton in The Goals 2000: Educate America Act. By 1990, Congress authorized a new geography assessment, to be conducted in 4th, 8th, and 12th grade by the National Assessment of Educational Progress (NAEP). And in 1994, and as part of the Goals 2000 initiative, a coalition of the U.S. Department of Education and four geographic associations published *Geography for Life* (Geography Education Standards Project, 1994), setting out 18 national geography standards specifying what students, at each grade level, should know and be able to do (Gandy & Kruger, 2004). Though the degree to which such initiatives have influenced what takes place in geography classrooms is still unclear (Bednarz, Downs, & Vender, 2003), they have nonetheless impacted geography education in some ways. In 1989 not one state had standards for geography, and only 13 states tested geography in their state exams; by 2004 all states, other than Iowa and Rhode Island, had established some form of geography standards (often under the umbrella of social studies), and the number of states including geography in their state exams had, by 2002, risen to 27. Additionally, more than 40 states now offer Advanced Placement Human Geography tests (Daley, 2003).[1]

Still, if one only looked at the research literature in social studies, one would be hard pressed to recognize that any of the changes in the U.S. scene have taken place—quite a paradox since geography is considered one of the field's core disciplines. *Theory & Research in Social Education*, the leading scholarly journal in social studies, has only published one article in the area of geography since 1990. While *Social Education* and *The Social Studies* have done better in that regard—the former published 35 articles and the latter 22—a large majority of those have been lesson plans for teachers or reflections by teachers about having taught a lesson/unit in geography. Research articles in/on geography education are a rare occurrence in either of those journals. In all, a review of those three journals reveals that, on average, pieces on geography—whether research-based or lesson plans—appear far less frequently that those about history, political science, or economics. In fact, they appear less often than articles on citizenship, multiculturalism, or technology. While we are unsure why research on geography appears so seldom in the social studies literature, we nevertheless believe this resounding silence about what is considered a core subject in the field sends a powerful message as to that which is missing from the literature in social education as well as a call to rectify the situation.

This, of course, does not mean that research in geography education is non-existent. Indeed, there is a large body of research literature within the discourse of geography education, much of it in journals. The *Journal of Geography*, published by the National Council for Geographic Education, is the major source of research in geography education in the U.S. Although it still largely comprises teaching strategies, the rate of such articles has decreased from 69% (1988–1993) to 38% (1994–1997), and articles on research have increased from 7.5% to 14.5% respectively (Bednarz et al., 2003). A newer journal, *Research in Geography Education*, inaugurated in 1999, is published by the Grosvenor Center for Geographic Education. Three journals in the area of geography education are published in Britain: *Primary Geography*, aimed at early elementary students; *Teaching Geography*, for late elementary to high school; and *Geography*, the most scholarly of the three, directed at advanced high school students, teachers, and undergraduates. *International Research in Geographical and Environment Education* is published by the Commission on Geographical Education of the International Geographical Union (Bednarz et al., 2003).

What becomes evident from reviewing the research literature are two trends: First, while there's an abundance of theoretical scholarship—mostly from the English-speaking world outside of the United States—about possible new directions for geography education on the one hand, and much practical literature regarding lesson and unit planning on the other, there is very little that theorizes the practical and few practical examples of applications of theory. In other words, the productive element of relating theory and practice in the process of meaningful research in/on geography education is the least substantive body of scholarship in the field. A second observation is that regardless of genre, much of the driving impetus for research has been existing curricula and pedagogy in K–12 geography education: Research in geography, even when attempting to push the field, is more often bound by that which is (or is proposed to be) implemented in schools rather than a critical examination of that which takes place in school classrooms. In light of the above, we have chosen to divide this chapter into three sections. The first section addresses the "state of geography" in K–12 education, mostly in the United States. The second section focuses on existing research on the former, with the intent of describing some of what has taken place as well as highlighting areas in which research is lacking. The third section points to new—mostly critical—directions for research in geography education.

THE STATE OF GEOGRAPHY IN K–12 EDUCATION

The goal of geography in schools is to introduce students to the discipline and provide a way of looking at the contemporary world. However, some suggest the move towards a standardized set of skills in geography emphasizes the former to the detriment of the latter (Harper, 1992). The origin and development of what came to be known as the *New Geography*[2] began in 1984 with a speech to the Association of American Geographers by Gilbert Grosvenor, Chairman of the National Geographic Society (NGS), appealing for a renewed commitment to geography in schools and for more collaboration between educators and professional geographers and organizations (Bockenhauer,

1993; Grosvenor, 1995; Harper, 1990). The result was the publication of the *Guidelines for Geographic Education* (1984). Building on the previous efforts of the High School Geography Project, 1969–1970 and curriculum guidelines from individual states and countries around the world, the hope was to establish standards and methods for helping teachers embrace an addition to the curriculum (Natoli, 1994). The NGS followed with national efforts at starting and supporting grassroots alliances between classroom teachers and professional geographers. The Geographic Education National Implementation Project (GENIP) began in 1985 to aid in applying the thematic work of the Guidelines to usable curriculum for social studies educators (Grosvenor 1995; Harper 1990).

In order to respond to state and national standards in addition to No Child Left Behind accountability measures, some departments of geography and education have begun collaborating (Gallavan & Knowles-Yanez, 2004; Kirman 2003; Zam & Howard, 2005). These efforts generally intend to address three key areas: (a) deficiencies in the geographic knowledge of preservice teachers; (b) an anticipation of more academic standards and assessment; and (c) a multidisciplinary effort to work towards improving instruction in geographic concepts (Zam & Howard 2005). Faculty involved crafted a course to address the demands of standards and accountability at both the public school level (i.e., Ohio Academic Social Studies Content Standards: 3-Geography) and the level of preservice certification (i.e., Praxis II: social studies subject matter knowledge). Following Bednarz's (2003) assertion that "little time or money [is expended] in ensuring that these documents [standards] are well understood and used uniformly by teachers…[and that] only when an implementation of education reform like the Standards is consistent with other educational initiatives will teachers find it advantageous to adopt them" (pp. 99, 101), these scholars propose that schools of education realign and collaborate with geography departments in order to more effectively prepare social studies teachers (Zam & Howard, 2005).

Geography in school curriculum

Secondary curricula in geography vary according to state but often are less-emphasized than traditional history (Thornton, 2003). Elementary level geography tends to focus on place vocabulary (Brophy, McMahon & Prawat, 1991; Thornton & Wenger, 1990), although some studies suggest that broader connections are being made in some classrooms (Sosniak & Stodolsky, 1993; Thornton, 2003). Standards related to geography for K–12 education can be found in 48 states—Iowa and Rhode Island have no standards or standards program—although they do not appear in consistent form. While much of the integration of geography into standards is found embedded in social studies or earth science courses, 28 states utilize standards specific to a geography curriculum for all grade levels. Across the curriculum, the most consistent representation of geography comes at the middle school level, following standard scope and sequence (Anthamatten, 2004). State standards follow the general guidelines laid out by the Five Themes of Geography and the more detailed *Geography for Life* (Bohem & Bednarz, 1994). Differing levels of local control on social studies curriculum create difficulties in painting a national picture. In the 2002–2003 *National Survey of Course Offerings and Testing in Social Studies,* 15 states listed no information, 18 reported no specifically required geography course, and 18 reported at least one required geography offering (Council of State Social Studies Specialists, 2002–2003). Bednarz et al. (2003) describe three curricular models for geography across the states: geography as part of social studies, geography as supplement to history, and least often, geography as stand alone subject.

Geography and teacher education

One of the concerns associated with reviving, much less transforming, geography education in schools is that many teachers are not adequately prepared to do so (Boehm & Petersen, 1994; Cirrincione & Farrell, 1989; Gregg & Leinhardt, 1994). Elementary teachers generally have only a few college courses in the social sciences, which may or may not include a geography course or two. Secondary social studies teachers normally major in one of the social sciences, with history and political science being more common majors than geography (Thornton, 2003). As a result, pre-service geography teachers may feel (and be) unprepared to adopt the kind of teaching practices recommended in the geography literature (Boehm & Petersen, 1994; Byklum, 2004). The picture is somewhat more promising with in-service teachers. Gandy & Kruger (2004), for instance, found that 84% of the teachers they surveyed received some form of geography content training (college, workshops, or self-study) one to three times. This represents a higher rate than the 55% reported by Farrell and Cirrincione (1989) and the 37% reported by Fitzhugh (1992). Still, while some research indicates a correlation among a teacher's subject area knowledge, the inclination to teach that subject, and the quality of instruction (Brophy, 1991; Gandy & Kruger, 2004; Gregg & Leinhardt, 1994), data in geography education does not explicitly indicate such a relationship (Barrett Hacking, 1996; Wolfe, 2002). Indeed, as the 2001 NAEP illustrates, students of teachers with less preparation in geography sometimes did as well as or better than students whose teachers took more courses in geography. It then seems reasonable to suggest that changing K-12 geography education entails more than simply requiring teachers to take more geography courses; it requires rethinking the nature of teachers' preparation in such courses and moving away from the recall of factual knowledge as the benchmark for assessing university students' geographic expertise (Rallis & Rallis, 1995).

The literature on rethinking geography and teacher education reveals two main trajectories: (a) how the inclusion of geography might change the practice of social studies teachers; and (b) how the changing nature of the world necessitates the addition of spatial thinking to teacher training. Some scholars propose that preservice teachers should explore physical spaces in hopes of building inquiry-based learning experiences that lead students to the skills necessary to understanding. Kirman (2003) further suggests that teachers adopt inquiry-based instruction, tying critical geography skills to contemporary environmental and spatial social problems. Defined as *transformative geography*, this approach grows out of the Association of American Geographers' *Statement of Professional Ethics* (1998) and posits an ethical engagement in spatial thinking. The AAG argues that geographers should "encourage consideration of the relationship between professional practice and the well-being of the peoples, places, and environments that make up our world" (1998, Section VIII). Kirman (2003) proposes, too, that connecting ethics and caring to the social studies curriculum holds transformative potential and might better motivate and engage students. Other scholars—both from the disciplines and from education—argue for a closer collaboration between schools of education and geography departments in hopes of increasing the spatial skills of educators (Bednarz, & Bednarz, 1995; Gallavan & Knowles-Yanez 2004; Kaufman 2004). This is not only because social studies teachers lack adequate training/certification in geography (Seastrom, Gruber, Robin Henke, McGrath, & Cohen, 2002), but also because the training students do acquire features introductory courses in physical and human geography that do not provide adequate conceptual training in spatial understandings for effective geography instruction (Gilsbach 1997; Kaufman 2004; Zam & Howard, 2005).

Suggestions for alleviating these problems include expanded work with place and location activities (Mackenzie & Sawyer, 1986), employing geographic literacy towards dispelling stereotypes (Scott, 1999), combining geographic study with multicultural literature (Berson, Ouztis, & Walsh, 1999), regional analysis (Stoddard, 1997), thematic units emphasizing the importance of place and difference (Gersmehl, 1992), and training teachers to plan instruction with a "geographic eye" (Gay, 1995).

NAEP: The national "report card" on geography and its education

The most comprehensive example of the state of K–12 geography education is presented by The National Assessment of Educational Progress (NAEP). First administered in geography in 1994, NAEP surveys the geographic knowledge and skill of students at grades 4, 8, and 12. Students are asked to recall, understand, analyze, interpret, and apply geographic information (Weiss, Lutkus, Hildebrant, & Johnson, 2002). Results from the 2001 NAEP, which assessed 25,000 students in both public and private schools, indicate an increase in scores compared to the 1994 assessment in grades 4 and 8, but not in grade 12. On average, however, only about 2% of students performed at the highest (Advanced) levels, compared with 23% at the Proficient level, 48% at the Basic level, and 27% at the Below Basic level. (While the Below Basic group did decrease in all three grades from 30–27%, that decrease shifted into the Basic level, which grew from 45–48%.)

Regardless of grade level, students in private schools out-performed public school students. Students in urban schools scored lower than students in suburban areas, towns, or rural areas, and students eligible for free or reduced lunch scored lower on average than other students (Stoltman, 2002). While there was no change from 1994 to 2001 in the average scores of either male or female students in any of the three grade levels, the 2001 results still show that gender does matter: Higher percentages of fourth- and eighth-grade male students are at or above Proficient and Advanced levels than their female counterparts. In grade 12, a higher percentage of male students scored at or above the Basic and Proficient levels. In all grades, White students scored higher on average than did minority students, with Asian/Pacific Islander students coming second, followed by Hispanics, American Indians, and African Americans respectively.[3]

An interesting, perhaps disturbing, aspect of geography education highlighted by NAEP is the relationship (or lack thereof) between the preparation of geography teachers and the number of geography classes taken by students and students' achievement. Only 7% of fourth grade students and 8% of eighth-grade students were taught by teachers who majored or minored in geography. In 2001 a higher percentage of students reported taking 3 years of geography, compared with 1994, and, conversely, a lower percentage reported taking no geography courses. The 2001 NAEP also reported a positive association between more course-taking and higher geography scores. (While this was true in grades 4 and 8, grade 12 students taking no geography courses in high school had higher average scores than those who had taken 2, 3, or 4 years of geography.)

As for what takes place in geography courses, NAEP reports instruction on map and globe skills as the most prevalent. Only about one-quarter of students surveyed received instruction in foreign countries and cultures at least once a week, while 29% received no instruction in foreign countries and cultures. Still, more instruction did not necessarily translate into higher student scores. For example, students in grades 4 and 8 whose teachers never or hardly ever taught about foreign countries and cultures scored as well as or better than those whose teachers taught those areas more often.

RESEARCH ON TEACHERS, TEACHING, AND LEARNING[4]

Research on teacher's conceptions of geography

Several studies in Britain examined preservice teachers' conceptions of geography and geography education. Walford (1996) found that prospective teachers' conceptions of geography fall into four categories: *interactionists* focus on the interdependence of and interaction between humans and their environment; *synthesizers* employ a multidisciplinary approach that focuses on developing a sense of global responsibility to manage the environment; *spatialists* focus on geography as spatial analysis of distribution, relations, processes, and consequences; and *placeists* explore why places are where they are, why they are like they are, and what that means. Though the emphasis on positivist spatial analysis in geography may have decreased in recent years, according to Walford, a significant proportion of students in the study (49%) "couched their definitions of the subject in a way akin to 'hard science.' For the majority, the traditional linkage of physical and human aspects of study seems to have survived any pluralist tendencies of their university courses" (p. 76). Barrett Hacking (1996) explored the "geographic persuasions" (a sense of geography drawn from personal experience, interests, and ideology) of secondary preservice teachers and their relationship to students' thinking about geography teaching. Despite the wide variety of geographic persuasions found, each affiliated with a different school of thought and invoking a distinct ideology, the study determined that prospective teachers tended to suspend those persuasions when planning and teaching—indeed, their lessons were remarkably similar; all followed a linear model. Martin (2000) conducted a similar study with elementary teachers and found that their ideas about pedagogy superseded their conceptual understanding of geography, drawing more heavily from educational theories about teaching and learning than from their own conceptual understandings of geography. When Catling (2004) asked 218 elementary prospective teachers "what is geography?" and "why teach geography to elementary children?", she found that participants' "images of geography appear to be limited to an information-oriented sense of geography as a subject that studies physical and human geography and the interrelationship between them" (p. 157).

Studies on maps, place location, and concepts of physical geography (Atwood & Atwood, 1995, 1996; Chiodo, 1993) have shown that preservice teachers hold the same misconceptions and often score no better than their future students (LeVasseur, 1999b). In a 3-year study, combining surveys of 100 preservice social studies teachers and interviews with practicing teachers to determine how much and what teachers know about Africa, Osunde, Tlou, and Brown (1996) found that the majority of respondents had a variety of misconceptions. Common beliefs about Africa included viewing its "inhabitants [as] wild natives who live in huts, their lifestyle involves hunting and gathering, its society struggles with famine and malnutrition, and wild animals wander everywhere. Many of those surveyed indicated that Africa is a country" (p. 120). Respondents had greater misconceptions about Africa than about the other five world regions (Asia, Europe, Middle East, North America, Russia) addressed in the survey (see also Brook, Field, & Labbo, 1995). While one might expect (though in no way accept) that prospective teachers know so little (and are so ill informed) about a far away continent such as Africa, a survey of Michigan social studies student teachers conducted by Segall (2002) found respondents almost equally ignorant about Canada, a country bordering Michigan and one most respondents had visited more than once.

In a qualitative study examining the geography-related schemata of three novice and three expert teachers and the nature and extent of their content knowledge and pedagogical strategies, Klein (1997) found that, in general, teachers demonstrated incomplete, fragmented geographic knowledge. Rogers (1997) surveyed 50 elementary teachers and interviewed 7 others to examine their knowledge of geography and geographic education. She found that teachers' understandings of geography and geographic education were limited to place names and locations instead of geographic relationships.

Research on teaching

Some research suggests that geography education has changed significantly in response to the various initiatives mentioned at the outset of this chapter. Marran (1994), for instance, argues that the "old" textbook-dependent, teacher-directed geography, focused on memorizing facts about principal products of world regions, is losing ground to a "new" emphasis on *doing* geography. New geography embraces constructivist ideas about best learning and teaching practice, particularly the value of hands-on, active learning and inquiry approaches (cf. Bednarz et al., 2003). Others, however, argue that despite various initiatives to make geography education more meaningful, classroom practice and student achievement remain much the same (Gandy & Kruger, 2004; Page, 1994). Thornton & Wenger (1990), for instance, found that the elementary teachers they studied "selected activities that emphasized factual recall and skills practice" and equated the geography curriculum with textbook coverage (p. 520). Regardless of the methodological approach adopted by teachers in this study, their pedagogical choices emphasized student absorption of facts and the practice of discrete skills as well as low-level factual knowledge. These practices were then legitimized through assessment and evaluation procedures. Still, although the teachers' priority was covering, not understanding, of subject matter, students' learning of factual information was seldom impressive. Even in classrooms where students sometimes engaged in activities entailing complex thinking, Thornton & Wenger add, tests mostly focused on recall of information. Rogers' (1997), too, found that while teachers reported introducing geographic concepts in their classrooms, classroom observations showed reliance on place names, locations, and map skills. Further, activities rarely strayed either from textbook suggestions or traditional paper and pencil formats; students rarely physically explored the world outside the classroom (see also Brophy et. al., 1991). On a positive note, a study by Sosniak & Stodolsky (1993) found that fourth-grade geography, though still taught as facts and skills, was connected to other areas of social studies as well as to language arts and to students' personal experience.

While the five themes of geography have, by now, been incorporated in "all geography textbooks and most social studies programs as a context for geographic education" (Boehm & Petersen, 1994, p. 211), there is little evidence that this has resulted in a more meaningful geography education. Some (e.g., Gersmehl, 1992) have suggested that when the five themes are used "as topics (nouns), rather than ways of organizing information about geography topics (verbs), they may constrain geographic inquiry rather than liberate it" (Gregg & Leinhardt, 1994, p. 349). Harper (1992) points out that while the themes can potentially provide students with tools to study the world in more meaningful ways, the way they are implemented—described by Boehm & Petersen (1994) as overly simplistic or even erroneous—may not actually help students gain sufficient understanding of the world around them. Sunal and Haas' study (1993) suggests that the use of the themes in school is mostly descriptive and that the first two—location and place—are the ones most often used (see also Hickey & Bein, 1996), leaving the other—more complex and relational themes—mostly unexamined (see Sunal, Christensen, & Haas, 1995).

RESEARCH ON STUDENTS' ATTITUDES AND MIS/UNDERSTANDINGS IN GEOGRAPHY

Students' attitudes toward geography

Research in general indicates that students' literacy rate and competence improve as their interest in the subject increases (Bloom, 1976). Sack and Petersen (1998) report of two studies, conducted in 1983 and 1993, that surveyed over 1,400 fourth-, fifth-, and sixth-grade students in Texas about their attitudes toward geography. In both studies, students rated geography their least favorite of the listed school subjects although there was a slight improvement in 1993. While in 1983 only 8% of students listed geography as their first or second favorite subject, that number rose to 14% in 1993. Another study, by Trygestad (1997), found that most students ranked geography "Good" (56%) or "Okay" (24%); few students thought geography was "Great" (14%) or "Boring" (6%). The 2001 NAEP reports that at grade 12, the percentage of students who preferred subjects other than geography increased from 63% to 72% between 1994 and 2001. Only 15% of students in 2001 chose geography as one of their favorite subjects. Inquiring about students' views about what constitutes geography education, Trygestad (1997) found that students "viewed geography learning as the acquisition of geographic literacy. Some students described geography as making maps or knowing locations and, therefore, considered the subject of limited use" (p. 13). When asked what constitutes the most beneficial learning in geography, students mentioned activities and projects. "Students felt they learned more and understood better when they were able to do something" and when presented with active and stimulating classroom lessons that challenge their thinking (p. 16).

Students' knowledge, conceptions, and misconceptions

According to several studies, U.S. students are not only "geographically illiterate, lacking essential knowledge, skills, and concepts in their physical and human environments, they also lack the ability to perform higher level cognitive thinking in geography" (Patrick, 1993; cf. Trygestad, 1997, p. 3; see also Marker & Mehlinger, 1992). The 2001 NAEP suggests that many elementary students lack such basic information as the name and location of their own state. While students in grades 8 and 12 have better definitional information, many were unable to analyze information related to an environmental issue, provide reasons for or consequences emanating from the issue, or suggest a possible solution to geographic issues or problems (Stoltman, 2002). Lash (2004) reports that 11% of young Americans could not locate the United States on a map. The location of the Pacific Ocean, Lash adds, was a mystery to 29%; Japan, to 58%; France, to 65%; and the United Kingdom, to 69%. Surveying 700 students from junior high through upper undergraduate levels (including prospective teachers) about their understandings and misunderstandings of relative locations of continents, states, and ocean size, Franeck, Nelson, Aron, and Bisard (1993) found misunderstandings persisting across all measured educational levels. Some included perceiving South America as being directly south of North America, Europe as being directly east of the contiguous United States, and Africa as primarily in the Southern Hemisphere. Answers regarding the relative size of oceans revealed that while a large majority correctly selected the Pacific Ocean as the largest, almost a quarter named the Atlantic Ocean, while 60% incorrectly chose the Indian Ocean as the smallest. Such findings have been substantiated by earlier studies in addition to overwhelming anecdotal reports from hundreds of college faculty, suggesting that "American students from kindergarten through graduate school were geographically incompetent" and globally unaware (Petersen et al., 1994, p. 206).

Other research demonstrates that, while elementary students have difficulty understanding nested geographical relationships (e.g., local community within the state, the region, the nation, the hemisphere), they can learn those relationships through exposure to map-based instruction (Harwood & McShane, 1996). As part of their investigation of K–3 students' knowledge about cultural universals, Brophy and Alleman (2005) identified several characteristics of children's thinking that mediate their understandings of geographical information. First, they tend to focus on individuals, families, and local settings and rarely make reference to effects of events on the nation, let alone the world or the human condition at large. Second, although students are familiar with human actions relating to cultural universals that are observable in their homes and neighborhoods, they usually know little or nothing about how and why these practices vary across locations and cultures. While students' answers to geographic questions, as might be expected, tend to reflect limited geographic exposure and a child's purview, some children, Brophy and Alleman suggest, did communicate clear misconceptions, such as the idea that rivers flow inland from the oceans or that highways are literally high (elevated above the surrounding land).

Hickey and Bein (1996) also report that students in the primary grades (K–2) struggle with concepts of location, directionality, and distinguishing between spheres and circles. In the intermediate grades (3–5) students' concepts about landforms, latitude and longitude, and layers of the earth are unformed or misinformed. Middle grade students struggle with concepts such as culture, climate, adaptation versus modification, and general map location and terminology. At the secondary level, the authors add, students are confused by graphs relating climatic information and the idea behind plate tectonics. In each case, Hickey and Bein found that relating new concepts to local landmarks and using visualizations, experiments, and demonstrations results in enhanced student learning, as does having students create models and design charts, graphs, or models. LeVasseur (1999b) reports that students were least knowledgeable about physical geography. While 93% of sixth-grade students and 90% of ninth-grade students were able to identify areas on a map as continents, students at both grade levels were unable to distinguish the topography of U.S. regions and had difficulty inferring relative temperature and elevations from a map. Only a quarter of respondents knew that a river could flow north. All students had difficulty identifying parts and characteristics of a city on a map. According to van der Schee, van Dijk, and van Westrhenen's (1992) study of seventh- through tenth-grade students, students tend to have few problems with declarative knowledge but have difficulty applying procedural knowledge. This, the researchers propose, may reflect the lack of focus on geography concepts in instruction. Scott (1999) investigated high school students' perceptions of the developing world, indicating ethnocentric perceptions such as "the superiority of the U.S. over the developing world, the substandard living conditions evident in many developing nations, the exotic nature of foreign cultures, and the perceived lack of relevance of the developing world for their lives as adolescents" (p. 263). While much of this, the author suggests, can be blamed on media portrayals of the developing world, a substantial number of students, according to Scott, "responded that they acquired their perceptions in school" (p. 264).

Regarding students' understanding of concepts underlying the five themes of geography, Trygestad (1997) reports that students "understood the concept of location (96%), place (80%), and region (82%), but had more difficulty identifying and using movement (49%) and interaction (44%)" (p. 11). Not only did 96% of the students identify or use the concept of location, it was the most frequently cited valuable concept, dominating "students' thinking of geography across achievement and grade levels" (p. 12).

Research on GIS and other technologies

While Geographic Information Systems (GIS) certainly influence how geographers view the world and manage the environment (Buzer, 2002), relatively little is known about how such systems influence younger learners. The growing body of literature examining this issue tends to focus on "whether" GIS make a difference, rather than how and with what consequences. GIS merge various layers of information in a computer environment that "offers enhanced capabilities for retrieval, storage, manipulation, analysis, and visualization" of geographic data (Donaldson, 2001, p. 147). Layers of data can be turned on or off, allowing geographic information to be viewed from various spatial perspectives (Audet & Paris, 1997; Nellis, 1995). Despite these possibilities, the incorporation of GIS in schools, while becoming more common (Bednarz & Ludwig, 1997), is still very limited (Brown, 1999; Donaldson, 2001; Kerski, 2000) as is its meaningful use in teacher preparation (Bednarz & Audet, 1999). Reasons range from inadequate teacher training (Bednarz & Audet, 1999; Brown, 1999), pressure to teach a given curriculum (Kerski, 2000), teacher reluctance to learn a new technology without institutional support (Audet & Paris, 1997; Bednarz & Ludwig, 1997), and teacher confusion as to whether to teach about or with GIS (Audet & Paris, 1997) to lack of appropriate curricula and access to hardware and software (Broda & Baxter, 2003; Kerski, 2000). Still, studies examining the use of GIS offer some hope regarding student learning. Keiper (1996), for instance, found that GIS in elementary classrooms help students practice geographic skills outlined in the National Standards and that they can be extremely motivating. Studying the impact of a GIS project that emphasized doing geography rather than only learning about it in a fifth-grade class, Keiper (1999) concluded that it "dramatically shifted the study of geography from memorization of places to the practice of geography skills," helping students "ask meaningful geographic questions that lead to students acquiring, organizing, and analyzing geographic information" (p. 57). Kerski (2000) also found that students using GIS performed significantly better on assignments than students using traditional methods. In a review of existing research, Lloyd and Bunch (2003) report that GIS develop spatial abilities (Goodchild, 1993; Thompson, Lindsay, Davis, & Wong, 1997), foster conceptual understanding (Mosely, 2001), enhance problem-solving skills, enable spatial analysis, and support interdisciplinary connections (Audet & Abegg, 1996; Gerber, 1995). However, comparing students' use of traditional maps and interactive maps—digital representations of maps allowing users to link additional information (photos, data, video clips, or sounds) for generating and presenting information—Linn (1997) found that, although students preferred working with interactive maps, there was no significant difference in results between students using interactive maps and those using traditional maps.

RESEARCH ON GENDER RELATED ISSUES

Examining geographic knowledge of males and females from junior high to college geography courses, Henrie, Aron, Nelson, and Poole (1997) found that males outperformed females at each level and in each of the subfields tested (physical geography, human geography, regional geography, and map skills), averaging 13% higher. The knowledge gap, they add, became wider and more consistent with increased education. Nonetheless, a comparison of final course grades at all levels showed no significant difference between males and females. Other studies (e.g., Cherry, 1991) also report that males generally score better than females when asked to locate places on a map and that females (and minorities) tend to score lower than White males on tests of geographic knowledge (Bein, 1990; Eve, Price, & Counts, 1994; NAEP, 2001), but at least one study found that differences between male and female performance in earlier grades disappeared at higher levels of education. Franeck et al. (1993) found significant differences in favor of males at the junior high school level, but these differences decreased in high school and virtually disappeared at the college level (for a counter-argument, see Eve et al., 1994; Schoenfeldt, 2000). Still other studies relate performance differences to specific areas of geographic understanding. For example, LeVasseur (1999b) reports that in his study of 23 geography classes in grades 6 and 9 on the skills and tools of geography, sixth grade male and female students scored equally well in their ability to interpret direction, distance, and symbols on a map. Males and females, Le Vasseur adds, also performed equally well when interpreting line graphs. Females out-performed males on interpreting bar graphs. More females than males were also able to use a grid to locate places on a map (see also LeVasseur, 1999a). Attempting to make sense of these often conflicting studies, Self and Golledge (1994) conclude that while "gender differences in spatial abilities do exist, they can often be significantly reduced or modified by training, reinforcement, and repeated trials." This, they add, "indicates that the lower performance by females is not necessarily due to a lack of ability, but because of a lack of opportunity to develop certain spatial skills or to the suppressive influence of sociocultural role expectations" (p. 236). J. S. Smith (2001) states that while there was no evidence that sex had influence on map skill and cognitive mapping abilities, the study illustrates that other factors, such as comfort with maps and computer games, where sex-related issues might play a role, were significant in determining student spatial abilities.

In a study examining everyday out-of-school geographic experiences of forty-six 13-year-olds in Oregon, Wridt (1999) found that male and female adolescents frequented different types of places, traveled in different ways, by different means, and with different companions as a function of their gendered social relationships. These gendered out-of-class experiences, Wridt suggests, may impact students' in-class geography learning. (For a study on changes in childhood geographies, 1940s–2000s, and their implication for education, see Wridt, 2001).

RESEARCH ON MAPS, MAP SKILLS, AND MAPPING

While there continues to be a dispute as to what ought to be taught in geography education, there is general consensus about the necessity to teach about maps and globes and the skills required to use them meaningfully (Gregg & Leinhardt, 1994). There is long-standing debate between two schools of thought—the Piagetian and the Non-Piagetian—as to what students, especially the very young, can do and, consequently, what meaningful instruction entails. While both agree that, on average, students' abilities to engage maps increase with age, they disagree on whether very young children have the abilities to make meaning of maps. Researchers influenced by the Piagetian theory of development (Downs & Liben, 1988; Downs, Liben, & Daggs 1988; Liben & Downs, 1989, 1997) suggest that young children are not yet able to engage maps in meaningful ways, while those belonging to the Non-Piagetian school of thought believe they are (Blaut, 1997; Blaut, Stea, Spencer, & Blades, 2003; Cox, 1991; Mehler & Dupoux, 1994; Sowden, Stea, Blades, Spencer, & Blaut, 1996). Studies by those adhering to the Non-Piagetian approach have illustrated that at about age two children can solve detour problems using an overhead view of obstacles (Rieser, Doxsey, McCarrell, & Brooks, 1986) and that 3-year-olds can use a very simple map to find hidden objects in a room and negotiate a maze (Spencer, Blades, & Morsley, 1989). The ability to interpret aerial photos has been observed in 5- and 6-year-olds (Blaut & Stea, 1971; Matthews, 1992. See also Robertson & Taplin, 2000). Whether one takes a Piagetian or Non-Piagetian approach, this debate (pursued further in Aitken, 2001; Boehm & Petersen, 1997; Gregg & Leinhardt, 1994; Matthews, 1992), as Sowden et al. (1996), among others, have pointed out, has important implications regarding how we structure students' experiences with maps when they enter school.

In a study that asked fifth- and seventh-grade students to generate questions for others about maps and then have those answered using the information on the map, Gregg (1997) found that students most often generated three types of questions: read symbol, infer latitude and longitude, and interpret scale. Problems with all three aspects of map content were common among both fifth- and seventh-grade students. In response to questions about exact longitude/latitude, none of the responses was complete. The accuracy of responses about questions regarding scale was also very low—more than 33% of responses of fifth graders were incorrect (dropping to 20% in grade 7). Students, regardless of grade, also had difficulty combining information from general and insert maps. Results also indicate that students had problems understanding the use of color in maps, often interpreting all of a map's colors as having meaning (e.g., assuming that sub-Saharan Africa was colored tan because it is a sandy area) and that students had difficulties reading national boundaries on the map. Another study by Gregg (1999) examined the relationship between students' understandings of maps and methods taught. In one classroom, using a didactic-analytic approach, students were asked to read maps of Canada, solve problems, and navigate as they responded to a set of exercises. Students in another classroom created their own maps of Canada. Gregg found that map-makers learned more than map-readers, especially with regard to symbols. She also points out that while map-reading maintained the level of achievement between high and low-scoring students in the pre-test, map-making strongly benefited students with the least amount of prior knowledge without negatively affecting the learning of students who began the study with more prior knowledge.

Leinhardt, Stainton, and Merriman Bausmith (1998) conducted a study with two seventh-grade classrooms where students constructed their own maps either individually or in groups. The study found that making maps in groups, more so than when students worked individually, forced students to make their thinking explicit and public and thus to justify and support their thinking. Consequently, and as the post-test indicated, students working in groups had a better understanding of map concepts than students who worked individually. A study by Merriman Bausmith and Leinhardt (1998) examined map construction by 12 middle-school students to determine "what actions influence the accuracy of their maps, how prior knowledge helps them to produce their maps, and what can be learned through map making" (p. 93). Results point to a relationship between student recognition of map element interconnections and subsequent map accuracy. Students with prior knowledge related to the maps being constructed, as well as about longitude and latitude, were more successful in placing the appropriate symbols and accurately drawing and labeling the longitude and latitude lines. Results also indicate two pedagogical issues: (1) focusing on recognition of interconnections of map elements can promote better map reasoning skills, and (2) map making is a more effective instructional activity for the development of coherent, interconnected mental representations and understanding of map elements when it is conducted in combination with instruction about basic map elements (e.g., scale, symbol, and projection).

A study on hand-drawn mental maps by Thomas and Willinsky (1999) asked more than a thousand students, grades 8 through 10, in 11 countries and two U.S. states (California and Hawaii) around the Pacific Ocean to hand draw and label a map of the Pacific region and to respond to a series of questions on various topics (e.g., community, culture, economics, education, history, language, and ethnicity) concerning the area. The purpose of the study was to examine whether (and how) students "see" the world. The study found that students' conceptions of the Pacific region—what it does and does not include, who is depicted more prominently, etc.—differed. Some students, most notably from the U.S. (California), placed the Pacific Ocean in the center of their maps. A majority of students drew the Pacific as longer than wider, thus placing Asia and the Americas closer together. Assuming a connection between students' maps and their perceptions of the world around them, the researchers suggest that a majority of students see countries on other sides of the Pacific as being at least geographically, if not culturally, close to their own. (For studies on adults' mental maps of the world, see Saarinen, 1999.)

ABSENCES IN EXISTING RESEARCH

In a review of research in geography education more than a decade ago, Downs (1994) stated that we have yet to establish a significant, empirically sound, and theoretically grounded body of research that can result in a practical, relevant knowledge base for the field of geography education. Without it, Downs cautioned, "we cannot build a cumulative structure of understanding, we cannot identify the missing links, we cannot generate provocative questions, we cannot assess the value of our answers, we cannot see where we are going and why we are going there" (p. 58). Regrettably, we believe, Downs' words still ring true today. Indeed, as Bednarz et al. (2003) point out, the existing body of research literature in/on geography education "can be characterized as small-scale (in terms of numbers of participants), largely asynchronous (few longitudinal studies), rarely controlled (re: formal experimental design), and often descriptive and anecdotal" (p. 29). Lash and Wridt (2002) claim that current research on geographic education largely ignores the fact that geography matters. Much of the research on students' understanding of geographic concepts, they add, relies on developmental psychology theory which is often accompanied "by a notion of childhood as *universal*, treats young people as human *becomings* rather than as human beings, and often does not situate the learning process within a particular social, cultural, or physical context" (p. 159). Additionally, Lash and Wridt claim, much of the research within geography education focuses only on "a *micro* setting or scale of analysis, such as the formal learning environment of the classroom" instead of investigating "the interconnections between home, community, and the larger socio-cultural contexts in which knowledge is produced" (p. 159). Another sort of critique, one relating to the absence of research on issues of difference—specifically in the *Journal of Geography*, the main research journal in geography education—has been leveled by Monk (1999). For the most part, Monk asserts, the underlying approach "has focused on a consensus view of disciplinary content and institutional issues rather than asking 'who are we teaching?' and what that might mean. Indeed, in all this ferment, attention to women, gender, children's daily lives and multicultural issues have been barely visible" (p. 250).

In addition to calling for more (and more substantive) research, we also encourage studies in those areas on which researchers are, largely, silent. More research is needed on the preparation of geography teachers—not simply on their perceptions and understandings, but on how their perceptions and practices are formed in, through, and against their teacher preparation. That is, to critically examine the various discourses prospective teachers encounter at universities and how those help "construct" particular understandings about geography, its purposes, and its pedagogy. Further studies should be conducted on what teachers, students, and parents believe should be taught in geography education, why, when, and to whom (Bednarz et al., 2003). And naturally, we encourage research that can provide thicker and deeper description and analysis of teaching and learning in classrooms and the relationship between them. Mostly absent from existing research on these issues are critical examinations of the implicit and null curriculum, of the enacted curriculum, of classroom discourse, of the kinds of questions asked (and not asked), of what constitutes "appropriate" responses (and by whom), of what is not asked (and why), and of the pedagogical implications of all of the above. We also suggest more research on students' thinking in/about geography rather than mostly on skills acquired. There is also a need for more studies about assessment in geography, examining the various large-scale assessments administered as well as more authentic, in-class procedures and the degree to which (and how) those might be reifying the very issues geography education has, for so long, attempted to transform: What messages do those assessments convey to students and teachers about what is and is not significant in geography, what and how one should (and should not) know in/about it and the degree to which those messages are then carried back into the classroom once the assessment is over? Research is also needed to better understand how institutional geography education impacts students' geographic understandings and engagements outside of school and vice versa. Attention ought to be paid to what and how geography students learn outside of school, particularly from popular culture, and its influence on students' in-class understandings. Despite the fact that geography is, more often than not, taught in the context of social studies, we know very little as to whether and how students are able (or are invited) to make cross- and inter-disciplinary connections and transfers both in geography education per se and when studying other areas in social studies (for an exception, see Gregg & Leinhardt, 1993).

FUTURE DIRECTIONS FOR RESEARCH

In the last quarter century, a variety of critical discourses—i.e., postmodernism, post-structuralism, feminism, and postcolonialism—have challenged disciplinary claims to universality, transparency, objectivity, and truth, critically examining them as social constructions that privilege particular understandings about the world. Yet while geography, as a discipline, has, in various ways, attempted to engage—respond to, accept, reject—such challenges, geography education and much of the research about it have not. We thus use the next section to suggest new avenues in which research in geography education might more closely address some of the pertinent issues facing geography, in light of the challenges posed by the above-mentioned critical discourses.

Geography as the maker of the world: Ideology, language, and representation

Despite geography's tendency to present itself as scientific and objective, the ideas that geography is value-free or that there is an epistemological vantage point from which the world can be described objectively have been widely refuted by critical geographers (e.g., Gregory, 1978, 1994; Harvey, 1973; Lefebvre, 1991; Massey, 1994; Rose, 1993; Said, 1978; Soja, 1996; Willinsky, 1998). These scholars suggest instead that geography is a humanly constructed discourse and that all forms of geography either reproduce or challenge particular knowledge and identity formations as well as the power relations that go along with them (Thornton, 2003). Each interpretation of the world, Thornton adds, carries with it a series of explicit, implicit, and null assumptions, values, and perspectives about what the world is and should be (see also Battimer, 1993; Davies & Gilmartin, 2002; Slater, 2001). Seen this way, geography is inherently a political and pedagogical enterprise. The questions researchers ought to ask should thus also be political and pedagogical in nature: What world does geography education make possible and intelligible, to whom, how, to what ends and with what consequences? How does it position students to inter/act (or abstain from it) in the world, at what scales, with what purposes? What understandings and power structures underlie the discourses made available in geography education? Who gets privileged by them? Who does not?

Claiming that geography is a socially constructed discourse implies paying attention to how ideology, language, and forms of representation work to construct the world and its people. By that we mean an examination of ideologies underlying the language and images used in geography education and the social relations advanced through them (Gilbert, 1989). For lack of space, we focus on only a few issues and what those might mean for research. In all, the intent is to examine the assumptions, values, and perspectives encoded in the explicit, implicit, and null messages conveyed as well as in the pedagogical opportunities made available to students.

Geography and/as the imperial project

While much has been written about the role geography has played in the West's project of empire-building and colonialism (Bhabha, 1994; Gregory, 1995; Jackson, 1989; Pratt, 1992; Said, 1978; Willinsky, 1998), there is little empirical research about whether or how the legacy of imperialism is still present in geography classrooms today. What we need to know more about are the lingering colonial concepts inherent in what is taught and what is glossed over or ignored in geography education and the degree to which (and how) those underlie students' learning to construct—and in that process also divide—the world (Willinsky, 1998). What, for example, does geography's focus on the nation state as a category of analysis "do" to students' geographic understandings growing up in a postcolonial world? How do European-generated terms such as the Middle East, Far East, the Orient, or Dark Africa still determine a Western sense of center and the power relations that underlie it? What do persisting European names of rivers, lakes, or mountains—ones appropriated and renamed in the effort to exploit, reconstruct, and control other lands (Crush, 1994; Edwards, 2001; Pahl, 1995)—both allow and inhibit in the construction of a "sense of place" (whose sense? whose place?) by different—say, European and aboriginal—students (Osborne, 1998)? Answers to such questions are important because how we divide and name the world has consequences for students' ways of seeing, for their mapping of identities and subjectivities, for the construction of their maps of meaning (Lambert, 2002) both inside and outside of the geography classroom.

Representations in/of geography

Examining the substance of geographical representations and their use (both in and out of classrooms) is an area we know little about. Yet it is through such representations that students obtain much of their information about the world and its people. For example, while Collins and Lutz (1993) provide an incisive critique of the *National Geographic* magazine and how prevalent notions of race in the United States help determine how various people of the world are depicted, and while this magazine is routinely used in geography classrooms, we are unaware of any research conducted on how and why it is used and with what consequences as to how students see the Other as well as how they see themselves in relation to the Other (or as a result of Othering). The same is true with regard to maps, where much research exists on how students use maps and the relationship of that use to their understandings in geography, yet there is very little research about how the maps used in classrooms position students to construct a place in the world and how they then view the world from such positions (Segall, 2003. Also see Black, 1997; Harley, 1988; Kaiser & Wood, 2001; MacEachren, 1995; Monmonier, 1991; Wood, 1992). Another form of textualizing the world much discussed in the literature in geography, but rarely submitted to research in its education, is the role and use of *landscapes*. Too often considered an innocently framed visual image of an environment, a landscape, Cosgrove (1985) points out, is more than a neutral material object; it is a way of organizing a perception of an environment, based on the cultural codes of the society in (and for) which it is produced (see also Mitchell, 1994). This emphasis, Osborne (1998) adds, encourages the exploration of landscape as an active verb rather than an objective noun. Such understandings, Barnes and Duncan (1992) suggest, mean exploring landscapes as complex systems of encoded meanings that need to be examined to better understand how societies construct—or, as Davies and Gilmartin (2002) suggest, reproduce—places and learn to live in them.

Geography and difference

While research exists on what and how male and female or majority and minority students perform or understand differently (or not) in geography education, very little of it has focused on gender and race—not as biological differences, but as socially constructed categories—in geography education or on geography education as a gendered, raced (Saunders, 1999; M. Smith, 2002), or classed endeavor. We thus suggest research that examines how gender, race, and other categories of difference are produced and reproduced through dominant understandings of what places and people are or should be and how ideas about nature, landscape, and the built environment produce and reproduce difference (Rose, Kinnaird, Morris, & Nash, 1997). That is, we encourage research on how geography education works to maintain, ameliorate, or aggravate race and gender inequalities (De Oliver, 1998), how it contributes to their categorization and to the racial and gendered power relations underlying them. For example, how does geography's use of social scientific masculinity and aesthetic masculinity—the former characterized by a quest for abstraction and for a detached objectivity, the latter by asserting male sensibilities to human experience of place (Rose, 1993)—encourage particular, gendered geographic imaginations among students (see also Massey, 1991; Deutsche, 1990)? How, and with what consequences to students learning, are notions such as the privileging of public over private spaces (Cope, 1997; Hanson & Pratt, 1995; Laws, 1994; Massey, 1994) or the exclusion of the body as a scale of analysis (Butler, 1993; Gregson, Rose, Cream, & Laurie, 1997; Weedon, 1999) maintained by ideas and practices currently prevalent in geography education? And how do common gendered terms about the environment such as *fertile* or *virgin* land, *mother* earth (see Weedon, 1999; see also Momsen, 2000; Plumwood, 1993; Shiva, 1989; Silvey, 1998; Warren, 1990) help construct a variety of ideas about appropriate gendered behavior and values not only *about* places but also in them?

Attention to race needs to be grounded in the racialized ideas and lives of students and how geography maintains and/or challenges them. This is because the constructions of race (as is true of gender and class) differences occur and are saturated in specific places, take shape over space, and "create spaces of inequality, fear, powerlessness, and discrimination" (Cope, 1997, p. 96). Issues to examine include how conceptions of spaces and borders—both physical and imagined—work to separate groups, keeping some invisible as they are marked and stereotyped (Johnston, 2002) or how places learned about as well those in which students live (including in their own school) are carved up along racial lines and how different groups construct identities (often oppositional ones) within such places as they get "used" (see Helfenbein, 2004a). Similarly, attention should be paid to how concepts and images used in geography education make real and immediate ideas about race and racism and the degree to which their use "serves to either naturalize, or make normal, or provide the means to challenge racial formations and racist practices" (Schein, 1999, p. 189; see also Domosh, 2000).

Geography and/as citizenship

Most research focusing on citizenship education does not perceive geography as an important factor in that domain, nor does research in geography education see citizenship as its province. But while citizenship may be a political concept, the maintenance and outcome of political processes and affiliations are spatially organized (Morgan, 2000).[5] Further, and regardless of what is taught in geography classrooms or how, geography education is inherently about helping students construct a sense of place, of belonging and affiliation, a basis from which to think of and act in the world—a foundation for citizenship. Whether students see themselves as citizens of a region, a nation, or the world, concepts and affiliations developed in geography classrooms will help determine not only at which scales students will choose to act as citizens, but also how. While today's students are growing up in a global world, to what degree, and how, does geography education prepare students to engage *globalization*—an inherently geographic phenomenon? How is the term used and examined, what forms of it are prevalent in textbooks and classroom discourse, and how do those influence students' understandings of globalization and its impacts (Chilcott, 1991; Conolly, 1996; Heilman, 2003; Kirkwood, 2001; Massey, 2002)? And how, if at all, does the above assist students, not only to make meaning in a global world, but also to live meaningful lives in it, in light of (despite?) the increasing lack of tolerance for those culturally and racially different; the uneven distribution of resources; ethnic conflicts (Chilcott, 1991) that accompany cross-cultural interactions; and the combination of riches, resources, and talents and the advancement in communication resulting from the emergence of the "global village"?

While some research, mostly in global education, has examined how textbooks and curricula position the "Other," we suggest research on who textbook writers believe is their implied reader and how language used creates and positions this reader—the student of geography—as knower (Slater, 1989). Attention should be given to the degree to which descriptions and explanations of social and environmental issues, often as historical "problems" in an otherwise functioning system of governance, invite students either to accept the world as given and beyond required action or to challenge the current order by asking important questions about power, politics, and social justice (Henley, 1989; see also Gilbert, 1989; Huckle, 2002; Kress, 1985). Similarly, we invite research on how writing is used in the geography classroom and the degree to which it allows students to move beyond the scientific, distancing language of the textbook and construct complex understandings of the world and to appropriate alternative—oppositional—spaces, to push boundaries and cross borders (Helfenbein, 2004b; Jones, 1989; Lee, 1996). Proposing that research explore how existing forms of geography education "reflect the identities, values and interests of the groups that have constructed the subject in particular ways" (Morgan, 2000, p. 66), as well as how it might be configured otherwise, can, we believe, help researchers evaluate and reconstruct geography as a subject and, at the same time, examine how it operates to construct its students as subjects.

NOTES

1. Trends similar and different have been felt elsewhere. For example, in England, geography was made a compulsory foundational subject for elementary and secondary students in the 1980s, even though a more recent curricula review resulted in a reduction in geography education in grade 10 (Conolly, 1996). For more on geography education in Britain, see Gardner and Craig (2002) and Morgan (2002). In Australia, geography is mandatory only in New South Wales and only for 100 hours, devoted mostly to Australian geography at some stage in seventh through tenth grades. In Tasmania and Western Australia, as well as in other territories, geography is not available at all in seventh through tenth grades. Seniors can take geography as an elective in all states and territories (Davey, 1996, p. 97). Additional sources of information on geography education include: Switzerland Reinfried, 2000), the Muslim world (Ibrahim & Saarinen, 2000), Korea (Yoon & Atman, 2000), and Canada (Fox, 1997).
2. It should be noted that the term *New Geography* itself is contested as to its relation to the Five Themes of Geography and how they are implemented (see Boehm & Peterson, 1994).
3. While the 2001 NAEP reports only 13% of White grade 4 students Below Basic, 56% of Black students were in that group; 29% of White students were at Proficient or Advanced, compared to only 5% of Black students.
4. Earlier informative reviews include: Boehm and Petersen (1997) on a variety of issues underlying geography education; Stoltman (1991) and Forsyth (1995) on research in geography

education; Stoltman (1997) and R. S. Bednarz (2002) on curriculum and instruction; Bettis (1997) on assessment and reform in geographic education; Bednarz et al. (2003) on the status of geography education; Gregg and Leinhardt (1994) on research on maps; Downs (1994) on the need for research in geography education; Self and Golledge (1994) on sexrelated differences in spatial abilities among students; and Matthews (1992) on children's conception understanding of/in space/place.

5. While international research on civic education (Hahn & Torney-Purta, 1999, Torney-Purta, Lehmann, Oswald, & Schulz, 2001) implies a significant role for geographic education within citizenship education, those connections, they add, are not explicit, and one must read between the lines to find them (Stoltman & DeChano, 2002, p. 141).

REFERENCES

Aitken, S. C. (2001). *Geographies of young people: The morally contested spaces of identity.* London & New York: Routledge.

Anthamatten, P. (2004). State geography standards in 2004. *Journal of Geography 103,* 182–184.

Association of American Geographers. (1998). *Statement on professional ethics.* Retrieved April 2, 2005, from http://www.aag.org/Publications/EthicsStatement.html.

Atwood, V. A., & Atwood, R. K. (1995). Preservice elementary teachers' conceptions of what causes night and day. *School Science and Mathematics, 95,* 290–294.

Audet, R. H. & Abegg, G. L. (1996). Geographic information systems: Implications for problem solving. *Journal of Research in ScienceTeaching, 33*(1), 21–45.

Audet, R. H., & Paris, J. (1997). GIS implementation model for schools: Assessing the critical concerns. *Journal of Geography, 96,* 293–300.

Barnes, T. J., & Duncan, J. S. (Eds.). (1992). *Writing worlds: Discourse, text, and metaphor in the representation of landscape.* London: Routledge.

Barrett Hacking, E. (1996). Novice teachers and their geographical persuasions. *International Research in Geographic and Environmental Education, 5,* 77–86.

Battimer, A. (1993). *Geography and the human spirit.* Baltimore, MD: John Hopkins University Press.

Bednarz, R. S. (2002). The quantity and quality of geography education in the United States: The last 20 years. *International Research in Geographical and Environments Education, 11* (2), 160–170.

Bednarz, S. W. (2003). Nine years on: Examining implementation of the national geography standards. *Journal of Geography, 56*(1), 99–109.

Bednarz, S. W., & Audet, R. H. (1999). The status of GIS in teacher preparation programs. *Journal of Geography, 98*(2), 60–67.

Bednarz, S. W., & Bednarz, R. S. (1995). Preservice geography education. *Journal of Geography, 94,* 482–486.

Bednarz, S. W., Downs, R. M., & Vender, J. C. (2003). Geography education. In G. Gaile & C. Wilmott (Eds.), *Geography in America at the dawn of the 21st-century* (2nd ed., pp. 463–480). Oxford: Oxford University Press.

Bednarz, S. W. & Ludwig, G. (1997). Ten things higher education needs to know about GIS in primary and secondary education. *Transactions in GIS 2*(2), 123–133.

Bein, F. L. (1990). Baseline geography competency test: Administered in Indiana universities. *Journal of Geography, 89,* 260–265.

Berson, M. J., Ouzts, D. T., & Walsh, L. S. (1999). Connecting literature with K–8 national geography standards. *Social Studies, 90*(2), 85-93.

Bettis, N. C. (1995). The renaissance in geography education in the United States, 1974–1994. *International Journal of Social Education, 10*(2), 61–72.

Bettis, N. C. (1997). Assessment and reform in geographic education: 1930–1997. In R. G. Boehm & J. F. Petersen (Eds.), *The first assessment: Research in geography education* (pp. 252–272). San Marcos, TX: The Gilbert M. Grosvenor Center for Geographic Education.

Bhabha, H. (1994). *Location of culture.* London: Routledge.

Binko, J. B., & Neubert, G. A. (1996). *Teaching geography in the disciplines.* Bloomington, IN: Phi Delta Kappa.

Black, J. (1997). *Maps and politics.* Chicago: University of Chicago Press.

Blaut, J. (1997). The mapping abilities of young children. *Annals of the Association of American Geographers, 87*(1), 152–158.

Blaut, J., & Stea, D. (1971). Studies of geographic learning. *Annals of the Association of American Geographers*, 61, 387–393.

Blaut, J., Stea, D., Spencer, C., & Blades, M. (2003). Mapping as a cultural and cognitive universal. *Annals of the Association of American Geographers*, 93(1), 165–185.

Bloom, B. S. (1976). *Human characteristics and school learning*. New York: McGraw Hill.

Bockenhauer, M. (1993). The National Geographic Society's teaching project. *Journal of Geography*, 92(3), 121–124.

Boehm, R. G. (1997). The first assessment: A contextual statement. In R. G. Boehm & J. F. Petersen (Eds.). *The first assessment: Research in geographic education* (pp. 1–17). San Marcos, TX: Grosvenor Center for Geographic Education.

Boehm, R. G. & Bednarz, S. (1994–*Geography for life: National geography standards*. Jacksonville, AL: National Council for Geographic Education.

Boehm, R. G., & Peterson, J. F. (1994). An elaboration of the fundamental themes in geography. *Social Education*, 58 (April-May), 211–232.

Boehm, R. G., & Petersen, J. F. (Eds.). (1997). *The first assessment: Research in geographic education*. San Marcos, TX: Grosvenor Center for Geographic Education.

Broda, H. W., & Baxter, R. E. (2003). Using GIS and GPS technology as an instructional tool. *The Social Studies*, 94(4), 158–160.

Brook, D. L., Field, S. L., & Labbo, L. D. (1995). South Africa's transformation as seen at school. *Social Education*, 59(2), 82–86.

Brophy, J. (1991). Teachers' knowledge of subject matter as it relates to their teaching practice. *Advances on research on teaching* (Vol. 2). Greenwich, CT: JAI Press.

Brophy, J., & Alleman, J. (2005). *Children's thinking about cultural universals*, Mahwah, N.J.: Erlbaum.

Brophy, J., McMahon, S., & Prawat, R. (1991). Elementary social studies series: Critique of a representative example by six experts. *Social Education*, 55, 155–160.

Brown, S. C. (1999). *Teaching with GIS using existing grade 7–12 curricula*. Unpublished doctoral dissertation, State University of New York.

Butler, J. (1993). *Bodies that matter*. New York: Routledge.

Buzer, S. (2002). Geography, technology and culture. In R. Gerber & M. Williams (Eds.), *Geography, culture and education* (pp. 41–50). Boston: Kluwer Academic.

Byklum, D. (2004). Charting a course: Directions in geography education. *Journal of Geography*, 103(5), 220–222.

Catling, S. (2004). An understanding of geography: The perspectives of English primary trainee teachers. *GeoJournal*, 60, 149–158.

Cherry, S. F. (1991). *Action research: Factors influencing recognition of geographical locations on a world map*. (ERIC Document Reproduction Service No. ED 343 825)

Chilcott, J. H. (1991). It is time to change the classroom maps. *The Social Studies*, 82(2), 44–48

Chiodo, J. J. (1993). Mental maps: Preservice teachers' awareness of the world. *Journal of Geography*, 92(3), 110–117.

Cirrincione, J. M., & Farrell, R, T, (1989). The content of the geography curriculum : A teacher's perspective. *Social Education*, 53(2), 105–109.

Collins, C. A., & Lutz, J. L. (1993). *Reading National Geographic*. Chicago: University of Chicago Press.

Conolly, G. (1996). Setting the curriculum: A place for geography. In R. Gerber & J. Lidstone (Eds.), *Developments and directions in geographic education* (pp. 37–51). Clevedon, UK: Channel View Publications.

Cope, M. (1997). Gender and geography: A political geography perspective. *Journal of Geography*, 96(2), 91–97.

Cosgrove, D. (1985). Prospect, perspective and the evolution of the landscape idea. *Transactions of the Institute of British Geographers*, 101(45–62).

Council of State Social Studies Consultants. (2003-2004). *National survey of course offerings and testing in social studies: Kindergarten– grade 12*. Retrieved June 9, 2005, from http://www.cssss.org/pdf/survey2003.pdf.

Cox, M. (1991). *The child's point of view*. New York: Guilford.

Crush, J. (1994). Post-colonialism, de-colonization, and geography. In A. Godlewska & N. Smith (Eds.). *Geography and empire*. Oxford: Blackwell.

Daley, R. (2003). *No geographer left behind: A policy guide to geography education and the No Child Left Behind Act of 2001*. (ERIC Document Reproduction Service No. ED 480174)

Davey, C. (1996). Advancing education through geography: A way forward. In R. Gerber & J. Lidstone (Eds.), *Developments and directions in geographic education* (pp. 93–115). Clevedon, UK: Channel View Publications.

Davies, W., & Gilmartin, M. (2002). Geography as a cultural field. In R. Gerber & M. Williams (Eds.), *Geography, culture and education* (pp. 13–30). Boston: Kluwer Academic.

De Oliver, M. (1998). Geography, race and class: A case study of the role of geography at an urban public university. *American Journal of Education, 106*, 273–301.

Deutsche, R. (1990, February). Men in space. *Artforum*, pp. 21–23.

Domosh, M. (2000). Cultural patterns and processes in advanced placement human geography. *Journal of Geography, 99*(3/4), 111–119.

Donaldson, D. P. (2001). With a little help from our friends: Implementing geographic information systems (GIS) in K-12 schools. *Social Education, 65*(3), 147–150.

Downs, R. M. (1994). The need for research in geography education: It would be nice to have some data. *Journal of Geography, 93*(1), 57–60.

Downs, R. M., & Liben, L. S. (1988). Through a map darkly: Understanding maps as representations. *Genetic Epistemologies, 16*, 11–18.

Downs, R. M., Liben, L., S., & Daggs, D. G. (1988). On education and geographers: The role of cognitive development theory in geographic education. *Annals of the Association of American Geographers, 78*(4), 680–700.

Edwards, G. (2001). A very British subject: Questions of identity. In D. Lambert & P. Machon (Eds.). *Citizenship through secondary geography* (pp. 109–121). London and New York: Routledge.

Eve, R. A., Price, B., & Counts, M. (1994). Geographic illiteracy among college students. *Youth and Society, 25*, 408–427.

Farrell, R. T., & Cirrincione, J. M. (1989). The content of the geography curriculum: A teacher's perspective. *Social Education, 53*(2), 105–108.

Fitzhugh. P. (1992, May). Geography needs assessment: A focus on teacher training and awareness. Paper presented at the annual conference of the National Council for Geographic Education. Santo Domingo, Dominican Republic. (ERIC Document Reproduction Service No. ED 355134)

Forsyth, A. (1995). Learning geography: An annotated bibliography of research paths. In *Pathways in geography* series (Title no. 11). Indiana, PA: National Council for Geographic Education.

Fox, M. (1997). Hope of a ripple effect: A Canadian perspective on geography in the curriculum. In R. G. Boehm & J. F. Petersen (Eds.). *The first assessment: Research in geography education* (pp. 191–200). San Marcos, TX: The Gilbert M. Grosvenor Center for Geographic Education.

Franeck, M. A., Nelson, B. D., Aron, R. H., & Bisard, W. J. (1993). The persistence of selected geographic misconceptions: A study of junior high through undergraduate college students. *Journal of Geography, 93*(6), 247–253.

Gandy, S. K., & Kruger, D. P. (2004). An assessment of influences on the implementation of the national geography standards. *Journal of Geography, 103*(4), 161–170.

Gallavan, N. P., & Knowles-Yanez, K. (2004). Co-mingling geographic education with social studies methods. *Journal of Geography, 103*, 64–75.

Gardner, R., & Craig, L. (2002). Is geography history? In M. Smith (Ed.). *Teaching geography in secondary schools: A reader* (pp. 273–279). London: Routledge/The Open University Press.

Gay, S. M. (1995). Making the connections: Infusing the National Geography Standards into the classroom. *Journal of Geography, 94*(5), 459–461.

Geography Education Standards Project (1994). *Geography for life: National geography standards*. Washington, D.C.: National Geographic Society.

Gerber, R. (1995). Geographical education for life based on technological and graphic literacy. *Geographical Education, 8*, 50–56.

Gersmehl, P. J. (1992). Themes and counterpoints in geographic education. *Journal of Geography, 91* (3), 119–123.

Gilbert, R. (1989). Language and ideology in geography teaching. In F. Slater (Ed.), *Language and learning in the teaching of geography* (pp. 151–161). London & New York: Routledge.

Gilsbach, M. T. (1997). Improvement needed: Preservice geography teacher education. *Social Studies, 88*, 35–38.

Goodchild, M. (1993). Ten years ahead: Dobson's automated geography in 1993. *The Professional Geographer, 45*, 444–446.

Gregg, M. (1997). Problem posing from maps: Utilizing understanding. *Journal of Geography,* *96,* 250–256.

Gregg, M. (1999). Mapping success: Reversing the Matthew effect. *Research in Geographic Education, 1*(2), 118–135.

Gregg, M., & Leinhardt, G. (1993). Geography in history: What is the where? *Journal of Geography, 92* 56–63.

Gregg, M, & Leinhardt, G. (1994). Mapping out geography: An example of epistemology and education. *Review of Educational Research, 64*(2), 311–361.

Gregory, D. (1978). *Ideology, science, and human geography.* London: Hutchinson.

Gregory, D. (1994). *Geographical imaginations.* Oxford: Blackwell.

Gregory. D. (1995). Imaginative geographies. *Progress in Human Geography, 19,* 447–485.

Gregson, N., Rose, G., Cream, J., & Laurie, N. (1997). Conclusions. In Women and Geography Study Group (Eds.), *Feminist geographies: Explorations in diversity and difference* (pp. 191–200). London: Longman.

Grosvenor, G. M. (1995). In sight of the tunnel: The renaissance of geography education. *Annals of the Association of American Geographers, 85*(3), 409–420.

Hahn, C., & Torney-Purta, J. (1999). The IEA civic education project: national and international perspectives. *Social Education, 65*(7), 425–431.

Hanson, S., & Pratt, G. (1995). *Gender, work and space.* New York: Routledge.

Harley, J. (1988). Maps, knowledge, and power. In D. Cosgrove & S. Daniels (Eds.), *The iconography of the landscape* (pp.277–312). Cambridge: Cambridge University Press.

Harper, R. A. (1990). Geography's role in general education. *Journal of Geography, 89*(5), 214–218.

Harper, R. A. (1992). At issue: What is geography's contribution to general education. *Journal of Geography, 91*(3), 124–125.

Harvey, D. (1973). *Social justice and the city.* London: Edward Arnold.

Harwood, D., & McShane, J. (1996). Young children's understanding of nested hierarchies of place relationships. *International Research in Geographic and Environmental Education, 5,* 3–29.

Heilman, E. (2003). How does the world work? Economic globalization in popular middle school textbooks. In L. Allen, D. Breault, D. Cartner, B. Setser, M. Hayes, R. Gaztambide-Fernandez, & K. Krasney (Eds.), *Third Curriculum and Pedagogy Conference (Decatur, GA): Curriculum and pedagogy for peace and sustainability.* Troy, NY: Educator's International Press.

Helfenbein, R. (2004a). Mapping space, place, and identity: A critical geography of the WELL–Unpublished doctoral dissertation, University of North Carolina-Chapel Hill.

Helfenbein, R. (2004b). A radical geography: Curriculum theory, performance, and landscape. *Journal of Curriculum Theorizing, 20*(3), 67–75.

Henley, R. (1989). The ideology of geographical language. In F. Slater (Ed.), *Language and learning in the teaching of geography* (pp. 162–171). London & New York: Routledge.

Henrie, R. L., Aron, R. H., Nelson, B. D., & Poole, D. A. (1997). Gender-related knowledge variations within geography. *Sex Roles, 36*(9/10), 605–623.

Hickey, G. M., & Bein, F. L. (1996). Students' learning difficulties in geography and teachers' interventions: Teaching cases from K-12 classrooms. *Journal of Geography, 95*(3), 118–125.

Huckle, J. (2002). Toward a critical school geography. In M. Smith (Ed.). *Teaching geography in secondary schools: A reader* (pp. 255–265). London: Routledge/The Open University Press.

Ibrahim, M. B., & Saarinen, T. S. (2000). The role of geographic education in shaping the Muslim image of the world. *Research in Geographic Education, 2*(2), 25–52.

Jackson, P. (1989). *Maps of meaning: An introduction to cultural geography.* London: Routledge.

Johnston, L. (2002). Borderline bodies. In L. Bondi, H. Avis, R. Bankey, A. Bingley, J. Davidson, R. Duffy, et al. (Eds.), *Subjectivities, knowledges, and feminist geographies* (pp. 75–89). London: Rowan & Littlefield.

Jones, A. (1989). The feeling tone of childhood: Children writing about their environment. In F. Slater (Ed.). *Language and learning in the teaching of geography* (pp. 141–148). London & New York: Routledge.

Kaiser, W. L., & Wood, D. (2001)–*Seeing through maps: The power of images to shape our world view.* Amherst, MA.: ODT.

Kaufman, M. (2004). Using spatial-temporal primitives to improve geographic skills for preservice teachers. *Journal of Geography, 103*(4), 171–181.

Keiper, T. A. (1996). Introducing a geographic information system to an elementary classroom: A case study. Unpublished doctoral dissertation, University of Missouri-Columbia.

Keiper, T. A. (1999). GIS for elementary students: An inquiry into a new approach to learning geography. *Journal of Geography, 98*(2), 47–59.

Kerski, J. J. (2000). The implementation and effectiveness of geographic information systems technology and methods in secondary education. Unpublished doctoral dissertation, University of Colorado at Boulder.

Kirkwood, T. F. (2001). Our global age requires global education: Clarifying definitional ambiguity. *The Social Studies, 92*(1), 10–15.

Kirman, J. M. (2003). Transformative geography: Ethics and action in elementary and secondary geography education. *Journal of Geography, 102,* 93–98.

Klein, P. H. (1997). Knowing and teaching geography: A qualitative study of pedagogical content knowledge and schemata in expert and novice teachers. Unpublished doctoral dissertation, Georgia State University.

Kress, G. (1985). *Linguistic processes in sociocultural practice.* Deakin, Vic.: Deakin University Press.

Lambert, D. (2002). Geography and the informed citizen. In R. Gerber & M. Williams (Eds.). *Geography, culture and education* (pp. 93–103). Boston: Kluwer Academic Publishers.

Lash, J. W. (2004). Finding our place: Thoughts on the value of geography. *Journal of Geography, 103*(5), 222–224.

Lash, J., & Wridt, P. (2002). Geography, culture and knowing: Hybridity and the production of social and cultural knowledge. In G. R. & M. Williams (Eds.). *Geography, culture and education.* Dordrecth, Netherlands: Kluwer Academic Publishers, GeoJournal Library Series.

Laws, G. (1994). Oppression, knowledge, and the built environment. *Political Geography, 13*(1), 7–32.

Lee, A. (1996). *Gender, literacy, curriculum: Re-writing school geography.* London: Taylor & Francis.

Lefebvre, H. (1991). *The production of space* (D. Nicholson-Smith, trans.). Oxford: Basil Blackwell.

Leinhardt, G., Stainton, C., & Merriman Bausmith, J. (1998). Constructing maps collaboratively. *Journal of Geography, 97*(1), 19–30.

LeVasseur, M. L. (1999a). *An analysis of selected barriers to achievement levels in geography of female students in grade six and grade nine.* Unpublished doctoral dissertation, University of South Florida.

LeVasseur, M. L. (1999b). Students' knowledge of geography and geographic careers. *Journal of Geography, 98*(6), 265–271.

Liben, L., & Downs, R. M. (1989). Understanding maps as symbols: The development of map concepts in children. *Advances in Child Development and Behavior–22,* 145–201.

Liben, L., & Downs, R. M. (1997). Can-ism and can'tianism: A straw child. *Annals of the Association of American Geographers, 87*(1), 159–167.

Linn, S. E. (1997). The effectiveness of interactive maps in the classroom: A selected example in studying Africa. *Journal of Geography, 96,* 164–170.

Lloyd, R., & Bunch, R. L. (2003). Technology and map-learning: Users, methods, and symbols. *Annals of the Association of American Geographers, 93*(4), 828–850.

MacEachren, A. (1995). *How maps work.* New York: Guilford.

Mackenzie, G., & Sawyer, J. (1986). Effects of testlike practice and mnemonics on learning geographic facts. *Theory and Research in Social Education, 14*(3), 201–209.

Marker, G., & Mehlinger, H. (1992). Social studies. In P. W. Jackson (Ed.), *Handbook of research on curriculum* (9th ed., pp. 830–851). New York: Macmillan.

Marran, J. F. (1994). Discovering innovative curricular models for school geography. In R. S. Bednarz & J. F. Petersen (Eds.). *A decade of reform in geographic education: Inventory and prospect* (pp. 23–30). Indiana, PA: National Council for Geographic Education.

Martin, F. (2000). Postgraduate primary education students' images of geography and the relationship between these and students' teaching. *International Research in Geographical and Environmental Education, 9,* 223–244.

Massey, D. (1991). A global sense of place. *Marxism Today* (June), 24–29.

Massey, D. (1994). *Space, place, and gender.* Minneapolis: University of Minnesota Press.

Massey, D. (2002). Geography matters in a global world. In M. Smith (Ed.), *Teaching geography in secondary schools: A reader* (pp. 266–272). London: Routledge/The Open University Press.

Matthews, M. H. (1992). *Making sense of place: Children's understanding of large-scale environments.* Savage, MD: Barnes & Noble.

Mehler, J., & Dupoux, E. (1994). *What infants know.* Oxford: Blackwell.

Merriman Bausmith, J., & Leinhardt, G. (1998). Middle-school students' map construction: Understanding complex spatial displays. *Journal of Geography, 97*(3), 93–107.

Mitchell, W. J. T. (1994). Introduction. In W. J. T. Mitchell (Ed.), *Landscape and power*(pp. 1–4). Chicago: University of Chicago Press.

Momsen, J. H. (2000). Gender differences in environmental concern and perception. *Journal of Geography, 99*(2), 47–56.

Monk, J. (1999). Geography: Whose world is it? *Journal of Geography, 98*(6), 250–252.

Monmonier, M. (1991). *How to lie with maps.* Chicago: University of Chicago Press.

Morgan, J. (2000). To which space do I belong? Imagining citizenship in one curriculum subject. *The Curriculum Journal, 11*(1), 55–68.

Morgan, J. (2002). Constructing school geographies. In M. Smith (Ed.). *Teaching geography in secondary schools: A reader* (pp. 40–59). London: Routledge/The Open University Press.

Mosely, W. G. (2001). Computer assisted comprehension of distant world: Understanding hunger dynamics in Africa. *Journal of Geography,100*, 32–45.

National Assessment of Educational Progress (2001). *NAEP 2001 geography report card*–Washington, D.C.: U.S. Department of Education: National Center for Educational Statistics.

National Geographic Society (1988). *Geography: An international Gallup survey.* Princeton, NJ: The Gallup Organization.

Natoli, S. J. (1994). Guidelines for geographic education and the fundamental themes in geography. *Journal of Geography, 93*(1), 2–6.

Nellis, D. M. (1995). Geography for life: Today's innovations as tomorrow's traditions. *Journal of Geography, 94*, 302–304.

Osborne, B. S. (1998). Some thoughts on landscape: Is it a noun, a metaphor, or a verb? *Canadian Social Studies, 32*(3), 93–97.

Osunde, E. O., Tlou, J., & Brown, N. J. (1996). Persisting and common stereotypes in U.S. students' knowledge of Africa: A study of preservice social studies teachers. *The Social Studies, 87*(3), 119–124.

Page, K. R. (1994). *The practice of geography instruction in American schools.* Unpublished doctoral dissertation, Kansas State University.

Pahl, R. H. (1995). The image of Africa in our classrooms. *The Social Studies, 86*(6), 245–247.

Patrick, J. J. (1993). *Achievement of goal three of the six national education goals.* (ERIC Document Reproduction Service No. ED 360 221)

Petersen, J. F., Natoli, S. J., & Boehm, R. G. (1994). The guidelines for geographic education: A ten-year retrospective. *Social Education, 58*(4), 206–210.

Plumwood, V. (1993). *Feminism and the mastery of nature.* London: Routledge.

Pratt, G. (1992). *Imperial eyes: Travel writing and transculturation.* London: Routledge.

Rallis, D. N., & Rallis, H. (1995). Changing the image of geography. *The Social Studies, 86*(4), 167–168.

Rieser, J., Doxsey, P., McCarrell, N., & Brooks, P. (1986). Wayfinding and toddlers' use of information from an aerial view of a maze. *Developmental Psychology, 18*, 714–720.

Robertson, M., & Taplin, M. (2000). Aerial photography, place related behaviour and children's thinking. *Research in Geographic Education, 2*(1), 37–61.

Rogers, L. K. (1997). *An examination of elementary teachers' knowledge of geography and geographic education.* Unpublished doctoral dissertation. State University of New York at Binghamton.

Rose, G. (1993). *Feminism and geography: The limits of geographical knowledge.* Cambridge, UK: Polity Press.

Rose, G., Kinnaird, V., Morris, M., & Nash, C. (1997). Feminist geographies of environment, nature and landscape. In Women and Geography Study Group (Eds.). *Feminist geographies: Explorations in diversity and difference* (pp. 146–190). London: Longman.

Saarinen, T. (1999). The Eurocentric nature of mental maps of the world. *Research in Geographic Education, 1*(2), 136–178.

Sack, D., & Petersen, J. F. (1998). Children's attitudes toward geography: A Texas case study. *Journal of Geography, 97*(3), 123–131.

Said, E. (1978). *Orientalism.* New York: Vintage.

Salter, C. L. (1986). Geography and California's educational reform: One approach to a common cause. *Annals of the Association of American Geographers, 76*(1), 5–17.

Saunders, R. H. (1999). Teaching rap: The politics of race in the classroom. *Journal of Geography, 98*(4), 185–188.

Schein, R. H. (1999). Teaching "race" and the cultural landscape. *Journal of Geography, 98*(4), 188–190.

Schoenfeldt, M. (2000). Spatial cognition of preservice teachers. *Research in Geographic Education, 2*(1), 18–36.

Scott, T. J. (1999). Student perceptions of the developing world" Minimizing stereotypes of the "Other." *The Social Studies, 90*(6), 262–265.

Seastrom, M. M., Gruber, K. J., Robin Henke, R., McGrath, D. J., & Cohen, B. A. (2002). *Qualifications of the public school teacher workforce: Prevalence of out-of-field teaching 1987–88 to 1999–2000.* (NCES 2002603). Retrieved April 2, 2005, from http://www. ncs.ed.gov/pubsearch/pubsinfo.asp?pubid=2002603

Segall, A. (2002). What do prospective social studies teachers in the U.S. know about Canada? *Michigan Journal of Social Studies, 14*(1), 7–10.

Segall, A. (2003) Maps as stories about the world. *Social Studies and the Young Learner, 16* (1), 21–25.

Self, C. M., & Golledge, R. G. (1994). Sex-related differences in spatial ability: What every geography educator should know. *Journal of Geography, 93*(5), 234–243.

Shiva, V. (1989). *Staying alive: Women, ecology and development.* London: Zed Press.

Silvey, R. (1998). Ecofeminism in geography. *Ethics, Place and Environment, 1,* 243–251.

Slater, F. (1989). Language and learning. In F. Slater (Ed.), *Language and learning in the teaching of geography* (pp. 11–38). London & New York: Routledge.

Slater, F. (2001). Values and values education in the geography curriculum in relation to concepts of citizenship. In D. Lambert & P. Machon (Eds.), *Citizenship through secondary geography* (pp. 42–67). London and New York: Routledge.

Shiva, V. (1989). *Staying alive: Women, ecology and development.* London: Zed Press.

Silvey, R. (1998). Ecofeminism in geography. *Ethics, Place and Environment, 1,* 243–251.

Smith, J. S. (2001). The influence of sex, spatial activity, geographic setting and geographic landscape on adolescent spatial abilities. *Research in Geographic Education, 3*(1&2), 107–117.

Smith, M. (2002). Inclusion in geography. In M. Smith (Ed.), *Teaching geography in secondary schools: A reader* (pp. 182–199). London: Routledge/The Open University Press.

Soja, E. W. (1996). *Thirdspace journeys to Los Angeles and other real and imagined places.* Cambridge, MA: Blackwell.

Sosniak, L. A., & Stodolsky, S. S. (1993). Making connections: Social studies education in an urban fourth-grade classroom. In J. Brophy (Ed.), *Advances in research on teaching (Volume 4): Case studies of teaching and learning in social studies* (pp. 71–100). Greenwich, CT: JAI Press.

Sowden, S., Stea, D., Blades, M., Spencer, C., & Blaut, J. (1996). Mapping abilities of four-year-old children in York, England. *Journal of Geography, 95,* 107–111.

Spencer, C. Blades, M., & Morsley, K. (1989). *The child in the physical environment: The development of spatial knowledge and cognition.* New York: John Wiley.

Stoddard, R. H. (1997). The world as a multilevel mosaic: Understanding regions. *Social Studies, 88*(4), 167–172.

Stoltman, J. P. (1991). Research on geography teaching. In J. P. Shaver (Ed.), *Handbook of research on social studies teaching and learning* (pp. 437–447). New York: Macmillan.

Stoltman, J. P. (1997). Geography curriculum and instruction research since 1950 in the United State. In R. G. Boehm & J. F. Petersen (Eds.), *The first assessment: Research in geography education* (pp. 131–170). San Marcos, TX: The Gilbert M. Grosvenor Center for Geographic Education.

Stoltman, J. P. (2002). *The 2001 National Assessment of Educational Progress in Geography.* ERIC Digest. ERIC Clearinghouse for Social Studies/Social Science Education, Bloomington, IN. (ERIC Document Reproduction Service No. ED468593, http://www.ericdigests. org/2003-3/2001.htm)

Stoltman, J., & DeChano, L. (2002). Political geography, geographical education, and citizenship. In R. Gerber & M. Williams (Eds.), *Geography, culture and education* (pp. 127–143). Boston: Kluwer Academic.

Sunal, C., Christensen, L., & Haas, M. (1995). Using the five themes of geography to teach about Venezuela. *The Social Studies, 86*(4), 169–174.

Sunal, C., & Haas, M. (1993). *Social studies for the elementary and middle school student.* Fort Worth, TX: Harcourt, Brace, Javanovich.

Thomas, L., & Willinsky, J. (1999). Grounds for imagining a Pacific community: Mapping across boundaries and great divides. *Journal of Geography, 98*(1), 1–13.

Thompson, D., Lindsay, F., Davis, P., & Wong, D. (1997). Towards a framework for learning with GIS: The case of Urban World, a hypermap learning environment based on GIS. *Transactions in GIS, 2*, 151–167.

Thornton, S. J. (2003, November). *Placing geography: Moving beyond the past in social studies education*. Paper presented at the annual meeting of the National Council for the Social Studies, Chicago.

Thornton, S. J., & Wenger, R. N. (1990). Geography curriculum and instruction in three fourth-grade classrooms. *The Elementary School Journal, 90*(5), 515–531.

Torney-Purta, J. Lehmann, R., Oswald, H., & Schulz, W. (2001). *Citizenship and education in twenty-eight countries: Civic knowledge and engagement at age fourteen*. Amsterdam: International Association of the Evaluation of Educational Achievement.

Trygestad, J. (1997, March). Students' conceptual thinking in geography. Paper presented at the annual meeting of the American Educational Research Association, Chicago.

van der Schee, J., van Dijk, H., & van Westrhenen, H. (1992). Geographical procedural knowledge and map skills. In H. Schrettenbrunner & J. van Westrhenen (Eds.), *Empirical research and geography teaching*. Utrecht: Koninklijk Nederlands Aardrijkskundig.

Walford, R. (1996). "What is geography?" An analysis of definitions provided by prospective teachers of the subject. *International Research in Geographical and Environmental Education, 5*, 69–76.

Warren, K. J. (1990). The power and the promise of ecological feminism. *Environmental Ethics, 12*, 125–146.

Weedon, C. (1999). *Feminism, theory and the politics of difference*. Oxford: Blackwell.

Weiss, A. R., Lutkus, A. D., Hildebrant, B. S., & Johnson, M. S. (2002). *NAEP 2001 geography report card*. Washington, D.C.: National Center for Education Statistics, Office of Educational Research and Improvement, U.S. Department of Education.

Willinsky, J. (1998). *Learning to divide the world: Education at empire's end*. Minneapolis: University of Minnesota Press.

Wolfe, L. J. E. (2002). Geography inservice education programs, teacher beliefs and practices, and student outcomes. Unpublished doctoral dissertation, Emory University, Atlanta, GA.

Wood, D. (1992). *The power of maps*. New York: Guilford.

Wridt, P. (1999). The worlds of girls and boys: Geographic experience and informal learning opportunities. *Journal of Geography, 98*(6), 253–264.

Wridt, P. (2001). Changing communities, changing childhoods: Playing, living and learning in New York City from the 1940s–2000s. *Research in Geographic Education, 3*(1&2), 113–117.

Yoon, S. H., & Atman, K. S. (2000). Learning styles and academic achievement in middle school geography students in Korea. *Research in Geographic Education, 2*(1), 1–17.

Zam, G. A., & Howard, D. G. (2005). Bridging the gap: Between geography and education standards at the University of Toledo. *Journal of Geography, 104*, 25–34.

16 Recent research on the teaching and learning of pre-collegiate economics

Steven L. Miller
The Ohio State University

Phillip J. VanFossen
Purdue University

INTRODUCTION

Why is economic literacy important? What is meant by economic literacy? How and where is economics taught in schools? What do we know about the effectiveness of various instructional approaches in teaching economics? These are among the questions this chapter addresses. The chapter begins by revisiting the conclusions and recommendations from the chapter on economic education by Schug and Walstad found in the 1991 edition of the *Handbook of Research on Social Studies Teaching and Learning* (hereafter, *Handbook*) to provide some context for interpreting more recent research. In the next major section, we revisit the case for economic literacy, seeking any new elements from advocates of economic education, and then what economic literacy means, in order to determine what economics students should be learning. Discoveries here lead to an examination of the curriculum to determine what economics content schools are attempting to implement, and to research on how well teachers are prepared to teach that curriculum. Next, this review summarizes research on student learning of economics, followed by a section on research about economics instruction in schools and a brief review of some of the research on economic education in countries with transition economies (e.g., nations of the former Soviet Union). The chapter concludes with a summary and recommendations for further research.

This review follows the formulation of Schug and Walstad (1991) concerning what research to include (p. 411). First, the focus is on major topics addressed by researchers in economic education; thus, not every issue is addressed. For example, the growing literature on student financial literacy and entrepreneurship education has been omitted since the content associated with these areas (which some in economic education do regard as part of the field) is typically not considered "social studies." For example, the "Thematic Strands" of the National Council for the Social Studies social studies standards contain no reference to common financial literacy topics (National Council for the Social Studies, 1994). Second, this review focuses primarily on sources that are readily available. We agree with our colleagues that most of the important findings in the field are not typically located in obscure sources. Third, our review concentrates on research in grades K–12. While there is an abundant and growing research literature on economics teaching and learning at the post-secondary level, especially in the principles courses, the focus of this volume is on elementary and secondary schools. We should also note that this review emphasizes research published since the last edition of the *Handbook*. The Schug and Walstad chapter was a comprehensive summary of economic education research through 1990, and therefore this review only occasionally includes references to earlier literature, typically to provide needed context.

One place to begin our updated review is to recall the status of research in economic education as Schug and Walstad saw it in 1991. They found significant progress in research about economics teaching and learning, but also some glaring gaps. They reached three major conclusions:

1. "Researchers have developed useful measures of economic knowledge and attitudes that have been normed using large national samples" (p. 417).
2. Some studies have shown that economic inservice programs for teachers resulted in gains in economic knowledge of both teachers and their students.
3. Studies provided information on how students who had not had economics reason about economic issues and problems, potentially useful information in the revision of curricula.

As we review more recent research, we should bear in mind the suggestions Schug and Walstad made for further research (1991, p. 417):

1. Research was needed to better determine the emphasis in economics curricula, especially between a focus on the learning of basic concepts versus the use of economic reasoning.
2. There was a great need for research on the effectiveness of different methods of instruction in teaching particular concepts at different grade levels, e.g. how the concept of demand might best be taught to sixth-graders.
3. Despite the research on how students reason with various economic concepts, many concepts had not been studied, especially in macroeconomics.
4. There was a need for researchers to rely less on state departments of education and teachers' self reports for research findings and to engage in more direct observation of classrooms.

WHY IS ECONOMIC LITERACY IMPORTANT?

The fundamental case for economic literacy—and by association, the definition of economic literacy—has changed only slightly in the decades since economic education emerged as a distinct area of study, as we will show in detail later. In the last *Handbook*, Schug and Walstad cited Stigler's two "basic reasons" that make the case for economic literacy "compelling:"

> *First*, we are a nation of people who want to think and talk about economic issues. These issues affect us in our roles as consumers, workers, producers, and citizens. Individuals and the nation benefit from education in the concepts, method, and logic that help in the analysis of economic issues. *Second*, economic decisions are made on a daily basis. In our society, the ability to apply an economic perspective to public and private concerns is an essential skill for all citizens. (Schug & Walstad, 1991, p. 411. Italics in the original)

It is worth emphasizing the salient characteristics of this case, as they recur in some version in almost every statement of the case for economic literacy:

- the value of economics in the various roles people play in society (e.g., consumers, savers, investors);

- the benefits of economic literacy to citizenship and decision-making on public issues;
- the importance of the application of economics and of economic reasoning, not merely knowledge of economic facts or concepts;
- the ubiquitous nature of economic phenomena.

These four themes appear again in one of the most recent and significant statements of the case for economic literacy. The introduction to the *Voluntary National Content Standards in Economics* (hereafter referred to simply as *Standards*) states:

> The principles of economics bear directly on the ordinary business of life, affecting people in their roles as consumers and producers. Economics also plays an important role in local, state, national, and international public policy. Economic issues frequently influence voters in national, state, and local elections. A better understanding of economics enables people to understand the forces that affect them every day, and helps them identify and evaluate the consequences of private decisions and public policies. Many institutions of a democratic market economy function more effectively when its citizens are articulate and well informed about economics. (National Council on Economic Education, 1997, p. 1)

The emphasis on citizenship and reasoning has been especially prominent in many statements of the case for economic literacy. For example, the American Economic Association's National Task Force on Economic Education (Bach et al., 1961) concluded that "everyone must, to some extent, act as his own economist... both he (sic) and the community will be better served if he is well informed and can think clearly and objectively about economic questions" (p. 13). Walstad (1998) concluded that the "development of basic economic literacy is an important goal for a democratic society that relies heavily on informed citizenry and personal economic decision-making."

It is significant to notice that some recent statements of the case for economic literacy have added two new dimensions to the rationale. The first is the claim that economic literacy actually enhances the functioning of a market system and democracy. Consider this statement from Alice Rivlin (1999), former Vice Chair of the Federal Reserve Board:

> First, a free market economy works well only when the participants—producers, consumers, savers, investors—have the information they need to make intelligent decisions... Second, democracy works well only when citizens participate, vote and make their views known to public officials... Without a basic understanding of how the economy works, what the essential terms and concepts are, the average citizen is likely to feel completely left out of any conversation, whether in the media or around the water cooler, about what is happening in the economy and what to do about it.

The introduction to the *Standards* noted above echoes this argument: "Many institutions of a democratic market economy function more effectively when its citizens are articulate and well informed about economics" (National Council on Economic Education, 1997). Interestingly, VanFossen (2000) found high school economics teachers actually held a range of goals and rationales, some that were incompatible with the widely held rationales noted above. Three broad themes emerged: high school economics as preparation for college economics, economics as life skills, and economics as good citizenship.

One might speculate that the emergence of the liberated republics of the former Soviet Union and satellite nations has heightened awareness of the role of economic literacy as an element in the transition process as the West has attempted to encourage these nations to convert to *both* democratic forms of government and market-oriented economies. The relationship between market economies and democracy has been presented by many scholars. (Dahl, 1990; Friedman, 1982; Patrick, 1996)

Another significant addition to the case for economic literacy in recent years is the recognition of the emergence of the global economy. For example, Miller (1993–94) argued the case for what he referred to as "global economic education" (p. 49). While earlier statements of the need for economic literacy seldom contained any reference to the world beyond the United States, emphasizing instead the benefits to American society, the more recent introduction to the *Standards* quoted above contains the explicit reference to the importance of economics in "international public policy."

WHAT ECONOMICS IS WORTH KNOWING?

What economic knowledge and understanding are essential for effective citizenship? What economic content and reasoning skills must citizens master in order to enhance the workings of a market system, to encourage democracy, or to participate in decisions related to international public policy? In their 1991 *Handbook* chapter, Schug and Walstad described a set of economic ideas that were worth knowing, beginning with the 1961 Task Force on Economic Education (TFEE) report noted above (Bach et al., 1961). The TFEE report described the "minimum understanding of economics essential for good citizenship and attainable by high school students" and recommended that high school students should master approximately 45 economic concepts (p. 4).

The TFEE report led directly to the creation of the Joint (now National) Council on Economic Education's *Framework for Teaching the Basic Concepts* (Hansen et al. 1977). The *Framework* distilled the TFEE's 45 economic concepts to a "set of 24 content categories (that) became the guide for numerous curriculum development efforts" (Schug & Walstad, 1991, p. 412). In its final revision (Saunders & Gilliard, 1995) the *Framework* was narrowed to 21 basic economic concepts in four general concept areas: fundamental, microeconomic, macroeconomic, and international.

As Schug and Walstad reported, however, this concept-based approach in the *Framework* has been criticized for a number of shortcomings. These included:

> ...a weak treatment of ideology (Heilbroner, 1987), the omission of significant microeconomic theory (Strober, 1987), an unrealistic view of international trade (Culbertson, 1987), and the fractured presentation of macroeconomics. (Galbraith, 1987).... (Schug & Walstad, 1991, p. 412)

In response to these criticisms, alternatives to the concept-based approach to economic literacy were proposed—specifically that the goal of economic education (and thus economic literacy) should be to help students learn to reason with economics, to develop the "economic way of thinking" (Wentworth 1987; Wentworth & Western, 1990). Dahl (1998) characterized this approach to economic literacy when he argued that in order to "evaluate trade-offs and reason economically," people must grasp six key ideas that form the foundation of an economic way of thinking (p. 2):

1. There is no such thing as a free lunch.
2. Thinking incrementally.
3. Markets coordinate consumption and production.

4. Relative price changes guide decision making.
5. Trade promotes growth.
6. Markets can fail.

The presence of this alternative approach led to Schug and Walstad's call for more research, noted earlier in this chapter; specifically to conduct studies comparing curriculum derived from each model.

Voluntary National Content Standards in Economics   One more evolution in defining economic literacy occurred in 1997, with the publication of the National Council on Economic Education (NCEE's) *Standards*. The *Standards* were developed to guide school districts, curriculum developers, and ultimately teachers in determining what content in economics should be taught and when (Meszaros & Siegfried, 1997, p. 324). The *Standards*—produced by a broad coalition including academic economists, economic educators, and various national organizations—consist of what economists call principles of economics rather than required performance levels on certain criteria (Siegfried & Meszaros, 1998). As such, they represented "the fundamental propositions of economics" (Siegfried & Meszaros, 1998, p. 139). The writing committee used six criteria to develop the *Standards*: (1) The economic concepts included had to be deemed essential; (2) The standards must reflect consensus in the discipline; (3) Standards had to be clearly stated; (4) Standards needed to reflect the best scholarship in economics; (5) Each standard was to be challenging, but attainable by 95% of high school graduates; and (6) Each standard had benchmarks that could be measured (Siegfried & Meszaros, 1998).

The *Standards* are primarily conceptual, and each consists of "an essential principle of economics that an economically literate student should understand and is accompanied by a statement of what that student should be able to do with that knowledge upon leaving" 4th, 8th, or 12th grades" (Siegfried & Meszaros, 1998, p. 141–142). The document contains 20 such standards (see Meszaros & Siegfried, 1997 for complete descriptions). While it remains true that the *Standards* continue to be voluntary, they have essentially replaced the *Framework* as the de facto definition of economic literacy. For example, all of the more recent classroom materials published by the NCEE reference the *Standards*.

As with the *Framework*, the *Standards* have not been without their critics (Becker, 1998). Pennar (1997) criticized the *Standards* as being too simplistic to be of much use. Hansen (1998) questioned whether the six criteria outlined above had indeed been met. For example, he argued that the focus on brevity would leave readers questioning what the *Standards* were all about and that "a major difficulty is the ambivalence about the meaning of the standards" (p. 151). Echoing Wentworth's (1987) critique of the *Framework* document, Hansen also expressed concern that the "almost exclusive focus on principles-based standards in economics ignores the need for an explicit skill standard" (p. 152). Others have called into question the assumption that general consensus (the second criterion) actually exists in the field of economics. For example, Fuller and Geide-Stevenson (2003) analyzed data from a 2000 survey of members of the American Economic Association. They found that while significant, broad consensus among economists did exist in some areas (e.g., the general efficiency of markets in allocating resources), "the degree of consensus varies between propositions that are international, macroeconomic, and microeconomic in nature" and that "macroeconomic propositions exhibit a lower degree of consensus" (p. 369).

However, disagreement among economists in the 2000 AEA survey related more to the complex economic theory found at the college level than to the more fundamental economics principles for K–12 students found in the *Standards*. The *Standards* are supported as meeting the criterion of "general consensus" by the diverse committee that drafted them and by the committee that designed the economics assessment for the National Assessment of Educational Progress, as noted later in this chapter.

Personal Finance and Consumer Economics Standards Traditionally, personal finance education (or consumer economics) has not been a part of the suggested content of economic education. Calderwood, Lawrence, and Maher (1970) summarized this distinction by concluding that "economics is not the same as personal finance" and that "although the consumer plays a vital role in the economy, an exclusive devotion to 'wise buying' or how to open a savings account is not itself 'economics'" (p. 4). Moreover, the *Standards* contain no explicit mention of personal finance or consumer economics.

More recently, however, "the chorus of advocates for more financial literacy grows louder every day" (Morton, 2005, p. 66). Among this chorus is former Federal Reserve Board Chairman Alan Greenspan, who stressed that "educators need to focus directly on providing youth with a foundation for understanding personal financial management" (2005, p. 64). The NCEE has also joined this chorus, pointing to "the spiraling rate of personal bankruptcies and credit card debt; the lack of understanding of the importance of saving and investing" among today's consumers (2005b, p.1). As many as 38 states have adopted standards that contain personal finance or consumer education concepts or topics, although only 7 states require students to take a course in personal finance and only 9 states require testing of students' knowledge of personal finance concepts (NCEE, 2005b).

Developed by a panel of professionals representing education, government, and financial service organizations, the Jump$tart Coalition's (2002) *National Standards in Personal Finance* (hereafter, NSPF) were issued to define the financial and consumer knowledge and skills students require. Morton (2005) argued that such personal finance standards should be part of what constitutes economic literacy and that economic education and personal finance education were complements rather than substitutes because "economics and personal finance are ultimately about choices and the consequences of those choices" and that "economics provides the organizing principles and logic" for personal finance education (pp. 66–67).

ECONOMICS IN THE CURRICULUM

Despite the emergence of the *Standards*, individual states still decide what economics to require, whether consumer or financial topics will be included, where economics will be placed in the curriculum, whether it will be taught in a separate course (a significant issue, as we shall see presently), and whether it will be part of a high-stakes testing program. The NCEE conducts a biennial survey of the states that gives some answers to these questions (NCEE, 2005a). For the most recent data (2004), the survey found:

- Forty-nine states plus the District of Columbia include economics in their standards. Some 45 of these claim to implement economics instruction K–12.
- Thirty-eight states (78% of those with standards) require implementation of economics standards.
- Seventeen states (34%) require an economics course to be offered.
- Fifteen states (30%) require students to take an economics course, including the four states with the largest number of students enrolled in public schools (California, Texas, New York and Florida). All of these economics courses are at the high school

level and are sometimes combined with another subject, e.g., Civics and Economics in North Carolina.

- Twenty-six states require testing of economics, although it is not clear from the survey whether such testing is part of graduation or promotion requirements.

In scanning the results for 2004 compared with the prior three surveys, there is little change from 2002, but generally more states required economics, an economics course, and economics testing in 2004 than in 1998.

The inclusion of economics K–12 is somewhat consistent with the *Standards*, which provide benchmarks for grades 4, 8, and 12. Ohio provides a reasonable example of how states attempt to implement standards. In Ohio's standard for economics (where most, but not all, economics content is found), there are benchmarks for grades K–2, 3–5, 6–8, 9–10, and 11–12 (Ohio Department of Education, 2002). In Ohio, as in most states, economics content is "integrated" or "infused" throughout the social studies curriculum. Although Ohio's model curriculum suggests an eleventh grade combined government and economics course, school districts need not require such a course if they meet the academic content standard another way, i.e. integration into another subject. It should be noted, however, that at least one study (Marlin, 1991) found a negative relationship between state-mandated courses in economics and student achievement. Marlin found that teachers held negative attitudes about teaching economics as a state-mandated course and that these attitudes influenced student outcomes.

How much economics students learn when the content is integrated into another subject area has been widely researched. As we discuss in greater detail in the following section on student learning of economics, it is clear that students learn significantly more economics in a separate course than through the integration of economic content with other courses. Researchers have speculated on possible reasons for this. One concern with an infusion approach is the inadequate (or to some degree inaccurate) treatment of economic content and concepts found in the curriculum of other social studies courses, as defined by the respective national standards for the disciplines that undergird these courses. For example, Buckles and Watts (1998) analyzed national standards in history, geography, social studies, and civics in order to "identify and evaluate the scope and accuracy of the economic content in the standards from the disciplines most closely related to economics" (p. 157). They concluded that the national standards in various social studies areas:

> …missed opportunities to include the economic concepts we believe are necessary to teach and learn the social studies. The civics standards missed opportunities to include more economics … Geography…concentrated on the importance of natural resources and the environmental cost of economic activity. If these documents were implemented in their current forms, we believe they would contribute to low levels of economic literacy among students taking only those courses and confuse students who take separate economics courses. (p. 165)

Other explanations have been offered as well. Miller (1988) analyzed social studies textbooks used to teach a variety of social studies courses and found inadequate treatment of economics, such as a lack of economic analysis, low-level explanations for economic events, factual errors, and the misapplication of economic content. Miller and Rose (1983) analyzed high school history textbooks and found significant inaccuracies in the treatment of the causes of the Great Depression, a condition still present in U.S. history texts 15 years later (Cargill & Mayer, 1998).

TEACHER PREPARATION IN ECONOMICS

Another possible reason for the relative lack of student learning in economics through infusion could be the amount of economics content knowledge social studies teachers themselves possess. Recall that one of the conclusions from Schug and Walstad (1991) suggested a positive relationship between teacher and student knowledge of economics, a finding confirmed by other researchers, as noted below. Setting aside the high school advanced placement course, in which more teachers have substantial coursework in economics (Scahill & Melican, 2005), most economics is taught in other social studies courses by teachers prepared to be comprehensive social studies teachers.

Thirty-nine states certify teacher preparation programs following guidelines established by the National Council for the Accreditation of Teacher Education (NCATE), which in turn uses the standards for teacher content preparation established by the relevant member associations (NCATE, 2002, p. 42). For integrated social studies, including economics, that association is the National Council for the Social Studies (NCATE, 2005). An examination of the NCATE standards indicated that for 'broad field' social studies licensure programs, NCSS (2000) does not require a specific number of hours for any particular social studies disciplines taught. The subject matter content course work for those licensed to teach social studies as a broad field:

- at the secondary school level should include no less than 40% of a total 4-year or extended-preparation program, with an area of concentration of at least 18 semester hours (24 quarter hours) in one academic discipline;
- at the middle school level should include no less than 30% of a total 4-year or extended-preparation program, with an area of concentration of at least 18 semester hours (24 quarter hours) in one academic discipline.

The available evidence indicates that the "area of concentration" for these teachers is not economics. Lynch (1994) found that, of social studies teachers not assigned to teach economics, nearly 70% of teachers in his study had taken two or fewer college-level courses in economics. Additional analysis by Lynch (1990) revealed that in order to have a significant impact on student learning, social studies teachers needed to have taken at least four courses in economics. Allgood and Walstad (1999) found the greatest increase in economic understanding occurred among students of high school teachers with at least six college-level economics courses. Walstad and Kourilsky (1999), however, reported that data from a Gallup Organization survey indicated that more than 80% of social studies teachers had taken four or fewer college-level economics courses. Further, Dumas, Evans, and Weible (1997) found that, of the 27 states that specify minimum coursework in various social studies disciplines as a requirement for licensure, the mean number of semester hours in economics was 3.9, slightly more than one semester-long course.

Even teachers assigned to teach the high school economics course are sometimes unlikely to have had substantial coursework in economics. Eisenhauer and Zaporowski (1994), in their study of New York state teachers who taught high school economics, discovered that 86% of the economics courses were taught by cross-disciplinary teachers. These teachers were not identified as economics teachers, but rather broad field social studies teachers who taught economics as a small proportion of their teaching load. Even more startling were the findings that those respondents identified as economics teachers had an average of 12.3 college-level economics courses, compared to only 2.49 courses for the cross-disciplinary teachers, with nearly 13% of all teachers in their study having *never* taken an economics course.

More recent studies may indicate that this situation is improving. For example, Aske (2000), in a survey of teachers of the high school economics course in Colorado, found their economic backgrounds to be somewhat stronger: "52% of the economics only teachers and 48% of the economics/government teachers had 5 or more college economics courses. Only 11% of the teachers had fewer than 2 economics courses" (p. 2). He did note that many of these teachers had substantially supplemented their economics backgrounds with economics courses after completing their initial teacher preparation programs.

RESEARCH ON STUDENT LEARNING OF ECONOMICS

Children's economic learning and understanding

Do young children have an understanding of their economic world? Can such understanding be increased through economic education? Since the 1950's, more than 35 studies have been conducted on how children's understanding of economics develops and how children learn economics content and concepts (Schug, 1994; Laney & Schug, 1998). Schug and Walstad (1991) reported that many of these studies followed a similar pattern in that they frequently interviewed young children about their understanding of an economic concept or idea (See, for example, Berti & Bombi, 1988; Schug & Birkey, 1985). These interviews, often done using props, were an attempt to capture "the spontaneous concept development that occurs as children experience economics in their daily lives" (Laney, 1993a, p. 228).

The findings of these and other more recent studies (e.g., Brophy & Alleman, 2002; Diez-Martinez & Ochoa, 2003; Laney, Moseley, & Pak, 1996; Sweeney & Baines, 1993; Webley & Plaiser, 1998) indicated that young children's economic thinking moved through "a series of levels or stages similar to those described by Jean Piaget" (Schug & Walstad, 1991, p. 414). Additionally, a number of studies have found that children often have significant misconceptions about basic economic concepts that remain if uncorrected (Armento, 1982, Kourilsky, 1993; Laney, 1990; Schug & Birkey, 1985). In their interview study of 216 K–3 students Brophy and Alleman (2002) investigated students' understanding of the economics of shelter and reported student misconceptions about the difference between buying and renting, about the value of property, and other key concepts; "some of this 'knowledge' (was) at least partly incorrect and involves naïve ideas or even clear misconceptions" (p. 460). Among other misconceptions held by primary students were: that work and income are not connected, that the size of the price tag determines the price of an item, that the value of money comes from its size, and that property is owned by those who are near it (Laney & Schug, 1998).

An example of both the stage development of children's economic reasoning and children's misconceptions about economics can be found in Schug and Lephardt (1992). The researchers asked 67 randomly selected children in grades one, six, and eleven questions about international trade. Their responses were transcribed and then classified into levels "approximating levels of cognitive development" (Schug, 1994, p. 27). Schug and Lephardt discovered that children's reasoning about international trade was characterized by three increasingly sophisticated types of responses: (1) Nations trade because "people want to have things from other countries"; (2) Nations trade because each nation benefits from the trade; and (3) Nation's "buy goods and services from other nations because the cost is less" (Schug, 1994, p. 27–28). Brophy and Alleman (2002) also reported evidence of such stage development as "noteworthy and usually statistically significant progressions" across grade levels of knowledge of economic concepts related to shelter (p. 461).

These studies examined stages of children's economic understanding, but research has indicated that children's economic knowledge and understanding can be improved via direct, purposeful instruction. For example, Morgan (1991) studied 300 first- through third-grade students whose teachers used the video series *Econ and Me* (Agency for Instructional Technology, 1989). Morgan administered pre- and post-tests designed to measure students' knowledge of the five basic economic concepts outlined in the *Econ and Me* series (goods and services, producers and consumers, scarcity, opportunity cost, and productive resources). Students' post-test scores were significantly higher than pre-test scores, indicating that the students in the study had increased their understanding of these economic concepts. Using a modified experimental design, Gretes, Piel, and Queen (1991) analyzed the impact of economic simulations on the economic knowledge of the students of 10 fifth-grade teachers. The authors claimed that those students who participated in the economic simulations scored significantly higher on the post-test measure of economic knowledge and that these gains held regardless of student ability group.

In perhaps the most complex examination of the impact of economic education on children's economic understanding, Sosin, Dick, and Reiser (1997) studied nine elementary classrooms (grades three through six) and eleven control group classrooms (same grade levels). The teachers in the experimental group were all enrolled in a graduate course focused on integrating economic concepts into their respective classrooms. The control group teachers agreed to teach no economic content during the course of the study. Results indicated that students in the classrooms where economics was explicitly taught scored significantly higher than their control group counterparts: On average, post-test scores were more than double. Using a learning (flow) production function model (as opposed to a 'level-of-understanding'—or stock—model), Sosin et al. (1997) examined student post-test scores to determine the extent to which various determinants contributed to post-test score gain. Estimates indicated that student race and gender had little impact on student's success on the post-test—with reading ability having a moderate interaction effect—but *all* students in the experimental groups learned economic concepts, and those students who were taught more economics learned more economics.

Studies of high school students economic learning

One could argue that, with few exceptions, no single area in the social studies has been as rigorously and quantitatively analyzed as the teaching and learning of economics at the pre-college, especially high school, level (Walstad, 1992). This is due in no small part to the nature of the discipline of economics as a social science, but it is also due to the existence of measurement tools noted in the Schug and Walstad (1991) conclusions cited earlier.

The Test of Economic Literacy, for example, was first developed in 1976 by the then Joint (later National) Council on Economic Education. This first iteration (TEL1) was revised in 1985 by a committee of economists, high school economics teachers, and test experts, who used the *Framework* as the basis for the revision (Lynch, 1994). This revised version (TEL2) was administered to more than 3,000 students from across the United States and from various socio-economic backgrounds. Analysis of these scores led to a standardization of the TEL2 that confirmed that it could "differentiate between students with more (economic) knowledge and those with less" (Lynch, 1994, p. 63). The TEL2 was subsequently revised in 2001 (TEL3) and was then nationally-normed, using a sample of more than 7,200 high school students in 36 states (Walstad & Rebeck, 2001c). Much of the research reported in this section of the chapter uses the TEL2.

While the TEL2 has been by far the most widely used test in pre-collegiate economic education, it has not escaped some controversy. Nelson and Sheffrin (1991), for example, criticized the TEL2 for its apparent ideological bias, especially with respect to what the authors describe as a naïve (or outdated) macroeconomic view. Similarly, Galbraith (1987) criticized the *Framework* (from which the TEL2 was drawn) for failing to address the value of fiscal policy in a Keynesian framework (also a macroeconomic issue). Lynch (1994), however, concluded that these and other criticisms of the TEL2 may result more from the "state of macroeconomic thought today than it does any bias in the TEL" (p. 68). Nonetheless, many researchers have found the various iterations of the TEL to be the best available research tools.

What then has research using the TEL2 (and more recently the TEL3) demonstrated about high school student's economic learning and understanding? Schug and Walstad (1991) provided a summary of research conducted using the TEL2 standardization sample (e.g., Soper & Walstad; 1988; Walstad & Soper, 1989) and reported that, of the 3,031 students in the sample who had taken both the pre- and post-test, students in consumer economics courses and students in social studies courses (with or without economics) scored virtually the same on TEL2 pre- and post-tests. Students who had taken an economics course, however, had significant gains in post-test scores. Evidence from recent studies—using data from the TEL3 standardization sample—showed similar conclusions: high school students who had taken an economics course scored significantly higher than students who had not taken economics (Walstad & Rebeck, 2001). Peterson (1992) suggested that the 'value-added' of high school economics may even have been understated in previous studies. Using a subset of the TEL2 standardization sample, Peterson conducted a 'switching' regression analysis that adjusted for students who took their high school economics course as an elective and concluded that uncorrected models had underestimated the impact of taking an economics course on student learning: "simply 'plugging in' a typical student's characteristics into an uncorrected ordinary least squares regressions...will understate the potential gain attributable to a (high school) course in economics" (p. 15).

Despite these positive findings, however, researchers have long noted the relatively low level of economic knowledge exhibited by high school students (Becker, Greene, & Rosen, 1990), even those who take a course in high school economics. In their analysis of TEL3 standardization sample, Walstad and Rebeck (2001) reported that students who completed an economics course were able to answer only 61% of the questions correctly, compared to 41% for students who had not taken economics. A 2005 survey by Harris Interactive confirmed this low level of economic knowledge among high school students: 2,242 U.S. students in grades 9–12 completed the 24- item survey, which was prepared by NCEE and covered each of the twenty standards from the economics *Standards* and some personal finance concepts. Of the high school students surveyed, 60% received a failing grade by answering less than 60 % of questions about economics correctly. Only 9% of high school students received either an A or B on the survey (Harris Interactive, 2005).

Student knowledge differs across the four broad categories of economic concepts in the *Framework* document: fundamental concepts, microeconomic concepts, macroeconomic concepts; and international economic concepts. The highest levels of achievement occur in the fundamental category—with economics students answering 67.0% of these questions on the TEL3 correctly—and microeconomic (62.3% correct) areas. Students who have taken high school economics do less well in macroeconomics (57.0% correct) and international economics (53.4% correct) (Walstad & Rebeck, 2001). Walstad and Rebeck attributed these differences to relative time spent on these various topics in the typical high school course: Most of the instructional time is devoted to fundamental concepts, with much less time spent on international concepts.

Researchers have also noted the incrementally small increase in test scores associated with taking an economics course. For example, Walstad and Rebeck (2001) reported that students who had taken a high school economics course answered (on average) only 8 more questions correctly (out of 40 on the TEL3) compared to students who had not taken economics. Walstad (1992) attributed these relatively low scores to a number of factors, "some associated with teacher and course characteristics, others related to social and education problems...others connected to measurement issues. The most important reason is the small amount of time devoted to economics throughout the school curriculum" (p. 2030). However, there are other possible explanations. For example, it could be argued that the relatively disappointing difference in TEL scores is a function of the relatively low teacher knowledge of economics discussed earlier.

The incrementally low increases in TEL2 and TEL3 scores have prompted some economists to question whether the expected average gain of "2 or 3 questions (on the TEL2) warrants the time, energy, and expense devoted to economic education" (Clark & Davis, 1992, p. 154). Clark and Davis used the TEL2 standardization sample data ($n = 3{,}031$) to create a data set that contained all students for whom TEL2 pre-and post-tests, and attitudinal and attitudinal sophistication data, were available ($n = 975$). They then parsed out students who had made either a net gain or no gain on the TEL2 post-test. According to Clark and Davis, this data analysis suggested "that average measurable gains from economics instruction are not only limited but also unlikely to be obtained in a great many instructional situations" (p. 153).

Whether economics knowledge from the high school course persists has been explored by studies in college economics courses. Myatt and Waddell (1990) found that students' grades in high school economics had a significant effect on grades in the university principles of economics course. Durden and Ellis (1995) concluded that students who had taken a high school economics course earned significantly higher grades in college-level principles of economics courses. Lopus (1997) determined that significant gains existed only for students whose high school courses had a recognizable micro- or macro-economic focus. This is consistent with Walstad and VanScyoc's (1990) finding that a high school course that focuses on "economic theory and principles, as opposed to a course where the focus is on the practical...will improve student understanding of basic economic concepts" (p. 51). Perhaps this finding is not as instructive as it would seem at first glance, however. One must recall that the TEL2 (and now the TEL3) was based on curriculum frameworks and content standards that are essentially principles-based. It is therefore not surprising that a student taught using a principles-based approach would do better on an instrument based on economic principles.

Walstad and VanScyoc (1990) examined the impact of textbooks on students' economic understanding and attitudes. They concluded that "textbooks seemed to improve economics learning and change attitudes towards economics" (p. 51). Certain types of textbooks were negatively correlated with student achievement. The authors argued against, for example, "the use of a one-semester college textbook" and "applied and 'free enterprise' high school texts" as these can have "a negative effect on the economics learning and attitudes of students" (p. 51).

It is important to note that from January to March 2006 the National Assessment of Economic Progress (NAEP) in economics was administered to high school seniors, the first time NAEP has tested this subject. The No Child Left Behind Act designated economics as one of the subjects for which assessment is to be conducted at "regularly scheduled intervals" (NAEP, n.d., p. 3). When the data become available, researchers will have a rich source of information with which to learn more about student learning of economics, partly because the assessment collects data on additional variables of interest, such as the teachers' instructional strategies and whether a student has taken an economics course (NAEP, n.d., p. 2). In addition the assessment framework corresponds to the *Standards*, which will make comparison with other research easier and provide results that correspond to the current conception of what economics students should know.

Studies of student economic attitudes

What is the relationship between students' economic attitudes and their economic learning? Does increased knowledge of economics content improve student attitudes toward economics, or is the reverse true? A number of studies have attempted to answer these questions. Indeed, Phipps and Clark (1993) reported that research in economic education has "been characterized by the development of increasingly sophisticated models of economics learning, with students' attitude toward economics a key variable in many of these models" (p. 195). Schug and Walstad (1991) noted that "the development of economic attitudes has been a long interest in economic education" (p. 415).

Measuring economic attitudes

Phipps and Clark (1993) noted that student attitude has typically been measured using the Survey on Economic Attitudes (SEA). The SEA was developed as a "two-part affective-domain instrument to measure student attitudes as a result of exposure to economics instruction" (Soper & Walstad, 1983, p. 4). The SEA was comprised of two dimensions: the Attitude Toward Economics (ATE) dimension, which measured student attitudes toward the subject of economics, and the Economic Attitude Sophistication (EAS) dimension, which assessed the degree of students' agreement with broad consensus positions of professional economists. The SEA was nationally normed in 1979, using a representative sample of high schools across the country, and subsequently renormed in 1986 (see Soper & Walstad, 1988). Internal consistency was relatively high (Cronbach's alpha = .88) for the ATE dimension of the SEA, and slightly lower for the EAS (Cronbach's alpha = .66).

Schug and Walstad (1991) summarized a number of studies (e.g., Jackstadt & Brennan, 1983; Soper & Walstad, 1983; Walstad, 1987) that indicated that the relationship between student economic knowledge and attitude formation was essentially uni-directional and concluded that "economic understanding appears to be related to student attitudes toward the economic system and to the degree of sophistication in assessing economic issues" (p. 416). For example, Schober (1984), in a study of 642 students of teachers who had participated in an economic education workshop and 423 students of teachers who had not, found that "economics achievement has a significant influence on opinion formation. However, economics opinions do not significantly influence economic achievement" (p. 292).

More recent studies have questioned the assumption that the SEA has a single dimension. Phipps and Clark (1993) applied factor analytic techniques to the SEA in order to "obtain insight into the dimensions of attitudes toward economics" (p. 207). Their results suggested that the ATE dimension of the SEA had three underlying factors: enjoyment, usefulness, and difficulty. They concluded that this factor analysis "provided additional insights into the impact of student, teacher, and school characteristics on students' affective learning of economics" (p. 208).

What of student attitudes toward economics as a course? Schug and Walstad (1991) noted that "for a long time the belief has been that economics achievement and attitude toward economics as a subject are related. That is, if students like economics, they will learn more, and if they learn more their attitude toward the subject will improve" (p. 416). Walstad and VanScoyc (1990) found a significant relationship between ATE post-test score and student TEL2 post-test score, implying that "after initial ATE level was controlled for, much of a student's attitude toward the subject of economics was shaped by what he or she knew about it; the greater the knowledge of economics, the more positive the attitude toward the subject" (pp. 50–51). Walstad and VanScoyc also found that, all else being equal, male students and students from higher socio-economic groups had more positive attitudes towards economics.

Studies of economic reasoning

As noted earlier, Schug and Walstad (1991) called for more research, including investigation of the efficacy of using an economic reasoning approach compared to a concept-centered approach. Unfortunately, no comparison studies have been conducted from which any research-based conclusions can be drawn. There have been, however, further attempts to define economic reasoning. VanSickle (1992) reported on experts' approaches to solving problems within their domain of expertise. He described differences in knowledge used by experts and noted that while experts obviously had greater declarative knowledge (e.g., content knowledge in economics), they also knew how to deploy that knowledge differently (procedural knowledge). The interconnection of declarative and procedural knowledge, along with the attendant assumptions and cross references to concepts on generalizations, forms schematic knowledge. VanSickle argued that "experts have more schemata than novices and experts' schemata are developed more fully in their areas of expertise" (p. 58). Thus, expert economic reasoning can be seen as using more highly developed economics schemata.

Miller and VanFossen (1994) studied the idea of relative expertise applied specifically to economics. Using a "think aloud" procedure, experts (PhD economists) and novices (high school students) each addressed three specific economic problems. Their statements were translated in a graphical model that displayed "the relevant attributes of economic problem solving and distinguish(ed) between expert and novice problem solvers" (p. 396). VanFossen (1995) analyzed the *talk-aloud* protocols of 6 groups—from high school students who had not taken an economics course through PhD economists—to the same three economic problems. Results indicated that experts in economic problem solving possessed and employed significantly more procedural knowledge (e.g., the use of economic models, re-ordering the problem, use of sub-problems, etc.) than novices. While this research literature is thin, this line of study has potential for other social studies disciplines generally and economic education specifically. Miller and VanFossen (1994) have suggested that perhaps rather than measuring gains in economic content knowledge on economics tests, researchers might focus on student acquisition of greater relative expertise in economic problem solving and on classroom instructional strategies that generated greater expertise.

CLASSROOM STRATEGIES FOR TEACHING ECONOMICS

Unfortunately, despite the call from Schug and Walstad (1991) for more studies of the relative effectiveness of different instructional strategies, especially focused on teaching specific concepts, little progress has been made in this regard. Most research on specific strategies has been conducted in college principles courses, perhaps because of greater access to larger numbers of students and ease in meeting the conditions of quasi-experimental designs. Most of the published literature on specific teaching strategies at the pre-collegiate level describes a particular method without providing much evidence of effectiveness.

In one study, Schug and Baumann (1991) identified methods used by experienced teachers to correct students' economic misconceptions. The researchers used surveys and interviews with 20 expert economics teachers, who were identified by a nominations process, to identify the most common student misconceptions about opportunity cost, the laws of supply and demand, gross national product (GNP), and the creation of money. Schug and Baumann also collected information on what these teachers felt were the most effective "teaching ideas" for correcting students' misconceptions.

Another study compared students' economic learning after the use of different approaches. Son and VanSickle (2000) investigated the effects of problem-solving instruction on knowledge acquisition and retention in a high school economics course. Using a quasi-experimental design, Son and VanSickle studied the intact high school economics classes of 6 teachers: half taught economics using a problem-solving approach, and half taught using an expository style. Results were mixed; no significant differences existed in economic knowledge structure, but the problem-solving approach led to higher knowledge acquisition and retention at significant levels.

ECONOMIC LITERACY IN TRANSITION COUNTRIES

As noted earlier, the recent emergence of the nations with transition economies (e.g., Russia and the nations of the former USSR) seemed to highlight the relationship between democracy and market economies, an important factor in the case for economic literacy outlined in this chapter. Indeed, there has been significant growth in the research on economic education in these transition nations, especially in countries of the former Soviet Union and satellite nations (hereafter, FSU nations). The case for economic literacy in these nations resembles aspects of that put forward in the United States. For example, Alenchikov (1993) stated, "One of the basic tasks of economic education is to shape young students' readiness for economic activity as a necessary condition for their participation in society" (p. 57). Shen and Shen (1993), writing about economic liberalization in the People's Republic of China, noted that "[t]he success of economic reform in socialist economies depends heavily on the thinking of the population" (p. 70). Watts, Walstad, and Skiba (2002) draw much the same conclusion, explaining that how "far the economic reforms in transition economies ultimately go...will depend to a large degree on what people in these post-communist nations think and understand about...how a market economy works" (p. 30). The NCEE, which is conducting what is likely the most sweeping of all the Western programs aimed at economic education in these nations with transition economies, notes that:

> [l]egislation for the CEEP (Cooperative Education Exchange Program) grew out of the conviction that economic and civic education are critically important to the economic health and political stability of the emerging democratic market economies of the former Soviet Union and central and eastern Europe... (2005a)

Alenchikov (1993) cites unnamed surveys of economic knowledge (circa 1990) of "teachers, masters of production training, school administrators, and organizers of school students' socially useful productive labor" from which he concluded that "90 percent of them are in need of economic training..." (pp. 57–58). More recent research has indicated that FSU nations have shifted the focus of academic economics (housed in universities and technical colleges) from a Marxist orientation to a more market-oriented theory (Kovzik & Watts, 2002; Phipps, Vredeveld, & Voikova, 2002). More importantly, other studies have indicated that, over the last decade, economic education—and a focus on economic literacy—has grown significantly in FSU nations (Watts & Walstad, 2002). Studies of student economic learning in FSU nations have reached the same conclusion as studies of students in the U.S. Specifically, that the students of teachers who are well-trained in economics (i.e., have a strong academic background or have had intense workshop training) had significant gains in economic knowledge (Walstad, 2002).

Walstad and Rebeck (2001b) sought to measure the effects of the NCEE's International Economic Education Program (IEEP) on the economic knowledge of students and teachers in four countries: Lithuania, Ukraine, Kyrgyzstan, and Poland. They used regression analysis on scores for a subset of the TEL2 for 77 teachers and 1953 students. Controlling for extraneous variables as well as could be expected under the circumstances, Walstad and Rebeck concluded that: (a) the IEEP program resulted in higher TEL scores for students of the participating teachers; and (b) a significant portion of that increase was a result of increased teacher knowledge of economics due to the IEEP. These results reinforced the importance of teacher content knowledge in economics, again consistent with the findings from studies in the United States cited earlier.

Shen and Shen (1993) surveyed students in elite high schools in the People's Republic of China (PRC) in 1989 and compared their attitudes with counterparts in some high schools in California. They noted that economic reform had been underway in China since 1978 and selected elite high schools because the students would be the future "opinion leaders and will have a significant impact on the future of reform" (p. 70). In general, they discovered surprisingly little difference between Chinese and American students, which they found encouraging for the future of reform and from which they concluded that intuition and "common sense" had prevailed over propaganda in China.

While the FSU and the PRC have provided new, fertile ground for researchers in economic education, much remains to be done. As Walstad (2002) noted, the research on "economic education in transition countries is only beginning to be given serious study. More research will be needed to advance our understanding of . . . student learning in economics" (p. 83).

CONCLUSIONS AND RECOMMENDATIONS FOR RESEARCH

Many conclusions could be drawn from such a large and diverse body of research literature. The authors of this chapter have decided to highlight four, several of which echo Schug and Walstad in 1991. First, while some progress has been made toward achieving economic literacy, much work remains to be done. For example, while 97% of American adults believe that knowledge of our economy is essential for citizens and that economics should be taught in high schools (Harris Interactive, 2005), only 38 states require economics' standards to be implemented, and only 15 states require students to take an economics course to earn a high school diploma. While standardized test data indicate that the economic literacy of high school students has improved—from a TEL2 mean of 52% correct to a TEL3 mean of 61% correct—students still receive, on average, failing grades on their economic knowledge (Harris Interactive, 2005). Presumably we will know more with the release of the data from the NAEP economics assessment. Moreover, to the degree that economics instruction occurs in schools, it is still predominantly integrated or infused in other subjects—an approach that research clearly demonstrates is less successful than requiring students to take a course in economics. This last finding is of particular interest in light of our second conclusion, that teacher knowledge of economic content is strongly related to how much economics students learn, a finding now supported by data from the transition economies as well as from the United States. Ironically, the available research on teacher knowledge of economics shows that social studies teachers have little coursework in the subject—even, in many cases, those social studies teachers responsible for teaching the high school economics course.

Third, the influence of the *Standards* is manifest and represents a next iteration in the process of defining what constitutes economic literacy. In spite of the historical distinction between personal finance (or consumer) education and economic education, it appears possible (even likely) that financial literacy will become an increasingly important part of economic literacy and thus economic education. It remains unclear what role social studies educators will have either in defining the financial literacy curriculum or in teaching it. Despite the arguments of some for its integration into economics, financial literacy might become the province of business and consumer science teachers. Finally, the research continues to raise concern over the treatment of economics in educational materials, including (and, perhaps, especially) history textbooks. The connections to economics are inadequate and some of the information and explanations are simply wrong.

There is a large, unfinished agenda in research in economics literacy, and many of the suggestions from Schug and Walstad in the last *Handbook,* noted in the introduction to this chapter, remain unfulfilled. First, we do not know enough about how students reason with economics, certainly not enough to settle the differing viewpoints on whether the emphasis in the economics curriculum should be on economic concept learning or on developing economic reasoning characterized by an *economic* way of thinking. Perhaps this question will prove a false dualism, as many economic educators, including the authors, believe that one is impossible without the other. Second, comparatively little progress has been made on the effectiveness of particular instructional strategies at the pre-collegiate level. Especially important is new research on the usefulness of technology. Computer simulations, Internet-based strategies such as the inquiry-oriented model WebQuest (Dodge, 1998), and access to current economics data and analysis using the Internet are all strategies teachers may now deploy, but we know little of their relative efficacy. For example, the NCEE has published more than 400 Internet-based lessons at its *EconEdLink* site (http://econedlink.org/), but, to date, no studies of the classroom use of these lessons have been done.

New research strands are also evident. For example, virtually everything that has been done in research in economic literacy must also be done with respect to financial literacy, assuming that it maintains its gathering momentum. Consider its increased significance as more people manage their own retirement portfolios, for example.

The transition economies continue to offer rich opportunities for researchers. We must examine the impact of economic education programs and compare research findings in the transition countries to those in the United States, along the lines begun by Walstad and Rebeck (2001a) noted above. The theorized link between democracy and market economics offers other fruitful lines of educational research. For example, what differences exist in economics knowledge and attitudes about the role of government in the economy when comparing countries that have liberalized *both* government and the economy with those that have attempted some economic reforms without similarly liberalizing how their nations are governed (e.g., the People's Republic of China)? This is especially important if one considers the possibility that transition nations may grow to include many in Asia, Africa, and Latin America.

REFERENCES

Agency for Instructional Technology. (1989). *Econ and Me: Teacher's guide.* Bloomington, IN: Author.

Alenchikov, I. N. (1993). Economics and the school. *Russian Education and Society, 35*(3), 57–65.

Allgood, S., & Walstad, W. (1999). The longitudinal effects of economic education on teachers and their students. *Journal of Economic Education, 30*(2), 99–111.

Armento, B. (1982). Awareness of economic knowledge: A developmental study. Paper presented at the Annual Meeting of the American Educational Research Association, New York, NY. Resources Information Center. ERIC Document number 219311.

Aske, D. R. (2000) Who is teaching economics to Colorado high school students? *Journal of Social Studies Research*. Winter. Accessed on May 15, 2005, from http://www.findarticles.com/p/articles/mi_qa3823/is_200004/ai_n8888432.

Bach, G., Bellack, A., Chandler, L., Lewin, B., Samuelson, P. Fraenkel, M., & Bond, F. (1961). *Economic education in the schools*. New York: Committee on Economic Development.

Becker, W. (1998). Standards and testing: Another view. *Journal of Economic Education, 29*(2), 183–186.

Becker, W., Greene, W., & Rosen, S. (1990). Research on high school economic education. *Journal of Economic Education, 21*(3), 231–45.

Berti, A., & Bombi, A. (1988). *The child's construction of economics*. Cambridge: Cambridge University Press.

Brophy, J., & Alleman, J. (2002). Primary-grade students knowledge and thinking about the economics of meeting families' shelter needs. *American Educational Research Journal, 39*(2), 423–468.

Buckles, S., & Watts, M. (1998). National standards in economics, history, social studies, civics, and geography: Complementarities, competition, or peaceful coexistence? *Journal of Economic Education, 29*(2), 157–166.

Calderwood, J., Lawrence, J., & Maher, J. (1970). *Economics in the curriculum: Developmental economic education program*. New York: Wiley.

Cargill, T. F., & Mayer, T. (1998). The great depression and history textbooks. *The History Teacher 31* (4) accessed on May 15, 2005, from http://www.fte.org/teachers/readings.htm.

Clark, J., & Davis, W. (1992). Does high school economics turn off too many students? *Journal of Education for Business, 67*(3), 152–155.

Culbertson, J. (1987). A realist international economics. *Journal of Economic Education, 18*(2), 161–176.

Dahl, D. (1998). Why Johnny can't choose: And what Johnny (and Jane) needs to know to understand the economy. *The Region, 12*(4), 5–11.

Dahl, R. (1990). *After the revolution: Authority in a good society*. New Haven, CT: Yale University Press.

Diez-Martinez, E., & Ochoa, A. (2003). Mexican children's and adolescent's development of occupational hierarchy related to consumption and saving. *Children's Social and Economic Education, 5*(3), 148–163.

Dodge, B. (1998). Some thoughts about Webquests. San Diego State University. Retrieved, September 15. 2006, from http://edweb.sdsu.edu/courses/edtec596/about_webquests.html.

Dumas, W., Evans, S.,& Weible, T. (1997). Minimum State Standards for Secondary Social Studies Teacher Licensure: A National Update. *The Social Studies, 88*(3), 163–166.

Durden, G. C., & Ellis, L. V. (1995). The effects of attendance on student learning in principles of economics. *American Economic Review, 85*(2), 343–346.

Eisenhauer, J., & Zaporowski, M. (1994). Cross-disciplinary teaching in high school economics. *Social Education, 58*(4), 226–229.

Friedman, M. (1982). *Capitalism and freedom*. Chicago, IL: University of Chicago Press.

Fuller, D., & Geide-Stevenson, D. (2003). Consensus among economists: Revisited. *Journal of Economic Education, 34*(4), 369–387.

Galbraith, J. (1987). On teaching fractured macroeconomic. *Journal of Economic Education, 18*(2), 213–226.

Greenspan, A. (2005). The importance of financial education today. *Social Education, 69*(2), 64–65.

Gretes, J., Piel, J., & Queen, J. A. (1991). Teaching economic concepts to fifth graders: The power of simulations. *Social Science Record, 28*(2), 71–83.

Hansen, W. L. (1998). Principles-based standards: On the Voluntary Content Standards in Economics. *Journal of Economic Education, 29*(2), 150–156.

Hansen, W., Bach, G., Calderwood, J., & Saunders, P. (1977). *Framework for teaching economics: Basic concepts*. New York: Joint Council on Economic Education.

HarrisInteractive.(2005). *WhatAmericanteensandadultsknowabouteconomics*.Retrieved,May 10, 2005, from http://ncee.net/cel/WhatAmericansKnowAboutEconomics_042605-3.pdf.

Heilbroner, R. (1987). Fundamental economic concepts: Another perspective. *Journal of Economic Education, 18*(2), 111–120.

Jackstadt, S., & Brennan, J. (1983). Economic knowledge and high school students' attitudes toward the American economic system, business, and labor. *Theory and Research in Social Education, 11*(3), 1–15.

Jump$tart Coalition for Personal Finance. (2002). *National standards in personal finance: With benchmarks, applications and glossary for k-12 classrooms.* Washington, DC: Author.

Kourilsky, M. (1993). Economic education and a generative model of mislearning and recovery. *Journal of Economic Education. 24*(1), 23–33.

Kourilsky, M., & Bruno, J. (1992). Implementing mandates in economics: A model and diagnostic protocol for teacher training. *Journal of Education for Business, 67*(3), 182–188.

Kovzik, A., & Watts, M. (2002). Reforming undergraduate economics instruction in Russia, Belarus, and Ukraine: Curriculum, personnel, and clientele issues. In M. Watts & W. Walstad (Eds.), *Reforming economics and economics teaching in the transition economies: From Marx to markets in classrooms.* Cheltenham, UK: Edward Elgar.

Laney, J. (1988). Can economic concepts be learned and remembered: A comparison of elementary students. *Journal of Educational Research, 8*(2), 99–105.

Laney, J. (1990). Generative teaching and learning of cost-benefit analysis: An empirical investigation. *Journal of Research and Development, 23*(3), 136–144.

Laney, J. (1993a). Experiential versus experience-based learning and instruction. *Journal of Educational Research, 86*(4), 228–236.

Laney, J. (1993b, May/June). Economics for elementary school students: Research-supported principles of teaching and learning that guide classroom practice. *The Social Studies,* 99–103.

Laney, J., Moseley, P., & Pak, L. (1996). Children's ideas about selected art and economic concepts before and after an integrated unit of instruction. *Children's Social and Economic Education, 1*(1), 61–78.

Laney, J., &Schug, M. (1998). Teach kids economics and they will learn. *Social Studies and the Young Learner,* November/December, 13–17.

Lopus, J. S. (1997). Effects of the high school economics curriculum on learning in the college principles class. *Journal of Economic Education, 28*(2), 143–53.

Lynch, G. (1994). High school economics: Separate course vs. the infusion approach. *International Journal of Social Education, 8*(3), 59–69.

Lynch, G. (1990). The effect of teacher course work on student learning: Evidence from the TEL. *Journal of Economic Education, 21*(3), 287–297.

Marlin, J. (1991). State-mandated economic education, teacher attitudes, and student learning. *Journal of Economic Education, 22*(1), 5–14.

Meszaros, B., & Siegfried, J. (Eds.). (1997). The voluntary national content standards in economics. New York: National Council on Economic Education, 1997. ED 416 165.

Miller, S. L. (1988). *Economic Education for Citizenship.* Bloomington, IN: ERIC Clearinghouse for Social Studies/Social Science Education.

Miller, S. L. (1993–94). Conceptualizing global economic education. *International Journal of Economic Education,* Winter, 8(3), 49–58.

Miller, S. L., & Rose, S. A. (1983). The great depression: a textbook case of problems with American history textbooks. *Theory and Research in Social Education, 11*(1), 25–39.

Miller, S. L., & VanFossen, P.J. (1994). Assessing expertise in economic problem solving: A model. *Theory and Research in Social Education. 22*(3), 380–412.

Morgan, J. (1991, September/October). Using *Econ and Me* to teach economics to children in primary grades. *The Social Studies,* 195–197.

Morton, J. (2005). The interdependence of economic and personal finance education. *Social Education, 69*(2), 66–69.

Myatt, A., & Waddell, C. (1990). An approach to testing effectiveness of teaching and learning of economics in high school. *Journal of Economic Education, 21*(3), 355–363.

National Assessment of Educational Progress. (n.d.). *Economics framework for the 2006 national assessment of educational progress.* Retrieved, June 14, 2006, from http://www.nagb.org/pubs/economics_06.pdf.

National Council for the Accreditation of Teacher Education (2002). *Professional standards: Accreditation of schools, colleges, and departments of education.* Retrieved, May 15, 2005, from http://www.ncate.org/documents/unit_stnds_2002.pdf.

National Council for the Accreditation of Teacher Education (2005) *Standards.* Retrieved May 15, 2005, from http://www.ncate.org/public/programStandards.asp?ch=4.

National Council for the Social Studies, 2000. *Teacher standards volume I: Programmatic standards.* Retrieved May 15, 2005, from http://www.socialstudies.org/standards/teachers/vol1/programmatic/.

National Council for the Social Studies, 1994. *Expectations of Excellence: Curriculum Standards for Social Studies.* Retrieved February 6, 2007, from http://www.socialstudies.org/standards/.

National Council on Economic Education. (1997). *Voluntary national content standards in economics.* New York: National Council on Economic Education. Retrieved May 14, 2005, from http://www.ncee.net/ea/program.php?pid=19.

National Council on Economic Education. (2005a). Economic education for democratic transformation: Background. Retrieved May 18, 2005, from http://www.ncee.net/ei/projects/eedt.php.

National Council on Economic Education. (2005b). Survey of the states: Economic and personal finance education in our nation's schools in 2004. Retrieved May 11, 2005, from http://www.ncee.net/about/survey2004/.

Nelson, J. A., & Sheffrin, S. M. (1991). Economic Literacy or Economic Ideology? *Journal of Economic Perspectives, 5*(3), 157–165.

Ohio Department of Education. (2002). *Academic Content Standards: K-12 Social Studies.* Columbus, OH. Retrieved May 14. 2005, from http://www.ode.state.oh.us/academic_content_standards/SSContentStd/PDF/SOCIAL_STUDIES.pdf.

Patrick, J. (1996) Principles of democracy for the education of citizens in former communist countries of central and eastern Europe. In R. C. Remy & J. Strzemieczny (Eds.), *Building civic education for democracy in Poland.* Washington, DC: National Council for the Social Studies.

Pennar, K. (1997, January 20). Economics made too simple. *Business Week,* p. 32.

Peterson, N. (1992). The high school economics course and its impact on economic knowledge. *Journal of Economic Education, 23*(1), 5–16.

Phipps, B., & Clark, J. (1993). Attitudes toward economics: Uni- or multidimensional? *Journal of Economic Education, 24*(3), 195–212.

Phipps, B., Vredeveld, G., & Voikova, A. (2002). Economic education reform in Bulgaria. In M. Watts & W. Walstad (Eds.), *Reforming economics and economics teaching in the transition economies: From Marx to markets in classrooms.* Cheltenham, UK: Edward Elgar.

Rivlin, A. M. (1999, May). On economic literacy. Speech presented at the Economic Literacy Conference, Federal Reserve Bank of Minneapolis, Minneapolis, Minnesota. Retrieved June 13, 2006, from http://www.federalreserve.gov/boardDocs/speeches/1999/199905132.htm.

Saunders, P., & Gilliard, J. (1995). *Framework for teaching the basic economic concepts.* New York: National Council on Economic Education.

Scahill, E. M., & Melican, C. (2005). The preparation and experience of advanced placement in economics instructors. *Journal of Economic Education. 36*(1), 93–98.

Schober, M. (1984). An analysis of the impact of teacher training in economics. *Theory and Research in Social Education, 13*(1), 31–42.

Schug, M. (1994). How children learn economics. *International Journal of Social Education, 8*(3), 25–34.

Schug, M., & Baumann, E. (1991). Strategies to correct high school students' misunderstanding of economics. *The Social Studies, 82*(2), 62–6.

Schug, M., & Birkey, C. (1985). Teaching economics to children. *Theory and Research in Social Education, 11*(3), 1–15.

Schug, M., & Lephardt, N. (1992). Development in children's thinking about international trade. *Social Studies, 83*(5), 207–211.

Schug, M., & Walstad, W. (1991). Teaching and learning economics. In J. Shaver (Ed.), *Handbook of Research on Social Studies Teaching and Learning.* New York: MacMillan Reference Books.

Shen, R., & Shen, T. Y. (1993). Economic thinking in China: Economic knowledge and attitudes of high school students. *Journal of Economic Education, 24*(1), 70–84.

Siegfried, J., & Meszaros, B. (1998). Voluntary economics content standards for America's schools: Rationale and development. *Journal of Economic Education, 29*(2), 139–149.

Son, B., & VanSickle, R. (2000). Problem-solving instruction and students' acquisition, retention, and structuring of economics knowledge. *Journal of Research and Development in Education, 33*(2), 95–105.

Soper, J., & Walstad, W. (1983). On measuring economic attitudes. *Journal of Economic Education, 14*(4), 4–17.

Soper, J., & Walstad, W. (1988). The economic attitudes of U.S. high school students: New norms for the Survey on Economic Attitudes. *Theory and Research in Social Education, 16*(4), 295–312.

Sosin, K., Dick, J., & Reiser, M. L. (1997). Determinants of achievement of economics concepts by elementary school students. *Journal of Economic Education*, 28(2), 100–121.

Strober, M. (1987). The scope of microeconomics: Implications for economic education. *Journal of Economic Education*, 18(2), 135–149.

Sweeney, J. A., & Baines, L. (1993). The effects of a video-based economics unit on the learning outcomes of third graders. *Social Science Record*, 30(1), 43–56.

VanFossen, P. (1995). *Relevant indicators of expertise in economic problem-solving: A factor analysis*. Paper presented at the American Educational Research Association Annual Meeting, San Francisco, CA. Resources Information Center. ERIC Document number 388 572.

VanFossen, P. (2000). Teachers' rationales for teaching economics. *Theory and Research in Social Education*, 28(3), 391–410.

VanSickle, R. L. (1992). Learning to reason with economics. *Journal of Economic Education*, 23(1), 56–64.

Walstad, W. (1987). Applying two-stage least squares. In W. Becker & W. Walstad (Eds.), *Econometric modeling in economic education research*. Hingham, MA: Kluwer Nijhoff.

Walstad, W. (1992). Economics instruction in high schools. *Journal of Economic Literature*, 30(4), 2019–2051.

Walstad, W. (1998). Why it's important to understand economics. *The Region*, Federal Reserve Bank of Minneapolis. Retrieved June 13, 2006, from http://minneapolisfed.org/pubs/region/98-12/walstad.cfm.

Walstad, W. (2001). Economic education in U.S. high schools. *Journal of Economic Education*, 15(3), 195–210.

Walstad, W. (2002). The effects of teacher programs on student economic understanding and market attitudes in transition countries. In M. Watts, & W. Walstad (Eds.), *Reforming economics and economics teaching in the transition economies: From Marx to markets in classrooms*. Cheltenham, UK: Edward Elgar.

Walstad, W., & Kourilsky, M. (1999). *Seeds of success: Entrepreneurship and youth*. Dubuque, IA: Kendall-Hunt.

Walstad, W., & Rebeck, K. (2000). The status of economics in the high school curriculum. *Journal of Economic Education*, 31(1), 95–101.

Walstad, W. , & Rebeck, K. (2001a). Assessing the economic understanding of U.S. high school students. *The American Economic Review*, 91(2), 452–457.

Walstad, W., & Rebeck, K. (2001b). Teacher and student economic understanding in transition economies. *Journal of Economic Education*, 32(1), 58–67.

Walstad, W., & Rebeck, K. (2001c). *Test of economic literacy, third edition: Examiner's manual*. New York: National Council on Economic Education.

Walstad, W., & Soper, J. (1983). Measuring economic attitudes in high school. *Theory and Research in Social Education*, 9(1), 41–54.

Walstad, W., & Soper, J. (1989). What is high school economics? Factors contributing to student achievement and attitudes. *Journal of Economic Education*, 20(1), 53–68.

Walstad, W., & Van Scyoc, L. (1990). The effects of textbooks on economics understanding and attitudes in high school economics courses. *Journal of Research and Development in Education*, 24(1), 44–52.

Watts, M., & Walstad, W. (Eds.). (2002). *Reforming economics and economics teaching in the transition economies: From Marx to markets in classrooms*. Cheltenham, UK: Edward Elgar.

Watts, M., Walstad, W., & Skiba, A. (2002). The academic transition from Marxism to market economics. In M. Watts & W. Walstad (Eds.), *Reforming economics and economics teaching in the transition economies: From Marx to markets in classrooms*. Cheltenham, UK: Edward Elgar.

Webley, P., & Plaisier, Z. (1998). Mental accounting in childhood. *Children's Social and Economic Education*, 3(2), 55–64.

Wentworth, D. (1987). Economic reasoning: Turning myth into reality. *Theory into Practice*, 26(3), 170–175.

Wentworth, D., & Western, R. (1990). High school economics: The new reasoning imperative. *Social Education*, 54, 78–80.

Part VI

Information ecologies: Technology in the social studies

17 Technology and social studies

Kathleen Owings Swan
University of Kentucky

Mark Hofer
College of William and Mary

INTRODUCTION

For more than a decade educators have witnessed a substantial infusion of technology in schools and increasing emphasis on technology in teacher preparation. Since 1998, student to computer ratio has decreased, from 1:12.1 to 1:3.8 in 2005 (Wells & Lewis, 2006). The percent of schools with Internet access has increased, from 35% in 1994 to 100% in 2005 (Wells & Lewis, 2006), and the number of school districts with student laptop computers has grown substantially. Additionally, over the last 7 years the federal government spent at least $4 billion annually on K–12 school technology infrastructure. However, despite these investments, educational technology has not produced the pedagogical revolution in K–12 classrooms (Anglin, 1995; Becker, 2000; Cuban, 2001; Pew Institute, 2002; Saettler, 1990).

The social studies literature reflects similar findings regarding the unrealized potential of various computer technologies. In 1997, for instance, Martorella identified technology as "the sleeping giant," noting its potential (but unrealized) impact on teaching and learning in the social studies. More recent reviews of the social studies and technology literature reach similar conclusions (Berson, 1996; Ehman & Glenn, 1991; Whitworth & Berson, 2003), noting that while pockets of exemplary activity exist, the anticipated widespread diffusion of technology in K–12 social studies has failed to materialize. In 1991, Ehman and Glenn described a "very thin knowledge base" derived from research on interactive technologies in the social studies (p. 520). Whitworth and Berson's (2003) exhaustive review of research produced between 1996 and 2001 came to a similar conclusion. According to Whitworth and Berson, of the 325 articles related to technology in the social studies published between 1996 and 2001, only eight were research studies.

This chapter examines the research base related to educational technology and social studies, focusing specifically on studies of classroom practice and teacher preparation. In addition, we discuss some of the methodological issues and gaps in the existing literature base and conclude with suggestions for further research.

DEFINING TECHNOLOGY

Defining educational technology can be a challenging endeavor. Taken broadly, technology can mean any tool or device used to assist human endeavors. A more narrow definition may consider only personal computer technologies employed to a particular educational purpose. Any definition of technology is fluid. Between 1972 and 2005, for instance, the Association for Educational Communications and Technology revised their definition of educational technology four times. Our definition builds on Ehman and Glenn (1991), and we expect continued evolution from this point forward. For this review, we limit our focus to *computer or networked tools and resources that directly support the teaching and learning of social studies.*

METHODOLOGY

Our review of the literature included articles published in the major social studies education journals, technology in education journals, and discipline-specific education journals published over a 17-year period (i.e., 1990–2006). We began our search with four major social studies education journals: *International Journal of Social Education, Social Education, Theory and Research in Social Education,* and *The Social Studies.* Further, we performed advanced searches on all journals with set search parameters including *social studies* and *technology.* We then reviewed citation indexes for each journal and identified specific articles addressing technology within the social studies.

Seven Association for the Advancement of Computing in Education (AACE) journals, the *International Journal of e-learning, Journal of Interactive Learning Research, Journal of Educational/Multimedia and Hypermedia, Journal of Technology and Teacher Education, Information Technology in Childhood Education Annual, Contemporary Issues in Technology and Teacher Education,* and *International Journal of Educational Telecommunications* were reviewed using the AACE database. For technology based journals, several search parameters were defined, including *social studies, history, geography, citizenship, global education, economics,* etc. All abstracts were reviewed and a list of applicable journal articles was produced. Four International Society for Technology in Education (ISTE) journals, the *Journal of Research on Technology in Education, Learning and Leading with Technology, Journal of Computing in Teacher Education,* and *Ed Tech* were reviewed using the same search parameters as defined for the AACE journals.

Finally, eight discipline-specific journals were reviewed using the ERIC database. These included the *Journal of Geography, OAH Magazine of History, Teaching History, History Computer Review, History Teacher, American Educational History Journal, Anthropology and Education Quarterly,* and *Journal of Educational Psychology.* For the social studies based journals, several search parameters were defined, including *technology, computer, Internet* and *web.* Moreover, reference lists of several literature reviews yielded additional studies in the area of social studies and technology. Based on this process, we identified research studies with quantitative and qualitative designs.

We divided the research into two major categories: K–12 social studies instruction and teacher preparation. Within K–12 social studies instruction, we further divided the research into discipline-specific categories (history, geography, citizenship education). We subdivided research on teacher preparation into four categories: the general and targeted modeling of technology in social studies methods courses, field experiences with technology, longitudinal studies of technology in teacher preparation, and preparing educators to facilitate discussion with technology tools.

TEACHING HISTORY WITH TECHNOLOGY

The majority of research that examines technology in the social studies focuses on the impact of technology on historical thinking and the instructional uses of technology in history teaching. In this section, we review 16 such studies: teacher and student.

The teacher section focuses on the contextual factors influencing teacher use of digital primary sources and/or educational technology in the history classroom. The student section examines the instructional experience and effectiveness of technology interventions within the history classroom.

Teacher use

The past several years, 2004–2006, mark increased attention to researchers examining the reasons why teachers incorporate technology into their instruction. This reflects the larger instructional technology research movement that has migrated from comparative studies, determining which media was superior (Clark, 1994), to lines of research that look at how to best leverage the properties of educational technology (Harris, 2005). The nine studies in this section that investigate teacher use of technology provide a starting place for understanding teachers' existing practice.

The first studies reviewed look at the way in which access influences a teacher's use of digital primary sources. Hicks, Doolittle, and Lee (2004) report on a survey of a random sample of high school teacher members of the National Council of the Social Studies (NCSS) to determine the extent to which secondary social studies teachers use both printed and web-based primary sources as tools for inquiry. Of the 395 surveys mailed out, 158 were returned, yielding a response rate of 40%. The authors report on findings from both descriptive and inferential statistical analysis that the majority of the respondents use classroom-based primary sources rather than web-based sources. While the teachers in the study acknowledged the accessibility of the digital sources, they indicated that the documents were not necessarily "easier to use, more flexible, more engaging or more dynamic" (p. 226) and required significantly more classroom preparation time.

Friedman (2006), too, investigated factors influencing the use of digital primary sources by six secondary world history teachers. Through an examination of teacher interviews, classroom observations, and teaching materials, Friedman reported that while specific training in content-based technology pedagogy, either in a professional development format or as part of the teacher's preparation program, was significant, access to equipment, especially a classroom projector, was the key factor in determining the frequency of digital primary source use. Marri (2005) also looked at the issue of technology access in his case study that examined the ways in which one secondary U.S. history teacher in an under-resourced, alternative high school used educational technologies to foster multicultural democratic education. Marri utilized an inductive coding procedure to analyze 3 weeks of classroom observation notes, three teacher interviews, and a range of teacher-generated materials to develop the case. His findings indicate that the Internet helped overcome significant resource constraints inside and outside of the classroom by providing an information-gathering mechanism that assisted students in data manipulation and critical thinking.

Overall, the current literature suggests that, while access to those resources does not necessarily streamline the delivery of the material to students, indeed a teacher may be more inclined to use an online source if one is not available in hard copy (Hicks et al., 2004; Marri, 2005). A classroom projector may require far less preparation and set-up than taking students to a computer lab and would also allow teachers to use a digital resource without having to make classroom copies (Friedman, 2006). These studies suggest that reducing the overhead required to retrieve and display primary source documents is a key factor in promoting their use within the history classroom. Efficiency in teaching has been measured in these studies by teacher perception. As a result, findings may be highly influenced by a teacher's technical skill set as well as their existing pedagogical practices, as the following teacher use studies suggest.

DeWitt (2004) developed a comparative case study of four secondary history teachers from an analysis of three sets of teacher interviews, observations of class meetings, and written and electronic communications from the teachers. In comparing the cases, DeWitt identified primary motivations for using technology in history instruction, including student engagement, access to resources, and instructional efficiency. While these teachers had adopted various technologies to enhance their practice, DeWitt asserts that their primary approach to teaching was what he called, "technology enhanced traditionalism." In other words, since the teachers in his study relied primarily on lecture and recitation, presentation software in conjunction with a projection device was used heavily in all four classrooms. Swan and Hicks (2007) also found that teachers' use of technology was informed by their pedagogical approach, in addition to the individual teacher's technical facility and access. The researchers employed a qualitative design in examining the practices of three self-identified "tech-savvy" U.S. History teachers and explored the extent to which the participants utilized technology to support historical thinking and citizenship education over a 6-month period, using classroom observations, teacher interviews, and instructional materials. While all three teachers in the study used technology in their classrooms, only two of the teachers used the tools to support historical thinking, including building historical knowledge through the use of primary sources, conducting historical inquiry and encouraging students to think historically (Kobrin, 1996; Levstik & Barton, 2001; Wineburg, 1991). Two of the teachers in the study understood this pedagogical approach and were able to effectively leverage technology by having students create historical archives, design presentations using various primary sources, and facilitate discussions using a variety of historical media.

Both DeWitt (2004) and Swan and Hicks (2007) indicate that teacher practice is not notably altered by the integration of technology, but rather that technology is most frequently used to enhance or extend existing instructional approaches. Indeed, teachers' existing practices appear entrenched, confirming findings from a number of studies in fields outside of social studies (Cuban, 2001; Ravitz, Becker, & Wong, 2000; Windschitl & Sahl, 2002). As has been the case with a number of previous innovations, technology alone seems unlikely to move traditional pedagogies towards more student-centered approaches.

To determine the pliability of teacher practice, several researchers have intervened in history classrooms by introducing pre-designed, technology-enhanced, inquiry-based history curriculum to determine its impact on a teacher's instructional approach. Saye and Brush's (1999, 2004, 2006) qualitative case studies examined the use of a multimedia tool, *Decision Point!*, and the extent to which it could mitigate obstacles a teacher might face when implementing problem-based curriculum in the social studies classroom. *Decision Point!* is a multimedia environment, housing a variety of digitized historical documents as well as pedagogical tools designed to help students analyze and synthesize materials in the collection. In the 1999 and 2004 case studies, the researchers observed one teacher over a 4-year period; collected observation notes, teacher materials, and student products; and conducted teacher interviews to understand how the teacher delivered the instructional materials and whether it had any impact on her general approach to instruction. They found that while the *Decision Point!* curriculum prompted the teacher to reconsider some aspects of her teaching, particularly with regard to giving students time for critical thinking, she was tentative in other aspects of inquiry-based instruction, including contextualizing her instruction and questioning. The researchers concluded that the *Decision Point!* environment could potentially serve as a support for those teachers who are willing but unable to manage the process of disciplined inquiry. In a more recent case study, Saye and Brush (2006) examined the use of the same *Decision Point!* curriculum with two less traditional and expository-oriented teachers. Both teachers center their practice on problem-based inquiry units. Again, the researchers examined how each teacher implemented the unit and collected data using pre- and post-unit teacher interviews, planning notes, teaching materials, and daily classroom observations over 15 hours of instruction. Not surprisingly, they found that the implementation of the multimedia curriculum depended on the teacher's pedagogical style, so that the more traditional teacher was less likely to encourage critical thinking through prompted inquiry than those teachers who, before the intervention, were much more facile with problem-based inquiry.

Hofer and Swan (2006) also examined the ways in which a traditional, textbook-oriented fifth-grade history teacher implemented a digital documentary project using an archive of digital primary sources. In a qualitative case study using several teacher interviews, surveys, daily classroom observations, teaching materials, and student products, the researchers documented the challenges the teacher faced integrating technology and having her students create multimedia historical narratives using Microsoft's *Moviemaker* software. The teacher's challenges fell into three categories including problems connecting the project with local curriculum standards, troubleshooting technical difficulties (i.e., Internet speed, school firewalls, etc.), and, most importantly, developing a comfort level with the open-ended nature of the project. As Saye and Brush (2006) concluded, the teacher pedagogical orientation was the key determinant in using new technologies.

Student use of technology

Seven studies report on issues and effectiveness related to the use of multimedia environments, databases, and instructional models to facilitate student inquiry in history classrooms. Of these studies, three focus on using digital historical materials to support students in historical thinking. Saye and Brush (1999) and Brush and Saye (2000, 2002) explore the use of a "scaffolded" multimedia environment to structure historical inquiry into multiple perspectives related to the U.S. Civil Rights Movement. In a quasi-experimental design, Saye and Brush (1999) compared two classes of 11th-grade American history students studying the same unit. One class were taught the unit using the teacher's normal instructional methods and resources and the other through the *Decision Point!* multimedia curriculum (see Teacher Use section for description). Through a qualitative analysis of pre-/post-tests of content, end-of-unit essays, classroom observations, student surveys, and teacher interviews, the researchers found no significant difference in factual recall between the groups. The experimental group did, however, demonstrate greater engagement with the content and better "historical contextualization" of information. The experimental group also used a greater number of persuasive arguments and more often referenced divergent points of view in a post-unit essay. Interestingly, Saye and Brush noted that while the *Decision Point!* environment offered a significant amount of "hard scaffolding" (the "static supports that can be anticipated and planned in advance based upon student difficulties with a task") most students did not make use of the available help (p. 2). In contrast, the teacher's "soft scaffolding" ("dynamic situation specific aid provided by the teacher or peer to help with the learning process") turned out to be the essential element in supporting the analysis process (p. 2).

In follow-up studies, Brush and Saye (2000) and Saye and Brush (2004) employed a generative case study approach to investigate a single class of 11th-grade American History students utilizing the *Decision Point!* environment as part of their study of the U.S. Civil Rights Movement. In both of these implementations of the *Decision Point!* software, the authors collected and analyzed classroom observation notes, student interviews, teacher debriefings and interviews, student products, and post-unit essays to develop a case study. As was the case with their 1999 study, teacher scaffolding, prompts, contextual essays, and other tools appeared most effective within the multimedia environment. Interestingly, too, students reported feeling overwhelmed by the amount of information and documents available in the multimedia environment. Nonetheless, researchers note that the students report that the multimedia context promoted empathy, engagement, and increases in content retention.

Other studies also investigate the impact of particular kinds of scaffolding on technology use in history. Lee and Calandra (2004) focused on embedded annotations within a website to scaffold students' analysis of the United States Constitution. In this case, they examined the responses from students in two 11th-grade U.S. History classes to four scenarios involving a Constitutional question: one group used an annotated version of a website; the other did not use annotations. The annotations consisted of additional explanatory or informative material in connection with challenging terms (e.g., Bill of Attainder). Student responses to the four questions were analyzed using the constant comparative method to develop the findings. Their findings suggest that scaffolding with annotations within a site can influence "the explanatory clarity, veracity, and depth of students' answers" (p. 74). Based on their findings, Lee and Calandra developed a classification system of functional and nonfunctional prompts to assist developers in providing thoughtful and informed annotations for student use. *Functional annotations* (annotations that aid students directly in answering questions) provided positive support to students when developing responses, whereas *nonfunctional annotations* (information that does not directly aid students in forming a response) provided little to no assistance and, in some cases, distracted the students from the immediate task.

In contrast to studies testing the effectiveness of customized digital learning environments, Lee and Clarke (2004) observed 64 eleventh-grade students engaging in an exercise using two rich and expansive digital archive websites on the Cuban Missile Crisis. In a qualitative study of student work samples, interviews with students, and classroom observations, they found that, while some students reported success in using the sites, more often participants expressed difficulty in accessing site-based content. Students described a variety of problems and limitations in the user interface and structure. The findings suggest the importance of incorporating pedagogical structure in the design of a digital archive for student use. In another qualitative case study, Milson (2002), too, found that sixth graders using WebQuest to study ancient Egypt benefited from the kind of soft scaffolding suggested in the Saye and Brush (2002) study. In Milson's study, the 2-week WebQuest activity was designed to guide students through the inquiry process and led to at least, modest success for a variety of students. Again, however, analysis of classroom observations, student interviews, and teacher reflections revealed that students benefited more from the soft scaffolding provided by the teacher than the hard scaffolding provided in the WebQuest.

Interestingly, Wolf, Brush, and Saye (2003) found a contrary result in their study of *Big 6* meta-cognitive strategies applied to using multimedia historical resources to help students construct a newspaper article. A class of eighth-grade social studies students investigated the march on Selma, Alabama, during the U.S. Civil Rights Movement and wrote a first-person newspaper account of the event. Students' pre-/post-tests of content knowledge, journal and work logs, classroom observations, and interviews with 3 of the 18 students were analyzed to create a case study of this 12-session project. Students were provided with significant hard scaffolding using the Big 6 process (see Eisenberg & Berkowitz, 1990) to structure their research and writing. In this case, students relied heavily on the planned scaffolding and were able to engage in meta-cognitive strategies throughout the process.

Studies that focus either on a teacher's instructional use of technology in the history classroom or investigate the use of technology to support student historical inquiry suggest some clear trends on technology use in the history classroom. First, technology plays primarily a peripheral role in history classrooms. While teachers may acknowledge the increased access to historical materials provided by the web, instructional use of technology tends to support traditional, teacher-centered instruction. Perhaps partly in response to this trend, developers increasingly design web-based environments, websites, and instructional models to leverage the potential of technology to facilitate an inquiry approach to history. While these methods and models promote increased student engagement and suggest promise for enhancing historical inquiry, much ultimately depends on the scaffolding, or teacher facilitation and questioning. This should not be see as a limitation, but rather as an area of focus for further inquiry.

Technology in geography and citizenship

Few researchers have examined the impact of technology in areas outside of teaching history or social studies teacher education. In geography, we identified three studies published since 1990. Kerski (1999) surveyed teachers in American high schools that have adopted geographic information system (GIS) software in order to gauge the kinds and levels of use being implemented. A random sample of teachers who own GIS software were sent a survey through the mail. Of the 1520 surveys mailed, 27% were returned. Results of the survey indicate that the majority of respondents (52%) were science teachers and only 28% of respondents were geography teachers. One third of the respondents had not used the software instructionally, and only 18% used it in more than one lesson in multiple classes. Kerski suggests that a combination of factors could account for this apparent lack of integration, including insufficient training, issues with technology infrastructure, and the complexity of the software itself.

Keiper (1999) investigated GIS use in a fifth-grade classroom. In a qualitative case study, he used field notes, documents, and interviews to determine the potential of GIS as a means for teaching geography to elementary students. Students in the study worked with a learning module that used GIS in determining the optimal location for a proposed park. He found that the GIS module afforded students considerable opportunity to practice geographic skills and that the GIS curriculum can be highly motivating. However, students struggled with the *Arc View* GIS software interface and with working collaboratively on only one computer.

Moving beyond GIS usage, Linn (1997) explored the use of interactive maps and their impact on students' understanding of geography concepts. In five seventh-grade geography classrooms, students produced maps using both traditional and computer technologies during a 2-week unit. A pre-/post-test of content knowledge was administered to all the students and analyzed using statistical methods. While there was no statistical improvement in students' understanding of geographic content as a result of using the technologies, an analysis of survey data and products generated from all students suggested that students' motivation was greater and they enjoyed their work with the computers.

Studies of technology in specific disciplines within the social studies focus on history and geography. We located only one study related to technology and civic education. In an exploratory, descriptive case study, Heafner (2004) describes an exercise in which students researched and created a campaign advertisement for a local senatorial candidate. Using PowerPoint, they conveyed their candidate's positions on relevant issues. Heafner noted the positive change in student engagement, enthusiasm and motivation as they began this activity. Like Keiper (1999) and Linn (1997), Heafner concluded that technology added value to social studies instruction by increasing motivation and engaging students in the learning process. More work needs to be undertaken in these areas to determine what benefit, if any, these kinds of technology implementation have on students' social studies content knowledge.

Training teachers to use technology

While some schools and colleges of education have emphasized the integration of technology in teacher preparation for more than a decade, the development of the Preparing Tomorrow's Teachers to Use Technology (PT3) grant program proved to be a significant catalyst to advance this effort, funding hundreds of teacher education programs to explore the integration of technology and teacher preparation. Beginning in 1999, the U.S. Department of Education provided more than $400 million in grants to teacher education programs aimed at preparing preservice teachers to infuse technology into their instruction. Perhaps not surprisingly, the majority of studies on training teachers to use technology have been published since the inception of the PT3 program. These studies focus on both general and targeted modeling of technology in social studies methods courses, field experiences with technology, longitudinal studies of technology in teacher preparation, and preparing educators to facilitate discussion with technology tools.

TECHNOLOGY INTEGRATION IN TEACHER PREPARATION

Despite calls for attention to technology integration throughout teacher education programs and particularly in teaching methods courses (Adamy, 1999; Beisser, 1999; Byrum & Cashman, 1993; Handler & Marshall, 1992; Wetzel, 1993), there is little evidence to suggest that this approach has been widely adopted (Mehlinger & Powers, 2002). A baseline survey on the use of technology in social studies methods courses was sent to the membership of the NCSS College and University Faculty Assembly (CUFA), yielding a 59% response rate (Bolick, Berson, Coutts, & Heineke, 2003). A statistical analysis of responses suggests that regular use of technology in social studies methods courses is infrequent, at least among survey respondents. Forty-two percent of respondents reported occasional use, 19.8% reported using technology periodically throughout the semester, and 6.2% reported use of technology in every class session. Bolick et al. suggest that faculty use of technology can be divided into two main categories: digital communications (word processed lesson plans, email, Internet information, and lesson plans) and instructional technologies (multimedia presentations, lessons with social studies software, web page creation, etc.). Of these two categories, digital communications were used significantly more often than instructional technologies, with word processing, email and the use of the Internet accounting for nearly all use. Respondents rarely included even nascent components of technology integration within the methods class.

In the only other national study of technology usage among social studies educators, Bednarz and Audet (1999) employed a qualitative design to investigate the status of geographic information systems (GIS) technology in teacher preparation programs nationally. They reported patterns similar to those noted by Bolick et al. (2003). Bednarz and Audet surveyed all 736 member programs of the Association of American Colleges of Teacher Education (AACTE) on whether GIS is currently incorporated into teacher preparation. The survey yielded a rate of 34%. Of the 253 programs that responded to the survey, only 26 reported that GIS was a part of the teacher preparation program. In semi-structured follow-up interviews with this sample, the authors report that only a "handful" of respondents exposed students to GIS technology in an intentional and meaningful way, and that, due to competing program demands and course requirements, this is unlikely to change.

General modeling of technology in methods courses

Two studies focus on the impact of modeling general technology use in social studies methods instruction on students' practice, confidence, and attitude towards technology. In the first of these, Keiper, Harwood, and Larson (2000) studied 58 preservice teachers in elementary and secondary social studies methods courses at two technology-rich teacher education programs. After engaging in a qualitative content analysis of responses to questionnaires completed by students during the methods course, Keiper et al. reported that students attributed a variety of benefits to technology, including data collection (88%), improving student computer skills (31%), instructional variety (29%), the ability to incorporate dynamic sound and images (22%), and using technology as a communication tool (21%). Obstacles to using technology in the classroom included accessibility of technology in the classroom (66%), differing student abilities with technology (35%), the difficulties in supervising students using technology (22%), and the reliability of technology (21%). It is important to note that these findings are student perceptions of technology in the social studies and are not tied directly to specific interventions or outcomes. In an earlier study, Bennett and Scholes (2001) conducted a pre-/post-test survey of 42 students enrolled in an elementary social studies methods course on students' experience with and attitudes towards using technology in education. During this course, students used technology in a variety of ways to access course materials, communicate with each other, submit their coursework, and conduct research using the Internet to develop social studies topics and lesson plans. In a descriptive statistical analysis of the survey responses, the authors report more positive attitudes toward technology and increased specificity in goals related to technology.

In a more narrowly focused qualitative study of 23 elementary education students and their methods instructor, Molebash (2002, 2004) examined the impact of a technology rich social studies methods course on the students' perceptions of social studies, teaching social studies, and integrating technology in the social studies. In this course, two-thirds of all the modeling activities incorporated technology in some way. Specifically, the instructor modeled the use of online digital archives to promote inquiry in the classroom, support a variety of classroom discussion techniques, engage students in interactive reading and explore the use of handheld computers in the social studies. Using a semester of classroom observations, multiple interviews with the instructor and students, and a content analysis of student products, he found that while students' prior experience with social studies impacted their perception of and attitude towards technology in social studies, the constructivist modeling of technology by the methods instructor positively influenced these perceptions. The students reported that this modeling of technology use in the methods course helped them to see how social studies can be taught in a more stimulating manner, leading to an increased desire to teach social studies. Students were also able to identify more uses of technology in teaching, beyond Internet research.

Diem (2002) also explored the effectiveness of technology training efforts in social studies methods courses in a mixed methods study of 108 preservice teachers over a 2-year period. Diem does not identify specific uses of technology in these courses, but he does report adequate access to computers, Internet connectivity, and social studies software. Qualitative data was collected from student interviews, classroom observations, written documents, and semi-structured weekly reflections from methods instructors and students. Diem also employed a causal-comparative quantitative design to supplement the qualitative data. Diem reported that student knowledge of and integration of technology in lesson planning both increased as a result of the methods course, but most technology integration was limited to Internet research, and a majority of the students were not able to effectively integrate technology in their actual instruction.

Targeted modeling in methods courses

One group of studies investigate demonstrating the use of various kinds of scaffolding to introduce preservice social studies teachers to integrating technology for historical inquiry. Lee and Molebash (2004), for instance, conducted an exercise for a social studies methods course of graduate-level students in which the students used web-based historical documents to assist them in developing their pedagogical content knowledge. The authors focused on the scaffolding necessary to enable preservice teachers to utilize web-based resources to engage their students in historical inquiry using three different scaffolding strategies (unstructured, semi-structured, and structured). The students were divided into three groups, each of which was provided a different research strategy to determine how the Cuban Missile Crisis was resolved. Surprisingly, the authors found the unstructured approach superior to the semi-structured approach. In the semi-structured approach, students used an expansive digital archive of 275 documents relating to the Cuban Missile Crisis. The authors conclude, however, that the structured approach was most effective for students both in their ability to explain and to provide the context for the answer to the question. In this activity, the students were able to experience the importance of structuring work with web-based documents to effectively engage students in historical inquiry.

Lee (2001), too, examined how students might use a similar web-based digital archive to facilitate historical inquiry. In this qualitative study of 20 students in a secondary social studies methods course, Lee studied how students deal with controversial and contradictory information on a topic in an online archive of materials on the American Civil War. After exploring the contents of the archive, students were challenged to develop instructional activities using the archive's resources. Through observations, interviews with students, and an examination of student-created instructional activities, Lee found that students recognized the potential for web-based documents to facilitate inquiry and historical interpretation but chose to downplay controversial resources in the archive. While the students acknowledged the challenge of these "problematic" documents, they generally designed activities that circumvented the need for students to grapple with them. In these two studies, Lee emphasizes the need for scaffolding when teaching historical controversies.

While the findings from the studies in this section are promising, they represent a relatively small sample of programs and participants, and the range of approaches to "modeling" varies considerably, making it difficult to draw broad conclusions about the impact of modeling.

Field experiences with technology

Two studies focus on how coursework prepares students to implement technology-integrated activities in field placements, in student teaching, and in the first year of teaching. In a qualitative study of 18 preservice teachers, Dawson and Nonis (2000) investigated a field-based collaborative project pairing the preservice teachers with teachers from a partner K–12 school system. Using this approach, the preservice teachers worked under the apprenticeship of practicing teachers to develop technology-enhanced learning activities over the course of a semester. In an analysis of students' reflective journals, weekly email correspondence, classroom observations, weekly technical competencies, and inservice teacher evaluations, Dawson and Nonis noted improved attitudes towards technology in teaching and increased knowledge and skill related to instruction among the preservice teachers. The researchers also identified facilitators (instructional flexibility, low student/teacher ratio, collegial environment, and curricular and technical support) and barriers (time and access) students experienced in implementing their projects in the field. In an extension of the Dawson and Nonis study, Mason Bolick (2002) studied eight preservice secondary social studies teachers participating in a similar field-based technology experience. Students were paired with inservice teachers to design, develop, and implement lessons using digital history resources. In an analysis of student-created lessons, email messages, classroom observations, reflective journals, and course evaluations, Mason Bolick found that students reported gains in confidence, knowledge, and skill related to history, technology, and pedagogy similar to the findings reported by Dawson and Nonis.

Longitudinal studies of technology integration in preservice teacher education

The final three studies conducted in teacher preparation programs explore how students' work with technology over time influences their teaching practice. Wilson (2003) examined the students' implementation of technology in a field placement during a teacher preparation program. In this program, technology was systematically integrated into the social studies methods course. The instructor modeled, and students practiced, various forms of technology integration, including online communication, web-based learning opportunities, the development of lesson plans incorporating technology, and the creation of electronic portfolios. Wilson reported the perceptions and practices of 16 secondary social studies preservice teachers regarding technology integration from methods courses through student teaching. Following an analysis of email communications from students, open-ended surveys regarding technology integration during the methods course and student teaching, and field notes of classroom observations, Wilson notes that students reported increased confidence and comfort using technology, reporting that 14 of 16 students frequently used technology in their teaching, despite facing some of the same barriers noted above. It is unclear, however, exactly how the instructor's modeling of technology impacted the students and how they incorporated technology into their own teaching.

Crowe (2004) also takes a longitudinal view of the development of technology skills over the span of three different courses in two semesters in a teacher preparation program. This qualitative self-study followed the experiences of 23 students in three different courses leading to their student teaching experience. Crowe found that modeling the use of technology positively impacts students' attitudes, willingness to try technology, and desire to learn more about technology. As evidence, she noted that, while it was not required, 12 of 23 students incorporated technology into their microteaching activity and 16 of the 23 used technology during their student teaching.

In an interpretive, multiple-case study, Doppen (2004) followed four first-year teachers as they navigated the use of technology in their teaching. Over the course of a school year, Doppen collected classroom observation notes and teacher- and student-created documents along with teacher and student interviews from the two middle and two high school history classrooms to determine how these novice teachers attempted to facilitate historical thinking and inquiry, multiple perspectives, and historical empathy in their students. Doppen reports that the philosophical and pedagogical beliefs of the teachers had a great impact on their student-centered approach and their intended use of technology in the classroom. And, while they believed they were well prepared to begin teaching, they experienced significant challenges, including good and reliable access to computer technologies and the necessary support to incorporate them into their teaching. Although the four teachers were committed to engaging their students in historical inquiry, they had difficulty doing so, particularly when using technology. They predominately used computers either to present PowerPoint presentations or to challenge their students to create their own presentations. Only one of the four learned over time how to effectively structure student work to encourage historical thinking. Doppen concludes that teacher preparation programs need to provide multiple structured experiences with technology, including opportunities to help students navigate the integration of technology in real classrooms. In addition, Doppen asserts that teacher candidates must be challenged to reconcile their philosophical, pedagogical, and classroom management beliefs with the integration of technology.

From this limited sample of technology use in teacher preparation, it appears that modeling technology use, engaging students in focused interventions utilizing technology, and involving students in technology integration in the field can positively affect their attitudes, confidence, and vision for the use of technology in their teaching, as well as increase their knowledge and skills related to technology. Three questions remain, however. In many of the studies, the specific interventions and modeling by the course instructors was either vague or unclear. This examination of specific interventions and their impact is an important step in helping us understand how technology can be modeled and what types of effects we might expect. Second, only Doppen explores how the teachers integrate technology in their teaching beyond the teacher preparation program. With adequate access to technology, support, and emphasis on technology integration in the context of a course or teacher preparation program, it is not surprising that the students would implement technology in their student teaching. To gauge how this emphasis on technology actually impacts teaching practice, it is important to follow these students into their induction years of teaching. Finally, merely using technology to support class presentations or student research does not necessarily translate to effective and powerful uses of technology in the K–12 classroom.

Preparing educators to facilitate discussion with technology tools

In recent years, researchers have also begun to investigate the use of threaded discussion, email and other computer-mediated technologies as a means of connecting students across distance and furthering preservice teachers' understanding of global perspectives and/or self reflection. Merryfield (2003) reported on a study of 92 practicing American teachers and 22 "cultural consultants" in multiple graduate courses focused on social studies and global education over a 3-year period. Each of the courses featured online interactions through email communication, a course listserv, online chats, and threaded electronic discussion boards. These discussions included assignments on personal experiences, research, literature, primary resources, instructional resources, and teachers' plans to use content from the courses in their teaching. In a qualitative content analysis of text archives of all the online interactions and formative and summative course evaluations, Merryfield found that using asynchronous discussion boards with structured frequency and response limits had a positive effect on preservice teachers' cross cultural understanding. By creating online communities consisting of methods students and "cultural consultants" from around the globe, Merryfield reported success in promoting reflection and deeper engagement with course content as well as furthering the diversity of the learning community. Merryfield also reports that chats and threaded discussions can facilitate conversation of difficult, emotional, or controversial issues. She finds that the "facelessness" (p. 161) of online interaction frees people from different cultures of some inhibitions that often interfere with face-to-face interaction.

Larson and Keiper (2002) also explore similarities and differences in face-to-face and electronic threaded discussion boards in one class of secondary social studies methods students. They utilized a qualitative approach to analyze field notes from two face-to-face discussions and the text record of one threaded discussion in an attempt to determine benefits for each approach. They conclude that both forms of discussion are promising and that the interactions between students vary depending on the approach. In face-to-face discussion, students quickly and naturally acknowledge and extend on other students' statements. In contrast, the process was slow and required encouragement and prompting by the instructor in the online discussion. Larson and Keiper also found that, if required to do so, all students contributed to the online discussions, which was not the case in the face-to-face discussions. And while the asynchronous nature of online discussions provided students more time to participate, they found them more labor intensive than face-to-face discussions. Both Merryfield (2003) and Larson and Keiper (2002) note the importance of providing appropriate scaffolds to facilitate an effective online discussion.

Mason and Berson (2000) report positive effects on engagement when using computer-mediated communication in their elementary social studies methods course. In this qualitative study of 47 students, the authors analyze student responses to an eight-item questionnaire at the end of the semester. They report that over the course of the semester, students found the computer-mediated communication approach meaningful as they engaged in reflective dialogue through class videoconference sessions and electronic threaded discussions. The students reported that the approach helped enrich their understanding of social studies pedagogy. While the students were apprehensive at first, their confidence and self-direction in using the discussion tool increased over the semester.

Zong (2002) studied two preservice teachers' experiences in a 5-week online international simulation that required students to use both asynchronous and synchronous online technologies and assessed the impact on their integration of global perspectives into the social studies curriculum and instruction. Zong developed an interpretive case study of two preservice teachers during their student teaching experience to determine how they integrated global perspectives into their teaching. She observed each student eight times during their student teaching, collected lesson plans, and conducted a series of unstructured interviews following each observation and a structured interview at the end of the semester. In addition to understanding the potential of the Internet in connecting students to others beyond the borders of the classroom, she found that the project allowed the students to "learn about diverse points of view among nations and motivated them to teach this perspective consciousness in their own classes" (p. 609).

While these four studies provide some evidence that electronic communication tools can benefit preservice teachers in their methods classes, increased discussion and exploration of how the tools may be structured and facilitated will advance our understanding of this approach.

METHODOLOGICAL ISSUES

Varied approaches to data collection can enrich our understanding of a field. While the surge of research in the area of technology and social studies education is promising, as with other areas of educational research, there are ways in which methodologies can be shored up and strengthened. As Ehman and Glenn (1991) noted 15 years ago, research on technology and social studies suffers from some methodological limitations, including descriptions of treatment and participants and follow-up on the retention and transfer of knowledge and skills.

Because so much of the research we reviewed employed qualitative designs, it is important to consider what such studies can offer and what limitations they may have. Denzin (1989) suggests that "thick description" is an important characteristic of qualitative research, enabling "judgments of transferability" by providing sufficient context for the reader to make comparisons to other settings (Lincoln & Guba, 1985, p. 359). Detailed descriptions of setting, context, participants, and results strengthen the trustworthiness of qualitative findings. Some of the studies reviewed within this chapter do not meet this standard. Unfortunately, page limits in research journals often constrain thick description. A number of the studies reviewed for this chapter lacked the kind of thick description that might lend further support to their findings (see Lee & Calandra,

2004; Milson, 2002). This was particularly the case in intervention studies which often lacked description of the context, technological environment, and structure and implementation of interventions. Such detail allows for replication in different settings and for more careful theorizing about the impact of context on teaching and learning.

A second issue relates to follow-up. A common finding in the studies reviewed here is that students' performance, skills, or understanding increase as a result of one intervention or another. While these are certainly important findings, we know little about how durable the learning gains are and how (if) skills transfer (Ehman & Glenn, 1991). Lee and Molebash's (2004) study represents one of the only instances where student retention of skills or transfer of higher-order thinking processes was part of the initial research design. For example, both Dawson and Nonis (2000) and the extension study by Mason Bolick (2002) find that preservice and inservice teachers made important gains in understanding how to use digital historical resources and in designing technology-enhanced instruction during a field-based experience with using technology. We don't know, however, if these gains are sustained or if and how teachers utilize technology in their later instruction.

The concerns noted above have persisted in the 15 years since the last *Handbook* chapter. In addition, we have identified other issues related to reliance on students' and teachers' self-reports of understanding and practice, the investigation of one's own practice, and the design of research questions.

Self-reporting

The "lack of use" studies (Bolick et al., 2003; Hicks et al., 2004; Bednarz & Audet, 1999) and many of the studies involving methods students (Crowe, 2004; Wilson, 2003) rely primarily on self-report in the form of surveys and student reflections of their current use of technology in teaching and/or attitudes and skills in using technology. While helpful, self-report data can be problematic, as participants may misreport their skill and the scope of their technology use. Second, while descriptive survey data is helpful in providing a snapshot of technology use, surveys alone cannot explain exactly what respondents mean by their responses or what they thought particular questions meant. Another, perhaps more fundamental problem with student self-report measures is that respondents may tell the researcher what they think is desired, particularly when the instructor is conducting the research. Students may report that they intend to use technology in their teaching, but they may actually make little use of technology when left to decide on their own, either because of time and access issues or because they may come to realize that they are not as prepared to integrate technology as they thought. To determine more accurately the impact of instructor modeling on preservice teachers' practice, longitudinal studies should be designed to follow participants into student teaching and through the induction years. These issues do not negate the importance of existing research; rather, they suggest ways of strengthening the research base.

Studying our own students

Perhaps a more intractable problem is studying our own students. Many of the studies reviewed here report on potentially promising efforts to enhance social studies teaching and learning or strategies to effectively prepare preservice teachers to use technology in teaching. Some of these studies were undertaken in the researchers' own social studies methods courses. Experimenting with technology in one's own course provides a convenient and controlled environment in which to develop intuitions and refine practice for technology integration. This is useful information and a significant contribution to the field. Relying so heavily on this approach, however, involves both logical and methodological problems. First, due to their lack of teaching experience, students may be unable to accurately report changes in skills and knowledge in enhancing teaching and learning with technology. While some students may genuinely perceive this gain, some may be reporting what their instructor hopes to find. Additionally, if students recognize that technology is a stated or implied focus of the methods course, they may be more inclined to incorporate technology into lessons than if technology were more in the background. For example, a majority of students may employ technology during field experiences because they perceive it as an expectation of the methods instructor, not because they have learned to appreciate its inclusion or to understand the value that technology might bring to a particular lesson.

Studies of our own practice are useful and informative, but insufficient, if we are to develop a strong case for what constitutes "promising practice" in incorporating technology in teacher education and in K–12 social studies instruction. Rather, researchers' next steps must be to test approaches in different settings with varied and larger populations, and to follow students and their teachers over time.

Research questions

With any new educational tool or strategy, it is easy to slide from research into advocacy. It is difficult to see potential in a new technology and not lead the charge to "revolutionize" the classroom. Brush and Saye (2000, 2002), Doppen (2004), Saye and Brush (1999, 2004, 2006), and Lee (2001) are notable for their balanced reporting of findings related to the potential *and* pitfalls of technology in the social studies classroom. In some studies, however, research questions seem to advocate rather than investigate. Researchers appear to assume that technology is preferable to traditional modes of instruction, that it can make a good teacher better, and that it leads to more student-centered (and therefore preferable) instruction. While any of these assumptions may prove to be the case, we might be better served to investigate how a particular strategy to integrate technology in a methods course affects students' performance, or how a particular technology-enhanced activity supports particular kinds of learning. As Ehman and Glenn (1991) duly note, "Improved research designs are important if the field is to move forward, however, better designs with the wrong questions will not help" (p. 519).

FUTURE DIRECTIONS

While still in its adolescence, the surge of technology research within the last 5 years has provided a foundation from which to further develop lines of inquiry in the field. One of the clearest trends found in many of the studies has been in the area of scaffolding. Specifically, many researchers exploring the use of technology in social studies classrooms have begun identifying the ways in which the range of instructional technologies (i.e., digital primary sources, discussion boards, online instruction, GIS, etc.) could be scaffolded for student and teacher use (Brush & Saye, 2000, 2002; Keiper, 1999; Kirman & Unsworth, 1992; Lee, 2001; Lee & Calandra, 2004; Lee & Clarke, 2004; Lee & Molebash, 2004; Merryfield, 2003; Milson, 2002; Saye & Brush, 1999, 2004, 2006; Wolf, Brush & Saye, 2003). To this end, researchers in history instruction have examined how embedded digital prompts can optimally support students' historical thinking. As a first step, they have begun categorizing types of scaffolds and have documented the level of effectiveness of each (see Brush & Saye, 2000; Lee & Calandra, 2004; Saye & Brush, 2002). For the vast majority of studies, however, scaffolding remains a latent and unexplored instructional component (Keiper, 1999; Larson & Keiper, 2002; Merryfield,

2003). We need research to continue defining types of cognitive supports for various thinking processes in a diversity of school settings, including appropriate sequencing, time allocation, and the gradual removal of instructional scaffolds.

Other researchers have chronicled the extent of technology use in teacher preparation programs (see Bernardz & Audet, 1999; Bolick et al., 2003) as well as in K–12 social studies classrooms (see Hicks et al., 2004; Kerski, 1999). Consistently, the findings have suggested that technology use in instruction in both K–12 and higher education is sparse and, consequently, technology has had little impact on social studies education. In an attempt to understand the barriers that exist in integrating technology, a number of scholars have chosen to look at the motivations and pedagogical approaches of those teachers who regularly utilize technology in their teaching (DeWitt, 2004; Friedman, 2006; Marri, 2005; Swan & Hicks, 2007). Over extended periods of time in the classroom, these researchers developed case studies of teachers who utilize a range of technologies, including projectors, software, hardware, and the Internet. The findings of these studies suggest that factors outside of time, training and access (Becker, 1998; Clark, 1994; Cuban, 2001; Cuban, Kirkpatrick, & Peck, 2001; Ehman & Glenn, 1991; Mehlinger, 1996) can account for the ways in which teachers use or do not use technology in social studies. According to DeWitt (2004), Marri (2005), and Swan and Hicks (2007), teaching practices are far more entrenched than perhaps scholars had originally suspected, and existing instructional practices and purposes may be a much stronger indicator of how a teacher does or does not use technology. The field would benefit from further exploration of how particular uses of technology support different pedagogical approaches and how teachers navigate the use of different types of tools and resources in their own practice.

Because more recent research in using technology focuses on historical thinking, methodologies developed to investigate historical thinking may provide a direction for the broader diffusion of technology in social education. While many recent theoretical and research pieces have touted technology as a mechanism to facilitate constructivist pedagogy and to transform social education (Berson, Lee, & Stuckart, 2001; Braun & Risinger, 1999; Bull, G., Bull, G., Garofalo, & Harris, 2002; Martorella, 1997; Mason, C., Berson, M., Diem, R., Hicks, D., Lee, J., & Dralle, T., 2000; NCSS, 1994; van Hover, Berson, Swan, & Bolick; 2004), the research in history instruction reminds us that technology can be used to simply augment and enhance existing promising practice. Rather than attempting to transform the way teachers teach, current technologies can be used by history teachers to efficiently access digital primary sources, to scaffold historical inquiry and to provide access to resources for students. Additionally, the myriad of studies which experiment with tools for K–12 students as well as preservice teachers helps create vision for how educational technologies can be used to support global education (see Larson & Keiper, 2002; Merryfield, 2003; Zong, 2002), and geography education (see Keiper, 1999; Kirman & Unsworth, 1992; Linn, 1997) as well as history education (see Lee, 2001; Mason Bolick, 2002; Milson, 2002). While providing educators with possibilities, it will become increasingly important to examine the ways in which K–12 teachers experience these technologies, particularly those teachers without the technology expertise. These types of studies might provide insight on creating sustainable change within K–12 settings.

Some of the most compelling research reviewed in this chapter shares common attributes that may help guide future inquiry in the field. First, a number of researchers spent the necessary time in the classroom to understand the complexity of teaching with technology and to gain greater perspective on both its potential and limitations. Saye and Brush (2004) for example, report findings from three different interventions with the same groups of students in a high school history class. This extended inquiry in the field helped them to move beyond the novelty effect and the challenge of introducing a new instructional strategy, both of which can skew technology research either positively or negatively. A related attribute in much of this work is the effort on the part of the researchers to align the intervention with the opportunities and constraints of the classroom and turn the instruction over to the classroom teacher (Saye & Brush, 1999, 2004, 2006). This gives the researchers insight into how the intervention may play out in real classroom settings. These small but focused steps, when taken together, effectively move the field forward by fostering specific skills and understandings and/or testing the effects of particular technologies or strategies. It is in this focused inquiry with teachers in the classroom that we can more effectively understand how to best leverage technology to support a variety of pedagogical approaches in the social studies classroom.

REFERENCES

Adamy, P. (1999). An analysis of factors that influence technology integration by math teacher educators. Unpublished doctoral dissertation, University of Virginia, Charlottesville.

Anglin, G. (Ed.) (1995). *Instructional technology*. Englewood, CO: Libraries Unlimited.

Becker, H. J. (1998). Running to catch a moving train: Schools and information technology. *Theory into Practice, 37*, 20–30.

Becker, H. (2000, July). Findings from teaching, learning, and computing survey: Is Larry Cuban right? *Teaching, Learning and Computing.* Retrieved April 5, 2006, from http://www.crito..uci.edu/tlc/findings/ccsso.pdf.

Bednarz, S. W., & Audet, R. (1999). The status of GIS technology in teacher preparation programs. *Journal of Geography, 98*(2), 60–67.

Beisser, S. R. (1999, March). Infusing technology in elementary social studies methods. Paper presented at the Society for Information Technology & Teacher Education. 10th Annual International Conference, San Antonio, TX. (ERIC Document Reproduction Service No. ED 432 294)

Bennett, L., & Scholes, R. (2001). Goals and attitudes related to technology use in a social studies method course. *Contemporary Issues in Technology and TeacherEducation, 1*(3), 373–385.

Berson, M. J. (1996). Effectiveness of computer technology in the social studies: A review of the literature. *Journal of Research on Computing in Education, 28*(4), 486–499.

Berson, M. J., Lee, J. K., & Stuckart, D. W. (2001). Promise and practice of computer technologies in the social studies: A critical analysis. In W. B. Stanley (Ed.), *Critical issues in social studies research for the 21st century* (pp. 209–229). Greenwich, CT: Information Age Publishing.

Bolick, C., Berson, M., Coutts, C., & W. Heinecke. (2003). Technology applications in social studies teacher education: A survey of social studies methods faculty. *Contemporary Issues in Technology and Teacher Education, 3*(3), 300–309.

Braun, J., & Risinger, F. (1999). *Surfing social studies*. Washington, D.C.: National Council for the Social Studies.

Brush, T., & Saye, J. (2000). Implementation and evaluation of a student-centered learning unit: A case study. *Educational Technology, Research and Development, 48*(3), 79–100.

Brush, T., & Saye, J. (2002). A summary of research exploring hard and soft scaffolding for teachers and students using a multimedia supported learning environment. *Journal of Interactive Online Learning*, [Online serial] 1(2). Retrieved July 12, 2006, from http://www.ncolr.org/jiol/issues/PDF/1.2.3.pdf

Bull, G., Bull, G., Garofalo, J., & Harris, J. (2002). Grand challenges: Preparing for the technological tipping point. *Learning and Leading with Technology, 29*(8), 6–12.

Byrum, D. C., & Cashman, C. (1993). Preservice teacher training in educationalcomputing: Problems, perceptions, and preparation. *Journal of Technology and Teacher Education, 1*(3), 259–274.

Clark, R. E. (1994). Media will never influence learning. *Educational Technology Research and Development, 42*(2), 21–29.

Crowe, A. (2004). Teaching by example: Integrating technology into social studieseducation courses. *Journal of Computing in Teacher Education, 20*(4), 159–165.

Cuban, L. (2001). *Oversold and underused: Computers in the classroom*. Cambridge, MA: Harvard University Press.

Cuban, L., Kirkpatrick, H., & Peck, C. (2001). High access and low use of technology in high school classrooms: Explaining an apparent paradox. *American Educational Research Journal, 38*(4), 813–834.

Dawson, K., & Nonis, A. (2000). Preservice teachers' experiences in a K-12/universitytechnology-based field initiative: Benefits, facilitators, constraints and implications for teacher educators. *Journal of Computing in Teacher Education, 17*(1), 4–12.

Denzin, N. K. (1989). *Interactive interactionism*. London: Sage.

DeWitt, S. W. (2007). Dividing the digital divide: Intsructional use of computers in social studies. *Theory and Research in Social Studies Education, 35* (2), 277-304.

Diem, R. A. (2002, April). An examination of the effects of technology instruction in social studies methods courses. Paper presented at the annual meeting of the American Educational Research Association, New Orleans, LA. (ERIC Document Reproduction Service No. ED346082)

Doppen, F. H. (2004). Beginning social studies teachers' integration of technology in the history classroom. *Theory and Research in Social Education, 32*(2), 248–279.

Ehman, L. H., & Glenn, A. D. (1991). Interactive technology in the social studies. In J. .Shaver (Ed.), *Handbook of Research on Social Studies Teaching and Learning* (pp. 513–522). New York: Macmillan.

Eisenberg, M., & Berkowitz, R. (1990). *Information problem solving: The Big Six skills approach to library and information skills instruction*. Norwood, NJ: Ablex.

Friedman, A. (2006). World history teachers' use of digital primary sources: The effect of training. *Theory and Research in Social Education, 34*(1), 124–141.

Handler, M., & Marshall, D. (1992). Preparing new teachers to use technology: One set of perceptions. In R. Carey, D. Carey, J. Willis, & D. Willis (Eds.), *Technology and Teacher Education Annual, 1992* (pp. 386–388). Charlottesville, VA: Association for the Advancement of Computing in Education.

Harris, J. (2005). Our agenda for technology integration: It's time to choose. *Contemporary Issues in Technology and Teacher Education, 5*(2), 116–122.

Heafner, T. (2004). Using technology to motivate students to learn social studies. *Contemporary Issues in Technology and Teacher Education, 4*(1), 42–53.

Hicks, D., Doolittle, P., & Lee, J. K. (2004). History and social studies teachers' use of classroom and web-based historical primary sources. *Theory and Research in Social Education, 32*(2), 213–247.

Hofer, M., & Swan, K. O. (2006, Spring). Standards, firewalls, and general classroom mayhem: Implementing student-centered technology projects in the elementary classroom. *Social Studies Research and Practice, 1*(1). Retrieved July 10, 2006, from http://www.socstrp.org/issues/viewarticle.cfm?volID=1&IssueID=1&ArticleID=13.

Keiper, T. A. (1999). GIS for elementary students: An inquiry into a new approach to learning geography. *Journal of Geography, 98*, 47–59.

Keiper, T., Harwood, A., & Larson, B. E. (2000). Preservice teachers' perceptions of infusing computer technology onto social studies instruction. *Theory and Research in Social Education, 28*(4), 566–579.

Kerski, J. (1999). A Nationwide analysis of the implementation of GIS in high school education, ESRI library [Online]. Retrieved April 5, 2006, from http://gis.esri.com/library/userconf/proc99/proceed/papers/pap202/p202.htm.

Kirman, J. M., & Unsworth, M. (1992). Digital data in the grade 6 classroom. *Journal of Geography, 91*(6), 241–246.

Kobrin, D. (1996). *Beyond the textbook: Teaching history using documents and primary sources*. Portsmouth, NH: Heinemann.

Larson, B. E. (2003). Comparing face-to-face discussion and electronic discussion: A case study from high school social studies. *Theory and Research in Social Education, 31*(3), 347–365.

Larson, B. E., & Keiper, T. A. (2002). Classroom discussion and threaded electronic discussion: learning in two arenas. *Contemporary Issues in Technology and Teacher Education*, available at: http://www.citejournal.org/vol2/iss1/socialstudies/article1.cfm, Vol. 2 No.1.

Lee, J. K. (2001). Pre-service social studies teachers "reckoning" with historical interpretations and controversy arising from the use of digital historical resources. *Journal for the Association of History and Computing* IV (2). Retrieved November 1, 2002, from http://mcel.pacificu.edu/JAHC/JAHCIV2/ARTICLES/lee/leeindex.html.

Lee, J. K., & Calandra, B. (2004). Can embedded annotations help high school students perform problem solving tasks using a web-based historical document? *Journal of Research on Technology in Education, 36*(4), 65–84.

Lee, J. K., & Clarke, W. G. (2004). Doing digital local history: The story of Asaph Perry. *Social Education, 68*(3), 203–207.

Lee, J. K., & Molebash, P. (2004). Outcomes of various scaffolding strategies on student teachers' digital historical inquiries. *Journal of Social Studies Research, 26*(1), 25–35.

Levstik, L. S., & Barton, K. (2001). *Doing history: Investigating with children in elementary and middle schools* (2nd ed.). Hillsdale, NJ: Erlbaum.

Lincoln, Y., & Guba, E. (1985). *Naturalistic inquiry.* Newbury Park, CA: Sage.

Linn, S. E. (1997). The effectiveness of interactive maps in the classroom: A selected example in studying Africa. *Journal of Geography, 96*(3), 164–170.

Marri, A. R. (2005). Educational technology as a took for multicultural democratic education: The case of one U.S. history teacher in an underresourced high school. *Contemporary Issues in Technology and Teacher Education, 4*(4), 395–409.

Martorella, P. (1997). Technology and social studies: Which way to the sleeping giant? *Theory and Research in Social Education, 25*(4), 511–514.

Mason Bolick, C. (2002). Digital history TIP: Preservice social studies teachers' experiences in a technology-rich field initiative. *Journal of Computing in Teacher Education, 19*(2), 54–60.

Mason, C. L., & Berson, M. J. (2000). Computer mediated communication in elementary social studies methods. *Theory and Research in Social Education, 28*(4), 527–545.

Mason, C., Berson, M., Diem, R., Hicks, D., Lee, J., & Dralle, T. (2000). Guidelines for using technology to prepare social studies teachers. *Contemporary Issues in Technology and Teacher Education, 1*(1), 107–116.

Mehlinger, H. (1996). School reform in the information age. *Phi Delta Kappan, 77*(6), 400–407.

Mehlinger, H. D., & Powers, S. M. (2002). *Technology and teacher education: A guide for educators and policymakers.* Boston: Houghton Mifflin Company.

Merryfield, M. (2003). Like a veil: Cross-cultural experiential learning online. *Contemporary Issues in Technology and Teacher Education, 3*(2), 146–171.

Milson, A. J. (2002). The Internet and inquiry learning: integrating medium and methodin a sixth grade social studies classroom. *Theory and Research in Social Education, 30*(3), 330–353.

Molebash, P. E. (2002). Constructivism meets technology integration: The CUFAtechnology guidelines in an elementary social studies methods course. *Theory and Research in Social Education, 30*(3), 429–455.

Molebash, P. E. (2004). Preservice teacher perceptions of a technology-enriched methods course. *Contemporary Issues in Technology and Teacher Education, 3*(4), 412–432.

National Center for Education Statistics. (2000, February). *Internet access in U.S. public schools and classrooms: 1994–1999.* National Center for Education Statistics (NCES 2000-086).

National Council for the Social Studies (1994*). Expectations of excellence: Curriculum standards for social studies.* Silver Spring, MD: National Council for the Social Studies.

Pew Institute (2002). *The digital disconnect: The widening gap between internet savvy students and their schools.* Retrieved November 5, 2003, from http://www.pewinternet.org/reports/toc.asp?Report=67.

Ravitz, J. L., Becker, H. J., & Wong, Y. T. (2000). *Constructivist-compatible beliefs and practices among U.S. teachers* (Report No. 4). Irvine, CA: Teaching, Learning and Computing. Retrieved June 5, 2005, from http://www.crito.uci.edu/TLC/findings/report4/startpage.html.

Saettler, P. (1990). *The evolution of American educational technology.* Englewood, CO: Libraries Unlimited.

Saye, J., & Brush, T. (1999). Student engagement with social issues in a multimedia supported learning environment. *Theory and Research in Social Education, 27*(4), 472–504.

Saye, J. W., & Brush, T. (2002). Scaffolding critical reasoning about history and social issues in multimedia-supported learning environments. *Educational Technology, Research and Development, 50*(3), 77–96.

Saye, J. W., & Brush, T. (2004). Scaffolding problem-based teaching in a traditional social studies classroom. *Theory and Research in Social Education, 32*(3), 349–378.

Saye, J. W., & Brush, T. (2006). Comparing teachers' strategies for supporting student inquiry in a problem-based multimedia-enhanced history unit. *Theory and Research in Social Education, 34*(2), 183–212.

Shulman, L. (1986). Those who understand: Knowledge growth in teaching. *Educational Researcher, 15*(2), 414.

Swan, K., & Hicks, D. (2007). Through the democratic lens: The role of purpose in leveraging technology to support historical inquiry in the social studies classroom. *International Journal of Social Education, 21*(2), 142–168.

van Hover, S. D., Berson, M. J., Swan, K. O., & Bolick, C. M. (2004). Implications of ubiquitous computing for the social studies. *Journal of Computing in Teacher Education, 20*(3), 107–112.

Wells, J., & Lewis, L. (2006). *Internet access in U.S. public schools and classrooms: 1994–2005* (NCES 2007-020). U.S. Department of Education. Washington, DC: National Center for Education Statistics.

Wetzel, K. (1993). Teacher educators' uses of computers in teaching. *Journal of Technology in Teacher Education, 1*(4), 335–352.

Whitworth, S. A., & Berson, M. J. (2003). Computer technology in the social studies: An examination of the effectiveness literature (1996–2001). *Contemporary Issues in Technology and Teacher Education, 2*(4), 472–509.

Wilson, E. K. (2003). Preservice secondary social studies teachers and technology integration: What do they think and do in their experience? *Journal of Computing in Teacher Education, 20*(1), 29–39.

Windschitl, M., & Sahl, K. (2002). Tracing teachers' use of technology in a laptop computer school: The interplay of teacher beliefs, social dynamics, and institutional culture. *American Educational Research Journal, 39*(1), 165–205.

Wineburg, S. S. (1991) On the Reading of historical texts: Notes on the breach between school and academy. *American Educational Research Journal, 28*(3), 495–519.

Wolf, S. E., Brush, T., & Saye, J. (2003). Using an information problem-solving model as a metacognitive scaffold for multimedia-supported information-based problems. *Journal of Research on Technology Education, 35*(3), 321–341.

Zong, G. (2002). Can computer mediated communication help to prepare global teachers? An analysis of preservice social studies teachers' experience. *Theory and Research in Social Education, 30,* 589–616.

Part VII
Teacher preparation and development

18 The education of social studies teachers

Susan Adler
University of Missouri

A body of research now exists which supports the premise that good teachers matter (National Commission of Teaching and America's Future, 1996; Sanders & Horn, 1998). This research points to the difference an effective teacher can make, even in very challenging circumstances. Teachers are far more than mere conduits of information or of curriculum developed by "experts." Teachers are the key to what happens in classrooms (Thornton, 1991, 2005). They, along with their students, are the implementers of the actual curriculum. Of course, rules and expectations, along with the specific contexts of teaching, make a difference. However, ultimately, it is the teacher who makes the decisions about what actually gets taught in the classroom and how it gets taught. It is the teacher who assesses what students have actually learned and what individual needs individual students may have. To use Thornton's (1991, 2005) term, teachers are the "curricular-instructional gatekeepers."

The preparation and education of good teachers would seem, therefore, to be of great importance. The basic premise of teacher education is that the knowledge, skills and perspectives of prospective teachers and, in the case of professional development, in-service teachers, will change (Banks & Parker, 1990). Research in teacher education should inform readers about best practices and strategies for the education of teachers. This is especially important at a time when there is considerable disagreement about what constitutes the best approach in teacher education and when this disagreement is being played out in the policy arena.

Disagreement about the best strategies and policies for teacher education is confounded in social studies by the persistent lack of consensus about the meaning of social studies itself (Armento, 1996; Evans, 2004; Nelson, 2001) and by the attack on social studies in the curriculum (Whitson, 2004). Conflicting views about the nature of social studies suggest conflicting ideas about the knowledge and skills needed by social studies teachers. Are teachers to be prepared as teachers of the academic disciplines or must they also develop the skills and knowledge to create curriculum that will facilitate learners attaining competence as citizens in a democratic society?

This chapter reviews recent research in social studies teacher education, with a primary focus on teacher preparation. It builds on previous recent reviews (Adler, 1991; Armento, 1996; Banks & Parker, 1990) and will examine the extent to which concerns and recommendations raised in earlier research have provided new research direction and increased our understanding of the education of social studies teachers. Adler (1991) was critical of the particularistic approach she found in her review of research in social studies teacher education. That is, the research appeared to be focused on an "array of unrelated or random aspects of teacher education" (p. 218). She was optimistic about an emerging body of research that explored interrelationships among teacher practices, the context of those practices, and teachers' beliefs and perspectives. Banks and

Parker (1990) reminded readers that most teacher educators are practitioners with little engagement in research. They encouraged social studies teacher educators to engage in research focused on their practice. In a 1993 article, Adler echoed Banks and Parker by encouraging teacher educators to balance the demands of teaching and research through reflective inquiry into their own practice. "Through the thoughtful description and reflection upon practice our understanding of the experiences of educating teachers may be broadened and deepened" (p. 166).

Armento (1996) concluded that current research, increasingly composed of qualitative studies involving small numbers, may present a distorted view of social studies teacher preparation. Like Banks and Parker (1990), Armento found little critical examination of interactions in the methods course, practica, or content courses. She found little sense of urgency among researchers about the preparation or professional development of social studies teachers. She called for greater attention to the dynamics of growth and learning and to the views of social studies that permeate programs.

Thus recent previous reviews of research in the area of social studies teacher preparation have lamented the limited scope or potential impact of this body of research. That is, the research has appeared to do little to inform teacher education practices or provide an understanding of just what happens in teacher education. From earlier reviews one can conclude that research has not given a clear picture of which practices seem to contribute to the development of effective teachers or what might be done to reform and improve the education of social studies teachers. This current research review will seek to synthesize research in the field to determine what might be learned about practices in social studies teacher education and the impact of these practices. It is important as well to examine the intersections of research in social studies teacher education with current research in teacher education more generally.

TRENDS IN RESEARCH IN TEACHER EDUCATION

In recent years, teacher education has been the subject of "blistering debate" (Cochran-Smith, 2005a, 2005b). Ideas about what constitutes the best approach in the preparation of teachers are hotly contested. Further, these ideas are often based on untested beliefs and competing ideologies. Cochran-Smith (2001) argues that there are at least three competing agendas in teacher education: professionalization, deregulation, and what some would designate as over-regulation. The professionalization advocates (see, for example, National Commission on Teaching and America's Future, 1996) focus on the self-regulation of teacher education. The work of the National Association for the Accreditation of Teacher Education (NCATE) and the Teacher Education Accreditation Council (TEAC) represent efforts to define standards and assessments by the professionals within the field: teacher educators and teachers. These advocates of professionalization argue that there is a body of research on good teaching and on good practices in teacher education and that this research can guide the professional oversight of teacher education programs. Furthermore, they argue, teacher educators themselves must assume the responsibility of assessing programs and advocating for continuous improvement.

On the other side are those who argue that teacher preparation is a matter simply of attaining subject- matter knowledge. Take bright people, with strong content background, the argument goes, and provide them with an apprenticeship of practice, not a university-based preparation program that precedes actual teaching (see, for example, Abell Foundation, 2001; Ballou & Soler, 1998; Paige, Stroup, & Andrade, 2002). Good teaching requires strong content knowledge; the rest will be learned through apprenticeship while on the job. Finally, there is the policy push at both the state and national levels, to improve student performance by placing a "highly qualified" teacher in every classroom. Legislation defining how we recognize a "high quality teacher," for example through test scores, creates regulations and testing that serve to shape the structure and practices of teacher education. Advocates of regulation look to the state to assure that the teachers in today's classrooms are competent and qualified.

Research in teacher education cannot be above the debates. To claim to be outside the realm of policy and politics is to give up a crucial role in shaping the forces that, in turn, shape teacher education. Both initial and sustained teacher education can make a difference to the skills and knowledge of classroom teachers (National Commission on Teaching and America's Future, 1996; Sanders & Horn, 1998). Research can contribute to designing, understanding and implementing practices that will prepare good teachers who will stay in the profession and who will continue to develop and change through their years as teachers.

Changing research directions

The past half century has seen a shift in the research agenda in teacher education. Questions about helping teachers develop sets of specific teaching skills had long been the focus of research in teacher education. This "training approach," which dominated research in teacher education from the 1950s to the 1980s, focused on providing teachers with a set of observable skills thought to be correlated to student success (Cochran-Smith, 2004, 2005b). By the 1970s and into the 1980s, a body of research on effective teaching seemed to be emerging, and with it was a hope that teacher education could be grounded in this knowledge-base of teaching (Galluzo, 1999). If researchers could identify teacher behaviors that correlated with student achievement, then teachers could be helped to master performances and behaviors that would result in improved student learning.

By the 1980s, however, this approach to research in teacher education was coming under attack. The empirical research on effective teaching strategies that lay the basis for this research was considered by critics to be lacking in robust empirical support (Cochran-Smith, 2004, 2005a, 2005b). Effective teaching research was criticized for being decontextualized, as though the same behaviors could be effective anywhere and as though the culture and politics of schools have little influence on what goes on there. Furthermore, research in teacher education appeared to take a mechanistic view of teaching and teachers (Galluzo, 1999). Behavior, after all, is a manifestation of knowledge, beliefs, and understandings. This research approach failed to acknowledge the role of the teacher as decision maker or the development of professional knowledge or judgment in teachers. The focus was on skill application, not on teacher decision-making (Lanier, 1982).

Cochran-Smith (2004, 2005a) describes the shift that began in the 1980s as one that shifted the focus from how teachers acquire the skills necessary for teaching to how teachers can learn to function as responsible decision makers. "The goal of teacher preparation programs was to design the social, organizational, and intellectual contexts wherein prospective teachers could develop the knowledge, skills and dispositions needed to function as decisions-makers" (Cochran-Smith, 2004, p. 296). Researchers in teacher education turned to a focus on the development of professional thinking and decision making, with less focus on skill acquisition.

In addition, the role of discipline-based differences began to emerge. The work of Shulman (1986) and others, made clear that it is not enough to know the concepts, skills, and processes of a discipline. Shulman suggests that in addition to knowing subject matter, teachers must understand what he called "pedagogical content knowledge," that knowledge "most germane to its teachability" (p. 9). Pedagogical content knowledge, then, is that knowledge that is most relevant to teaching a particular subject. Teachers need to be able to represent the course content in ways that are appropriate to learners; they must be able to offer a variety of explanations; and they must be able to give examples. How pedagogical content knowledge plays out in different disciplines became a focus for research.

This shift acknowledges the role of the teacher as "curricular-instructional gatekeeper" (Thornton, 1991, 2005). If it is the teacher who controls classroom curriculum and instructional activity, the question for teacher educators then becomes one of helping teachers develop the capacity for making professional, thoughtful decisions while engaged in teaching itself. This would not obviate the need for skill development but asks questions about how teachers learn to use these skills. Of what use, after all, are skills that are not effectively and appropriately applied? Since teachers ultimately must interpret the official curriculum, their understandings of methods, and of the curriculum itself, become important. This focus of teacher education research on the development of teachers' knowledge, skills, and dispositions has been criticized by some as failing to attend to issues of student learning (Cochran-Smith, 2004). Researchers have made few links between the development of teachers and student learning.

More recently, teachers and researchers have responded to criticisms of schools, teachers, and teacher education by looking for the empirical links between teacher practices and teacher education and student outcomes. This approach to teacher education is one that seeks to influence policy and the mandates to which teachers and teacher educators must respond. Student outcome, as part of a political problem in the United States, has been tied to easily measurable achievement scores. In the United States, the questions that most concern many social studies educators and researchers, questions about the education of thoughtful and effective citizens, have garnered little attention as problems of policy. This raises an additional question for researchers in social studies teacher education. Developing knowledge, skills, and dispositions is important. Helping teachers to become thoughtful decision makers, or reflective practitioners, is also important. Linking the development of teachers to the education of young people is crucial. But, in addition, what role should research play in the policy and political debates surrounding teacher education and who decides what constitutes effective research?

Zeichner (1999) discusses other important changes in the direction of research in teacher education that are worth noting. There has been an increase in case studies of teacher education programs; this approach provides a close-up look at particular teacher education programs, generally from the perspectives of students and faculty. Another trend has been a focus on learning to teach in different settings. This research points to how difficult it is to change the beliefs and attitudes preservice teachers bring to teacher education. This work has also pointed to practices which do have an impact on prospective teachers. Promising practices include organizing prospective teachers into cohort groups, having closer connections between campus experiences and school experiences, service learning, and the experience of developing portfolios.

Another significant trend that has emerged in recent years is that of "self-studies." Heeding earlier calls for teacher educators to engage in critical inquiry into their own practice, increasing numbers of published studies reflect teacher educators studying their own work. Self-study is the "intentional and systematic inquiry into one's own practice" by those who prepare teachers (Dinkelman, 2003). It is probably no coincidence that as interest increased in creating teacher education programs that would support the development of the "reflective practitioner," so too did interest in teacher educators being reflective themselves. Supporters of the self-study approach point out that such research models the reflective practice that we hope preservice teachers will learn (Dinkelman, 2003; Hamilton & Pinnegar, 2000). Furthermore, self-study could, argue its proponents, provide the potential for developing a deeper understanding of the practices of teacher education by making the tacit theories of teacher education practitioners public and explicit and by subjecting those beliefs and practices to careful study, data collection, and reflection.

So what do we know about the education of teachers? A report of the American Educational Research Association Panel on Research and Teacher Education (Cochran-Smith & Zeichner, 2005) indicates that there are some aspects of teacher education programs that are known to contribute to the education of successful teachers. First, collaborations between university programs and local school districts have a positive impact on teacher and student learning, although more needs to be known about the precise conditions under which these outcomes are enhanced. Second, there is no clear evidence that any one program type (e.g., 4-year vs. 5-year) makes a difference; however, articulating a clear, consistent vision of teaching and learning is related to teacher quality. Third, strategies used in teacher education programs, such as case studies and teaching portfolios, can result in changes to teacher candidates' knowledge and beliefs. Fourth, course work and field work can positively affect candidates' attitudes, knowledge, beliefs, and confidence about teaching culturally diverse learners.

QUESTIONS

Research on social studies teacher education contributes to the broader research on teacher education and reflects the general trends found there. For purposes of this research review, studies from 1994 to 2005 were reviewed. The focus of this review was on teacher preparation, although some reference will be made to studies on the professional development of teachers. The latter, however, is discussed more fully in another chapter of this volume. This research review will focus on the following key questions:

- What are current practices in social studies teacher education and what impact do they have on preservice teacher beliefs, attitudes, and practices?
- What do we know about the beliefs and attitudes of social studies teacher candidates and teachers, and what do we know about factors that may contribute to a restructuring of those beliefs and attitudes?
- What do we know about the content knowledge and the development of pedagogical content knowledge of social studies teacher candidates?
- What is known about social studies teacher educators, and what can be learned from self-studies conducted by teacher educators?
- How have policy initiatives and politics affected teacher education programs and participants?

These questions provide a way to organize recent work on the education of social studies teachers. Finally, this chapter will provide a synthesis of what has been learned and recommendations for where the field of research in social studies teacher education needs to go.

CURRENT PRACTICES

Few studies can be found that provide us with an over-arching view of the current state of social studies teacher education. The most recent studies of social studies teacher preparation programs were conducted by Dumas (1993, 1995). In his study of the preparation of social studies teachers at major research universities, he found that while most of these programs followed the National Council for the Social Studies (NCSS) standards for teacher preparation, which called for some course work across the social sciences, most teacher candidates had deficiencies in their course work in some areas (Dumas, 1993). In a second study, looking at the preparation of middle school social studies teachers at major state universities, Dumas found that these candidates generally took fewer content courses than were mandated by the NCSS standards (Dumas, 1995).

Research tells us little about the demographics of those who choose to enter social studies teacher preparation programs or about those who are actually hired. We know little, in a comprehensive way, about the nature of the programs in which preservice social studies teachers are involved. For example, what courses in the disciplines are required in social studies teacher preparation programs? Given the concerns about the content knowledge of teachers and the argument that content knowledge is central to good teaching, what do we know about the content knowledge of the teacher candidates in social studies teacher education programs? What fields do secondary social studies teachers actually major or minor in? Do those who graduate with a major in education have a substantial number of upper-division courses in one or more of the social sciences? How do those teacher candidates who are completing a social studies education program score on tests of subject matter? Are most social studies programs focusing on certifying broad field social studies teachers? What courses in history and the social sciences do candidates preparing for a broad field certification actually take, and what difference does that make to their performance as teachers? In the political climate in which both social studies and teacher education have found themselves in recent years, these would seem to be important questions for social studies educators themselves to investigate. We need to move beyond ideological disputes, such as social studies vs. the disciplines, and examine what social studies teacher candidates know about their teaching field(s) and what difference this makes to their teaching.

There are, however, a good number of studies focusing on particular components of social studies teacher education. Much of this research examines practices in the social studies methods course. There are also a number of studies reporting on the effects of field experiences, on preparing teachers to work with diverse learners, and on promoting reflection by preservice teachers. A major change from previous reviews of research is the attention paid to technology in the education of teachers. Furthermore, social studies teacher educators appear to have heeded recommendations to study their current practice (Adler, 1993; Banks & Parker, 1990). Although self-study by social studies teacher educators will be discussed more thoroughly later in this chapter, many of the studies that examine current practices are, in fact, descriptions of and inquiries into the particular experiences of practitioner teacher educators.

The methods course

In their definition of social studies the National Council for the Social Studies states that the purpose of social studies is to enable the development of effective citizens: "to help young people develop the ability to make informed and reasoned decisions for the public good as citizens in a culturally diverse, democratic society in an interdependent world" (NCSS, 1994, p.3). As noted in the introduction, the emphasis on preparing people to make informed and reasoned decisions for the public good is often contested. However, for those who accept this premise, few current empirical studies exist that might provide guidance in educating teachers to better accomplish this end. Avery (2003) presents a review of literature in civic education. Based upon this, she makes several suggestions to improve courses in the teaching of social studies methods. Avery concludes from her review of the literature in civic education that preservice teachers ought to get extensive practice facilitating class discussions about controversial issues. She argues that there is a need for assignments to help teachers understand how young people think about political concepts and issues. Further, she argues that beginning teachers should be helped to understand that the development of civic identity is a dynamic process that takes place in social and cultural contexts. Finally, she points to the importance of helping teachers learn to analyze civics textbooks and materials. In a later review of literature on preparing teachers in an era of globalization, Avery (2004) argues that citizenship education ought to take place within a context of understanding globalization, including developing the skill of perspective taking. Avery provides a framework for examining practices in the methods course; however, neither of these were empirical studies.

Jongewaard (2000) sought to identify characteristics of universal citizenship and to use this as one core of his combined elementary and secondary social studies methods course. From a review of the literature on cross-cultural communication and citizenship characteristics, Jongewaard derives six "cultural universals." His study reports on his effort to "engage students in pedagogical approaches to concept development that are likely to facilitate the learning and application of the characteristics of universal citizenship" (p. 5) which he had derived through the use of structured activities and assignments. Using pre- and post-test scores from two measures of universal citizenship as well as follow-up questionnaires, Jongewaard concluded that characteristics of universal citizenship can be defined, taught, and measured. Adler and Confer (1998) found that explicit teaching focusing on a rationale for social studies had an effect on participants' articulation of citizenship and citizenship goals. Furthermore, in two follow-up case studies which were part of this same research, one of two beginning teachers reported that her implementation of curriculum had been very much influenced by her methods course experience. The studies by Adler and Confer and by Jongewaard both suggest that a clear focus on facilitating an understanding of citizenship and appropriate pedagogies can make a difference in preservice teachers' attitudes and beliefs. However, only one case study suggests that this might make a difference in teaching practice.

Social studies may be seen as an interdisciplinary field in itself and/or a school subject that can serve as the core for interdisciplinary teaching. Schools and districts can sometimes promote interdisciplinary teaching, especially at the middle school level. Two studies examined the experience of developing interdisciplinary curriculum in the context of a methods course. In response to the 1990 Kentucky Education Reform Act, which called for connecting and integrating experiences in schools, Combs and White (2000) worked with their secondary methods classes with English, foreign language, and social studies majors to facilitate the development of interdisciplinary instruction. The preservice teachers received carefully planned instruction on the creation of interdisciplinary units, along with guidance as the units were developed. An analysis of the units produced showed that the students were able to link "targeted content across disciplines in natural ways that are interesting and, therefore, motivational" (p. 4). Another important finding, based on student self-report, was that these preservice teachers developed an enhanced appreciation of professional relationships from the team experience of curriculum development.

In an action-research study with elementary preservice teachers, Milson and King (2001) report on their efforts at engaging preservice teachers in a science-technology-society project in both their social studies and their science methods courses. The teacher candidates not only learned about the theme of science-technology-society (STS), which is part of both the NCSS standards and science standards, but they participated in an STS project as well. Using class discussion, final exams, and self-evaluations as data, Milson and King concluded that their students had accepted the rationale for STS and saw the value of integrative approaches in elementary school curriculum. However, few of these preservice teachers actually chose to create lessons based on STS themes.

One explanation for this was that STS topics were often deemed too controversial and the preservice teachers were more comfortable sticking with traditional topics (such as "Native American Cultures") regarded as safe. Furthermore, many of the preservice teachers had difficulty with the processes of scientific inquiry and civic decision making. Their findings reinforce the notion that it is not enough for teachers to understand something (such as the rationale for STS); they, themselves, need the skills to implement a different approach within real-life contexts.

Other studies of practices found in the social studies methods class similarly report on the role of experiential learning for preservice teacher. Ross (1996) reported on his experiences implementing portfolio evaluation in his social studies methods class. He provides a descriptive account of his efforts and describes how assessment practices can shape learning. An assessment of the portfolios showed that his students were able to construct a more holistic image of teaching and decision-making than they had previously. Byer and Dana-Wesley (1999) found that the use of active teaching strategies that engaged students in the methods course resulted in higher ratings for the instructors and the report of greater understanding on the part of the participants. Research on social studies methods classes is based almost entirely on action research projects of teacher educators. The studies reviewed here suggest that focused efforts can make a difference in the beliefs and attitudes of preservice social studies teachers. However, an exclusive reliance on action research, or self-study, leaves us with a thin research base from which to draw generalizations about the social studies methods course. Furthermore, there is little evidence that apparent changes in or refinement of a set of beliefs actually results in congruent teacher practice. Where there is data on follow-up into student teaching, the daily routines and expectations of classrooms appear to overwhelm the novice teacher.

Field experiences

Although limited, research on the field experience component of teacher education programs supports the findings that collaboration between schools and universities can have a positive effect on the beliefs and practices of both inservice and preservice teachers. Two studies that used a survey approach to determine the impact of school university collaboration on field experiences on beliefs and self-efficacy (Carey, Fannin, Morford, & Wilson, 2000; Wingfield, Nath, Freeman, & Cohen, 2000) found positive growth in the self-efficacy and sense of confidence of preservice teachers. Shaver, Stallworth and Wilson (2001) investigated another kind of school-university partnership. In this study, a team of school-based and university-based faculty selected a common piece of young adult literature to use as the core of an integrated unit on civil rights. The novel was read in the methods classes as well as in high school social studies and middle school English classes. The preservice teachers worked with their instructors to develop lessons around the novel and the broad theme of civil rights. Interviews and survey data were collected before, during, and after teaching the novel. As a result of their experience, the preservice teachers had an enhanced vision of integrated curriculum and the use of fiction in a social studies class. Data indicated as well that both the teachers and the preservice teachers were very positive about the process of collaboration; classroom teachers indicated that the process made them feel valued by the university.

A study by Owens (1997) provided a broad description of the early field experience at one institution. Owens examined the nature of the placements (for example, urban and suburban, grade levels) and preservice teachers' responses to their placements. His findings confirm the importance of carefully selecting mentor teachers. Montgomery (1994) reflects on her experiences as a student teacher mentor. Her description of her role as a mentor teacher and her growth in the process of mentoring could serve as a guide for others taking on that important role. Her experiences suggest that, thoughtfully done, mentoring preservice teachers can be an important form of professional development for teachers.

Diversity

Several studies investigated the impact of particular program experiences on preservice teachers' beliefs and practices around issues of diversity. McCall (1995) and Smith (2000) point to the importance of the beliefs and attitudes that preservice teachers bring with them to their education. Both these studies examined the meanings and assumptions that preservice teachers held and the effect of their backgrounds in the development of those beliefs. Both studies raise the question of what experiences are needed to broaden or change preservice teacher beliefs about diversity.

Several other studies suggest that experiences, moving beyond reading and classroom discussion, can have an effect on beliefs and behaviors. Boyle-Baise and Kilbane (1999) discuss a community service learning project working with minority youth and its impact on the participants. In their qualitative study they found that the preservice teachers did tend to "play it safe." Such strategies included focusing on the task at hand (e.g. providing help with homework), keeping comments to the students with whom they worked positive, and responding rather than initiating interactions with youth. However, their data revealed that there were positive results, nonetheless. The experience disrupted stereotypes and provided realistic knowledge of culture groups. Preservice teachers took advantage of the opportunity to "hang-out" with the youth and developed comfortable, companionable relationships. This description of one program experience does have implications for teacher preparation. The Boyle-Baise and Kilbane studies suggest that it is not enough to "play it safe." Situations and experiences need to be problematized; additionally, the perspective of providing a service to those who "lack" needs to be questioned. The data does indicate the potential of an in-depth experience with culturally diverse youth and also the importance of creating mechanisms for debriefing and questioning the experiences.

Wade and Raba (2003) describe another type of in-depth experience and the potential such experiences can carry. In this case, the preservice teachers, many of whom came from rural areas, participated in a week long internship in Chicago. The intention was to engage preservice teachers in "border crossings" in order to unlearn racism and develop some insight into urban teaching. The authors concluded that a week-long experience is too short to move beyond the telling of interesting stories. The authors conclude that the development of "critical cultural awareness" (Gay & Howard, 2000) would entail a more comprehensive approach, including having teacher educators examine their own beliefs and attitudes as well as providing experiences and self-reflection opportunities for preservice teachers.

Percival (2000) describes his experience in building a community of learners in his methods class. Experience with community building enabled the preservice teachers to actually apply this in their own classrooms. In a study focusing on global rather than multicultural perspectives, Wilson (2001) reports that experiences in the methods class and during student teaching can contribute to a deeper understanding of a global perspective. Consistent with studies discussed above, Wilson reports that previous experiences and beliefs do make a difference. Preservice teachers with international experience learned how to apply the beliefs they already held. Experiences in the methods class, such as acquiring and using knowledge about other countries and peoples, and interactions with a Ghanaian doctoral student did lead to growth toward teaching with a global perspective in all students, as demonstrated in their writing, observation, and teaching. Students reported that their coursework and methods in particular had influenced the way they thought about teaching from a global perspective.

Taken together, these studies contribute to a body of literature that points both to the difficulty of changing the previously acquired beliefs of preservice teachers and to the possibilities, through a variety of experiences, in changing those beliefs. Recommendations for engaging preservice teachers in the community, particularly in culturally diverse communities, as part of their pre-service education (Boyle-Baise, 2003; Gay, 2004) need to be taken seriously. However, those who reported on the ways they engaged their preservice teachers in multicultural experiences were both encouraged by the potential for change and discouraged by the difficulty of change.

Technology

Perhaps the biggest change in research on social studies teacher education is the large increase in the number of studies of technology and teacher preparation. This is no surprise, of course; as Bennett noted in a 2000 review of technology standards and their implementation, the possibilities of technology have led to calls for teacher educators to rethink the way they prepare teachers (Bennett, 2000/2001, p. 9). Bennett suggests that the power of new technologies is in their potential to create more student-centered classrooms in which the teacher serves as a guide and students work together collaboratively at learning stations. In a review of social studies methods textbooks published between 1977 and 2000, Johnson (2000) found that all the textbooks were limited regarding specific ways in which the teaching of social studies could be enhanced through technology. He concludes that more needs to be done in the methods course itself and provides methods instructors with some guidelines and recommendations. The studies reviewed here focus primarily on preservice teachers' perceptions of experiences with technology, their attitudes toward technology integration and use, and the acquisition of technology skills. None of these studies followed the preservice teachers into schools as beginning teachers in order to investigate their implementation of technology.

Several studies reported the use of technology in particular programs to promote collaboration among preservice teachers and between the teacher education program and school sites (Keiper, Myhre, & Pihl, 2000/ 2001; Mason, 2000; Mason, 2000/2001; Mason & Berson, 2000; Merryfield, 2000; Riley & Stern, 2001). Based upon these reports, technology can be used to promote thoughtful and reflective interactions. Merryfield (2000) found that threaded discussions in a graduate course in social studies added to the development of a culturally diverse learning community and deepened meaningful discussions of sensitive and controversial issues. Mason (2000; 2000/2001) and Mason and Berson (2000) also found that through Web-based dialog, opportunities for collaboration and reflection and self-initiated professional dialog were enhanced. They found high levels of trust and openness among participants, as well as a scaffolding of reflective inquiry. Riley and Stern (2001) report similar findings in their description and analysis of Web-supported instruction engaging preservice teachers in dialog across two campuses. Similar collaboration was found in a study of technology-enabled communication between a university program and school sites (Keiper et al., 2000/2001). Not only was communication facilitated, but more collaborative interactions developed, breaking down some of the school-campus barriers.

Preservice teachers' conceptions of technology and technology integration, as well as their skill acquisition, have also been investigated. Once again, these studies reported on particular experiences at the researchers' work sites and relied primarily on preservice teacher questionnaire responses, along with analyses of their assignments. Owens' (1999) students provided positive feedback about the convenience and usefulness of the Internet. Diem's (2002) study was one of the few that involved participants across multiple course sections at a large university. He found that technology training in the social studies methods classes increased preservice teachers' knowledge and use of technology. In fact, Diem found that the greatest use of technology was Internet use, which had largely replaced going to the library. Preservice teachers also reported that their school sites were technologically ahead of the university. Keiper, Harwood, and Larson (2000) looked at preservice teachers' perceptions of the benefits of integrating technology into social studies classrooms. These teachers did note a number of benefits including the ability to obtain information and data, enhance communication, and motivate through dynamic sound and visuals. Lipscomb and Doppen (2002) report on the implementation of a course specifically focused on integrating technology into social studies. Course participants showed growth in their proficiency with technology and recognized the possibilities of integrating technology into their teaching.

Two studies investigated the use of Web-based modules as a means of content delivery (Ehman, 1999, 2001; Sunal & Sunal, 2003). Sunal and Sunal investigated preservice teachers' conceptions of guided inquiry following the use of a Web-based module while Ehman investigated knowledge of technology integration as a result of using a Web-based module on that topic. Both studies reported growth in student knowledge related to the module. But as Ehman noted, it was not clear whether the free standing module was any more efficacious in the development of student knowledge and understanding than other teaching methods.

White (1996) addressed Bennett's (2000/2001) later assertion that technology could and should be used to create more student-centered, constructivist classrooms. Using a survey sent to over 400 preservice social studies teachers at two major universities, White found that nearly all the respondents reported that a student-centered approach was "definitely important" to making social studies more relevant to learners and that the use of technology could facilitate such a goal. However, there is no report on the extent to which these respondents actually sought to create student-centered classrooms or integrate technology in their teaching. Several studies did investigate the use of technology by preservice teachers in classrooms and pointed to problems and obstacles. Preservice teachers tended to report that time was an obstacle in the implementation of technology integration (Lipscomb & Doppen, 2002; Sunal & Sunal, 2003). Concern about the differing ability levels of students and the dependability of both hardware and the Internet were also reported as concerns by preservice teachers (Keiper at al, 2000; Mason & Berson, 2000).

Reflection

By the 1980s teacher education programs had become increasingly focused on "educating the reflective practitioner." Originally grounded in the work of Donald Schön (1983, 1987) this program emphasis is consistent with a view of teachers as decision makers described above. Given this concern, teacher educators began to ask what experiences would promote reflective inquiry among preservice teachers. Problem Based Learning (Hughes, Sears, & Clarke, 1998), foundations courses focusing on reflection (Riley & Stern, 1997), the use of online journals, (Bennett, 2001; Mason, 2000), and focusing a methods course on critical discussions of democracy and curriculum building (Dinkelman, 1999a, 1999b) are shown to promote some reflection in particular instances.

It is difficult to generalize from these studies, first, because each is a self-study of a particular experience. But, even more important, there is no clear agreement on how the researchers defined reflection. Dinkelman (1999a, 1999b), in his case study research of three students in his social studies methods class, focused on critical reflection. Building on the work of VanManen (1977) and Liston and Zeichner (1991), he defined critical reflection as "deliberation about the moral and ethical dimensions of education" (1999b, p. 331). Hughes (1997) built on the work of Newmann (1990, 1991) to focus on thoughtfulness and the characteristics Newmann developed to define a thoughtful classroom. Hughes' students were given a survey in which they were asked to rate the problem-based course, other education courses, and courses outside education. Results show that the participants perceived the Problem Based Learning course as providing a significantly more thoughtful learning environment than other courses. Bennett (2001) looked at reflection as a running log of thoughts and reactions. Riley and Stern (1997) looked at reflection as the ability to understand and apply the link between theory and practice.

These studies do suggest that university course experiences can have some impact on the thoughtfulness and reflection of students, although the concept itself remains ambiguous (McAninch, 2004). Dinkelman's case studies remind readers that having a predisposition toward thoughtfulness or reflection is also important. In fact, he found no discernable transformation of the students' views; rather, the course gave the students a vocabulary and a focus for their reflection. Finally, no studies make the longitudinal link that experiencing thoughtful classrooms, reflecting on experience, or being engaged in critical inquiry makes a difference in the practice of these students as beginning teachers. Given the commitment of so many teacher educators to "educating the reflective practitioner," it seems important to clarify what is meant by reflective teaching in social studies. Further, it would be significant to know whether teacher education programs really help beginning teachers to be more reflective *in practice*. Finally, does reflection help them as teachers and make a difference to student learning?

What do we know?

Research on the practices and experiences of social studies teacher education draw largely on the self-study of teacher educators. Apparently heeding the call to engage in critical inquiry into their own practice, social studies teacher educators collected data on their experiences. That data provided the stuff of reflection and analysis to be shared with the larger community. Action research in teacher education is premised on the assumption that it can provide teacher educators with ideas for their own practice and a greater understanding of the assumptions and tacit theories of teacher education practitioners. On the other hand it is difficult to generalize from such studies. Many suggest that the experiences of a teacher education program can make a difference in the expressed attitudes of prospective teachers. We know much less, however, about whether and how these expressed attitudes translate into practice.

There is also limited evidence that prospective teachers are being asked to "imagine otherwise" (Segall, 2002). Prospective teachers are engaged in somewhat limited ways in what Segall refers to as "otherwise experiences" (p. 161). Through such experiences as service learning, technology integration, and urban internships, some prospective teachers are being asked to imagine a different way of teaching and learning. But these efforts are baby-steps within traditional social studies teacher education programs that remain largely unchanged. The research described above can provide ideas for particular experiences, but there is little that actually re-visions social studies teacher education.

THE INNER LIVES OF TEACHERS

At the heart of the conception of teachers as decision makers, is the conception that teachers' knowledge, thinking, beliefs, and attitudes affect how teachers make sense of events and the contexts of their work. Further, it is assumed that teachers' knowledge, beliefs, thinking, and attitudes serve as the basis for the decisions they make about their practice and student learning. As seen by the studies already reviewed, a good deal of the research in social studies teacher education examines changes in teacher thinking, beliefs, and attitudes. Researchers over the past decade have asked about the beliefs and attitudes that prospective teachers hold when they enter teacher preparation programs and have inquired about the extent to which the experiences of a program affect teachers' beliefs. Many of the studies reviewed above used "belief" or "attitude" as outcome measures. Some of those studies will be referred to again in this section. Although it is somewhat arbitrary, the research reviewed in this section had an explicit focus on changing teacher beliefs, attitudes, or conceptions. As will be discussed later, there is considerable "muddiness" in the use of these various terms.

Given the nature and purpose of social studies, one place to begin inquiring into teacher beliefs is to ask about prospective teachers' beliefs about the nature of social studies and citizenship. Owens (1996) and Slekar (1995, 1998) found that the prospective elementary teachers in their programs held fairly negative views of social studies. Their own experiences as learners in school settings had helped to mold this negative view. Once again we see the power of past experiences in shaping teacher beliefs (see also McCall, 1995; Smith 2000). In Slekar's case study of two preservice teachers in elementary social studies he found that their experiences with history had come largely from an objectivist epistemology. Each of the two preservice teachers did express a desire to teach differently, to be less didactic. However, Slekar did not follow these two teachers into the classroom.

Kubow (1997) and Wilkins (1999) examined preservice teachers' attitudes toward and understandings of the concept of citizenship. In his survey of 43 preservice teachers, Kubow found that they held only a vague conception of citizenship and concluded that more needs to be done in social studies teacher preparation to enable preservice teachers to refine their conceptions. Wilkens examined the conceptions of citizenship among 669 post-graduate preservice teachers in two of the largest teacher education programs in the United Kingdom. Like Kubow, he found a lack of clarity about what it means to be a "good citizen." He also found a high degree of political disengagement, a view that "racism is here to stay," and a backlash to what the respondents referred to as "political correctness." In fact, the concept of citizenship was tainted with negative imagery and with suspicion about values being imposed from "above." Such findings should raise a concern in the United Kingdom, at least, where, at the time of Kubow's study, citizenship education was beginning to assume greater importance.

Adler and Confer (1998) found that few prospective teachers began the social studies methods class with clearly articulated conceptions of citizenship. Over the semester of the class, the dominant concept of citizenship education that emerged was one of empathy and perspective-taking; in addition, the course participants were able to more clearly state a rationale for social studies. A case study of two of the participants into their first year of teaching, found that both sought to put their beliefs into practice, with varying degrees of success. Both teachers had entered their teacher preparation program with a strong concern for cultural diversity. Both had expressed this as an important component of citizenship education. The teacher who appeared to be, and believed herself to be, more successful at turning her beliefs into practice, credited the methods class with helping her to refine, articulate, and implement her beliefs. The other participant in the case study indicated that the methods course had little influence on his practice.

Angell's (1998) study explored the question of belief restructuring, probing the interaction of program experiences and existing beliefs. She found that beliefs can serve to both facilitate professional growth and to inhibit new conceptualizations. She found that overlapping messages from multiple sources can influence the beliefs held by preservice teachers, thus lending support to the importance of having a clear conceptual framework across a teacher preparation program. At the same time, however, these overlapping messages "must find receptivity in the individual learner, a willingness to expose vulnerabilities, to admit incomplete understandings and to consider change" (p. 527).

Not only are prior beliefs important, but school-based experiences also have an influence on teacher beliefs. Fehn and Koeppen (1998) addressed the importance of building program experiences that are connected with the contexts of teaching, when he noted that his students' positive attitudes about document based instruction remained, but were often overwhelmed by the perceived understandings of classroom realities. Other studies also report the extent to which beginning teachers' beliefs may be overwhelmed by actual teaching experiences. The participants in a study by Milson and King (2001) reported that they valued dealing with science-technology-society issues. In practice, however, they were overwhelmed by concerns of coverage and management. Similarly, beliefs about the potential of using technology to change the nature of social studies teaching and learning are often overwhelmed by concerns about the technology itself, the time available for implementing new approaches, and concerns about management of diverse students (Keiper et al., 2000; Keiper et al., 2000/2001; Lipscomb & Doppen, 2002).

Chant's case study (2001, 2002) of three beginning teachers both looked more broadly at the belief systems of his participants and followed them into their first year of teaching to see how these beliefs played out in practice. Chant investigated the personal practical theories, theories which guide teachers in their instructional action and decision-making, of three beginning social studies teachers. As part of their social studies methods class, each of the three participants had identified an operational set of personal theories that they believed would guide their practice. During the preservice program, these participants collected data from their field experience and student teaching to determine the congruence of their personal theorizing with their practice. Chant then followed the three participants into their first year of teaching. These teachers each had an explicit understanding of their personal practical theories when they began teaching, and each attempted to use these to guide their practice. In fact, two of the three participants continued to refine their personal theories as they sought to improve their practice. One of the three, however, deviated from her beliefs. Her perceptions of student behavior, her desire to establish order, and the focus of her colleagues on issues of discipline made it difficult for her to act on most of her expressed beliefs. Chant suggests that we need to learn more about the ways in which contextual factors help to shape teachers' theorizing in practice.

A major problem in this area of research is the lack of clarity around the constructs themselves. Pajares notes (1992) that "teacher beliefs is a messy construct," and the same can be said for teacher attitudes, conceptions, and knowledge. Researchers use different terms to denote similar constructs and similar terms to look at different constructs. Much of the research reviewed here failed to carefully define the construct being examined. Furthermore, beliefs need to be considered as a cluster; that is, decision-making is rarely a straight forward movement from a belief about one thing, such as the nature of social studies, to classroom practice. Beliefs are embedded in a system of other beliefs, values, and knowledge which, taken together in particular contexts, influence decision-making. Much of the research reviewed examined only one aspect of the prospective teachers' belief systems, such as citizenship, technology or diversity, with Chant's work being an exception. Few of these studies actually explore the ways in which teacher beliefs are played out in practice, when the broad set of beliefs and knowledge would come into play.

PEDAGOGICAL CONTENT KNOWLEDGE

What do *social studies teachers* need to know and be able to do that is unique to teaching social studies? Shulman's (1986) conception of pedagogical content knowledge suggests that teaching any subject is about more than knowing content and developing generic teaching skills. Teachers must have the skills to be able to transform *particular* subject matter into meaningful curriculum. Research on the development of pedagogical content knowledge among social studies teachers focuses primarily on the teaching of history. Learning to think historically as one component of the social studies methods course was explored in several studies.

Fehn and Koeppen (1998) describe their efforts at teaching a history intensive social studies methods course with an emphasis on document based instruction. Data from interviews, lesson plans, and the written reflections of their 11 students suggest that focused experiences in methods classes can have an impact on the beliefs of preservice teachers, but not necessarily on their practice. Interviews indicated that all 11 teacher candidates left methods class with "positive regard for document-based instruction" (p. 475). On the other hand, during student teaching this enthusiasm appeared to be diminished by the socializing process at their field sites. Positive attitudes remained, but tempered by the "realities" of needing to "cover" a body of material and to fit in with predetermined plans. Thus, despite the impact of the methods class on preservice teachers' desire to teach with documents, their efforts in student teaching were tempered by what they perceived as the realities of teaching.

Yaeger (1997) reported that the secondary methods course can build on previous historical knowledge and serve as a foundation for planning lessons that emphasize historical thinking. The preservice teachers, however, interpreted the idea of historical thinking in different ways, from reading sources for information to evaluating, analyzing, and synthesizing sources. During student teaching, some of the participants in the study made efforts to incorporate their conception of historical thinking into their lessons, although those who did so felt they were taking a risk. Given their different conceptions of historical thinking, it is no surprise that they incorporated the concept in differing ways. For some, historical thinking in practice meant reading documents for comprehension. Others adopted a more didactic approach as more "efficient." This study suggests that, in addition to exposure to and understanding of historical thinking, student teachers' perceptions of the maturity level of their pupils influenced their decisions to incorporate document-based activities.

Hauessler-Bohan and Davis (1998) investigated the historical thinking student teachers' construction of historical events. Focusing on three case studies, common themes emerged from their analysis of the data. The three participants were inexperienced with historical writing and inquiry. In analyzing documents they failed to consider context or the time period. They dealt with documents on a factual rather than analytical level. The researchers concluded that teachers of history "could benefit from more systematic and deliberate engagement and practice with historical thinking and writing in their history courses" (p. 190). Mayer's (2003) study supports this conclusion. Mayer investigated the impact of a course on the methods and philosophy of history. His data suggest that such courses can make a difference not only on preservice teachers' understanding of history, but on their conceptualization of teaching as well. This study did not, however, examine the actual practice of the participants. Similarly, Seixas (1998) found that preservice teachers developing lessons around the use of primary source documents encountered a number of problems—choosing appropriate documents, making the issues or themes significant to learners today, and developing pedagogically meaningful exercises for hypothetical students. Yet, as Seixas points out, the preservice teachers in his study were unlikely to have other structured experiences in which they could focus on learning to teach with documents.

These studies raise a number of questions about the content knowledge and the pedagogical content knowledge of preservice teachers and the relationship of that knowledge to classroom teaching. The relationship between content and pedagogy is more complex than a linear arrangement of courses (first content, then methods) would suggest (Segall, 2004). Furthermore, Barton and Levstik (2004) point out that the research to date on pedagogical content knowledge of history teachers indicates that—while a strong history background and knowledge of pedagogical skills may be a prerequisite to teaching history in an investigative, interpretative manner—it does not assure that this will be done. The expectations that teachers maintain control and cover the material are more powerful than any teacher's individual pedagogical content knowledge (Barton & Levstik, 2004). However, teachers who develop a strong sense of purpose about why social studies should be taught are more likely to teach in ways that engage learners in deep study of historical content and processes (Barton & Levstik, 2004).

It has not always been the case that content and pedagogy were taught separately; indeed, earlier teachers colleges sought to closely connect the teaching of content and pedagogy (Thornton, 2005). A stronger relationship between methods and content might help preservice teachers approach curriculum with a sense of purpose, rather than conceiving of teaching activities and the content to be taught as somehow separate. Considering a sense of purpose gets at the purpose of social studies itself. Teaching the academic disciplines is not the same as teaching social studies for civic competence (Whitson, 2004). Civic competence requires dealing with complex and controversial issues. In what ways will improved preparation in history, or in the other social sciences, contribute to educating young people to engage in the social world, to become informed and active citizens? As Whitson (2004) notes, the considerations of what content knowledge teachers need to know "forces us to recognize that the struggle over definitions cannot be abandoned" (p. 29). What appears to be needed are more clear analyses of the content and pedagogical content knowledge necessary to teach for civic competence.

TEACHER EDUCATORS AND SELF-STUDY

Nearly all of the studies reviewed above can be considered action research studies. Action research is a process through which practitioners systematically collect and analyze data to better understand the effects of their practice. It is the systematic inquiry of one's own teaching practice, students, or context. The goals of action research include gaining information and insight into how particular programs operate in order to develop more reflective practice and to effect positive change in the learning environment (Miller, 2003). Much of the action research reviewed for this chapter reports on outcomes of student changes and learning. Some studies are more consciously "self-studies;" that is, they are personal, critical reflections of the researchers' own experiences. (See Johnston, 2006 for a discussion of the similarities and differences between action research and self-study.) Several such studies report on the experience of collaboration in teaching; others focus on some tensions, problems, or concerns in their own practice.

Kirkwood-Tucker and Bleicher (2003) and Hohenbrink, Johnston, and Westhoven (1997) conducted studies of collaboration in teaching. These researchers examined the disagreements, frustrations, and compromises involved in collaborative teaching. And both studies report on personal gains, such as greater understanding and a renewal of spirit, that occurred from the collaboration. Koeppen and Griffith (2003) reflect on their failure to recognize the diversity of their students and the tensions between traditional and non-traditional students in the methods class. Percival (2000) reflects on successful efforts to build a community of learners and to influence the perspectives of preservice teachers.

Little of the action research reviewed for this chapter takes a critical look at the process of educating social studies teachers. It is based on assumptions that a particular method or strategy of teaching will help teacher candidates become better teachers. But those assumptions are often taken for granted and not questioned or explored. Boyle-Baise (2003) and Wade (1999) take a different approach in their examination of the tensions and struggles of striving to teach democratically. This seems to be a particularly significant area of reflection for social studies teacher educators who may want to model, in their teaching, how democracy works. As Boyle-Baise (2003) notes: "How many of us ponder what it [democracy in our teaching] really means? How many of us actually do it" (p. 66). Accordingly, she provides a framework for democratic teaching and describes her efforts in her methods class. Wade (1999) similarly reflects on what democracy means and how it might be implemented in teaching and reports on the issues and challenges that emerge from attempts to share power and decision-making. She concludes that her "efforts to teach democratically were sometimes successful, sometimes not, yet always challenging and interesting" (p. 88). She notes, as well, that what had been helpful to her were the stories of other democratic educators who write of their struggles, determination, and frustration (p. 89). It is just such sharing of stories to which self-study, or action research, can contribute in a systematic, reflective way.

Policy initiatives

The decade under review has seen ideological policy debates swirling around education and teacher education. While teacher educators seek to create and implement professional standards, legislatures impose regulations, such as testing, while others argue that teacher education isn't necessary at all. Despite these policy debates, with some exception, little research in social studies teacher education has sought to examine the debates, or to use research to take a position on these debates.

One exception to this is Gerwin's 2003 study. This action research study reviewed 38 lesson plans from five student teachers, along with observations and focus groups. Gerwin describes how following the mandated lesson format affected the student teachers' thinking about history and about how adolescents understand it. The lesson plans were characterized by fragmentation, omission, and defensive simplification, and even the way the student teachers expressed their conceptions of history showed a lack of understanding about why people should study their past.

It is somewhat surprising that in a decade characterized by legislated reforms and accountability, so little work has been done to examine the effects of these reforms on the education of social studies teachers. While policy makers work to define a "highly qualified" teacher through test scores, many social studies educators hold a different concept of highly qualified. If one extrapolates from the research done on social studies teacher education, a highly qualified social studies teacher is one who can actively engage diverse learners and can use technology appropriately. Such a teacher is a reflective decision maker who understands social studies goals and is responsive to the children in the classroom. This image of teaching provides a counter to the image of teacher as simply a content expert. But few researchers have explicitly sought to counter the policy image and to make the case that what is learned in teacher preparation makes a difference to children.

CONCLUSIONS

Much of the research over the past decade is made up of reports of practitioners studying their own practice. This approach to research has engaged teacher education practitioners both in systematic reflection on their work and in contributing to the body of research in the field. However, research on one's own practice easily becomes little more than individualistic studies of particular practices. That is, there is little to date which links these individual studies and allows readers of the research to consider broader generalizations. In Adler's 1991 review of research on the education of social studies teachers she critiqued the research as being particularistic, "an array of unrelated or random aspects of social studies teacher education…" (p. 218). This randomness seems to have been little changed. Even with the increased focus on teachers' understandings and beliefs, it is difficult to make generalizations about teacher beliefs, beyond the importance of acknowledging the beliefs they bring with them to the teacher education experience. Little of the research examines the interrelationships among participants and contexts and even less considers impact on the pupils of the teachers being studied. Cochran-Smith and Zeichner (2005) conclude their review of research on teacher education by suggesting that research is needed to study the complex relationships among teaching strategies used by teacher educators, the practices of beginning teachers, and the learning of their pupils.

Rather than random, individualistic studies, it seems time to consider larger-scale studies that might link the work of individual teacher educators. Design-based research is suggestive about the possibilities for future work. Design-based research is based upon several key premises (Design Research Collective, 2003). The first premise is that the central goals of designing learning environments and developing theories of learning are intertwined. The second premise is that development and research take place through continuous cycles of design, enactment, analysis, and redesign. The third premise is that research must lead to sharable theories to help communicate relevant implications to practitioners. Fourth, research must account for interactions with environments. Fifth, the processes under study must connect to outcomes of interest (p. 4). In short, design-based research is detached neither from contexts nor from the complex nature of outcomes. "We view educational interventions holistically-we see interventions as enacted through the interactions between materials, teachers, and learners" (Design-based Research Collective, 2003, p. 5).

Linking research method to a concern for teachers' understandings, learner outcomes, and the contexts of practice is a tall order. However, such research could build on design-based interventions in existing classrooms. Preservice teachers, for example, could participate in the intervention under study, engaging with the researcher and other practitioners in seeking to produce change in particular contexts. Examinations of similar interventions across multiple sites would aim at a more complex understanding of implementing educational change. What are the effects of diverse teacher beliefs and local contexts on the implementation of educational innovations? How are the skills and knowledge of preservice teachers impacted by participating in such research, and how does this influence their work as beginning teachers?

Shaver (2001) argues that clarifying the goals of research in education will help to alleviate the apparent "mindlessness" of much current research. Zeichner (2005) suggests an agenda for research in teacher education that social studies teacher educators might heed. Their recommendations for priority research include:

- Identifying the factors in teacher education that contribute to student achievement;
- Examining the effectiveness of policies such as teacher testing and state and national accreditation on teacher learning, teacher practice, and student learning;
- Studying the ways in which teachers are prepared for cultural diversity, working with English Language Learners, and teaching children with disabilities, and how those experiences impact their actual practice.

Social studies teacher educators might also focus specifically on aspects of teacher education unique to social studies. For example, what are ways of facilitating the growth of pedagogical content knowledge, and how do these impact classroom teaching? How might understanding of democracy and citizenship be developed, and how might that impact classroom practice?

Shaver (2001) argues that the major goal of research in education ought not to be knowledge for its own sake. We ought to be seeking, he argues, to develop thoughtful classrooms (p. 245). In short, the major goal in educational research is, or ought to be, improved practice in education. And the major goal for research in social studies education ought to be the development of thoughtful social studies classrooms. Rather than a diffuse, random study of whatever interests a particular researcher, and whatever will contribute to promotion and tenure, social studies teacher educators should seek to find ways to make a difference in social studies classrooms. The appropriate professional goal, argues Shaver, "is to help social studies teachers, regardless of their teaching area or their position or lack of position on the nature of social studies, meet their instructional challenges" (p. 247).

If we are really to understand and improve teacher education, longitudinal studies and coordination of data will be necessary. Educators and researchers working together could facilitate research that is more complex and meaningful. For example, coordinating data collection and developing standards for comparison of research findings could serve to link otherwise isolated, particularistic, and short-term studies. Research on social studies teacher education ought to contribute to improved practice. But understanding how this happens means looking at more than the impact of particular strategies taught or the development of teacher attitudes and beliefs. It's important to remember that ultimately, the goal of teacher education is about improved learning in classrooms. If teacher educators cannot make the case that teacher education matters to young people and to the nation, research in teacher education may not matter at all.

REFERENCES

Abell Foundation. (2001). *Teacher certification reconsidered: Stumbling for quality*. Baltimore, MD: The Abell Foundation.

Adler, S. A. (1991). The education of social studies teachers. In J. Shaver (Ed.), *Handbook of research on social studies teaching and learning* (pp. 197–209). New York: Macmillan.

Adler, S. A. (1993). Teacher education: Research as reflective practice. *Teaching and Teacher Education, 9*(2), 159–167.

Adler, S. A., & Confer, B. J. (1998, February). A practical inquiry: Influencing preservice teachers' beliefs toward diversity and democracy. Paper presented at the annual meeting of the American Association of Colleges of Teacher Education, New Orleans, LA.

Angell, A. V. (1998). Learning to teach social studies: A case study of belief restructuring. *Theory and Research in Social Education, 26*(4), 509–29.

Armento, B. J. (1996). The professional development of social studies educators. In J. Sikula (Ed), *Handbook of Research on Teacher Education* (2nd ed., pp. 485–502). New York: Macmillan.

Avery, P. (2003). Using research about civic education to improve courses in the methods of teaching social studies. In J. J. Patrick, G. E. Hamot, & R. Leming (Eds), *Civic learning in teacher education: Vol. 2. International perspectives on education for democracy in the preparation of teachers*. Washington, DC: Office of Educational Research and Improvement. (ERIC Clearinghouse for Social Studies/Social Science Education, Bloomington, IN)

Avery, P. (2004). Social studies teacher education in an era of globalization. *Critical issues in social studies teacher education* (pp. 37–58). Greenwich, CT: Information Age Press.

Ballou, D., & Soler, S. (1998, February). *Addressing the looming teacher crunch: The issue is quality*. Retrieved from Progressive Policy Briefing Institute Web site: http://www.ppionline.org.

Banks, J. A., & Parker, W.C. (1990). Social studies teacher education. In W. R. Houston (Ed.), *Handbook of research in teacher education* (pp. 674–86). New York: Macmillan.

Barton, K. C., & Levstik, L. S. (2004). *Teaching history for the common good*. Mahwah, NJ: Erlbaum.

Bennett, L. (2000/2001). Technology standards for the preparation of teachers. *International Journal of Social Education, 15*(2), 1–11.

Bennett, L. (2001). Online journals to reflecton teaching in an elementary social studies course. *The International Social Studies Forum, 1*(1), 17–31.

Boyle-Baise, M., & Kilbane, J. (1999, November). What really happens: Community service learning for multicultural teacher education? Paper presented at the annual meeting of the college and university faculty assembly of the National Council for the Social Studies.

Boyle-Baise, M. (2003). Doing democracy in social studies methods. *Theory and Research in Social Education, 31*(1), 51–71.

Boyle-Baise, M., & Grant, G. (2004). Citizen/community participation in education. In S. Adler (Ed.), *Critical Issues in Social Studies Teacher Education* (pp. 145–164). Greenwich, CT: Information Age Press.

Byer, J., & Dana-Wesley, M. (1999). Students' response to active instructional approaches in a social studies methods course. *Southern Social Studies Journal, 24*(2), 57–70.

Carey, S., Fannin, K., Morford, T., & Wilson, A. (2000, November). The impact of one social studies department on preservice social studies teachers. Paper presented at the annual meeting of the National Council for the Social Studies, San Antonio, TX.

Chant, R. (2001, November). The impact of personal theorizing on beginning teaching: A case analysis of three social studies teachers. Paper presented at the annual meeting of the National Council for the Social Studies, Washington, D.C.

Chant, R. H. (2002). The inpact of personal theorizing on beginning teaching: Three social studies teachers. *Theory and Research in Social Education, 30*(4), 516–540.

Cochran-Smith, M. (2001). Reforming teacher education. *Journal of Teacher Education, 52*(1), 263–265.

Cochran-Smith, M. (2004). The problem of teacher education. *Journal of Teacher Education, 55*(4), 295–299.

Cochran-Smith, M. (2005a). The politics of teacher education. *Journal of Teacher Education, 56*(3), 179–180.

Cochran-Smith, M. (2005b). Researching teacher education in changing times: Politics and paradigms. In M. Cochran-Smith, & K. M. Zeichner (Eds.). *Studying teacher education: The report of the AERA panel on research and teacher education* (pp 69–110). Washington, D.C.: AERA

Cochran-Smith, M. & Zeichner, K. M. (2005). Executive summary. In M. Cochran-Smith, & K. M. Zeichner (Eds.). *Studying teacher education: The report of the AERA panel on research and teacher education* (pp 1 –36). Washington, D.C.: AERA.

Combs, D., & White, R. (2000). There's madness in these methods: Teaching secondary methods students to develop interdisciplinary units. *The Clearing House, 73*(5), 282–286.

Design-based Research Collective (2003). Design-based research: An emerging paradigm for educational inquiry. *Educational Researcher, 32*(1), 5–8.

Diem, R. (2002, April). *An examination of the effects of technology instruction in social studies methods classes*. Paper presented at the annual meeting of the American Educational Research Association, New Orleans, LA.

Dinkleman, T. (1999a). An inquiry into the development of critical reflection in secondary student teachers. *Teaching and Teacher Education, 16*(2), 195–222.

Dinkleman, T. (1999b). Critical reflection in a social studies methods seminar. *Theory and Research in Social Education, 27*(3), 329–357.

Dinkelman, T. (2003). Self-study in teacher education: A means and ends tool for promoting reflective teaching. *Journal of Teacher Education, 54*(1), 6–18.

Dumas, W. (1993). Preparation of social studies teachers at major research universities. *International Journal of Social Education, 7*(3), 59–65.

Dumas, W. (1995). Preparation of middle school social studies teachers in major state universities. *Teacher Education and Practice, 11*(1), 58–64.

Ehman, L. H. (1999, November). Adding instruction about technology infusion to the secondary social studies course with web-based modules. Paper presented at College and University Faculty Assembly of the National Council of the Social Studies, Orlando, Florida.

Ehman, L. H. (2001). Using stand-alone web modules to integrate technology into secondary social studies methods instruction. *Journal of Research on Technology in Education, 34*(1), 39–50.

Evans, R. W. (2004). *The social studies wars: What should we teach the children?* New York: Teachers College Press.

Fehn, B., & Koeppen, K. E. (1998). Intensive document-based instruction in a social studies methods course and student teachers' attitudes and practices in subsequent filed experiences. *Theory and Research in Social Education, 26*(4), 461–84.

Galluzo, G. (1999). Consensus and the knowledge base for teaching and teacher education. In J. D. Raths & A. C. McAninch (Eds), *Advances in teacher education* (Vol. 5, pp. 69–84). Stamford, CT: Ablex Publishing.

Gaudelli, W. (2001, November). Professional development, global pedagogy and potential: Examining an alternative approach to the episodic workshop. Paper presented to the College and University Faculty Assembly of the National Council for the Social Studies, Washington, DC.

Gay, G. (2004). Social studies teacher education for urban classrooms. In S. Adler (Ed.), *Critical issues in social studies teacher education* (pp. 75–96). Greenwich, CT: Information Age Press.

Gay, G., & Howard, T. (2000). Multicultural teacher education for the 21st century. *The Teacher Educator, 36*(1), 1–16.

Gerwin, D. (2003). A relevant lesson: Hitler goes to the mall. *Theory and Research in Social Education, 31*(4), 435–465.

Hauessler-Bohan, C., & Davis, O. L. (1998). Historical constructions: How social studies student teachers' historical thinking is reflected in their writing of history. *Theory and Research in Social Education, 26*(2), 173–917.

Hamilton, M. L., & Pinnegar, S. (2000). On the threshold of a new century: Trustworthiness, integrity, and self-study in teacher education. *Journal of Teacher Education, 51*(3), 234–240.

Hohenbrink, J., Johnston, M., & Westhoven, L. (1997). Collaborative teaching of a social studies methods course: Intimidation and change. *Journal of Teacher Education, 84*(4), 293–300.

Hughes, A. S., Sears, A. M., & Clarke, G. M. (1998). Adapting problem-based learning to social studies teachers education. *Theory and Research in Social Education, 26*(4), 531–548.

Johnson, F. E., (2000). Social studies methods textbooks and computing technology: A call for integration. *International Journal of Social Education, 15*(1), 39–61.

Johnston, M. (2006). The lamp and the mirror: Action research and self-studies in the social studies. In K. Barton (Ed.), *Research methods in social studies education* (pp. 57–84). Greenwich, Conn: Information Age Publishing.

Jongewaard, S. (2000). The six characteristics of universal citizenship: Their development and measurement in preservice teachers. Paper presented at the annual meeting of the College and University Faculty Assembly of the National Council for the Social Studies, San Antonio, TX.

Keiper, T., Harwood, A., & Larson, B. (2000). Preservice teachers' perceptions of infusing computer technology into social studies instruction. *Theory and Research in Social Education, 28*(4), 566–579.

Keiper, T., Myhre, O., & Pihl, P. (2000/ 2001). Enhancing school-university collaboration through technology. *International Journal of Social Education, 15*(2), 62–75.

Kirkwood-Tucker, T. F., & Bleicher, R. (2003). A self-study of two professors team teaching a unifying global issues theme unit as a part of their separate elementary social studies and science preservice methods classes. *The International Social Studies Forum, 3*(1), 203–217.

Koeppen. K. E., & Griffith, J. B. (2003, January). Non-traditional students and their influence on teacher education. Paper presented at the annual meeting of the Association for Colleges of teacher Education, New Orleans, LA.

Kubow, P. K. (1997, March). Citizenship education for the 21st century: Insights from social studies teacher preparation students in three countries. Paper presented at the annual meeting of the American Educational Research Association, Chicago, IL.

Lanier. J. (1982). Teacher education: Needed research and practice for the preparation of teacher professionals. In D. Corrigan (Ed.), *The future of teacher education: Needed research and practice* (pp. 13–35). College Station, TX: College of Education, Texas A&M University.

Lipscomb, G. B., & Doppen, F. H. (2002, November). Climbing the STAIRS: Social studies teachers' perceptions of technology integrations. Paper presented at the Annual Meeting of the College and University Faculty Assembly of the National Council for the Social Studies.

Liston, D. P., & Zeichner, K. M. (1991). *Teacher education and the social conditions of schooling.* New York: Routledge Press.

McAninch, A. C. (2004). Reflection in social studies teacher education. In S. Adler (Ed.), *Critical issues in social studies teacher education* (pp. 59–74). Greenwich, CT: Information Age Press.

McCall, A. L. (1995). "We were cheated." Students' responses to a multicultural, social reconstructionist teacher education course. *Equality and Excellence in Education, 28*(1), 15–24.

Mason, C. L. (2000). On-line teacher education: An analysis of student teachers' use of commuter-mediated communication. *International Journal of Social Education, 15*(1), 19–38.

Mason, C. L. (2000/2001). Collaborative social studies teacher education across remote locations: Students experiences and perceptions. *International Journal of Social Education, 15*(2), 46–61.

Mason, C. L., & Berson, M. J. (2000). Computer mediated communication in elementary social studies methods: An examination of students' perceptions and perspectives. *Theory and Research in Social Education, 28*(4), 527–545.

Mayer, R. H. (2003, April). Learning to think historically: The impact of a philosophy and methods of history course on three preservice teachers. Paper presented at the annual meeting of the American Educational Research Association, Chicago, IL.

Merryfield, M. M. (2000). Using electronic technologies to promote equity and cultural diversity in social studies and global education. *Theory and Research in Social Education, 28*(4), 502–526.

Miller, G. E. (2003). *Action research: A guide for the teacher researcher* (2nd ed.). Upper Saddle River, NJ: Merrill.

Milson, A. J., & King, K. P. (2001). Investigating science-technology-society issues with prospective elementary school teachers. *The International Social Studies Forum, 1*(2), 77–87.

Montgomery, J. (1994). Silkworms, schedules and mummy spices: Experiences that are a success with student teachers. *Social Studies Review, 33*(3), 12–15.

National Commission on Teaching and America's Future (1996). *What matters most; Teaching for America's Future.* New York: Report of the National Commission on Teaching & America's Future.

National Council for the Social Studies (1994). *Expectations of Excellence,* Washington, DC: National Council for the Social Studies.

Nelson, J. L. (2001). Defining social studies. In W. Stanley (Ed.), *Critical issues in social studies research for the twentieth century* (pp. 15–38). Greenwich, CT: Information Age Publishing.

Newmann, F. M. (1990). Qualities of thoughtful social studies classes: An empirical profile. *Journal of Curriculum Studies, 22*(3), 253–275.

Newmann, F. M. (1991). Promoting higher order thinking in social studies: Overview of a study of sixteen high school departments. *Theory and Research in Social Education, 19,* 324–340.

Owens, W. T. (1996). The status of social studies among preservice elementary teachers, *Southern Social Studies Journal, 22*(1), 17–28.

Owens, W. T. (1997). Investigating a social studies field experience for preservice elementary teachers prior to student learning. *Southern Social Studies Journal, 23*(1), 30–44.

Owens, W. T. (1999). Preservice teachers' feedback about the Internet and the implications for social studies educators. *The Social Studies, 90*(3), 133–140.

Paige, R., Stroup, S., & Andrade, J. R. (2002). Meeting the highly qualified teachers challenge. *The secretary's annual report on teacher quality.* Retrieved from: www.ed.gov/offices/OPE/News/teacherprep/indix.html

Pajares, M. F. (1992). Teacher beliefs and educational research: Cleaning up a messy construct. *Review of Educational Research, 62*(3), 307–322.

Percival, J. E. (2000). A true and continuing story: Developing a culturally sensitive, integrated curriculum in college and elementary classrooms. *The Social Studies, 91*(4), 151–158.

Riley, K. L., & Stern, S. S. (1997, October). Understanding cultural influence: Using authentic assessment and qualitative methodology to bridge theory and practice. Paper presented at the fourth annual AATC Conference, Indianapolis, IN.

Riley, K. L., & Stern, B. S. (2001, November). Problems and possibilities of Web-based instruction: Transforming social studies methods and practice. Paper presented at the annual meeting of the National Council for the Social Studies, Washington, D.C.

Ross, E. W. (1996). The role of portfolio evaluation in social studies teacher education. *Social Education, 60*(3), 62–66.

Sanders, W., & Horn, S. (1998). Research findings from the Tennessee Value-added Assessment System (TVAAS) database: Implications for educational evaluation and research. *Journal of Personnel Evaluation in Education, 12*(3), 247–256.

Schön, D. A. (1983). *The reflective practitioner: How professionals think in action.* New York: Basic Books.

Schön, D. A. (1987). *Educating the reflective practitioner: Toward a design for teaching and learning in the professions.* San Francisco: Jossey-Bass.

Segall, A. (2002). *Disturbing practice: Reading teacher education as text.* New York: Peter Lang.

Segall, A. (2004). Blurring the lines between content and pedagogy. *Social Education, 68*(7), 479–482.

Sexias, P. (1998). Student teachers thinking historically. *Theory and Research in Social Education, 26*(3), 310–341.

Shaver, J. P. (2001). The future of research on social studies—for what purpose? In W. Stanley (Ed.), *Critical issues in social studies research for the twentieth century* (pp. 231–252). Greenwich, CT: Information Age Publishing.

Shaver, K., Stallworth, J. B., Wilson, E. (2001, January). Interdisciplinary teaching and learning in a Professional Development School. Paper presented at the annual meeting of the Holmes Partnership, Albuquerque, NM.

Shulman, L. S. (1986). Those who understand: Knowledge growth in teaching. *Educational Researcher, 15*(2), 4–14.

Slekar, T. D. (1995). Preservice teachers' attitudes concerning elementary social studies instruction. Unpublished master's thesis.

Slekar, T. D. (1998). Epistemological entanglements: Preservice elementary school teachers "apprenticeship of observation" and the teaching of history. *Theory and Research in Social Education, 26*(4), 435–507.

Smith, R. W. (2000). The influence of teacher background on the inclusion of multicultural education: A case study of two contrasts. *The Urban Review, 32*(2), 155–176.

Sunal, C. S., & Sunal, D. W. (2003). Teacher candidates' conception of guided inquiry and lesson planning in social studies following web-assisted instruction. *Theory and Research in Social Education, 31*(2), 243–264.

Thornton, S. J. (1991). Teachers as curricular-instructional gatekeepers in social studies. In J. Shaver (Ed.), *Handbook of research on teaching and learning in social studies* (pp. 237–248). New York: Macmillan.

Thornton, S. J. (2005). *Teaching social studies that matters: Curriculum for active learning.* New York: Teachers College Press.

VanManen, M. (1977). Linking ways of knowing with ways of being practical. *Curriculum Inquiry, 6*(3), 205–228.

Wade, R. C. (1999). Voice and choice in a university seminar: The struggle to teach democratically. *Theory and Research in Social Education, 27*(1)70–92.

Wade, R., & Raba, S. (2003). The Chicago Experience: Border crossing for social studies preservice teachers. *Theory and Research in Social Education, 31*(2), 153–173.

White, C. (1996). Relevant social studies education, *Journal of Technology and Teacher Education, 4*(1), 69–76.

Whitson, J. A. (2004). What social studies teachers need to know. In S. Adler (Ed.), *Critical Issues in Social Studies Teacher Education* (pp. 9–35). Greenwich, CT: Information Age Press.

Wilkins, C. (1999). Making 'good citizens': The social and political attitudes of PGCE students. *Oxford Review of Education, 25*(1&2), 217–230.

Wilson, A. (2001). Growing toward teaching from a global perspective. *The International Social Studies Forum, 1*(2), 127–143.

Wingfield, M., Nath, J., Freeman, L., & Cohen, M. (2000, April). The effect of site-based preservice experiences on elementary social studies, language arts and mathematics teaching self-efficacy beliefs. Paper presented at the annual meeting of the American Educational Research Association, New Orleans, LA.

Yaeger, E. A. (1997). Teaching historical thinking in the social studies methods course, *Social Studies, 88*(3), 121–26.

Zeichner, K. M. (1999). The new scholarship in teacher education. *Educational Researcher, 28*(9), 4–15.

Zeichner, K. M. (2005). A research agenda for teacher education. In M. Cochran-Smith & K. M. Zeichner (Eds.), *Studying teacher education: The report of the AERA panel on research and teacher education* (pp 737–760). Washington, DC: AERA.

19 The professional development of social studies teachers

Stephanie van Hover

University of Virginia

INTRODUCTION

Growing evidence demonstrates that effective teachers exert a powerful, long-lasting influence on their students and directly contribute to pupil achievement and learning growth (Bransford, Darling-Hammond, & LePage, 2005; Sanders & Rivers, 1996; Smith & Niemi, 2001; Stronge, 2002). This research is emerging within a context of standards and high-stakes accountability, a context in which, as Stanley and Longwell (2004) note, "social studies continues to be seen as relatively less important (in terms of what is tested and what students are held accountable for) than the other major areas of the curriculum" (p. 211). In this shifting and complex landscape, social studies teachers are serving as instructional gatekeepers, making day-to-day decisions about subject matter and instruction (Thornton, 1991) and directly influencing how and what students learn about social studies (Smith & Niemi, 2001). And, as Bransford et al. (2005) argue, these teachers need to be "increasingly effective in enabling a diverse group of students to learn ever more complex material and to develop a wider range of skills" (p. 2) within a high-stakes environment.

As goals for student learning become increasingly ambitious, education reform movements and educational policy makers call for changes in classroom practice and, to facilitate these changes, call for increased professional development opportunities for teachers (Borko, 2004; Fullan & Miles, 1992). The federal No Child Left Behind Act, for example, calls for states to ensure the availability of "high quality" professional development for all teachers (Hess & Petrilli, 2006/2007). Evidence does suggest that effective professional development can lead to teacher learning and improvements in classroom practice (Borko, 2004; Borko & Putnam, 1995; Desimone, Porter, Garet, Yoon, & Birman, 2002; Garet, Porter, Desimone, Birman, & Yoon, 2001; Louis & Marks, 1998); however, the current state of professional development has been described by Borko (2004) as "woefully inadequate" (p. 3) and by Sykes (1996) as "the most serious unsolved problem for policy and practice in American education today" (p. 465). What is the state of professional development in social studies education? What do we, as a field, know about professional development? How does social studies professional development affect teacher learning? How does social studies professional development affect student learning? This chapter explores these questions through a review of social studies literature from the mid- 1990s to the present. For the purposes of this chapter, "professional development" includes attention to the spectrum of learning opportunities available to practicing K–12 social studies classroom teachers.

Adler, in her 1991 review of this topic, characterized the extant literature on the professional development of inservice social studies teachers as "particularistic and unsystematic" (p. 211) and found much of the work to focus on outcomes of particular interventions—whether teachers had learned new knowledge, skills, or dispositions— rather than insight into whether teachers became better teachers as a result of professional development. Armento (1996), writing a chapter on the professional development of social studies educators for the *Handbook of Research on Teacher Education*, observed that the literature appeared to be non-cumulative. She argued that discussing the status of research in this area is complicated by several factors (Armento, 1996), one of which is that the "social studies professional community has yet to rally around a consensus view of the field" (p. 485). As Stanley and Longwell (2004) note, "external and internal debates over the definition and purposes of social studies teacher education have been a persistent feature of the field" (p. 193). So how do we determine, then, what social studies teachers need to know, what they need to learn? What are the purposes and processes of the professional development of social studies teachers?

The goal of this chapter is to examine the professional development of social studies teachers by synthesizing, reviewing, and critically assessing the current literature on this topic and to offer suggestions for future research. An extensive review of the literature from the mid-1990s to the present yields papers, dissertations, book chapters, books, presentations, monographs, reports, and web-based articles addressing some aspect of the professional development of social studies teachers. This chapter also includes attention to papers from the larger world of educational research in order to contextualize the discussion of the education and professional development of inservice social studies teachers. However, as Armento (1996) cautions, authors apply subjective criteria to the inclusion or exclusion of sources, and, in many cases, miss or omit relevant works. Thus, while this chapter attempts to provide an intensive and extensive review of the extant literature, some works may be missing or overlooked.

The chapter begins with an examination of the research on the professional development of beginning teachers—the induction of social studies teachers in their first years of teaching. Then, the chapter provides a brief overview of the literature that describes and examines principles of effective professional development as informed by research on teacher learning, socialization, and development. Next, the chapter reviews existing research on more "traditional" modes of professional development— workshops and summer institutes, for example—across the different social studies content areas. Finally, the chapter concludes with a synopsis of the literature and suggestions for future research.

PROFESSIONAL DEVELOPMENT OF BEGINNING TEACHERS

The first years of teaching exert a tremendous impact on the personal and professional life of a teacher (Gold, 1996, p. 548). Beginning teachers often face myriad challenges, including heavy teaching loads, multiple preparations, the "least desirable" classes, extracurricular duties, few instructional resources, little collegial support, discipline issues, professional isolation, inadequate salaries, high parent expectations, poor administrative support, unfamiliarity with routines and procedures, and a disconnect between their expectations of teaching and the realities of the classroom (Bullough, 1986, 1987; Darling-Hammond, 1998a; Gold, 1996; Gold & Roth, 1993; Rosenberg, Griffin, Kilgore, & Carpenter, 1997; van Hover & Yeager, 2003, 2004) Novice teachers may also struggle with stress, loneliness, isolation, disillusionment, and fatigue (Gold, 1996, p. 562). Even under the best of conditions, new teachers are a "fragile and valuable resource" requiring "care and support" (Rosenberg et al., 1997, p. 302). Given this context, the learning curve for beginning teachers is enormous (Brownell, Yeager, Sindelar, van Hover, & Riley, 2004; Feiman-Nemser, 2001; Thornton, 1991).

Education reformers consistently call for support and professional development for new teachers during their formative years (Darling-Hammond, 1998a, 1998b, 1999; Darling-Hammond, Berry, Haselkorn, & Fideler, 1999; Darling-Hammond & McLaughlin, 1999; Feiman-Nemser, 2001, 2003). According to these researchers, careful attention to induction can potentially increase retention rates of new teachers, promote professional and psychological well-being, and improve instructional practice (Gold & Roth, 1993; Patterson, 2002; Patterson & Luft, 2004). Feiman-Nemser (2003) describes quality induction as a continuum of support from preservice teacher education programs through the first years of teaching. She argues that new teachers require social and emotional support, but also need mentoring in implementing curricula, addressing specific students' needs, creating safe learning environments, engaging students in worthwhile learning, working well with parents, and basing instructional decisions on assessment data (p. 28). In other words, beginning teachers require unique and targeted professional development in their first years of teaching.

The beginning years of teaching offer, as Patterson and Luft (2004) suggest, a rich opportunity to study the nature of teacher change and to explore influences on beginning teachers' instructional decision-making. Other research documents the ways in which beginning teachers' beliefs and experiences, coursework, and perceptions of curriculum, students, and pedagogy mediate teaching practices (Cochran-Smith & Zeichner, 2005; Pajares, 1992; Richardson, 1996). The relative influence of teacher education appears to depend on a complex confluence of factors, including how messages sent by teacher educators mesh with prospective teachers' beliefs and attitudes, and the level of congruence between teacher education experiences and field experiences (Clift & Brady, 2005) That is, teachers' prior educational and life experiences, combined with beliefs about the nature of history and student abilities, influence how they interpret content and implement instruction (Adler, 1991; Angell, 1998; Fehn & Koeppen, 1998; Grossman, 1991; Thornton, 1991; Wineburg, 2001). A few studies within social studies education examine teacher development and socialization in the first years of teaching (Barton, McCully, & Marks, 2004; Chant, 2002; Hartzler-Miller, 2001; Hicks, 2005; van Hover, 2006; van Hover & Yeager, 2003, 2004, 2005; Yeager & van Hover, 2006)

Yon & Passe (1994), for example, conducted a case study in which they examined the relationship between an undergraduate elementary social studies methods course and an elementary teachers' (Shannon's) perspectives on social studies over a 3-year time period. Interviews, journals, and observations from Shannon's undergraduate methods course, her student-teaching experience, and her first year of teaching revealed that her definition of social studies and her description of the purpose of social studies remained constant. However, other perceptions/beliefs changed over the 3-year period, including the importance of social studies as a subject, the importance of integrating social studies into other topics/subjects, the importance of systematic planning for specific social studies goals, and the importance of using the text as a guide for planning instruction. Yon and Passe (1994) found that the culture of the school exerted a strong influence on Shannon's perceptions of social studies and changed the way she viewed the role of social studies in the elementary school curriculum.

van Hover and Yeager (2003) examined the instructional practice of a secondary beginning history teacher, Angela Talbot, who graduated from a social studies masters/certification program. The strongest student in her class, Angela could articulate a sophisticated conception of historical thinking and appeared to possess "exemplary" pedagogical content knowledge. Nonetheless, her classroom practice revealed that Angela did not incorporate the historical inquiry and historical thinking approaches, including the use of multiple perspectives and sources that were discussed in her methods course. Angela's understandings about the interpretive nature of history were not evident in her instruction. Rather, Angela's instruction was highly "self-oriented"; she lectured in a narrative fashion that allowed her to present her own interpretations of history and to control the conclusions she thought should be drawn from the material (van Hover & Yeager, 2004, 2005).

Other research on the socialization and learning of beginning teachers includes attention to teachers' personal theorizing (Chant, 2002), understanding and implementation of historical inquiry (Hartzler-Miller, 2001), experiences with high-stakes testing and accountability contexts (van Hover, 2006), and international comparisons (Barton et al., 2004; Hicks, 2005). These studies offer glimpses into the complex confluence of factors that influence beginning teachers' instructional decision-making. All call for a continuum of professional development that extends beyond teacher education into the early years of a teachers' career. And while an increasing number of states and school districts have developed and implemented induction programs (Darling-Hammond, Berry, Haselkorn, & Fideler, 1999), very few studies have examined how professional development, or induction, of beginning teachers' affects social studies teachers in their first years in the classroom.

Patterson and Luft (2004) described their work with Project: Alternative Support for the Induction of Secondary Teachers (ASIST). This induction program served 15 beginning teachers, 4 of whom were social studies teachers. Project: ASIST offered monthly full-day workshops that focused on inquiry-based instruction as well as on general topics, including management, planning, and assessment. Participants also received individualized attention in adapting content in the workshops for their own particular teaching context and were observed once a month. The project funded trips to the state social studies conference and established an online discussion group. The beginning teachers found the mentoring provided by Project: ASIST very helpful, and the support allowed them to become aware of and negotiate some of the dilemmas of implementing inquiry-based instruction in a social studies classroom. The induction program allowed the participants to experiment with new instructional approaches and to reflect with peers and mentors about their experiences (p. 148). Patterson and Luft (2004) argue that such induction programs clearly offer a way to systematically bridge the gap between teacher education programs and public schools, to teach and reinforce research-based best practices (like inquiry) to beginning teachers, and to offer meaningful professional development to teachers struggling to survive in their first years of teaching.

While other research on the professional development of beginning social studies teachers exists, it is typically embedded in studies on other topics. For example, studies of the formation of teacher community include attention to how the existence of a learning community helps support beginning teachers (Brownell et. al., 2004; Thomas, Wineburg, Grossman, Oddmund, & Woolworth, 1998). This area of study, the professional development of beginning social studies teachers, is an area ripe for further research. Intensive, sustained study of induction programs and social studies teachers' experiences in those induction programs would add to our understanding of teacher learning and change, as would studies that investigate the impact of induction programs on teachers' practice and student learning.

PROFESSIONAL DEVELOPMENT AND SOCIAL STUDIES EDUCATION

Unfortunately, our knowledge of the professional development of social studies teachers is idiosyncratic and there exists no "big picture" of social studies professional development across the country. A plethora of professional development opportunities exist for social studies teachers, but they vary wildly in format, content, and quality. The majority of offerings in social studies follow the traditional format of workshop (half-day, whole day, after school) or institute—approaches often described in the research as weakly conceived and poorly delivered—and without attention to how teachers learn (Grant, 2003, p. 200). The current literature on professional development includes a great deal of attention to principles for designing effective professional development (Borko, 2004; Borko & Putnam, 1995; Hawley & Valli, 1999; Little, 1999; Putnam & Borko, 1997; Rhine, 1998; Sykes, 1996, 1999; Valli & Stout, 2004; Wilson & Berne, 1999). Valli and Stout (2004), for example, assert that for professional development to be effective:

> Professional development must help teachers understand the discipline they are teaching together with the content standards and the assessments, connect teachers with adequate resources, give clear guidance on what students are expected to do, and provide a continuous and supportive framework for their reform efforts. (p. 184)

Sykes (1999) argues further that delivery of teacher professional development should include attention to five general guidelines: (a) select and design professional development based on the teacher-student learning connection; (b) ensure that professional development is embedded in the specific content of the curriculum; (c) integrate the examination of student learning into professional development; (d) attend to student learning associated with the implementation of curricular and/or instructional innovations; and (e) reference both formative and summative evaluation of professional development to student learning (p. 161).

These, and other authors, situate their suggestions within the research on teacher learning and teacher socialization. They assert that workshops and other professional development opportunities too often ignore what we know about how teachers learn. Effective professional development attends to the beliefs and prior knowledge of teachers, models ambitious teaching and learning practices, and is sustained over a period of time with mentoring and support (Borko & Putnam, 1995; Guskey, 1995; Hawley & Valli, 1999; Little, 1999). Additionally, researchers suggest that the school culture and school structures should be closely analyzed and reorganized in ways that facilitate teacher community, collaboration, and learning (Little, 1999; Louis & Marks, 1998; Newmann, King, & Youngs, 2000).

Teacher community

Research and writings describing effective professional development also include attention to the importance of creating learning communities that support teachers in sustained school-based professional development that focuses on instructional practices, student achievement, and development of subject matter knowledge (Little, 1999; Smylie, 1995; Wilson & Berne, 1999). Most of the work in this area examines school-based collaboration projects that may include some component related to social studies teaching and learning, but typically focus on other issues. The Teacher Learning Cohorts (TLC) project, for example, established and studied teacher collaboration in two urban elementary schools with the purpose of fostering teacher learning among general educators and providing professional development in how to reach the needs of students identified with disabilities (Brownell, Adams, Sindelar, Waldron, & van Hover, 2006; Brownell, Yeager, Rennells, & Riley, 1997; Brownell et. al., 2004). Other work focuses on collaboration between teachers working in professional development schools (PDS) (Bossard et al., 1996; Silva, 2000, 2003; Silva & Dana, 2001; Silva & Fichtman, 2004; Silva, Gimbert, & Nolan, 2000; Silva & Tom, 2001) or in other school-university partnerships (Brandes & Seixas, 1998, 2000; Seixas & Brandes, 1997). A few studies, however, focus exclusively on social studies and the formation of teacher community (Bossard et al., 1996; Grossman, Wineburg, & Woolworth, 2000a, 2000b, 2001).

The Community of Teacher Leaders project (Grossman, Wineburg, & Woolworth, 2000a, 2001; Thomas et. al., 1998; Wineburg & Grossman, 1998, 2000), funded by a grant from the James S. McDonnell Foundation of St. Louis, brought together teachers in a large urban high school and educators/researchers from a nearby university in a 2½-year study of the development of teacher community. Twenty-two English and social studies teachers, as well as a special educator and an English as second language (ESL) teacher, met after school every other week, met twice a month for a full day, and, in the summer, participated in a 5-day retreat. In these meetings teachers read and discussed books, conversed and reflected about teaching and learning, and worked on an interdisciplinary curriculum. The university-based educators served as facilitators and researchers for this project and collected multiple forms of data documenting the development of teacher community, including interviews, think-alouds, transcripts of project meetings, self-reports, records of e-mail correspondence, and ethnographic field notes.

Based on their analysis of the data and on their own experiences as facilitators, the researchers offered initial ideas for a model of the formation of a teacher professional community, including formation of group identity and norms of interaction; understanding differences; negotiating the essential tension between improving practice, enhancing student learning, and continuing intellectual development in a subject matter; and taking communal responsibility for individuals' growth (Grossman et. al, 2000b, p. 45). From the researchers' perspective, the "book club" format allowed them to investigate how the teachers in their study interacted and thought about subject matter. They concluded that, through participation in the learning community, the teachers began to think more deeply about the nature of history and literature (Wilson & Berne, 1999; Wineburg & Grossman, 1998). They also noted that teachers at different points in their careers experienced the formation of teacher community in different ways (Thomas et. al., 1998). The project appeared to exert the strongest influence on experienced teachers, who enjoyed being part of a learning community engaged in discussion of subject matter. Experienced teachers also appeared to recognize that collaboration sometimes engenders conflict and, as a result of their participation in the project, engaged in renewed political activism. New teachers asserted that participation in the learning community reduced the isolation they felt and helped them move beyond day-to-day survival. Student teachers from a nearby university, who got to see a learning community at work, said they realized they could make a contribution to the learning community and saw a direct connection between teacher education programs and this community.

This study offers interesting insight into the challenges inherent in creating a community of learners over a long period of time in a secondary public school. The extensive qualitative data provides insight into the messiness of teacher learning and the conflict involved in collaboration. However, as the researchers recognized, they did not examine how or what teachers took into the classroom (Grossman et al., 2000b). In addition, the link to practice and to student achievement is missing. Rather, the researchers relied on self-report data for anecdotal stories about how professional development affected classroom practice. This makes it difficult to know what participants learned in this professional development opportunity and whether they were able to translate their new knowledge to the classroom.

Research examining different types of school-university partnerships also includes attention to the development of teacher community (Bossard et al., 1996; Brandes & Seixas, 1998, 2000; Seixas & Brandes, 1997). Bossard et al. (1996), for example, identified factors associated with an effective professional development school network and examined issues, concerns, and challenges to maintaining a professional community. They investigated a Professional Development School Network in Social Studies established in Ohio in 1991; the leadership team consisted of eight high school teachers and a university professor. The Network redesigned a teacher education program, developed a team-taught, field-based social studies methods course, facilitated inservice workshops for colleagues, and presented/published work related to the PDS. Bossard and her colleagues found that challenges to maintaining a collaborative community included the time commitment required to sustain collaboration, the diversity of schools and teachers involved in the project, and the difficulties of dealing with university cultures. The experience, however, taught the participants the importance of learning communities and collaboration. In a study investigating a different type of school-university partnership, Brandes and Seixas (1998, 2000) explored issues that emerged from a 1-year interdisciplinary school-university collaboration in which a cohort of teachers became full-time university students and participated in a series of interdisciplinary humanities courses at a local university. The project culminated in a teacher curriculum project. The participants struggled with contradictory demands and expectations as well as the complex relationships between schools and universities.

This research suggests that the formation and maintenance of teacher learning communities is time and labor intensive for participants as well as researchers. Yet, this work offers a glimpse at the potential for teacher communities to influence teacher learning. More research in this area is warranted, however, to examine the immediate and longer-term impact of teacher communities on classroom practice and student learning.

WORKSHOPS, INSTITUTES, AND THE CONTENT AREAS

While debate continues over the nature and purpose of social studies (Stanley & Longwell, 2004), a review of the relevant literature indicates that most social studies professional development opportunities focus on particular content areas or topics, including history, geography, civics, global education, multicultural education and social justice. These professional development programs, for the most part, follow the traditional model of workshops and summer institutes (Borko, 2004; Humphrey et al., 2005; Wilson & Berne, 1999). And while critics refer to the "workshop program"—the fragmented and serendipitous nature of teacher learning that typically occurs in traditional inservice programs (Ball & Cohen, 1999; Grant, 1997; Valli & Stout, 2004; Wilson & Berne, 1999)—this approach remains the most common approach to professional development. A number of research studies in social studies education examine workshops and institutes; this section reviews the research conducted on these content-specific professional development opportunities.

History

Professional development opportunities abound in history education—from one-day workshops to institutes lasting several weeks—offered by myriad organizations, including the American Historical Association, the Colonial Williamsburg Foundation, the Smithsonian Institute, the National Council for History Education, the National Council for the Social Studies, the Gilder Lehrmann Institute of American History, the National Council on Public History, the Organization of American Historians, college and university history departments, colleges of education, and many other entities. Additionally, since 2001, the Teaching American History (TAH) grant program, funded by the U.S. Department of Education (DOE), has led to a proliferation of professional development opportunities for history teachers (Humphrey et al., 2005). The

TAH Grant program supports local educational agencies who collaborate with university history departments, colleges of education, museums, and other entities to develop professional development programs designed to raise student achievement by improving teachers' knowledge, understanding, and appreciation of American history (Humphrey et al., 2005; Stein, 2003). The DOE awarded 60 grants in 2001, 114 in 2002, 114 in 2003, 122 in 2004, and 129 in 2005 (Ed.Gov, 2006). The awards vary from $500,000 to $2,000,000 and are available to granters for up to 3 years. Despite the plethora of opportunities for history teachers' professional development, very few systematic studies investigate the impact of these workshops, institutes, and curricular training on teachers' classroom instruction or on student achievement. The few studies that do exist tend to focus on content mastery and teacher self-report data rather than classroom-based observation or data on student achievement.

While a growing number of papers focus on professional development activities supported by TAH grants (Carpenter, Dublin, & Harper, 2005; Hudson & Santora, 2003; Moyer, Onosko, & Forcey, 2003; Pesick & Weintraub, 2004; Zeisler-Vralsted, 2003), the majority simply describe the type of history professional development provided/to be provided and offer teachers' responses to this training. Most of these grants are in the first year or two of implementation, and researchers have not yet collected classroom data or student achievement data. Rather, the studies focus on teachers' understandings of history content or their general experiences with the professional development programs.

Hudson and Santora (2003), for example, discuss their TAH grant-supported 8-day *American History as Dialogue* Summer Institute, which focused on historical inquiry through oral history. The authors videotaped sessions and asked teachers to keep reflective logs during the institute. These data provide insight into teachers' developing sense of what constitutes history and historical understanding, as well as information about teachers' habits of mind, specifically their enthusiasm about the project, their innate interest and curiosity about each other as agents in history, and their proclivity to engage in collecting oral histories (p. 218). The authors recognize that a great deal of work lies ahead as they move the research to the classroom in order to investigate the impact of the institute on teachers' instruction. Other examples of TAH grant-related papers include reports on collaborative projects in New York (Carpenter, Dublin, & Harper, 2005), New Hampshire (Moyer et al., 2003), Oakland, California (Pesick & Weintraub, 2004), and Wisconsin (Zeisler-Vralsted, 2003).

In 2002, SRI International conducted an evaluation of the effectiveness of the TAH program (Humphrey et al., 2005). The authors of the report conducted a review of the current research and policies on teaching and learning American history, surveyed all TAH project directors, surveyed a sample of teachers participating in TAH project activities, and systematically collected and analyzed the training materials produced by a sample of TAH grantees (Humphrey et al., 2005) The evaluation yielded several key findings (Humphrey et al., 2005). Rather than the anticipated outcome of serving high numbers of beginning teachers or teachers with weak content backgrounds, the majority of TAH participants were fully certified, experienced teachers with academic backgrounds in history (p. ix). The projects covered a wide range of historical content, thinking skills, and methods. Data indicated that while teachers appeared to gain factual knowledge, teacher work products revealed participants' limited ability to analyze and interpret historical data (p. xv). And although the majority of project directors and participants reported positively on the effectiveness and quality of TAH grants, the SRI evaluators assert that internal evaluations lacked the rigor to accurately measure the projects' effectiveness—in part due to the heavy reliance on teacher self-report data (p. xiv). The evaluators also observe that, even though most TAH project activities included some attention to characteristics of effective professional development, the lack of research on this topic in the teaching and learning of history hampered project director's abilities to make evidence-based decisions in developing activities that would increase teacher knowledge and improve student achievement (p. xvi).

Outside the world of TAH grants, very few research studies exist that examine the impact of history professional development (Mintrop, 2004; Wolpow, Johnson, & Wognild, 2002). In a study of an inservice program funded by the National Endowment for the Humanities, Wolpow et al. (2002) examined the impact of a series of Holocaust education workshops. These workshops were designed to familiarize teachers with key issues and content in Holocaust studies, to teach teachers how to integrate genocide-related materials into their curricula and classroom instruction, to develop interdisciplinary approaches to teaching about the Holocaust and genocide, and to identify historical resources (primary and secondary sources, media) for teacher use. Participating teachers attended 72 hours of workshops facilitated by scholars in Holocaust studies. The researchers explored the self-efficacy of teachers in terms of knowledge and skills and examined key issues/concepts and methods/sources participants identified as important for implementation into grades 6–12. Not surprisingly, they found that participating teachers' self-efficacy scores were higher than non-participants. And, after analyzing essay questions completed by teachers, the authors discovered that participants believed that they should teach their students about the scope of the Holocaust, the important names/dates/events, and the roles of those who persecuted as well as those who suffered; that participants believed students should learn about the nature of the Holocaust and the nature of humanity through study of first-hand accounts and video and literature of the Holocaust and other genocide; and that students should learn the role of the media as a source of complicity in an atrocity. The researchers did not collect demographic/background data on their participants or any data that documented the impact of this workshop on actual classroom teaching practice and, by extension, students' understandings of the Holocaust and genocide.

Overall, the majority of research in professional development for history offers interesting insight into the different types of workshops/institutes available for teachers and provides anecdotal and self-report evidence that teachers enjoy and learn from these experiences. What is missing from this work, however, is systematic evidence that demonstrates whether these workshops/institutes affect classroom instruction and student achievement/understanding of history.

Civics

In civics education as in history, opportunities for professional development abound. National and international programs hosted by a number of different organizations— Street Law, Center for Civic Education, and the Bill of Rights Institute, to name a few— offer a variety of ways for teachers to engage in and learn about teaching civics. The majority of research on professional development in civics education, however, focuses on three programs offered or administered by the Center for Civic Education: *We the People… Project Citizen, We the People… the Citizen and the Constitution*, and CIVITAS. For example, in their report "What Works in Middle School," the National Staff Development Council identified *Project Citizen* and *We the People* as exemplary professional development programs that influence student achievement (Killion, 2006). *Project Citizen* is a service-learning program that emphasizes active citizenship and engagement in community affairs. *We the People,* a textbook series, focuses on students' knowledge of American constitutional democracy and the contemporary relevance of the Bill of Rights (Vontz & Leming, 2005). For both programs, state coordinators for the Center for Civic Education distribute curricular materials and provide professional development to teachers. Training varies from 1-hour presentations to weeklong institutes. A

1991 Educational Testing Service (ETS) evaluation of *We the People* and *Project Citizen* revealed that students who participated in these programs scored significantly better on a test of knowledge of history and principles of the U.S. Constitution than students who participated in other constitutional instructional programs (Killion, 2006).

Several studies examine the work of CIVITAS, an international civic education exchange program administered by the Center for Civic Education and funded by the United States Department of Education's Office of Educational Research and Improvement, with cooperation of the United States Department of State (Cornett, Dziuban, & Abisellan, 2002; Quigley & Hoar, 1997). Most of these papers have emerged from program evaluations of international partnerships with Russia, Lithuania, Poland, the Dominican Republic, South Africa, Macedonia, Hungary, Kyrgyzstan, and the Ukraine (Cornett et al., 2002; Craddock, 2003; Hamot & Misco, 2004; Mason, 2004; Patrick, Vontz, & Metcalf, 2003; Polozhevets, Schecter, & Perelmuter, 1997). These papers provide in-depth descriptions of the nature and extent of partnerships, the professional development opportunities provided, and data measuring some aspects of program impact.

Cornett et al. (2002), for example, describe the work of a partnership between CIVI-TAS@Hungary and the Florida Law Related Education Association, Inc., the State Bar of Texas-Law Related Education, Inc., and the Mississippi *We the People* state coordinator. This partnership offers professional development through teacher training institutes, lesson development and testing, implementation of student-centered academic competitions, and professional exchanges. A series of institutes focused on the content of democracy and training in teaching methodologies, including introducing teachers to academic competitions and the *Project Citizen* program. The grant evaluators collected data (surveys and questionnaires) on the academic competitions and found that the participants' students feel the competition improved their knowledge and skills related to understanding Hungarian democracy, improved their attitudes toward democracy, and increased their political tolerance. The researchers also collected observational data that provided insight into classroom practice and helped inform future professional development efforts.

The research examining the impact of CIVITAS and other civic education professional development opportunities provides cases that delve into some of the complex issues of democracy and teaching for democracy. It would be interesting and useful to have large-scale studies of the impact of this professional development across cases, however.

Geography

In the 1980s, the National Geographic Society launched a multi-million dollar campaign designed to improve teachers' knowledge of geography through the creation of a national professional development network of Geographic Alliances. These Alliances, comprised of geography professors, teacher educators, and K–12 teachers, have been established in all 50 states as well as the District of Columbia and Puerto Rico and provide teachers with a variety of opportunities to learn geographic concepts and skills (Bednarz, Bockenhauer, & Walk, 2005; Englert & Barley, 2003; Kenreich, 2002, 2004). National Geographic's Education Foundation supports these Alliances while also offering grant monies for professional development institutes, engaging in outreach to educators through dissemination of print and electronic curriculum resources, and lobbying Congress for geographic education initiatives at the national level (Kenreich, 2002; NationalGeographic.Com, 2007). Research in this area examines different facets of the impact of the professional development outreach of the National Geographic Society (NGS) on geography teachers, with particular emphasis on the state alliances

(Bednarz, 2002; Berry, 1992; Binko, Neubert, & Madden, 1997; Cole & Ormrod, 1995; Jurmu, Jurmu, & Meyer, 1999; Kenreich, 2000, 2004; Teseniar, 1998; Widener, 1996; Wolfe, 1994).

The state alliances offer intensive professional development opportunities in the summer, Alliance Summer Geography Institutes (ASGIs). The geography community considers graduation from an ASGI a rite of passage, and upon graduation, teachers are given the title "Teacher Consultants" (Kenreich, 2002). Several studies have investigated the impact of these state ASGIs on various aspects of teacher consultants' instruction and student achievement. Berry (1992), for instance, investigated the impact of ASGI training on Alabama and Mississippi teachers' perceptions of geography education. He used three forms of the Perceptions of Geography Education Survey to collect pre-ASGI, post-ASGI and delayed post-ASGI on 45 teachers. Findings indicated that the 2-week institutes heightened teachers' perceptions of geography education in terms of geography curricula and methodology as well as personal knowledge. Perceptions of personal knowledge, however, decreased significantly between the post-test and delayed post-test.

In a study that examined the effectiveness of ASGIs in classroom teacher behaviors, Cole & Ormrod (1995) found that ASGI graduates do alter their classroom instruction as a result of attending institutes and also conduct high-quality inservices that lead to changes in the teaching practice of their colleagues. The authors also assessed the content of ASGIs—using Shulman's notions of pedagogy, content, and pedagogical content knowledge—and asserted that the summer training programs are responsive to and do incorporate "best practices." Jurmu et al. (1999) focused their study of ASGIs on teachers' mastery of content. They evaluated two, 2-week training experiences (one offered in 1993, one offered in 1994) that focused on an environmental theme. After observing the 1993 institute, the authors developed six modifications to implement for the 1994 institute, including changes in format, the daily evaluation form, the group investigation process, staff-presented lessons, consultation by faculty, and geography students as participants. They measured the impact of the institutes and of the alteration to institute content. They found that, after both institutes, teachers reported feeling better prepared in terms of content and pedagogy, and that the confidence levels were higher after the second institute.

Widener (1996) explored the influence of the Missouri Geographic Alliance on geography competence of students in Missouri public schools. She compared Teacher Consultants to teachers who had not attended ASGIs. She found that Teacher Consultants did employ strategies, methods, and materials developed and distributed by the Missouri Geographic Alliance, while other teachers did not. Also, students in schools directly impacted by the Missouri Geographic Alliance scored significantly higher on a commercially published, competency-based geography test than students in non-Alliance schools did. Teseniar (1998) collected quantitative and qualitative data to investigate the influence of a South Carolina ASGI on middle school teachers. The quantitative data, a survey, asked a sample of institute and non-institute teachers to report their level of participation in professional development and professional organizations. Surveys revealed that institute teachers tended to belong to a greater number of professional organizations than non-Institute teachers. Teseniar also collected observation and interview data about six teachers over the course of a year—before, during and after the institute. Findings indicated that ASGI training helped middle school teachers develop a more comprehensive and integrative perception of geography, introduced teachers to a broad range of innovative teaching strategies, and led teachers to reflect on their practice. And, although some changes in teaching practice were evident, they were not as dramatic or systematic as the changes in teachers' perceptions of geography.

Bednarz (2002) explored the possible effects of infusing an action research component into professional development of geography teachers participating in an institute hosted by the Texas Alliance for Geographic Education. Ten of the twenty institute participants chose to undertake an action research project and conducted studies that investigated student perceptions of geography, of tests, and student study habits. Teachers collected data through questionnaires, surveys, student interviews, and analysis of results of a performance assessment. According to Bednarz, her findings indicate that teachers appeared to gain skills, confidence, and useful knowledge through the implementation of action research projects and also appeared to enjoy sharing their findings with their colleagues.

Kenreich (2000, 2004) conducted a survey of 98 participants of an Ohio NGS Alliance Summer Geography Institute in order to collect demographic data as well as examine the impact of the Institutes on teachers' beliefs, classroom practices, and professional development activities in geographic education. The study included participants who had attended an ASGI from 1 to 8 years before they participated in the survey. He found that participants tended to be upper elementary or middle school teachers who are White females, teaching at a public school for at least 20 years, with fewer than two college-level courses in geography (p. 155). The survey revealed that changes in beliefs and practices did take place for the vast majority of teachers. Teachers' confidence with geography content increased, and the teachers reported spending more instructional time on geographic concepts and skills and utilizing geographic resources (maps, globes, etc.) more frequently. Additionally, about two-thirds of the survey respondents reported conducting professional development seminars at the school and/or district level for colleagues. Kenreich asserts that his findings indicate that the ASGIs do exert an influence on teachers' classroom beliefs, classroom practices, and professional development activities but highlight the need to recruit a more diverse population of teachers to the Alliances.

Englert and Barley (2003) used the NAEP geography test to compare the results of teachers who had gone through NGS Alliance professional development training with those who had not. Focusing on a sample of 62 eighth-grade teachers across 18 geographically dispersed states, the authors found that students who had Alliance members as teachers performed statistically significantly higher on NAEP tests. Additionally, item-analysis revealed that Alliance students outperformed non-Alliance students on NAEP questions related to understanding U.S. geography, reading maps, and drawing and interpreting maps. Englert and Barley (2003) also collected background information on the Alliance teachers, including level of participation in the NGS Alliance program, years of teaching, and hours of general professional development. Regression analysis revealed that "frequency of participation in the NGS Alliance Summer Institutes" was the only variable that significantly impacted student achievement. The authors argued that the results demonstrate that the professional development programs of the NGS Alliance appear to be exerting an important impact on student achievement and knowledge of geography, as measured by the NAEP.

In a study with a slightly different focus, Kenreich (2002) examined how the NGS professional development alliance system facilitates the professional growth of teacher leaders, specifically focusing on how secondary teachers constructed their identities as advocates. He conducted an in-depth qualitative study of an 8-day NGS Alliance Leadership Academy, held at the NGS headquarters in Washington, D.C. This academy offered geography content presentations but also featured sessions designed to teach advocacy skills. All attendees received a 3-ring notebook entitled *From Awareness to Action: A How-To Kit for Geography Advocates* (Kenreich, 2002, p. 386) Through interviews, observations, and content analysis of the advocacy binder, Kenreich found that, while most teachers initially became involved in the NGS Alliance system due to an interest in geography education and a desire for more content knowledge, their active participation in Alliance activities fostered interest in becoming teacher leaders and engaging in political advocacy. The teachers conceptualized advocacy in different ways, using both political and non-political terms and identifying a variety of different stakeholders in geographic advocacy, including the media, the state legislature, community/civic organizations, educational administration, and the business community. Kenreich offered evidence that, through certain models of professional development, teacher leaders can view themselves as change agents for educational reform.

In summary, the research on geography professional development utilizes a variety of research approaches to explore the impact of NGS summer institutes on teachers' perceptions, instruction, participation in professional development, and action research skills, as well as some insight into whether professional development influences student understandings of geography and student achievement on standardized tests. Some studies rely solely on teacher self-report data or utilize anecdotal evidence for data sources, but as compared to other disciplines within social studies education, the geography research community has included attention to research that documents the impact and influence of summer institutes on teachers' instruction and student achievement.

GLOBAL EDUCATION, MULTICULTURAL EDUCATION, & SOCIAL JUSTICE EDUCATION

A few papers discuss or call for professional development geared towards enriching teachers' knowledge about and dispositions toward multicultural education and education for social justice (Boyle-Baise & Washburn, 1995; Crocco, 2002; Fabillar & Jones, 2002; Ketter & Lewis, 2001; Sleeter, 1992), but these studies often do not focus specifically on social studies teachers. More work exists that examines different facets of professional development in global education. Since the 1960s, global education has emerged as an important component of social studies education and, in the interest of infusing global perspectives into K–12 classroom teaching, many professional development opportunities in global education exist (Adler, 1991; Boston, 1997; Gaudelli, 2006; Kirkwood-Tucker, 2004; Merryfield, 1997, 1998). Groups including the Bay Area Global Education Program, the International Studies Education Project of San Diego, the Consortium for Teaching Asia and the Pacific in Schools, and the Center for Human Interdependence have all structured a variety of professional development programs for teachers (Boston, 1997; Gaudelli, 2006). Research in global education professional development includes attention to professional development schools (PDS), as well as workshops, institutes, and other learning opportunities.

Gaudelli (2006), for example, explored how teachers experience professional development about global education through a study of six teachers, at various career stages, who were involved in the World Teaching Institute (WTI). The actual institute lasted for 1 week, but was followed by monthly face-to-face meetings and continued opportunities for online, asynchronous dialog. The institute focused on reframing teachers' existing knowledge around core global values and ideas, offering approaches to infuse global education into the curriculum, and fostering conversations/dialog among teacher participants. Analysis of interviews, group meetings, observations, and teacher reflections revealed that teachers reported a greater interest in teaching about controversial issues and that they now paid more attention to engaging English as second language learners. Also, many participants mentioned feeling overwhelmed by how much they did not know about the world and expressed concern about not having enough time to think about resources and applicability of global education in the classroom. Participants also reported that they planned and implemented new teaching activities as a result of the institute and that they viewed teaching in a different way, one that included greater attention to student inquiry. Gaudelli cautioned that changes in outlook of participants were highly individualized, but the teachers' experiences did appear to center on some common themes—feeling overwhelmed, planning/implementing pedagogical change, encountering controversial issues, and engaging English to Speakers of Other Languages (ESOL) students. Future global education professional development opportunities, Gaudelli argued, should include attention to characteristics that made the WTI a positive experience—dialogue, diversity of offerings, interdisciplinary effort—but that for professional development to be truly successful, experiences should include experiential global learning and school-based administrative support. Gaudelli's work reflects most of the research on global education and professional development—rich, qualitative work that investigates teachers' experiences in workshops or working together through professional development networks.

PROFESSIONAL DEVELOPMENT AND HIGH-STAKES TESTING

The emphasis on standards and accountability at the state and national level has led to the construction of new curriculum frameworks at the state level. These proposals promote new visions of classroom teaching practices yet offer little insight into how teachers will learn to teach differently (Grant, 1997, 2003). Almost no research in social studies education examines the professional development opportunities surrounding high stakes testing. One exception is Grant's 1997 study in which he explored the range of opportunities available for New York elementary, middle, and high school teachers to learn about a new social studies curriculum framework, the content and pedagogy of those sessions, and teachers' responses to the framework and the professional development sessions they attended (p. 259). He observed 16 professional development sessions related to the framework. Findings revealed that, despite the access to multiple learning opportunities about the framework, teachers attended very few sessions and most of those were of local origin. Also, the sessions offered were one-shot deals rather than ongoing occasions for learning. The content of these workshops was fragmented and thin, and the pedagogy was presenter-centered. Teachers viewed the professional development offered by the state as unhelpful and irrelevant and expressed little regard for the new framework. Grant (1997) argues that this study highlights the need to rethink professional development for teachers, that effective professional development would include a well-organized, coherent curriculum with ideas that engage teachers as learners. Additionally, the presenters/facilitators would model ambitious teaching and wise practice and teach in ways that reflect an understanding of teacher learners. Given the current high-stakes context, more research should attend to professional development and teacher learning in an age of accountability.

CONCLUSIONS

The body of research on social studies professional development has grown over the past decade. Many of the studies provide insight into specific cases and tend to be either descriptive or qualitative in nature. Thus, the research in social studies education reflects the growing trend noted by Zeichner (1999), who has observed a shift from an exclusive reliance on positivistic studies to the "use of a broader variety of research methodologies," including naturalistic and interpretive research methodologies and critical, feminist, and post-structural analyses, as well as the "investigation of a much broader range of research questions" (p. 8). Yet, the majority of the research reviewed remains idiosyncratic and specific to particular cases. There still exists no big picture of social studies professional development, nor any sense of how work in this area is connected. The professional development opportunities under study are tied to a particular time and place—and often, a particular grant—and are not contextualized within the larger framework of professional development. Additionally, research in this area is confounded by the fact that the field does not possess clearly elucidated purposes and goals for professional development. What, then, are next steps for research on social studies professional development?

In her article exploring the terrain of professional development, Borko (2004) analyzed existing research by organizing research programs into three phases. Phase I research programs, she asserts, focus on individual professional development programs at a single site, and researchers study the program, the participants' learning, and the relationship between the program and teacher learning. Phase II research programs study a single professional development program implemented by more than one facilitator at more than one site, and the relationship among facilitators, the program, and the participants' learning is studied. Finally, Phase III research compares multiple professional development programs enacted at multiple sites (p 4). All phases include attention to impact of professional development on student learning.

In social studies education, we have research in Phase I—examining an individual program at one particular site—but the majority of this research fails to examine the impact of professional development on teacher practice and student achievement and relies heavily on teacher self-report through exit interviews, exit surveys, reflective journals, or anecdotal conversations. Future research in this phase should focus on what happens in the classroom following professional development and whether/how professional development impacts teacher learning and student learning over time. And, while qualitative research offers rich detail and interesting insight into the nuances of professional development under study, more attention to mixed methods might add another layer to our understanding of teacher learning (Zeichner, 1999). No research exists in social studies that meet the parameters of Borko's Phases II and III. Social studies research is typically underfunded, but researchers could consider creative ways to collect data across sites and examine the large-scale impact of professional development in classrooms. Another interesting idea offered by Borko (2004) is to examine existing professional development programs in other subject areas and see if they can be adapted to social studies education. For this to be effective, however, the field must engage in conversation about what we believe is important for teachers to learn and what social studies "best practice" looks like—in other words, in order for us to figure out what types of professional development programs can help us achieve our goals, we need to clarify our goals.

Research in professional development should also include greater attention to the principles of effective professional development outlined in the research. As Grant (2003) notes, "the standard inservice program is weakly conceived and poorly delivered," and the "mix of messages broadcast from one professional development session to another can seem incoherent and only distantly related to teaching and learning" (p. 200). We should either attempt to fix the "workshop problem" or move beyond it and begin developing, implementing, and studying new approaches to professional development, approaches that incorporate attention to effective approaches for teacher learning, socialization, and change.

The research reviewed provides some insight into the processes of the professional development of social studies teachers but, ultimately, fails to answer key questions: What are the overall goals of professional development? How do we know, as a field, that professional development of social studies teachers affects change in classrooms? And, as a field, how do we define/conceive of "making a difference" in a classroom? We need to systematically investigate the complexities of teacher professional development, to build upon one another's work in order to be able to respond to the question that is particularly important in the current political climate: How does social studies professional development make a difference?

In the current context of "highly qualified teachers," "evidence-based decision-making," and standardized tests, we need to conduct research that investigates topics that we value as a field, but we also need to examine how what we value directly influences student achievement and student understandings of social studies. Unless social studies researchers determine, based on empirical research, what an effective teacher looks like and can document how social studies professional development contributes to that, we risk the chance that an increasingly intrusive federal government may impose their own definitions of a "highly qualified" social studies professional development onto the field.

REFERENCES

Adler, S. (1991). The education of social studies teachers. In J. P. Shaver (Ed.), *Handbook of research in social studies teaching and learning* (pp. 210–221). New York: MacMillan.

Angell, A. V. (1998). Learning to teach social studies: A case of belief restructuring. *Theory and Research in Social Education, 26,* 509–529.

Armento, B. J. (1996). The professional development of social studies educators. In J. Sikula, T. G. Buttery, & E. Guyten (Eds.), *Handbook of research on teacher education* (2nd ed., pp. 485–502). New York: Macmillan Library Reference.

Ball, D. L., & Cohen, D. K. (1999). Developing practice, developing practitioners: Toward a practice-based theory of professional education. In L. Darling-Hammond & G. Sykes (Eds.), *Teaching as the learning profession: Handbook of policy and practice* (pp. 3–32). San Francisco: Jossey-Bass.

Barton, K., McCully, A. W., & Marks, M. J. (2004). Reflecting on elementary children's understanding of history and social studies: An inquiry project with beginning teachers in northern Ireland and the United States. *Journal of Teacher Education, 55*(1), 70–90.

Bednarz, S. W. (2002). Using action research to implement the national geography standards: Teachers as researchers. *Journal of Geography, 101*(3), 103–111.

Bednarz, S. W., Bockenhauer, M. H., & Walk, F. H. (2005). Mentoring: A new approach to geography teacher education. *Journal of Geography, 104*(3), 105–112.

Berry, W. E. (1992). *The relationship between teachers' perceptions of geography education and their participation in the Alabama and Mississippi Geographic Summer Geography Institutes.* University of Southern Mississippi.

Binko, J. B., Neubert, G. A., & Madden, M. (1997). Writing and Geography provide lessons for other disciplines. *Journal of Staff Development, 18*(4), 11–15.

Borko, H. (2004). Professional development and teacher learning: Mapping the terrain. *Educational Researcher, 33*(8), 3–15.

Borko, H., & Putnam, R. T. (1995). Expanding a teacher's knowledge base: A cognitive psychological perspective on professional development. In T. R. Guskey & A. M. Huberman (Eds.), *Professional development in education: New paradigms & practices* (pp. 35–66). New York: Teachers College Press.

Bossard, K., Chase, S., Dove, T., Hoover, S., Merryfield, M., Norris, J., et al. (1996). *Can our learning community survive? Teachers examine the long-term effectiveness of their PDS Network in social studies and global education* (No. ED 415 130).

Boston, J. A. (1997). Professional development in global education. In M. Merryfield, E. Jarchow, & S. Pickert (Eds.), *Preparing teachers to teach global perspectives: A handbook for teacher educators* (pp. 168–188). Thousand Oaks, CA: Corwin Press.

Boyle-Baise, M., & Washburn, J. (1995). Coalescing for change: The coalition for education that is multicultural. *Journal of Teacher Education, 46*(5), 351–359.

Brandes, G. M., & Seixas, P. (1998). Subjects and disciplines: Assymetries in a collaborative curriculum development project. *Teachers and Teaching: Theory and Practice, 4,* 95–114.

Brandes, G. M., & Seixas, P. (2000). "...So that the two can mix in this crucible": Teachers in an interdisciplinary school-university collaboration in the humanities. In S. Wineburg & P. L. Grossman (Eds.), *Interdisciplinary curriculum: Challenges to implementation* (pp. 153–170). New York: Teachers College Press.

Bransford, J. D., Darling-Hammond, L., & LePage, P. (2005). Introduction. In L. Darling-Hammond & J. D. Bransford (Eds.), *Preparing teachers for a changing world: What teachers should learn and be able to do* (pp. 1–39). San Francisco: Jossey-Bass.

Brownell, M. T., Adams, A., Sindelar, P. T., Waldron, N., & van Hover, S. (2006). Learning from collaboration: The role of teacher qualities. *Exceptional Children, 72*(2), 169–185.

Brownell, M. T., Yeager, E. A., Rennells, M., & Riley, T. (1997). Teachers working together: What Teacher educators and researchers should know. *Teacher Education and Special Education, 20*(4), 340–359.

Brownell, M. T., Yeager, E. A., Sindelar, P. T., van Hover, S., & Riley, T. (2004). Teacher learning cohorts: A vehicle for supporting beginning teachers. *Teacher Education and Special Education, 27*(2), 174–189.

Bullough, R. V. (1986). *First-year teacher: A case study*. New York: Teachers College Press.

Bullough, R. V. (1987). Planning and the first year of teaching. *Journal of Education for Teaching, 13*, 231–250.

Carpenter, J., Dublin, T., & Harper, P. (2005). Bridging learning communities: A summer workshop for social studies teachers. *The History Teacher, 38*(3), 361–369.

Chant, R. H. (2002). The impact of personal theorizing on beginning teaching: Three social studies teachers. *Theory and Research in Social Education, 30*(4), 516–540.

Clift, R. T., & Brady, P. (2005). Research on methods courses and field experiences. In M. Cochran-Smith & K. Zeichner (Eds.), *Studying teacher education: The report of the AERA Panel on Research and Teacher Education* (pp. 309–424). Mahwah, NJ: Erlbaum.

Cochran-Smith, M., & Zeichner, K. (2005). Executive Summary. In M. Cochran-Smith & K. Zeichner (Eds.), *Studying teacher education: The report of the AERA Panel on Research and Teacher Education* (pp. 1–36). Mahwah, NJ: Erlbaum..

Cole, D. B., & Ormrod, J. E. (1995). Effectiveness of teaching pedagogical content knowledge through summer institutes. *Journal of Geography, 94*, 427–433.

Cornett, J. W., Dziuban, C. D., & Abisellan, E. (2002). Civic education project in Hungary: A CIVITAS partnership with Florida, Texas, and Mississippi. *International Journal of Social Education, 17*(2), 69–86.

Craddock, A. (2003). Civic learning in teacher education through an American-Urkainian partnership. In J. J. Patrick, G. Hamot, & R. S. Leming (Eds.), *Civic learning in teacher education: International perspectives on education for democracy in the preparation of teachers.* (pp. 139–156). Bloomington, IN: ERIC Clearninghouse for Social Studies.

Crocco, M. S. (2002). Homophobic hallways: Is anyone listening? *Theory and Research in Social Education, 30*(2), 217–232.

Darling-Hammond, L. (1998a). Learning to teach in the 21st century. *Principal, 78*(1), 23–25.

Darling-Hammond, L. (1998b). Teacher learning that supports student learning. *Educational Leadership, 55*(5), 6–11.

Darling-Hammond, L. (1999). Target time toward teachers. *Journal of Staff Development, 20*(2), 31–36.

Darling-Hammond, L., Berry, B. T., Haselkorn, D., & Fideler, E. (1999). Teacher recruitment, selection, and induction: Policy influences on the supply and quality of teachers. In L. Darling-Hammond & G. Sykes (Eds.), *Teaching as the learning profession: Handbook of policy and practice* (pp. 183–222). San Francisco: Jossey-Bass.

Darling-Hammond, L., & McLaughlin, M. W. (1999). Investing in teaching as a learning profession: Policy problems and prospects. In L. Darling-Hammond & G. Sykes (Eds.), *Teaching as the learning profession: Handbook of policy and practice* (pp. 376–412). San Francisco: Jossey-Bass.

Desimone, L. M., Porter, A. C., Garet, M. S., Yoon, K. S., & Birman, B. F. (2002). Effects of professional development on teachers' instruction: Results from a three-year longitudinal study. *Educational Evaluation and Policy Analysis, 24*, 81–112.

Ed.Gov. (2006). Teaching American history awards. Retrieved February 27, 2006, from http://www.ed.gov/programs/teachinghistory/awards.html.

Englert, K., & Barley, Z. (2003). National Geographic Society Alliance Study. *Journal of Geography, 102*(2), 80–89.

Fabillar, E., & Jones, C. (2002). Interdisciplinary connections: Teacher and student empowerment through social and cultural history, critical pedagogy, and collaboration. *Radical Teacher, 65*(Winter 2002/2003), 18–22.

Fehn, B., & Koeppen, K. E. (1998). Intensive document-based instruction in a social studies methods course and student teachers' attitudes and practice in subsequent field experiences. *Theory and Research in Social Education, 26*, 461–484.

Feiman-Nemser, S. (2001). From preparation to practice: Designing a continuum to strengthen and sustain teaching. *Teachers College Record, 103*(6), 1013–1065.

Feiman-Nemser, S. (2003). What new teachers need to learn. *Educational Leadership, 60*(8), 25–29.

Fullan, M. G., & Miles, M. B. (1992). Getting reform right: What works and what doesn't. *Phi Delta Kappan, 73*, 725–752.

Garet, M. S., Porter, A. C., Desimone, L. M., Birman, B. F., & Yoon, K. S. (2001). What makes professional development effective? Results from a national sample of teachers. *American Educational Research Journal, 38*(4), 915–945.

Gaudelli, W. (2006). Professional development for global education: Possibilities and limitations. *Policy and Practice in Education, 11*(2).

Gold, Y. (1996). Beginning teacher support: Attrition, mentoring, and induction. In J. Sikula, T. G. Buttery & E. Guyten (Eds.), *Handbook of research on teacher education* (pp. 548–593). New York: MacMillan.

Gold, Y., & Roth, R. A. (1993). *Teachers managing stress and preventing burnout: The professional health solution.* London: Falmer Press.

Grant, S. G. (1997). Opportunities lost: Teacher learning about the New York State social studies framework. *Theory and Research in Social Education, 25*(3), 259–287.

Grant, S. G. (2003). *History lessons: Teaching, learning, and testing in U.S. high school classrooms.* Mahwah, New Jersey: Erlbaum.

Grossman, P. L. (1991). Overcoming the apprenticeship of observation in teacher education coursework. *Teaching & Teacher Education, 7*(4), 345–357.

Grossman, P. L., Wineburg, S., & Woolworth, S. (2000a). *What makes teacher community different from a gathering of teachers?* University of Washington: Center for the Study of Teaching and Policy.

Grossman, P. L., Wineburg, S., & Woolworth, S. (2000b). *What makes teacher community different from a gathering of teachers?: An occasional paper co-Sponsored by the Center for the Study of Teaching and Policy and Center on English Learning and Achievement (CELA).* University of Washington: Center for the Study of Teaching and Policy.

Grossman, P. L., Wineburg, S., & Woolworth, S. (2001). Toward a theory of teacher community. *Teachers College Record, 103*(6), 942–1012.

Guskey, T. R. (1995). Professional development in education: In search of the optimal mix. In T. R. Guskey & A. M. Huberman (Eds.), *Professional development in education: New paradigms and practices* (pp. 114–132). New York: Teachers College Press.

Hamot, G., & Misco, T. (2004). An examination of kyrgyz educators views of moral education. Paper presented at the annual conference of College & University Faculty Assembly of the National Council for the Social Studies. Baltimore, MD, November, 2004.

Hartzler-Miller, C. (2001). Making sense of "best practice" in teaching history. *Theory and Research in Social Education, 29*, 672–695.

Hawley, W. D., & Valli, L. (1999). The essentials of effective professional development: A new consensus. In L. Darling-Hammond & G. Sykes (Eds.), *Teaching as the learning profession: Handbook of policy and practice* (pp. 125–150). San Francisco: Jossey-Bass.

Hess, F. M., & Petrilli, M. J. (2006/2007). *No Child Left Behind: A Peter Lang Primer.* New York: Peter Lang.

Hicks, S. (2005). Continuity and constraint: Case studies of becoming a teacher of history in England and the United States. *International Journal of Social Education, 20*(1), 18–51.

Hudson, L. E., & Santora, E. D. (2003). Oral history: An inclusive highway to the past. *The History Teacher, 36*(2), 206–220.

Humphrey, D. C., Chang-Ross, C., Donnelly, M., Hersh, L., Skolnik, H., & International, S. (2005). *Evaluation of the Teaching American History Program*: United States Department of Education, Office of Planning, Evaluation and Policy Development (http://www.ed.gov/rschstat/eval/teaching/us-history/teaching-exec-sum.html).

Jurmu, M. C., Jurmu, J. M., & Meyer, J. W. (1999). Mastery of content and pedagogy: Evaluation of strategies for teacher institutes. *Journal of Geography, 98*, 14–22.

Kenreich, T. W. (2000). *Teacher consultants in the Ohio Geographic Alliance: Their beliefs, classroom practices, and professional development activities.* The Ohio State University.

Kenreich, T. W. (2002). Professional development becomes political: Geography's corps of teacher leaders. *Theory and Research in Social Education, 30*(3), 381–400.

Kenreich, T. W. (2004). Beliefs, classroom practices, and professional development activities of teacher consultants. *Journal of Geography, 103*(4), 153–160.

Ketter, J., & Lewis, C. (2001). Already reading texts and contexts: Multicultural literature in a predominantly White rural community. *Theory into Practice, 40*(3), 175–183.

Killion, J. (2006). What works in the middle: Results-based staff development. from http://www. nsdc.org/midbook/index.cfm.

Kirkwood-Tucker, T. F. (2004). Empowering teachers to create a more peaceful world through global education: Simulating the United Nations. *Theory and Research in Social Education, 32*(1), 56–74.

Little, J. W. (1999). Organizing schools for teacher learning. In L. Darling-Hammond & G. Sykes (Eds.), *Teaching as the learning profession: Handbook of policy and practice* (pp. 233–262). San Francisco: Jossey-Bass.

Louis, K. S., & Marks, H. M. (1998). Does professional community affect the classroom? Teachers' work and student experiences in restructuring schools. *American Journal of Education, 106*(4), 532–575.

Mason, T. (2004). From the Balkans to the Baltics: Challenges for civic education in Eastern Europe. Paper presented at the annual conference of the College & University Faculty Assembly of the National Council for the Social Studies, November, 2004.

Merryfield, M. (1997). A framework for teacher education in global perspectives. In M. Merryfield, E. Jarchow & S. Pickert (Eds.), *Preparing teachers to teach global perspectives: A handbook for teacher educators* (pp. 1–24). Thousand Oaks, CA: Corwin Press.

Merryfield, M. (1998). Pedgagogy for global perspectives in education: Studies of teachers' thinking and practice. *Theory and Research in Social Education, 26*(3), 342–379.

Mintrop, H. (2004). Fostering constructivist communities of learners in the amalgamated multidiscipline of social studies. *Journal of Curriculum Studies, 36*(2), 141–158.

Moyer, J., Onosko, J., & Forcey, C. (2003). History in Perspective (HIP): A collaborative project between the University of New Hampshire, SAU #56, and 13 other school districts. *The History Teacher, 36*(2), 186–205.

NationalGeographic.Com. (2007). National Geographic Education Foundation. Retrieved February 27, 2007, from http://www.nationalgeographic.com/foundation/.

Newmann, F. M., King, M. B., & Youngs, P. (2000). Professional development that addresses school capacity: Lessons from urban elementary schools. *American Journal of Education, 108*(4), 259–299.

Pajares, M. (1992). Teachers' Beliefs and Educational Research: Cleaning up a messy construct. *Review of Educational Research, 62*, 307–332.

Patrick, J. J., Vontz, T. S., & Metcalf, K. K. (2003). Learning democracy through Project Citizen in Lithuania, Latvia, and Indiana. *International Journal of Social Education, 17*(2), 49–68.

Patterson, N. C. (2002). *Impacts of teacher induction: A longitudinal cross-case comparison of beginning teachers in a content-specific program.* University of Arizona.

Patterson, N. C., & Luft, J. A. (2004). Creating a continuum: Considering induction programs for secondary social studies teachers. *Theory and Research in Social Education, 32*(2), 138–152.

Pesick, S., & Weintraub, S. (2004). DeTocqueville's ghost: Examining the struggle for democracy in America. *The History Teacher, 36*(2), 231–251.

Polozhevets, P., Schecter, S. L., & Perelmuter, R. (1997). Civic education and the future of democracy in Russia. *International Journal of Social Education, 12*(2), 84–100.

Putnam, R. T., & Borko, H. (1997). Teacher learning: Implications of new views of cognition. In B. J. Biddle, T. L. Good & I. F. Goodson (Eds.), *The international handbook of teachers and teaching* (pp. 1223–1296). Dordrecht, The Netherlands: Kluwer.

Quigley, C. N., & Hoar, J. N. (1997). CIVITAS: An international civic education exchange program. *International Journal of Social Education, 12*(2), 11–26.

Rhine, S. (1998). The role of research and teachers' knowledge base in professional development. *Educational Researcher, 27*(5), 27–31.

Richardson, V. (1996). The role of attitudes and beliefs in learning to teach. In J. Sikula, T. G. Buttery & E. Guyten (Eds.), *Handbook of research on teacher education* (2nd ed.). New York: Simon & Schuster Macmillan.

Rosenberg, M. S., Griffin, C. C., Kilgore, K. L., & Carpenter, S. L. (1997). Beginning teachers in special education: A model for providing individualized support. *Teacher Education and Special Education, 20*, 301–321.

Sanders, W. L., & Rivers, J. C. (1996). *Cumulative and residual effects of teachers on future student academic achievement.* Knoxville: University of Tennessee Value-Added Research and Assessment Center.

Seixas, P., & Brandes, G. M. (1997). A workshop in uncertainty: New scholarship in the humanities and social sciences as a basis for professional and curricular development. *Journal of Curriculum and Supervision, 13*, 56–69.

Silva, D. Y. (2000). Collaborative curriculum encounters. *Journal of Curriculum and Supervision, 15*(4), 279–299.

Silva, D. Y. (2003). Triad journaling: A tool for creating professional learning communities. *Teacher Education Quarterly, 30*(4), 69–82.

Silva, D. Y., & Dana, N. F. (2001). Collaborative supervision in the professional development school. *Journal of Curriculum and Supervision, 16*(4), 305–321.

Silva, D. Y., & Fichtman, N. (2004). Encountering new spaces: Teachers developing voice within a professional development school. *Journal of Teacher Education, 55*(2), 128–140.

Silva, D. Y., Gimbert, B., & Nolan, J. F. (2000). Sliding the doors: Locking and unlocking possibilities for teacher leadership. *Teachers College Record, 102*(4), 779–804.

Silva, D. Y., & Tom, A. R. (2001). The moral basis of mentoring. *Teacher Education Quarterly, 28*(2), 39–52.

Sleeter, C. E. (1992). *Keepers of the American Dream*. London: Falmer Press.

Smith, J., & Niemi, R. (2001). Learning history in school: The impact of course work and instructional practices on achievement *Theory and Research in Social Education, 29*(1), 18–42.

Smylie, M. (1995). Teacher learning in the workplace: Implications for school reform. In T. R. Guskey & A. M. Huberman (Eds.), *Professional development in education: new paradigms and practices* (pp. 92–113). New York: Teachers College Press.

Stanley, W. B., & Longwell, H. (2004). Ideology, power, and control in social studies teacher education. In S. Adler (Ed.), *Critical issues in social studies teacher education* (pp. 189–230). Greenwich, CT Information Age Publishing.

Stein, A. (2003). The Teaching American History Program: An introduction and overview. *The History Teacher, 36*(2), 178–185.

Stronge, J. H. (2002). *Qualities of effective teaching*. Alexandria, VA: Association for Supervision and Curriculum Development.

Sykes, G. (1996). Reform of and as professional development. *Phi Delta Kappan, 77*, 465–467.

Sykes, G. (1999). Teacher and student learning: Strengthening their connection. In L. Darling-Hammond & G. Sykes (Eds.), *Teaching as the learning profession: Handbook of policy and practice* (pp. 151–180). San Francisco: Jossey-Bass.

Teseniar, M. F. (1998). *The 1997 South Carolina Geographic Alliance Summer Geography Institute: A Study of geographic perceptions, teaching strategies, and teacher professional development*. University of South Carolina.

Thomas, G., Wineburg, S., Grossman, P. L., Oddmund, M., & Woolworth, S. (1998). In the company of colleagues: An interim report on the development of a community of teacher learners. *Teaching & Teacher Education, 14*(1), 21–32.

Thornton, S. J. (1991). Teacher as curricular-instructional gatekeeper in social studies. In J. P. Shaver (Ed.), *Handbook of research on social studies teaching and learning*. New York: MacMillan Publishing Company.

Valli, L., & Stout, M. (2004). Continuing professional development for social studies teachers. In S. Adler (Ed.), *Critical issues in social studies teacher education* (pp. 165–188). Greenwich, CT: Information Age Publishing.

van Hover, S. (2006). Teaching History in the Old Dominion: The impact of Virginia's accountability reform on seven secondary beginning history teachers. In S. G. Grant's (Ed.), *Measuring history: Cases of state-level testing across the states* (pp. 211–226). Greenwich, CT: Information Age Publishing.

van Hover, S., & Yeager, E. A. (2003). "'Making' students better people?" A case study of a beginning history teacher. *International Social Studies Forum, 3*(1), 219–232.

van Hover, S., & Yeager, E. A. (2004). Challenges facing beginning history teachers: An exploratory study. *The International Journal of Social Education, 19*(1).

van Hover, S., & Yeager, E. A. (2005). "I want to use my subject matter to...": The role of purpose in one secondary U.S. history teachers' instructional decision-making. Paper presented at the annual conference of the American Educational Research Association. Montreal, Canada, April 2005.

Vontz, T. S., & Leming, R. S. (2005). Designing and implementing effective professional development in civic education. *International Journal of Social Education, 20*(2), 67–88.

Widener, B. (1996). *The influence of the Missouri Geographic Alliance on geography competence of students in Missouri public schools*. University of Missouri-Columbia.

Wilson, S., & Berne, J. (1999). Teacher learning and the acquisition of professional knowledge: An examination of research on contemporary professional development. *Review of Research in Education, 24*(1999), 173–209.

Wineburg, S. (2001). *Historical thinking and other unnatural Acts: Charting the future of teaching the past*. Philadelphia: Temple University Press.

Wineburg, S., & Grossman, P. L. (1998). Creating a community of learners among high school teachers. *Phi Delta Kappan, 79*(January), 350–353.

Wineburg, S., & Grossman, P. L. (2000). Scenes from a courtship: Some theoretical and practical implications of interdisciplinary humanities curricula in the comprehensive high school. In S. Wineburg & P. L. Grossman (Eds.), *Interdisciplinary curriculum: Challenges to implementation*. New York: Teachers College Press.

Wolfe, L. J. (1994). *The effectiveness of an inservice geography institute on participating teachers*. Emory University.

Wolpow, R., Johnson, N. N., & Wognild, K. N. (2002). Designing, implementing, and evaluating a teacher in-service program enabling 6th–12th grade rural teachers to integrate Holocaust studies into their curricula: A case study. *Theory and Research in Social Education, 30*(4), 563–588.

Yeager, E. A., & van Hover, S. (2006). Virginia vs. Florida: Two beginning history teachers' perceptions of the influence of high-stakes tests on their insturctional decision-making. *Social Studies Research and Practice, 1*(3).

Zeichner, K. (1999). The new scholarship in teacher education. *Educational Researcher, 28*(9), 4–15.

Zeisler-Vralsted, D. (2003). The Wisconsin Collaborative United States History Professional Development Program. *The History Teacher, 36*(2), 221–230.

Author Index

Subject Index